Methodos Series

Methodological Prospects in the Social Sciences

Volume 15

This Book Series is devoted to examining and solving the major methodological problems social sciences are facing. Take for example the gap between empirical and theoretical research, the explanatory power of models, the relevance of multilevel analysis, the weakness of cumulative knowledge, the role of ordinary knowledge in the research process, or the place which should be reserved to "time, change and history" when explaining social facts. These problems are well known and yet they are seldom treated in depth in scientific literature because of their general nature.

So that these problems may be examined and solutions found, the series prompts and fosters the settingup of international multidisciplinary research teams, and it is work by these teams that appears in the Book Series. The series can also host books produced by a single author which follow the same objectives. Proposals for manuscripts and plans for collective books will be carefully examined.

The epistemological scope of these methodological problems is obvious and resorting to Philosophy of Science becomes a necessity. The main objective of the Series remains however the methodological solutions that can be applied to the problems in hand. Therefore the books of the Series are closely connected to the research practices.

More information about this series at http://www.springer.com/series/6279

Jörg Blasius • Frédéric Lebaron • Brigitte Le Roux
Andreas Schmitz

Editors

Empirical Investigations of Social Space

 Springer

Editors
Jörg Blasius
Institute of Political Science & Sociology
University of Bonn
Bonn, Germany

Frédéric Lebaron
Department of Social Sciences
Ecole normale supérieure Paris-Saclay
Cachan, France

Brigitte Le Roux
MAP5 - University Paris Descartes
Paris, France

Andreas Schmitz
Institute of Political Science & Sociology
University of Bonn
Bonn, Germany

Methodos Series
ISBN 978-3-030-15386-1   ISBN 978-3-030-15387-8   (eBook)
https://doi.org/10.1007/978-3-030-15387-8

This Springer imprint is published by the registered company Springer Nature Switzerland AG.
The registered company address is: Gewerbestrasse 11, 6330 Cham, Switzerland

Foreword

In October 1998, the first international conference on *Empirical Investigation of Social Space*, held in Cologne, Germany, brought together social scientists, statisticians, and other researchers interested in the principles and methodology behind Bourdieu's empirical work. This conference was organized by Jörg Blasius (working at the time in Cologne), Brigitte Le Roux (Paris), and Henry Rouanet (Paris, † 2008), in cooperation with Pierre Bourdieu (Paris, † 2002). A particular focus was put on methodological and statistical research using correspondence analysis and its application within the social sciences. At this conference, Bourdieu presented a paper entitled "Construction of social space and correspondence analysis," where he discussed his use of simple and multiple correspondence analyses.

Seventeen years later, a subsequent conference was organized by Jörg Blasius (Bonn), Frédéric Lebaron (Versailles), Brigitte Le Roux (Paris), and Andreas Schmitz (Bonn), in cooperation with Loïc Wacquant (Berkeley), held in Bonn in 2015 (see Blasius and Schmitz 2017 for a conference report), in order to continue the earlier discussions. Both conferences attracted a large number of international researchers, especially those involved in the empirical work of Bourdieu. For this edited volume, we gathered participants of both conferences as well as further experts who were not able to participate at the conference.

This book would not have been possible without the help of numerous persons who helped us with proof-reading the papers and organizing its publication. We, the editors, are pleased to thank Silvia Arnold (Bonn), Manuela Schmidt (Bonn), and Will Tayler (Bamberg). Finally, we would like to thank the Thyssen Foundation for their generous support of the second conference.

Bonn, Germany	Jörg Blasius
Cachan, France	Frédéric Lebaron
Paris, France	Brigitte Le Roux
Bonn, Germany	Andreas Schmitz

Contents

Contributors

Christian Baier, Dr. rer. pol., is a research associate at the Bavarian State Department of Statistics (Bayerisches Landesamt für Statistik) in Fürth. His research interests include sociology of science, relational methods, and statistical text analysis.
Email: christian.baier@uni-bamberg.de Web: https://www.uni-bamberg.de/soztheorie/personen/mitarbeiterinnen/christian-baier/publikationen/

Ylva Bergström is Associate Professor of Sociology of Education in the Department of Education at Uppsala University, Sweden. Her main research interests are sociology of education and politics, and applications of geometric data analysis. She is a member of the research unit Sociology of Education and Culture (SEC).
Email: ylva.bergstrom@edu.uu.se Web: http://www.skeptron.uu.se/pers/ylvab

Gunn Elisabeth Birkelund is Professor of Sociology at University of Oslo, Norway. Her main research interests are labor market studies and studies of social inequalities related to gender, ethnicity, and socioeconomic status. She presently works on a comparative project of labor market discrimination, and a project on ethnic school and neighborhood segregation.
Email: g.e.birkelund@sosgeo.uio.no Web: https://www.sv.uio.no/iss/personer/vit/gunnb/

Jörg Blasius is Professor of Sociology at the Institute for Political Science and Sociology, University of Bonn, Germany. His main research interests are explorative data analysis, especially correspondence analysis and related methods, data collection methods, sociology of lifestyles, and urban sociology.
Email: jblasius@uni-bonn.de Web: https://www.politik-soziologie.uni-bonn.de/de/institut/lehrkoerper/blasius

Philippe Bonnet is a social psychologist and statistician, now retired from CNRS. His main research interests are in geometric data analysis of quantitative, qualitative, and textual data with emphasis on structured data and applications to behavioral and social sciences.

Email: philippe.bonnet@parisdescartes.fr Web: http://recherche.parisdescartes.fr/VAC_eng/Membres/BONNET-Philippe

Mikael Börjesson is Professor in Sociology of Education at Uppsala University, Sweden, and is co-director of the research unit Sociology of Education and Culture (SEC). His main research domains are fields of education, transnational strategies, and the internationalization of higher education, elites and elite education, cultural consumption and social spaces, and applications of geometric data analysis.
Email: mikael.borjesson@edu.uu.se Web: https://mp.uu.se/web/profilsidor/start/-/emp/N96-2267

Donald Broady has, since 1997, held chairs at different departments at Uppsala University. Today he is Professor Emeritus in the Department of Sociology. Also, since 1988 he has been a research fellow in the Department of Numerical Analysis and Computing Science, Royal Institute of Technology (KTH), Stockholm. Broady's research has focused on cultural fields, elites, the sociology and history of education, mark-up languages, and Internet applications.
Email: donald.broady@soc.uu.se Web: http://www.skeptron.uu.se/broady/

Frédérik Cassor is Engineer Assistant at the Centre for Political Research in Sciences Po (CEVIPOF), Sciences Po University, Paris, France. His research interests are mainly focused on data collection methods, explorative data analysis, geometric data analysis, especially correspondence analysis and related methods, sociology of political behaviors, electoral studies, and quantitative methodology watching.
Email: frederik.cassor@sciencespo.fr Web: http://www.cevipof.com/fr/l-equipe/l-equipe-administrative/bdd/equipe/157

Tobias Dalberg is a doctoral student in the Department of Education, Uppsala University, Sweden. His main research interests are sociological and historical studies of science and education, geometric data analysis, and sequence analysis.
Email: tobias.dalberg@edu.uu.se Web: http://www.skeptron.uu.se/pers/tobiasd

Rainer Diaz-Bone is Professor of Sociology in the Department of Sociology, University of Lucerne. His main research areas are sociological methodology, survey methods and philosophy of science, statistics (especially categorical data analysis), sociological theory (structuralism and pragmatism), and economic sociology.
Email: rainer.diazbone@unilu.ch Web: https://www.unilu.ch/fakultaeten/ksf/institute/soziologisches-seminar/mitarbeitende/rainer-diazbone/

Stine Thidemann Faber is Associate Professor of Sociology in the Department of Culture and Global Studies, Aalborg University, Denmark. Her main research interests are sociology of families, social inequalities, social categories, classification struggles, symbolic boundaries, and qualitative analysis.
Email: stf@cgs.aau.dk Web: http://vbn.aau.dk/da/persons/stine-thidemann-faber(80b7a894-3f71-446c-bf4b-c72985b50bd9).html

Magne Flemmen is a postdoctoral fellow in the Department of Sociology and Human Geography, University of Oslo, Norway. His research interests lie in the areas of class analysis, social stratification, and inequality. His work focuses on the theory and model of social space, as well as the cultural and political components of class divisions.
Email: magne.flemmen@sosgeo.uio.no Web: http://www.sv.uio.no/iss/english/people/aca/magneof/

Håkan Forsberg is Senior Lecturer in Sociology of Education in the Department of Education, Uppsala University, Sweden. His main research interest concerns social differentiation in relation to school choice, marketization of education, and migration.
Email: hakan.forsberg@edu.uu.se Web: https://katalog.uu.se/profile/?id=N10-501

Jürgen Friedrichs was Professor Emeritus at the Institute of Sociology and Social Psychology at the University of Cologne; he passed away at the age of 80 on February 19th, 2019. His main research interests were migrant integration, urban sociology, neighborhood effects, poverty areas, and gentrification.
Web: http://www.iss-wiso.uni-koeln.de/institut/personen/f/prof-em-dr-juergen-friedrichs/

Michael Gemperle is Lecturer at the Institute of Sociology, University of St. Gallen, Switzerland, and Senior Researcher at the Zurich University of Applied Sciences. His main research areas are sociology of work, sociology of education, and sociology of intellectuals.
Email: michael.gemperle@unisg.ch Web: https://www.alexandria.unisg.ch/persons/2348

Olaf Groh-Samberg is Professor of Sociology at the Research Center on Inequality and Social Policy, University of Bremen, Germany. He is also Dean of the Bremen International Graduate School of Social Sciences (BIGSSS) and DIW Research Professor at the DIW Berlin. His main research interests are social inequalities.
Email: ogs@bigsss-bremen.de Web: http://www.socium.uni-bremen.de/ueber-das-socium/mitglieder/olaf-groh-samberg/

Johs Hjellbrekke is Professor of Sociology at the University of Bergen and Director of the Norwegian University Center in Paris. His main research interests are social stratification, class analysis, social mobility, the sociology of elites, geometric data analysis, and statistical analysis of categorical data.
Email: Johs.Hjellbrekke@uib.no Web: https://www.uib.no/en/persons/Johs..Hjellbrekke

Vegard Jarness is a senior researcher at the NIFU – Nordic Institute for Studies in Innovation, Research and Education in Oslo, Norway. His research interests include social class, cultural stratification, political divisions, and education.
Email: vegard.jarness@nifu.no Web: https://www.nifu.no/en/employees/vegard-jarness/

Dominique Joye is Professor of Sociology at the Institute for Social Sciences, Faculty of Social and Political Sciences of the University of Lausanne, associated with the NCCR Lives "Overcoming Vulnerability: Life Course Perspective" and to FORS, the Swiss Center of Expertise for the Social Sciences. His main research interests are social inequalities as well as survey methodology.
Email: Dominique.joye@unil.ch Web: https://applicationspub.unil.ch/interpub/noauth/php/Un/UnPers.php?PerNum=8278&LanCode=37

Olav Korsnes is Professor Emeritus of Sociology at the University of Bergen, Norway. His main areas of research and publication are sociology of work and education, social mobility, social stratification, and elites.
Email: olav.korsnes@uib.no Web: https://www.uib.no/personer/Olav.Korsnes

Brigitte Le Roux is Maître de Conférences at the Laboratoire de Mathématiques Appliquées (MAP5), CRNS (the French National Center for Scientific Research) Université Paris Descartes and Associate Researcher at the Political Research Center of the Sciences Po, Paris (CEVIPOF/CNRS). She is an assistant director for the journal *Mathématiques & Sciences Humaines*, and she serves on the editorial board of the journal *Actes de la Recherche en Sciences Sociales*. She completed her doctoral dissertation with Jean-Paul Benzécri in 1970 at the Faculté des Sciences de Paris.
Email: Brigitte.LeRoux@mi.parisdescartes.fr Web: http://www.math-info.univ-paris5.fr/~lerb/

Frédéric Lebaron is Professor of Sociology at Ecole normale supérieure Paris-Saclay (member of University Paris-Saclay) and Researcher at Institutions et Dynamiques Historiques de l'Economie et de la Société, IDHES (CNRS). He specializes in economic sociology, political sociology, stratification and inequality, social science methodology, especially Bourdieu, and geometric data analysis.
Email: frederic.lebaron@uvsq.fr Web: http://lebaron-frederic.e-monsite.com/

Yannick Lemel is General Inspector of INSEE, and Senior Researcher at CREST, France. His main research interests are statistical modeling for social sciences, and studies of social inequalities related to socioeconomic status. Presently, he works on cultural activities in France, and on a comparative project about prestige in postindustrial societies.
Email: Yannick.Lemel@ensae.fr Web: https://www.gemass.fr/yannick-lemel?lang=fr

Ida Lidegran is Senior Lecturer in Sociology of Education at Uppsala University, Sweden. She is a member of the research unit Sociology of Education and Culture (SEC). Her research area covers domains such as educational strategies, elites and elite education, migrant studies, and applications of geometric data analysis.
Email: ida.lidegran@edu.uu.se Web: http://katalog.uu.se/empinfo/?id=N99-1570

Katharina Manderscheid is Professor of Sociology in the Department of Socioeconomics, University of Hamburg, Germany. Her current research focuses on spatial mobility and the future of the automobile, urban sociology, conduct of life, and

sustainability and social inequality. She also teaches qualitative and quantitative methods and is interested in the role of methods in the process of social research.
Email: Katharina.manderscheid@uni-hamburg.de Web: https://www.wiso.uni-hamburg.de/fachbereich-sozoek/professuren/manderscheid

Richard Münch is Senior Professor of Social Theory and Comparative Macrosociology at Zeppelin University Friedrichshafen and Emeritus of Excellence at Otto Friedrich University Bamberg. His main research interests are focused on societal change in the context of globalization and European integration, academic capitalism and the education-industrial complex in the field of education.
Email: richard.muench@uni-bamberg.de Web: https://www.uni-bamberg.de/en/soztheorie/staff/emeritus/

Martin Munk is Professor of Sociology in the Department of Political Science, Aalborg University, Denmark. He is a selected Visiting Fellow at The Max Planck Sciences Po Center on Coping with Instability in Market Societies (MaxPo) in the academic year 2018–2019. His research focuses on social stratification, educational choices, intergenerational mobility, social reproduction, labor markets, returns to different forms of capital, the transformation of societies and welfare states, statistical techniques, and population data.
Email: mdm@dps.aau.dk Web: http://personprofil.aau.dk/110005

Fionn Murtagh is Professor of Data Science, Department of Computer Science at the University of Huddersfield, England. He is Director of the Institute of Mathematics and Data Science, which is being established.
Email: fmurtagh@acm.org Web: http://www.multiresolutions.com/home/

Jérôme Pacouret is a PhD Candidate in sociology at Ecole des hautes études en sciences sociales (Centre européen de sociologie et de science politique). His research interests include copyright law, authorship, the global film industry, professional hierarchies, and transnational approaches.
Email: pacouret.jerome@gmail.com. Web: http://cse.ehess.fr/index.php?1446

Mikael Palme, born 1950, has recently retired from his position as associate professor in sociology of education in the Department of Education at Uppsala University, Sweden and is a member of the Swedish SEC research group (Sociology of Education and Culture). He has written on the social structure of the Swedish education system, on the impact of globalization on education and on families' educational strategies. He is one of the scholars who introduced Pierre Bourdieu's sociology in Scandinavia in the 1980s. Along with Francois Denord and Bertrand Réau he is the editor of *Researching Elites. Theory, Method, Analyses* (Springer, forthcoming).
Email: mikael.palme@edu.uu.se Web: http://katalog.uu.se/empinfo/?id=N8-1595

Myrtille Picaud is a postdoctoral fellow at the Centre Européen de Sociologie et de Science Politique, Paris Sciences et Lettres, France. Her main interests lie at the crossroads of urban, cultural, and political sociology, with a special emphasis on reflecting about data collection methods and analysis.
Email: myrtille.picaud@hotmail.fr Web: http://cessp.cnrs.fr/spip.php?rubrique322

Annick Prieur is Professor of Sociology at Aalborg University in Denmark. Her main interests are sociology of culture and studies of different dimensions of social differentiation as well as social marginalization and criminology.
E-mail ap@socsci.aau.dk Web: http://vbn.aau.dk/da/persons/pp_e0bae3f7-41ae-4717-9a0e-b3d0ea9661ca/publications.html

Nicolas Robette is a lecturer in sociology in ENSAE (Université Paris Saclay), researcher in CREST-LSQ, Palaiseau, France. His main interests are sociology of lifestyles and cultural tastes, and quantitative methods in social sciences.
Email: nicolas.robette@uvsq.fr. Web: http://nicolas.robette.free.fr/

Lennart Rosenlund (Dr. Philos.) is Professor Emeritus at the University of Stavanger (Institute of Media and Society). His overall research is centred on issues of social differentiation. He has engaged in community studies, sociology of culture, and issues within the methodology of the social sciences.
Email: lennart.rosenlund@uis.no Web: http://www.uis.no/article.php?articleID=103298&categoryID=11198

Olivier Roueff is a permanent researcher at CRESPPA-CSU (French National Centre for Scientific Research, Paris, France). His main research interests are the activities and struggles of intermediaries in art and politics (Europe, India), the social spaces of lifestyles in France and in India, and the exploration of qualitative and quantitative methods.
Email: o.roueff@free.fr Web: http://www.cresppa.cnrs.fr/csu/equipe/les-membres-du-csu/roueff-olivier

Gisèle Sapiro is Professor of Sociology at Ecole des hautes études en sciences sociales and Research Director at the CNRS (Centre européen de sociologie et de science politique). Her research interests include the sociology of culture, literature, intellectuals, translation and publishing, as well as the historical sociology and epistemology of the human and social sciences.
Email: sapiro@ehess.fr Web: http://cse.ehess.fr/index.php?585

Heinrich Schäfer is Professor of Sociology and Protestant Theology at Bielefeld University and member of the Center for the Interdisciplinary Research on Religion and Society (CIRRuS). His research interests are focused on the explorative analysis of qualitative data and the development of HabitusAnalysis, as well as sociology of religion and Latin American societies.
Email: heinrich.schaefer@uni-bielefeld.de Web: https://www.uni-bielefeld.de/theologie/forschung/religionsforschung/personen/schaefer.html

Christian Schmidt-Wellenburg is Assistant Professor at the Chair of Sociology, Faculty of Economic and Social Sciences, University of Potsdam, Germany. His main research interests are methodologies of field- and discourse-analysis, sociology of Europe, economic sociology, and sociology of knowledge.
Email: cschmidtw@uni-potsdam.de Web: https://www.uni-potsdam.de/de/allg-soziologie/team/schmidt-wellenburg.html

Andreas Schmitz is Assistant Professor in the Department of Sociology at the University of Bonn, Germany. His main research interests are relational social theory, relational methodology, applied statistics, and generalized field theory.
Email: andreas.schmitz@uni-bonn.de Web: https://www.politik-soziologie.uni-bonn.de/de/institut/lehrkoerper/blasius/mitarbeiter-1/andreas-schmitz

Leif-Hagen Seibert works as a postdoctoral researcher at the Center for the Interdisciplinary Research on Religion and Society (CIRRuS), Bielefeld University, Germany. His main research interests are religion and conflict, theories and methods of sociology of religion, and criticism of religion and ideology.
Email: leif.seibert@uni-bielefeld.de Web: http://www.uni-bielefeld.de/theologie/forschung/religionsforschung/personen/seibert.html

Adrian Tovar Simoncic is an independent sociologist and anthropologist and an external collaborator of CIRRuS, at the University of Bielefeld in Germany. His main research areas are sociology of religion, religious diversification in Latin America, late-modern individualism, as well as theory and method in HabitusAnalysis.
Email: atovar@uni-bielefeld.de

Jakob Skjøtt-Larsen is Associate Professor of Sociology in the Department of Sociology and Social Work, Aalborg University. His main research interests are social differentiation, social class and lifestyles, social class and political attitudes, correspondence analysis and related methods, and mixed methods.
Email: jsl@socsci.aau.dk Web: http://vbn.aau.dk/da/persons/jakob-skjoettlarsen(f3b7a428-f753-4bb9-b4d3-aa2733543db9).html

David Swartz, following retirement from full-time teaching, is now Visiting Researcher in the Department of Sociology at Boston University. He is also Senior Editor and Book Review Editor of *Theory and Society*. His most recent book is *Symbolic Power, Politics, and Intellectuals: The Political Sociology of Pierre Bourdieu* (University of Chicago Press, 2014). His research interests include social theory, education, culture, stratification, and political sociology.
Email: dswartz@bu.edu Web: http://people.bu.edu/dswartz/

Loïc Wacquant is Professor of Sociology at the University of California, Berkeley, and researcher at the Center for European Sociology, Paris. His interests include urban marginality, penality, carnality, and the politics of reason.
Email: loic@berkeley.edu Web: www.loicwacquant.net

Nora Waitkus is a doctoral researcher at the Research Center on Inequality and Social Policy at the University of Bremen, Germany. Her main research interests are class analysis, wealth inequality, and accumulation dynamics.
Email: waitkus@uni-bremen.de Web: http://www.socium.uni-bremen.de/about-the-socium/members/nora-waitkus/en/

Chapter 1
Investigations of Social Space: Introduction

Jörg Blasius, Frédéric Lebaron, Brigitte Le Roux, and Andreas Schmitz

Introduction

More than 15 years after his death, Pierre Bourdieu (1930–2002) is without question one of the leading social scientists of the twentieth century. Not only has his work been cited to an almost unparalleled degree; the principles guiding his research are increasingly employed across many disciplines within and outside the social sciences. However, even today, this comprehensive reception of Bourdieusian concepts, and the research carried out using them, suffers from a relative lack of attention to the methodological implications and foundations of his work. The aim of this book is to explicate the research principles and methodology of Bourdieusian sociology and to contribute to its continuing systematic elaboration.

For a great number of researchers from the social sciences and neighboring disciplines, Bourdieu is especially appreciated for his theoretical work, his critical stance, and his impassioned approach to practicing science. In his early Algerian studies, as well as in the *The Weight of the World* (Bourdieu 1999a), his intention was to ensure that the living worlds (and world views of the suffering population) were made visible by his research; ultimately, the goal was to contribute to improving their life conditions. Consequently, Bourdieu argued that sociological

J. Blasius (✉) · A. Schmitz
Institute for Political Science & Sociology, University of Bonn, Bonn, Germany
e-mail: jblasius@uni-bonn.de; andreas.schmitz@uni-bonn.de

F. Lebaron
Department of Social Sciences, Ecole normale supérieure Paris-Saclay, Cachan, France
e-mail: frederic.lebaron@ens-cachan.fr

B. Le Roux
University Paris Descartes, Paris, France
e-mail: Brigitte.LeRoux@mi.parisdescartes.fr

© Springer Nature Switzerland AG 2019
J. Blasius et al. (eds.), *Empirical Investigations of Social Space*,
Methodos Series 15, https://doi.org/10.1007/978-3-030-15387-8_1

analyses need to adequately grasp the actors' subjectivity (in order to escape the pitfalls of 'social physics') by way of participant *objectivation* (Bourdieu 2003).

As a matter of fact, objectivation is a core aspect of Bourdieu's sociology: In his concept of research, it is essential to break with one's everyday understanding of the actors (including scientific actors) in order to prevent a reproduction of one's everyday ideologies (Bourdieu 2006[2001]). This condition can be fulfilled by systematically objectifying the respective phenomena, thus revealing the relational system in which they manifest themselves. At this point, the concepts of social spaces and fields come into play: These key theoretical terms do not merely constitute analytical means of thinking; their usefulness only emerges in immediate interaction with empirical field work. Although he was opposed to rigid methodological fetishism, Bourdieu's empirical research was based on the *relational construction* of fields and spaces. This core facet of his methodology motivates a specific type of statistical data analysis: the construction of social spaces using the techniques from *L'Analyse des Données* (Benzécri et col. 1973; with respect to social spaces: Rouanet et al. 2000; Lebaron 2009), or Geometric Data Analysis (GDA) (Le Roux Rouanet 2004).

In *La Distinction* (1984[1979]), which is sometimes regarded as Bourdieu's most important work, he described the correspondence between professional fractions and lifestyle information based on statistical analyses of survey data. In his field-theoretical work *Homo Academicus* (1988[1984]), he undertook a formal construction of the Parisian academic field using multiple correspondence analysis (MCA), which is a major part of GDA. Finally, in one of his most recent articles – *Une Révolution Conservatrice dans L'Édition* (1999b), on the decline of French publishing culture – he combined MCA with clustering techniques.

This specific methodological program of quantification and formalization is the consequence of a critical reflection on the limitations of traditional quantitative techniques. Bourdieu's research practice of relating modern social theory with advanced statistical modeling would have been impossible without the contributions of Jean-Paul Benzécri, and his colleagues and followers, who provided Bourdieu with the tools necessary for the objectivation of social spaces and fields.

In this introductory chapter, we will first outline the principles of Bourdieusian reasoning. We will then discuss the methodological implications of his paradigm with a particular emphasis on the concept of relation. Finally, we give a short overview of the contributions to this edited volume.

Fundaments of Bourdieusian Sociology

Bourdieu's research is characterized by a consistently relational view: With his dictum "the real is relational" (Bourdieu 1998: 15), he put relations as constituents of (social) reality – in the foreground. Thus, (human) entities or (interpersonal) structures, which are traditionally at the forefront of sociological thinking, have a secondary analytical value compared to the relational constitution of the (social) reality:

> I must, at every stage, make sure that the object I have given myself is not enmeshed in a network of relations that assign its most distinctive properties (Bourdieu and Wacquant 1992: 228).

From an epistemological point of view, Bourdieu emphasized a relational mode of object construction; that is, a process of identifying and modeling similarities and differences between entities and their characteristics. This fundamental epistemological concept of difference and similarity is addressed by the concepts of "social spaces" and "social fields", which are defined as the totality of mutually external positions.

> The notion of space contains, in itself, the principle of a relational understanding of the social world. It affirms that every "reality" it designates resides in the *mutual exteriority* of its composite elements (Bourdieu 1998: 31).

This stance characterizes Bourdieu's conception of the social: His theoretical concept of social spaces (that is, his conception of society itself) and social fields (as an expression of differentiated social spheres) are the basis of his research program. Social spaces and fields are characterized by their endogenous structuration – structures of congruity and oppositions that are conceptualized as specific capital dimensions and class (or group) relations. Social spaces and fields also have specific meanings, orientations, and rules, which are expressed by concepts such as *illusio*, *nomos*, and *doxa*.

Bourdieu's concept of action is that of practice, thus emphasizing the practical meaning of everyday action. This model of practice challenges both structuralist notions of automatic compliance with rules and the idea of autonomous action (cp. Lamaison 1986). An essential feature of Bourdieu's paradigm is to analytically and practically transcend both the traditional structure-practice dichotomy and the distinction between the macro and the micro level.

The concept of habitus illustrates this relational and integrative position: Habitus means a bundle of patterns of perception, evaluation, and action (dispositions) which can be analytically located within a space or field (or position). In the context of the social space, Bourdieu constructed class habitus relationally; for instance, the habitus of the middle classes is constructed in contrast to those of both the upper and the lower classes. He further focused on the interrelations between male and female habitus and on the intersections of classes and gender (as well as, among other things, ethnicity). Likewise, he described social fields in the context of 'ideal-type' forms of habitus and their interrelations: For example, in the context of the academic field, he compares the habitus of (more autonomous) scientists to that of (more heteronomous) research managers (Bourdieu 1988[1984]).

Based on their acquired habitus, actors exhibit particular practices in their responses to current environmental conditions. Their habitus are oriented to certain social fields and result in practices that fulfil the requirements of these fields. However, it is possible for incompatibilities between habitus and social fields or social spaces to become a new basis for social practice: Within social fields and spaces, actors and groups of actors (classes) engage in conflicts (and co-operation) over goods and objects of interest, as well as for definitional sovereignty over rules and values. At the same time, social fields and social spaces are also characterized by the fact that actors install themselves in material and meaningful niches, acknowledging (and, under certain circumstances, misunderstanding) their own position in the social space. This (sociological) view of social conflicts is based to a considerable degree on mechanisms of cognitive theory: The objective structural conditions of social spaces and social fields are incorporated into the perceptual structures of the actors, so that the actors perceive the social world through them and reproduce them in their practice. Bourdieu summarized these phenomena as relations of symbolic power between actors.

These basic concepts and their relational architecture guide the Bourdieusian approach to conducting research.

Methodology

The fundamental principle of Bourdieu's empirical work follows the same 'logic of relation' that was previously noted as being central to Bourdieu's stances on social theory. First, relationality manifests itself in terms of an epistemology in the tradition of Karl Mannheim and Gaston Bachelard; the social position of the researchers, as well as their position in the disciplinary field, is understood to also be a genuine factor in their own position-takings, and thus in the production of scientific goods itself.

Second, this relational logic also manifests itself in the form of a particular closeness between theoretical and empirical work, that is, their reciprocal combination. In fact, the common differentiation between theory and empirical work is replaced by an integrated understanding of scientific research.

Third, the process of object construction is based on a relational logic: Social fields and social spaces are empirically constructed, beginning with the collection of the data and continuing until their analysis (Le Roux and Rouanet 2004; Blasius and Schmitz 2014; Lebaron 2018; Lebaron and Le Roux 2015). With respect to the practice of research, the logic of relation – and the relational concepts (such as fields, habitus, or practice) derived from it – served Bourdieu as (implicit) hypotheses for the control of observation and questioning. In this process, the theoretical concepts introduced above play a crucial role in selecting the most important aspects from the infinite variety of social reality. An empirical investigation requires 'feature carriers' (statistical units such as humans or institutions) in order to describe with regard to their objective and subjective features – features that are not simply observed or measured, but rather identified in relation to each other. Thereby, the collection of suitable data is characterized by a process of recursive, mutual categorization of actors (or institutions). Even in his early field work in Algeria, Bourdieu's approach can be characterized by its inclusion of the relational collection and coding of various types of data, in order to identify relations and representations of social structures (Blasius and Schmitz 2014).

Fourth, in doing so, data types and data collection comprise both 'quantitative' and 'qualitative' connotations. In fact, Bourdieu was an early proponent of mixed methods and triangulation.

Fifth, one of Bourdieu's goals in the objectification of any particular phenomenon was to apply an 'epistemic rupture', i.e., a break with the perceptions and dispositions of the investigated actors to whom the relational analysis is being applied, but also a break with the researcher's own views and presuppositions. Despite the relevance Bourdieu ascribed to qualitative data, such objectification requires "statistical analysis", which "is the only means of manifesting the structure of the social space" (Bourdieu 1985: 725). Even in his early Algerian studies, he was already analyzing complex data; in this case he used punch cards, which he marked in order to map simultaneously occurring or mutually exclusive characteristics, thus enabling the visualization of contrasting and equivalent relations (Bourdieu 1990: 8). His main problem was the evaluation of more than a small number of oppositions within each analysis. Although Bourdieu applied several graphical visualization techniques and different statistical approaches, he could not find a satisfactory representation of dimensionally structured relations, as embedded in his theoretical concept. Being deeply convinced that the world is multi-dimensional, he rejected all forms of linear approach, such as ordinary regression models: These methods usually have the goal of explaining a dependent variable over a series of independent variables, and were thus methodical approaches that did not match the methodological principles of his theory. Consequently, his research was quite unlike the usual practice of statistical modelling: Instead of constraining the data with strong assumptions such as linearity between variables (and between categories), he focused on the relational structure of the data by using geometric modeling (construction and interpretation of geometric maps).

In the same period of the 1960s, Benzécri started his work on *L'Analyse des Données*, focusing especially on simple and multiple correspondence analysis (CA, MCA) (Benzécri et col. 1973); his underlying idea was that a "model should follow the data and not vice versa" (cp. Blasius and Greenacre 2006: 6). CA and MCA differ from traditional statistics, which involve significance tests, normality assumptions, and attempts to fit the data to a previously specified model. CA and MCA identify the structure of data without fitting the data to a statistical model; this was the non-linear technique Bourdieu was searching for:

> If I make extensive use of correspondence analysis, in preference to multivariate regression for instance, it is because correspondence analysis is a relational technique of data analysis whose philosophy corresponds exactly to what, in my view, the reality of the social world is. It is a technique which "thinks" in terms of relation, as I try to do precisely with the notion of field (Bourdieu and Wacquant 1992: 96).

From the geometric point of view, as is typical for the French tradition in the GDA framework, any data set is conceptualized as clouds of points, and thus a social space that relates these points and these clouds to each other. Although CA and

MCA interpretations are usually based on maps (social spaces), and (geometric) distances within these maps, the underlying geometric model provides a numerical solution that can be interpreted much like the well-known principal component analysis (PCA). In fact, MCA can be understood as PCA applied to qualitative data. From the mid-1970s to the present day, Bourdieu and his adherents have used CA and MCA to empirically objectify the relational conception of the social – both methods transform data into (two-dimensional) maps (for a differentiation between these two methods in the Bourdieusian framework, see Blasius and Schmitz 2014). The formally constructed social space allows social scientists to interpret non-linear relations between indicators (for example lifestyle indicators), between individuals (for example academics Bourdieu 1988[1984] or economists (Lebaron 2008) or between groups of individuals (or example groups of class fractions (Bourdieu 1984[1979]).

A core difference between relational methodology and individualist methodology is that the former does not assume theoretical and statistical independence of the analyzed entities. Even advanced 'causal' approaches, such as fixed and random-effect regression models, assume the independence of entities, reducing causality to the 'averaged internal mechanisms' of artificially separated individuals. As a consequence, individualistic perspectives fail to reveal causality between agents; that is, relational causality (cp. Schmitz 2016). CA and MCA, in contrast, 'rehabilitate' the individual and its interdependencies within the world of statistical modeling as entities, and their relational positions become genuine objects of analyses.

Bourdieu used CA in *Anatomie du Goût* (Bourdieu and De Saint-Martin 1976) as well as in *La Distinction* (Bourdieu 1984[1979]). The aim of these publications was to develop an integrative vision of the French social space with a particular emphasis on the dominant classes. With increasing computational power and new possibilities for analyzing complex data (Benzécri 2006), Bourdieu later primarily applied MCA, e.g. in *La Patronat* (Bourdieu and De Saint-Martin 1978) and in *Homo Academicus* (Bourdieu 1988[1984]), but he was also interested in extending the set of methodical tools within the framework of GDA (cp. Rouanet et al. 2002).

In sum, Bourdieu's work resulted in a powerful sociological research program that provides social sciences with comprehensive insights, while preserving the impulse to develop it further. All attempts to do so should keep in mind its paradigmatic core: methodological relationality.

Following Lebaron (2011: 87ff.), a modern relational research program based on a Bourdieusian perspective aims to: (1) Reveal the structure of a social field and/or of a specific social space. Here, descriptive procedures should always come first, while an inference procedure should follow as a 'natural' extension of descriptive conclusions (Rouanet and Le Roux 2010: Chapter 5). (2) Show possible structural homologies between different social fields and/or social spaces, such as the (varying) positional homology between producers and consumers of cultural goods. (3) Determine the relative autonomy of social fields and/or social spaces. Bourdieu put a particular emphasis on the relations between social fields, where the first step of the analysis is to consider the embedding of the social fields within the field of power (Bourdieu and Wacquant 1992; Schmitz et al. 2017). (4) Study subspaces within a global social space. For example, a social class can diverge from an overall capital structure, and is structured by the composition of different forms of capital, for example, cultural and economic capital (Bourdieu 1984), as well as by the weighted sum of capitals, i.e., the capital volume (for the relation between the forms of capital, capital volume, and the composition of capitals within a (two-dimensional) social space, see Blasius and Friedrichs 2008). (5) Explain social practices such as position-takings. A good example is the necessity for objectifying the scientific subject within Bourdieusian sociology. Even seemingly scientific statements can be (partially) traced back to objective positions within both the social space and the scientific field. (6) Assess the importance of various effects, especially field effects. This includes the effects social fields may have on the habitus of *their* individuals, as well as effects on individuals of different social fields. (7) Study the dynamics of social fields: Bourdieu's concepts genuinely involve historicity and change. Issues of dynamics can be found in many of his empirical investigations: for example, the transformation of Algerian society, reforms in the French educational sector, trajectories of classes, and changes in the dominant capital forms.

These aims are realizable with the application of the techniques and concepts of GDA, which have been available since sociologists first began to construct social spaces. New theoretical considerations motivate the further developments of statistical techniques – for example, specific MCA (Le Roux and Rouanet 2004, 2010) and class-specific MCA (Le Roux and Rouanet 2004, 2010).

Contributions of the Authors

The book is organized in three parts. Part one deals with the social space and its construction, part two is devoted to social fields as sub-segments of the social space, and part three addresses methodological and methodical questions.

Social Spaces

The first section of the book is devoted to the construction and analysis of social spaces; that is, entire societies, thus treating societal core issues such as class relations and capital distributions.

The first section starts with *Loïc Wacquant's* contribution, which argues that the triad of 'habitus, capital, and field' can be replaced by the dyad of 'social space and symbolic power'. This shift from a triad to a dyad of analytical core concepts illuminates the inner logic of Bourdieu's concepts, and also serves to re-orient observers towards the ways the symbolic is woven into comprehensive societal power relations. Following Bourdieu's work on the *grandes écoles, Ida Lidegran, Mikael Börjesson, Donald Broady & Ylva Bergström* analyze the field of elite education in Sweden by revealing the structural interplay of study orientations, educational capital, and gender of upper secondary school pupils in Uppsala. The third paper, written by *Johs. Hjellbrekke & Olav Korsnes,* applies MCA and class-specific MCA to survey data in order to analyze structural homologies within the Norwegian field of power. *Jörg Blasius & Jürgen Friedrichs* show how lifestyle items, as originally formulated by Bourdieu in *La Distinction*, and reformulated to apply to contemporary German culture, can be used to differentiate old and new inhabitants of a neighborhood of Cologne. Using data from a dwelling panel, the authors show how lifestyle patterns can change over time in the process of gentrification. *Nora Waitkus & Olaf Groh-Samberg* analyze capital portfolios and accumulation strategies in Germany using latent class analysis. Based on disaggregated measures, they construct a 'space of capital' and analyze class mobility over time. The paper by *Stine Thidemann Faber, Annick Prieur, Lennart Rosenlund & Jakob Skjøtt-Larsen* discusses, using as an example class structure in contemporary Denmark, five ways to apprehend classes: as structures of distribution, as forms of the habitus, as symbolic boundaries, as symbolic structures of domination, and as consciousness or identity. *Nicolas Robette & Olivier Roueff* discuss cultural domains and class structure by assessing homologies and cultural legitimacy. The authors test several hypotheses related to the social differentiation of lifestyles, and examine whether a structural homology exists between the entirety of social and cultural spaces. Starting from the observation that, today, reproduction strategies are no longer limited to national boundaries, but rather operate across borders, *Martin Munk* focuses on the intergenerational reproduction of transnational and national cultural capital, and shows how educational reproduction and mobility occur within the global space of university institutions. The concluding paper of section A, by *Magne Flemmen, Vegard Jarness & Lennart Rosenlund*, investigates class, lifestyles and politics. Referring to Bourdieu's homology thesis, in their empirical analyses the authors reveal structural similarities in both the space of lifestyles and the space of political stances.

Social Fields

Section B comprises the conceptualization of societal spheres within the social space, the social fields with relative autonomy. Social fields such as the academic field, the cultural field, the economic field, and the field of the labor market will be discussed in detail.

The section starts with a contribution from *David Swartz* on the use of Bourdieu's field concept in English-speaking literature. The contribution illustrates the extensive and widespread use of the concept of field and its appurtenant analytical concepts in current English-speaking social sciences. *Richard Münch* gives a comprehensive summary of his research on academic capitalism, utilizing Bourdieu's conceptualization of the scientific field and the transformations it has undergone in the last decades. *Christian Schmidt-Wellenburg* shows how internationalization affects the position-takings of German-speaking economists on crisis issues by reconstructing the field of economists, its historical changes, and the economists' involvement in academic, political, and professional practices. Applying and differentiating Bourdieu's concept of cultural capital, *Myrtille Picaud, Jérôme Pacouret & Gisèle Sapiro* construct a social space of the public of a literary festival using MCA, thus gaining insights into the structured interplay of the literary market and the corresponding audiences. *Håkan Forsberg, Mikael Palme & Mikael Börjesson* discuss education as both field and market, using as an example upper secondary schools in Stockholm. According to their findings, the educational market created in upper secondary education through state intervention resulted in a large expansion of the supply of education in terms of schools and study programs. *Michael Gemperle* analyzes work orientations using the example of nursing, applying the concept and methodology of the social space paradigm. Using specific MCA, he analyzes how the work orientations of nurses correspond to their position within the occupational group's social space. *Tobias Dalberg* analyses the dynamics of inequality in the field of Swedish human scientists by comparing two cross-sections: human scientists who held a position at Swedish universities and university colleges in 1945 and in 1965. *Christian Baier & Andreas Schmitz* conclude the section by proposing a Bourdieusian approach to institutional fields, using the example of German universities. Applying Multiple Factor Analysis, they show how this institutional field changed from 1995 to 2012 in reaction to heteronomous intrusions.

Methodology and Methods

Section C focuses on methods within the Bourdieusian framework, and includes both quantitative and qualitative contributions. A particular focus is placed on further developments of GDA, such as analyzing temporal and process data, and analyzing (sub-) classes within the social space.

The section starts with a paper written by *Brigitte Le Roux & Frédérik Cassor* studying changes over time, using GDA methods (MCA and clustering) applied to the French *Barometer of Political Trust*. Using different techniques within the GDA framework, they demonstrate the advantages of visualizing dynamic structures. Building on a Bourdieusian approach to the social, *Fionn Murtagh* focuses on the geometry and topology of data and information in the analysis of processes and behaviors using three examples: the challenges and opportunities presented by big data analysis, the narrative analysis of sentiments, and the sphere of mental health and depression. Using the European judicial field as an example, *Frédéric Lebaron & Philippe Bonnet* discuss class-specific MCA, a further development within the framework of GDA that allows scientists to analyze the spatial structure of sub-groups within an overall social space. *Rainer Diaz-Bone & Katharina Manderscheid* reflect on how to establish correspondence analysis in sociology in German-speaking universities. They argue that for German university researchers who adopt a Bourdieusian sociology, GDA should be a standard procedure; however, this is not yet the case. Comparing the social and cultural spaces of France, Norway, and Switzerland, *Dominique Joye, Gunn Elisabeth Birkelund & Yannick Lemel* compare approaches to nominal, ordinal, and metric data within the GDA framework, and declare themselves in favor of canonical correlation as a general analytical approach. The final paper, written by *Heinrich Schäfer, Leif-Hagen Seibert & Adrian Tovar Simoncic*, proposes a qualitative methodology derived from Bourdieu, consisting of a conceptualization of the habitus as an analytical third layer of 'socioanalysis', and as a promising complement for the statistical construction of social spaces and fields using GDA.

References

Benzécri, J. P. (2006). L'analyse des données: Histoire, bilan, projects, …, perspective. In memoriam: Pierre Bourdieu. *Revue MODULAD, 35*, 1–5.

Benzécri, J. P. et col. (1973). L'analyse des données. In *L'analyse des correspondances*. Paris: Dunod.

Blasius, J., & Friedrichs, J. (2008). Lifestyles in distressed neighborhoods. A test of Bourdieu's "taste of necessity" hypothesis. *Poetics, 36*, 24–44.

Blasius, J., & Greenacre, M. (2006). Multiple correspondence analysis and related methods in practice. In M. Greenacre & J. Blasius (Eds.), *Multiple correspondence analysis and related methods* (pp. 3–40). Boca Raton: Chapman & Hall.

Blasius, J., & Schmitz, A. (2014). Empirical construction of Bourdieu's social space. In J. Blasius & M. Greenacre (Eds.), *Visualization and verbalization of data* (pp. 205–222). Boca Raton: Chapman & Hall.

Bourdieu, P. (1984[1979]). *La Distinction*. Paris: Les éditions de Minuit. (*Distinction. A Social Critique of the Judgement of Taste*. 1984. Cambridge, MA: Harvard University Press.)

Bourdieu, P. (1985). The social space and the genesis of groups. *Theory and Society, 14*, 723–744.

Bourdieu, P. (1988[1984]). *Homo Academicus*. Paris: Les éditions de Minuit (*Homo Academicus*, 1988, Stanford: Stanford University Press).

Bourdieu, P. (1990). *The logic of practice*. Stanford: Stanford University Press.

Bourdieu, P. (1998). *Practical reason: On the theory of action*. Stanford: Stanford University Press.

Bourdieu, P. (1999a). *The weight of the world*. Cambridge: Polity.

Bourdieu, P. (1999b). Une Révolution Conservatrice dans L'Édition. *Actes de la recherche en sciences sociales, 126-127*, 39–59.

Bourdieu, P. (2003). Participant objectivation. *Journal of the Royal Anthropological Institute, 9*(2), 281–294.

Bourdieu, P. (2006[2001]). *Science de la science et réflexivité*. Paris: Raisons d'agir Éditions. (*Science of Science and Reflexivity*. Cambridge: Polity Press).

Bourdieu, P., & Saint-Martin, M. (1976). Anatomie du goût. *Actes de la Recherche en Sciences Sociales, 5*, 1–110.

Bourdieu, P., & Saint-Martin, M. (1978). La patronat. *Actes de la Recherche en Sciences Sociales, 20–21*, 3–82.

Bourdieu, P., & Wacquant, L. J. (1992). *An invitation to reflexive sociology*. Chicago: University of Chicago Press.

Lamaison, P. (1986). From rules to strategies: An interview with Pierre Bourdieu. *Cultural Anthropology, 1*(1), 110–120.

Le Roux, B., & Rouanet, H. (2004). *Geometric data analysis: From correspondence analysis to structured data analysis*. Dordrecht: Springer.

Le Roux, B., & Rouanet, H. (2010). *Multiple correspondence analysis*. London: Sage.

Lebaron, F. (2008). Central bankers in the contemporary global field of power: A 'social space' approach. *The Sociological Review, 56*(1_suppl), 121–144.

Lebaron, F. (2009). How Bourdieu "quantified" Bourdieu: The geometric modelling of data. In K. Robson, C. Sanders, & C. (Eds.), *Quantifying theory: Pierre Bourdieu* (pp. 11–29). Milton Keynes: Springer.

Lebaron, F. (2011). Geometric data analysis in an social science research program: The case of Bourdieu's sociology. In M. G. Summa, L. Bottou, B. Goldfarb, F. Murtagh, C. Pardoux, & M. Touati (Eds.), *Statistical learning and data science* (pp. 77–89). Boca Raton: CRC Press.

Lebaron, F. (2018). Pierre Bourdieu, geometric data analysis and the analysis of economic spaces and fields. In *Forum for social economics* 47, 288–304.

Lebaron, F., & Le Roux, B. (2015). *La méthodologie de Pierre Bourdieu en action*. Paris: Dunod.

Rouanet, H., & Le Roux, B. (2010). *Multiple correspondence analysis* (Vol. 163). Thousand Oaks: Sage.

Rouanet, H., Ackermann, W., & Le Roux, B. (2000). The geometric analysis of questionnaires: The lesson of Bourdieu's La distinction. *Bulletin of Sociological Methodology/Bulletin de Méthodologie Sociologique, 65*(1), 5–18.

Rouanet, H., Lebaron, F., Le Hay, V., Ackermann, W., & Le Roux, B. (2002). Régression et analyse géométrique des données: réflexions et suggestions. Mathématiques et sciences humaines. *Mathematics and Social Sciences, 40*(160), 13–45.

Schmitz, A. (2016). *The structure of digital partner choice: A Bourdieusian perspective*. Cham: Springer.

Schmitz, A., Witte, D., & Gengnagel, V. (2017). Pluralizing field analysis: Toward a relational understanding of the field of power. *Social Science Information, 56*(1), 49–73.

Part I
Construction of the Social Space

Chapter 2
Bourdieu's Dyad: On the Primacy of Social Space and Symbolic Power

Loïc Wacquant

Introduction

Despite longstanding, intense, and recurring clarifications there are still countless misinterpretations when it comes to the basic principles of Bourdieusian sociology.

By some, Bourdieu is seen as the 'reproduction theorist', whereas his first three books were about the cataclysmic transformation of a colonial society at war; Bourdieu purportedly 'ignores agency', whereas the very purpose of habitus is to repatriate the inventive agent at the heart of social analysis; some contend that Bourdieu 'didn't theorize the linkages between fields' whereas one of his most distinctive concepts, the field of power, is designed especially for that; others allege Bourdieu is 'blind to ethnicity', whereas he wrote extensively on cultural gradations of (dis)honor, and his regional origins and years in Algeria gave him an innate sense of ethnicity in French society, and so on. The problem gets compounded when it comes to interpretations that are specific to national contexts: The Turkish Bourdieu is not the Brazilian Bourdieu is not the Norwegian Bourdieu, or the French Bourdieu for that matter. Each country has evolved its own selective version suited to the structure and history of its intellectual field (according to principles delineated by Bourdieu in his discussion of "The Social Conditions of the International Circulation of Ideas," (Bourdieu 1999[1990])).

Now, there are many ways to introduce, spotlight, or encapsulate Bourdieu's sociology, but by far the most common and popular one in the major European languages (French, German, English, and Spanish) is to refer to the conceptual triad 'habitus-capital-field'. Countless articles, primers, and theoretical discussions of the

L. Wacquant (✉)
University of California, Berkley Researcher, Berkeley, CA, USA

Centre de Sociologie européenne, Paris, France
e-mail: loic@berkeley.edu

© Springer Nature Switzerland AG 2019
J. Blasius et al. (eds.), *Empirical Investigations of Social Space*,
Methodos Series 15, https://doi.org/10.1007/978-3-030-15387-8_2

French sociologist take it as axiomatic that these three notions adequately sum up his framework and capture its originality.

In this chapter, I use and further develop an earlier work of mine (esp. Wacquant and Akçaoğlu 2017) to argue that this characterization is flawed for three reasons: The triad is *redundant, incomplete, and misleading*. It obscures the analytic primacy of social space over the concept of the field and the correlative limitations of the term 'field' to a specific (and empirically rare) subset of social universes (see also Swartz in this volume). Further, it muddies the specificity of the concept of field as a monopolistic cosmos, thus leading to the uncontrolled multiplication of fields, emptying the notion of any rigorous meaning. Finally, this approach effaces Bourdieu's most original and potent concept, that of symbolic power. By contrast, I will contend that the dyad *social space and symbolic power* captures the two pillars at the foundation of his sociology.

Bourdieu's 'Three Rs'

Bourdieu's reasoning can be characterized by the 'three Rs': a rationalist epistemology, a relational ontology, and a reflexive methodology that continually questions itself in the very movement in which it is employed (cp. Wacquant and Akçaoğlu 2017). This relational and reflexive reasoning is especially threatening to scholars who have *rigid mental structures* and construe social inquiry as the pre-reflective application of mechanical formulas prescribed by an all-encompassing theoretical creed – and on this front, the last Marxists vie hard with the surviving Parsonians.

Bourdieu's mentor in the philosophy of science. Gaston Bachelard (1949), teaches us that scientific knowledge emerges not by filling a void but by breaking with "spontaneous knowledge" that is already there, and it is no different when it comes to classical works of sociology as they travel across borders. His notion of epistemological vigilance prompts us to establish the source of our problems, to pose our own questions, to forge robust analytic constructs instead of borrowing the soft and pliable notions of common sense (including scholarly common sense), to methodically question our methods, and to adopt a proactive stance when it comes to data production. The first commandment that every sociologist should live by is to *never accept a prefabricated object* (cp. Wacquant 2018: 5f).

When Bourdieu's concepts and analytic principles are the foundation for actual research operations, they can help us to articulate new questions and depict the empirical landscape in new ways, as does Tom Medvetz' (2012) in his model inquiry into the rise of *Think Tanks in America*. Medvetz goes beyond the limitations of studies of the elite and of policy-making to grasp the intrinsic ambiguity of this organizational animal and to diagnose its opaque role in the US field of power.

The most widely employed simplification is the conceptual triad of "habitus-capital-field." This triad offers at best an incoherent and incomplete condensation of Bourdieu's thought.

However, I contend here that this conceptual triad of habitus, capital, and field represents at best an incomplete and uncoordinated encapsulation of Bourdieu's philosophy: Capital and field are mutually redundant, since a field is simply the space where capital is concentrated. Habitus, conversely, is the embodiment of capital and can also be understood as the somatization of cognitive and cathectic categories, that is, as the imprinting of symbolic power onto the socially structured organism (cp. Wacquant 2016).

If you carry out the semantic equivalent of 'smallest space analysis' à la Guttman (1968) and Lingoes (1965) on Bourdieu's framework, you find that the dyad or the duet of *social space and symbolic power* suffices to regenerate all the other concepts he uses and thence to capture all manners of phenomena. Their articulation constitutes the most parsimonious and irreducible conceptual core of his theory of practice.

Social Space as a Core Category

The concept of 'social space' is the generic concept from which logically derives the *specific concept of field*, as a specialized social space arising when a domain of action and authority becomes sufficiently demarcated, autonomized, and monopolized. Realizing that social space (and not field) is the general construct that "faces" the concepts of habitus and capital to generate practice clears up recurrent difficulties and dissolves myriad false problems (cp. Wacquant and Akçaoğlu 2017). First, we are reminded that fields are relatively *rare historical phenomena* that exist only in certain realms of activity, and only in advanced social formations that have undergone sufficient differentiation – it is with good reason that Bourdieu so frequently invokes the Durkheimian concept of *differentiated societies*, instead of modern, capitalist, or postindustrial societies. Craig Calhoun (1993) spotlighted the narrow historicity of fields in his astute contribution to *Bourdieu: Critical Perspectives*, but he saw it as an unresolved tension in the theory of practice, rather than as a misspecification of the relationship between field and social space. For example, Bourdieu does not use the term 'field' when revisiting his youthful fieldwork in *Le Sens pratique* (*The Logic of Practice*, published in 1980 (1990)): There were no fields in colonial Kabylia because forms of capital had not been disentangled and sorted out into distinctive institutional tracks. This was no mere oversight, coming as it did a full decade after he produced his first robust elaboration of field with article on the "Structure and Genesis of the Religious Field" (1971[1991]), which provides a template for all the other fields.

The vast majority of social action unfolds in social spaces that are just that: social spaces, multidimensional distributions of socially efficient properties (capitals) which stipulate a set of patterned positions from which one can intelligibly predict strategies. However, they are not fields because they have no institutionalized boundaries, no barriers to entry, and no specialists in the elaboration of a distinctive source of authority and sociodicy. This definition allows us to avoid the comical multiplication of fields and forms of capital *ad infinitum* – hardly a month goes by without some scholar proposing a new species! Thus there is no "sexual field" (pace Illouz 2012; Green 2013) and no "racial field" (sorry for Matt Desmond and Mustafa Emirbayer 2015) for the simple reason that neither sex nor race as denegated ethnicity are monopolized by a nexus of distinct institutions and agents who elaborate them for consumption by others, (as a form of denegated ethnicity) are monopolized by a nexus of distinct institutions and agents whose role it is to reify these objects for the consumption by others (as, for example, priests do for the laity or politicians for voters). These objects' sociological importance emanates from the very fact that they cut across microcosms and pattern social space at large through the formation of habitus: They are principles of social vision and division that have *not been corralled into fields*. More broadly, the promotion of social space as anchor category is coterminous with Bourdieu's reformulation of question of group-making after Distinction (which he considered crude and obsolete on this front) that drops the presumption of the existence of classes to pave the way for a radically historicist ontology of social collectives (cf. Wacquant 2013).

Part of the confusion around the relationship of field and social space was sown by Bourdieu himself in two ways. First, between 1968 and 1977, he developed the narrower notion of field, before he hit upon and fully elaborated the broader category of social space which began to supersede it, beginning in 1975, and through the 1980s and beyond.

Given that Bourdieu honed all his concepts for the purposes of specific empirical inquiries for each new research project, this is unsurprising; his analyses were never intended as part of some grandiose Parsonian meta-vision with a preconceived set of analytic categories. Second, Bourdieu had to encounter, learn, and adapt Jean-Paul Benzécri's techniques of multiple correspondence analysis to operationalize the notion of social space and thence machine it conceptually. Lebaron and Leroux (2015) show this in *La Méthodologie de Pierre Bourdieu en action*. Third, Bourdieu is often quite sloppy in his own use of the two terms, even after elaborating the concept of social space: He sometimes talks of a social field, or of the family as a field, and of various settings that mix plain social space with the intersection of multiple fields as fields, which they are not. *Stricto sensu, Stricto censu*, one can argue also that the field of power, so-called, is really not a field (it is not the locus of concentration and distribution of a distinctive species of capital, it does not have a specific *nomos*, and it does not secrete a set of distinctive cognitive constructs, etc.) but a *meta-field* as a multilayered kind of social space.

Symbolic Power as a Core Category

Just as the concept of social space, the concept of symbolic power is epicentral and truly original to Bourdieusian sociology. It addresses the capacity for *consequential categorization*, the ability to make the world -to preserve or change it- by fashioning and diffusing symbolic frames, collective instruments of cognitive construction of reality. It is more capacious, multifaceted, ramifying, and powerful than habitus, capital, and field put together and squared. It anchors the triad of *cognition-recognition-misrecognition* that captures Bourdieu's view of the social agent as a "symbolic animal," to use the language of Ernst Cassirer, who is the major inspiration behind Bourdieu's thinking on this front (here, the key book to ponder is Cassirer's majestic *An Essay on Man: An Introduction to a Philosophy of Human Culture* [1944]), but an embodied and embedded agent who exists first and last in the eyes of others, via a recursive "game of mirrors" in which social fictions becomes reality insofar as they rest on shared categories and common beliefs that ground consonant action.

Symbolic capital also captures Bourdieu's notion that power is never so efficient (and dangerous) as when it disguises itself, and gets paradoxically activated by the subordinate, so that it proceeds via a cognitive relationship of assent opaque to itself obviating the expenditure of material suasion. Symbolic violence is that effortless force that molds the world via communication without us even noticing it; it tricks dominant and dominated alike, as in *Masculine domination* (Bourdieu 2001 [1998]).

Symbolic power is a concept that Bourdieu elaborates over the full spectrum of his scientific life, from his youthful investigations into honor in Kabylia and kinship in Béarn, to his works on art, education, and social suffering, to his later forays into politics and eventual return to science itself. It is expressed most compactly in the sociological pragmatics of *Language and Symbolic Power* (Bourdieu 1982) and in *Pascalian Meditations* (Bourdieu 2000[1997]).

A striking illustration of symbolic power is found in Bourdieu's lecture course *On the State* (Bourdieu 2014[2012]). Pivoting toward the state was necessitated by Bourdieu's intensifying focus on symbolic power during the decade of the 198s, which logically pushed him to confront the grand 'symbolic alchemist' of the modern era. You can detect that, for instance, in the historical chapter on the linguistic unification of France at the behest of political authorities that opens *Ce que parler veut dire* (Bourdieu 1982), which demonstrates that "the production and reproduction of legitimate language" operates in tandem with the building of the central state, first by the absolutist royalty and later by the republican bourgeoisie, whose power relies increasingly on the transmission of state-validated cultural capital, that is, educational credentials. In his lecture course *On the State*, Bourdieu offers an analytic dissection of state theories (something he did for no other topic), a bold reinterpretation of the historical transition from "the house of the king" to the "reason of state," and a novel model of the state as organizing power anchored by the concept of bureaucratic field and the notion of the 'monopolization of legitimate symbolic violence'. And he correlates the forging of the modern Leviathan, based on the bureaucratic mode of reproduction, with the coining of the public sphere, the simultaneous advance and private appropriation of the universal, and the rise of cultural capital. In doing so, the state emerges as being at once the product, the site, the target, and the referee of struggles to make reality: the 'paramount symbolic power', the 'supreme fetish', and the 'warrant of all fetishes'.

Conclusion

In this contribution, it has been shown that the triad of habitus, capital, and field can be fruitfully replaced by the duet of social space and symbolic power. This shift from the triad to the duet not only clears up common mistakes but also sheds light on the inner logic of Bourdieu's project, and can help us extend it further. Social space and symbolic power are crucial concepts for what Bourdieu called *socioanalysis* (cp. Bourdieu and Wacquant 1989, Wacquant 1990): a perspective that unveils the social unconscious, lodged in bodies and institutions, which governs us all. and which thus fosters the 'return of the repressed'. This is most visible in *The Weight of the World* (1999[1993]), and in Bourdieu's dissection of the three social microcosms that shaped him: the village society of Béarn in which he grew up, in *The Ball of Bachelors* (2006[2002]); the academic system through which he rose, in *Homo Academicus* (1988[1984]); and the philosophical institution from which he broke, in *The Political Ontology of Martin Heidegger* (1994[1988]), which is a manner of an exorcism of the philosopher he could have become.

References

Bachelard, G. (1949). *Le rationalisme appliqué*. Paris: Presses Universitaires de France.

Bourdieu, P. (1982). *Ce que parler veut dire. L'économie des échanges linguistiques*. Paris: Fayard (modified and expanded tr. *Language and Symbolic Power*. Cambridge: Harvard University Press, 1991).

Bourdieu, P. (1988[1984]). *Homo Academicus*. Cambridge: Polity Press.

Bourdieu, P. (1989). Social space and symbolic power. *Sociological Theory, 7*(1), 14–25.

Bourdieu, P. (1990[1980]). *The logic of practice*. Cambridge: Polity Press.

Bourdieu, P. (1991a). *The craft of sociology*. New York: Walter De Gruyter.

Bourdieu, P. (1991b). Genesis and structure of the religious field. *Comparative Social Research, 13*, 1–44.

Bourdieu, P. (1994[1988]). *The political ontology of Martin Heidegger*. Cambridge: Polity Press.

Bourdieu, P. (1999[1990]). The social conditions of the international circulation of ideas. In R. Shusterman (Ed.), Bourdieu: A critical reader (pp. 220–228). Oxford: Basil Blackwell.

Bourdieu, P. (2000[1997]). *Pascalian meditations*. Cambridge: Polity Press.

Bourdieu, P. (2001[1998]). *Masculine domination*. Cambridge: Polity Press.

Bourdieu, P. (2006[2002]). *The ball of bachelors*. Cambridge: Polity Press.

Bourdieu, P. (2014[2012]). *On the state*. Cambridge: Polity Press.

Bourdieu, P., & Wacquant, L. J. D. (1989). For a socioanalysis of intellectuals: On Homo Academicus. *Berkeley Journal of Sociology, 34*, 1–29.

Bourdieu, P., & Wacquant, L. J. D. (1992). *An invitation to reflexive sociology*. Chicago/Cambridge: University of Chicago Press/Polity Press.

Bourdieu, P., et al. (1999[1993]). *The weight of the world: Social suffering in contemporary society*. Cambridge: Polity Press.

Calhoun, C. (1993). Habitus, field, and capital: The question of historical specificity. In C. Calhoun, E. LiPuma, & M. Postone (Eds.), *Bourdieu: Critical perspectives* (pp. 61–88). Chicago: University of Chicago Press.

Cassirer, E. (1944). *An essay on man: An introduction to a philosophy of human culture*. New Haven: Yale University Press.

Desmond, M., & Emirbayer, M. (2015). *The racial order*. Chicago: University of Chicago Press.

Green, I. A. (2013). *Sexual fields: Toward a sociology of collective sexual life*. Chicago: University of Chicago Press.

Guttman, L. A. (1968). A general nonmetric technique for finding the smallest coordinate space for a configuration of points. *Psychometrika, 33*(4), 469–506.

Illouz, E. (2012). *Why love hurts: A sociological explanation*. Cambridge: Polity Press.

Lebaron, F., & LeRoux, B. (Eds.). (2015). *La Méthodologie de Pierre Bourdieu en action. Espace culturel, espace social et analyse des données*. Paris: Dunod.

Lingoes, J. C. (1965). An IBM 7090 program for Guttman-Lingoes smallest space analysis. *Behavioral Science, 10*, 183–184.

Medvetz, T. (2012). *Think tanks in America*. Chicago: University of Chicago Press.

Wacquant, L. J. D. (1987). Symbolic violence and the making of the French agriculturalist: An enquiry into Pierre Bourdieu's sociology. *Journal of Sociology, 23*(1), 65–88.

Wacquant, L. J. D. (1990). Sociology as socioanalysis: Tales of homo Academicus. *Sociological Forum, 5*(4), 677–689.

Wacquant, L. J. D. (2013). Symbolic power and group-making: On Pierre Bourdieu's reframing of class. *Journal of Classical Sociology, 13*(2), 274–291.

Wacquant, L. J. D. (2016). A concise genealogy and anatomy of habitus. *The Sociological Review, 64*(1), 64–72.

Wacquant, L. J. D. (2018). Four transversal principles for putting Bourdieu to work. *Anthropological Theory, 18*(1), 3–17.

Wacquant, L. J. D., & Akçaoğlu, A. (2017). Practice and symbolic power in Bourdieu: The view from Berkeley. *Journal of Classical Sociology, 17*(1), 55–69.

Chapter 3
High-Octane Educational Capital: The Space of Study Orientations of Upper Secondary School Pupils in Uppsala

Ida Lidegran, Mikael Börjesson, Donald Broady, and Ylva Bergström

Introduction – Elite Education and Educational Capital in Sweden

> – My sister has studied here, my mother also and some of my relatives are alumni. And it felt like it is very close to home. ... The school is like distanced from the city. So it has a very good location. And, then, I know that they have very good teachers. (Female pupil, the natural science programme at Lundellska skolan, Uppsala)

By international comparison, the Swedish educational system is more egalitarian than most. On upper secondary level there are hardly any equivalents to the *grands lycées* in France, or renowned public schools in England or liberal arts colleges in the US (Börjesson et al. 2016a; Börjesson and Broady 2016; Maxwell and Aggleton 2016; van Zanten 2016). No study fees are allowed, neither at private nor at municipality schools. All upper secondary programmes are 3 years long and up until 2011, all of them had given general eligibility for higher studies. The admission to tertiary studies is centralised, not entrusted to individual universities, and what counts is school grades from upper secondary schools, alternatively scores obtained at the Swedish Scholastic Aptitude Test.

Electronic supplementary material The online version of this chapter (https://doi.org/10.1007/978-3-030-15387-8_3) contains supplementary material, which is available to authorized users.

I. Lidegran (✉) · M. Börjesson · Y. Bergström
Department of Education, Uppsala universitet, Uppsala, Sweden
e-mail: ida.lidegran@edu.uu.se; mikael.borjesson@edu.uu.se; ylva.bergstrom@edu.uu.se

D. Broady
Department of Sociology, Uppsala universitet, Uppsala, Sweden
e-mail: donald.broady@soc.uu.se

© Springer Nature Switzerland AG 2019
J. Blasius et al. (eds.), *Empirical Investigations of Social Space*,
Methodos Series 15, https://doi.org/10.1007/978-3-030-15387-8_3

Nevertheless, though not always acknowledged as such, there exists an elite education space within the Swedish system – both in the sense that it hosts a large portion of the offspring of current elites and in the sense of being a site for the formation of future elites (Börjesson et al. 2016a). The interview quote above expresses the attractive forces that such schools and programmes exert upon privileged or high-aiming families.

In relation to educational capital the interviewed girl is positioned at the summit of three different hierarchies. Firstly, she is enrolled in the natural science programme, which in the Swedish system functions as the 'royal road' in the original literal sense, a road reserved for the privileged, and also in sense more common today, a path leading to elevated social positions (Broady et al. 2009). Secondly, she has been selected to one of Uppsala's top secondary schools (Lidegran 2009; Bertilsson 2014). Finally, among all Swedish regions, Uppsala (Lund is not far behind) exhibits the highest concentration of educational capital, hosting the oldest university in the Nordic countries, founded in 1477, a large university hospital with its corps of medical doctors, the national direction of the Church, many authors and intellectuals, knowledge-intensive high tech firms, especially in the bio-sciences, etcetera (Lidegran 2009).

The case of Uppsala, with its exceptional concentration of cultural capital, offers certain opportunities to research how educational capital is produced, reproduced, distributed and legitimised, and its contribution to the production, reproduction, distribution and legitimation of other assets, be it economic or symbolic assets – what is often for short, and a bit too narrow, termed as 'social reproduction'. In this chapter, we focus on the relation between two of the hierarchies mentioned, the programme structure and the school hierarchy. Our empirical basis is a survey of upper secondary pupils in Uppsala.

Objective and Questions

The general objective of this study is to contribute to the understanding of the structure – especially the polarities and hierarchies – of elite education in Sweden (see also Forsberg et al. in this volume). Our main source of inspiration has been the research on French *grandes écoles* undertaken in the 1980s by Pierre Bourdieu, Monique de Saint Martin and their collaborators (Bourdieu and de Saint Martin 1987; Bourdieu 1989), though, of course, we choose our data and methods to avoid the presumption that the same structure – i.e. the clear-cut opposition 'economic capital versus cultural capital' – should necessarily be found in Sweden. Our main questions are the following:

- How are the study orientations of upper secondary pupils in Uppsala structured? To be more precise: What is the structure of the space defined by the distribution of indicators of the pupils' educational capital in its embodied state, namely indicators of their study practices and attitudes towards teaching, teachers, grades, subjects, and the attended school and programme?

- How is this structure related to inherited (primarily from the parental home) educational capital and to gender?
- How is this structure related to the pupils' own acquired objectivised and institutionalised educational capital, such as being enrolled in prestigious programmes or schools?

Background

The Swedish Space of Secondary Education and Its Elite Subspace

In the profound transformations of the Swedish school system during the last three decades the turning point was the beginning of the 1990s when marketisation and privatisation were introduced (Lindensjö and Lundgren 2000). The deregulation and especially the extremely far-reaching voucher system favoured independent schools, many of them for-profit and today owned by venture capitalists (Forsberg 2015).

However, our previous and on-going studies have revealed a remarkably stable over-all social structure of the upper secondary school after, and also before, the introductions of market mechanisms and in spite of numerous subsequent reforms aiming at 'democratisation' – recently a new grading system, a new programme structure and a new curriculum. In the run of the decades we have observed the same two main dimensions of this educational space, a first gender division, and a second social hierarchical one (Broady and Palme 1989; Palme 2008; Bertilsson 2014; Forsberg 2015; Börjesson et al. 2016a). The space displays a triangular shape. At the base, there are the vocational programmes predominantly populated by children of the working class; the daughters chose programmes in health and caring and the sons in construction and industry. The upper middle and upper class children, and especially those from culturally rich fractions (as opposed to the economically affluent), are concentrated in the natural science programme at the apex of the triangle. This domain could, roughly, be regarded as an elite education subspace. The middle classes fall in between. The most important change during the last decades – in Sweden as in many other countries (cf. Baudelot and Establet 1992) – has been the influx of female students into the most prestigious programmes, but the gendered and social structure shows no signs of fundamental change or even reforms. In the national perspective the natural science programme's position is unthreatened.

Uppsala – A City with a High Density of Educational Capital

The study was conducted in the old university city of Uppsala. Here, unlike almost everywhere else in Sweden, the cultural or educational elites are able to dominate the economic elite. The university defines the city to a considerable extent, and the space of secondary schools is also heavily influenced by the presence of the university.

(Lidegran 2009) For a study on the content and dimensions of educational capital, Uppsala is a privileged site, where it is most likely to find educational capital in its most condensed and refined form.

Upper Secondary Schools in Uppsala

Uppsala differs significantly from the adjacent Stockholm, 40 min away by train, with its much clearer dominance of economic capital over cultural. In Stockholm, you also find a very large independent and privately owned school sector (Forsberg 2015). In Uppsala, such schools have been and still are of marginal importance. All six secondary schools included in our study are public and municipal schools. However, there are major differences between them.

Katedralskolan, a previous grammar school, claims to have been funded in 1246, well over 200 years before the university. It is located in a building from the 1800s in the central academic part of Uppsala. The programmes preparing pupils for higher education dominate the offer and include, besides the natural science and the social science programmes, also the international baccalaureate (IB). At Katedralskolan, the pupils may choose additional courses in music, such as choir singing, and in mathematics, in collaboration with Uppsala University. A trademark of the school is the language orientation of the programmes. Both the natural science and the social science programme offer optional German, French and Spanish profiles.

Lundellska skolan, Uppsala's other, though much younger (founded in 1892), previous grammar school resides in a modern building located outside of the city centre in a secluded, close to nature environment. Lundellska skolan is also dominated by programmes preparing for further studies. All pupils are offered laptops and the school also distinguishes itself by the fact that all teachers are certificated and all teaching is teacher-led. Besides the natural science programme, Lundellska skolan offers an economic orientation of the social science programme, which Katedralskolan does not have, and buzz words such as 'entrepreneurship' and 'business' are emphasised at the website.

Fyrisskolan, *Linnéskolan* and *Bolandsskolan* are more recent schools, offering a variety of programmes, especially vocational programmes in the case of Bolandsskolan. Fyrisskolan is the only school offering the technology programme, and its social science programme has a computer orientation profile. Linnéskolan and Bolandsskolan are the only two schools included in our study without natural science programme.

Finally, *Rosendalsgymnasiet* is the youngest. The school started in 2005 and is located close to the Uppsala University's Science Park Campus. It exclusively offers programmes preparing for higher education. In the marketing, the school promises close contacts with the universities, and it states that some teachers are half-time employed at the university. Thus Rosendalsgymnasiet acts as modern-day challenger of the two hitherto dominating grammar schools. The fact that there are no vocational programmes at Rosendalsgymnasiet might be an advantage in the competition for pupils from well-to-do homes and with outstanding educational merits.

Research Approach

When performing this kind of research, a rule of thumb is to construct a space *without* using data on the species of assets that seem most interesting in as much as that they promise to be good explanation candidates, in our case for example social origin and gender, factors that might be expected to explain major differences among pupils' lifestyles, orientations, and trajectories through the educational system. For this article, we have tried to catch the structure of the space by using indicators on the students' perception of and orientation towards their studies. Thereafter, once this structure is established, we project (as so called supplementary categories, which do not affect the structure) information on, for example, the parents' educational level, the gender of the pupils, and their school credentials and choice of school and programme.

Some basic research in this vein was conducted at the Centre de sociologie européenne in Paris, starting with the famous study by Pierre Bourdieu and Monique de Saint Martin (1976, also presented in Bourdieu 1979a) on 'the anatomy of taste.' Here, indicators of tastes and lifestyles were used to grasp the structure of the space of social groups in France, before information on occupations, salaries, educational level etcetera were projected into this space.

Educational Capital

We have (inspired by for example Bourdieu 1979b, see also Serre and Wagner 2015) found it useful to consider the different 'states' of capital (Börjesson et al. 2016b). (Bourdieu focused on cultural capital, but we prefer to talk about educational capital since it is not obvious that education and culture are as intertwined in the Swedish society as they are in the French.) As a chemical compound might exist in different states – a solid, a liquid and a gaseous one, for example H_2O as ice, fluid water or vapour –, a capital such as the educational might also be (1) embodied into people's minds and capacities, (2) institutionalised in, for example, the educational organisations, and (3) objectified in grades or exams.

The embodied state implies the ability to master the educational system, know how to navigate among different options of programmes and schools, subjects and fields of study, but also to be able to study efficiently and most importantly to perform at tests and examinations. The embodied state can also include attitudes, perceptions and values – more subjective sides of educational capital. Second, the objectified state is to some extent conflated with the institutional state and consists mainly of both grades and results of tests and examinations and of degrees and diplomas. All these are granted by educational institutions.

A further distinction can be made between inherited and acquired educational capital (Lidegran 2009). The first is commonly measured by the highest level of education of the parents, but it also implies the whole educational trajectories of the parents, siblings, the grandparents, and the wider family. Occasionally, the municipal educational administration is called by parents who are furious because their offspring have not been admitted to the school at which three generations of family have studied. Acquired capital is educational merits, grades, scores and diploma, tied to the individual. Since the educational system has merit-based selection, there is no direct transfer of educational capital, which is possible for economic capital. The offspring have to acquire the necessary merits themselves to enter the desired programmes and schools.

In our study, we will predominantly relate the embodied state of educational capital, especially its subjective and 'soft' dimensions in the form of orientations and perceptions, to indicators of educational capital in the objective state, including both acquired (such as grades, degrees and schools), and inherited, implying the highest level of the parents' education.

Educational Spaces

In Bourdieu and collaborators' studies on education and culture, there was a shift from an initial focus on correlations between students' educational trajectories and their social origin and gender, and the use of basic descriptive statistics (cf. Bourdieu and Passeron 1964), towards more fine-tuned studies of educational fields of institutions on the basis of questioners and statistical data analysed by different versions of correspondence analysis (Bourdieu and de Saint-Martin 1987; Bourdieu 1989). These latter studies have educational fields or spaces as the main research object, comprising the relations between educational institutions and educational programmes.

Specific Multiple Correspondence Analysis

The technique used for analysing the questionnaire is specific multiple correspondence analysis (specific MCA), which is appurtenant to the family of geometric data analysis (GDA) (Le Roux and Rouanet 2004, 2010). This technique allows us to sort out the most important differences in the data material, and it presents the relations between the categories and individuals in a multidimensional geometric space. This is apparently in line with the theoretical framework of Bourdieu's and his collaborators' spatial understanding of social spaces and fields (Lebaron and Le Roux 2015).

When applying this technique, we separated three different types of variables and categories. First, the active variables and categories used to establish the structure of the space, namely variables concerning the embodied state of educational capital including study practices and orientations towards teaching, teachers, grades, subjects and the attended school and programme were active. Second, the supplementary variables were projected into the space once constructed. As supplementary variables we used gender and indicators of educational capital in its objective state – both acquired (grades, study programmes and schools) and inherited (parents' highest educational level). Third, specific MCA gave us the possibility to handle no-answers as passive categories (Le Roux and Rouanet 2004: 237). This implies that the variable is active, but not all its categories.

Construction of a Space of Educational Orientations of Upper Secondary School Pupils in Uppsala

A questionnaire with 52 questions covering current and earlier studies, social origin, practices and attitudes in various areas was answered by 589 pupils in upper secondary schools in Uppsala in the period from 2007 to 2008. Four upper secondary programmes preparing for further studies (the natural science programme, the social science programme, the specially designed programme and the technology programme) at six different schools in Uppsala (Bolandsskolan, Fyrisskolan, Katedralskolan, Linnéskolan, Lundellska skolan and Rosendalsgymnasiet) were included in the study (for the study design see Bergström 2015).

Variables and Categories

The questions were grouped in four themes or headings, fairly balanced in the numbers of categories. Questions related to the perception of the **School and Programme** include four variables (in total 11 active categories) relating to their rationales for choosing the programme (degree of preparation for university studies and interesting subjects) and their perception of the school attended (quality of the teachers and the reputation of the school). Attitudes towards **Teachers/Teaching** form the second heading containing 5 questions including 15 categories. With regard to teaching, two questions measured the importance of taking in large text materials in short time and of training public speeches. For teachers, three variables are used: a friendly relation to the pupils, making simple test and the ability to uphold discipline in the class room. Attitudes towards **Grades and Study practices** constitute the third heading, which includes five variables and 16 categories: two relating to grades (in defence of viz. opposing grading) and three concerning the studies (that the studies are demanding, the number of hours spent on homework during the weekend, and the number of hours spent of preparing for tests). The fourth heading, finally, assembles questions on **Subjects**, more precisely the perceived level of difficulty of mathematics, science, Swedish and English (4 questions, 12 categories). In total, 18 variables and 54 categories are active in the construction of the space (see Table 3.1 in the Online Appendix).

A Space with Three Dimensions

The result of the specific MCA, the space of educational orientations of upper secondary school pupils in Uppsala, is presented below. We have interpreted the first three axes given by the specific MCA.

By analysing the decrease of the variance of the axes, we can see that the first axis is clearly the more important one and well separated from the second axis (0.144 >> 0.113), which in turn is separated from the third axis (0.102). The third axis is visibly separated from the fourth axis (0.086). After the fourth, there are small decreases of variances. Moreover, the modified rate (Le Roux and Rouanet 2010: 39) for the first axis is 0.39, for the second axis 0.19, and for the third axis 0.13. The cumulated modified rate of the first three axes sums up to 70%, thus indicating the importance of those axes (see Table 3.2 and Fig. 3.9 in Online Appendix).

The first step in the analysis of the space is to study the contribution of the headings to the variance of the first three axes (see Table 3.3 in Online Appendix). To the first and also the most important axis, the heading 'Programme and school' (36%) contributes the most, followed by 'Grades and studies' (29%) and 'Teachers and teaching' (27%). The heading 'Subjects' primarily orients along the second axis (63%), followed by 'Grades and studies' (27%). For the third axis, the heading 'Teachers and teaching' and 'Grades and studies' has the largest contribution (40 and 39%). Studying the different headings, it becomes clear that the contribution of 'Programme and school' is concentrated to the first axis, 'Subjects' to the second, 'Teachers and teaching' to the first and the third, and 'Grades and studies' to all three.

In the next step, we interpret the axes one by one. In order to do so we select all the categories with contributions to the current axis exceeding the average contribution (1/54 = 1.85%).

Axis 1: A General Axis of Educational Commitment

The interpretation of axis 1 is based on 23 categories that contribute over average (see Fig. 3.1 below and Table 3.4 in the Online Appendix). These categories account for 82% of the variance of the axis. As indicated by Table 3.3 in the Online Appendix, all headings but 'Subjects' contribute to the first axis. The opposition can be summarised as a cleavage between positive versus negative or indifferent attitudes towards the school, the programme, teachers, teaching, grades and studies. In short, it expresses a dimension of belief in and orientation towards education, or a general commitment to the value of educational capital. At the positive pole (left in Fig. 3.1), the opinions that the programme prepares for university studies and that the school has a good reputation go together with the statement that the school has good teachers, positive attitudes towards grades, and that it is important to learn to master large text materials, to train oral presentation and that teachers uphold

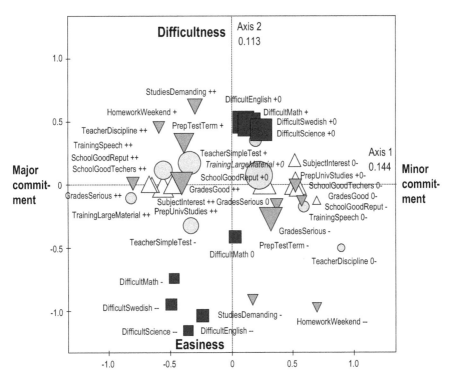

Fig. 3.1 The space of educational orientations of upper secondary school pupils in Uppsala Axes 1 and 2. Contributing categories

discipline in the classroom. This is also paired with investments in studies in the form of many hours spent on homework during the weekends and on preparing for tests. At the opposite pole (right in Fig. 3.1) negative or indifferent attitudes towards these themes are found expressing a lack of commitment to conquer educational capital. For instance, one is less inclined to have chosen the programme for its ability to prepare for further studies and one does not adhere to the idea that the school has a good reputation. Time-investments in the studies are sparse. A sceptical stance towards grades is expressed.

Axis 2: Subjects and Studies: 'Easiness' Versus 'Difficultness'

Fourteen categories are used for the interpretation of the second axis, which sum up to 86% of the variance of the axis. The second axis is primarily related to 'Subjects' (the four variables on subject account for 63% of the contribution to the axis) and to some extent to 'Grades and studies' (see Fig. 3.1 above and Table 3.3 in the Online Appendix). It contains an opposition between a pole of 'easiness' and a pole of 'difficultness'. At the first dimension (bottom of Fig. 3.1), shows Swedish, English, mathematics and science as easy subjects (or at least not difficult). In addition, little time invested in the studies is distinctive. The latter pole is characterised by holding the mentioned subjects difficult or very difficult. This is combined with spending a lot of time on homework during the weekend and preparing for tests (top of Fig. 3.1). Since the time invested in the studies is clearly of lesser importance than the level of difficulty of the subjects and since the time aspect in addition is more important for the orientation of the third axis, we choose to give priority to the difficult/easy-dimension when summarizing the second axis.

Axis 3: Studies and Teaching: Large versus Minor Investments

The interpretation of the third axis is based on 21 categories that contribute over average, accounting for 84% of the variance to the axis. This axis is primarily oriented by the variables under the headings 'Grades and studies' and 'Teachers and teaching' (see Table 3.3 in Online Appendix). More precisely, it is a focus on the studies and the teachers. Time invested in the studies and the perception of the demand on study efforts account for 32% of the contribution to the axis. To some extent, it is a correction to the first two axes and especially the second one. The axis associates on the one hand strong investments in the studies (many hours spent on homework during the weekends and preparing for test) with a positive stance towards teachers and teaching (important to train public speech and a good teacher upholds discipline in the class), but it also stresses that the teacher should not be a buddy or offer too simple tests (bottom in Fig. 3.2), and on the other hand less clear investments in the studies (less hours spent on homework during the weekends and preparing for tests) are paired with stressing the importance to train public speech and that point that the teacher upholds the discipline in the class, is friendly and offers simple tests (top in Fig. 3.2). Given the overall importance of time spent on studies, we have chosen to summarize the axis as an axis of investments in the studies.

A summary: The first axis represents juxtaposition between very positive attitudes towards education, teaching, teachers and studies and indifferent or negative attitudes. The second axis separates a pole of 'easiness' and a pole of 'difficultness' with regard to the most important subjects. The third axis separates important from modest investments in the studies.

The individuals are well-dispersed in the space (see Figs. 3.10 and 3.11 in the Online Appendix). In the plane of axes 1 and 2, there is a larger concentration of individuals in the upper right quadrant, where the most negative or least positive stances combined with regarding the main subjects as difficult are found. The individuals are more dispersed in the other quadrants, where more positive attitudes are located (the two quadrants to the left), and where the less frequent categories of

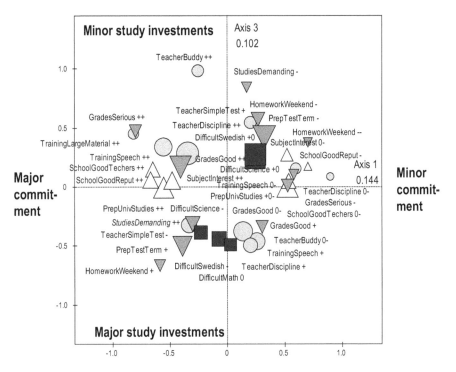

Fig. 3.2 The space of educational orientations of upper secondary school pupils in Uppsala Axes 1 and 3. Contributing categories

investing very little time in the studies are positioned (the lower right). A similar pattern of concentration is visible in the plane of axes 1 and 3, with a higher concentration of individuals in the lower right quadrant than in the other quadrants, which contains more rare categories than the first one.

Inherited and Acquired Educational Capitals and Gender

So far, we have only dealt with the active variables, i.e. those used in the construction of the space. The technique of supplementary variables enables us to explore how the space of educational orientations of upper secondary school pupils in Uppsala is related to their other properties. First, we notice differences between male and female pupils. Then, we will analyse the inherited aspects of educational capital (here measured by parents' highest level of education and to some extent by their occupation). Finally, we introspect the acquired educational capital indicated by the grades and the attended programmes and schools.

A Gendered Space

The deviation between boys and girls is negligible on axis 1, but noticeable on axes 2 and 3 (see Figs. 3.12 and 3.13 and Table 3.5 in the Online Appendix). Along the second axis, male pupils are oriented towards the pole of 'easiness', and the female pupils towards the pole of 'difficultness'. Also along the third axis, girls are oriented towards the pole of heavy investments in studies, downwards, while boys are drawn more to the pole of more modest investments, upwards. This general gender pattern is in line with national surveys of the pupils' opinions where girls are more engaged in the school work, more oriented towards further studies, but also more stressed over grades and their performance (Skolverket 2010).

Inherited Educational Capital – Differences among the Male and Female Pupils

There is a minor correspondence between the space and the parents' highest educational level, but not as important as one could have expected given the in general close relationship between parents and their offspring when it comes to educational investments (see for instance van Zanten 2015, for a study discussing more pedagogical and softer aspect of education in relation to school choices). However, the weak result is to some extent dependent on the noticeable gender differences among the pupils. Thus, a division of the educational level by gender has been used (see Figs. 3.3 and 3.4 below and Table 3.5 in the Online Appendix). The educational level of the parents of the female pupils is compared to male pupils more hierarchically organised in the space, going from a low level in the upper right quadrant to a high level to the left. For the female pupils, the level of education of the parents is thus more clearly aligned with their own orientation towards education. Also in the plane of axes 1 and 3, the educational level of the parents of female pupils is more 'logically' dispersed, where the educational level rises as we move downwards to the lower left quadrant mainly defined by a high level of investments in the studies. For the male pupils, all educational levels of the parents are concentrated in the upper right quadrant, associated with small investments in the studies, and form no linear pattern (Figs. 3.6 and 3.7).

Schools and Study Programmes Structuring the Space

In the final step of the analysis, the schools, the study programmes and the combination of study programmes and schools will be examined. These variables represent an acquired educational capital in its objectified and institutionalised state of importance for the accumulation of further educational capital such as diplomas

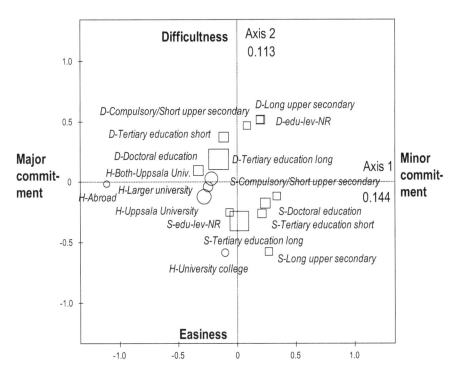

Fig. 3.3 The space of educational orientations of upper secondary school pupils in Uppsala Axes 1 and 2. Parents highest level of education as supplementary variables for all pupils (H−); Divided by gender: Sons (S−), Daughters (D−). Symbol proportional to size

and degrees in higher education. To start with programmes and schools separately (see Figs. 3.5 and 3.6 below and Table 3.6 in the Online Appendix), a fundamental cleavage between the two major programmes, the natural science programme and the social science programme, appears with the former along the first axis positioned at the side of a strong orientation towards and investments in education, and the latter at the pole of less commitment to education. Furthermore, the natural science programme is drawn to the region of the space where we find an overrepresentation of pupils who don't find the subjects difficult, in the lower left quadrant in the plane of axes 1 and 2, while the social science programme appears in the upper right quadrant, where the subjects are found difficult. Also along the third axis, the natural science programme is oriented towards the pole of larger time investments in the studies, while the social science programme is associated with lesser investments. Thus in all three dimensions, the natural science programme expresses the most clearly educational capital-oriented position, whether it comes to commitment (axis 1), easiness (axis 2) or investments (axis 3).

The two other programmes, the technology programme and the international baccalaureate programme, are very much smaller and take different positions in the space. With regard to the first axis, the IB-programme is found in the most

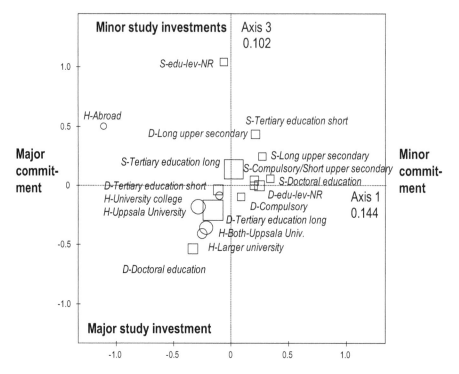

Fig. 3.4 The space of educational orientations of upper secondary school pupils in Uppsala Axes 1 and 3. Parents highest level of education as supplementary variables for all pupils (H−); Divided by gender: Sons (S−), Daughters (D−). Symbol proportional to size

extreme position to the left, expressing a very large commitment to education, clearly exceeding also the position of the natural science programme, while the technology programme is positioned at the opposite, less educationally oriented pole, in a similar position as the social science programme. In the plane of axes 1 and 2 they form an orthogonal axis to the natural science programme and social science programme, with the technology programme at the position of small time investments in the studies (male dominated) and the IB-programme at the pole of large time investments (female dominated).

The positions of the schools are largely defined by their programme structure. The two schools that do not offer the natural science programme, Bolandsskolan and Linnéskolan, are the only ones distinctively positioned at the right, dominated side along axis 1. The four other schools, all offering the natural science programme, are either in the middle (Fyrisskolan and Rosendalsgymnasiet) or, in the case of the most traditional and prestigious schools, Lundellska skolan and Katedralskolan, more leaning towards the dominant pole, to the left. Along the second axis, a differentiation appears between the two schools offering the two programmes most clearly distinguished by the second axis, Fyrisskolan with the technology programme at the bottom, 'easiness' and male dominated position, opposed by

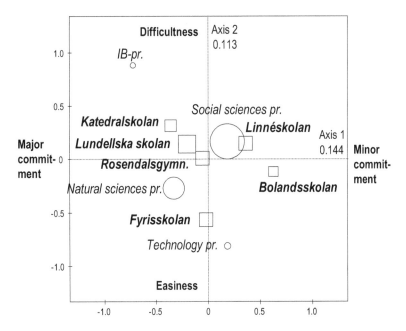

Fig. 3.5 The space of educational orientations of upper secondary school pupils in Uppsala Axes 1 and 2. Schools (Quadrant) and programme (circle) as supplementary variables. Symbol proportional to size

Katedralskolan, giving the IB-programme, and in addition having a very strong language profile in general, in the upper left quadrant defined large investments in the school work and an overrepresentation of female pupils. In the plane of axes 1 and 3, Katedralskolan once again upholds the most extreme position in direction of the most dominant pole (large investments), downwards, while along the first axis, Bolandsskolan and Linnéskolan, take the opposite, less dominant position (small investments in the studies).

In order to further elaborate on the relation between study programme and school, and to better understand the differentiation mechanisms in upper secondary schools, we have used the precise information of the programme and its orientation and divided the programmes by school (Figs. 3.7 and 3.8 and Table 3.6 in the Online Appendix).

First, the natural science programme takes the most extreme position along the first axis, oriented towards the dominant educational capital pole for three out of four schools offering the programme, implying that the social science programme is often oriented towards the least dominant pole. Second, the dispersion of the programmes between the schools differs. For Rosendalsgymnasiet and Katedralskolan there are large differences between the programmes in the plane of axes 1 and 2, while Bolandsskolan, Lundellska skolan and Fyrisskolan show smaller differences.

Switching the perspective from the schools to the programmes, it is obvious that the programmes have similar properties. All natural science programmes are close to each other in the space, in the lower left quadrant of both the plane of axes 1 and 2 and the plane of axes 1 and 3. It is further interesting to notice that they are also differentiated internally according to school. The natural science programme is divided by a female pole consisting of the Lundellska skolan and Katedralskolan and a male pole defined by Rosendalsgymnasiet and Fyrisskolan. A similar differentiation is found within the social science programmes. The gendered profile of the schools is manifested in that the generally female dominated social science programme at the male dominated Fyrisskolan has a computer orientation and is positioned at a more male oriented position in the space than the natural science programme at the female oriented Katedralskolan, which also has a language orientation of its natural science programme.

Conclusions

In research on the social space or social fields, the concept educational capital is often reduced to a one-dimensional variable separating social groups with different highest levels of education. Educational capital sometimes serves merely as an indicator of possessions of cultural capital and seldom attracts the attention that it is worth. This chapter presents a more differentiated approach.

Our starting point was the construction of the space of orientations that upper secondary school pupils (n = 589) in Uppsala express towards their studies. This old university town distinguishes itself by an extraordinarily high concentration of educational and cultural capital, which offers opportunities to grasp these species of capital in a rather 'pure' form. To put it in more sociological terms: this is a community were educational capital is extremely crucial for the social reproduction of dominant groups.

The space was defined by the pupils' answers to questions on their study practices and their positive or negative attitudes towards teaching, teachers, grades, subjects, and the attended school and programme. The outcome of the specific multiple correspondence analysis was the following: The first axis (the most important opposition in the space) represented a division between positive and negative attitudes towards their schooling and their teachers. It might be called a school commitment axis. The second axis opposed the statements that the studies are 'easy' and that they are 'difficult'. The third axis stretched between the pupils' declarations of investing much and little time into the studies.

This constructed space represents the *embodied* state of educational capital, as inscribed in the pupils' minds, perceptions and habits, and played out in their study practices, as reported by the pupils themselves.

In the next step we introduced numerous supplementary variables, i.e. variables that do not alter the already constructed structure of the space, but are positioned in it according to their distribution among the students. Thereby we got a clear answer to one of our initial questions, on how gender differences and inherited (from the parental home) educational capital appear in the space. Especially the second and the third axis are characterised by gender differences. The boys tend to be drawn to the poles of 'easiness' and of lesser time invested in the studies, and the girls to the 'difficultness' pole and the intensive investments' pole. The space is also structured by inherited educational capital to some extent. Larger resources tend to go with the more extensive investments in the studies and a general positive attitude towards education. When divided by gender, it becomes clear that the inherited educational capital is configured differently for female and male pupils. Girls follow the logic of the space more closely than the boys do.

In order to trace the educational capital's *institutionalised* state (schooling institutions, study programmes, etcetera), we continued to project relevant information into the space as supplementary variables and categories. It is obvious that programmes and schools, as well as the interaction between the two, shape the educational space of Uppsala upper secondary school. The dominance of the natural science programme over the social science programme is expressed along all the three first axes, with the former consequently leaning more towards the dominant pole in comparison to the latter. In previous studies, we have disclosed a similar distinction between pupils taking natural sciences viz. social sciences. With regard to political preferences, the natural sciences pupils showed an inclination for international issues on human rights, international rights of employees, a strong trust in the EU and other supranational institutions, but they were more reluctant to position themselves on issues on redistribution, positions takings that marked the difference among the large group of pupils in social science and technology (Bergström 2015; Bergström and Dalberg 2014).

The positions of the schools are largely defined by their educational offer; schools without the natural science programme are located in the dominated regions of the space. However, finer differences between the schools that offer the natural science programme can be observed. First, traditional grammar schools are found in the most dominant positions, by contrast to relative newcomers. The former is also more female-oriented, while the latter are more oriented towards the male dominated parts of the space.

The intersection of school and programme thus becomes the most crucial structural determinant of the space. The first axis is differentiating the social science programme (the least socially and meritocratically selective programme) at the least prestigious school, principally a vocational school, from the natural science programme (most socially and meritocratically selective) at the oldest and most prestigious former grammar school, were there are few vocational programmes and a strong dominance of programmes preparing for university studies and so called cutting-edge programmes. These programmes and schools are also positioned as extremes along the third axis, representing the oppositions between heavy and minor time investments.

To summarise: The space of upper secondary education in Uppsala is primarily characterised by an opposition (axis 1) between stronger vs. weaker commitment to schooling. At finer levels, indicated by axes 2 and 3, the hierarchies differ, and the differences between boys and girls become apparent. Among male pupils, dominant positions are expressed in statements postulating that the school subjects are easy to learn, while a dominant position among female pupils is compatible with the conces-sion of investing much time in the studies. The former self-representation rimes well with an image of the intellectually gifted disciple capable of learning effortlessly, while the latter is more oriented towards the perception of studies as a laborious task, and of success as the result of the input of a sufficient amount of work.

Finally, our results give us key insights in the dominance of the natural science programme in the Swedish upper secondary school. Not only is the programme at the top of the hierarchy of *institutionalised* educational capital, epitomised by the fact that the programme recruits the largest shares of offspring from the cultural fractions of the upper middle class, but it is also the programme occupying the most prominent position with regard to *embodied* educational capital in three different dimensions as spelled out by our analysis: in a general commitment to schooling and to the value of education, in the perception of the subjects as neither difficult nor demanding, and finally as a strong dedication to invest a lot of time in the studies. Increasingly, these values are upheld by the female students. This result calls for further research on the implications of the feminisation of educational capital.

References

Baudelot, C., & Establet, R. (1992). *Allez les filles!* Paris: Seuil.

Bergström, Y. (2015). *Unga och politik. Utbildnings, plats, klass och kön.* Stockholm: Premiss.

Bergström, Y., & Dalberg, T. (2014). Education, social class and politics. The political space of Swedish youth in Uppsala. In M. Grenfell & F. Lebaron (Eds.), *Bourdieu and data analysis: Methodological principles and practice* (pp. 227–252). Bern: Peter Lang Publishing.

Bertilsson, E. (2014). *Skollärare. Rekrytering till utbildning och yrke 1977–2009.* Uppsala: Uppsala universitet.

Börjesson, M., & Broady, D. (2016). Elite strategies in a unified system of higher education. The case of Sweden. *L'Année Sociologique, 66,* 115–146.

Börjesson, M., Broady, D., Dalberg, T., & Lidegran, I. (2016a). Elite education in Sweden. A contradiction in terms? In C. Maxwell & P. Aggleton (Eds.), *Elite education. International perspectives* (pp. 92–103). London: Routledge.

Börjesson, M., Broady, D., Le Roux, B., Lidegran, I., & Palme, M. (2016b). Cultural capital in the elite subfield of Swedish higher education. *Poetics, 56,* 15–34.

Bourdieu, P. (1979a). *La distinction. Critique sociale du jugement.* Paris: Éditions de Minuit.

Bourdieu, P. (1979b). Les trois états du capital culturel. *Actes de la recherche en sciences sociales, 30,* 3–6.

Bourdieu, P. (1989). *La noblesse d'État : Grands corps et grandes écoles.* Paris: Éditions de Minuit.

Bourdieu, P., & de Saint Martin, M. (1976). Anatomie du goût. *Actes de la recherche en sciences sociales, 5,* 2–82, 89–112.

Bourdieu, P., & de Saint Martin, M. (1987). Agrégation et ségrégation. Le champ des grandes écoles et le champ du pouvoir. *Actes de la recherche en sciences sociales, 69,* 2–50.

Bourdieu, P., & Passeron, J. C. (1964). *Les héritiers: Les étudiants et la culture.* Paris: Minuit.

Broady, D., & Palme, M. (1989). *Högskolan som fält och studenternas livsbanor.* Paper presented at the symposium "Självbiografi, kultur och livsform", Esbo, Helsingfors, 10–12 March 1989.

Broady, D., Börjesson, M., Bertilsson, E., Larsson, E., Lidegran, I., & Nordqvist, I. (2009). Skolans kungsväg. Det naturvetenskapliga programmets plats i utbildningssystemet. In *Resultatdialog 2009. Aktuell forskning om lärande* (pp. 25–31). Stockholm: Vetenskapsrådet.

Forsberg, H. (2015). *Kampen om eleverna. Gymnasieskolors och familjers tillgångar och strategier på gymnasiefältet i Stockholm, 1992–2011.* Uppsala: Uppsala universitet.

Le Roux, B., & Rouanet, H. (2004). *Geometric data analysis: From correspondence analysis to structured data analysis*. Dordrecht/Boston/London: Kluwer.

Le Roux, B., & Rouanet, H. (2010). *Multiple correspondence analysis*. London: Sage.

Lebaron, F., & Le Roux, B. (Eds.). (2015). *La méthodologie de Pierre Bourdieu en action. Espace culturel, espace social et analyse des données*. Paris: Dunod.

Lidegran, I. (2009). *Utbildningskapital. Om hur det alstras, fördelas och förmedlas*. Uppsala: Uppsala universitet.

Lindensjö, B., & Lundgren, U. P. (2000). *Utbildningsreformer och politisk styrning*. Stockholm: Liber.

Maxwell, C., & Aggleton, P. (2016). Introduction: Elite education. International perspectives. In C. Maxwell & P. Aggleton (Eds.), *Elite education. International perspectives* (pp. 1–12). London: Routledge.

Palme, M. (2008). *Det kulturella kapitalet. Studier av symboliska tillgångar i det svenska utbildningssystemet 1988–2008*. Uppsala: Uppsala Universitet.

Serre, D., & Wagner, A. C. (2015). For a relational approach to cultural capital: A concept tested by changes in the French social space. *The Sociological Review, 63*, 433–450.

Skolverket (2010). *Attityder till skolan 2009*. Rapport 344. Stockholm: Skolverket.

Van Zanten, A. (2015). A good match: Appraising worth and estimating quality in school choice. In J. Beckert & C. Musselin (Eds.), *Constructing quality: The classification of goods in markets*. London: Oxford University Press.

Van Zanten, A. (2016). Introduction. La formation des élites : pour une approche généraliste, compréhensive et comparative. *L'Année Sociologique, 66*, 73–80.

Chapter 4
Field Analysis, MCA and Class Specific Analysis: Analysing Structural Homologies Between, and Variety Within Subfields in the Norwegian Field of Power

Johs. Hjellbrekke and Olav Korsnes

In the social sciences, multiple correspondence analysis (MCA) owes much of its fame to the work of the late Pierre Bourdieu (1930–2002). Now classic works like *L'anatomie du gout* (Bourdieu and de St. Martin 1976), *Le patronat* (Bourdieu and de St. Martin 1978), *Distinction* (Bourdieu 1984[1979]), *Homo Academicus* (Bourdieu 1984) and *State Nobility* (1996[1989]) all relied heavily on the use of either simple correspondence analysis (CA) or multiple correspondence analysis (MCA). By subjecting data on various forms of capital distributions to CA or MCA, field structures were objectified and the homology thesis, i.e. fields in the modern French society was structured in similar ways.

The problem of homology has been a returning question in the reception and the attempts of replicating Bourdieu's work, both within and outside of France (see Robette & Roueff and Flemmen et al. in this volume). In this chapter, we'll discuss how this hypothesis can be investigated statistically by turning to two variants of geometrical data analysis: MCA and class specific MCA (Le Roux and Rouanet 2010; Hjellbrekke 2018). In particular, class specific MCA (hereafter CSA) is a methodological innovation that allows us not only to explore the relation between the field of power and its subfields, but also to discuss how Bourdieu's homology thesis may be scrutinized.

J. Hjellbrekke (✉) · O. Korsnes
Department of Sociology, University of Bergen, Bergen, Norway
e-mail: Johs.Hjellbrekke@uib.no

© Springer Nature Switzerland AG 2019   43
J. Blasius et al. (eds.), *Empirical Investigations of Social Space*,
Methodos Series 15, https://doi.org/10.1007/978-3-030-15387-8_4

Social Space, Social Field, Field of Power and Subfield

Analytically, the term 'social space' refers to a theoretically weighted synthesis of the main principles of stratification in any given society. In the disciplinary history of sociology it was Pitirim A. Sorokin who first associated the term with a synthesis of various forms of social stratification (Sorokin 1959 [1927]), but arguably, it is Pierre Bourdieu's use of the term that has attracted most scholarly attention during the last decades. While Sorokin primarily used the term in order to demonstrate how various dimensions of stratification can be related analytically, Bourdieu used it in order to develop an alternative to Marxist class analyses. According to Bourdieu, the social space is structured by differences in volume and composition of capitals, and as these differences provide the basis for various forms of power and domination, one will find hierarchical divisions between dominating and dominated agents in the social space, and classes are identified on the basis of these hierarchical relations. But these are only classes 'on paper' – i.e. sets of positions and relations between them that are more or less likely to produce real classes and class actions only under certain conditions. Constructing a social space according to this logic may support analyses of the basis of class formation, but it does not substitute analyses of real class behavior (Bourdieu 1992: 229–251).

Usually, this social space is constructed on the basis of indicators of three main types of capital: economic, cultural and social capital. The agents' positions in the space are located according to their capital volume and profile, and the position of each agent must therefore be interpreted relationally, i.e. in relation to the location of all other positions in the space (Bourdieu 1992: 229–251). Positions with relatively similar capital volumes and profiles will be located close to each other, while positions with different capital volumes and profiles will be located more distant from each other.

The same relational principles of interpretation apply to the social space as to what Bourdieu conceptualized as a 'field' (see also Swartz in this edited volume). A field can also be perceived as a structured space of oppositions between a set of specific positions, and the structure of the field may be determined on the basis of the distribution of capitals between the agents that engage in the struggles over power in the specific field, whether it is the political field (Hjellbrekke and Osland 2010; Bourdieu 1991a: Part III), the journalistic field (Hovden 2008; Marchetti 2002), the religious field (Bourdieu 1991b), or the academic field (Bourdieu 1984). On the basis of capital volume and composition, hierarchical divisions between dominant and dominated agents may also be uncovered, both within field positions, between field positions in the same field, and between positions in different fields.

The concept 'field of power' was developed as an alternative to 'classical' sociological elite theories (Bourdieu and de St. Martin 1978, Bourdieu 1996). Analytically, the field of power is located in the area of the space where the overall volumes of capital are highest. It is conceptualized as a field in which agents in dominant positions of various fields are engaged in struggles over the power relations between, and the hierarchically ordering of the fields. And because different types of capital will be valued differently in different fields, the struggles in the field of power are also about the general value and distribution of different types of capital, and about the right to dictate what shall be the legitimate, i.e. dominating principles of domination.

Also, the relation between the field of power and its constituting fields may be characterized as a relation between a field and a subfield: The structural oppositions which permeate the struggles are not necessarily replicated in identical ways in the internal field struggles, e.g. in the bureaucratic or the political field. In an exhaustive field analysis this is rather something that must be explored empirically.

There are, however, no easy and straightforward ways to analyze the relation between structures in the field of power and its subfields empirically, which duly respect the fundamental relational logic that underpins the field constructions. The field of power and its subfields must be constructed on the basis of distributions of the same types of capital, but when analyzing and interpreting the results of an analysis of a subfield, one must bear in mind that the subfield is *always already situated* in the structures of a more global field. An adequate analysis of a subfield must take this relation into account.

The purpose of this chapter is to explore how this may be done in an analysis of the Norwegian field of power and three of its subfields – the subfields of politicians, higher civil servants, and business leaders.

The Construction of a Field of Power

The field of power was constructed on the basis of data from The Leadership Survey which was part of the Norwegian Study of Power and Democracy (1998–2003) commissioned by the Norwegian Government. The survey was distributed to an 'area selected sample' of 1710 individuals in ten different sectors (see Gulbrandsen et al. 2002). The data were not produced with the ambition of constructing a field in the Bourdieusian sense, but contained variables which made it possible to do so, and 30 variables were chosen for constructing a field of power (see Hjellbrekke et al. 2007). The active variables were grouped into five main categories: economic capital, inherited and personal cultural capital, inherited and personal social capital (Table 4.1).

Briefly summarized, MCA revealed a space with three main dimensions, summing up to 75% of the variance (Benzécri's modified rates).

– Axis 1 was interpreted as an economic capital axis, contrasting high and low volumes of economic capital.
– Axis 2 was interpreted as a seniority and social mobility axis, separating high and low volumes of both inherited cultural and social capital, and also as describing an opposition between high volumes of educational capital and high volumes of political capital.
– Axis 3 was interpreted as a capital structure axis, where high volumes of inherited social capital and low volumes of personal educational capital are contrasted to high volumes of both personal educational and inherited economic capital.

Table 4.1 Active variables, construction of a field of power

Economic capital	Inherited and personal cultural capital
Personal income, 3 categories: – 25%, 26–74%, 75%+	Father's education: 5 categories (lowest to highest)
Income on capital, savings, stocks etc., 3 categories: – 25%, 26–74%, 75%+	Partner's education: 5 categories (lowest to highest)
Fortune, 3 categories: – 25%, 26–74%, 75%+	Own education: 5 categories (lowest to highest)
	Studied abroad: 1 year, 2 years+, No Worked abroad: Yes/No
Personal social capital (Categories: Yes/No)	**Inherited social capital (Categories: Yes/No)**
Board member, Private company	Father/mother, Board member, Private/Public Company
Board member, Gen. Assembly, Private company	Father/mother, Board member, Managerial Org.
Board member, Election Committee, Private company	Father/mother, Board member, Trade Union
Board member, Public company	Father/mother, Board member, NGO
Board member, Managerial Org.	Father/mother, Member of Parliament
Board member, Trade Union	
Board member, NGO	
Professional Experience/Field trajectory (categories: Yes/No)	
Civil Service	Defense
Research/Higher Education	Organizations
Politics	Church
Police/Justice	Media
Business	Culture

When the variable on sectorial belonging was projected into this space as a supplementary variable, a tripolar opposition between positions in business, in politics, in research and in the church was revealed in factorial plane 1–2. The sectors' positions in the space are shown in Fig. 4.1.

Horizontally, along axis 1, there is a clear opposition between the business positions and all the other positions. Whereas all the business positions are located to the right in the plane, almost all the others are located to the left. However, when the *full* set of 48 positions was projected as a supplementary variable into this space, there were also clear indications of sector internal oppositions. For instance, the positions of leaders of public companies and of cooperatives, with career trajectories that also depend on the accumulation of political capital and on political consecration, are located much closer to the political positions in the field (see Hjellbrekke et al. 2007; Hjellbrekke and Korsnes 2016).

Vertically, along axis 2, we find a clear-cut opposition between religious positions and positions in higher education and research (upper left quadrant) and the political positions (lower left quadrant). With respect to social mobility, positions in politics seem more 'readily' available for newcomers in the field than positions in academia

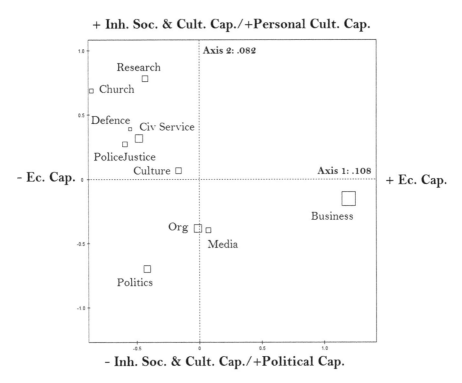

Fig. 4.1 Sectorial Positions in the Field of Power

or in the church. But at the same time, the axis might also describe an internal capital hierarchy in the political field. Whereas the mean positions for the state secretaries are located near the barycenter, the position of the MPs is located at the bottom of the quadrant.

Axis 3 (not shown, see Hjellbrekke et al. 2007) reveals an opposition between judicial and military positions on one side of the axis, and a figuration of positions in politics, including trade unions and professional organizations, NGOs and public and private cultural institutions on the other side of the axis.

However, this analysis is still not able to tell us what capital oppositions prevail *internally* in a subfield, e.g. in the political field, the administrative field, or the academic field. Are these field-internal structures much the same as those in the global construction of the space, or do other types of capital generate field-internal lines of divisions, among politicians, civil servants, or among business leaders, which we find in analyses of the divisions in the global field of power? In Bourdieusian terms, this is a question about structural homologies between the oppositions in the field of power and the various subfields, and in order to explore such structural homologies we shall apply CSA (Le Roux 2014: 264–69).

Subfields in the Field of Power: Field Homologies and Class Specific Multiple Correspondence Analysis (CSA)

A subfield may be perceived as a subspace constituted by a certain group or a subsample within the frames established through the construction of the global space. The characteristics of the dimensions in this subspace depend upon the internal oppositions in the group that is analyzed. To reveal these dimensions, the most straightforward procedure would be to conduct an analysis of only the sub-sample, *without* taking the global space as a point of reference, neither analytically nor statistically. This, however, would imply separating these individuals from the structures of the global space, and not to analyze their internal oppositions within this structure. If their relations to the other individuals and positions in this space shall be taken into account, this is not a feasible solution.

By way of a class specific MCA, this problem can be overcome, as the distance between two individuals, say *Hillary* and *Donald*, is defined by the positions they have on *all* the axes in the global space. These axes which are used as variables in the CSA, will again be determined by all individuals in this space, and not just those in the subgroup. A CSA can be compared to running a non-normed PCA (Principal Component Analysis), or a PCA on the covariance matrix, on this subset of individuals, where the individuals' factorial coordinates are the values on the active variables. The distances between the individuals are thus defined in the original space, but we search for new axes within the given nested subcloud. In this way, one can analyze statistically whether or not the individuals in the given subgroup are similar to, or different from the individuals in the reference group. In our case, this reference group is constituted by all the individuals in the above outlined elite sample, i.e. the global cloud. Each subcloud belongs to the same space as the global cloud, making direct comparisons between the results from different subclouds statistically legitimate (Le Roux 2014: 264–69 and 391–394, Bonnet et al. 2015: 120–29).

Briefly summed up, the more the distributions for the individuals in the subsample are close or similar to those of the individuals in the *global* sample across the active set of variables, the more similar will the results from the CSA be to the results from the MCA, both in terms of dimensionality and in terms of the interpretation of the individual axes. Conversely, the more the distributions in the subsample differ from the ones in the global sample, the more will also the results from the CSA differ from those obtained in the global MCA, not only when it comes to how the axes are to be interpreted, but in most cases also in terms of the dimensionality of the solution.

Table 4.2 shows the eigenvalues of the original MCA (N = 1710), of the CSA of the politicians (n = 190), of the higher civil servants (n = 197) and of the business leaders (n = 390), three subgroups whose mean points are located in different sectors of the factorial plane shown in Fig. 4.1.

As Table 4.2 indicates, the oppositions revealed in the CSAs of the three subsamples are not identical to the ones structuring the global space. Firstly, the eigenvalues, and also the dimensionality, differ between the three CSAs. Whereas four dimensions should be retained for interpretation in the MCA space, there are three dimensions to interpret among the civil servants and in the business elite, but only two among the politicians. There might, however, be a secondary factorial plane to interpret among the latter, i.e. a plane constituted by lower order axes (axes 3 and 4).

Secondly, the strength of axis 1 varies from subsample to subsample. Among the politicians and the business leaders, axis 1 is clearly the most important axis. This is not at all as clear among the civil servants. The differences between axes 2 and 3 are also systematically smaller in the CSAs than in the original MCA space. The oppositions in the subsamples might therefore not be as clear cut as in the global sample.

Table 4.2 does not, however, tell us anything about how similar or dissimilar the axes found in the CSAs are to those we have found to structure in the global field of power. To what degree is this the case? And to what degree do field-specific types of capital generate field-specific structural oppositions? In other words: are the axes from the various CSAs oriented through the respective sub-clouds in similar ways? The cosines for the angle between the 'old' and the 'new' axes which can be interpreted in the same way as correlation coefficients, give us a first indication on this; the respective values are given in Table 4.3[1]:

Table 4.2   Axes 1–5, MCA and CSA

	MCA	CSA	CSA	CSA
	Global analysis	Politicians	Civil Servants	Business
Axis 1	.1078	.1061	.0881	.1105
Axis 2	.0841	.0789	.0709	.0799
Axis 3	.0669	.0733	.0633	.0736
Axis 4	.0603	.0697	.0572	.0604
Axis 5	.0542	.0556	.0557	.0572

Table 4.3   Cosines, axes from specific MCA and CSA

MCA, Global Analysis	CSA, Politics Axis 1	CSA, Politics Axis 2	CSA, Politics Axis 3	CSA, Civ Serv Axis 1	CSA, Civ Serv Axis 2	CSA, Civ Serv Axis 3	CSA, Business Axis 1	CSA, Business Axis 2	CSA, Business Axis 3
Axis 1	.1252	.3790	−.1097	.2301	.0588	−.0700	−.7419	−.2943	−.2215
Axis 2	.7298	.1980	−.0100	.7450	−.3860	.2333	−.4674	.6415	−.0023
Axis 3	.1953	.1588	−.5475	.4947	.3743	−.4391	−.1948	.0289	.3658

---

[1]Terminologically, there is a difference between those who emphasize the geometric properties in CA and MCA (see Le Roux and Rouanet 2010) and those with a standpoint closer to matrix algebraic approaches (e.g. Greenacre 2017). Our position is closer to the geometric approach, and for this reason, we favor the use of cosines over correlations.

The closer the cosine or the correlation is to $+1$ or -1, the sharper is the angle between an old and a new axis, and the more similar is also the given axis from the CSA to the axis from the MCA. The closer the cosine is to 0, the closer to orthogonal are also the axes, and the more different are also the orientations of the given axes through the cloud. If the value of the cosine $= 0.0$, the axis from the CSA will be at an angle of 90 degrees to the axis from the MCA. From Table 4.3, we find that both among the politicians and the civil servants the new axes 1 display clear similarities to the old axis 2, i.e. the mobility and seniority axes. In other words, in both of these subfields, the most distinct opposition is found between 'inheritors' and 'newcomers'. But as we know from Table 4.2, this opposition is stronger, or more dominant, in the political subfield than in the administrative subfield. This said, the structural correspondence is not perfect. A cosine of .75 indicates that the angle between the new first axis and the old axis 2 is approx. 40 degrees. This might in turn indicate that there are two different versions of the mobility or seniority oppositions at work in the subsamples. Furthermore, as far as can be judged from the cosines, the new axes 2 in the CSAs are also different. The field internal structures are thus also different.

This may be explained by the fact that historically the careers and trajectories that lead to top positions in politics and in the civil service have not been identical, and the qualifications and capital assets needed for entering the two fields have differed. Even though the educational heterogeneity increased in the civil service in the decades from 1976 to 1996, in 1996, 27% did not hold the equivalent of a master degree or higher (see Christensen et al. 2001). The educational level has been lower among the politicians, and even though there are good reasons to ask whether or not the Norwegian MPs constitute a social elite (Hellevik 1969), the hurdles a politician must pass on his or her way to a top position are different from those a civil servant must pass on his or her way to the top of the administrative hierarchy.

The structural oppositions in the business elite, however, prove to be other than in the political and in the administrative elite. Of the three CSAs presented in Table 4.3, the resultsfrom the CSA of the business elite is closest to the results from the global analysis. Firstly, the new axis 1 displays a clear similarity to axis 1 in the global analysis. We have therefore reasons to expect that the dominant opposition among the business leaders is an opposition linked to economic capital assets, i.e. to the dominant form of capital in this subfield. Secondly, the cosine between axis 2 in the Business CSA and axis 2 in the global analysis is .6415, i.e. an angle of 50 degrees between the two axes. Whereas, to a certain degree, axis 2 in the CSA describes an 'inheritors' vs. 'newcomers' opposition, this opposition does not have the exact same orientation as it does in the global cloud. Most likely, also in this case, we'll find field specific variations over the more general principle. Finally, in the subset of business leaders, axis 3 describes an opposition not found in the MCA space. It might therefore describe an opposition that is specific to the business elite.

In order to get a more precise idea of the field specific oppositions, the contributions from the individual categories to the most important axes must be examined in greater detail. This is done in Tables 4.4, 4.5 and 4.6 and in Figs. 4.2, 4.3 and 4.4, where only categories with contributions above the average contribution, i.e. $> 1/K$, are included.

Table 4.4 Points with contributions >1/K, axes 1 and 2. CSA, Higher Civil Servants. Contributions to axes

	Axis 1	
	Left	**Right**
Inherited Social Capital	FM, Private, No: 3.1	FM, Trade Union, Yes: 13.2
	FM, NGO, No: 3.1	FM, Managerial Assoc, Yes: 12.6
	FM, Trade Union, No: 2.6	FM, NGO, Yes: 9.7
	FM, Managerial Assoc. No: 2.3	FM, Priv. Comp, Yes: 7.7
	SUM: 11.1	FM, MP, Yes: 5.4
		SUM: 48.6
Personal social capital	BM, Public Company, No: 2.4	BM, Public Company, Yes: 4.5
Inherited and personal cultural capital		Father, Univ 5 years +: 6.1
		Partner Univ 5 years +: 3.1
		Studied Abroad, Yes: 2.3
		SUM: 11.5
Professional experience/field trajectory		NGO, Yes: 3.5
		Politics, Yes: 1.4
		SUM: 4.9
SUM	Left side: 13.5	Right side: 69.5
SUM, both sides	83.0	
	Axis 2.	
	Left	**Right**
Inherited social capital		FM, MP, Yes: 3.9
Personal social capital		BM, Public Company, Yes: 2.2
		BM, NGO, Yes: 2.1
		SUM: 4.3
Inherited and personal cultural capital	Worked abroad, Yes: 9.8	Worked abroad, No: 5.4
	Studied abroad, Yes: 7.3	Partner, No Diploma: 3.3
	Partner, Univ 5 years+: 5.4	Studied abroad, No: 3.0
	Univ 7 years: 4.7	Father Comp. Educ: 2.6
	SUM: 27.2	SUM: 14.3
Professional experience/field trajectory	Research, Yes: 13.2	Justice, Yes: 9.0
		Politics, Yes: 6.3
		Research, No: 4.7
		SUM
SUM	Left side: 40.4	Right side: 42.5
SUM, both sides	82.9	

Table 4.5 Points with contributions >1/K axes 1 and 2. CSA, Politicians

	Axis 1.	
	Left	**Right**
Inherited social capital	FM, Private, No: 2.0	FM, MP, Yes: 6.8
		FM, Priv. Comp, Yes: 5.6
		FM, NGO, Yes: 4.9
		FM, Trade Union, Yes: 4.6
		FM, Managerial Assoc, Yes: 3.0
		SUM: 24.9
Inherited and personal cultural capital	Diploma: 35.3	Father, Uni 5 years +: 2.5
	Partner, Diploma: 4.0	Partner Univ 5 years +: 1.8
	Father, Comp. Ed: 3.6	Studied Abroad, Yes: 1.5
	SUM: 42.9	SUM: 5.8
Professional experience/field trajectory		NGO, Yes:1.4
SUM	Left side: 44.9	Right side: 32.1
SUM, both sides	77.0	
	Axis 2.	
	Left	**Right**
Economic capital	Capital income, Low: 11.5	Fortune, Medium: 3.8
	Fortune, Low: 11.5	Capital Income, High: 2.1
	Income, Low: 2.0	SUM: 5.9
	SUM: 25.0	
Inherited social capital		FM, MP, Yes: 3.8
		FM Manag. Assoc. Yes: 2.4
		FM, Trade Union, Yes: 2.2
		FM, NGO, Yes: 1.9
		FM, Private, Yes: 1.4
		SUM: 11.7
Personal social capital	BM, Private, No: 2.8	BM, private, yes: 2.8
Inherited and personal cultural capital	Univ. 3–4 years: 9.9	Diploma: 5.6
	Partner, Univ., 3–4 years: 2.4	Univ. 1–2 years: 4.3
	SUM: 12.4	Partner, No Diploma: 1.8
		SUM: 11.7
Professional experience/field trajectory	Business, NO: 4.1	Business, Yes: 4.1
		Politics, Yes: 1.9
		SUM: 6.0
SUM	Left side: 44.2	Right side: 38.1
SUM, both sides	82.3	

Table 4.6 Points with contributions >1/K, axes 1 and 2. CSA, CEOs in Business

	Axis 1.	
	Left	**Right**
Economic capital	Capital Income, High: 12.0	Capital Income, Medium: 2.3
	Property, High: 4.7	Fortune, Medium: 2.2
	Income, High: 4.3	SUM: 4.5
	SUM: 21.0	
Inherited social capital	FM, Managerial Assoc. Yes: 10.4	FM, Priv. Comp, No: 2.2
	FM, Private, Yes: 5.5	FM, NGO, No: 1.5
	FM, NGO, Yes: 4.9	FM, Managerial Assoc, No: 1.9
	FM, Trade Union, No: 3.3	SUM: 5.6
	SUM: 24.1	
Personal social capital	Election Committee, Yes: 13.2	
	General Assembly, Yes: 7.3	
	Managerial Ass, Yes: 7.3	
	SUM: 27.8	
Inherited and personal cultural capital	Studied Abroad, Yes: 2.9	
SUM	Left side: 75.8	Right side: 10.1
SUM, both sides	85.9	
	Axis 2.	
	Left	**Right**
Economic capital	Income, High: 4.3	
Inherited social capital	FM, Priv. Comp., No: 2.6	FM, Manag. Assoc. Yes: 6.6
		FM, Priv. Comp, Yes: 6.4
		FM, NGO, Yes: 2.4
		FM, Trade Union, Yes: 2.3
		FM, MP, Yes: 1.7
		SUM: 19,4
Personal social capital	Election Committee, Yes: 6,8	BM, Public Company, Yes: 2.2
		BM, NGO, Yes: 2.1
		SUM: 4.3
Inherited and personal cultural capital	Partner, Diploma: 6.4	Father, Univ. 5 years+: 4.6
	Univ. 3–4 years: 3.3	Father, Univ. 3–4 years: 2.9
	Father, Cont. Ed. 1–3 years: 1.9	Univ., 5–6 years: 2.5
	SUM: 11.6	Partner, Univ. 2.3
		SUM: 12.3
Professional experience/field trajectory	Managerial Assoc. Yes: 15.4	Managerial assoc. No: 4.3
	Trade Union, Yes: 3.9	
	SUM: 19.3	
SUM	Left side: 44.6	Right side: 40.3
SUM, both sides	84.9	

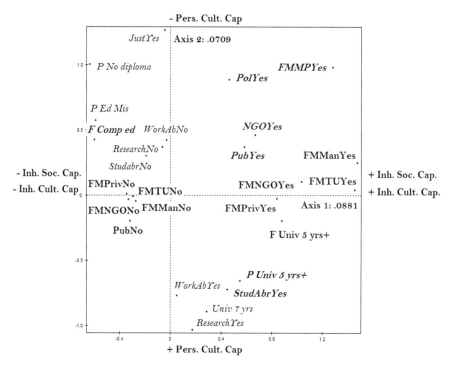

Fig. 4.2 CSA, higher civil servants. Categories with contributions >1/K to axis 1 in bold, to axis 2 in italics and to both axis 1 and 2 in bold and italics. (Legend: FM = Father/Mother, P = Partner, F = Father)

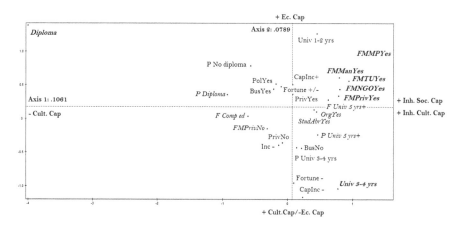

Fig. 4.3 CSA, politicians. Categories with contributions >1/K to axis 1 in bold, to axis 2 in italics, and to both axis 1 and 2 in bold and italics. (Legend: FM = Father/Mother, P = Partner, F = Father)

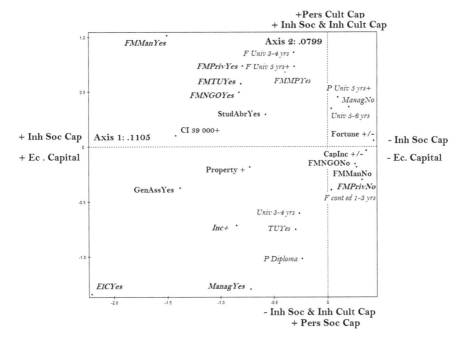

Fig. 4.4 CSA, business executives. Categories with contributions >1/K to axis 1 in bold, to axis 2 in italics and to both axis 1 and 2 in bold and italics. (Legend: FM = Father/Mother, P = Partner, F = Father)

Starting with the higher civil servants, axis 1 is not only skewed; the contributions from points on the right hand side are far higher than from those on the left hand side. It is also strongly dominated by an opposition between high and low inherited social capital, two categories stand out with a combined contribution of 25.8% having a father or mother who at a national level has served at the board of either a trade union or a managerial association. In this way, the dominant opposition between insiders and outsiders is more clearly linked to having or not having had parents with board memberships in key organisations and associations in the Norwegian tri-partite system of industrial relations. Among the higher civil servants, the parental opposition in a central arena for concertation manifests itself in the next generation as a structural opposition between newcomers and inheritors to powerful positions in the Norwegian state apparatus.

The central opposition on axis 2 is one between high volumes of personal and inherited cultural capital. It can also be interpreted as an axis of endogamy. Popular origins, having partners with low educational levels, relatively high volumes of personal social capital and experience from politics and/or justice stand in a clear opposition to categories indicating high volumes of both personal and inherited cultural capital. These oppositions are displayed in Fig. 4.2.

In Fig. 4.2, axis 1, the horizontal axis, describes an opposition between high and low volumes of inherited cultural capital and partly also inherited social capital. Even though the contributions to the axis are strongly skewed, the axis is 'balanced' in that the contributions stem from these two main types of capital. The axis can therefore be interpreted as a general volume axis for these two types of capital; a volume axis that is specific to the higher administrative field.

Figure 4.2 confirms that axis 2 must be interpreted as a volume axis with respect to educational capital, and also an endogamy axis. Higher civil servants without the highest educations, with popular origins and also partners with lower educations will more often be found in the upper quadrants of Fig. 4.2. Civil servants with the opposite properties are more often located in the two lower quadrants.

When we turn to the political subfield, the results (Table 4.5) seem at first clearly different. Firstly, one single category, having 'Diploma' as one's highest education, has a contribution of 35.3% to axis 1. However, categories indicating higher own educations do not have a contribution over the threshold. Instead, the category of low own education stands in opposition to categories indicating high volumes of inherited *social* capital and partly also inherited *cultural* capital. It is therefore a nearby conclusion that in the political field, axis 1 describes an opposition between a group that constitutes a 'political nobility', i.e. a group of individuals with a 'right of inheritance' to the positions once held by their parents, and a group of 'newcomers' with far less 'exclusive' backgrounds and with far more restricted capital profiles. The latters' potential for capital conversion is probably lower than that of the inheritors, and their dependency on the political field is therefore also higher (see Denord et al. 2011).

In contrast, axis 2 is not only far better balanced, in that no single category stands out with an extremely high contribution. It is also more of a capital composition axis, discriminating relatively high volumes of cultural capital (left side) from high volumes of inherited social capital (right side). Low volumes of economic capital are also contrasted to relatively high volumes of economic capital (Capital Income Low vs. Capital Income High).

The structures in the political subfield are shown in Fig. 4.3: whereas axis 1 is clearly defined by an opposition between politicians with the lowest educations and the others, i.e. a version of the 'newcomers' vs. 'inheritors' opposition (see also Lie Andersen 2014), axis 2 is a more complex-structure axis.

The dominant oppositions in the administrative and in the political field are therefore not identical. But even so, in both cases, the CSA has revealed an opposition linked to social mobility that structures these two subfields within the field of power. Whereas the axes from the CSAs describe oppositions between different forms of capital, the general, structuring principle is the same; one between 'newcomers' and 'inheritors'.

And the same overall principle of division is found to structure the oppositions among the business executives, although in yet another and also slightly more complex version. Table 4.6 shows the contributions to axes 1 and 2 in the CSA of the CEOs in the business sector.

Firstly, and as could be expected, axis 1 describes an opposition between high and low volumes of economic capital. But this opposition is also one between inheritors and newcomers in terms of volume of field-specific 'inherited social capital', e.g. having parents that were board members in private companies and/or managerial associations. Furthermore, having or not having held key positions in the field, e.g. being a 'gatekeeper' as member of an election committee or being member of a general assembly, two key indicators on field specific 'consecration' and on personal social capital, is also polarised along the same axis. Whereas 'outsiders' are systematically located to the right, the 'insiders' are located to the left in Fig. 4.4. As the axis is also separating between high and low volumes of economic capital, it can therefore be interpreted as a general volume axis, where the 'haves' are contrasted to the 'have not so muchs'.

But the opposition between inheritors and newcomers is not structured uni-dimensionally, which can be seen clearly from Fig. 4.4.

Also, axis 2 can be interpreted as an axis describing an opposition between a group of 'double' inheritors, located in the two upper quadrants, and the most powerful newcomers in the lower left quadrant. Categories indicating high volumes of inherited social and of both personal and inherited cultural capital are located in the upper quadrants, and experience from organisations – both managerial associations and trade unions – are located on the lower left side. Thus, one may partly interpret the axis as describing an opposition between personal social capital and inherited social and cultural capital. The homogamy pattern is also distinct: executives with partners with high educations are more often found in the upper quadrants and executives with lower educations and partners with low educations more often found in the lower quadrants.

Not having access to more detailed data on individual positions in the political field (e.g. party leader, MP, mayor etc.) or on exact positions in the hierarchies in the civil service or on what companies the business executives lead, we cannot analyze whether or not these oppositions also manifest themselves in, and correlate with other hierarchies. Even so, oppositions regarding capital volume and capital composition will in many cases also be indicators on power and dominance relations both within and between various fractions of the power elite.

Field Analysis, GDA and Field Homologies

When we conduct specific field analyses of these three subgroups of the field of power, we observe that the oppositions in the subfields are not identical with those we find in the global field of power. This is not surprising, as there are many reasons to believe that the relations of power and domination one finds, e.g. in the political field, are quite different from those one will find e.g. in the economic field. Nevertheless, we claim that there are clear tendencies of homology in the oppositions in the global field and the subfields. In our understanding, the homology thesis does not imply that the relations of power and domination in different social spaces and fields are identical, but structured according to the same basic social logic. This means that in the global field, as well as in the subfields, one should expect that the oppositions between the positions, and the relations of power and domination between them, are related to inequalities in the volume and composition of the same basic types of capital. And this is clearly the case. Moreover, structural oppositions specific to the Norwegian field of power seem to repeat themselves in various, non-identical ways across the subfields – this applies in particular to oppositions relating to social mobility and field seniority, between 'newcomers' and 'inheritors'. This further strengthens the homology argument, and the purpose of doing field analysis of subfields – which CSA makes possible to do statistically – is exactly to demonstrate that oppositions in the field of power must be understood as oppositions between subfields that are inter and intra-relationally structured by similar, but non-identical oppositions of relations of power and domination.

The same argument pertains to comparative studies of fields of power. In Bourdieu's analyses of the French field of power, the homology thesis refers to a structural coincidence between capital oppositions in the field of *Grandes écoles* and the French field of power (Bourdieu 1996). The analyses also reveal that agents with high volumes of inherited cultural capital are less often oriented towards the economic pole of the field of power, while agents in dominating sectors of the field are less preoccupied with intellectual and cultural 'temptations' (Bourdieu 1989: 234–235). To assume, in line with an empiricist interpretation of the homology thesis, that this will automatically also be the case in states that have not institutionalized a system of higher education similar to the French one, is quite absurd for obvious reasons. Nevertheless, a field theoretical research program may have more universally relevance, e.g. in elite studies, as long as it is not assumed to imply that fields of power always display the same structure, comprise the same positions, and must be constructed on the basis of exactly the same capital indicators, and that the relations between the types of capital must be identical. Such an assumption would imply a de-contextualization of the object of research, and make the analysis a-historical. And it would amount to a preconstruction of the research object of the sort Bourdieu repeatedly warned social scientists against (Bourdieu et al. 1968).

The same empiricist interpretation of the homology thesis, and the analytical weaknesses that follow from this, can be found in studies of relations between structures of class inequalities and differences in life styles that relate to Bourdieu's Distinction (Bourdieu 1979). Concerning the very simplistic positions one can find in the debate about this issue (see Jarness 2013, 2015; Hjellbrekke et al. 2015), it is also necessary to point out that relations between structures of class inequalities and differences in life styles may be very similar across contexts, even if the objects or the variables that constitute the differences may vary a lot. The implication of the homology thesis is that more or less consistent sets of preferences in taste correspond to oppositions between the location of different positions in the capital structures that make up the structures in different social spaces; not that these preferences and oppositions are the same across contexts and time.[2]

Capital structures may be perceived as universal principles of structuration of both class and life styles, but they are combined in ways that may result in national as well as field specific variations and variants, when it comes to field structures, field trajectories, and structuring of the habitus of persons that are placed in similar, but never identical positions. A comparative approach is necessary in order to reveal such variations, but must take into account the distinction between universal and societal-specific factors, and between the epistemological and ontological status of the research object. If not, one runs the risk of confusing empirical and theoretical generalizations, e.g. by generalizing Bourdieu's findings in France to other countries, and pretend to test the homology thesis by mechanically moving around constructions of social space (Hjellbrekke and Korsnes 2013).

References

Bonnet, P., Lebaron, F., & Le Roux, B. (2015). L'espace culturel des Français. In F. Lebaron & B. Le Roux (Eds.), *La méthodologie de Pierre Bourdieu en action* (pp. 99–130). Paris: Dunod.

Bourdieu, P. (1979). *La distinction*. Paris: Éditions de Minuit.

Bourdieu, P. (1984[1979]). *Homo academicus*. Paris: Éditions de Minuit.

Bourdieu, P. (1989). *La noblesse d'État*. Paris: Editions de Minuit.

Bourdieu, P. (1991a). *Language and symbolic power*. Cambridge: Polity Press.

Bourdieu, P. (1991b). Genesis and structure of the religious field. *Comparative Social Research, 13*, 1–44.

Bourdieu, P. (1992). *An invitation to reflexive sociology*. Chicago: The University of Chicago Press.

Bourdieu, P. (1996[1989]). *The state nobility*. Cambridge: Polity Press.

Bourdieu, P., & de Saint-Martin, M. (1976). L'anatomie du goût. *Actes de la recherche en sciences sociales, 5*, 2–112.

Bourdieu, P., & de Saint-Martin, M. (1978). Le patronat. *Actes de la recherche en sciences sociales, 20/21*, 3–83.

Bourdieu, P., Chamboredon, J. C., & Passeron, J. C. (1968). *Le métier de sociologue*. La Haye: Mouton/EHESS.

Christensen, T., Lægreid, P., & Zuna, H. P. (2001). *Profesjoner i regjeringsapparatet*. Oslo: Makt- og demokratiutredningens rapportserie.

Denord, F., Hjellbrekke, J., Korsnes, O., Lebaron, F., & Le Roux, B. (2011). Social capital in the field of power: The case of Norway. *The Sociological Review, 59*(1), 86–108.

Greenacre, M. J. (2017). *Correspondence analysis in practice* (3rd ed.). Boca Raton: Chapman & Hall.

Gulbrandsen, T., Engelstad, F., Klausen, T. B., Skjeie, H., Teigen, M., & Østerud, Ø. (2002). *Norske makteliter*. Oslo: Gyldendal.

Hellevik, O. (1969). *Stortinget – en sosial elite?* Oslo: Pax.

---

[2]This thesis does *not* imply that members of the upper class or the elites acquire a predefined set of "high brow" cultural objects and activities, and that they shun "low brow" objects and activities. Even though the preferences for objects and activities might have changed drastically compared to the situation in the 1960s and 1970s, one might still find structural homologies between class relations and life styles.

Hjellbrekke, J. (2018). *Multiple correspondence analysis for the social sciences*. London: Routledge.

Hjellbrekke, J., & Korsnes, O. (2013). Héritiers et outsiders. *Actes de la recherché en sciences sociales, 200*, 85–103.

Hjellbrekke, J., & Korsnes, O. (2016). Women in the field of power. *Sociologica Italian Journal of Sociology Online*, 2/2016. https://doi.org/10.2383/85291.

Hjellbrekke, J., & Osland, O. (2010). Pierre Bourdieu – maktkritikk som sysifosarbeid. In J. Pedersen (Ed.), *Moderne politisk teori* (pp. 273–293). Oslo: Pax forlag.

Hjellbrekke, J., Le Roux, B., Korsnes, O., Lebaron, F., Rosenlund, L., & Rouanet, H. (2007). The Norwegian field of anno 2000. *European Societies, 9*(2), 245–273.

Hjellbrekke, J., Jarness, V., & Korsnes, O. (2015). Cultural distinctions in an 'Egalitarian' society. In P. Coulangeon & J. Duval (Eds.), *The Routledge companion to Bourdieu's 'Distinction'* (pp. 187–206). London: Routledge.

Hovden, J. F. (2008). *Profane and sacred. A study of the Norwegian journalistic field*. Dr. polit. Thesis, Institute for Information and Media Studies, University of Bergen, Bergen

Jarness, V. (2013). *Class, status, closure. The Petropolis and cultural life*. PhD-thesis, Department of Sociology, University of Bergen, Bergen.

Jarness, V. (2015). Cultural vs economic capital: Symbolic boundaries within the middle class. *Sociology, 51*(2), 357–373. https://doi.org/10.1177/0038038515596909.

Le Roux, B. (2014). *Analyse géometrique des données multidimensionnelles*. Paris: Dunod.

Le Roux, B., & Rouanet, H. (2010). *Multiple correspondence analysis* (Series: Quantitative applications in the social sciences #163). Thousand Oaks: Sage Publications.

Lie Andersen, P. (2014). Den norske politiske eliten. In H. Korsnes & J. Hjellbrekke (Eds.), *Elite og klasse i et egalitært samfunn* (pp. 144–164). Oslo: Universitetsforlaget.

Marchetti, D. (2002). Les sous-champs spécialisés du journalism. *Réseaux, 1*, 22–55.

Sorokin, P. A. (Ed.). (1959[1927]). *Social and cultural mobility*. Glencoe: Free Press.

Chapter 5
Changes of Lifestyles in the Social Space: The Case of Gentrification

Jörg Blasius and Jürgen Friedrichs

Introduction

Using Bourdieu's 'social space' approach ([1979], 1984), we show how lifestyles change over time in a neighborhood as it is gentrified. In conventional panel studies such as the Panel Study of Income Dynamics (PSID), the British Household Panel Study (BHPS), or the German Socio-Economic Panel (GSOEP), the sample is based on households and/or persons in households. For example, in case of migration, the studies attempt to follow panel members to their new location. This is most appropriate when the research question refers to persons (or households) and the changes over time in their living conditions and attitudes. However, if the focus of research is on changes within a neighborhood, (for example, if one is interested in how in-movers differ from out-movers in terms of socio-demographic characteristics and lifestyle indicators), it is not helpful to follow former target persons when they move out of the neighborhood.

According to the stage theory of gentrification, an improvement of the neighborhood is expected to be accompanied by a change in the residents (Clay 1979; Kerstein 1990; Ley 1996; Lees et al. 2008): The new residents entering the neighborhood will have a relatively high income and a relatively high educational level, while the out-movers will have a relatively low income, insufficient to cover the increasing rents and other costs of living in the neighborhood. To test this theory, there is a need to compare in-movers and out-movers. For a valid comparison, one has to construct a new sample that includes the out-movers' replacements.

J. Blasius (✉)
Institut für Politische Wissenschaft und Soziologie, University of Bonn, Bonn, Germany
e-mail: jblasius@uni-bonn.de

J. Friedrichs (deceased)
Institute of Sociology and Social Psychology, University of Cologne, Cologne, Germany

© Springer Nature Switzerland AG 2019
J. Blasius et al. (eds.), *Empirical Investigations of Social Space*,
Methodos Series 15, https://doi.org/10.1007/978-3-030-15387-8_5

With conventional panel data, changes in the neighborhood can only be described by examining stayers and out-movers; there is no information on the in-movers replacing them. When replacing the out-movers with a random sample of inhabitants in the same neighborhood, the question of how to construct the new sample remains. We must take into account the fact that the out-movers are not a random sample of former residents; according to the theory of gentrification they are being displaced from the residential area (Palen and London 1984; Le Gates and Hartmann 1986). To solve this sampling problem, and to ensure an adequate substitution of out-moving residents in the neighborhood, we change the sample unit: Instead of persons (households), we use dwellings (single family houses) as sample units. In the first wave, there is no difference from a conventional panel study: One can start with a random sample drawn in the neighborhood where gentrification is expected; in our case we received addresses from the Office for Statistics and Inhabitants (*Amt für Statistik und Einwohnerwesen*) of the City of Cologne.

Following single family houses is simple since they have a unique address that can easily be recorded. For target persons living in multi-family houses, we marked the exact location of the dwelling within the building. In case of migration between the first and the second wave we asked randomly selected members of the new households in the same dwellings where the out-movers had lived. The same holds for changes occurring between the second and the third and between the third and the fourth wave; we did not follow persons or households as in conventional panel studies, but asked the in-movers in the previously selected dwellings (for more details, see Friedrichs and Blasius 2015).

The advantage of the dwelling panel is that it enables a comparison of in-movers and out-movers within each sample unit, for example with respect to their lifestyles and socio-demographic characteristics. While in conventional panel studies some of the individual factors are fixed (for example, sex and age), and while other characteristics can change only in one direction (for example, the educational level can only increase), these effects are not fixed in the dwelling panel; for example, a man can replace a woman, and a young person can replace an old person. Changes in these characteristics and especially in income indicate whether the neighborhood is becoming gentrified, and give an insight into the process of gentrification. Changes in attitudes, behaviors, and lifestyles can be studied while also analyzing changes in socio-demographic characteristics.

Lifestyle indicators will be used to construct a social space with dimensions of the composition of economic and cultural capital, as well as capital volume Bourdieu ([1979] 1984), or, after 45° rotation, as cultural and economic capital (see Blasius and Friedrichs 2008). For creating the social space, Bourdieu and his scholars most often applied multiple correspondence analysis (MCA) as part of geometric data analysis (Le Roux and Rouanet 2010). We also apply this technique, constructing the social space using indicators such as where respondents bought their furniture, the kinds of meals they served to guests, and general characteristics of the dwelling. Furthermore, socio-demographic characteristics are included as passive (or supplementary) variables (Bourdieu called these variables "illustrational") to confirm the interpretation of the axes in the social space.

Finally, we defined those social groups who are the main actors in the process of gentrification and also included them into the social space.

The empirical part of this paper is based on data from two residential areas of Cologne, Germany, (Deutz and Mülheim), in which we expect gentrification to be taking place (Blasius et al. 2016a, b; Blasius and Friedrichs 2016; Friedrichs and Blasius 2016). The first wave of the dwelling panel (collected in 2010) comprises 1009 cases, the second (2011) 878 cases, the third (2013) 810 cases, and the fourth wave (2014) has 747 cases; all data were collected in face-to-face interviews.

The Process of Gentrification

In the literature on gentrification, a common distinction refers to the forces of supply and demand in the process (for an overview, see Lees et al. 2008). While the supply side refers to the available urban land and buildings, the demand side refers to the social groups involved in the process (cf. Blasius et al. 2016a). Here, we will concentrate on the demand side, and examine both the economic and cultural structure of the households that predominantly drive the process of gentrification, and of those that are instead victims of the process.

Multiple authors have performed analyses of the social groups moving into a gentrifying neighborhood, often referring to them as 'pioneers' and 'gentrifiers'. Ley (1996: 35) describes gentrifiers as "well educated, upwardly mobile in a public or, perhaps less commonly, a private-sector occupation in a professional or managerial capacity, single or living with a working partner, and with adequate discretionary income to engage in the rituals of culture consumption, expressing the canons of good taste in a designer market place".

The term 'good taste' signifies a characteristic which is part of Bourdieu's concept of social distinction Bourdieu (1983, [1979] 1984). More explicitly, Bridge (2001) also makes reference to Bourdieu, defining the new middle class via their capability as "taste-makers", and argues: "New middle-class gentrifiers recognize the need for a historical marker, but also need to be at the edge of taste-making. This balance of the old and the new is at the heart of the socially differentiating nature of gentrification aesthetics" (Bridge 2001: 94).

Aesthetics as the differentiating feature of the new middle class – those who are expected to move into a gentrified neighborhood – has also been mentioned by other authors (for example, Butler 1997; Ley 1996: 18). Zukin (1982, 2010) posits that gentrification is driven by a search for authenticity, encapsulated and symbolized by the old, i.e., Edwardian and Victorian, buildings, be they residential or industrial, converted into lofts. Hence, Zukin (1987: 131) views gentrification as a movement "toward the social diversity and aesthetic promiscuity of city life". Jager (1986: 80) argues in a similar way: "the middle classes have to defend themselves against pressures from the dominant classes and ... must continue to demarcate themselves from the lower classes". Distinction is acquired through aesthetics: "The ambiguity and compromise of the new middle classes is revealed in their aesthetic tastes. It is through facade restoration work that urban conservation expresses its approximation to a former bourgeois consumption model in which prestige is based upon a 'constraint of superfluousness'" (Jager 1986: 80).

The second social group that is usually mentioned in the process of gentrification are the pioneers. This group is usually described as consisting of young and well-educated persons with low incomes. Typical pioneers are students and unestablished artists looking for cheap accommodation close to the city center; they live in various types of households, but have no children (Blasius et al. 2016a). The initial phase of the gentrification process is driven by pioneers; after they have 'discovered' the neighborhood, gentrifiers who have better incomes and who are somewhat older than pioneers enter the area (Ley 1996).

Another approach to distinguish pioneers and gentrifiers from old residents is to look at the time of their move into the neighborhood, i.e., at which stage in the gentrification process (Bridge 2001). Referring to Bourdieu's distinction between cultural and economic capital, Bridge (2001: 93) argues that persons with high cultural capital move in first, followed by those with high economic capital. "In this sense, 'taste' has been converted into 'price'", and "low paid professionals (teachers, academics, nurses) are followed by higher paid professionals".

Lifestyle indicators are useful to describe the distribution of social groups in different neighborhoods (Blasius and Friedrichs 2011). To explain the distribution (and thus: segregation), we turn to Bourdieu's concept of distinction, using his social space approach. We apply it to the gentrification process.

Operationalizations

In *La Distinction*, Bourdieu ([1979] 1984) is mainly interested in identifying and distinguishing different groups of French society in the late 1960s. In this work he first subdivided the society into three classes, namely upper, middle, and lower. In a further step he subdivided these classes into several class fractions, operationalized by occupation, because he wanted to establish the differences within classes; for example, within the upper classes, between artists and managers. In order to distinguish these class fractions, he used lifestyle attributes such as preferences for clothing, food served to guests, and preferred artists, which he combined with elements of traditional stratification research such as age (groups) and educational level. Bourdieu developed the concept of the 'social space' to visualize the relations between class fractions and their associated lifestyles.

Although there is widespread discussion of gentrification in the international field, there is very little literature on how to operationalize the social groups involved in the process. Early descriptions of gentrifiers are given by Glass (1964) and Clay (1979), and taken up again by Ley (1996: 35): "middle-class households ... small and usually childless; often unmarried; primarily under 35 years of age; employed overwhelmingly in the advanced services, that is, the quaternary category of professional, administrative, technical, and managerial occupations; highly educated, with a majority having at least one university degree; receiving moderate or high incomes despite their youthful age; and containing small portions of racial or non-English-speaking minorities".

To operationalize this concept, we made more explicit the vague typologies prevalent in the literature, and derived a classification based on household type, income, age, and family status (Blasius et al. 2016a, b), based on prior studies of gentrification in Hamburg and Cologne (Dangschat and Friedrichs 1988; Blasius 1993). This classification is shown in Table 5.1. The discussion of the operationalization of social groups is specifically German, and thus involves slightly different, nationally appropriate versions of this universal typology.

We define a person, or better the respective household, as being a pioneer if the interviewee is not older than 35 years and has an educational level sufficient for admission to higher education (or at least 12 years of schooling). The size of the household may differ: A pioneer is childless, and no longing living with their parents, but may otherwise live alone, with their partner, or share the apartment with friends. As a threshold for monthly income we use 1500 Euro for a single person, which is close to the median equivalent income in Germany. For any further person resident in the dwelling of 15 years and older, we add another 750 Euro; this corresponds to the OECD (2009) criteria for defining the equivalent income. If the variable income is not available because the respondent refused to answer this question, we used the indicator *student* as a proxy for classifying a person as a pioneer.

The second group are gentrifiers. They have a higher equivalent income and are (on average) older than pioneers. Many of the gentrifiers have an academic education, but this is not a decisive criterion. Relevant literature sources distin-

Table 5.1 Typology of Pioneers and Gentrifiers

Characteristic	Pioneers	Early Gentrifiers	Established Gentrifiers	Others	Elderly
Age	≤35 years	≤45 years	≤45 years	≤64 years	>65 years
Years of schooling	12 years	no definition	no definition	No pioneers or gentrifiers	By age criteria, no pioneers or gentrifiers
Household size	any	1 or 2 person, max. one child	1 or 2 person, max. one child		
Children	no	max. 1	max. 1		
Income[a]	<1.500€	≥1500 to <2500 €	≥2.500 €		

[a]Household equivalence income, calculated by OECD-Scale: first adult = 1.0, other persons ≥ 15 years = 0.5, below 15 years: 0.3

guish between gentrifiers and super-gentrifiers, sometimes also called super-rich financiers (Zukin 2010), but by definition this group is very small, and few of them live in gentrified areas. In a qualitative research design it might be interesting to ask for their lifestyles, but in quantitative research this group is too small to identify its members, and so we distinguish between two groups of gentrifiers by their income instead: early and established gentrifiers. According to the theory of gentrification, we assume that most of the lower-income gentrifiers moved into the neighborhood before the higher-income gentrifiers, since the latter are more risk-averse. Both groups of gentrifiers may live alone or with their partner, and they may have one child, but not two or more. Both groups of gentrifiers, as well as the pioneers, include migrants or minorities, provided that the respective persons fulfill the defined criteria.

The remainder of the residential population can be subdivided into different groups, depending on the specific aspect one wishes to study (for example, native and migrant groups). In this paper, we distinguish between two groups: those who are 65 years and older ('elderly'), mainly including households that have lived in the area for many years or even decades, and the remainder of the population (neither pioneers nor gentrifiers), who we call 'others'. It should be noted that this typology was developed for German cities. When focusing on another country, the income thresholds in particular should be adjusted to the economic conditions in the respective country.

Sample and Methods

To construct the social space, we use data from a survey in two neighborhoods in Cologne, Germany. Both are close to the city center on the east bank of the river Rhine; for details of the selected neighborhoods, see Friedrichs and Blasius (2016). The survey is a random sample of residents drawn from the Population Register of Cologne; in the first wave it comprised 1009 interviews. While contacting the target persons during the first wave, the exact position of the dwelling in the house they lived in was marked by the interviewers in the contact sheet. Prior to the implementation of the second and subsequent waves, an assistant of the project team confirmed all addresses; in case of out-movers, the assistant recorded the new name on the doorbell, the new household was invited via an official letter from Cologne University, and a randomly selected person in this new household replaced the previous resident. For more details on the dwelling panel, see Friedrichs and Blasius (2015).

These four waves allow us to study changes in lifestyles and socio-demographic characteristics in the neighborhood. Interviews were performed face-to-face; field work for the first wave began in mid-2010, and the response rate was 45.7%; the last wave took place in 2014 (for more details, see Friedrichs and Blasius 2015).

Results

New residents are expected to have new lifestyles. In the first wave, all respondents had been asked questions concerning their lifestyles; in the following three waves only new residents received this part of the questionnaire. We used indicators first formulated by Bourdieu (1979, see also Bourdieu and Saint-Martin 1976), reformulated and adapted to German culture (Blasius and Winkler 1989, see also Blasius and Friedrichs 2008; Blasius and Mühlichen 2010). It should be noted that some of the lifestyle indicators include a specifically national factor: For example, while in Germany meals prepared in the traditional German style are associated with low cultural capital, traditional French cuisine (the functional equivalent of this variable category in France) in Germany is associated with high economic and cultural capital.

Of the three questions we used for this survey, the first asks where respondents buy their furniture: department store, antique dealer, specialized dealer, built myself, craftsmen, flea market, auction, internet, furniture shop, designer, inheritance, and mail order. The second question characterizes the respondents' dwellings: clean and tidy, comfortable, stylish, plain, warm, easy to clean, modern, rustic, harmonic, refined, full of fantasy, practical and functional, and cosy. The third question – "What kind of meals do you serve when entertaining guests?" – comprises the following categories: simple but nicely decorated, fine and exquisite, substantial and rich, improvised, nutritious, original, exotic, traditionally German, healthy, I never have guests, and I invite them to restaurants. Following Bourdieu ([1979] 1984), every question admits a maximum of three categories.

When using these items, we do not assume that all respondents perceive all items in the same way: Furthermore, the perception of the items depends on the culture of the country. For example, the category *clean and tidy*, which in Germany is associated with low cultural capital, was not necessarily understood to mean the same thing by all respondents. Where a respondent chose this category, it does not automatically mean that their home actually is clean and tidy; the choice of this category only implies that it was important for the respondent to refer to their dwelling clean and tidy. Conversely, if a respondent did not prioritize this item, it does not imply that their dwelling was dirty and untidy. It might go without saying that the dwelling is clean and tidy; certainly, the interviewer can see that it is clean and tidy; in any case, it was not important to the interviewee to mention it. A similar objection holds for the category *warm*, which could mean that the dwelling is warm in a physical sense, but could equally mean that it is warm in an emotional sense. Another category is *traditional German cuisine* – young well-educated persons, for example pioneers, rarely use this descriptor, but they may still serve their guests sausages (a traditional German food); they may call the same meal original or exotic. In contrast, older and less-educated persons would describe the same meal as traditionally German (compare also Blasius and Friedrichs 2008; Blasius and Mühlichen 2010).

The potential diversity of connotations may at first glance impair an adequate measurement. But Bourdieu ([1979] 1984) makes use of this diversity of meanings, since it constitutes a basis for his assessment of differences *between* and *within* the upper, middle and lower classes when constructing his social spaces. Like Bourdieu, we are interested in constructing a (two-dimensional) social space with the dimensions capital volume and composition of cultural and economic capital, or economic capital and cultural capital. In fact, both sets of labels for the two axes are the same – movement from one description to the other can be achieved simply by a rotation of 45° (Blasius and Friedrichs 2008). Applying MCA will exhibit the categories that can be understood as indicators of economic and cultural capital, be it high or low. Where both forms of capital are high (or both are low), the capital volume is high (or low); where one form capital is high and the other is low, the differences can be seen in the composition of economic and cultural capital.

Table 5.2 shows the chosen indicators for the first wave applying listwise deletion (N = 979, see first column). We also show the same indicators for those residents who moved into the neighborhood between waves 1 and 4 (in-movers, N = 262), and those residents who stayed in the neighborhood (N = 735). Where the new residents did not take part in the survey, we kept the information from the residents of the previous wave, which could be either from the first wave (stayers) or, in cases of a second out-mover within the same dwelling, from other, formerly new residents (in-movers). The attached chi-square statistics belong to the two independent groups of stayers and in-movers.

We start with a reading example for Table 5.2: In the first wave, 34.4% of the respondents chose a specialized dealer as a source for furniture. Those residents who moved out between waves 1 and 4 chose this indicator relatively rarely; the relative percentage for the stayers is, at 37.0%, somewhat higher than for all residents from the first wave. Of the in-movers (new residents), only 27.5% chose the antique dealer as a source of furniture; the difference between 37.0 and 27.5% (and between the 63.0 and 72.5% who did not choose this indicator) is statistically significant at the 1% level.

Table 5.2 shows that (1) there are only a few differences between the stayers and out-movers (compare columns 1 and 2) and that (2) only a few indicators are statistically significant (compare columns 2 and 3). Because we simultaneously test a large number of indicators, some of them are significant just by chance; in the literature, this phenomenon is discussed under the term alpha-adjustment for multiple testing (Holm 1979). Without going into detail on how to adjust the level of significance, we consider only effects that are significant at least at the 1% level; consequently, none of the characteristics of the dwellings shows a difference between the two groups being examined here. With respect to purchasing furniture, in contrast to our assumptions, the new residents relatively rarely mentioned designer, antique, and specialized dealers; all three are indicators of high economic capital. In agreement with our assumptions, however, three of the indicators describing cultural capital were mentioned more often by the new residents: internet, built myself, and flea market. With respect to the meals served for guests, the indicator *improvised* was mentioned relatively often, while traditional German food was mentioned less often

Table 5.2 Lifestyle indicators, first wave and waves 2–4, values are given in percentages

	First Wave (N = 979)	Stayers (N = 735)	In-movers (N = 262)	Statistics
Sources of Furniture				
Department store	16.1	15.6	14.1	$\chi^2 = 0.3$, n.s.
Antique dealer	10.2	10.3	7.3	$\chi^2 = 2.1$, n.s.
Specialized dealer	34.4	37.0	27.5	$\chi^2 = 7.8$, p<.01, CV = .09
Built by myself	15.7	15.9	23.3	$\chi^2 = 7.1$, p<.01, CV = .09
Craftsman	6.3	7.6	4.6	$\chi^2 = 2.8$, n.s.
Flea-market	12.0	10.6	20.6	$\chi^2 = 16.8$, p<.001, CV = .13
(*)Auction	1.8	1.9	1.1	$\chi^2 = 0.7$, n.s.
Internet	15.2	13.3	32.8	$\chi^2 = 48.8$, p<.001, CV = .22
Furniture shop	83.4	82.3	84.0	$\chi^2 = 0.4$, n.s.
Designer	7.9	8.2	2.7	$\chi^2 = 9.3$, p<.01, CV = .10
Inherited	20.4	19.0	22.9	$\chi^2 = 1.8$, n.s.
Mail order house	9.4	9.0	7.6	$\chi^2 = 0.4$, n.s.
Characteristics of dwelling				
Clean, tidy	45.4	46.8	42.0	$\chi^2 = 1.8$, n.s.
Comfortable	20.9	19.6	17.9	$\chi^2 = 0.3$, n.s.
Stylish	17.8	17.6	24.0	$\chi^2 = 5.2$, p<.05, CV = .07
(*)Plain	5.4	4.5	5.3	$\chi^2 = 0.3$, n.s.
Warm	22.7	22.8	21.4	$\chi^2 = 0.2$, n.s.

(continued)

Table 5.2 (continued)

	First Wave (N = 979)	Stayers (N = 735)	In-movers (N = 262)	Statistics
Easy to clean	23.0	23.5	17.2	$\chi^2 = 4.6$, p<.05, CV = .07
Modern	11.6	12.0	18.3	$\chi^2 = 6.5$, p<.05, CV = .08
(*)Rustic	1.9	2.4	0.8	$\chi^2 = 2.8$, n.s.
Harmonic	20.7	19.6	24.0	$\chi^2 = 2.3$, n.s.
Refined	16.4	15.9	13.7	$\chi^2 = 0.7$, n.s.
Full of fantasy	9.5	9.5	11.1	$\chi^2 = 0.6$, n.s.
Praktical, functional	38.0	37.3	37.8	$\chi^2 = 0.2$, n.s.
Cosy	56.7	57.4	56.9	$\chi^2 = 0.3$, n.s.
Meals for guests				
Simple, but nicely decorated	39.3	38.1	43.9	$\chi^2 = 2.7$, n.s.
Fine and exquisite	16.5	16.6	14.9	$\chi^2 = 0.4$, n.s.
Substancial, rich	38.7	39.4	40.8	$\chi^2 = 0.2$, n.s.
Improvised	28.9	25.1	37.4	$\chi^2 = 14.4$, p<.001, CV = .12
Nutritious	18.1	19.6	19.8	$\chi^2 = 0.0$, n.s.
Original	27.6	26.3	30.5	$\chi^2 = 1.7$, n.s.
Exotic	16.1	15.0	14.1	$\chi^2 = 0.1$, n.s.
Traditional German	23.2	25.9	15.3	$\chi^2 = 14.4$, p<.001, CV = .11
Healthy	38.1	38.3	41.2	$\chi^2 = 0.7$, n.s.
(*)Don't have guests	4.4	4.4	2.3	$\chi^2 = 2.3$, n.s.
Invite in Restaurant	8.7	9.8	6.1	$\chi^2 = 3.3$, n.s.

by the new residents; both findings can be understood as indicators of gentrification. Four of the indicators are marked with a star, meaning they were mentioned by fewer than 5% of all interviewees; for this reason we excluded them from further analyses.

In the next step we ran MCA on the indicator matrix, using the lifestyle indicators as active variables, as described in Table 5.2. The first MCA is based on all respondents from the first wave from whom we have full information on the three variables (column 1, N = 979). Included as supplementary variables in the social space are the socio-demographic indicators education (edu1 to edu5; no formal education, elementary school, secondary school, college, university), equivalent income according to the OECD criteria (OECD 2009) (I1 to I6; below 500 Euro, 500 to 999 Euro, 1000 to 1499 Euro, 1500 to 1999 Euro, 2000 to 2499 Euro, 2500 Euro and more), age groups (A1 to A6; up to 25 years, 26–35, 36–45, 46–55, 56–64, 65 years and older) and the five social groups (pioneers, early gentrifiers, established gentrifiers, others, and elderly); these variables do not affect the geometric orientation of the axes, but they can be interpreted together with the active variables. The supplementary variables are also used to confirm the interpretation of the axes of the social space based on the active variables. Figure 5.1 shows the social space of the active variables, and Fig. 5.2 shows the supplementary variables.

The lifestyle indicators have two categories each (*mentioned* and *not mentioned*): Since both are perfectly negatively correlated, we only show the categories mentioned in the social space. The category *not mentioned* is opposed to the respective category *mentioned* for each variable in each dimension; both categories can be connected by a straight line which goes through the centroid of the social space, shown by the cross of axes. The distance to the centroid on each axis is a function of the masses (the relative percentage of the respective variable category); by applying the barycentric system of correspondence analysis (Greenacre 1984), it becomes apparent that the squared distance to the centroid times the mass is balanced on each dimension.

The first axis (horizontal dimension) reflects low cultural capital on the negative part and a high cultural capital on the positive part. Projecting the categories on a 90° angle onto this axis, we see indicators such as *mail order*, *traditional German cuisine*, *department store*, and *clean and tidy* in the negative part; all of them have been established as indicators of low cultural capital in previous studies (for example, Blasius and Friedrichs 2008; Blasius and Mühlichen 2010). The only indicator that might not fit this interpretation is *invite to restaurant*, but with fewer than 10% of selections, this indicator is used relatively seldom (see Table 5.2). Further, the negative part of the first axis is also populated by older persons (A6), and since the entire neighborhood is assumed to be gentrified, and therefore relatively rich, it may be that the elderly prefer to invite their guests to a restaurant instead of cooking the meals by themselves. The upper half of dimension one is associated with exotic and original meals, a dwelling that is characterized as full of fantasy, and with furniture that is purchased from the flea market, from the antique dealer, or from the designer, or which they built on their own or inherited. These indicators have been ascribed high cultural capital in previous studies. With respect to the

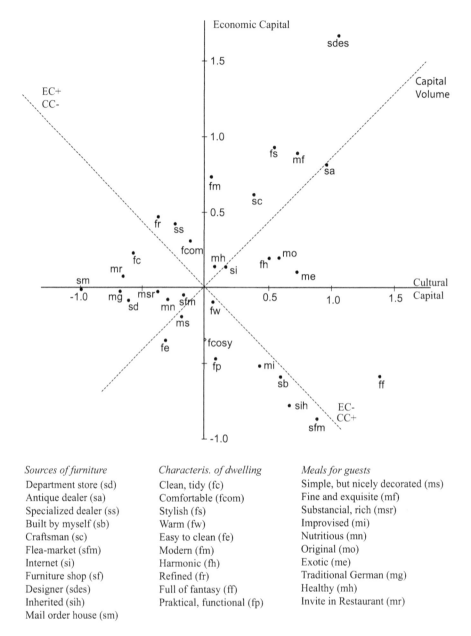

Fig. 5.1 Active variables of the social space, wave 1

Sources of furniture	Characteris. of dwelling	Meals for guests
Department store (sd)	Clean, tidy (fc)	Simple, but nicely decorated (ms)
Antique dealer (sa)	Comfortable (fcom)	Fine and exquisite (mf)
Specialized dealer (ss)	Stylish (fs)	Substancial, rich (msr)
Built by myself (sb)	Warm (fw)	Improvised (mi)
Craftsman (sc)	Easy to clean (fe)	Nutritious (mn)
Flea-market (sfm)	Modern (fm)	Original (mo)
Internet (si)	Harmonic (fh)	Exotic (me)
Furniture shop (sf)	Refined (fr)	Traditional German (mg)
Designer (sdes)	Full of fantasy (ff)	Healthy (mh)
Inherited (sih)	Praktical, functional (fp)	Invite in Restaurant (mr)
Mail order house (sm)		

socio-demographic characteristics, we find middle-aged residents (36 to 45 and 46 to 55) and residents with higher educational levels (college and university degree) on the positive part of the first axis; the negative part shows residents with low

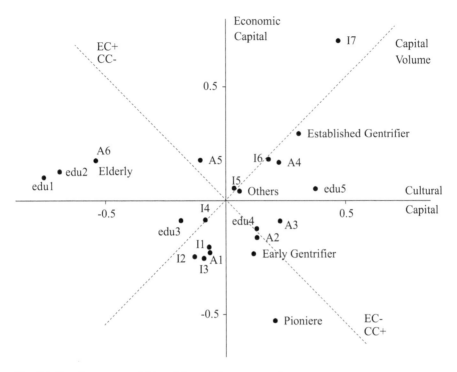

Fig. 5.2 Supplementary variables of the social space, wave 1

education (no formal education, elementary school) and residents aged 65 years and older. These passive indicators cross-confirm the interpretation of dimension 1, based on the active lifestyle indicators, as cultural capital.

Axis 2 (vertical dimension) reflects the economic capital, with a high level on the positive part and a low level on the negative part. Four indicators that were assigned to high cultural capital also indicate low economic capital: the furniture categories *flea market*, *inherited*, and *built myself*, and the category *full of fantasy* for characterizing the dwelling. Together with the dwelling characteristic *practical/functional*, these indicators are located in the negative part of dimension 2. On the positive part of this dimension, we find the designer and the antique dealer as sources for furniture; the characteristics of the dwellings are described as stylish and modern, and meals for guests are referred to as fine and exquisite. The interpretation as an economic dimension can be confirmed by projecting the seven indicators of equivalent income (Fig. 5.2) onto this dimension. While the first three groups of low income are located close to each other on the negative part on dimension 2, the other four indicators are located along the second dimension in the expected successive order.

Including a super-dimension between the two axes at 45°s in Fig. 5.1 (dashed line), representing the capital volume, and subsequently projecting the lifestyle indicators on this dimension, we find the following results: The designer as a source for furniture has the highest value, followed by the antique dealer, then the category *fine and exquisite* in meals for guests, and then the category *stylish dwelling*. This corresponds to Bourdieu's theory Bourdieu ([1979] 1984) that capital volume is the weighted sum of economic and cultural capital – it is high when both kinds of capital are high. For example, when people buy their furniture from the designer or an antique dealer, they need both a sufficient amount of money (economic capital) and sufficient knowledge to recognize the value of the furniture (cultural capital). Low capital volume is associated with mail order and the department store as sources for furniture, along with serving traditional German meals and having clean or *easy to clean* dwellings. With respect to the composition of cultural and economic capital, Fig. 5.1 shows that especially the categories *flea market, inherited*, and *built myself*, for furniture, and *improvised* meals for guests are indicators of relatively high cultural but relatively low economic capital. Overall, the entire solution is close to those reported by Blasius and Friedrichs (2008) and Blasius and Mühlichen (2010).

With respect to the five social groups included into the social space as supplementary variables (Fig. 5.2), established gentrifiers have the highest capital volume, pioneers have the lowest economic capital but relatively high cultural capital, while early gentrifiers are located between these two participants in the process of gentrification. Finally, the elderly have relatively low cultural capital and above-average economic capital, while the 'others' are located close to the centroid; both forms of their capital are close to average.

Figure 5.3 shows the space of individuals from the first wave. The figure is subdivided into six parts; the part on the upper left shows all five social groups together, the upper right part the established gentrifiers, and the lower right part the elderly. With respect to the established gentrifiers, it can be seen that they are concentrated in the upper right sector of the social space, i.e. the part which is associated with a high capital volume. However, it can also be seen that some of the established gentrifiers have a lifestyle that largely distinguishes them from the majority of their social group. Early gentrifiers and especially pioneers are concentrated in the lower right part of the social space, that is, they have high cultural and (relatively) low economic capital. The fact that the members of both groups of actors participating in the gentrification process are concentrated in the same area of the social space might be due to the fact that former pioneers do not immediately change their lifestyles when adopting the status of (early) gentrifiers. The change in their formal status may occur from one day to the next; for students, for example, by definition after completion of their university studies and upon beginning their first job as an academic. It may take some time until they actually implement their new status as early gentrifiers and start to change their lifestyles according to their improved financial situation.

In the next step we show the changes of lifestyles over the four waves, running MCA on the entire data set as it was during the fourth wave (N = 997, consisting of N = 735 stayers and N = 262 in-movers, cf. Table 5.2), with all lifestyle indicators being set as active. In addition, the sub-samples of old and new residents (see columns 2 and 3 in Table 5.2) were used as supplementary variables. Subsequently,

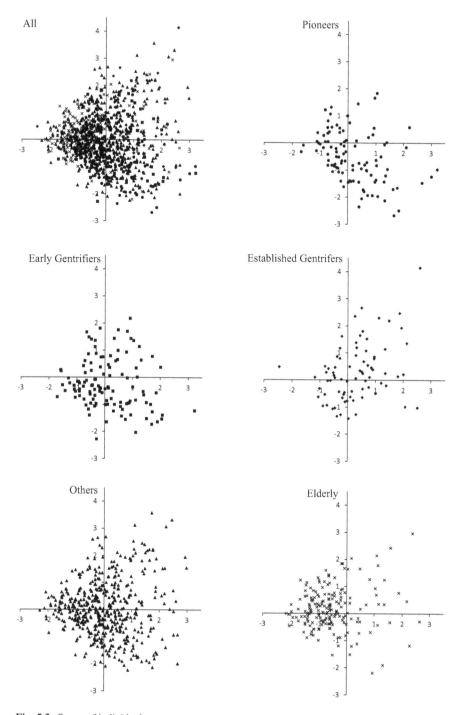

Fig. 5.3 Space of individuals

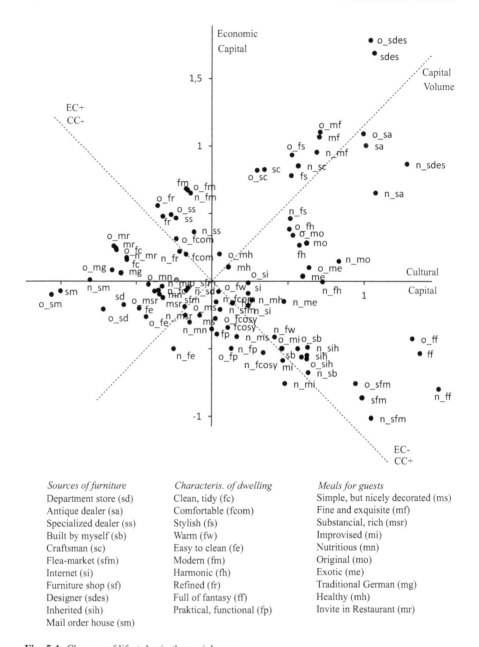

Fig. 5.4 Changes of lifestyles in the social space

Sources of furniture	Characteris. of dwelling	Meals for guests
Department store (sd)	Clean, tidy (fc)	Simple, but nicely decorated (ms)
Antique dealer (sa)	Comfortable (fcom)	Fine and exquisite (mf)
Specialized dealer (ss)	Stylish (fs)	Substancial, rich (msr)
Built by myself (sb)	Warm (fw)	Improvised (mi)
Craftsman (sc)	Easy to clean (fe)	Nutritious (mn)
Flea-market (sfm)	Modern (fm)	Original (mo)
Internet (si)	Harmonic (fh)	Exotic (me)
Furniture shop (sf)	Refined (fr)	Traditional German (mg)
Designer (sdes)	Full of fantasy (ff)	Healthy (mh)
Inherited (sih)	Praktical, functional (fp)	Invite in Restaurant (mr)
Mail order house (sm)		

we use the same variables three times: First, based on all 997 cases; second, based on new residents (N = 262); third, based on the 'stayers' (N = 735). This procedure allows us to show changes in lifestyles over time. Figure 5.4 shows the social space

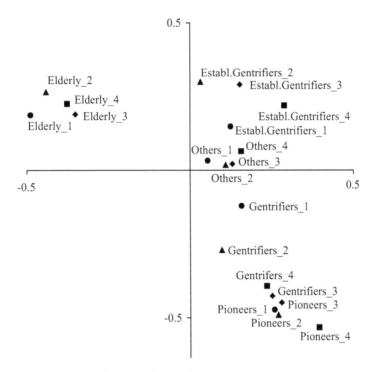

Fig. 5.5 The actors of gentrification in the social space over time

of this solution (a leading "o_" refers to the old residents and a leading "n_" refers to the new residents); the three respective indicators are located on a straight line, with the entire sample located between the two sub-samples. Large differences indicate that there were significant changes in the choice of lifestyle indicators over time.

As Fig. 5.4 shows, the respective lifestyle indicators are close to each other in most cases, which indicate that there are few changes in the use of lifestyle indicators over time. Most obvious are the distances between the three groups with regard to the indicators *designer* and *antique dealer*: Although both indicators were chosen relatively rarely by the in-movers (see Table 5.2), their respective categories are located closer to the centroid than is the case with the stayers (compare "o_sdes" with "n_sdes", and "o_sa" with "n_sa", projecting the respective categories by 90° on the axis 'capital volume'). The respective categories are still indicators of a high capital volume, but both have lost – at least partly – their distinctive position in the social space. In terms of Bourdieu ([1979] 1984), one can conclude that from the first to the fourth wave the labels lost their symbolic power as an indicator for high capital volume – they are no longer important signs of distinction. In the final step we included the five social groups from all four waves as supplementary variables in the social space (Fig. 5.5).

Comparing the locations of the pioneers over time shows that their positions do not change significantly; they maintain a relatively low level of economic capital and a relatively high level of cultural capital. The capital volume of the established gentrifiers increases over time, which is an indicator for at least some gentrification in the neighborhood. Furthermore, the early gentrifiers moved towards the pioneers, a movement that might be caused by the fact that some pioneers turned into gentrifiers without changing their lifestyles over time (in the given case within a maximum of 4 years). The others group remains close to the centroid over time; over all four waves they represent an average lifestyle. Finally, the elderly move slightly towards increasing cultural capital, but their cultural capital is still clearly below average in the fourth wave.

Conclusion

In a four wave dwelling panel study on individuals' dwellings, we documented the process of gentrification in Cologne using lifestyle indicators. To our knowledge this is the first study applying Bourdieu's concept of social space to gentrification research. Operationalizing the actors of gentrification and using lifestyle indicators similar to those first introduced by Bourdieu ([1979] 1984), and later reformulated for German culture (Blasius and Winkler 1989; Blasius and Friedrichs 2008; Blasius and Mühlichen 2010), we show how lifestyles in the two Cologne neighborhoods Deutz and Mülheim changed over time. Some of our findings can be interpreted as changes in the use of symbols of distinction, such as the categories *antique dealer* and *designer* as sources for furniture: Both indicators lose some of their distinctive power, their economic capital decreases. With respect to the category *full of fantasy* as a dwelling characteristic, and the flea market as a source of furniture, we observe a change in the composition of capital: Cultural capital increases, economic capital decreases. Overall, we were able show that Bourdieu's theories can be successfully applied to the study of gentrification.

References

Blasius, J. (1993). *Gentrification und Lebensstile. Eine empirische Untersuchung.* Wiesbaden: Deutscher Universitätsverlag

Blasius, J., & Friedrichs, J. (2008). Lifestyles in distressed neighbourhoods. A test of Bourdieu's "taste of necessity" hypothesis. *Poetics, 36*, 24–44.

Blasius, J., & Friedrichs, J. (2011). Die Bedeutung von Lebensstilen für die Erklärung von sozial-räumlichen Distanzen. In J. Rössel & G. Otte (Eds.), *Lebensstilforschung, Sonderheft 51 der Kölner Zeitschrift für Soziologie und Sozialpsychologie* (pp. 399–423).

Blasius, J., & Mühlichen, A. (2010). Identifying audience segments applying the "social space" approach. *Poetics, 38*, 69–89.

Blasius, J., & Winkler, J. (1989). Gibt es die "feinen Unterschiede"? Eine empirische Überprüfung der Bourdieuschen Theorie. *Kölner Zeitschrift für Soziologie und Sozialpsychologie, 41*, 72–94.

Blasius, J., Friedrichs, J., & Rühl, H. (2016a). Pioneers and gentrifiers in the process of gentrification. *International Journal of Housing Policy, 16*, 50–69.

Blasius, J., Friedrichs, J., & Rühl, H. (2016b). Gentrification in zwei Kölner Wohngebieten. *Kölner Zeitschrift für Soziologie und Sozialpsychologie, 68,* 541–559.

Blasius, J., & Friedrichs, J. (2016). Gentrification in Köln. In J. Friedrichs & J. Blasius (Eds.), *Gentrifizierung in Köln* (pp. 57–91). Opladen: Barbara Budrich Verlag.

Bourdieu, P. ([1979], 1984). *La distinction.* Paris: Editions de Minuit. *Distinction. A social critique of the judgment of taste.* Cambridge, MA: Harvard University Press.

Bourdieu, P. (1983). The forms of capital. In J. Richardson (Ed.), *Handbook of theory and research for the sociology of education* (pp. 241–258). New York: Greenwood Press.

Bourdieu, P., & de Saint-Martin, M. (1976). Anatomie du goût. *Actes de la Recherche en Sciences Sociales, 5,* 1–110.

Bridge, G. (2001). Estate agents as interpreters of economic and cultural capital: The gentrification premium in the Sydney housing market. *International Journal of Urban and Regional Research, 25,* 87–101.

Butler, T. (1997). *Gentrification and the middle classes.* Aldershot: Ashgate.

Clay, P. L. (1979). *Neighbourhood renewal. Middle-class resettlement and incumbent upgrading in American neighbourhoods.* Toronto: Lexington.

Dangschat, J., & Friedrichs, J. (1988). *Gentrification in Hamburg. Eine empirische Untersuchung des Wandels von drei Wohnvierteln.* Hamburg: Gesellschaft für Sozialwissenschaftliche Stadtforschung.

Friedrichs, J., & Blasius, J. (2015). The dwelling panel – A new research method for studying urban change. *Raumforschung und Raumordnung, 73*(6), 377–388.

Friedrichs, J., & Blasius, J. (2016). Die Kölner Gentrification-Studien. In J. Friedrichs & J. Blasius (Eds.), *Gentrifizierung in Köln* (pp. 7–27). Opladen: Barbara Budrich Verlag.

Glass, R. (1964). Introduction. In Center for Urban Studies (Ed.), *London: Aspects of change* (pp. XIII–XVII). London: MacGibbon & Kee.

Greenacre, M. J. (1984). *Theory and applications of correspondence analysis.* London: Academic.

Holm, S. (1979). A simple sequentially rejective multiple test procedure. *Scandinavian Journal of Statistics, 6,* 65–70.

Jager, M. (1986). Class definition and the esthetics of gentrification: Victoriana in Melbourne. In N. Smith & P. Williams (Eds.), *Gentrification of the city* (pp. 78–91). Boston: Allen & Unwin.

Kerstein, R. (1990). Stage models of gentrification. An Examination. *Urban Affairs Quarterly, 25,* 620–639.

Lees, L., Slater, T., & Wyly, E. (2008). *Gentrification.* Oxon/New York: Routledge.

Le Gates, R. T., & Hartmann, C. (1986). The anatomy of displacement in the United States. In N. Smith & P. Williams (Eds.), *Gentrification of the city* (pp. 178–200). Boston: Allen & Unwin.

Le Roux, B., & Rouanet, H. (2010). *Multiple correspondence analysis.* Thousand Oaks: Sage.

Ley, D. (1996). *The new middle class and the remaking of the Central City.* New York: Oxford University Press.

OECD. (2009). *What are equivalence scales?* Retrieved December 10, 2017, from http://www.oecd.org/eco/growth/OECD-Note-EquivalenceScales.pdf

Palen, J. J., & London, B. (Eds.). (1984). *Gentrification, displacement and neighbourhood vitalization.* New York: University of New York.

Zukin, S. (1982). *Loft-Living: Culture and capital in urban change.* New Brunswick: Rutgers University Press.

Zukin, S. (1987). Gentrification: Culture and capital in the urban core. *Annual Review of Sociology, 13,* 129–147.

Zukin, S. (2010). *Naked City. The death and life of authentic urban places.* Oxford/New York: Oxford University Press.

Chapter 6
The Space of Economic and Cultural Capital: A Latent Class Analysis for Germany

Nora Waitkus and Olaf Groh-Samberg

Introduction

Bourdieu's concept of the social space is a powerful tool for analyzing social inequality in contemporary societies (Bourdieu 1984). His theory combines a structural dimension of various types of resources – called capitals – with a theory of social and cultural practices. As a relational approach, it refers to the relative differences of resources (here: capitals) and elements of cultural practices between individuals or social groups, rather than the absolute level of resources or substantial forms of cultural practices. Bourdieu's central argument is that the structural dimension of the social space is homologous to the system of differences and oppositions that underlie and structure the social and cultural practices, i.e., the space of lifestyles. This homology is caused by socialization effects which are inherent to the processes of attaining and reproducing various forms of capitals by individuals or families. This theoretical framework allows for a dynamic understanding of social classes: Social classes can be understood as groups of individuals which share similar experiences of acquiring and reproducing certain sets of capitals, via both family socialization and status attainment processes over the life course.

Research following Bourdieu has mainly focused on the concept of cultural capital (see Lareau and Weininger 2003; Prieur and Savage 2013) and the space of cultural practices or lifestyles (Bennett et al. 2009; Le Roux et al. 2008).

Electronic supplementary material The online version of this chapter (https://doi.org/10.1007/978-3-030-15387-8_6) contains supplementary material, which is available to authorized users.

N. Waitkus (✉) · O. Groh-Samberg
University of Bremen (BIGSSS/SOCIUM), Bremen, Germany
e-mail: waitkus@uni-bremen.de; ogs@bigsss-bremen.de

© Springer Nature Switzerland AG 2019
J. Blasius et al. (eds.), *Empirical Investigations of Social Space*,
Methodos Series 15, https://doi.org/10.1007/978-3-030-15387-8_6

With regard to Bourdieu's approach to capitals, cultural capital has been much more extensively discussed and employed than economic capital. Accordingly, little attention has been paid to the entire distribution of economic and cultural capital and, thus, the structural dimension of the social space. Following Bourdieu's original methodological approach, Multiple correspondence analysis (MCA) has been applied to indicators of cultural practices and preferences in order to explore the structuring of the space of lifestyles (for an overview see Coulangeon and Duval 2014). The resulting structure of the space of lifestyles is assumed to simply mirror the structure of the space of capitals. Empirically, this assumption is often tested, or merely illustrated, by plotting indicators of education, occupations or income onto the space of lifestyles (e.g. Bourdieu 1984: 262).

Our analysis in this chapter deviates from these approaches in several respects. First, we aim at directly assessing the structural dimension of the social space, as a space of capitals. We argue that the concept of the social space provides a multidimensional approach to social stratification research, combining economic and cultural capital, which has been largely neglected so far (but see e.g. Savage 2015; Savage et al. 2013). Second, a main advantage of Bourdieu's concept of the social space is that it easily allows integrating various dimensions of economic capital, including wealth. This is particularly important since classical approaches to social class have acknowledged wealth only as business assets, but not as a decisive dimension of social stratification (Savage 2014; Savage 2015; Waitkus and Groh-Samberg 2018). Occupation-based approaches to social class (for example Erikson and Goldthorpe 1992; Weeden and Grusky 2005, Wright 1997) exert particular difficulties in acknowledging wealth as a crucial dimension of social class, simply because wealth is more independent of occupations than (labor) income (Savage 2015). Thirdly, our analysis focuses on the horizontal dimension of the social space as defined by the relative composition of economic and cultural capital. For Bourdieu, the differences in the relative composition of capitals build the main determinant for socio-cultural and socio-political conflicts *within* the "ruling classes", between its (dominated) cultural and (dominating) economic poles. While these horizontal disparities or class cleavages have been neglected in uni-dimensional or gradational approaches to social stratification (or have been misunderstood as status inconsistencies), we follow Bourdieu's argument that cultural and economic capital represent two distinct and even conflicting forms of legitimate power in contemporary capitalist societies (Bourdieu 1987). While we cannot test this assumption to its full extent, we nevertheless, fourthly, take into account the dynamic perspective on the social space by assessing intra-generational class mobility over time. Finally, we use latent class analysis (LCA), rather than MCA, for our empirical analysis. LCA is a clustering approach based on categorical variables – in our case, various dimensions of economic and cultural capital – that allows for identifying social classes based on their specific capital portfolios (see Savage et al. 2013 for a similar approach).

This chapter is structured as follows: First, we discuss Bourdieu's concept of the social space and highlight the main features for the purpose of our analysis. Section two describes data and methods. In section three we present our results. We first describe the nine social classes obtained from LCA of cross-sectional capital portfolios. Subsequently, we exploit the longitudinal nature of the data and present mobility patterns over time. Section four concludes our piece of work.

Theoretical Outline: The Space of Capital

We propose an empirical approach to social classes based on a direct assessment of the structural dimension of the social space, as a space of capital. In the following, we first briefly discuss Bourdieu's theoretical understanding of the social space before we offer a conceptualization for an empirical assessment of the space of capital.

The Structure of the Social Space

In *Distinction* (1984), Bourdieu established the concept of the social space as a distinct approach to social class analysis. Bourdieu himself, and most of the research following him, employed correspondence analysis to various measures of cultural practices and tastes. He argues that the resulting "space of lifestyles" is homologous to the space of social positions. This argument was empirically supported by plotting some direct indicators of economic resources (namely income) and formal educational qualifications onto the space of lifestyles (Bourdieu 1984: 262).

Bourdieu argues that the two main axes of the space can be interpreted as a vertical axis representing the overall capital volume, and a horizontal axis representing the composition of the two most dominant types of capital, namely economic and cultural capital. A third axis of the social space is characterized as the 'social trajectory', capturing the intergenerational as well as life-course mobility of individuals (Bourdieu 1987: 4). An important feature of Bourdieu's social space is that the horizontal differentiation between the cultural and the economic pole becomes stronger as one moves upwards along the vertical axis. It is thus within the upper classes where the division into an economic and a cultural fraction is most pronounced, represented by the ascetic and highly cultured practices of arts and intellectuals on the one hand, and the conspicuous luxury consumption of the rich, on the other (Bourdieu 1989). Whereas the middle classes are stratified along this horizontal axis as well – reflecting their strong orientations towards the bourgeoisie classes – the horizontal divide is almost absent in the working classes.

The horizontal differentiation into a dominantly cultural and a dominantly economic pole of the ruling classes refers not only to symbolic distinctions, but also to the underlying struggles about the legitimate principles of domination. For the "dominated fractions of the dominating classes" (Bourdieu 1984: 470), this is money, but in its legitimized forms of successful economic entrepreneurship, industrialism, and venture capital, representing the productive forces that bring all the progress and fortune to modern societies. For the "dominated fractions of the dominating classes" (ibid.), the most legitimate principle of domination is knowledge, expertise, culture, in its most exceptional forms of universal reason and its strongest institutional manifestation in the modern state, or the "state nobility" (Bourdieu 1996). While Bourdieu is very clear about the dominance of economic capital over cultural capital, he has never given a sound explanation for this brutal fact (Bourdieu 1996: 270). However, as a matter of social struggles, the relative weight of economic vs. cultural capital is not predefined at a fix rate. This leads to a crucial problem of Bourdieu's concept of capital and the social space: While the labeling of the two axes of the social space (capital volume and its composition) suggests or even requires that the two types of economic and of cultural capital are measurable in distinct quantities and can be added up and related to each other, there is no straightforward way how such a conversion rate between economic and cultural capital might be derived (Bourdieu 1984: 125 ff.).

While the empirical strategy of detecting the structure of the social space departs from a relational (correspondence) analysis of cultural practices and tastes, his theoretical explanation runs in the opposite direction, thereby introducing the concept of habitus as a mediator between structure and praxis: In order to explain the structure of the social space, Bourdieu argues that it is basically the concrete capital portfolio, and the individual trajectory of capital endowment and accumulation over time, that shapes the habitus, which then shapes the cultural practices and tastes (Bourdieu 1989). Thus, in his theoretical model, the space of capital is the fundamental and determining structure of social inequality, which basically produces the cultural practices. We do not engage here with the theoretical controversies over Bourdieu's theory of the habitus, which has been criticized for being too deterministic and static (Jenkins 1992).

Yet, Bourdieu has never provided an attempt to measure the social space directly as a space of capital. He further never quantified something like the "overall volume of economic and cultural capital" and the "ratio" of the capital composition – and to our knowledge this has also not been attempted by others. Although we do not propose directly to quantify measures of economic and cultural capital either, we put forward an approach that at least allows deriving social classes based on a direct assessment of various types of economic and cultural capital.

A Direct Approach to Measuring the Space of Capital

The theoretical idea behind this direct operationalization of the space of capital is to understand capital portfolios – i.e., the clustering of specific portfolios of various types of economic and cultural capital – as the outcome of class-specific types of investment strategies. Specific capital portfolios are assumed to represent distinct social strategies of investing into social status: strategies to attain, reproduce, and accumulate capital portfolios. While we cannot measure the underlying investment preferences (and the class habitus) directly, we take the actual clustering of capital portfolios as the outcome of successfully realized investment strategies.[1] In this way,

---

[1] This strategy ignores the fact that strategies of capital accumulation may simply fail, so that the actual capital composition of a given household may not represent its original strategies. While this is true at the individual level, our analyses operates at the level of social groups, or classes.

we retain and reinterpret the practical and dynamic nature of Bourdieu's notion of capital. Capital portfolios thus serve as proxies for class-specific strategies of resource accumulation (Savage et al. 2005).

To this end, we need to disaggregate capital as far as possible. For instance, economic capital exists in specific forms of labor earnings, home ownership, stocks or business assets, etc. We assume that these various forms of capital involve different strategies and preferences. For example, home ownership, building loans or life insurances are types of economic capital that typically fulfill an insurance function. They might be accompanied by long-term saving strategies, while savings are obtained from labor income. On the contrary, financial assets, real estate or business property involve high risks (chances for profit and risks of losing) and require a stock of wealth that can be invested in the first place. However, it is the specific combination of various types of capital, i.e. the 'capital portfolio', which indicates a distinct logic of social practices, or a class-specific habitus. For example, academic education can serve different social strategies when combined with different sets of economic capital. Academic titles either serve as a prerequisite or collective legitimization strategy for entering managerial positions, positions that are accompanied by high labor incomes and financial assets that are invested on the stock market. Or, in contrast, higher education can serve as an entrance to academic professions that earn a high income because they deserve it – in other words, as a gratification and acknowledgement of the value of education as such. In this case, higher education is likely combined with high social security, an outright owned bourgeois house, and probably some financial assets that are safely invested in long-running funds. If we only consider single measures of income and education, it is often unclear which one serves the other. Combined with other sets of economic and cultural capital, like wealth and high-brow cultural practices, the underlying investment strategies become apparent, at least in terms of probabilities. Therefore, we focus on the portfolio of disaggregated and comprehensive sets of economic and cultural capital. Based on such an account, social classes can be understood more thoroughly as groups which share certain social strategies and capital endowments. This approach comes close to what Savage and colleagues pointed out: Applying *capital* as an analytical entity to social class analysis enables investigating how inequalities evolve and how classes accumulate and protect their benefits relative to others (Savage et al. 2005: 43).

Data and Methods

For our analysis, we draw on German household panel data that contain rich information on households' socio-economic resources, including different forms of wealth. The German Socio-economic Panel Study (GSOEP) was initiated in

---

The likelihood of failures, or of any other type of individual deviations between social strategies and actual outcomes of capital accumulation, is part of the overall probability distribution of class membership.

1984 in West Germany and expanded to East Germany right after the fall of the wall in 1989 (Wagner et al. 2007). All household members older than 17 years are personally interviewed on a yearly basis. Today, the survey covers more than 30,000 individuals living in over 11,000 households. In the years 2002, 2007 and 2012, a detailed wealth module was implemented, permitting for in-depth analysis of individuals' (and households') wealth endowments (Frick et al. 2010). The period of investigation covers the years 2002–2012 and thus allows us to further analyze class mobility patterns over time.

We restrict our sample to couples and singles aged 25–60, which may or may not have children. We thus focus on prime age adults living in single, couple or nuclear family households, excluding more complex household types that contain more than two adults. The individuals in these excluded households amount to 16.5% of all adults aged 25–60 in each of the three years. This is done to ease the aggregation of economic and cultural capital at the household level. All information is aggregated on the household level, assuming couples pool and share their respective individual capitals (This assumption is certainly a simplification of the inequalities within households, in particular with respect to within-couple wealth inequality – see Grabka et al. 2015.). All sorts of economic capital are adjusted for inflation and household size. Wealth components are divided by two for couple households, and incomes are adjusted according to the new OECD equivalence scale. We assume cultural capital to benefit each partner in a couple undividedly, so that the highest value of each cultural capital component is assigned to both partners of a couple. Our final sample comprises 22,630 person years (with 8655 persons in 2002, 7749 persons in 2007 and 6226 persons in 2012).

We include different sorts of economic as well as cultural capital in our analysis. The model contains five indicators for economic capital:

- Net household income; we use households' total net income minus income from asset flows
- Income from capital
- Net value of home ownership
- Net value of assets (financial assets, business assets, tangible assets and further real estate)[2]
- Market values of building loans and insurances.

We add four indicators for cultural capital:

- Highest educational level in the household (highest qualification)
- Highest human capital in the household (measured via working experience weighted by the level of required qualification)[3]

---

[2]The net value of assets is constructed as follows: net value of further real estate + market value of financial assets + market value of business assets + market values of tangible assets + property debt – other debts.

[3]The proxy for human capital is the type of employment (0 = not working; 1 = sporadic employment, 2 = part-time employment, 3 = fulltime employment) multiplied by educational

- Highest activity level of highbrow cultural practices[4]
- Highest activity level of popular cultural practices[5]

To group households according to their specific capital portfolios, we apply latent class analysis (LCA) based on the categorical coding of the various types of capital reported above. LCA is a probabilistic type of cluster analysis for categorical variables and well-suited for detecting groups with specific configurations or portfolios of capital (Vermunt and Magidson 2004). Methodologically, it builds on the statistical concept of conditional independence, meaning that individuals are clustered that the correlation of the various variables within each cluster is zero. LCA is foremost an explorative method that requires substantial interpretation of the results to derive the final model. Formally, the best cluster solution is obtained when the information criteria reach the minimum. Nonetheless, it is even more important that the cluster solution is sense making, stable and valid (Vermunt and Magidson 2004). The model-fit statistics (see Online Appendix Table 6.1) reveal the conventional finding of a decreasing log-likelihood, as well as AIC (Akaike information criteria) and BIC (Bayesian information criteria) with the number of classes increasing. However, the ten-class solution is rather unstable and the log-likelihood thus cannot be replicated. The nine-class model is stable and shows the smallest (stable) information criteria. Based on the comparison of model fit statistics and the inspection and interpretation of different numbers of classes, we thus opt for a nine-class model.

We pool the data for the 3 years 2002, 2007 and 2012, assuming that the overall structure of the social space is constant over this period of time.[6] We use cross-sectional weights as delivered with the SOEP (accounting for the oversampling of various groups and the different sampling and attrition probabilities) for reporting the results. The wealth data in the SOEP are checked, edited and multiply imputed for missing values (Frick et al. 2013). We use all five replicates and therefore repeated each step of the analysis five times. All reported results refer to the mean value of results over the five replicates.

---

level needed for the employment performed (0 = no education, 1 = basic briefing, no education, 2 = formal instructions or classes, 3 = vocational training, 4 = higher vocational training/lower tertiary degree, 5 = tertiary education).

[4]This proxy for highbrow cultural activities is the mean of (1) attendance of opera, theatre, classical concerts or exhibitions and (2) being culturally active in music, theatre, drawing, photography, or dancing. Both variables are measured on a scale from 1 (never) to 4 (daily). The highest mean is assigned to all household members.

[5]The proxy for popular cultural practices is the most frequent attendance of cinema, pop concerts, disco, sport events of a household member from never (1) to daily (4).

[6]As a robustness check, we performed the LCA using only one single point of observation (i.e., 2002, 2007 and 2012). The results are pretty robust, with some smaller deviations for the first year of 2002.

Results: The Space of Capital in Germany, 2002–2012

We start with presenting the nine latent classes obtained from a cross-sectional analysis of the pooled data. While our analysis is based on the above-mentioned set of indicators, we also describe the resulting classes in terms of additional socio-demographic characteristics. In a second step, we make use of the longitudinal nature of the underlying data and assess class mobility over time. A main focus of the analysis lies on the vertical and horizontal structuring of the classes.

The Class Structure of Capital Portfolios: Results from a Latent Class Analysis

As indicated in Table 6.1, the *Lower Class* is about 12% of our sample (for the full model see Online Appendix Table 6.2). Members of this class have very low incomes and negative assets, home ownership, building loans and insurance or income from capital. Further, they perform lowest on all forms of cultural capital (Table 6.2) with almost no one reporting a tertiary education and almost 60% having not more than basic vocational qualification as the highest educational level in the household. Age is above average, and 60% are not employed. We find a comparably high number of retirees (10%) and mainly low-skilled manual and low-skilled service workers (26% and 25%).

The small *Cultural Lower Class* (6%) differs from the *Lower Class* mainly in terms of cultural capital. The economic differences are rather low, as both groups show low incomes and almost no wealth. This latent class shows that the highest

Table 6.1 Nine-class solution with selected indicators for economic capital

	Size	Total income	Total assets	Home owner-ship	Build. loans & insurances	Income f. capital
Lower class	12%	6.807	−2.667	3.187	604	30
Cultural lower class	6%	6.966	2.377	9.447	2.777	317
Lower middle class	18%	22.634	−3.311	8.946	4.597	113
Cultural middle class	10%	31.892	3.997	13.010	6.218	188
Economic middle class	8%	24.306	12.477	36.108	16.224	550
Middle class	25%	33.041	12.554	42.041	16.496	522
Cultural upper middle class	12%	52.418	32.401	53.057	22.869	1.333
Economic upper middle class	6%	39.624	197.608	119.973	42.031	5.945
Elite	3%	83.165	355.931	139.205	51.505	12.237
Total	100%	29.942	31.070	35.238	14.016	1.152

Note: Weighted calculation based on pooled SOEP data, waves 2002, 2007, and 2012. Only household heads and partners aged 25–60 years in nuclear family households. Mean results from five imputed wealth replicates

Table 6.2 Nine-class solution with indicators for cultural capital and age

	Size	Tertiary degree	Human capital	Highbrow cult. practices	Popcultural practices	Age
Lower class	12%	4%	1,6	1,3	1,4	43
Cultural lower class	6%	21%	1,8	2,3	2,6	38
Lower middle class	18%	5%	3,0	1,8	2,2	39
Cultural middle class	10%	91%	4,0	2,4	2,5	38
Economic middle class	8%	7%	2,7	1,2	1,2	46
Middle class	25%	8%	3,4	2,1	2,4	42
Cultural upper middle class	12%	87%	4,1	2,4	2,4	43
Economic upper middle class	6%	15%	3,1	2,1	2,2	47
Elite	3%	91%	4,2	2,5	2,3	46
Total	100%	28%	3,1	1,9	2,2	42

Note: Weighted calculation based on pooled SOEP data, waves 2002, 2007, and 2012. Only household heads and partners aged 25–60 years in nuclear family households. Mean results from five imputed wealth replicates

pop cultural practices but also highbrow practices are frequent. Further, this group is the youngest among our sample, typically lives in single households (58%), is unmarried (55%) and half of its members are not working. If working, we find mainly low skilled service occupations (24%).

Above these two lower classes, we find a *Lower Middle Class* (18% of the sample). Compared to the Cultural Lower Class, this group is characterized by higher average income (although total assets are negative) and a stronger work orientation indicated by higher values for human capital acquired on job, while formal education and cultural practices are lower than in the Cultural Lower Class. A skilled manual worker in fulltime employment is the most common employment type in this latent class. This group is comparably young and mostly married (58%).

Next, we find three fractions of the middle classes which are characterized by a similar overall level though different composition of capital: The *Cultural Middle Class* is defined by its broad endowment with cultural capital. This group is highly educated (91% have tertiary education) and shows a strong human capital alongside with high intensity of cultural practices. Unsurprisingly, we find mainly socio-cultural professionals and semi-professionals (together 30%) as well as technical experts (19%) in this latent class. While the household's income is well on average, reflecting high returns from cultural capital, all other sorts of economic capital are considerably lower than in the other two middle classes. The Cultural Middle Class is one of the classes with a very high share of full time work (71%).

Compared to the Cultural Middle Class, the *Economic Middle Class* possesses less cultural capital, but we observe a considerable increase in the amount of net worth. Though income from labor is below average, the high overall net worth is mainly due to home ownership and building loans and insurances – thus, it is predominantly wealth that fulfills a security function (see Table 6.A1). Accordingly, we mainly find skilled and low-skilled manual workers of older ages.

The large *Middle Class* is about 25% of our sample. Compared to the Economic and the Cultural Middle Class, it combines the higher incomes of the Cultural Middle Class with the wealth level of the Economic Middle Class, while the endowment with cultural capital is more in-between. Especially the tertiary degree rate is low, while practices are higher than for the Economic Middle Class. This also holds for the mean age which is close to the overall average of our sample. In terms of occupational positions, the Middle Class consists of a broad variety of skilled occupations like routine skilled office workers, skilled manual workers, as well as junior mangers.

Subsequently, we identify two Upper Middle classes, again a more cultural and a more economic fraction:

The *Cultural Upper Middle Class* (CUMC, 12%) shows particular high incomes from labor, and more than twice as much financial assets than the Middle Class. However, home ownership is of central importance, as are building loans and insurances. Higher grade manuals and technical experts are found here, together with socio-cultural (semi-)professions. This mid-aged group performs high on all sorts of cultural capital, with 87% having tertiary education.

By contrast, the relatively small *Economic Upper Middle Class* (EUMC, 6%) is defined by strong wealth portfolios with much less cultural capital. This group has a diversified wealth portfolio and owns not only profound home ownership, but financial assets as well as building loans and insurances. In fact, this class possesses twice as much financial assets than the Cultural Upper Middle Class. It is the only group (except for the Elite) that owns considerable business assets and real estate. However, income from labor is lower than in the Cultural Upper Middle Class. In terms of occupations, we find mainly the petite bourgeoisie with and without employees as well as managers and even some manual workers (11%). This group is the oldest group in our sample and mainly consists of West Germans. In sum, this class combines the high and diversified economic capital portfolio of the Elite with only average performance on cultural capital which rather resembles the Middle Class.

Finally, the *Elite* makes up about 6%. This group performs "best" on all sorts of economic and cultural capital. It shows a highly diversified pool of wealth, including business assets, financial assets, home ownership, further real estate, as well as high incomes. The Elite combines both the high and diversified economic portfolio of the Economic Upper Middle Class with the strong performance on cultural capital of the Cultural Upper Middle Class. Again, this class is almost completely West German. Most adults here are either self-employed, large employers or higher-grade managers.

Overall, we find that the nine latent classes are strongly stratified vertically according to the overall volume of capital. In line with Bourdieu's concept of the social space, we also find a horizontal differentiation representing the relative composition of cultural and economic capital. Contrary to the absence of any horizontal differentiation in Bourdieu's portrait of the lower classes, we do find a horizontal differentiation between the Lower and the Lower Cultural Class. This is probably due to the increased importance of cultural capital that consequently induced new divisions in the lower classes, e.g. between industrial and service occupations, compared to the 1960s and 1970s (see for example Kriesi 1989, Oesch 2006). This horizontal differentiation in the relative importance of economic versus cultural capital is also strong in the middle and the upper middle classes. From the nine classes, three classes have a predominant cultural profile, found at the lower, the middle and the upper middle level, while two classes have an economic profile, found at the middle and the upper middle level. On the other hand, we do not find a horizontal differentiation at the very top. Rather, the Elite class shows exceptionally high values of both economic and cultural capital. This is somewhat at odds with Bourdieu's understanding that the horizontal differences are strongest at the very top. Of course, this claim probably pertains much more to the symbolic cleavages and struggles between the dominant and the dominated fraction of the dominating classes. This might not be visible based on the more structural indicators of economic and cultural capital that we use. However, in terms of occupational groupings, we also do not find a strong difference between the socio-cultural professions on the one hand and the managers on the other. Hence, the interesting question arises of whether the strategies of capital accumulation and investments in the highest layer of the social space have changed over the recent decades in such a way that it blurred the traditional cleavages between the "dominated fractions and dominant fractions within the dominant class" (Bourdieu 1984: 470). This might be due to educational expansion and the increased relevance of education and cultural capital for the economic elites, but also due to the economization of cultural capital and socio-cultural occupations, and the increased relevance of wealth for all higher social classes. One possible route to get more insights into the role and stability of the horizontal differentiation is to look at the class mobility over time.

Class Mobility

Given the longitudinal nature of our data, we can assess mobility patterns over time. This is only possible for those who participated in at least two of the three waves of the SOEP in which wealth information was collected. Given that the mobility patterns appear to be similar for the two periods from 2002 to 2007 and from 2007 to 2012, we pooled the data. Table 6.3 shows the transition matrix (row percentages) between one point in time (2002 or 2007) to 5 years later (2007 or 2012, respectively).

The cells at the diagonal of the transition table indicate the percentages of individuals from each of the nine classes that had remained in the same class 5 years later. The most *stable* classes are found at the very bottom of the social space (Lower Class, 74%) and above the Middle Class. In general, mobility is restricted to neighboring classes along the vertical axis. Yet, we also observe mobility to appear *within the horizontal regions* of the space of capital. Individuals from the

Table 6.3 Mobility across social classes in t (2002 or 2007) and t + 5 (2007 or 2012)

	Lower Class	Cultural Lower Class	Lower Middle Class	Cultural Middle Class	Economic Middle Class	Middle Class	CUMC	EUMC	Elite	Total
Lower Class	74	5	12	1	5	3	0	0	0	100
Cultural Lower Class	13	33	18	19	5	6	5	1	1	100
Lower Middle Class	9	6	51	3	6	23	1	1	0	100
Cultural Middle Class	2	3	5	49	1	10	29	1	1	100
Economic Middle Class	13	3	21	0	34	22	1	5	0	100
Middle Class	1	2	13	3	5	65	5	5	0	100
Cultural Upper Middle Class	0	1	0	10	0	9	69	2	10	100
Economic Upper Middle Class	0	3	6	1	3	21	7	54	5	100
Elite	0	0	0	4	1	2	28	6	59	100
Total	11	5	18	9	7	28	14	6	4	100

Note: Upstream (row) percentages. Weighted calculation based on pooled SOEP data, waves 2002–2007, and 2007–2012. Only household heads and partners aged 25–60 years in nuclear family households. Mean results from five imputed wealth replicates

Cultural Lower Class, for instance, are highly mobile and mainly move within the lower part of the distribution, as well as to the Cultural Middle Class. The Cultural Middle Class itself moves primarily into the Cultural Upper Middle Class. But very little mobility appears between the cultural and the economic classes, even within the same vertical layer. For all three classes with a cultural profile, the odds to move into one of the other two cultural classes are far higher than to move into one of the two economic classes, even within the same vertical layer. The same holds true for the mobility of the two classes with predominantly economic capital, although to a much lesser degree. For them, however, we also observe significant downward mobility. Individuals from the Economic Middle Class tend to move mostly into the Middle Class and Lower Middle Class, whereas their richer counterparts, namely individuals from the Economic Upper Middle Class, predominantly move downwards, into the Middle Class.

Upward mobility into the Elite is rather limited. Overall, downward mobility rates amount to 34% and 37% for the Economic Middle and Economic Upper Middle Classes, respectively. For the corresponding predominantly cultural classes, downward mobility amounts only to 10% and 20%. This might indicate the stronger risks involved in the strategies of dominantly economic capital accumulation. Accordingly, mobility into the Elite is more likely for members of the Cultural Upper Middle Class than for Economic Upper Middle Class. This emphasizes that a prerequisite for entering elite positions is not only economic capital, but the combination of high economic and high cultural capital.

As expected, we also observe intra-generational mobility to follow a life course pattern. In general, the younger classes of the Cultural Lower Class, Lower Middle Class exert higher mobility rates and most likely still "move" within the social space until members get settled. Additional analyses show that these mobility patterns are similar for men and women and for people with migratory background vs. German natives, with increasing stability of the Lower Class when only considering men. Even though the horizontal pattern is similar for different age groups, we observe the youngest group in our sample (<35 years) to be more mobile, whereas the oldest group (>45) is pretty stable and moves exclusively within their respective capital portfolio, if at all.

To sum up, class mobility occurs mainly along the vertical axis but within the distinct horizontal layers of the social space. Cross-profile mobility from e.g. the cultural to the more economic pole is rare to nonexistent. The predominantly cultural classes are particularly unlikely to alter their relative capital composition, are more upwardly mobile than the economic classes, and do serve as the main recruiting pool for elite positions.

Conclusions

The aim of this chapter is to construct the 'space of cultural and economic capital' based on disaggregated measures of capital portfolios, and to analyze the dynamics of class mobility over time. Given the difficulties of extracting single dimensions of economic and cultural capital, we opted for LCA that allows us to directly derive classes based on the distinct clustering of concrete capital portfolios. When interpreting the nine latent classes, we find clear evidence for the two main axis of the social space, namely the vertical axis of the overall volume of capitals, and the horizontal axis representing the composition of capitals in terms of the relative weight of economic and cultural capital. Further exploration of class mobility reveals the horizontal axis to be stable over time. Most mobility occurs along the vertical axis of the social space, while there is only little horizontal mobility, indicating that individuals rarely change their investment and accumulation strategies.

Other than expected from Bourdieu's empirical results on the social space of France in 1960s, we did not find the horizontal differentiation to increase with the overall volume of capital. We rather found the horizontal division to be present already in the lower social classes, and we could not detect a horizontal cleavage at the very top. The former finding that a horizontal differentiation is already present at the lower layer of the social space is most likely due to educational expansion and the increased importance of cultural capital for lower social classes is due to de-industrialization and new class divisions, e.g. between industrial and service occupations (Hertel 2017, Oesch 2006). The latter finding that the elite class is characterized by both the highest economic *and* cultural capital is more challenging to understand. On the one hand, the absence of any horizontal division at the top might be due to the low resolution of the cultural capital indicators, which are not capable of grasping major differences and cleavages in cultural practices and symbolic boundaries. For instance, using more detailed information on field of study instead of simply educational levels, or more concrete items on the type of cultural activities and tastes, instead of simply the frequency of highbrow and popular cultural activities (both of which seem to be quite similar) would have allowed to zoom deeper into horizontal divisions of the type of cultural capitals prevalent at the top of the class hierarchy. On the other hand, our findings reveal a particularly strong relevance of cultural capital, even though we only use rather limited indicators of cultural practices. The absence of horizontal differences at the top might, therefore, also reflect important social changes at the top. Cultural capital has gained relevance with the ongoing educational expansion and the rising levels of academic qualifications in top managerial and other elite positions, not the least as a collective legitimation strategy to obtain and defend elite positions (Khan 2011). The absence of marked differences in the capital portfolios at the top of the German social space might also, to some extent, reflect peculiarities of the German class system, with its strong civil servants ('Beamtentum') who obtain high wages based on academic qualifications, allowing constant wealth accumulation over time and – thanks to the strong educational inequalities – across generations.

The empirical findings also suggest that social classes that predominantly invest in economic capital, without parallel strong investments in cultural capital, face greater risks of downward mobility (Waitkus and Groh-Samberg 2018). This is very different from social classes with predominantly cultural capital, which exert higher upward mobility rates, even into the elite class, and are particularly prone to maintain their cultural profile over time. At the same time, we clearly find that economic capital is more diversified at higher layers of the social space. In the middle classes, wealth is mostly held in home ownership, building loans and life insurances. Hence, wealth is mostly serving an insurance function in the middle classes, and goes hand in hand with high labor incomes and cultural and human capital investments. More diversified wealth portfolios are a characteristic of those classes focusing primarily on economic capital – with the corresponding risks involved – or the elite. This issue remains an area of highly interesting research.

Appendix

Table 6.A1 Economic capital across social classes (means in €)

	Income f. labor	Net wealth	Home ownership	Building loans and insurances	Income f. Capital	Financial assets	Business assets	Real estate	Overall debts
Lower class	6.807	1.123	3.187	604	30	157	50	314	5.303
Cultural lower class	6.966	14.600	9.447	2.777	317	2.948	404	816	5.235
Lower middle class	22.634	10.232	8.946	4.597	113	951	673	101	13.316
Cultural middle class	31.892	23.225	13.010	6.218	188	4.901	2.939	851	20.227
Economic middle class	24.306	64.808	36.108	16.224	550	6.353	4.006	4.877	19.640
Middle class	33.041	71.091	42.041	16.496	522	8.192	4.665	2.713	27.136
Cultural upper middle class	52.418	108.327	53.057	22.869	1.333	19.990	5.587	9.353	39.531
Economic upper middle class	39.624	359.613	119.973	42.031	5.945	40.253	71.540	91.919	60.981
Elite	83.165	546.640	139.205	51.505	12.237	110.656	120.970	134.382	98.080
Total	29.942	80.324	35.238	14.016	1.152	11.832	10.820	12.243	25.215

Source: Weighted calculation based on pooled SOEP data, waves 2002, 2007, and 2012. Only household heads and partners aged 25–60 years in nuclear family households. Mean results from five imputed wealth replicates

References

Bennett, T., Savage, M., Silva, E., Warde, A., Gayo-Cal, M., & Wright, D. (2009). *Culture, class, distinction*. London: Routledge.

Bourdieu, P. (1984). *Distinction*. Cambridge: Harvard University Press.

Bourdieu, P. (1987). What makes a social class? On the theoretical and practical existence of groups. *Berkeley Journal of Sociology, 32*, 1–17.

Bourdieu, P. (1989). Social space and symbolic power. *Sociological Theory, 7*(1), 14–25.

Bourdieu, P. (1996). *The state nobility: Elite schools in the field of power*. Stanford CA: Stanford University Press.

Coulangeon, P., & Duval, J. (Eds.). (2014). *The Routledge companion to Bourdieu's 'distinction'*. London/New York: Routledge.

Erikson, R., & Goldthorpe, J. H. (1992). *The constant flux. A study of class mobility in industrial societies*. Oxford: Clarendon Press.

Frick, J., Grabka, M. M., & Markus, J. (2013). *SOEP 2007 – Editing und multiple Imputation der Vermögensinformation 2002 und 2007 im SOEP*. SOEP Survey Papers, 146.

Frick, J., Grabka, M. M., & Markus, J. (2010). *Editing und multiple Imputation der Vermögensinformation 2002 und 2007 im SOEP*. SOEP Survey Papers, 146.

Grabka, M. M., Marcus, J., & Sierminska, E. (2015). Wealth distribution within couples. *Review of Economics of the Household, 13*(3), 459–486.

Hertel, F. R. (2017). *Social mobility in the 20th century*. Wiesbaden: VS Verlag für Sozialwissenschaften.

Jenkins, R. (1992). *Pierre Bourdieu*. New York: Routledge.

Khan, S. R. (2011). *Privilege. The making of an adolescent elite at St. Paul's school*. Princeton/Oxford: Princeton University Press.

Kriesi, H. (1989). New social movements and the new class in the Netherlands. *American Journal of Sociology, 94*(5), 1078–1116.

Lareau, A., & Weininger, E. B. (2003). Cultural capital in educational research: A critical assessment. *Theory and Society, 32*(5), 567–606.

Le Roux, B., Rouanet, H., Savage, M., & Warde, A. (2008). Class and cultural division in the UK. *Sociology, 42*(6), 1049–1071.

Oesch, D. (2006). *Redrawing the class map. Stratification and institutions in Britain, Germany, Sweden and Switzerland*. New York: Palgrave Macmillan.

Prieur, A., & Savage, M. (2013). Emerging forms of cultural capital. *European Societies, 15*(2), 246–267.

Savage, M. (2014). Piketty's challenge for sociology. *The British Journal of Sociology, 65*(4), 591–606.

Savage, M. (2015). Introduction to elites. From the 'problematic of the proletariat' to a class analysis of 'wealth elites'. *The Sociological Review, 63*(2), 223–239.

Savage, M., Devine, F., Cunningham, N., Taylor, M., Li, Y., Hjellbrekke, J., Le Roux, B., Friedman, S., & Miles, A. (2013). A new model of social class? Findings from the BBC's great British class survey experiment. *Sociology, 47*(2), 219–250.

Savage, M., Warde, A., & Devine, F. (2005). Capitals, assets, and resources: Some critical issues. *The British Journal of Sociology, 56*(1), 31–47.

Vermunt, J., & Magidson, J. (2004). Latent class analysis. In M. S. Lewis-Beck, A. Bryman, & T. F. Liao (Eds.), *The SAGE encyclopedia of social science research methods* (Vol. 1, pp. 550–553). Thousand Oaks: Sage Publications, Inc.

Wagner, G., Frick, J., & Schupp, J. (2007). The German socio-economic panel study (SOEP)-evolution, scope and enhancements. *SOEP paper*, 1.

Waitkus, N., & Groh-Samberg, O. (2018). Beyond meritocracy. Wealth accumulation in the German upper classes. In O. Korsnes, J. Hjellbrekke, J. Heilbron, F. Bühlmann, & M. Savage (Eds.), *New directions in elite studies* (pp. 198–220). London: Routledge.

Weeden, K. A., & Grusky, D. B. (2005). The case for a new class map. *American Journal of Sociology, 111*(1), 141–212.

Wright, E. O. (1997). *Class counts: Comparative studies in class analysis.* Cambridge: Cambridge University Press.

Chapter 7
Five Ways to Apprehend Classes

Stine Thidemann Faber, Annick Prieur, Lennart Rosenlund, and Jakob Skjøtt-Larsen

Introduction

This chapter assesses the importance of class differences in contemporary Denmark and at the same time seeks to entangle the many different understandings of class that are communicated in the debate on class differences. We will argue that a reason for this apparent confusion is that class actually manifests itself in different ways, and we will here seek to systematize these manifestations in five different forms. For this purpose, we will use Pierre Bourdieu's class model from *Distinction* (1984 [1979]) as an inspiration and a starting point. Bourdieu regarded a society's class structure as multidimensional and related to the possession of different forms of capital (see also Waitkus & Groh-Samberg in this volume). The primary principles of differentiation are the total volume of capital (the 'sum' of the main forms of capital: economic and cultural) and the composition of capital, or the relative weight of respectively economic and cultural capital.

As the empirical foundation for Bourdieu's model was France in the 60s and 70s, it is relevant to ask whether the model can be put to work in another society

S. T. Faber (✉)
Department of Culture and Global Studies, Aalborg University, Aalborg, Denmark
e-mail: stf@cgs.aau.dk

A. Prieur
Aalborg University, Aalborg, Denmark
e-mail: ap@socsci.aau.dk

L. Rosenlund
Institute of Media and Society, University of Stavanger, Stavanger, Norway
e-mail: lennart.rosenlund@uis.no

J. Skjøtt-Larsen
Department of Sociology and Social Work, Aalborg University, Aalborg, Denmark
e-mail: jsl@socsci.aau.dk

© Springer Nature Switzerland AG 2019
J. Blasius et al. (eds.), *Empirical Investigations of Social Space*,
Methodos Series 15, https://doi.org/10.1007/978-3-030-15387-8_7

and in another historical period. This question is particularly pertinent in a society like the Danish, where a strong welfare state attenuates some of the consequences of economic inequalities, while education is free of charge, and the number of industrial working places has been dwindling.

Although *Distinction* has become a classic text for sociologists, the attempts to replicate Bourdieu's class model empirically in other social settings are rare. Among the most comprehensive studies are Rosenlund's (2000, 2017) from Stavanger in Norway, where the basic structure from *Distinction* was found to be working. In a very comprehensive British study – Bennett et al. (2009), based on survey data and interviews – the authors here found that while the total volume of capital accounts for most of the differences observed, the significance of composition of capital seems to be limited in the UK.

In the following, we will present the main insights from a Danish study[1]; a study that supports Rosenlund's conclusion, but also adds some nuances. The differences between Bennett's and our findings may, however, stem from differences in analytic design (cf. Prieur & Savage 2011).

Our analysis draws on a flourishing tradition inspired by Bourdieu, but also by British cultural studies and other sources, represented in particular by the mentioned Bennett et al. (2009), but also by Devine, Savage et al. (2013), Devine et al. (2005), Skeggs (1997), and the Canadian Lamont (1992). They have all examined the effects of class on daily lives and identities, thereby underlining a main point in Bourdieu's understanding: Class cannot be reduced to economic relations, but involves a range of cultural, social and symbolic aspects as well.

The case for our study is Aalborg, the third largest municipality in Denmark. In the first half of the twentieth century, Aalborg thrived first and foremost from commerce and industrial production. Today, and just like other major cities in Denmark, Aalborg has a post-industrial economy, with decreasing number of citizens employed in production or crafts and a rapidly increasing level of education. Aalborg is diversified, with industrial sites, businesses, high-tech R&D companies, public administration, a university and several cultural institutions together with rural areas within its borders. Thereby Aalborg may serve as a micro-cosmos of the nation.

The Sociological Debates on Post-industrialization

Already in 1959, Robert Nisbet predicted *The Decline and Fall of Social Class,* which was also the title of his famous book. Since then, many followed suit. In *The Coming of Post-Industrial Society* (1973), Daniel Bell addressed the social changes expected from new technologies, among them a substantial growth in knowledge-

---

[1] The title of the study was *Contemporary Patterns of Social Differentiation; The Case of Aalborg* (COMPAS). Further information can be found at: http://www.en.compas.aau.dk/

and service intensive vocations at the expense of those related to agriculture and industrial production, and a subsequent rapid growth in groups of highly educated professionals.

The occupational structure of Denmark as well as of the City of Aalborg has obviously undergone changes associated with post-industrialisation. Less than 1/5 of the Danish population work within the production industry, while the majority work within service- and knowledge intensive sectors. It is, however, less obvious that class society has withered, as expected by Nisbet and Bell. In a Danish setting Juul (2012) shows that in 2010 almost 35% of young people from homes where the parents had extensive higher education, were themselves (at the age of 25) undertaking similar studies or had already completed them. The corresponding figure for those whose parents were non-skilled workers was only 3%. Several studies also confirm that even in a generous welfare state, knowledge and education appear to work as a form of capital that, just like economic capital, is often inherited between the generations (Holm and Jæger 2007; Karlson and Jæger 2011).

This striking inertia of mobility related to education and other signs of inequality does not necessarily affect people' perceptions. For Ulrich Beck (1992), increased affluence, women's entry into the labour market, individualization of employees' contracts, differentiation of working conditions etc. were new social traits that all led to a transformation of conditions of existence; they became individualised and thereby undermined the collectivism of industrial society. Anthony Giddens (1991) also linked the reflexivity of late modernity to individuals' life trajectories, which become the object of active planning. Pre-defined identities – like being a worker – are not simply adopted. Instead, identities and biographies are continuously constructed and revised.

We may follow Beck's observation that nowadays life tends to be experienced as determined more by individual circumstances and choices than by collective destinies. We also agree with Giddens' characterisation of contemporary societies as post-traditional, as individual identity-projects are not pre-given. However, we are less convinced that individuals have become free and disconnected from the structures of class society. A withering of class society would imply a reasonably fair distribution of opportunities, and also that different lifestyles- and identity figurations were perceived as having equal value, with no lifestyle figuration, types of vocations and attitudes perceived as more legitimate and worthy than others. We doubt that this is the case.

Our findings are more attuned with the British sociologist Mike Savage (2000) who claims it is the way class operates that is changing, rather than the significance of class. While the idea of the free-setting of the individuals is appealing, there is little evidence in favour of it, and it may even lead people in less privileged positions to blame themselves instead of seeing their situations as results of social injustices.

The question of class should be addressed empirically, but how? We suggest to depart from a realisation that social classes are complex entities. We will try to organize this complexity into five different manifestations of social classes, and thereafter discuss how these manifestations are connected. We want to show how a growing sense of individualisation and a lacking identification with traditional categories of social class, may go hand in hand with inequalities and dominance. Our findings have previously been presented in different articles (e.g. Prieur et al. 2008; Harrits et al. 2010; Skjott-Larsen 2012; Prieur and Savage 2011, 2013); as well as in a Danish-language book titled *The Hidden Class Society* (Det skjulte klassesamfund) (Faber et al. 2012). In this chapter, we sum up and connect the different manifestations of class uncovered in our earlier work.

Danish Distinctions: Data and Analytic Approach

While a broad understanding of what social classes are and how they may appear is easy to justify theoretically, it represents challenges empirically. Our empirical material stems from two different sources: From a representative sample of 1600 persons between 18 and 75 years old, drawn from the population of the municipality of Aalborg, 1174 persons (73.4%) were interviewed for a survey covering lifestyles and various background questions (fall 2004).[2] The questions ranged from the uses of the city's cultural facilities or events, preferences of TV programmes, taste in music, attitudes towards the arts, home interior, culinary preferences, political attitudes and voting, to reading habits and preferences. Furthermore, the survey covered various social background questions: gender; age; marital status; education of the respondents, the partners and their parents; household income and a number of other important economic indicators; the vocations of the respondents, of their partners and their parents.

Thereafter we carried out 36 qualitative interviews with people who had previously responded to the survey, selected in order to represent the diversity of the different positions of the social space. These interviews made it possible to shed light on the subjective dimensions, including the emotional experiences, of social class.

As mentioned, our analysis has, in a simultaneously theoretical and empirical manoeuvre, dealt with five different manifestations of social class. These are to some extent intertwined and partially overlapping, but will be presented here separately:

- Classes as distributional divisions.
- Classes as habitus (experiences, memories, bodily apprehensions etc.).
- Classes as symbolic boundaries.
- Classes as consciousness and identities.
- Classes as structures of symbolic dominance.

---

[2]The questionnaire can be found at: http://www.en.compas.aau.dk/. See also Prieur et al. (2008).

Classes as Distributional Divisions

Our first approach to social classes consists of conceiving them as emerging from divisions with regard to socially valuable resources. Inspired by Bourdieu we look at how cultural capital, in tandem with economic capital, create divisions between groups of people.

When working in the tradition from Bourdieu, social classes are not defined and delineated in advance, as in the class scheme approaches of Erikson and Goldthorpe (1992) or Wright (1997). Instead of defining a set of theoretical classes a priori, we describe the structure of society in terms of a two-dimensional space where classes and fractions are represented in different domains without distinct borders. Multiple correspondence analysis (MCA) has been the tool in constructing this model of the social space.

Figure 7.1 below, visualizes our construction of the local social space based on 10 different variables related to economic and cultural capital and occupation, with in all 51 different categories (see Prieur et al. 2008 for more details and Rosenlund 2000 for a discussion of this particular use of MCA). MCA results come in the form of graphs and tables. The figure contains "the space of categories" where the categories are distributed in the map according to their coordinates along the two first dimensions. Answers frequently occurring together (like possessing expensive cars and holding a managerial position) are situated close to each other, while answers rarely found together are situated far from each other (like having a high income and living in a rented housing). The map thereby provides a quite intuitive representation of statistical differences. Next step in the analysis is to interpret the main axes of the map based on to what degree the various categories contribute to the constitution of the two axes.

The horizontal axis represents the principal dimension of the space. It has a hierarchical structure in the sense that all indicators of both cultural and economic capital have their highest values at the left side and their lowest values at the right side. The three variables *Father's education*, *Household income* and *Value of car* all have their lowest value on the right-hand side and increase monotonously when moving leftward. Further, attributes associated with low social positions are found to the right (*Father unskilled worker, Pensioner, Education basic level*) and those associated with high social positions are to the left (*Manager, Father manager, Teacher university/high school*). This axis thereby seems to correspond to a traditional representation of a social hierarchy, being a dimension of over-all *volume of capital* in Bourdieu's terminology.

The second dimension in the model appears vertically, revealing the relative weight of the two forms of capital. In the top domain, economic capital outweighs cultural capital; in the bottom, cultural capital outweighs economic capital. At the top, we find the highest values on the indicators of economic capital (top left: *Summer house > DKK 800,000, Car value > DKK 500,000, Private pension* etc.) together with the lowest on cultural capital (top right: *Father's education basic level*). At the bottom, we find the opposite: the lowest values on economic capital

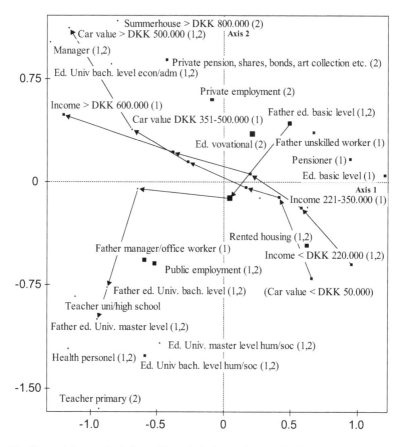

Fig. 7.1 The social space in Aalborg. Plane 1–2. Categories contributing the most to axis 1 and 2. Numbers in parentheses (1 or 2, or both) indicate to which. Markers are proportionated to the frequencies of the categories

indicators (bottom right: *Household income < DKK 220,000, Car value < DKK 50,000*) go together with the highest on cultural capital (bottom left: *Father's education university master level, (respondent's) Education university master and bachelor level hum/soc*). The figure thus displays a two-dimensional space where the horizontal axis reflects differences between individuals related to their overall amount of capital (*capital volume*) and the vertical axis reflects differences related to which of the two forms of capital that dominates their capital accounts (*capital composition*).

In this constructed space, we can loosely delineate three domains or three 'poles' with stark opposing characteristics: In the bottom-left corner, we find privileged individuals with access to cultural resources (for instance professors within higher education institutions). In the top-left corner, we find individuals with access to financial resources (for instance executives and managing directors). Finally, to the right we find individuals characterised by being less privileged and with a lack of access to resources (for instance unskilled workers). Between these three poles, the most important oppositions are played out with regard to their volume and composition of socially valuable resources. As we will show, these oppositions with regard to access to the two forms of capital also structure the social universe of political attitudes and moral issues, cultural consumption, taste orientations and lifestyles. Furthermore, these analyses will also indirectly reveal how different class habitus(es) are distributed in the social space.

Class as Habitus

The perhaps most important element in Bourdieu's understanding of how class distinctions function in contemporary societies, is his concept of habitus. Habitus can be defined as a way of living or inclinations to act in certain ways, disposing people for acting, thinking and navigating in the social world based on their past social experiences (Bourdieu 1984: 169–225). It produces a sense of belonging to certain environments and a sense of strangeness in others, as we tend to reproduce the social world we come from and may feel discomfort in unfamiliar social settings. Habitus can also, in the right social setting, function as a form of capital. This applies for instance when children from highly educated families meet a school system organized in accordance with the experiences and the type of knowledge that these children already know from home (Bourdieu and Passeron 1996).

Thus, habitus is shaped and structured by objective living conditions while, simultaneously; it shapes and structures the practices of those who have incorporated it. Modest conditions of existence are likely to be accompanied by a 'taste for necessity' i.e. a taste for affordable and filling types of food. Privileged conditions of existence, on the other hand, are likely to be accompanied by tastes characterised by their rarity, extravagance and/or refinement (Bourdieu 1984).

All of us put our habitus into play in our daily lives (see also Schäfer et al. in this volume). More or less automatically, we choose which newspaper to read in the morning, we serve certain types of food for our guests, listen to certain genres of music and participate in certain types of leisure activities, choose certain places to live, choose our friends, partners or spouses in certain ways, etc. While we tend to consider such lifestyle choices as personal, many others, with similar conditions of existence and similar positions in the social space, make similar lifestyle choices as we do. We all deploy certain acquired dispositions of a certain class habitus. At the same time, lifestyle choices and preferences are also imbued with symbolic meanings. They become part of our individual identities and communicate to others who and how we are, and not least, who and how we are *not*. Thereby they serve as markers of underlying class distinctions. Our taste is the best expression of our social position, according to Bourdieu (1984).

Bearing this in mind, a starting point for exploring class as habitus is to chart how life style choices, preferences and attitudes are distributed in the social space. In

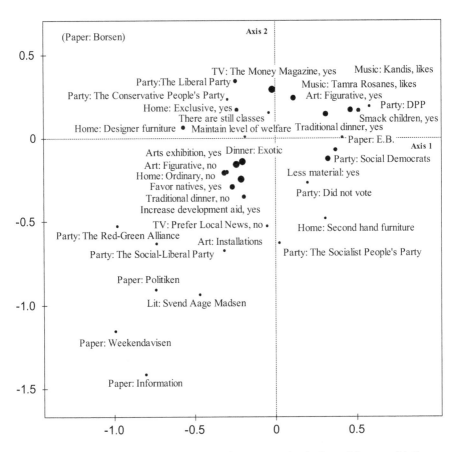

Fig. 7.2 Selected indicators of lifestyles as supplementary points in the social space of Aalborg

Fig. 7.2 we have inserted a few simple examples of patterns uncovered in our survey: indicators of both cultural preferences and moral-political views inserted in the very same social space as in Fig. 7.1. Here, the first axis – the dimension of volume of capital – separated the privileged (on the left side of the graph) respondents from the less privileged positioned to the right. The second axis – the dimension the capital composition – separated those with a capital account dominated by economic capital at the top from those with a capital account dominated by cultural capital at the bottom of the graph.

For every lifestyle element inserted, the point now indicates the geometric mean point of those individuals who are characterized by a given practice or attitude. Comparing the positions of the various elements of lifestyles therefore illuminates how the objective distribution of economic and cultural capital intersects with people's values and tastes.

This figure shows that it is among the privileged, especially among the culturally privileged, that we find readers of *Svend Åge Madsen's* books (Danish author),

Weekendavisen, *Information* and *Politiken* (three Danish newspapers). It is also among them that we find people who like conceptual art (*Art: Installations)* and who do not need to recognise the motive of a painting (*Art: Figurative-no)* in order to like it. The economically privileged primarily distinguish themselves by an interest in businesses (for instance reading the business magazine *Børsen*) as well as in preferences related to home decoration, describing their taste as exclusive (*Home: Exclusive, yes*) and directed towards architect-designed or designer furniture (*Home: Designer furniture*). These choices are opposed to the preferences among the less privileged groups, at the right side. With regard to home decorations they for instance enjoy 'flea market style' (*Home: Second hand furniture)*, while they at the same time make a virtue of necessity by describing themselves as people who are not concerned with material goods *(Less material, yes)*. Those with a high amount of cultural capital do not appear as clearly oriented towards the classical culture as the corresponding groups in Bourdieu's French studies. However, there is also in our Danish study a significant cleavage in taste preferences between the privileged and the less privileged. This is revealed in a lower interest in, and sometimes disapproval of, specific entertainment programs on television (e.g. reality TV), food culture (e.g. traditional Danish food), light pop music or country & western (here exemplified by *Kandis* and *Tamra Rosanes*), preference for figurative art, for tabloid newspapers (*Paper: E. B*) as well as certain choices in literature (e.g. *Danielle Steel* and *Jane Aamund*. The taste of those with a high amount of capital is perhaps not so exclusive, but it is none the less quite excluding.

Concerning moral-political attitudes, it is among those with a high amount of capital we find people who would like to *increase development aid*, who don't think that Danes should have a priority to get employment before immigrants (*Favour natives, no*), and who don't agree that it is acceptable to give children a small smack once in a while (*Smack children, no*). Those with low amount of capital tend to hold opposite attitudes. With regard to political voting, we assume that in the industrial époque the dividing line between left- and right-wing voting followed economic distribution between the rich (the bourgeoisie) and the poor (the proletariat). However, it is interesting to observe that the current dividing line – between those voting for right-wing parties (*The Liberal Party, The Conservative People's Party and The Danish People's Party*) and those voting for left-wing parties (The Social Democrats, The Socialist People's Party, The Social-Liberal Party and the Red-Green) – is much better explained by composition of capital than by total amount of capital (volume).

Among the less privileged at the right side it is, however, more difficult to distinguish between voters for The Social Democrats and voters for The Danish People's Party. It is also here that we find the most frequent occurrence of people not having voted, reflecting a more general observation that it is among the less privileged that we find most people who do not participate in any of the types of the cultural activities included in the survey.

Differences in terms of cultural and moral attitudes may make mobility between different groups difficult. When moving to another corner of the space, one runs the risk of encountering distaste towards the culture and morality that one has grown up with and learnt to enjoy and respect. Tension related to this appears in the interviews with the less educated interviewees as feelings of shame, feelings of inferiority and physical discomfort, as we soon will show. They also appear in the interviews with people having experienced upward social mobility. In one interview, the interviewee, Marianne, talks about how she has had to learn new cultural codes, such as those related to consumptions. Coming from a position as an employee in the cleaning business to work as an intermediary in a large IT company she and her husband now have more money, new friends and acquaintances, and new consumer habits:" *I do believe that it is related to our new lifestyle, but well yes – then you get your nails done, or you get a luxurious spa treatment or you buy a really nice bottle of red wine although you could have bought the cheaper one since it is just going to be poured down anyway, right?"* The example reminds of Bourdieu's understanding of the *nouveaux riches* as driven by a wish to display abundance.

Classes as Symbolic Boundaries

A reason why Bourdieu was critical towards the commonly used class schemes was that they constructed classes a priori (Bourdieu 1987) and independently of people's own perceptions. The social structure exists in a multidimensional space of economic, social, cultural and other differences, but it demands an act of perception and classification for such differences between positions in a social space to become differences between groups that perceive and construct themselves as being separate groups. The contours of such constructions are possible to discern in our data. In our survey, we found that the privileged distance themselves from the less privileged through tastes in music, food, politics and more. Signs of such construction work, however, is more explicitly expressed in the qualitative interviews.

When we analyse how the interviewees mark boundaries between themselves and others, we draw on Beverley Skegg's (1997) and her use of the concept of positioning to show how different discourses were used for identity work among young British working-class women. Their low position in society played a major role in their identity formation, even though they did not accept a working class identity. We also draw on Michèle Lamont (1992) who, based on interviews in male white, upper middle class in France and the United States, found that these men not only drew boundaries based on socioeconomic criteria (include economic success) and cultural criteria (related to assessed intelligence, manners and tastes), but also based on moral criteria (emphasising characteristics such as honesty, work ethics and integrity).

Only few of our interviewees describe themselves in explicit class terms, and even fewer admit to judge other people based on such criteria. When class(ed) identities were expressed in our interviews, it was often through subtle dis-identifications, in the form of distaste, distance and symbolic boundary drawings, with reference to cultural preferences, attitudes to politics, choice of residency in the city or social contexts where people meet across social divides.

Carsten, an upper secondary school teacher, represents the culturally privileged position in our sample, and he quite explicitly draws symbolic boundaries toward others based on cultural distinctions. For example, it appears in a comment, where Carsten explains that he notices the types of books in the bookcase, when he enters someone's home. *"It gives me a hint of what kind of topics that could be relevant to address"*, he says, so that it is possible to avoid *"getting into a situation where the social intercourse becomes strained"*.

The other interviewees, who like Carsten represent the culturally privileged, are, however, more likely to draw symbolic boundaries based on moral and political distinctions. This is seen, for example, in the interview with Jens, a teacher holding a managerial position at a large educational institution. Asked if there are types of people he would rather avoid sitting next to at a social event, he explains: *"I like to discuss with people who want to talk about things in a reasoned manner, but if people are too shallow, too stereotypical and way too loud; and you can see that it will not lead to a reasonable conversation ... If they are too racist or discriminatory, for example, I won't just sit there and listen to it."* We find similar morally based boundary drawing in an interview with a high school teacher, Terese, who disassociates herself from people who are *"a little Danish People's Party-like"*, as she thinks this reflects differences in level of education, thereby linking such statements to the socially less privileged positions: *"I look somewhat more nuanced on things than they do – they are often very black and white and have a very generalist approach; that is, if they've seen one person do something, they assume everyone does that sort of thing."*

Among the economically privileged, we have interviewed Thomas, who runs a communication company. Thomas is not particularly inclined to distance himself from any groups, but he respects people who have the ability to manage and achieve something despite of the odds:" *I've met a man who I once helped to learn how to read and spell and write and calculate. He is self-employed today. He has a remarkable business empire, and about him we had said, "Well, he will never amount to anything". I fully respect his achievements."*

Among the less privileged groups, we also find a number of symbolic boundary drawings towards other social groups. An example would be Poul, an electrician, who marks a distance towards people showing off. For Poul, standing out is not a virtue: *"I do not dare to lead others and say 'you do this and you do that' (. . .). It's not me at all. I'd rather blend in; be a bit anonymous and just go about doing what I need to do."* Bente and Lisbeth, both working as child-minders, also disregard people who show off. Bente explains how she prefers to interact with people who, like herself, are *"down-to- earth"*. And Lisbeth describes herself as someone who *"works on the floor"* as opposed to the more privileged in society, like the corporate directors who often have *"these big arm movements and attitude: "Listen! (. . .) What I say is important"*. She sympathises with *"the little man"* who is often overlooked and does not get *"his part of the cake"*. Several of the less privileged interviewees directly express how they lack the recognition and social influence enjoyed by others, for instance Joan, who is unskilled and on cash benefits. She also describes a sense of impotence towards the privileged; for instance the politicians:

"Those who are in the parliament – and it makes me so angry – they are sitting there and they get the world's biggest wages and are just being plain greedy (...). Those from the parliament should try to have one-two weeks where they lived like us."

Several of the less privileged interviewees distinguish between social status and wealth, on the one hand, and personal values and integrity on the other hand. They emphasise the importance of being decent, wholesome and hardworking people who take care of their families and value their abilities to cultivate close personal relationships. The argument that money and status symbols are not the most important in life, can be illustrated by the gardener Heidi, who states: *"I would also like a new bath room with spa, but I believe that the money for such things are hard-earned money."* And later in the interview: *"We don't need to travel to Mallorca to be able to have a good time and relax together."*

These are just a few examples of the different types of symbolic boundary drawings encountered in our interviews. Some boundaries are drawn based on economy and extravagance, others express a preference for the ordinary rather than the sophisticated, and yet others emphasize certain personality traits as attractive (e.g. being down-to-earth, having a strong work ethic, not "showing off" or being fake). We also hear explicit prejudices about specific people or particular groups of people, especially towards immigrants, managers and single mothers.

The multidimensional space of social and cultural distinctions is thus likely to serve as material for the drawing of symbolic boundaries, through which people in their everyday life associate with, distance themselves from, value or devaluate others. Such patterns of taste and distaste are one of the most important ways that class manifests itself in contemporary societies. People enjoying different music, different literature, different food and different television programmes, or valuing different demeanours, etc. are less likely to interact and spend time together. If these differences in preferences are related to the distribution of recognition and of material wealth, then preferences turn into privileges and we may then speak of classes (at least in a weak sense of the word) of people living parallel lives and enjoying different privileges.

Classes as Consciousness and Identifications

The fourth manifestation of classes concerns class-consciousness, identifications and dis-identifications. We will here draw both on Bourdieu's idea that classes may appear as subtle differences in everyday life, and on Skeggs (1997), who has shown that class identity more often appears as negative than as positive markers.

A main finding from our study is that identities linked to certain social positions are rarely expressed directly and positively as *"I am a worker"* or *"I belong to the working class"*. Class belonging is not central to people's narratives about their own lives or vision of other people. Still, a consciousness about a social hierarchy does exist. When we in our survey asked a randomly selected sample of citizens whether they agree in the statement *"There are no longer social classes in Denmark"*, three out of four actually disagree (53% disagree completely and 22% disagree to some extent).

Social inequalities are, however, not worded so frequently or loudly. Overall, our interviewees seem to regard class as a normative issue, as if it deals with whether a social position is merited or not, or whether one sees oneself as superior or inferior to other people. Many react to questions about class in a somewhat evasive way, or become defensive. Their reactions may be quite telling about how classes work at a micro-level. The relatively privileged interviewees tend to downplay the significance of class while class for the relatively under-privileged seem to be quite visible and tangible.

Another reason for the silencing of class – both in public debate, in research and in daily life – may be that we simply do not have a relevant and updated language for the landscape of social divisions we all tacitly navigate through in our daily encounters with other people. When the survey respondents were invited to place themselves in either the working, the middle or the upper class, more than three out of four placed themselves in the middle class; less than one out of five in the working class and only three out of hundred in the upper class. This distribution points to the idea of a society where few have too much and even fewer do not have enough. It is noticeable that almost all survey respondents (96%) actually accept to answer this question and place themselves within one of the three class categories, as our face-to-face interviews clearly reveal that the interviewees themselves extremely rarely use class categories. Class belonging is obviously not a part of a self-presentation, and probably not part of a conscious identity. When three out of four still agree we live in a classed society, it may simply express a recognition that we live in a society with social differences and inequalities.

In the interviews it is not surprising that everybody are able to notice and articulate that there are cultural and economic differences in what and how much people own, and most people also seem to agree that social differences do have an impact on people's opportunities and limitations as well as on how life is lived. It appears however, to be much more difficult for the interviewees to sense and to articulate moral and symbolic differences in how and when some cultural preferences are attributed a higher value than others.

Class as Symbolic Structures of Domination

The last manifestation of classes to be dealt with here is symbolic dominance. As it is quite possible to imagine a society where structures of distribution and the formation of groups separated by symbolic boundaries and with different forms of the habitus exist without relations of subordination, domination can never be taken for granted, but has to be empirically demonstrated.

While "good taste" may appear as something naturally given and self-evident, it is dependent on social judgments and is clearly linked to possession of capital. As "good taste" defines "bad taste", to have "good taste" may serve as a distinguishing strategy marking distances to other social groups: *"In matters of taste, more than anywhere else, all determination is negation; and tastes are perhaps first and foremost distastes, disgust provoked by horror or visceral intolerance ('sick-making') of the tastes of others"* (Bourdieu 1984: 56). Judgments of taste therefore express relations of domination. Those who are privileged with capital have the authority to define their own taste as good taste and other groups' taste as bad taste. They may even, to a certain degree, obtain the less privileged groups' recognition of these judgments so that the latter end up devaluating themselves. Social dominance regards the power over categories of perception, over how the world is perceived, evaluated and represented (Bourdieu 1977; Bourdieu and Wacquant 1992; see also Wacquant in this edited volume). Representations of the social world, or the imageries of this world, are supported by a structure of distribution of wealth, power and influence. Thereby categories of perception and mental structures are linked to distributions of wealth and power. This is how symbolic systems and social representations come to work indirectly as oppressive regimes. Through actions of perception and recognition that tacitly accept the limits instituted by domination, the dominated contribute themselves to their own domination. This is what Bourdieu terms symbolic violence, *"a gentle violence imperceptible and invisible even to its victims"* (Bourdieu 2001: 1). This deployment of power is accepted by the dominated (the victims), because they have the same cognitive dispositions as the dominating. In spite of having a personal preference for light pop tunes over classic music, or for an action movie from Hollywood over a Palme d'Or winner from Cannes, most people know well that the latter is the most valued and recognized.

Designating such differences with class terms highlights that they are not just innocent differences between equally recognized life forms. The cultural and moral boundaries that people draw between each other end up having serious consequences. The lower classes' lifestyles are attributed less value and people who represent these classed choices may be ignored, problematized or attacked. Such attributions of value have therefore to do with class, or, perhaps more accurately, with *The Hidden Injuries of Class*, as Sennett and Cobb (1972) termed it.

Class relations in a Danish context appear as less loaded with domination and subordination than in the sociological literature from the US, from UK or from France. However, also in our study we encountered painful memories of class-related experiences among the less privileged interviewees, like Margit, who explains that when she worked as a cleaner, she could enter a room and notice that people kept on talking as if she were not present, or as if her presence did not count. Margit describes a gaze that is even more powerful than the judgmental gaze described by Bourdieu, which is to be overlooked: She was not even worthy to be judged. Also, it is evident that she experiences the effects of her social position as a permanent state of bodily insecurity. Her stomach hurts, she tells: *"If I am among people where I don't feel I belong, I get stomach pains, because I feel deficient."* Thus, the embodiment of the symbolic violence makes Margit's body betray her whenever she perceives herself to be in a position of inferiority.

Most expressions of class-related devaluation are, however, of a subtler character. Almost all interviewees provide rather positive narratives of their lives, presenting their trajectories with dignity and as chosen by themselves. When we still claim to see signs of dominance in some of these narratives, it is because we quite often hear about class ambivalences, unease and feelings of shame or inferiority among the less privileged. Thereby their narratives betray their sense of an objective social hierarchy that positions them in the lower end.

Identity Formation in a World of Opportunities and Inequalities

Summing up, we conclude that class differences in our case can be seen as structures of distribution, as forms of the habitus and as symbolic boundaries. To a certain degree, we have also found class as symbolic structures of domination, while we have not found expressions of class as consciousness or identity.

So, do classes really exist and what do they look like in a contemporary Danish setting? In our study, we point to three main poles within the social space: people privileged with access to cultural resources, with access to financial resources, and people lacking access to most resources. People residing at these different poles of the social space do usually not identify themselves as belonging to such a position or such a class. By combining the distant gaze on connections between the social positions and the lifestyles identified by the aid of multiple correspondence analysis on the one hand with the different forms of boundary drawing and feelings of domination expressed by our interviewees on the other hand, we do, however, see the contours of a classed society.

If, in spite of an experience that our lifestyles express personal choices, the choices we end up making are the same as the choices that other people influenced by the same social conditions are likely to make. We need to understand why this is so. One obvious explanation is that opportunities are unevenly distributed so that external conditions that put limitations on our choices. This has, however, also to do with how such conditions become deeply embodied in the individuals. Individualization and new principles for differentiation have undoubtedly led to a questioning of the relevance of the class categorizations of industrial society. Class divisions have taken new shapes, become less visible, and are more rarely worded. But they are still there.

References

Beck, U. (1992). *Risk society*. London: SAGE.
Bell, D. (1973). *The coming of post-industrial society*. New York: Basic Books.
Bennett, T., Savage, M., Silva, E. B., Warde, A., Gayo-Cal, M., & Wright, D. (2009). *Culture, class, distinction*. Oxon: Routledge.
Bourdieu, P. (1977). *Outline of a theory of practice*. Cambridge: Cambridge University Press.

Bourdieu, P. (1984). *Distinction. A social critique of the judgement of taste*. London: Routledge & Kegan Paul.

Bourdieu, P. (1987). 'What makes a social class?' On the theoretical and practical existence of groups. *Berkeley Journal of Sociology, 32*, 1–17.

Bourdieu, P. (2001). *Masculine domination*. Cambridge: Polity Press.

Bourdieu, P., & Passeron, J. C. (1996[1979]). *Reproduction in education, society and culture*. London: SAGE.

Bourdieu, P., & Wacquant, L. J. D. (1992). *An invitation to reflexive sociology*. Chicago: University of Chicago Press.

Devine, F., Savage, M., Scott, J., & Crompton, R. (Eds.). (2005). *Rethinking class. Culture, identities and lifestyle*. New York: Palgrave Macmillan.

Erikson, R., & Goldthorpe, J. H. (1992). *The constant flux: A study of class mobility in the industrial societies*. Oxford: Clarendon Press.

Faber, S. T., Prieur, A., Rosenlund, L., & Skjøtt-Larsen, J. (2012). *Det skjulte klassesamfund*. Aarhus: Aarhus Universitetsforlag.

Giddens, A. (1991). *Modernity and self-identity*. Cambridge: Polity Press.

Harrits, G. S., Prieur, A., Rosenlund, L., & Skjøtt-Larsen, J. (2010). Class and politics in Denmark. Are both old and new politics structured by class? *Scandinavian Political Studies, 33*(1), 1–27.

Holm, A., & Jæger, M. M. (2007). Does parents' economic, cultural, and social capital explain the social class effect on educational attainment in the Scandinavian mobility regime? *Social Science Research, 36*(2), 719–744.

Juul, J. S. (2012). Social arv i Danmark. Arbejderbevægelsens erhvervsråd.

Karlson, K. B., & Jæger, M. M. (2011). Kassen, kulturen og kontakterne: Økonomisk, kulturel og social kapital i to generationer. *Dansk Sociologi, 22*(3), 61–80.

Lamont, M. (1992). *Money, morals and manners. The culture of the French and the American upper-middle class*. Chicago: The University of Chicago Press.

Nisbet, R. (1959). The decline and fall of social class. *Pacific Sociological Review, 2*(1), 11–17.

Prieur, A., Rosenlund, L., & Skjøtt-Larsen, J. (2008). Cultural capital today: A case study from Denmark. *Poetics, 36*(1), 45–70.

Prieur, A., & Savage, M. (2011). Updating cultural capital theory. *Poetics, 39*(6), 566–580.

Prieur, A., & Savage, M. (2013). Emerging forms of cultural capital. *European Societies, 15*(2), 246–267.

Rosenlund, L. (2000). *Social structures and change: Applying Pierre Bourdieu's approach and analytic framework* (Working papers 85/2000). Stavanger: Stavanger University College.

Rosenlund, L. (2017). Class conditions and urban differentiation – Applying *distinction's* methodology to the Community. *Bulletin de Méthodologie Sociologique, 135*, 5–31.

Savage, M. (2000). *Class analysis and social transformation*. Buckingham: Open University Press.

Savage, M., Devine, F., Cunningham, N., Taylor, M., Li, Y., Hjellbrekke, J., Le Roux, B., Friedman, S., & Miles, A. (2013). A new model of social Class? Findings from the BBC's great British class survey experiment. *Sociology, 47*(2), 219–250.

Sennett, R., & Cobb, J. (1972). *The hidden injuries of Class*. New York: Vintage Books.

Skeggs, B. (1997). *Formations of class and gender. Becoming respectable*. London: SAGE.

Skjott-Larsen, J. (2012). Cultural and moral Class boundaries in a Nordic context. *European Societies, 14, 660–683*.

Wright, E. O. (1997). *Class counts*. Cambridge: Cambridge University Press.

Chapter 8
Cultural Domains and Class Structure: Assessing Homologies and Cultural Legitimacy

Nicolas Robette and Olivier Roueff

Introduction

It is well known that the figures representing the French social space in *Distinction* (Bourdieu 1979) are based on several partial analyses. This means that one of Pierre Bourdieu's central hypotheses – the structural homology between social and cultural spaces as wholes – was not empirically tested by way of correspondence analysis (although Bourdieu did perform such an analysis for the bourgeoisie and petite bourgeoisie). Furthermore, many of the sociological discussions of cultural practices which have appeared since the publishing of *Distinction* use data describing a single taste domain, often music. This is beginning to change, as large-scale surveys have been conducted for Australia (Bennett et al. 1999), Norway (Rosenlund 2000), Porto in Portugal (Borges Pereira 2005), Aalborg in Denmark (Prieur et al. 2008), Great Britain (Bennett et al. 2009) – but not for France. Furthermore, as it has never been empirically tested, it is not obvious that cultural tastes constitute a homogeneous universe of practices. They can be structured by domains, depending on the relative autonomy of their respective fields of production: taste in music is not necessarily distributed in the same way as taste in books, and their relation to the social space may also differ. The French survey on cultural practices *Pratiques culturelles des Français* (Pratiques Culturelles des Français 2008)[1], enables new implementations and tests of these hypotheses through empirical analysis.

---

[1] See all details here: http://www.pratiquesculturelles.culture.gouv.fr/doc/08methodologie.pdf

---

N. Robette (✉)
ENSAE, Palaiseau, France
e-mail: nicolas.robette@uvsq.fr

O. Roueff
Centre de recherches sociologiques et politiques de Paris – CRESPA, Paris Cedex 17, France

© Springer Nature Switzerland AG 2019   115
J. Blasius et al. (eds.), *Empirical Investigations of Social Space*,
Methodos Series 15, https://doi.org/10.1007/978-3-030-15387-8_8

We first tested empirically the hypothesis of a homology between different domains of the most detailed tastes in the dataset – TV, reading, cinema and music. Multiple correspondence analysis (MCA) allows us to *compare* the four tastes' spaces, while multiple factor analysis (MFA) is employed as a method to *test* their homology.

Further analyses deal with the homology between these tastes' spaces and the whole space of social positions. Indeed, quantitative works often conclude that the cultural practices that are most associated with social class are also distributed by age and by sex (Philippe 2003; Bennett et al. 2009; Christine 2011; Octobre 2011; Christin 2012; Roose et al. 2012). The assumption is sometimes made that, today, the distribution of tastes is structured equally by age and sex and by social class (Bennett et al. 2009), and even that we can observe the weakening of cultural class divisions in favour of generational cultural divisions (Hervé and Michel 2009). In order to shed some light on this question, we untangled the web of factors – e.g. education, sex and age – structuring lifestyles in France by using several geometric data analysis techniques (Le Roux and Rouanet 2004), including standardized factor analysis (Bry et al. 2015). The research questions we intend to answer include: has age supplanted class membership in importance? If this is the case, should it be interpreted in terms of each individual's actual age, or with regard to their membership of a generational group? Has the opposition between economic and cultural capital lost its relevance? And is the axis ordering volumes of capital a good proxy for the scale of cultural legitimacy, as is usually postulated by sociologists?

Finally, after exploring these issues at the scale of the whole social space, we ask whether the results apply to a smaller scale by 'zooming' in on different social classes using class specific analysis (CSA). Does the level of heterogeneity in social classes' tastes increase at the higher levels of the social space, due to a broader range of practices among the upper classes (Peterson and Kern 1996)? Does the opposition between legitimate and popular culture organise the symbolic antagonism between classes from opposite ends of the social space? If so, is it invariably the same tastes that transmit this opposition?

The present chapter offers a set of results, albeit without going into great detail. Our goal is merely to present a sociological approach comprising statistical tools taken from the geometrical data analysis family, and sometimes elsewhere. Statistical algorithms are chosen (or created) to answer a sociological question depending on what exactly they *do* with data. First, each question demands an exploration of the tools to be chosen or created; the best tools are rarely the most obvious, and the answer will not be preordained (a MCA for representing a social space, a hierarchical clustering analysis for quickly obtaining a typology, and so on). Second, most questions are better dealt with if several tools are used, as each tool offers a very specific and narrow view on data, and rarely corresponds exactly to the sociological question. Statistical tools – whether geometrical or inferential – only describe data by reducing and organising information (as do algorithms) in multiple ways, and offer only partial clues (and only sometimes convincing ones) to help develop a sociological explanation of the statistical observations.

The Homology Between Domains of Practices

The fact that cultural tastes constitute a homogeneous universe of practices cannot be taken for granted. They are structured by cultural domains, depending on the relative autonomy of fields of production specialised in a particular type of symbolic good. Tastes in music are not necessarily organised in the same way as tastes in television, since the field of music operates in a quite different way from the field of television, and the social uses of music are different from the social uses of television. Thus the hypothesis of a structural homology between each of the fields in question, which would represent the main statistical proof of the relative homogeneity of consumption habitus, should be tested empirically.

Several methods are possible. The first is to perform four separate Multiple Correspondence Analyses (MCA) – that is to say, one for each domain of practices – and to compare their structuring factors and the distribution of categories. This method has the advantage of respecting the specific structuring principles in every domain: it accounts for these principles with no interference from the other domains. But it is really only appropriate for an initial investigation: the four domains are *roughly* similar. It is difficult to go beyond a superficial comparison – with the naked eye, so to speak – of the four series of plots (of individuals and/or categories) and any potential aids to interpretation; the coordinates of the taste variables and the correlations between the variables which determine social position are not strictly comparable from one domain to another, as they are produced by distinct processes of MCA.

The second method is to perform a single MCA combining the four groups of variables. This has the advantage of allowing a direct comparison: the categories are scattered on the same plot, and aids to interpretation rank the variables and categories of the four domains all together. However, there is no assurance that the domains will contribute to the results of the MCA in a balanced way. A domain can have more weight, dominating others – for example due to a greater number of variables – which is not justified from an analytical point of view: we want instead for all domains to contribute equally to the construction of the space of tastes.

We turn therefore to a third method, multiple factor analysis (MFA), which was developed by Brigitte Escoffier and Jerome Pagès in the 1980s (Escofier and Pagès 1990, 2008; see also Baier & Schmitz in this volume). It fruitfully combines the benefits of the previous two approaches: from the same data set, it balances the contributions of several groups of variables (here the four domains of taste) to the construction of the space. In this way it accounts for the correlations *within* each domain and *between* whole domains, whereas MCA does not allow us to weigh up the influence of each group of variables; this is thus a way to superimpose the four spaces of tastes over one another. Technically, MFA involves performing a separate MCA for each domain, combining individuals' coordinates on the axes of the MCA, resulting in a principal component analysis (PCA) from these coordinates weighted by the variance of the first axis of the domain. We can then switch between observing each isolated space (by 'deleting' the others) and the global space of the four domains all together (Fig. 8.1).

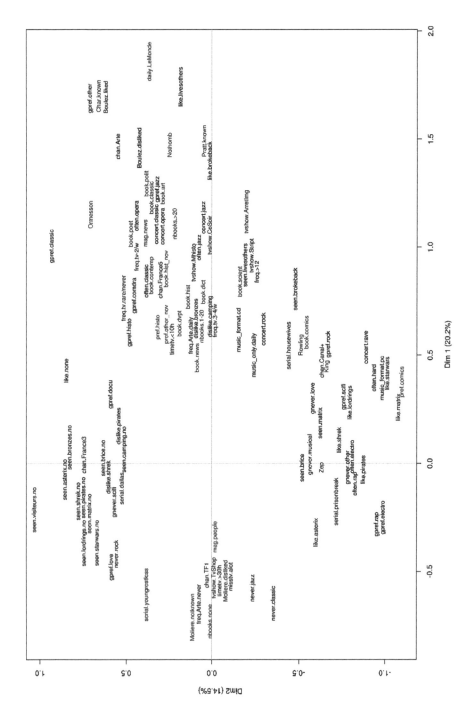

Fig. 8.1 MFA of the tastes in music, cinema, television, and reading

It is worth mentioning that all the correspondence analyses performed here are 'specific'. This will set some categories of variables as 'passive' so that they do not contribute to the construction of the space, especially in the case of 'junk' categories such as 'other' or 'not specified', or categories with low frequencies; these might weigh artificially on the construction of the space (Le Roux and Rouanet 2004). We used R software and the GDAtools package, which has all the geometric data analysis tools used here (MFA, specific MCA, CSA, ellipses, and so on. http://cran. r-project.org/web/packages/GDAtools/index.html).

The comparison of the four 'universes' of tastes constructed by the MFA confirms the overall homology between the four spaces (Robette and Roueff 2017). This comparison relies less on the plots than on the selection of the most significant categories (by axis and by domain). For a given axis, the categories are considered 'notable' if their coordinates are greater than 0.5 or less than −0.5, meaning that the category is at a remove of at least 0.5 relative to 0: this is a "rule of thumb" suggested by Le Roux and Rouanet (2010: 59) for categories projected as supplementary. Due to the two-stage process of the MFA (separate MCAs and then PCA), taste variables are considered as supplementary from a statistical point of view (even if they remain active from an interpretive point of view), hence the use of this rule of thumb rather than of the contributions to axes (valid with active variables only). Bolded categories are those whose coordinates on the axis are greater than 1 or less than −1: we consider these categories 'highly notable'.

Axis 1 combines, for the four domains, categories of intensity of practice (high on the right side, low on the left side) and categories of taste that can be interpreted as bourgeois (to the right) or popular (to the left). This is confirmed by the projection of individual social characteristics as supplementary variables. The respondent's own educational level "explains" 31% of the variance of axis 1, their PCS (i.e. the French *profession et catégorie socioprofessionnelle*) 29%, the mother's educational level 16% and the PCS of the head of household 16%. Age explains 28% of the variance of axis 2, and sex 9%.

For the four domains, the most notable categories are often ones that denote singular works rather than cultural genres (Table 8.1) – which is probably due to their rarity, but is also an indication of the strength of the interpretation (Robette and Roueff 2014). They are also all grouped on the right, suggesting legitimate, bourgeois tastes, while the left side exhibits far fewer notable categories. Thus, the axis objectivizes proximity vs remoteness to culture in general, and to bourgeois culture in particular – on the left, the only notable positive categories are TF1 (the main commercial TV channel), the soap opera *Les Feux de l'Amour* (*The Young and the Restless*), teleshopping programmes and gossip magazines.

As for axis 2, it is not related to intensity of practice (Table 8.2), with the exception of the category *never or seldom television*. On the other hand, it is notably associated with taste categories, especially for singular works. The four domains exhibit similar overall profiles: at the bottom of the Figure are emerging (new) tastes, at the top are established (old) tastes.

The advantage of MFA is not only its ability to confirm the homology between the four domains, but also that it allows us to study any potential small variations. Indeed, this approach ensures that these variations do not result from an imbalance

Table 8.1 Notable (and highly notable) categories for axis 1, by domain

Axis 1	Left	Right
Reading	Nb books read = none, don't know Molière, don't like Molière, read people magazines	**Read Le Monde, know Char, read Pratt, read Nothomb, read politics, art and classic books, ever read d'Ormesson, nb books read > 20, read news magazines, read poetry**, read historical, contemporary, science or history books, dictionaries, self-help books, other genres of novels, nb books read 11–20, prefer history books, ever read Rowling, read news books
Cinema	–	**Like The Lives of Others, preferred genre = other, like Brokeback Mountain**, have seen The Lives of Others, more than 12 times a year, have seen Brokeback Mountain, comedy-drama, dislike Camping, dislike Les Bronzés, like historical movies
Music	Never listen to classical music or jazz	**Like Boulez, don't like Boulez, preferred genre = jazz, often listen to opera, jazz concerts, classical concerts, opera concerts, preferred genre = classical**, often listen to jazz or classical, rock concerts, CD format, preferred genre = rock, rave parties, music only every day
Television	Never Arte, like The Young and the Restless, week time >30 h, teleshopping, miss TV a lot, TF1	**Arte, Arrêt sur Images, Ce Soir ou Jamais**, Strip Tease, 1–2 times a week, Mercredis de l'Histoire, France 5, rarely/never, 3–4 times a week, Arte every day, week time<10 h, Desperate Housewives

Table 8.2 Notable (and highly notable) categories for axis 2, by domain

Axis 2	Bottom	Top
Reading	**Preferred genre = comics**, ever read Stephen King, Zep, read comics, ever read Rowling	Like d'Ormesson, know Char
Cinema	**Like Matrix, like Star Wars**, like Pirates of the Caribbean, gjms autre, like The Lord of the Rings, preferred genre = science-fiction, like Shrek, have seen Matrix, have seen Astérix et Obélix, never watch romance or musical movies, have seen Brice de Nice	**Haven't seen Les Visiteurs**, aime aucun, haven't seen Astérix et Obélix / Les Bronzés / Shrek / Pirates of the Caribbean / Matrix / The Lord of the Rings, preferred genre = other, haven't seen Star Wars / Brice de Nice, dislike Shrek, preferred genre = documentaries, preferred genre = romance, never watch science-fiction, dislike Pirates of the Caribbean, haven't seen Camping, preferred genre = historical movies
Music	Computer format, preferred genre = electronic or hip hop, often listen to heavy metal, rave parties, often listen to hip hop or electronic, preferred genre = rock	Preferred genre = classical, like Boulez, never listen to rock
Television	Prison Break, Canal+	France 3, Arte, Dallas, rarely/never

of contributions of each domain, as they were standardized on the first axis: the comparison is based on a statistical foundation.

Thus, for axis 1, the differences between domains concern the presence, for movies only, of two categories of distaste on the left side (distaste for the lowbrow comedies *Camping* and *Les Bronzés font du ski*), the presence, for TV and reading only, of positive categories on the right side, and above all the absence of categories on the right side for movies only. Distaste for the music of the composer Pierre Boulez, on the left side, can be interpreted differently: this category is very close to the one of taste for Boulez, so it is the fact of knowing Boulez and thus being able to express a taste or distaste for his music which is distinctive. The same phenomenon is observed by Duval (2011) and Savage and Gayo (2011). For the category *cinema*, all movies' categories on the right side have coordinates lower than 0.5: individuals who are distant from bourgeois culture are more likely to express a taste for romance or action movies, *Titanic* or *Les Bronzés font du ski*; however, these categories are not notable, probably because they are common, in contrast to more distinctive expressions of tastes such as not reading books; disliking jazz; never watching Arte (the main cultural TV channel) but often TF1 (the main commercial TV channel); or enjoying gossip magazines or *Les Feux de l'Amour* (*The Young and the Restless*), where the distances are all much greater. Cultural tastes that stray from the bourgeois legitimacy are more likely to be weakly held; cultural tastes which can be classified as 'legitimate' are also more likely to be strongly held.

For axis 2, the differences between domains are visible only in the predominance of the categories taste in movies. Notable here is the presence of many categories of *no activity*, particularly at the top of the axis: the fact of not having seen these films can be thought of as a form of classifying, even if we cannot consider these categories as expressions of distaste. However, axis 2 is not a replica of the axis 1 opposition between bourgeois and popular tastes. Television tastes at the bottom are not necessarily those with the largest audience, but are popular with young respondents. One can even determine details such as the fact that the commercial channel Canal+ and the American serial drama *Prison Break* are favoured in particular by relatively young graduates. Conversely, the established series *Dallas* is at the top of the space. Among other emerging tastes appear comics in the reading category, and for the genres electro, rap, hard and rock for music (while tastes for international varieties and French varieties are specifically popular, at the right of axis 1, and not distinctive on axis 2). Finally, movie tastes at the top of the axis can mostly be characterised by their remoteness to the movies and genres to be found at the bottom (action movies, science fiction, comedy); those at the top include the taste for documentary and historical films, but also for romance movies. It is especially evident in the cinema category that axis 2 opposes simultaneously emerging to established tastes, as well as male to female tastes. A gendered pattern of opposition can be established, for example, regarding a lack of interest in romance or musicals and a lack of interest in science fiction. Similarly, when one lowers the threshold for notability with this interpretation in mind, other gendered categories can also be found in the categories reading and television: the female taste for reading the romantic *Harlequin* paperback series vs. the male taste for the celebrity talkshow *La méthode Cauet*, for example.

The Homology Between Social Space and the Space of Tastes

The Homology Between Class Tastes

A level of structural homology has been established for tastes. What about social properties? We will not examine in detail here the homology between the space of tastes and the social space as a whole – instead, we will return to this overarching theme later, refining the basic verification of the presence of homology by adding supplementary variables correlated to the first two axes. We are first interested in the spaces of social classes: are the cultural universes of the bourgeois, intermediate and popular classes structured by the same principles? It may be the case that correspondence analyses, which give more weight to rare categories (thus, here, to the bourgeois classes), combined with a relatively 'legitimistic' questionnaire specifically detailing the practices which the dominant perspective defines as cultural, lead to a space entirely defined by the properties of the bourgeois classes. We intend to show that this is not the case, or rather that the undeniable bias produced by the questionnaire and the technique must be interpreted differently. On the one hand, it is essentially the distance to legitimate culture that is being measured, even if one does not measure that exclusively. We will point out some clues of the relative autonomy of popular tastes, organised according to other logics than merely their relation to legitimate or intellectual culture (Grignon and Passeron 1989; Fabiani 1995). On the other, however, it is possible *by this very method* to observe how the distribution of cultural tastes are similar from one social class to another, even for the popular classes: legitimate culture produces a scale of legitimacy that organises, at least in part, the tastes of all social classes, including those social groups which are the most remote from the bourgeois centre of the production of legitimacy. The benefit of such an analysis is therefore again to observe both the overall replication of the same structure and local variations within the overall structure.

   In conducting such a comparison, the difficulty is similar to that encountered in the case of homologies between cultural domains: how can we avoid both the separate construction of specific spaces for each class – which would thus be statistically incommensurable – and the imbalance of respective weights of the classes? With this in mind, as an initial approach we plot on the cloud of individuals of the overall MFA the ellipses of concentration of the subpopulations corresponding to each class (Fig. 8.2). For the convenience of this cursory review of results, social classes are simply defined based on occupational categories (the French *catégories socio-professionelles* (CSP), as defined by INSEE): the bourgeoisie category is *cadres* (executives), meaning intellectual professions, and managers of companies

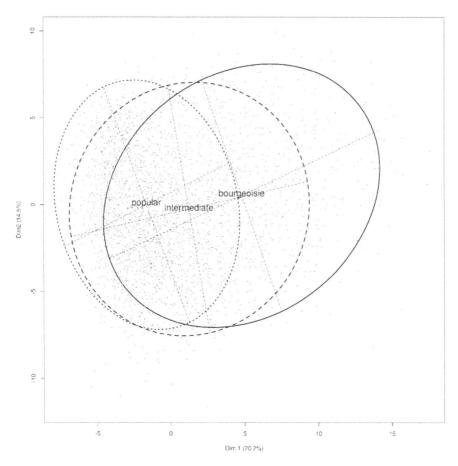

Fig. 8.2 Ellipses of concentration of social classes (on MFA cloud of individuals)

with more than ten employees; for intermediate groups, the category is *profession intermédiaires* (middle employees), which includes craftsmen, and retail traders; the category for the popular classes encompasses lower-level employees and labourers.

While the distribution of individuals on the axis 2 is relatively similar from one class to another, the dispersion on axis 1 – which indicates both intensity of cultural practices and proximity to legitimate culture – increases with the volume of capital. This is unsurprising, but we must also consider that there is a non-insignificant dispersion within the working classes themselves – and therein lies one of the interesting facets of the ellipses. The popular classes are not only non-consumers of bourgeois culture, with some class fractions exhibiting oppositions according to their relationship to bourgeois culture – bourgeois culture really is the heart of legitimacy, scaling taste in the overall social space even though it does not exhaust all the dimensions. In other words, we observe here an index of the social authority or the symbolic power of the bourgeoisie in cultural matters.

Table 8.3 Contributions to social class specific MFA axes of the domains of tastes (%)

Classes	Axes	Music	Movies	Television	Reading	Total
Bourgeois	1	21,6	**35,5**	22	20,9	100
	2	14,3	**54**	26,1	5,6	100
Intermediary	1	**27,7**	23,8	18,3	**30,2**	100
	2	16,7	**69,4**	7,2	6,7	100
Popular	1	28,7	**36,6**	11,8	22,9	100
	2	**42,1**	15,8	15,7	26,4	100

Reading: for popular classes, music contributes to 42,1% of the construction of axis 2

To go further, we turn to class specific analysis (CSA), because it helps to build a space for a subpopulation taking into account the distribution of categories in the subpopulation *and* in the total population (Le Roux and Rouanet 2004). It is particularly important, when constructing the space of a social class, to bear in mind the fact that this space does not exist in isolation, but is part of a broader space – that is, defined in relation to the rest of the population. In our case, we construct the space of tastes of active individuals in a given social class according to the space of the entire population in the survey. We build the CSA from the global MFA, to continue to compare the four domains of taste and the social classes simultaneously. We can then study – in addition to the plots – the contributions to the axes of each domain according to social class, the coordinates of the supplementary variables describing social properties (such as degree or income, again according to social class), and finally the categories which contribute the most to the axes, both by domain of taste and social class. These data enable us to describe in detail each class's tastes, and the way in which the different domains of tastes are structured for each social class. However, their interpretation must be informed by both sets of previous results. For lack of space, we only present the most interesting results.

First, we compare the contributions of the variables of each cultural domain to the first two axes of the CSA of each social class, built from the global MFA (Table 8.3).

For the bourgeois classes, the contributions of the four domains are relatively balanced on axis 1: internal differentiations in the bourgeois classes involve all cultural tastes. The relative prominence of movies on both axes is, however, notable. It is probably related to the distinguishing effect of even going to the cinema: the most established part of the bourgeois classes distinguishes itself by its distance from the cinema. Moreover, axis 1 is essentially correlated with cultural capital indicators (table with eta^2 available from authors): the interviewee's PCS summarizes 10% of the variance, the mother's educational level 9.8%, the interviewee's own educational level 9%, and the father's PCS 6.8%. Income and assets are negligible. There is also a slight effect of the distinction between public and private sector (3% of the variance), which is absent (or almost) in the other social classes: it may be the result of the presence in this class of occupations dealing directly with information and entertainment, and the scientific and teaching professions (except for primary and secondary education). The second axis, meanwhile, is clearly associated with age (16.5% of the variance).

On axis 1 (Table 8.3), the intermediate classes are differentiated primarily by reading tastes and then, in descending order, by music, movies, and television tastes: it seems safe to say that there is a capital composition effect here, the volume of cultural capital having perhaps the strongest distinguishing effect in this central region of social space – where the boundaries between graduates and non-graduates and between durations in higher education are the most significant. Meanwhile, axis 2 is constructed mainly by cinema, movies thus being more associated with variations in sex and/or age than with variations in capital in the middle of the social space. Indeed, the correlations (i.e. eta^2) between variables which determine social position support these interpretations. The variance on axis 1 is can mainly be explained by the respondent's own educational level (17.8%), followed far behind by the mother's educational level (8.6%), the father's PCS (7.4%) and age (5.9%). The variance of axis 2 is summarized first by age (17.2%), then by sex (9.4%).

For the popular classes, they are separated, on axis 1, primarily by their relationship to movies, and then by music and reading (in that order); on the axis 2, they are distinguished mainly by taste in music and, secondarily, reading (Table 8.3). Cinema and reading are less accessible than television and music, for rather different reasons: visits to the cinema are determined by their economic cost and the respondents' leisure habits; reading is determined by one's ability to 'read codes'. In addition, music contributes here strongly to the axis associated with age: juvenile music and ancient music could constitute a significant division within the popular classes. In fact, again, the variance of the axis 1 is summarized not only by the respondents' educational level, but also (indeed primarily) by age – which dominates axis 2 as well.

Note also that television seems the least distinguishing practice on axis 1, and less and less when passing from the bourgeois to the popular classes, as if the distinctive consumption (and absence of consumption) of television only existed among those most endowed with cultural capital. Following the same logic, on axis 1, it is among the intermediate classes that reading contributes the most and that movies contribute the least: reading practices, highly correlated to school experience, seem to have a considerable distinctive influence in an area where variations in cultural capital are at their strongest (it is also the case, as we have seen, among the intermediate classes that education correlates most strongly with axis 1). Conversely, the relationship to cinema, less framed by educational institutions and more correlated with age (and sex) than with education, exhibits comparatively little variance.

Another noteworthy variation is the fact that the male/female balance of tastes differs from one class to another. Sex has little structural influence among the bourgeois classes (whatever the axis), but it is correlated with age on axis 2 for the intermediate classes and it is also present, albeit secondarily, on the first two axes for the popular classes. The popular classes are thus distinguished by a strong association of sex, age and cultural capital effects (via education on axis 1 and SES on axis 2) in the structuration of their tastes, while for the other classes cultural capital seems to be clearly distinct from age (and sex in the intermediary classes). We will return to this discussion using other methods.

The Scale of Cultural Legitimacy: A Truly Multidimensional Social Space

An Empirically Grounded Scale

We now proceed to further analyse the homology between social space and the space of tastes. Our initial approach involves an exploration of the scale of cultural legitimacy. Usually, the first axis of factorial spaces of tastes is considered a satisfying representation of this scale, because this axis is correlated with indicators of economic and cultural capital. We will establish that this is a good proxy, but also that it is worth going into detail.

We have tested elsewhere several techniques for constructing scales of legitimacy empirically (Robette and Roueff 2014). One point must be retained here. The mutual ranking of tastes and social positions varies significantly according to their indicators: for tastes, indicators of participation, of abstract claims, of knowledge, all related to artistic genres or to individual artists or works; for social positions, indicators of income, of degree, of occupational category (and sometimes of age, and of racial or sexual self-identification). One of the main benefits of geometric data analysis (GDA) is that it enables the combination of these various indicators in order to study the structuring effects of their interactions. Rather than choosing only one, or considering them as competing and ranking their specific effects, GDA is able to better account for the artificiality of statistical variables: any indicator is only an approximation of reality, and techniques that calculate their interactions' effects offer to minimize this approximation.

A "U" Shape: A Multidimensional Scale

On the MFA of tastes, cultural and economic capitals are highly correlated with the first axis, and age and sex with the second axis: the latter are of lesser weight, but still important (Fig. 8.3). Besides, it has been established that cultural and economic capitals are not completely independent from age and sex. One can then expect that indicators of social class will not be strictly aligned with axis 1, and that indicators of sex and age will not be strictly aligned with axis 2. This presents us with a simple question: which social space is the space of tastes homologous with? Is the social space the space of class relations only, or do class relations interact with other power relations such as those of age and sex? One way to translate this question into a statistical inquiry involves looking at the exact shape of the scale of cultural legitimacy, beyond the proxy of axis 1.

All class indicators form a curve, more precisely an elongated U, or bell curve, from north-east to north-west, through the south of the geometrical plane. In addition, the most elongated variables according to this U are those indicating cultural capital. The distribution of the occupational categories (CSP) is less obvious, because we used detailed categories (see legend under Fig. 8.3). Thus, more typically female categories are at the top of the figure (lower-level employees, personal services, mid-level social sector employees, primary school teachers, etc.); more typically male categories are at the bottom (engineers, labourers, trained manual workers . . .). Still, following the U, one finds workers and employees, then mid-level occupations, then higher-level professionals.

This observation in mind, the bell curve appears more clearly than before on the space of tastes (Fig. 8.1). In the upper right (or north west?) of the figure, we see the absence of participation and the most shared, established (old) and female tastes. In the upper left, we find the highest degrees of participation and legitimacy. The bottom of the curve (and thus the middle of the U) is neither lowbrow nor highbrow, but characterised by emerging and male tastes. In summary, the dominant scale of cultural legitimacy, defined through the homology between the distribution of capitals and the distribution of tastes, forms a bell curve corresponding simultaneously to the power relations of class and to the power relations of sex and age. This does not challenge the usual approximation through which the scale is identified with the first axis of factorial analyses, or with the simple cross-tabulation of social positions and tastes. These remain good proxies. But we demonstrate here that the scale of cultural legitimacy is structured not only by social positions, but also by positions of sex and age, without any linear effect of the interaction of these last two variables. This point might be explored further, through the study of structural effects and then the study of interactions between the variables class, sex and age.

Studying Structural Effects

However, a more precise and refined exploration is possible thanks to regression analyses, if well used. Regression modeling and GDA are usually considered to represent two opposing, incompatible statistical 'philosophies' (see introduction of this volume). Adherents of the one approach might claim that regression modelling is able to uncover causal relations beyond the observed correlations, while the GDA is only really useful for inductive description or exploration of data. Those on the other side would argue that the former method merely imitates experimental sciences, their protocols for purifying the contexts of observation, and their quest for the strongest causal effect, while the latter respects both the multidimensionality of sociological explanations, and the inexhaustibility and historicity of social contexts. However, from a statistical point of view, both sets of techniques are based on

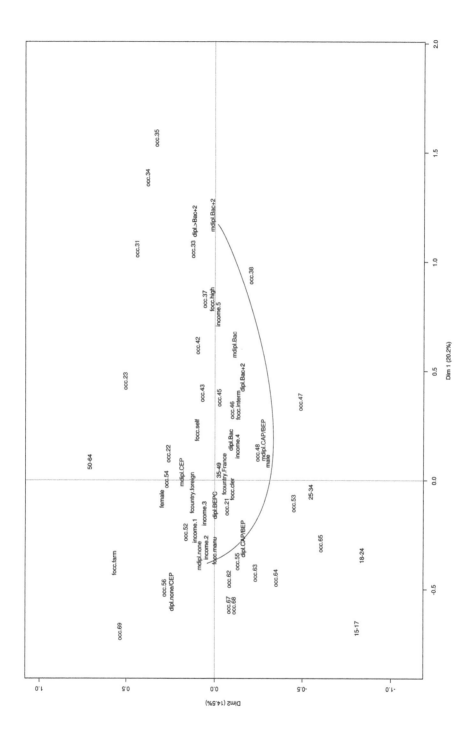

Fig. 8.3 Projection of social characteristics on the MFA of tastes

Prefix "occ" stands for interviewee's occupation, "dipl" for interviewee's diploma, "mdipl" for mother's diploma, "focc" for father's occupation, "fcountry" for father's country of origin The categories for interviewee's occupation are: 21 = craftsman, 22 = shopkeeper, 23 = business owner, 31 = professional, 33 = public sector executive, 34 = teacher, 35 = information, art and show business, 37 = administration or trade business executive, 38 = business engineer or technical executive, 42 = primary school teacher, 43 = health or social service intermediate occupation, 45 = public sector administrative intermediate occupation, 46 = business administrative and trade intermediary, 47 = technician, 48 = foreman, 52 = public sector clerk, 53 = policeman or serviceman, 54 = business administrative clerk, 55 = trade clerk, 56 = private service worker, 62 = industry skilled worker, 63 = craft skilled worker, 64 = driver, 65 = handling, storage and transport skilled worker, 67 = industry worker, 68 = craft worker, 69 = farm worker the same mathematical principles: correlations between variables (for PCA and linear regression) or simple cross-tabulations (for MCA and logistic regression). From an epistemological point of view, both approaches face the same possibilities and limitations: for instance, they may reveal correlations and hidden structures, which can only be interpreted as 'clues for causality', but never as 'mathematical evidence'.

We then propose a method to use regression analysis in the framework of GDA in order to study structural effects. Another method already exists, enabling the visualisation of the results of a regression by projecting the multidimensional space constructed from the independent variables of the model, and then the dependent variable as a supplementary: the global and partial effects of the independent variables can thus be compared (Rouanet et al. 2002). We call our method *Standardized Factorial Analysis* (Bry et al. 2015). This name is derived from the standardization methods used in demography (Léridon and Toulemon 1997; Deauvieau 2011). It is able to standardize a factorial space by one or more variables whose effect is isolated (i.e. controlled) through a linear regression. More precisely:

- First, we start with a traditional correspondence analysis (MCA, PCA, MFA, etc.), designed to build a new data table (called C) with the coordinates of the individuals on each axis of this analysis (here MCA). This results in the table Individuals x Coordinates, with i rows and p columns (i is the number of individuals and p is the number of principal components of the MCA). At this stage, one can choose to retain only the first principal components, those that contain the most information.
- Then, p linear regressions are performed, i.e. one for each column of the previous table C. The coordinates of the individuals of the MCA (i.e. the variables of C) are used one after the other as the dependent variable, with (for example) sex and age as independent variables.
- The residuals are retained for each of the regressions; resulting in a new table (called R) with i rows and p columns. The quantitative variables of R correspond to the coordinates of individuals in the initial MCA, net the sex and age structure.
- A PCA is then performed on table R, which provides a new cloud of individuals, i.e. a new space.
- The variables that were used to build the original MCA are then projected onto this space as supplementary variables: what appears is the factorial space of originally active variables, net the sex and age structure of the population. To the extent that the PCA is not performed directly on the variables of the original MCA, one cannot obtain the contributions of these variables. However, all other tools for the interpretation of supplementary variables may be used (cos^2, v-test, eta^2).

For a short illustration, Figs. 8.4 and 8.5 show the space of tastes for movies before and after the standardization of age and sex – knowing that the first axis, correlated with the volume of capitals, reflects the intensity of practice (high at left, low at right) and that the second axis, correlated with age and sex, reflects – apparently – the legitimacy of tastes (Bry et al.). The surprise with the traditional

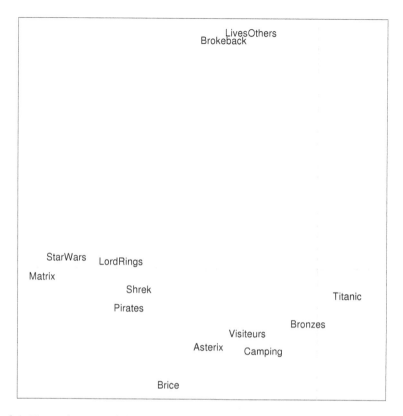

Fig. 8.4 The movies « especially liked » in the space of tastes for cinema (axes 1–2; « classical » MCA)

MCA (Fig. 8.4) is to see *auteur* movies in the centre of the first axis: legitimate taste is related to a less intense practice than a taste for Hollywood action and science fiction movies.

However, after performing the SFA (Fig. 8.5), the result is clear. Both figures present the three same groups of relatively similar films. Now, though, the French comedies have slightly moved to the right of the first axis. Moreover, the two *auteur* movies are now at the extreme left of the graph, at the same level of intensity as the action and science fiction movies. The comparison of the two spaces, one with structural effects and one without, thus shows that highbrow *cinéastes*' practices are as intense as those of action-movie lovers when sex and age are equivalent. Or, to put it differently, the observed association between the taste for art films and a relatively limited level of practice is the result of the sex and age structure of the population, as women and older people tend to watch fewer movies in general, while at the same time having more legitimate tastes.

SFA also raises a more general set of questions. The many applications we have attempted all point to the same phenomenon: when structural effects are neutralized,

Fig. 8.5 The movies « especially liked » in the space of tastes for cinema (axes 1–2; Standardized Factor Analysis)

the initial multidimensional space remains almost the same in its general pattern. Some categories may move, such as *auteur* movies in the example shown here, but the overall structure of the cloud of categories and the interpretation that can be given of its different factors survive the neutralization, including when controlling for several highly explanatory variables (such as social class, sex, age, and educational level). This probably illustrates a more general epistemological assumption: social determinisms observed through statistical variables, even when well established, are probabilistic and not mechanical, and moreover they are partial in the sense that they produce their effects only when associated with each other.

Conclusion

In this chapter, we have tested several hypotheses related to the social differentiation of lifestyles: whether there exists a structural homology between the entirety of the social and cultural spaces as wholes, by categorising four cultural domains (TV, reading, cinema and music); whether the same structural homology applies at the scale of the different social classes; and the extent of the associations between the factors structuring lifestyles (volume and composition of capital as well as sex and age).

While the results are not analysed in full detail here (although they are in other papers, see Robette and Roueff 2017, 2018), we have argued for the use of unusual or innovative statistical tools – such as MFA, CSA and SFA – which could open new avenues for future investigations in the field of lifestyles and cultural tastes and practices.

References

Bennett, T., Emmison, M., & Frow, J. (1999). *Accounting for tastes: Australian everyday cultures.* Cambridge: Cambridge University Press.

Bennett, T., Savage, M., Silva, E., Warde, A., Gayo-Cal, M., & Wright, D. (2009). *Culture, class, distinction.* London/New York: Routledge.

Borges Pereira, J. V. (2005). *Classes e Culturas de Classe das Famílias Portuenses. Classes sociais e «modalidades de estilização da vida» na cidade do Porto.* Porto: Afrontamento/Instituto de Sociologia da Faculdade de Letras da Universidade do Porto.

Bourdieu, P. (1979). *La distinction. Critique sociale du jugement.* Paris: Minuit.

Bry, X., Robette, N., & Roueff, O. (2015). A Dialogue of the deaf in the statistical theater? Adressing structural effects within a geometric data analysis framework. *Quality & Quantity, 50*(3), 1009–1020.

Christine, D. (2011). Des shonens pour les garçons, des shojos pour les filles ? Apprendre son genre en lisant des mangas. *Réseaux, 4*(168–169), 165–186.

Christin, A. (2012). Gender and highbrow cultural participation in the United States. *Poetics, 40*(5), 423–443.

Deauvieau, J. (2011). Est-il possible et souhaitable de traduire sous forme de probabilités un coefficient logit ? Réponse aux remarques formulées par Marion Selz à propos de mon article paru dans le BMS en 2010. *Bulletin de Méthodologie Sociologique, 112*(1), 32–42.

Duval, J. (2011). L'offre et les goûts cinématographiques en France. *Sociologie, 2*(1), 1–18.

Escofier, B., & Pagès, J. (1990). Multiple factor analysis. *Computational Statistics & Data Analysis, 18*, 121–140.

Escofier, B., & Pagès, J. (2008). *Analyses factorielles simples et multiples. Objectifs, méthodes et interprétation.* Paris: Dunod.

Fabiani, J. L. (1995). *Lire en prison. Une étude sociologique.* Paris: BPI.

Grignon, C., & Passeron, J. C. (1989). *Le savant et le populaire. Misérabilisme et populisme en sociologie et en littérature.* Paris: Gallimard/Seuil/EHESS.

Hervé, G., & Michel, P. (2009). La "tablature" des goûts musicaux : un modèle de structuration des préférences et des jugements. *Revue Française de Sociologie, 50*(3), 599–640.

Le Roux, B., & Rouanet, H. (2004). *Geometric data analysis: From correspondence analysis to structured data analysis.* New York: Springer.

Le Roux, B., & Rouanet, H. (2010). *Multiple correspondence analysis*. Thousand Oaks: Sage.

Léridon, H., & Toulemon, L. (1997). *Démographie. Approche statistique et dynamique des populations*. Paris: Economica.

Octobre, S. (2011). Du féminin au masculin. Genre et trajectoires culturelles. *Réseaux, 180*, 102–124.

Peterson, R. A., & Kern, R. M. (1996). Changing highbrow taste: From snob to omnivore. *American Journal of Sociology, 61*(5), 900–907.

Prieur, A., Rosenlund, L., & Skjott-Larsen, J. (2008). Cultural capital today: A case study from Denmark. *Poetics, 36*, 45–71.

Philippe, C. (2003). La stratification sociale des goûts musicaux. *Revue Française de Sociologie, 44*(1), 3–33.

Robette, N., & Roueff, O. (2014). An eclectic eclecticism: Methodological and theoretical issues in the quantification of cultural omnivorism. *Poetics, 47*, 23–40.

Robette, N., & Roueff, O. (2017). L'espace contemporain des goûts culturels. Homologies structurales entre domaines de pratiques et entre classes sociales. *Sociologie, 8*(4), 369.

Robette, N., & Roueff, O. (2018). *Une légitimité multidimensionnelle. L'échelle de légitimité culturelle et les interactions entre diplôme, âge et sexe*. Unpublished manuscript.

Rosenlund, L. (2000). Cultural change in Norway: Cultural and economic dimensions. *International Journal of Contemporary Sociology, 37*(2), 245–275.

Rouanet, H., Lebaron, F., Hay, V. L., Ackermann, W., & Le Roux, B. (2002). Régression et analyse géométrique des données: réflexions et suggestions. *Mathématiques et Sciences Humaines, 160*, 13–46.

Roose, H., van Eijck, K., & Lievens, J. (2012). Culture of distinction or culture of openness? Using a social space approach to analyze the social structuring of lifestyles. *Poetics, 40*, 491–513.

Savage, M., & Gayo, M. (2011). Unravelling the omnivore: A field analysis of contemporary musical taste in the United Kingdom. *Poetics, 39*(5), 337–335.

Chapter 9
Intergenerational Reproduction of Distinctive Cultural Capital: A Study of University Education Obtained Abroad and at Home

Martin D. Munk

Introduction

Cultural and social reproduction strategies are no longer limited to nation states but now operate across borders. A number of scholars have noted that investments in foreign elite education have become increasingly attractive (e.g., Wagner 2007), but supporting evidence is limited due to a lack of suitable data. An increasing number of students are enrolling in and completing university programmes, including in Denmark; however access is characterised by social selection, which particularly implies horizontal differentiation (Munk and Thomsen 2018). This social selection could affect the willingness to invest in education abroad. I suggest that the acquisition of this type of distinctive cultural capital abroad is viewed as an intergenerational reproduction strategy that supplements the portfolio of other strategies. Thus, I investigate whether migrants who graduate from elite universities abroad constitute a socially selected group. Prior research provides ample evidence of the effect of family background on the likelihood of obtaining higher education in domestic universities, and previous studies have demonstrated that family background is still a vital condition in educational attainment, especially with regard to elite education. However, whether social origin also increases the probability of obtaining higher education abroad remains unresolved. Therefore, I examine how family background affects the likelihood of obtaining a degree from an elite or non-elite university abroad compared to obtaining a university education at home, with no university as the reference category. This design is unique in the literature on international students because this line of research has lacked a comparison group in the home country to assess whether there is an effect

Martin D. Munk (✉)
Department of Political Science, Aalborg University, Copenhagen, Denmark
e-mail: mdm@dps.aau.dk

© Springer Nature Switzerland AG 2019
J. Blasius et al. (eds.), *Empirical Investigations of Social Space*,
Methodos Series 15, https://doi.org/10.1007/978-3-030-15387-8_9

that differs from social selection in domestic universities. The tool that currently defines elite and non-elite universities is university ranking lists, inspired by the study published by Wendy Espeland and Michael Sauder in the *American Journal of Sociology* in 2007. The merging of survey and register data has made it possible to compare migrants with non-migrants with regard to a set of common covariates. The combination of high-quality register data containing information on parental background and a weighted sample of emigrants makes it feasible to answer these questions. I restrict the sample to Danes who emigrated in the period between 1987 and 2002 and who had lived abroad for at least 5 years.

Only a few previous studies link the literature on educational or cultural reproduction to the literature on global higher education and migration. Munk (2009) analyses the acquisition of informational capital in prestigious foreign educational institutions as measured by Erasmus student mobility. He reveals that students from the upper and upper-middle social classes (measured by parental occupation) are more likely than students from other social classes to pursue transnational investments, although students from the middle and working classes have entered the competition. Other studies, such as Jasso (2011), link migration and admission into educational institutions. This gap in the literature is unsurprising because the vast majority of the existing social stratification literature was developed at a time when very few people studied abroad. In this chapter, I find that having highly privileged parents—often with abundant cultural capital and transnational orientations—increases the likelihood of obtaining a university education at home and abroad.

Theory

In the theory of reproduction strategies, Pierre Bourdieu posits that families possessing a high stock of capital strategically invest in credentials that have the highest distinctive and transferrable value (Bourdieu 1996) either at home or abroad. Because the venue for cultural reproduction is for the most part the horizontal dimension of the university system and because student mobility across borders has been increasing (Börjesson 2017), I focus on universities, both at home and abroad. Admission requirements for elite universities are demanding and studying abroad can be costly; thus it is likely that individuals from affluent and socially privileged families are particularly attracted to universities that are highly ranked on international ranking lists (Espeland and Sauder 2007; Sauder and Espeland 2009; see also Börjesson 2017).

Most studies of the reproduction of higher education analyse the patterns and intergenerational correlations within nation states as most students previously remained in their home country. Studies of social stratification and theories of social reproduction were mainly developed at a time when the key terms in theories of reproduction—education and social class—were relatively stable (Brown and

Lauder 2009). A central contribution in this area of research is the theory of cultural and social reproduction by Bourdieu, who developed his theories in a national context by focusing on the social conditions of exclusion from and selection into the educational system. In particular, he studied distinct Grandes Ecoles, elite schools at the top of the French university hierarchy (Bourdieu 1996; Munk 2009). Access to these elite schools is understood to be highly unequal, which ultimately results in unequal outcomes (Alboury and Wanecq 2003). In the US case, Karabel (2005) focused on the strong link between an elitist origin and admission to the Big Three: Harvard, Yale, and Princeton. According to Bourdieu (1996), families maintain their social position or existence through a multi-dimensional set of reproduction strategies. The classic example of an education strategy is the conversion of economic capital to cultural capital by families who are alert to the need for their children to obtain an education that will result in potentially advantageous pathways and prestige. This strategy is especially utilised by the upper class, but to a growing extent, it is also used by the upper-middle classes and other groups who are aware of the importance of education. However, Bourdieu focused on elite schools at home and did not directly examine the acquisition of distinctive education abroad and emigration as such. His long-standing collaborator Abdelmalek Sayad (1991, 2004) studied strategies of emigration and immigration, but from the perspective of a poor country (Algeria) rather than emigration from a European country to study in other Western countries.

Different aspects of transnational strategies are highlighted in Wagner (1998, 2007), Munk (2009), Brown and Lauder (2009), and Soehl and Waldinger (2012). Most of these studies do not relate to social origin or compare outcomes in national settings. However, the tendency of international student mobility to be socially selective is noted in empirical studies (e.g., Netz and Finger 2016). Both economic and sociological approaches suggest that children with socially advantaged origins invest more in international education, especially distinctive elite education. Consequently, they become part of the Zones of Prestige (Collins 2001) to distinguish themselves and maximise their opportunities, both abroad and at home. Following Bourdieu, the term cultural capital refers to various forms of knowledge, educational credentials, language, dispositions, and materialised advantages that provide social recognition (Bourdieu 1984). In this chapter, I consider cultural capital transmitted from parental education and language and cultural capital that can be attained by a migrant. The term cultural capital has been used primarily in national contexts. Nonetheless, in the global space of higher education institutions (Börjesson 2017) – which has a particular distribution of distinctive cultural capital that is typically displayed and highlighted by the world rankings of these institutions (Espeland and Sauder 2007) – education is increasingly acquired or applied abroad. Cultural capital can therefore become relevant for transnational aspirations and strategies to expand the stock of capital or to gain distinctive cultural capital abroad, sometimes conceptualised as cosmopolitan capital (cf. Weenink 2008), which involves the same dimensions as the aforementioned definition of cultural capital. What I want to stress with regard to distinctive cultural capital acquired abroad is the fact that it goes beyond the national educational field; emigrants are investing in capital outside of their national context.

However, there is a potential caveat: the majority of the migrants I analyse have prior experience of being abroad with their parents; thus, it seems appropriate to consider the degree to which they are truly bound to a national context. They certainly have a level of experience with other countries, which implies that some of these individuals are actually positioned between a national and a transnational context. Furthermore, many of them probably belong to what other scholars concep-tualise as transnational families (or cosmopolitan families). These individuals are prone to study abroad because they have been exposed to international environments during their upbringing, and they already possess good language skills and have an international circle of friends (Palloni et al. 2001).

From the perspective of cultural capital, obtaining a university degree abroad functions as a cultural reproduction strategy. This is the case especially for individuals who went abroad with their parents during their upbringing and have therefore adopted transnational orientations and accumulated distinctive cultural capital abroad. Alternately, they may simply have become more disposed to invest in cultural capital abroad, making the choice of a university programme abroad quite natural (Weenink 2008: 1092). Therefore, I present three scenarios to interpret investment strategies in education abroad and at home to explain and understand people's endeavours to obtain a degree abroad, sometimes with the ambition of finding a transnational position. The formation of transnational elites occurs especially in the United States (Kim 2016) and the United Kingdom. Capital acquired in the Zones of Prestige can, in turn, contribute to the creation of a transnational class or power elite (Weenink 2008; Brown and Lauder 2009; Caroll 2010). However, I do not consider transnational positions in this chapter.

One scenario comprises a tradition in internationally minded families holding cultural capital that makes them more likely to take advantage of educational opportunities abroad. The idea is that children from the most privileged social classes spend time in foreign countries to acquire the skills, qualifications, and knowledge required to maintain the family's position nationally or perhaps even transnationally (Johnson et al. 2011). In this sense, tradition latently prescribes that the new generations of the privileged classes go abroad to maintain the familys' social status. Therefore, the aim of studying abroad is not only to obtain valuable knowledge but also to obtain a distinctive asset needed to maintain the family position. At the same time, children in these families may be prone to migrate because their parents migrated as well, and they therefore have stronger dispositions towards out-migration.

In another and newer scenario, children from upper-middle-class families obtain elite education abroad as a new means of obtaining distinctive capital because increased enrolment in national universities has reduced the social advantage that national education used to provide (Wagner 2007). Under these new conditions, with an increasingly competitive environment, it is argued that upper-middle and upper-class students and their families must find new ways to reproduce their social advantage through investments in overseas education (Brooks and Waters

2009: 1086–1087). This novel tendency raises the question of the evolution of the intergenerational reproduction of higher education. Therefore, I compare two types of university education obtained abroad with two types of university education obtained in a national setting.

A third scenario presents an even newer tendency in which children pursue social mobility (a compensatory strategy). Specifically, students apply to universities abroad and acquire distinctive cultural capital that can potentially compensate for a lack of cultural capital in the home country to gain occupational prestige or simply to climb the social ladder at home or abroad. Some researchers suggest that upward social mobility, rather than social reproduction, is the driving force behind some parents' propensity to provide their children with cosmopolitan capital (Weenink 2008: 1103). According to this reasoning, attending international programmes is related to social ambitions more than to social reproduction. A study by Favell (2008) suggests that mobility may be more likely to be pursued by less privileged people than their peers from more privileged backgrounds. Less privileged young people may gamble with spatial mobility in their education and careers abroad to improve their social mobility opportunities, which are otherwise blocked at home (Brooks and Waters 2011). In particular, it may be that non-elite institutions abroad recruit from classes with primarily economic capital as a means to improve their social position.

Data

I analyse education abroad using two surveys of Danes who emigrated in the period between 1987 and 2002. These surveys were organised by Martin D. Munk and Panu Poutvaara in the Danes Abroad project and were conducted by Statistics Denmark.[1]

The survey data are from Danish citizens who emigrated from Denmark in 1987, 1988, 1992, 1993, 1997, 1998, 2001 or 2002 and who were between 18 and 59 years of age when they emigrated. For the eight selected years, emigrants are split into those who were still abroad and those who were again residing in Denmark according to the migration register as of December 31, 2007.

A total of 17,309 individuals emigrated in the selected emigration years and had not returned to Denmark. A major challenge in reaching people living abroad is that there are no data on their addresses in the Danish population register. To address this problem, Statistics Denmark first contacted parents or siblings who were residing in Denmark. They found contact information for a relative in Denmark for 54% of the cases or 9415 emigrants. Seven percent of these people did not provide contact information for their emigrated relative. The primary reasons were that the relative was no longer in contact with the emigrated person or the relative

[1] I thank Mette Foged for excellent research assistance. Financial support from the Danish Council for Independent Research Fund Social Sciences (FSE) is gratefully acknowledged.

refused to participate. This left a group of 8749 emigrants with available contact information. Those with only an address and telephone number were contacted and asked to provide their e-mail address. Final validation of the collected emails showed that 6984 emails were valid, and only people for whom email addresses were available were contacted. The data collection was performed using a web-based questionnaire. After several tests, the final questionnaire was sent to the 6984 emigrants in mid-June 2008, followed by three rounds of reminders to those who had not answered. When the data collection was closed, 4260 emigrants (N_1) had answered the questionnaire.

For returned migrants, the sampling process was simpler. These migrants were stratified into six groups. Because shorter migration spells constitute the majority of migrations from Denmark, we undersample short durations abroad such that they do not constitute most of the final survey data.[2] The resulting selected population contained 5700 return migrants, and contact information was obtained for 4600 of these return migrants. Data collection for return migrants started towards the end of September 2008. The return migrants 4600 received a letter with information on the survey, the website address and a password. Those who did not complete the web questionnaire were later contacted by phone, if was possible. The interviews lasted 45 minutes on average. A total of 70% of the 3065 replies (N_2) were received through the Internet. Similar to the 'stayers', the response rate for 'returners' was very high compared to similar surveys, at 67%.

We focus on individuals who had either stayed abroad at the time the surveys were conducted in 2008 or had returned to their home country after being abroad for more than 5 years. In the surveys, respondents were asked whether they had studied abroad; if so, a number of questions related to their studies were asked.

This section describes the data sources and sample restrictions and how we measure and quantify international elite education. Survey data on emigrants and return migrants are used and combined with population register data. The survey data include information on whether the respondent had obtained a degree abroad and if so, where. The application of register data allows for the construction of a proper comparison between groups of people who did not attend universities and people who had enrolled in Danish universities.

Combining Survey and Register Data

After excluding emigrants to Greenland and the Faroe Islands, the sample included 4126 respondents who had not returned to Denmark by 2007 and 2597 respondents who had returned to Denmark by 2007. In total, 983 migrants had obtained

---

[2]The applied sampling weights were 2%, 4%, 4%, 12%, 20% and 60% from the group with the shortest to the longest duration abroad (up to 6 months, 6–12 months, 1–3 years, 3–5 years, 5–10 years and 10 or more years abroad, respectively).

Table 9.1 Survey observations

Duration	Returners		Stayers		Total	
	Degree abroad	All	Degree abroad	All	Degree abroad	All
0 to 6 months	4	112			4	112
6 to 12 months	22	433			22	433
1 to 3 years	22	429			22	429
3 to 5 years	38	349			38	349
5 to 10 years 10 years or longer	61	507	768	3857	829	4364
Number of observations	147	1830	768	3857	915	5687

university degrees abroad. The analysis is restricted to people who at the time of their emigration were between 18 and 39 years of age at the time of their emigration as almost all respondents who had obtained a degree abroad belonged to this age group. Only 16 older respondents were deleted.

Table 9.1 shows the number of respondents and the number who had obtained a degree abroad according to the duration of their stay abroad. Ultimately, *N target* was 829 people who had obtained a university education abroad. Of this group, 768 were still abroad, and 61 had returned in 2007.

The same restrictions that were applied to the survey respondents were applied to the remaining register data to form a comparison group of those who had attended Danish universities and those who had not attended university at all.

Measuring Elite Education

For all migrants who had obtained a degree abroad, detailed information is available on the specific country, year, degree and university, and this information is applied in the statistical analysis. I divide universities into elite and non-elite institutions using the detailed information and international ranking lists. Although international ranking lists are not an objective measure of the best and most prestigious foreign universities, they are likely to be indicative of the perceptions held by Danish migrants. Moreover, some authors argues that these lists currently dominate global university systems (Sauder and Espeland 2009; Kauppi and Erkkilä 2011). The ranking lists are QS-Times' Higher Education's Annual World University Ranking 2004 (http://www.timeshighereducation.co.uk/hybrid. asp?typeCode=153) and the Financial Times' Ranking of the best MBA schools in the world in 2004 (see http://rankings.ft.com/businessschoolrankings/global-mba-rankings-2004). QS-Times' rankings are based on academic peer reviews, citations per faculty member, faculty-student ratio, global employer review, international study ratio, and international faculty ratio, in that order. An alternative is the Shanghai Ranking List, which relies on the number of Nobel Prize recipients among employees and students and the number of publications in journals such as Science and Nature. Both sets of rankings confirm the reputations of the leading American and British universities, such as Harvard, Stanford, Yale, Berkeley, MIT, Cambridge, and Oxford. Some of the elite universities abroad most frequently represented in the data are the University of London, Oslo University, the University of Oxford, Stockholm University, Lund University, University College London, College of Europe, London Business School, the University of Cambridge, the London School of Economics, King's College, Columbia University, and the University of Chicago. The elite universities at home are the University of Copenhagen, Aarhus University, and the Technical University of Denmark.

Method

In the statistical analysis, I compare Danes who had obtained a degree abroad to Danes with no university education and Danes who had attended universities in Denmark. The survey data provide information on whether respondents had obtained a university degree abroad at the time they answered the survey. Educational attainment for non-migrants in 2007 is taken from Danish register data. In this way, it is possible to divide our population into five groups: no university education, non-elite university in Denmark, elite university in Denmark, non-elite university abroad and elite university abroad. This section explains the weighting scheme and the multinomial logistic model with weighted data used to analyse the five distinct types of educational attainment.

Weighting Scheme

Respondents are made representative of migrants in the survey years by inverse probability weights.[3] The probability of being in the survey is estimated separately for men and women and for returners and stayers to account for differences in response behaviour and differences with respect to how the data were collected. The probability models are kept simple to avoid making the results overly sensitive when small subgroups are analysed. All models control for emigration year, age at emigration and country groups, which are defined as English-speaking countries,

---

[3]Inverse probability weighting is a statistical technique for calculating statistics standardised to a population that is different from the population in which the data were collected. Study designs with a disparate sampling population and population of target inference (target population) are common in application (cf. Robins et al. 1994). Here, the applied weights are the inverse probabilities of being in the survey. In inverse probability-weighted data (IPW data), parameter estimates are calculated based on the idea that each observation represents a number of individuals in the underlying population.

other Nordic countries, the rest of Europe, and the rest of the world. As explained previously, respondents who were still abroad were contacted through their parents. The analysis displays significant selection at the parental education level for this group; therefore, parental education levels are included in the probability models for stayers. Parental education is not significant for returned migrants, which makes sense given the differences in how the data were gathered. On the other hand, given that the migrants' education level is not controlled in the simple probability models used and education level is known to often play a role in response propensities, it is perhaps surprising that parental education is not significant for returners as a proxy for the migrants' own education level. Most emigrants who study abroad are young people who have yet to complete their education. Therefore, there is no control for educational level. To account for different sampling weights in the two duration groups (5–10 years and 10 years or more), a duration group dummy is included in the probability models for returned migrants. One returned respondent represents on average 9.3 emigrants, and one stayer represents 4 emigrants who stayed abroad.

Model

The model setup is a weighted maximum-likelihood multinomial logit specification, implying that the individual likelihood contributions are weighted by the inverse sampling probabilities. The calculation of inverse sampling probabilities is made possible by linking the survey respondents to the underlying population from which they are sampled. Robust standard errors are calculated to account for the uncertainty introduced by the fact that respondents with education abroad are represented by survey data. A multinomial logit model is a natural choice because our education groups cannot be ordered. In addition, these models are chosen such that the results can be compared with other results on access to universities (e.g., Munk and Thomsen 2018). The results are likely to reflect a two-dimensional capital hierarchy beyond the traditional distinction between academic and non-academic education. To obtain disjunctive groups, all individuals who emigrated in the survey years with university education in Denmark are excluded.

The reported model estimates are relative risk ratios (RRRs), which is a generalisation of odds ratios to multinomial models. These RRRs are provided to convey a sense of the net effects rather than the marginal effects. All covariates are included as dummy variables. Thus, the RRR is the ratio of the relative probability of the outcome in question (compared to the reference outcome) when the dummy variable changes from zero to one. An RRR of 2.5 means that if the dummy variable equals one, the likelihood of the outcome in question compared to the reference outcome is 2.5 times more likely than if the dummy variable equals zero. More generally, an RRR < 1 implies that the dummy variable in question reduces the likelihood of the outcome, while an RRR > 1 implies a higher likelihood of the outcome relative to the reference outcome of no university education.

Cultural Capital and Social Capital Abroad

In this section, I present facts about respondents' pre-emigration situation with regard to their families, their own experiences living abroad, and their friends living abroad. To measure a crucial dimension of cultural capital abroad, I specifically scrutinise three key items. The first item is whether, the respondents had lived abroad with their parents before emigrating. The second item is whether the respondents' parents had lived or studied abroad, and the third item is whether the respondents' parents spoke English. These items are similar to those applied by Weenink (2008), who measures parents' international behaviour by their frequency of business trips abroad; their work-related use of oral and written English; whether they hosted foreign guests at home; whether they visited foreign friends; and whether they read foreign books and newspapers. The results are reported separately for men and women and for elite and non-elite education given that I expect a gender difference.

Table 9.2 reports the degree of cultural and social capital the respondents' parents and graduates possessed distributed by whether the respondents had acquired an elite or non-elite university degree abroad. Unsurprisingly, the findings show that the number of English-speaking parents is higher among elite university graduates. Additionally, the likelihood of being elite university alumni is typically higher if the respondents' parents had worked or studied abroad. A slightly higher fraction of men from non-elite universities had lived abroad with their parents than had men from elite universities, while the opposite holds for women. Generally, those from elite universities more frequently have friends or relatives in the country to which they emigrate; this is the case for almost four out of ten men and for more than half

Table 9.2 Indicators of cultural capital and social capital abroad held by graduates and parents

		Men		Women	
		Non-elite	Elite	Non-elite	Elite
Had lived with parents abroad		9.3	8.2	7.7	10.9
Had friends or relatives in the destination country before emigrating		34.0	38.8	41.7	54.4
Had friends or relatives in the destination country before emigrating, first time emigrants		32.4	44.4	31.5	60.7
Mother	Speaks English	63.4	64.6	65.1	71.7
	Had studied abroad	13.9	18.4	10.6	13.0
	Had worked abroad	25.8	27.2	29.1	37.7
	Had worked or studied abroad	32.5	36.1	32.6	39.7
Father	Speaks English	64.4	75.7	66.7	73.2
	Had studied abroad	15.5	17.7	14.3	13.0
	Had worked abroad	38.1	40.8	36.3	41.3
	Had worked or studied abroad	42.8	48.3	40.3	43.5
Number of observations		194	147	350	138

Source: Survey data
Note: Column percentages

of the women. For non-elite university students, the situation is less striking: this is the case for only one-third of the men and four out of ten women.

In summary, the above results indicate that respondents who study abroad tend to have a significant stock of social capital, including an international circle of friends and relatives. In particular, women with more social capital abroad are more inclined to study at elite universities.

In addition to these factors, men are more often motivated by academic quality than women. Likewise, those who study at elite universities are more often motivated by academic quality than those who study at non-elite universities. Nearly half of the men and one-quarter of the women who obtain an elite university education abroad make the choice in part because, based on their evaluation, the foreign university is academically better. Additionally, two out of five men who obtain an elite education abroad favour valuable labour market skills, and approximately the same percentage favour prestige, while one-third cite better job opportunities abroad (Munk et al. 2011).

Respondents who studied in the US or UK stated more often than other respondents, that the university they attended was more prestigious and offered a higher academic level than universities in their home country. This pattern is especially pronounced for women. This result supports the Zones of Prestige thesis proposed by Collins (2001), which suggests that students are attracted to zones in specific countries partially because of prestige but also because of the perceived higher quality of the institutions. The study by Munk (2009) explains that the attraction is also driven by favourable academic capital.

Cultural Reproduction

In this section, I examine intergenerational cultural reproduction. First, I determine the proportion of men and women who earn a degree from abroad. The survey data show that 43% of men and 28% of women earned a degree from elite institutions abroad. When respondents in 2008 were asked to state their current highest level of education, 31% reported a bachelor's degree, 40% reported a master's degree, 20% reported a PhD or equivalent, and 9% reported an MBA. The data show that 76% of respondents have only one degree from abroad, 20% have two degrees and the remainder have three degrees, except for four persons who have four degrees from abroad.

Second, I analyse five outcomes in the same regression analysis and restrict the analysis to respondents for whom there is information on the education of both parents. This restriction is natural because in the analysis I focus on the intergenerational transmission of cultural capital. If the educational level of at least one parent is missing, there is a risk of misclassification of the highest parental education. The migrants' own education is measured by the survey data for migrants and the register data for non-migrants. Table 9.3 shows the distribution of parental education for the five aforementioned educational groups. Comparing the first three columns shows that parental education is strongly correlated with the likelihood of obtaining a non-elite or elite university education in Denmark. In particular, the fraction of those with university-educated mothers is eight to 11 times larger among women with university education at home than among to those with no university education. The distribution of parental educational levels for migrants who obtain a non-elite university education from abroad is similar to the distribution of parental educational levels for individuals with a non-elite university education from Denmark. Respondents who obtain an elite university education abroad have slightly better educated parents than respondents who obtain an elite university education in Denmark (and from non-elite universities abroad); this is the case particularly for women. It is striking that almost one-fifth of the women who attend elite institutions abroad have a mother with a university education, and one-fourth have a university-educated father. For men with an elite education abroad, one-tenth of their mothers and one-third of their fathers had obtained a university education. This pattern is found for generations for which only 5–6% of fathers and 1–2% of mothers obtained a university education. In summary, this means that both women and men who earn an elite degree abroad or at home have extremely well-educated families and hence a high degree of cultural capital, even compared to people who obtain a university degree at home.

With regard to elite education abroad, fathers appear to be role models for men and mothers appear to be role models for women. In fact, the analysis shows that the educational level of the parent of the same gender plays a substantial role in the outcome of the decision of whether to study abroad. The fraction of mothers with a university education is 9–12 percentage points higher for women who obtain an elite education abroad than for women who obtain an elite or non-elite university education in Denmark or a non-elite university education abroad. The same results apply for men with respect to their fathers' highest education.

In Tables 9.4 and 9.5, I present multinomial models of the effects of birth cohort, parental education and history of living abroad before the age of 18 on the likelihood of obtaining a university education at home or abroad. Note that multinomial logistic regression models should stand up to the independence of irrelevant alternatives (IIA) assumption, but the feasibility of IIA tests is disputed (Long and Freese 2006: 243–246). Dow and Endersby (2004) posit that estimating substitution patterns is often hypothetical, so the model is an approximation (Train 2009). Therefore, I describe a preference structure in the choice of universities without making causal claims based on the models. The purpose of the current study is mainly to study reproduction patterns that are not typically revealed in these types of studies (see Munk and Thomsen (2018) for a similar argument).

The statistical analysis confirms the social and gender differences found in Table 9.3. Overall, I find that family educational background strongly affects the likelihood of obtaining a university degree, for both men and women. The level of parental education increases the likelihood of obtaining an elite university degree *both* at home *and* abroad, most clearly for women. The distribution of parental education among those who obtain a non-elite education abroad does not differ from the distribution among those who obtain a non-elite university education in

Table 9.3 Distribution of parental education for five different education groups

	Men					Women				
	No degree	Non-elite Denmark	Elite Denmark	Non-elite abroad	Elite abroad	No degree	Non-elite Denmark	Elite Denmark	Non-elite abroad	Elite abroad
Education of mother:										
Basic school	56.1	28.6	22.6	27.1	19.8	56.2	28.3	21.7	24.2	11.6
Upper secondary	0.9	2.6	4.2	1.1	5.6	0.9	2.9	3.6	4.9	6.2
Vocational education	30.3	33.8	27.2	28.3	20.6	31.0	34.1	30.2	27.8	25.6
Short higher	2.1	5.1	6.5	7.3	8.7	2.2	5.5	6.5	4.9	9.3
Medium higher	9.7	24.1	31.5	31.1	34.1	9.1	23.8	30.3	32.0	30.2
University degree	0.9	5.9	8.1	5.1	11.1	0.7	5.4	7.7	6.2	17.1
Number of observations	20,290	1460	1179	177	126	18,962	1341	1100	306	129
Education of father:										
Basic school	42.0	20.4	15.4	14.1	15.9	41.5	21.2	16.3	18.6	15.5
Upper secondary	1.2	2.8	4.4	2.3	3.2	1.1	3.4	4.2	4.9	5.4
Vocational education	42.5	34.1	29.4	35.6	20.6	43.1	37.1	29.5	30.1	23.3
Short higher	3.1	4.4	2.4	4.0	3.2	3.1	3.7	3.0	4.6	2.3
Medium higher	8.0	21.3	21.3	26.0	24.6	7.7	16.5	23.3	22.2	28.7
University degree	3.2	17.0	27.1	18.1	32.5	3.5	18.2	23.8	19.6	24.8
Number of observations	20,290	1460	1179	177	126	18,962	1341	1100	306	129

Source: Register data and survey data

Note: For each gender, the three first columns are based on 0.5% population register data without the migrants, and the last two columns are based on survey data on the migrants. Observations are deleted if the education of one or both parents is missing

Table 9.4 Multinomial model of the probability of different university education choices, men

Reference: No university degree		Non-elite Denmark		Elite Denmark		Non-elite abroad		Elite abroad	
		RRR	z	RRR	z	RRR	z	RRR	z
Birth cohort 1951–1959		.812*	−1.65	1.673***	3.73	1.011	0.02	.712	−0.64
Birth cohort 1960–1965		.935	−0.65	1.203	1.51	2.001	1.38	1.040	0.10
Birth cohort 1966–1971		.957	−0.44	1.046	0.37	2.945**	2.22	1.208	0.52
Birth cohort 1972–1977		.988	−0.12	1.270**	1.96	3.620***	2.61	2.844***	2.85
Mother	Upper secondary	2.229***	3.99	3.629***	6.33	.764	−0.33	2.649*	1.72
	Vocational education	1.749***	7.56	1.822***	6.60	1.201	0.79	.970	−0.07
	Short higher education	2.777***	7.24	4.181***	9.36	2.112**	2.24	2.374*	1.68
	Medium higher education	2.492***	9.99	3.815***	12.98	1.973***	2.82	1.924	1.42
	University degree	4.140***	8.87	5.511***	10.27	3.451**	2.50	3.402**	2.37
Father	Upper secondary	2.848***	5.18	4.468***	7.21	3.113	1.46	2.523	1.56
	Vocational education	1.310***	3.44	1.406***	3.65	1.444	1.45	1.070	0.20
	Short higher education	2.063***	4.89	1.346	1.43	1.777	1.24	2.463	1.55
	Medium higher education	3.310***	12.50	3.605***	11.58	2.953***	4.01	3.999***	2.76
	University degree	5.531***	15.31	9.157***	18.72	5.152***	4.67	9.267***	5.71
Had lived abroad before turning 18		1.269	1.06	1.685**	2.21	4.656***	3.81	3.138**	2.29
Number of observations		23.232							
Pseudo R²		0.103							

Source: Register data and IPW survey data

Note: ***, ** and * indicate significance at the 1%, 5%, and 10% level, respectively. Reference: Born 1978–1983, has not lived abroad before the year of turning 18, and mother and father have basic schooling. Robust standard errors have been used

Table 9.5 Multinomial model of the probability of different university education choices, women

	Non-elite Denmark		Elite Denmark		Non-elite abroad		Elite abroad	
Reference: No university degree	RRR	z	RRR	z	RRR	z	RRR	z
Birth cohort 1951–1959	.640***	−3.18	.806***	−1.47	.196***	−4.07	.543	−1.32
Birth cohort 1960–1965	.658***	−3.75	.589***	−4.24	.441****	−3.64	.547	−1.49
Birth cohort 1966–1971	.952	−0.47	.777	−2.16	.579***	−2.57	.916	−0.24
Birth cohort 1972–1977	1.034	0.31	1.023	0.19	.882	−0.62	1.580	1.34
Mother Upper secondary	3.162***	5.44	3.806***	5.74	4.656***	4.60	17.806***	4.61
Vocational education	1.782***	7.50	1.969***	7.16	1.415**	2.00	2.524**	2.29
Short higher education	2.972***	7.48	3.789***	8.39	2.333***	2.73	10.066***	4.61
Medium higher education	2.860***	11.02	3.763***	12.12	2.759***	5.22	5.462***	3.97
University degree	5.412***	9.67	7.691***	11.45	4.256***	4.76	30.520***	7.29
Father Upper secondary	2.151***	3.52	3.708***	6.19	2.807****	3.31	1.404	0.63
Vocational education	1.254***	2.87	1.251***	2.30	1.046	0.25	.934	−0.20
Short higher education	1.498**	2.47	1.494**	1.99	2.049**	2.36	.737	−0.49
Medium higher education	2.301***	8.13	3.747***	11.48	2.480***	4.40	2.547***	2.90
University degree	4.659***	13.58	6.602***	15.11	3.489***	5.86	2.562***	2.81
Had lived abroad before turning 18	.906	−0.42	1.009	0.04	1.211	0.49	2.328**	2.42

Number of observations	21.838
Pseudo R²	0.103

Source: Register data and IPW survey data

Note: ***, ** and * indicate significance at the 1%, 5%, and 10% level, respectively. Reference: Born 1978–1983, has not lived abroad before the year of turning 18, and mother and father have basic schooling. Robust standard errors have been used

Denmark. Mothers seem to matter more for women and fathers seem to matter more for men in the decision of whether to obtain a university education. If the parent of the same gender has a university education, the likelihood of a respondent obtaining an elite education abroad increases strikingly, especially for women. This result is in line with previous research on nation states. Earlier studies have found that noblesse and wealthy families are reproduced through the mother's family (Schijf et al. 2004).

Both men and women who live abroad before the age of 18 are more than twice as likely to obtain an elite education abroad than those who do not, all else being equal. Men who live abroad before the age of 18 are almost five times more likely to obtain a non-elite university education abroad in comparison with men without experience living abroad in their early lives. Among women, no statistically significant effect on the likelihood of obtaining a non-elite education is found. Having lived abroad is generally associated with a higher probability of obtaining a university education abroad for men, whereas for women, only those with an elite education are statistically significantly different from the reference group with respect to early international experience. Therefore, women require transnational aspirations from their family to go abroad to obtain an elite degree. Some educational mobility is observed. (The analysis yields similar results when parental occupation are included).

The results are qualitatively similar if I use a stricter definition of elite education in which a university is required to be included in the ranking lists in both 2004 and 2005 to be defined as an elite university. The social selection of elite education abroad is consistent with the idea that investment in internationally recognised higher education is predominantly an applied strategy in upper-class elite families (measured by university parents) as well as in upper-middle-class families (measured by medium higher education (college) parents). Hence, intergenerational cultural reproduction as understood from national studies also operates in the transnational arena. Here, it should be noted that the evolution of transnational elite strategies for education does not imply that a strictly national elite reproduction process has ceased to exist as we also observe in the analysis. The vast majority of university graduates never study outside national (or even local) institutions (approximately one-third of the men who earn a degree abroad also earn a degree from home). Thus, the Zones of Prestige, where the space of elite universities leads to investments in distinctive cultural capital, should be perceived as an important supplement to, rather than a substitute for, nationally oriented strategies of reproduction.

I conduct a sensitivity analysis of the parameter estimates with respect to three alternative ways of tightening the definition of elite. The first alternative requires that the university is included in the ranking list for two consecutive years. The second alternative requires inclusion among the top 100 instead of the top 200 universities. Finally, MBA schools are omitted. The first modification tests the sensitivity of the results of small changes in the list from year to year since universities that shift in and out of the bottom of the list are omitted. The second modification tightens the definition of elite by moving the cut-off point up, while the last modification investigates the sensitivity with respect to categorising the MBA schools. Individuals recruited to top 100 universities and to universities compared to those recruited to MBA schools, are more often selected in terms of parental education. Hence, selection in terms of parental background is stronger when elite is defined more narrowly, but top 200 inclusion is chosen as the preferred definition considering the number of observations.

Discussion and Conclusion

Overall, I find that children with highly privileged parents are much more likely to seek an elite education abroad than children with less educated parents. In particular, children of upper-class parents with university degrees are much more likely to attend a higher-ranked university either at home or abroad.

The effect of parental background is much stronger with regard to obtaining an elite education abroad than with regard to obtaining a non-elite education abroad or a non-elite university education at home. These effects are slightly larger than those for elite universities at home, especially for women. Additionally, close to 40–50% of individuals pursuing an elite education abroad have parents who have studied or worked abroad. Hence, the intergenerational transmission of distinctive cultural capital operates within transnationally oriented families. The role of the father's education is more vital for men; likewise, the role of the mother's education is more vital for women, especially among women pursuing an elite education. These relations are probably rooted in socialisation patterns in families. In this study, I find a remarkably strong association between parental characteristics and the likelihood of obtaining a university degree abroad. Furthermore, the finding that the likelihood of attending an elite university is much higher for individuals from families with parents who themselves are university graduates is in line with other scholars' findings on national dynamics. One study shows that social origin has a clear, direct and persistent impact on the choice of a selective elite university education in the United States. One reason for this finding is that people from privileged social backgrounds are able to more easily adapt to the necessary behaviours and competencies: "Being attuned to the changing circumstances, the privileged devote considerable effort to cultivating their own stock of currencies required for entry into lucrative positions" (Alon 2009: 750).

I find that for women, having a mother with a university degree increases the probability of obtaining an elite university education abroad more than it increases the probability of obtaining an elite university education in Denmark and much more than it increases the probability of obtaining a non-elite university education abroad or at home. In addition, individuals who live abroad before the age of 18 are more likely to obtain a university education abroad than those who do not, even after controlling for parental education (and occupation, not presented), especially for men. Parents who live with their children abroad or send them abroad to study or work seem to stimulate their children to adopt an international habitus in their early life, which becomes evident through good language skills, strong international networks, and probably the motivation to acquire valuable skills and prestige. In fact, children from this type of family tend to pursue a trajectory in which the academic quality is considered to be higher.

The reason for this behaviour could be that early-life socialisation stems from a conscious strategy in families with high levels of cultural capital with possible transnational aspirations, or it could simply be that children from families who are used to the global scene are likely to pursue foreign education because it is easier and more natural for them than for respondents who lack experience in international environments. The transmission process seems to be that parents' pass on cultural capital and some social capital to their children, including a willingness and ability to look beyond borders that can eventually become relevant for transnational prospects. This argument is in line with the study by Soehl and Waldinger (2012), who contend that "socialisation in the parental household is powerful, transmitting distinct home country competencies, loyalties and ties, but not a coherent package of transnationalism." In this chapter, I document the reproduction of educational privileges in a transnational context, thus partly rejecting the idea that investments in distinctive cultural capital abroad merely imply social mobility. Although I find some evidence of social mobility, the overall pattern shows that elite education is highly restricted in terms of parental background.

A number of sociologists currently suggest that a global system of higher education, or even a global space (not a global field, as noted by Börjesson 2017), has emerged in which the most prestigious universities recruit elite students globally. Brown and Lauder (2009: 136) state that educational credentials, which were once mostly acquired nationally, now have a significant global dimension. The division between elite and non-elite institutions is noted by Bourdieu (1996) in a study of higher education in a national context. He distinguishes between very selective to through elite schools (grande porte) and less selective entrance to other universities (petite porte). His findings show a connection between graduating from elite universities and obtaining major posts within society as well as a connection between graduating from less selective universities and obtaining minor posts within society, but still at the higher end of the social ladder. This pattern is termed structural homology.

This chapter specifically contributes to the literature by showing that educational reproduction and mobility can work through the global space of university institutions. In particular, it shows that young people from a privileged background are more likely to attend elite universities abroad and to see most of the world as their field of study and work place. This phenomenon may have nothing to do with the increased access to universities in Denmark but rather may be related to the fact that families with abundant cultural capital accumulate more distinctive cultural capital in terms of the finest academic qualifications from prestigious universities at home and abroad, primarily in the United States and the United Kingdom. These findings support the Zones of Prestige hypothesis, which Randall Collins (2001, see also Karabel 2005) introduced as a way to understand the major attraction of students to elite universities in the US. Conclusively, in the case of migrants attending elite universities, it is not simply a matter of pursuing transnational strategies abroad but rather a question of accumulating distinctive cultural capital.

References

Alboury, V., & Wanecq, T. (2003). Les inégalités sociales d'accès aux Grandes Écoles. *Économie et Statistique, 361*, 27–47.

Alon, S. (2009). The evolution of class inequality in higher education: Competition, exclusion, and adaptation. *American Sociological Review, 74*(5), 731–755.

Bourdieu, P. (1984[1979]). *Distinction: A social critique of the judgement of taste*. Cambridge, MA: Harvard University Press.

Bourdieu, P. (1989). *La noblesse d'état, Grandes Ecoles et esprit de corps*. Paris: Les Editions de Minuit (*State Nobility,* Cambridge: Polity Press 1996).

Brooks, R., & Waters, J. (2009). A second chance at 'success': UK students and global circuits of higher education. *Sociology, 43*(6), 1085–1102.

Brooks, R., & Waters, J. (2011). *Student mobilities, migration and the internationalization of higher education*. Basingstoke: Palgrave Macmillan.

Brown, P., & Lauder, H. (2009). Globalization, international educations, and the formation of a transnational class? *Yearbook of the National Society for the Study of Education, 108*(2), 130–147.

Börjesson, M. (2017). The global space of international students in 2010. *Journal of Ethnic and Migration Studies, 43*(8), 1256–1275.

Carroll, W. K. (2010). *The making of a transnational capitalist class: Corporate power in the 21st century*. London: Zed Books.

Collins, R. (2001). Civilisations as zones of prestige and social contact. *International Sociology, 16*(3), 421–437.

Dow, J. K., & Endersby, J. W. (2004). Multinomial probit and multinomial logit: A comparison of choice models for voting research. *Electoral Studies, 23*(1), 107–122.

Espeland, W. N., & Sauder, M. (2007). Rankings and reactivity: How public measures recreate social worlds. *American Journal of Sociology, 113*(1), 1–40.

Favell, A. (2008). *Eurostars and Eurocities: Free movement and mobility in an integrating Europe*. Oxford: Blackwell.

Jasso, G. (2011). Migration and stratification. *Social Science Research, 40*(5), 1292–1326.

Johnson, C. H., Sabean, D. W., Teuscher, S., & Trivellato, F. (2011). *Transregional and transnational families in Europe and beyond: Experiences since the middle ages*. New York: Berghahn Books.

Karabel, J. (2005). The chosen. In *The hidden history of admission and exclusion at Harvard, Yale, and Princeton*. Boston: Mariner Books, Houghton Mifflin Company.

Kauppi, N., & Erkkilä, T. (2011). The struggle over global higher education: Actors, institutions, and practices. *International Political Sociology, 5*(3), 314–326.

Kim, J. (2016). Global cultural capital and global positional competition: International graduate students' transnational occupational trajectories. *British Journal of Sociology of Education, 37*(1), 30–50.

Long, J. S., & Freese, J. (2006). *Regression models for categorical dependent variables using Stata*. College Station: StataCorp.

Munk, M. D. (2009). Transnational investments in informational capital. A comparative study of Denmark, France, and Sweden. *Acta Sociologica, 52*(1), 5–23.

Munk, M. D., Foged, M., & Mulvad, A. M. (2011). Familiers kosmopolitiske uddannelsesstrategier – Et spørgsmål om migration og investering i distinktiv kapital (Families' cosmopolitan educational strategies, a question of migration and investment in distinctive capital). *Dansk Sociologi, 22*(3), 31–58.

Munk, M. D., & Thomsen, J. P. (2018). Horizontal stratification in access to Danish university Programmes. *Acta Sociologica, 61*(1), 198–210.

Netz, N., & Finger, C. (2016). New horizontal inequalities in German higher education? Social selectivity of studying abroad between 1991 and 2012. *Sociology of Education, 89*(2), 79–98.

Palloni, A., Massey, D. S., Ceballos, M., Espinosa, K., & Spittel, M. (2001). Social capital and international migration: A test using information on family networks. *American Journal of Sociology, 106*(5), 1262–1298.

Robins, J. M., Rotnitzky, A., & Zhao, L. P. (1994). Estimation of regression coefficients when some regressors are not always observed. *Journal of the American Statistical Association, 89*(427), 846–866.

Sauder, M., & Espeland, W. N. (2009). The discipline of rankings: Tight coupling and organizational change. *American Sociological Review, 74*(1), 63–82.

Sayad, A. (1991). *L'immigration ou les paradoxes de l'altérité*. Bruxelles: De Boeck & Lancier.

Sayad, A. (2004). *The suffering of the immigrant*. Cambridge: Polity Press.

Schijf, H., Dronkers, J., & van den Broeke-George, J. (2004). Recruitment of members of Dutch noble and high-bourgeois families to elite positions in the 20th century. *Social Science Information, 43*(3), 435–475.

Soehl, T., & Waldinger, R. (2012). Inheriting the homeland? Intergenerational transmission of cross-border ties in migrant families. *American Journal of Sociology, 118*(3), 778–813.

Train, K. E. (2009). *Discrete choice methods with simulation*. Cambridge, UK: University Press.

Wagner, A. C. (1998). *Les nouvelles élites de la mondialisation. Une immigration doree en France*. Paris: PUF.

Wagner, A. C. (2007). *Les classes sociales dans la mondialisation*. Paris: La Découverte, Collection Repères.

Weenink, D. (2008). Cosmopolitanism as a form of capital: Parents preparing their children for a globalizing world. *Sociology, 42*(6), 1089–1106.

Chapter 10
Class, Lifestyles and Politics: Homologies of Social Position, Taste and Political Stances

Magne Flemmen, Vegard Jarness, and Lennart Rosenlund

Introduction

A central point in Bourdieu's writings in general, and *Distinction* (1984) in particular, is the notion of homology (see also Hjellbrekke & Korsnes and Robette & Roueff in this volume). In fact, the concept appears so inextricably linked to Bourdieu's writings that much debate on the contemporary relevance of his work centres on it (see e.g. Chan and Goldthorpe 2007; Coulangeon and Lemel 2009; Flemmen 2014; Rosenlund 2014). However, the concept itself is not given a very concise definition by Bourdieu, and – perhaps adding to the confusion – is used for slightly different purposes throughout his work. It is perhaps small wonder, then, that the ensuing debates have been confused, because a lack of clarity surrounds both the concept itself and its methodological implications.

In this chapter, we discuss Bourdieu's homology model in detail and point to unfortunate yet widespread misinterpretations. The crux of our argument is that the so-called homology thesis (as it is advanced in *Distinction*) must be

Electronic supplementary material The online version of this chapter (https://doi.org/10.1007/978-3-030-15387-8_10) contains supplementary material, which is available to authorized users.

M. Flemmen (✉)
Department of Sociology and Human Geography, University of Oslo, Oslo, Norway
e-mail: magne.flemmen@sosgeo.uio.no

V. Jarness
Centre for the Study of Professions (SPS), Oslo Metropolitan University, Oslo, Norway
e-mail: vegard.jarness@oslomet.no

L. Rosenlund
Institute of Media and Society, University of Stavanger, Stavanger, Norway
e-mail: lennart.rosenlund@uis.no

© Springer Nature Switzerland AG 2019   155
J. Blasius et al. (eds.), *Empirical Investigations of Social Space*,
Methodos Series 15, https://doi.org/10.1007/978-3-030-15387-8_10

understood as a model of relations between social structures, not as a mechanical relationship between certain class positions and certain cultural goods and practices. Expanding on Bourdieu's work, and drawing on our previous studies (Flemmen 2014, Rosenlund 2014), we advance a novel approach to a strict assessment of the structural similarities between three structures: a social space, a space of lifestyles and a space of political stances. This is accomplished by means of specific multiple correspondence analysis (MCA) (Le Roux and Rouanet 2010). We focus on the case of present-day Norway and exploit the unique possibilities of the 2011 round of *Norsk Monitor*, carried out by Norwegian Ipsos MMI (see also Hjellbrekke & Korsnes in this volume).

We show that the distinct social universes of class, lifestyles and politics exhibit strikingly similar structures. The structure of the social space – with a primary division between high and low volumes of capital, and a secondary chiastic division between cultural and economic capital – is echoed in both the space of lifestyles and the space of political stances. The chapter not only unveils the persistence of class-structured lifestyles and political attitudes, it also develops methodological tools to move beyond the substantialist fallacy often implicated in assessing the homology thesis.

Structural Homologies

In evolutionary biology, homology refers to "likeness in structure between parts of different organisms (as the wing of a bat and the human arm)" (Merriam-Webster 2016). In the sociology of cultural stratification it has a similar meaning, depicting affinities between social structures. Bourdieu used the notion of homology for seemingly different purposes throughout his work, but the concept is probably most famous from the way it is used in *Distinction* (1984), in which it is argued that there is a homology between what Bourdieu calls a social space and a space of lifestyles. That is to say, there is a correspondence or a basic structural similarity between the social class structure and status divisions, so that these may in fact be more congruent than what is suggested by conventional Weberianism.

In Bourdieu's (1984, 1991) usage social class is not operationalised in terms of position in market or productive relations, but in social relations more broadly. Sayer (2005: 72–74) has noted that this understanding of class is more concrete than Marxist or Weberian ones, as it tries to approach class in terms of the resources or capital actors may mobilise in social life to achieve certain ends. With the concept of social space, Bourdieu constructs a model of the class structure, as shaped by the distribution of, and relation between, key forms of capital. In social space, the geometric distance in the map reflects difference in the endowment of the forms of capital 'in the real world'. His portrayal of the class structure of France of the 1960s is three-dimensional one: First, classes are delineated by the overall volume of capital – that is, the amount of scarce 'marketable' resources that agents possess. Second, classes are fractioned by *capital composition*, that is, the relative weight of cultural and economic capital in their overall holdings creates divisions within the classes. Finally, a last cross-cutting division is trajectory, that is, changes over time in the volume and composition of capitals of individuals and/or groups and fractions (Bourdieu 1984: 114–143).

A core point is that the relation between the social space and the space of lifestyles is one of homology: "the spaces defined by preferences in food, clothing or cosmetics are organised according to the same fundamental structure, that of the social space determined by volume and composition of capital" (Bourdieu 1984: 208). The space of lifestyles is shaped by differences in lifestyles, encompassing not only cultural consumption, but broader tastes in terms of shopping preferences, sport and leisure activities, etc. Bourdieu argues that the principal division in the space of lifestyles is between a 'taste of freedom' and a 'taste of necessity', corresponding to the volume of capital; and a secondary division between the 'ascetic' and the 'luxurious', which corresponds to the chiastic division between cultural and economic capital.

A much neglected, but nevertheless crucial, aspect of the model advanced in *Distinction* is that Bourdieu argues for the existence of a third space – a political space, or a space of political stances – that also corresponds to the structure of the social space (Bourdieu 1984: 451–453). The space opposes the political left and right along both dimensions of the social space. The propensity to vote for the right increases with higher capital volumes and with the preponderance of economic capital, whereas the propensity to vote for the left increases with lower capital volumes and the preponderance of cultural capital. Thus, the homology extends to a field of political consumption, meaning that the structure of political attitudes and party affiliations correspond systematically to both the structure of social space and the structuring of cultural tastes.

Bourdieu's homology thesis is properly understood as pertaining to the relationship between distinct *structures* – social and symbolic – and one cannot "reduce the homologies between systems of differences to direct, mechanical relationships between groups and properties" (Bourdieu 1984: 126). Indeed, Bourdieu repeatedly warned against what he called a 'substantialist' and 'naively realist' way of reading and assessing the validity of the model in other empirical cases, for instance expecting to find that contemporary upper classes in Norway or Japan are distinguished by their taste for the very same cultural goods, or the very same political stances, as did their French counterparts some 40 years ago. This, Bourdieu argues, would be to commit a substantialist fallacy of confusing the *context-specific manifestations* of classed lifestyle divisions for the class-structured divisions as such. The truly relational way of assessing the homology thesis, then, is seeing whether and how the space of lifestyles and the space of political stances is structured in correspondence with the structures of the social space.

However, despite this explicit warning, substantialist readings of the homology thesis are still widespread. This is particularly evident in the 'cultural omnivore' debate, in which scholars have read *Distinction* as a book about how the upper and middle classes exclusively consume 'highbrow' culture. Employing a methodology aimed at measuring the 'broadness' of people's taste, and/or seeing whether people straddle a divide between 'highbrow' and 'lowbrow' culture, findings of upper- and middle-class people exhibiting broad and eclectic tastes are taken as a rebuttal of the homology thesis (for further critique of omnivore methodology, see Atkinson

2011; Flemmen et al. 2017; Jarness 2015; Robette and Roueff 2014; Savage and Gayo 2011).

There is also a second aspect of Bourdieu's model that has caused some confusion: the degree of fit between the structures. On a superficial reading, the scheme gives the impression of a rather immediate and instantaneous reflection of *current* social position in lifestyle, as if one's position in the space has 'caused' one to have a corresponding lifestyle. However, according to Bourdieu, the effects of homology operate *through the habitus*: people in a similar position in the social space share lifestyles because their socially structured habitus is broadly similar. Bourdieu (1984: 172–173) holds that "systematicity is found in the opus operatum because it is in the modus operandi", meaning that tastes for particular goods and practices appear as class structured because they are manifestations of the dispositions embodied in the classed habitus, that have been shaped by histories of differential conditions of existence (i.e. unequal endowment and access to the various forms of capital). However, these dispositions are put into play in different social fields, which abide by their own distinct logics, and to partake in these fields means 'playing by the rules' current in them. This means that there is no automatic transference of position in social space to position-takings in, say, the field of political consumption.

Moreover, peoples' habitus are not simply shaped by their current conditions of existence: "The habitus, a product of history, produces individual and collective practices – more history – in accordance with the schemes generated by history" (Bourdieu, 1990: 54). Accordingly, the conditions of existence that shape the habitus must necessarily, and to some considerable extent, vary with social trajectory – social origin, inter- and intragenerational mobility, as well as the changing positions of groups in social space. The historical mediations of the habitus do perhaps imply that, at least in the context of rising standards of living as well as sizeable absolute social mobility, considerable parts of the population have found themselves facing conditions of existence that differ significantly from what faced them in their formative years. This might be one factor that implies that the overall 'fit' between the social space of conditions of existence and the space of lifestyles is less than perfect – and not a 'one-to-one correspondence' as imagined by for instance Coulangeon and Lemel (2009: 48).

Analytical Strategy and Data

The relational assessment of the homology thesis raises complex issues of operationalisation. Bourdieu was careful to underline that his methodological approach is fundamentally at odds with the standard operations in quantitative sociology, which in the case of both cultural stratification and political sociology would amount to statistically using lifestyle or attitudes as a dependent and class as an independent variable. Instead of the 'linear thinking' implied in this, Bourdieu favoured a methodology aimed at mapping structural homologies. A remarkable feature of this approach is the intrinsic affinity between the theorisation of the correspondence between the social space and the space of lifestyles, and the method by which to study this relationship: "correspondence analysis is a relational technique of data analysis whose philosophy corresponds exactly to what, in my view, the reality of the social world is" (Bourdieu and Wacquant 1992: 96).

In the analysis of upper and middle-class tastes in *Distinction*, (sub-)spaces of lifestyles were constructed and capital indicators were projected onto the spaces as supplementary variables. In this way, the maps were used as 'visual regression analysis' (Lebart et al. 1984) – 'predicting' indicators of position in the social space as a function of 'position-takings' in the space of lifestyle. In other publications (e.g. *Homo Academicus* (1988) and *State Nobility* (1996)), Bourdieu used correspondence analysis the other way around: the structure of social fields were constructed by using indicators of capital as active categories, and subsequently projecting indicators of various position-takings (i.e. practices, attitudes, etc.) onto that structure as supplementary categories. On a whole, the work of Bourdieu demonstrates the fruitfulness of doing both types of constructions, i.e. what Lebart et al.'s (1984: 108) has called a 'reciprocal approach' to using MCA in survey data analysis. In the analyses reported here, we use a variant called specific MCA, which lets us set some categories as passive, meaning they are given no mass in the analysis, thereby not affecting the structure of the space (Le Roux and Rouanet 2004, 2010). This is especially useful for categories such as *missing*.

In our analysis, we expand on this reciprocal approach by way of an approach developed by Rosenlund (2009, 2014) to assess the homology thesis. We proceed by constructing three spaces – a social space, a space of lifestyles and a space of political stances – with separate correspondence analysis procedures before comparing their structures. This has the advantage of providing a stricter assessment of the homology thesis, since it directly deals with the question of whether the structures in question are in fact similar. Moreover, it also respects the autonomy of social class relations and lifestyle differentiation, treating neither as a simple 'dependent' variable. Finally, in separating between a space of lifestyles and a space of political stances, our analysis goes even further in the assessment of whether and how different aspects of lifestyles – the cultural-aesthetical and the political – do in fact follow similar logics of differentiation.

To construct these spaces, it is necessary to draw on rich data with both ample indicators of the forms of capital and a wide range of variables on lifestyles and political stances. We know of no other social science survey that could offer this, so we have opted for the 2011 round of *Norsk Monitor*, carried out by the market research organization Norwegian Ipsos MMI (the data have been provided by the Prism Project, a joint research project on social change, carried out by University of Stavanger and IRIS). Respondents were selected by simple random sampling from telephone directories, and recruited through telephone calls. An interviewer asked introductory questions, and the bulk of the survey was conducted through self-completed questionnaires. The response rate for the telephone interviews was approximately 25% and another 10% filled out and returned the questionnaires, amounting to 3980 respondents. As would be expected from this relatively low response rate, the resulting sample was socio-demographically skewed. For our analysis, we correct for this with weights by gender, age, geographical region, educational level and the number of rooms in the home. This makes our sample nationally representative. To assess external validity, we found two relevant questions in other, high quality surveys that we could compare with. First, we compared the question on the political party voted for at the last election with the same question from the 2012 round of the European Social Survey. When both surveys are weighted, the distribution of this question is practically identical. The other question was about the frequency of checking newspapers online, which we compared with the 2012 round of Statistics Norway's survey about culture and media use. For this question, we obtained an identical distribution. This suggests that our weighting is fairly successful, at least in terms of the types of questions addressed in this chapter.

For the construction of the social space, we use 12 questions as indicators of economic and cultural capital. These variables, their appurtenant categories and relative frequencies are shown in Appendix A. To account for economic capital, we use questions about bank deposits, fund savings, the estimated value of one's home, ownership of second homes, personal gross income and the possession of a holiday home. For cultural capital, we use measures of both the embodied state and the institutionalised state (Bourdieu 1986). We construct 'embodied' cultural capital through two questions that tap into the home milieu, one question about the highest educational level of one's parents and one about to the extent one was surrounded by legitimate culture in the formative years. For this, we use one question about the degree to which the respondent grew up in a home surrounded by books, music, art and cultural interests. We construct 'institutionalised' cultural capital by using respondents' own educational levels as well as their educational field; this lets us differentiate cultural capital of the 'scientific or technical type' from its other manifestations. We supplement this with occupation, which taps into both forms of capital and constituting a central 'mechanism' through which educational capital is converted into economic capital.

In the construction of the space of lifestyle we use a wide range of indictors in order to move beyond the unduly narrowing of scope in much previous research and its fixation at cultural consumption. We thus follow Bourdieu's (1984: xxiv) broad focus on 'culture' in the 'anthropological sense', and heed Scott's (2002) warning that many analysts of cultural stratification have an unduly narrow understanding of Weber's notion of *Lebensstil*. Notably, we use indicators of both cultural and material consumption preferences, as well as more mundane everyday-life activities: music, reading, newspaper topics, movies, household equipment, holidays, physical activities, cooking, gambling practices, as well as set of questions that taps attitudinal aspects of lifestyle more broadly.

In our construction of the space of political stances we focus on both 'old' and 'new' politics. The choice of questions is inspired by earlier research (Borre 1995: 190; Harrits et al. 2010) but is expanded upon to produce a richer picture. Questions thus tap core ideological issues such as egalitarianism and state control over business, as well as core 'new politics' issues such as immigration, environmentalism and Christian values. The variable categories used in the construction of all three spaces can be found in Online Appendices A, B and C.

The Social Space

With two dimensions, we reach a cumulated rate of Benzécri's modified eigenvalues of 53.7%. The positions of all categories of our active variables – the cloud of categories – are shown in Fig. 10.1, with the first axis shown vertically and the second horizontally. The structure is strikingly similar to the model of the social space advanced by Bourdieu (1984: 128–129). Both axes are shaped almost equally by economic and cultural capital, so that both axes reflect differences in the possession of both forms of capital. A table of contributions is provided in Appendix A.

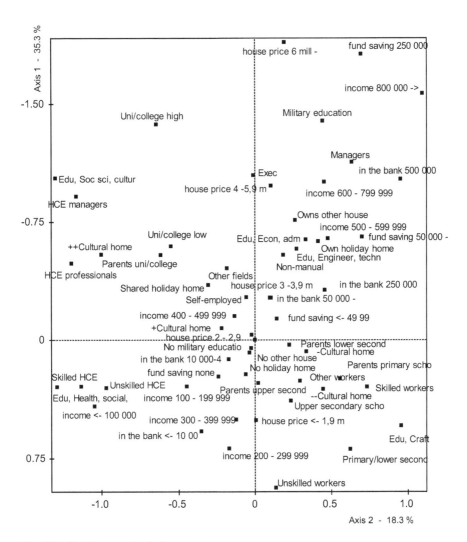

Fig. 10.1 Social space, cloud of categories

The first axis depicts differences in the *volume of capital*. At the bottom of the figure, we find all categories indicating low volumes of capital: Low incomes, low education levels, parents' low educational levels, low amounts or no money in banks and fund savings, not having grown up in a cultured home, no holiday home, no other home and a low to moderate estimated value of one's home. The bottom of our space can thus be seen as the bottom of the social class structure. Moving from the bottom and upwards in the space, the total volume of both cultural and economic capital the respondents possess increases. At the top we find high incomes, lots of money in fund savings and bank accounts, expensive homes, high levels of education, highly educated parents and having grown up in a home with lots of books, music and culture.

The second axis, shown horizontally, is an axis of *capital composition*. The division between a preponderance of cultural capital and a preponderance of economic capital is most clearly expressed in the top of figure, that is, among those endowed with high volumes of capital. We find those richest in cultural capital on the left of the map: They grew up in a cultured home, have highly educated parents and have high levels of education themselves, notably within the 'soft' disciplines (the social sciences, and the arts and humanities). On the right side of the map, we find their opposites, those rich in *economic* capital: They have the highest incomes, large amounts of money in banks and fund savings, valuable homes, as well as holiday homes and other properties. Thus, the second axis depicts a chiastic structure of capital composition: Moving from left to right in the space, the relative preponderance of *cultural* capital decreases, while the relative preponderance of *economic* capital increases.

For the purpose of assessing Bourdieu's idea of structural homologies in the final stage of the analysis, we store the coordinates of the respondents obtained in the construction of the social space. We group these into nine class categories by slicing each axis into three equally-sized groups and then cross these with each other. In the final operation, these categories will be projected as supplementary points onto the space of lifestyles and the space of political stances. We emphasise that the construction of these categories is heuristic, in the sense that the construction is an analytical procedure conducted for the purpose of projecting coordinates from one space onto the two others. The categories are thus not to be considered as 'realized' classes, in the sense that we assume a priori that there exists social and/or symbolic boundaries between them.

The construction of the nine class categories is demonstrated in Fig. 10.2, depicting the cloud of individuals. First, the respondents are divided into three equally-sized social classes along the capital volume axis (axis 1). Second, each of the classes is divided into three class fractions, according to the capital composition principle (axis 2). The categories can thus be interpreted as three vertically differentiated classes according to different volumes of overall capital (upper, lower and middle), each divided into horizontally differentiated fractions according to the composition of capital in their overall holdings (preponderance of either cultural or economic capital, or balanced capital portfolios).

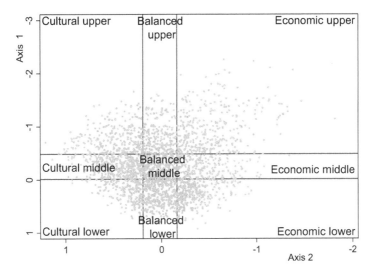

Fig. 10.2 Construction of nine class categories based on the social space (the cloud of individuals, factorial plane 1–2)

The Space of Lifestyles

With three axes, we reach a cumulated rate of Benzécri's modified eigenvalues of 67.3%. For present purposes, we focus on axes 1 and 3. Due to limited space, we only focus on the axes that correspond to the structures of the social space. The omitted axis 2 depicts a division between an established, legitimate lifestyle characterised by a taste for canonised items and a more culturally savvy and emerging lifestyle, characterised by a taste for alternative and as yet uncanonised items. This axis is strongly influenced by age differences (more detailed interpretations are available on request).

Variables on literature, newspapers, cookery and television have the highest contributions to axis 1 (see Table 10.1). Figure 10.3 shows the categories that have contributed above average to the axis. It depicts a division between a taste for legitimate items and a taste for items that are considerably less so. At the top of the figure we find categories expressing strong interest in items from the legitimate domains of culture and aesthetics, i.e. cultural goods that are institutionally recognised and canonised by the state and/or in the field of cultural production. These items include legitimate books (art and culture, poetry, foreign contemporary literature, debate, wine culture), newspaper topics (culture, wine, op-ed, in-depth articles, letters, business, work/career), television programmes (arts, politics, education, news and documentary), movies (drama, 'serious quality') and music (classical). A taste for these items goes hand in hand with a taste for fairly expensive material consumption goods that also have an aura of legitimacy attached to them: travels abroad, mountain holidays, French cookery, wine, e-book reader/iPad, as well as a general interest in following fashion.

Table 10.1 Contributions of blocks of variables
(domains of lifestyles) to the space of lifestyles

Domains	Axis 1	Axis 2	Axis 3
TV	10.39	10.84	14.90
Cookery	15.86	5.20	6.04
Physical activites	3.22	12.79	9.90
Music	8.02	9.26	7.05
Cinema	4.90	18.24	3.08
Newspaper topics	19.17	3.66	16.65
Litterature	22.65	8.06	14.55
Vacation	7.82	4.86	4.28
Home equipment	2.13	12.41	7.02
Attitudes	4.65	14.51	13.62
Gambling	1.20	0.17	2.90

See Appendix B for a full table of contributions

The taste for such legitimate items go together with a taste for items that are in a sense more popular and more accessible to a wider public, but that nevertheless have an aura of the savvy, hip and alternative attached to them. These include: modern jazz music, world music, urban holidays, Interrail/backpacking, vegetarian food, Japanese, Moroccan and Indian cuisine, a general interest in trying new dishes and self-development books. Crucially, however, this does not imply an open embracement of all forms of 'popular culture', as is reflected in the distaste for several symbolically loaded and typically denigrated types of cultural products and activities, such as microwave cookery and country and western music.

At the top of the map, we also find clear indicators of a sporty lifestyle, reflected in items like exercise and diet books, swimming, cross-country skiing, jogging, weight training, as well as a general interest in staying healthy and fit. This further underscores the impression of a generally legitimate lifestyle, which also encompasses the domains of sports and outdoor activities, and which is invested in good health and taking care of the body.

At the opposite end of axis 1 we find diametrical opposite cultural-aesthetical orientations. Here, negative responses – not liking, disliking or disinterest in – of many of the culturally legitimate items found at the upper part of the axis. Negative responses also include disliking or not engaging in many of the *savvy* and *alternative* items found at the top or the map, as well as no interest in several fairly expensive goods and activities.

Disliking all these items does not, however, indicate a wholly 'passive' or 'disengaged' lifestyle, since several positive responses can be identified. These include: Swedish and Norwegian *dansband* music, country and western music and gambling (Vikinglotto). Crucially, however, these items include goods and activities that lack the institutional recognition associated with the tastes prevalent at the opposite side of the axis. Some of these goods and activities are even frequently

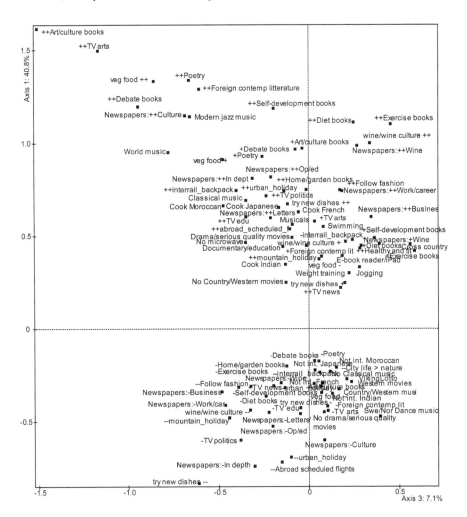

Fig. 10.3 Space of lifestyles, explicative points for Axis 1 (factorial plane 1–3)

denigrated and mocked by scientists, cultural 'experts' and other prominent figures in the media.

Axis 3 receives the highest contributions from the variables on newspapers, television, literature and general attitudes (see Table 10.1). Figure 10.4 depicts a division between an ascetic, intellectually oriented lifestyle on the left of the map, and, an excitement-seeking, bodily oriented and expensive lifestyle on the right of the map.

On the left side we find strong interest for legitimate and institutionally recognised cultural goods and activities: classical music, art/culture books, foreign contemporary literature and educational television programmes. We also find preferences for typically cosmopolitan and culturally 'savvy' items: world music,

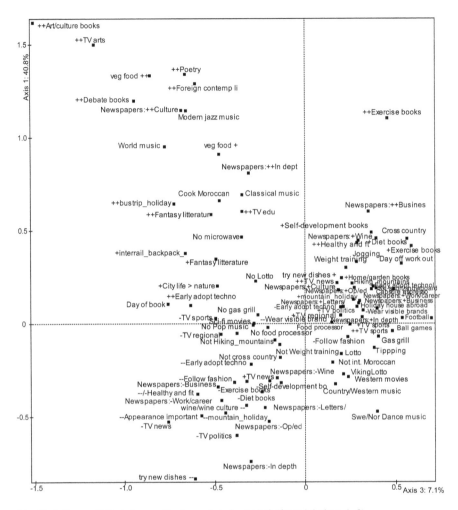

Fig. 10.4 Space of lifestyles, explicative points for Axis 3 (factorial plane 1–3)

vegetarian and Moroccan cookery, fantasy books and Interrail/backpacking holidays. This eclectic combination of the traditional and the hip, or the established and the emerging, can be seen as an expression of an intellectual and knowing style of cultural consumption that playfully straddles cultural divides.

It is also important to note the reported rejection of typically 'popular' goods and activities that lack institutional recognition: pop music, microwave cookery, various gambling games and watching sports on television. This underscores the importance of the dynamics of rejection and distaste for certain denigrated types of cultural products (Bryson 1996).

The intellectually oriented lifestyle found on the left of the map is also accompanied by a distinctive non-interest in sporty and bodily oriented activities (mountain hiking, cross-country skiing), not reading diet and exercise books, strongly disagreeing that appearance is important, and not believing in staying healthy and fit. Moreover, a non-interest for a range of fairly expensive goods and activities indicates that this intellectually oriented lifestyle is linked to material asceticism: not owning a gas grill, not being an early adopter of new technology, not wearing visible brands, as well as no interest in mountain holidays and following fashion.

On the right side of the map we find the opposite lifestyle. First, a range of expensive goods and activities are indicative of a sort of economic hedonism: holiday house abroad, mountain holidays, espresso machine, gas grill, being an early adopter of new technology, interest in trying new dishes and indulging in various gambling activities. This economically demanding lifestyle is also distinctly bodily oriented, reflected in a range of 'sporty' activities and interests: ski sport/snowboarding, cross country, mountain hiking, ball games, football, jogging, weight training, reading exercise and diet books, watching sports on TV, spending days off work outdoors and believing in staying healthy and fit.

While there is a slight interest for cultural consumption, the items preferred are markedly less legitimate and institutionally recognised than those found at the opposite pole, some of which are typically denigrated as being in 'bad taste': Swedish and Norwegian *dansband* music, western movies, watching sports on TV and indulging in various gambling activities.

The Space of Political Stances

With three axes, we reach a cumulated rate of Benzécri's modified eigenvalues of 79.8%. Plane 1–2 exhibits a Guttman effect (Le Roux and Rouanet 2004: 220–221), as the second axis represents a sort of 'intensity of opinion' dimension, distinguishing between those who hold their views – irrespective of content – strongly and those with more moderate attitudes. For present purposes therefore, we focus on axes 1 and 3. Both of these can be considered general axes, insofar as they are roughly equally shaped by variables on both 'old' and 'new' politics, i.e. stances related to economic and value issues (Flanagan and Lee 2003).

Figure 10.5 shows the cloud of categories in factorial plane 1–3 and depicts categories with above average contribution to axes 1 and 3. Axis 1 (displayed horizontally) appears to be a generalised left-versus-right axis, fusing aspects of 'old' and 'new' politics (see table of contributions in Appendix C). On the left of the figure, we find stances associated with the political left in Norway: opposing privatisation and private schools/hospitals, support for higher taxation to support public services, opposition to letting businesses decide too much, and disagreement

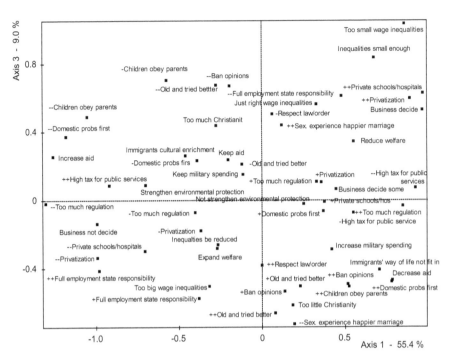

Fig. 10.5 The space of political stances, explicative points for axes 1 and 3 (factorial plane 1–3)

with the view that state regulation is an interference with business autonomy. Moreover, we also find disagreement with the claim that children should obey their parents, disagreement that we should solve domestic problems first, the view that developmental aid should be increased, and support for the view that immigration represents a cultural enrichment for the country. On the right of the map, we find the opposite of these views. This includes position-takings associated with the political right, both in terms of old politics (e.g. agreeing with privatisation and private schools) and new (e.g. disagreeing that immigrants way of life represents a cultural enrichment for the country).

Axis 3 (displayed vertically) cross-cuts the more established left-versus-right axis, and can be dubbed a liberal-versus-traditional axis. At the top of the figure, we find strong disagreement that old and tried ways are better than new, strong disagreement that one should ban certain opinions, disagreement that it is important to respect law and order, and the view that there is too much emphasis on Christianity in society. We also find disagreement that we should solve domestic problems first, disagreement that children should obey parents, and the view that immigrants represent cultural enrichment. Moreover, there is also strong support for privatisation, disagreement that the government is needed to secure full employment, strong support for private schools and hospitals, and the view that welfare services should be reduced. At the bottom we find more a traditionalist opposition to these views, for instance strong agreement that old and tried ways are better than new, strong agreement that it is important to respect law and order, and the view that there too little emphasis on Christianity in society.

Reading the map as a whole, we can retrace the dimensions of old and new politics along the diagonals of the space. The upper left quadrant corresponds to a liberal 'new left' fraction; the upper right to a more traditional right-wing on economic issues; the lower right is more typical 'new right' with authoritarian and anti-immigrant views; and the lower left quadrant more 'old left' with emphasis on traditional social-democratic policies.

Homologies

To assess Bourdieu's idea of structural homologies, we compare the characteristics of the three independently constructed spaces. For this purpose, we project the nine class categories constructed on the basis of the social space as supplementary points onto the space of lifestyles (Fig. 10.6) and the space of political stances (Fig. 10.7). As we might remember, the space of lifestyles is shaped by, on the one hand, a vertical division between high and low levels of cultural legitimacy, and, on the other, a horizontal division between an intellectual-ascetic and a bodily oriented and materialist way of life. The space of political stances is characterised by a horizontal division between leftist and rightist stances, and a vertical division between liberal and traditional stances.

The figures clearly show that both dimensions of the two separately constructed spaces correspond to the structures of the social space: The capital volume and the capital composition principles of differentiation are at work in these two distinct social 'microcosms' of human expression. In the space of lifestyles, the capital volume dimension can be traced along one of the diagonals of the space, and the capital composition dimension can be traced along the other. The space of political stances is even more congruent with the structures of the social space: The first dimension is structured according to composition of capital and the second dimension is structured according to volume of capital.

The distances between the supplementary points can be used to assess the strength of the relationships between the spaces. In the space of lifestyles, the correspondence to the capital volume dimension is strong: the distance between the cultural upper class and the economic lower class is 1.4 standard deviations (SDs) in plane 1–3, way above the threshold for a large deviation (Le Roux and Rouanet 2010: 59). Similarly, in the space of political stances, the distance between the upper class fraction with balanced capital portfolio and the lower economic lower class is

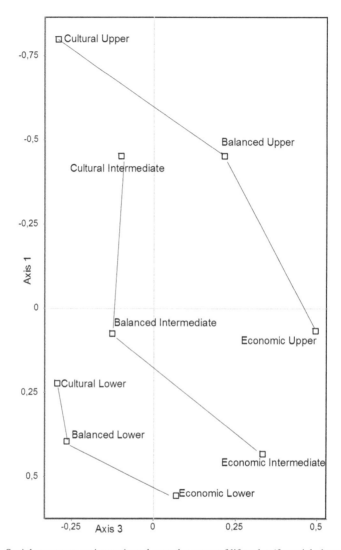

Fig. 10.6 Social space categories projected onto the space of lifestyles (factorial plane 1–3)

1.0 SDs, also above the threshold for a large deviation (please note that all distances are measured two-dimensionally in plane 1–3 in both spaces.)

The correspondence to the capital composition dimension is also strong: The distances between the cultural and the economic fractions of the upper class are large in both the space of lifestyles and the space of political stances: 1.2 and 1.0 SDs respectively. Moreover, the distance between the cultural and economic middle class is notable in the space of lifestyles: 0.7 SDs.

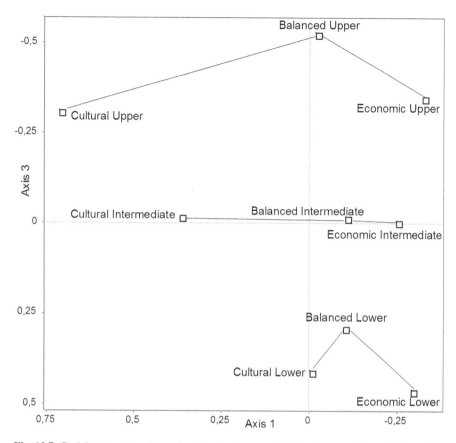

Fig. 10.7 Social space categories projected onto the space of political stances (factorial plane 1–3)

Conclusion

This chapter has demonstrated the continued relevance of the homology thesis put forward by Bourdieu (1984, 1985, 1989): the social space exhibits structural similarities with both the space of lifestyles and the space of political stances. While we recognise that the concept of homology may be understood in different ways, we have emphasised here the understanding of it as a claim about a specific relationship between social structures. Our analytical approach of constructing three separate spaces and the subsequent assessment of their structural similarities has allowed us to bring out their homologous interrelationships in a striking, visual way. While the employment of MCA to assess the social structuring of lifestyles has become more widespread lately, the attempts to properly assess the homology thesis have been somewhat limited. Indeed, while constructions of the space of lifestyles are widespread, assessments of its correspondence to the social space is almost non-existent (though see Cvetičanin et al. 2012; Faber et al. 2012; Rosenlund 2009, 2014). The usual analytical strategy seems to be to project various 'background' variables (e.g. education, income and social class) onto the space as supplementary variables, in some cases bringing the methodologies close to a 'sociology of the variable' (Blumer 1956), which was repeatedly criticised by Bourdieu. Using, say, occupational class, education and gender as supplementary variables means running the risk of inspecting the relationship between *isolated* aspects of the social space and the space of lifestyles. If so, this would involve moving the analysis closer to an analysis characterised by 'linear thinking' that considers homology as a mechanical relationship between singular categories. But it is only by comparing "system to system" (Bourdieu, 1998: 6) that the specific claims of structural homologies can be ascertained.

Obviously, our results unveil the persistence of class-structured lifestyles, despite the supposed rise of 'omnivorous' tastes among the privileged (Chan and Goldthorpe 2010; Peterson and Kern 1996). It also sits uneasily with once-popular claims that class is 'dead' in politics (Beck and Beck-Gernsheim 2002; Clark and Lipset 2001) – claims which always rested on over-simplistic models of class. We have moved beyond this by showing that while both culture and politics can be seen as distinct microcosms, their internal structuring suggest that they both function as complex mediations of social class divisions. This chimes with the qualitative work of Jarness (2013, 2017), who has shown how cultural-aesthetic and moral-political symbolic boundaries are seamlessly interweaved in symbolic struggles, not only between classes, but also between fractions within them. For instance, 'vulgar' consumption styles and 'racist' attitudes are typically seen as two sides of the same coin when members of the upper class disparage and distance themselves from their lower-class counterparts. This suggests that the homologous relationship between class, culture and politics that we see clear traces of at the aggregate level in our analysis is also manifested at the individual level, in terms of subjectively perceived and enacted class-cultural boundaries.

More generally, political and cultural differentiation according to the structures of the social space suggests a reflection of the power struggles linked to the unequal distribution of cultural and economic capital. Leftist politics and intellectual-ascetic tastes can be understood as a challenge to the power and legitimacy of economic capital, whereas rightist politics and bodily oriented and materialist tastes can be understood as affirmations of economic capital and a challenge to the power and legitimacy of cultural capital. In other words, political and cultural differentiation can be seen as a dual strategy of usurpation (Parkin 1979): In the first instance as an attempt to politically limit the enemy, and in the second as an attempt to negate its symbolic form.

References

Atkinson, W. (2011). The context and genesis of musical tastes: Omnivorousness debunked, Bourdieu buttressed. *Poetics, 39*(3), 169–186.

Beck, U., & Beck-Gernsheim, E. (2002). *Individualization: Institutionalized individualism and its social and political consequences*. London: Sage.

Blumer, H. (1956). Sociological analysis and the 'variable'. *American Sociological Review, 21*(6), 683–690.

Borre, O. (1995). Old and new politics in Denmark. *Scandinavian Political Studies, 18*, 187–205.

Bourdieu, P. (1984). *Distinction: A social critique of the judgement of taste*. Cambridge: Harvard University Press.

Bourdieu, P. (1985). The social space and the genesis of groups. *Theory and Society, 14*(6), 723–744.

Bourdieu, P. (1986). The forms of capital. In J. Richardson (Ed.), *Handbook of theory and research for the sociology of education* (pp. 241–258). New York: Greenwood.

Bourdieu, P. (1988). *Homo Academicus*. Stanford: Stanford University Press.

Bourdieu, P. (1989). Social space and symbolic power. *Sociological Theory, 7*, 14–25.

Bourdieu, P. (1990). *The logic of practice*. Stanford: Stanford University Press.

Bourdieu, P. (1991). First lecture. Social space and symbolic space: Introduction to a Japanese reading of Distinction. *Poetics Today, 12*(4), 627–638.

Bourdieu, P. (1996). *The state nobility: Elite schools in the field of power*. Stanford: Stanford University Press.

Bourdieu, P. (1998). *Practical reason: On the theory of action*. Stanford: Stanford University Press.

Bourdieu, P., & Wacquant, L. J. D. (1992). *An invitation to reflexive sociology*. Chicago: University of Chicago Press.

Bryson, B. (1996). "Anything but heavy metal": Symbolic exclusion and musical dislikes. *American Sociological Review, 61*, 884–899.

Chan, T. W., & Goldthorpe, J. H. (2007). Social stratification and cultural consumption: Music in England. *European Sociological Review, 23*(1), 1–19.

Chan, T. W., & Goldthorpe, J. H. (2010). Social status and cultural consumption. In T. W. Chan (Ed.), *Social status and cultural consumption* (pp. 1–27). Cambridge: Cambridge University Press.

Clark, T. N., & Lipset, S. M. (2001). *The breakdown of class politics: A debate on post-industrial stratification*. Washington, DC: Woodrow Wilson Center Press.

Coulangeon, P., & Lemel, Y. (2009). The homology thesis: Distinction revisited. In K. Robson & C. Sanders (Eds.), *Quantifying theory: Pierre Bourdieu* (pp. 47–60). Springer.

Cvetičanin, P., Nedeljković, J., & Krstić, N. (2012). Social space in Serbia. In P. Cvetičanin (Ed.), *Social and cultural capital in Serbia* (pp. 53–69). Nis: Centre for Emprical Cultural Studies of South-East Europe.

Faber, S., Prieur, A., Rosenlund, L., & Skjøtt-Larsen, J. (2012). *Det skjulte klassesamfund* [The Hidden Class Society]. Aarhus: Aarhus University Press.

Flanagan, S. C., & Lee, A. R. (2003). The new politics, culture wars, and the authoritarian-libertarian value change in advanced industrial democracies. *Comparative Political Studies, 36*(3), 235–270.

Flemmen, M. (2014). The politics of the service class: The homology of positions and position-takings. *European Societies, 16*(4), 543–569.

Flemmen, M., Jarness, V., & Rosenlund, L. (2017). Social space and cultural class divisions: Forms of capital and contemporary lifestyle differentiation. *British Journal of Sociology*. https://doi.org/10.1111/1468-4446.12295.

Harrits, G. S., Prieur, A., Rosenlund, L., & Skjott-Larsen, J. (2010). Class and politics in Denmark: Are both old and new politics structured by class? *Scandinavian Political Studies, 33*(1), 1–27.

Jarness, V. (2013). *Class, status, closure: The Petropolis and cultural life*. Bergen: University of Bergen.

Jarness, V. (2015). Modes of consumption: From 'what' to 'how' in cultural stratification research. *Poetics, 53*, 65–79.

Jarness, V. (2017). Viewpoints and points of view: Situating symbolic boundary drawing in social space. *European Societies*. https://doi.org/10.1080/14616696.2017.1371317.

Le Roux, B., & Rouanet, H. (2004). *Geometric data analysis: From correspondence analysis to structured data analysis*. Dordrecht: Kluwer.

Le Roux, B., & Rouanet, H. (2010). *Multiple correspondence analysis*. London: Sage.

Lebart, L., Morineau, A., & Warwick, K. M. (1984). *Multivariate descriptive statistical analysis: Correspondence analysis and related techniques for large matrices*. New York: Wiley.

Merriam-Webster. (2016). *Homology*. Retrieved from http://www.merriam-webster.com/dictionary/homology.

Parkin, F. (1979). *Marxism and class theory: A bourgeois critique*. New York: Columbia University Press.

Peterson, R. A., & Kern, R. M. (1996). Changing highbrow taste: From snob to omnivore. *American Sociological Review, 61*(5), 900–907.

Robette, N., & Roueff, O. (2014). An eclectic eclecticism: Methodological and theoretical issues about the quantification of cultural omnivorism. *Poetics, 47*, 23–40.

Rosenlund, L. (2009). *Exploring the city with Bourdieu: Applying Pierre Bourdieu's theories and methods to study the community*. Saarbrücken: VDM Verlag.

Rosenlund, L. (2014). Working with Distinction: Scandinavian experiences. In P. Coulangeon & J. Duval (Eds.), *The Routledge companion to Bourdieu's 'Distinction'* (pp. 157–187). London: Routledge.

Savage, M., & Gayo, M. (2011). Unravelling the omnivore: A field analysis of contemporary musical taste in the United Kingdom. *Poetics, 39*(5), 337–357.

Sayer, A. (2005). *The moral significance of class*. Cambridge: Cambridge University Press.

Scott, J. (2002). Social class and stratification in late modernity. *Acta Sociologica, 45*(1), 23–35.

Part II
Modeling Social Fields

Chapter 11
Bourdieu's Concept of Field in the Anglo-Saxon Literature

David L. Swartz

Introduction

The concept of field is being used globally more and more today. This chapter reviews Bourdieu's understanding of the concept and key elaborations and applications found today in the Anglo-Saxon social scientific literature. The concept now appears in numerous substantive areas of investigation. While by no means an exhaustive review of all the work inspired by Bourdieu's concept, this chapter offers illustrative references for a diverse range of substantive areas, such as culture, education, economics, intellectuals, media, organizations, politics, religion, social movements, stratification, and globalization. The chapter opens with a brief discussion of the origins and key characteristics of the concept. It then illustrates how Bourdieu and others have used and elaborated the concept of field in selected substantive areas of investigation. For each substantive area we identify those writings of Bourdieu that have been most relevant.

Overview of the Concept

The concept of field originates in the physical sciences where one finds varied expressions in electromagnetism, Newtonian gravitation, and Einstein's theory of general relativity. The concept describes motion among objects without some substantive medium such as through the forces of gravity, electricity, or magnetism. Unlike the conventional understanding of causality where variable A directly

D. L. Swartz (✉)
Department of Sociology, Boston University, Boston, MA, USA
e-mail: dswartz@bu.edu

© Springer Nature Switzerland AG 2019   177
J. Blasius et al. (eds.), *Empirical Investigations of Social Space*,
Methodos Series 15, https://doi.org/10.1007/978-3-030-15387-8_11

impacts B, field theory understands motion as structured by a set of forces whose relations create effects that do not reduce to the properties of individual units. In his philosophy of science, Cassirer (1953) best articulated this shift from substantialist to relational thinking in modern science where the object of investigation becomes the system of force relations rather than the properties of particular substances. Martin (2003) offers an analytical review of field perspectives in which he identifies and discusses three major and distinct if overlapping variants of field theory in the social sciences: the social-psychological perspective of *Gestalt* theory associated with Lewin (1951), the stratification and domination emphasis in Bourdieu's field theory, and the interorganization relations institutionalism associated with DiMaggio and Powell (1983). The latter is a benchmark statement identifying reasons for transorganizational consistencies that renewed institutional analysis in the study of organizations. While the DiMaggio and Powell paper exercises considerable influence in organization studies and draws upon Bourdieu, it is Bourdieu's conceptualization that currently informs the broadest range of substantive areas of sociological investigation. Moreover, as Martin and Gregg (2015) argue, it is Bourdieu more than anyone else who offers an exemplary field theoretic framework for research in the social sciences today. Martin (2003) identifies the formal properties of field analysis, highlights Bourdieu's field analytical approach, both its strengths and weaknesses, and compares fields to institutions. His central concern focuses on the nature of social scientific explanation offered by field theory, which he finds superior to conventional approaches for understanding the regularity of human behavior.

Bourdieu's Conceptualization of Field

Field (*champ*) is a key spatial metaphor in Bourdieu's sociology (see also Wacquant in this volume). Compared to his widely recognized conceptual language of cultural capital, habitus, practices, strategies, and reproduction, Bourdieu formalized somewhat later in his work the concept of field. Bourdieu first applied the concept to the French intellectual and artistic worlds as a way to call attention to the specific interests governing those cultural worlds of disinterest (Bourdieu 1971, 1983, 1985). The concept is developed from the conjuncture in the late 1960s of Bourdieu's research in the sociology art with his reading of Weber's sociology of religion (Bourdieu 1991), particularly the idea of independent "spheres of value." Bourdieu (Bourdieu and Wacquant 1992: 97) defines a field as "a network, or configuration, of objective relations between positions. These positions are objectively defined, in their existence and in the determinations they imposed upon their occupants, agents, or institutions, by their present and potential situation (*situs*) in the structure of the distribution of species of power (or capital) whose possession commands access to the specific profits that are at stake in the field, as well as by their objective relation to other positions (domination, subordination, homology, etc.)." For Bourdieu, fields denote arenas of production, circulation, and appropriation and exchange of goods, services, knowledge, or status, and the competitive positions held by actors in their struggle to accumulate, exchange, and monopolize different kinds of power resources (capitals). Fields may be thought of as structured spaces that organize around specific types of capitals or combinations of capital. Fields are structured to a significant extent by their own internal mechanisms of development and thus hold some degree of autonomy from their external environments. But their autonomy is usually relative, checked by heteronomous forces often economic or political in nature. In fields actors strategize and struggle over the unequal distribution of valued capitals and over the definitions of just what are the most valued capitals. Like a magnetic field, the effects of social fields on behavior can be far reaching and not usually apparent to actors.

A field perspective stands in sharp contrast to broad consensual views of social life even though actors within a field share common assumptions (the *Doxa*) about the worth of the struggle and the rules by which it is to be carried out. The concept of field stands as an alternative analytical tool to institutions, organizations, markets, individuals, and groups though all of these can be key components of fields. Field analysis brings these separate units into a broader perspective that stresses their relational properties rather than their intrinsic features and therefore the multiplicity of forces shaping the behavior of each.

For Bourdieu, field is an abstract concept—a heuristic tool—that permits the researcher to construct methodologically a space of activity that emerged historically and is structured by opposing positions in function of specific types of capital (power resources) and by a dynamic of struggle among the occupants of those positions. The positions are defined relationally by structured oppositions that distribute across different types of capital. Bourdieu (1993b: 72) speaks of the "invariant laws" or "universal mechanisms" that are structural properties characteristic to various degrees of all fields. Bourdieu's concept of field obtains its full significance within a broader conceptual program that includes the ideas of *habitus, capital, social space, field of power, doxa*, and *illusio*. Embedded in the concept is a critical methodology, a view of action, a view of power, and a political vision for sociology absent from other social scientific approaches using the language of field. Swartz (2013a) elaborates this understanding by showing how Bourdieu's concept of field is situated within a broader theoretical framework of metaprinciples that guide how Bourdieu thinks sociological analysis should be undertaken. A special issue of Bourdieu's journal *Actes de la recherche en sciences sociales* (December 2013) includes transcripts of some of Bourdieu's lectures on the concept. Presentation of key features of the concept can be found in Swartz's (1997: 117–142) widely cited introduction to Bourdieu's sociology, which identifies the structural properties of fields and the methodological orientation Bourdieu uses in constructing them. In *The Logic of Fields*, Bourdieu and Wacquant (1992: 94–115) offers in a readily accessible interview format responses by Bourdieu on how he has employed field analysis in his own research. It gives a good sense of the structural properties of fields and the methodological techniques employed in their construction. Finally, besides the current volume, one of the best English language collections of field analysis is (Hilgers and Mangez 2015) that reviews and critically assesses the theoretical background of Bourdieu's field analyses and offers several illustrative field analyses of culture, education, literature, and state formation and public policy.

Cultural Fields in Bourdieu's Work

Cultural production is where Bourdieu elaborated his field analysis most fully. He first forged his concept of field for the literary sphere (Bourdieu 1971) but went on to develop an analysis of the religious field before applying the concept to the scientific world (Bourdieu 1975) and then other spheres of cultural production, especially the worlds of art and literature (Bourdieu 1983, 1985, 1993a, 1996[1992]). Bourdieu (1975) proposes a field analysis of science that offers a more differentiated and conflict-laden view than found in the standard sociology of science (see also Münch in this volume). In (Bourdieu 1971) he formulates intellectual field analysis in contrast to the traditional focus by art historians on individual biography to understand the origins of artistic expression. Bourdieu (1996[1992]) is his best-known analysis of the origins and structure of the French literary field, notably his analysis of Gustave Flaubert's *Sentimental Education*, and includes pointers for a social scientific analysis of works of art more generally. Here Bourdieu develops his field perspective for the artistic field but makes it clear that this approach should apply to other kinds of fields as well. Bourdieu (1983) situates the field of cultural production within the "field of power" (described below under "Stratification, Field of Power, and the State"). Two opposing dynamics characterize fields of cultural production: the struggle for cultural autonomy (e.g. art for art's sake) against the heteronomy of commercial interests. He thus describes the different interests and dynamics characterizing fields of cultural production for restricted audiences compared to those for mass audiences (1985). In doing so, he (1993a) brings together some of his most important writings on the sociology of cultural production, Flaubert and the French literary field, and the sociology of artistic perception.

Cultural Field Analyses

Bourdieu's work has inspired hundreds of cultural studies. The few studies mentioned here elaborate fairly closely Bourdieu's model and illustrate the diversity in potential application. Heise and Tudor (2007), for example, take a comparative look at the film-as-art movements in the 1920s and 1930s in Brazil and Britain. The study finds that the consecration of art and artists is much more centralized under authoritarian regimes in Brazil at that time and more diverse in Britain. The heteronomy/autonomy opposition is found to be useful, though in Brazil the heteronomous forces are more political than in Britain. Anheier et al. (1995) finds that German writers and literati in the city of Cologne are differentiated in their literary field positions particularly by amounts of social and cultural capital. The authors use blockmodeling procedures and make a connection between field as a social topography and the concept of structural equivalence in network analysis. They find that elite and marginal writers are sharply differentiated relative to social and particularly cultural capital, which further separates high and low culture in the periphery sector of writers. Economic capital plays a lesser role. Ley (2003) examines the role of artists in contributing to gentrification in Toronto, Montreal, and Vancouver. Lipstadt (2003) offers one of the few field analyses in architecture, where she examines the *field effects* of several architectural competitions from 1401 to 1989. Meuleman and Savage (2013) explores Dutch cosmopolitan cultural tastes in music, films, and books. The study shows that taste for cosmopolitan items is multifaceted with distinct social differences among respondents for specifically Dutch cultural items, European forms of culture, and American popular culture. Oware (2014) examines the position of rap music in the field of cultural production and finds that underground rap music blurs the boundaries between restricted and large-scale production as represented by noncommercial and commercial rap respectively. Sapiro (2003) looks at the historical change in relationship between the French state and literary market, and Sapiro (2010) brings a field perspective to the globalized market of literary translations in the United States and France. Savage and Silva (2013) introduce a special issue of *Cultural Sociology* on field analysis and identify key features and central ambivalences of the concept of field for cultural analysis, particularly in the case of newly emerging popular forms such as pop music, and comedy. Finally, Heilbron (2015), in this award winning book, employs field as a heuristic framework for analyzing the history of French sociology. He is able to show the advantages of a field perspective over systemic, interactionist, and institutionalist accounts of knowledge production. Stressing field relationality, Heilbron shows how French sociology is shaped by the national systems of higher education, research, and publishing and the international circulation of ideas.

Food

The production and consumption of food can take on cultural field–like properties as has been the case of gastronomy (the pursuit of culinary excellence) in France. Ferguson (1998) and Ferguson (2006) examine the historical rise in the nineteenth century of French gastronomic practices and their elaboration in the twentieth century. These works show the analytical distinctiveness of the concept of field in comparison to related notions of 'culture' and 'world'. The 2006 book elaborates well beyond the 1998 work by showing the importance of writings and texts in the formation of an expansive and nationalized culinary discourse of enduring significance. Fantasia (2010) explores the more recent trends in which the field of *haute cuisine* grows in autonomy as a cultural field yet is increasingly oriented by big business concerns. He documents the recent interpenetration of 'industrial cuisine' and 'haute cuisine' so that the traditional autonomy associated with the latter takes on more and more today a symbolic facade.

Economic Sociology

Some of Bourdieu's (e.g., Bourdieu 1964; Bourdieu and Sayad 1964) earliest work that employs his concepts of habitus and capital enters into critical dialogue with economic views of action and markets (see also Schmidt-Wellenburg in this volume). But it is his concept of field that is receiving considerable attention today in economic sociology. In his posthumous book on the French housing market, Bourdieu (2005[2000]) situates his thinking relative to key perspectives in contemporary economic sociology such as network analysis and the embeddedness of action. He challenges fundamental assumptions of orthodox economics and proposes a broader constructionist sociology and anthropology of economic transactions. The key conceptual section "Principles of an Economic Anthropology" in (Bourdieu 2005[2000]) outlines how he conceptualizes the economic field. That book also offers an empirical analysis of public policy and the housing market in France. Bourdieu (1996[1989]: 300–369) looks at the social and educational background of big business CEOs and their role in the field of economic power in France. Swedberg (2011) reviews the ensemble of Bourdieu's writings for relevant economic sociology topics, particularly interactions between sellers and buyers, and notes how he subordinates the logic of markets to that of fields. In a widely cited work, Fligstein and McAdam (2012) draws some inspiration from Bourdieu to formulate their own general field framework, however they tend to conceptualize fields first and foremost from the actors' points of view. Hanappi (2011) outlines the key theoretical assumptions of Bourdieu's field and habitus approach to the economy and relates it to the embeddedness tradition in economic sociology. In particular, his paper examines how to conceptualize economic agency, including different notions of uncertainty, in light of Bourdieu's conceptual framework.

Education

The concepts of cultural capital, forms of symbolic power, and habitus have been the most influential of Bourdieu's concepts in educational research (see also Wacquant and Munk in this edited volume). Still, Bourdieu (1988[1984], 1996[1989]) employed the concept of field in key analyses of French education and the concept now inspires considerable educational research. The 1988 work offers a field analysis of the French university professorate at the time of the May 1968 student revolt. The 1996 book gives a conceptual and detailed empirical analysis of the relationship between the elite French *grandes écoles*, the field of power, and big business leadership. The growing interest in employing the concept of field in the sociology of education is illustrated by the numerous papers in the *British Journal of Sociology of Education* since 2000 (see in particular Grenfell and James 2004). Karabel's (2005) landmark book on elite college admissions offers a social and cultural history that employs the concept of field to analyze the struggle over admissions at Harvard, Yale, and Princeton that was formative of the particular system of college admissions in the United States today. Brosnan (2010) argues that medical education in the United Kingdom can be conceptualized as a field within which medical schools compete for different forms of capital, such as students, funding, and prestige. Competition within the field helps to maintain inter-school differences with respect to curricula, reputations, and types and levels of resources. Ferrare and Apple (2015) argues for connecting the micro experiences of actors to the macro structures of educational fields. The focus is on how students construct, experience, and struggle over meaning relative to perceptions of track/curriculum choices in the local contexts of schools and universities as shaped by macro structures. By contrast, Rawlings and Bourgeois (2004) uses field analysis to explore institutional niches of agriculture schools in US higher education.

Intellectuals

The sociology of intellectuals represents a central concern in Bourdieu's sociology (Swartz 2013b). Intellectuals occupy an important if dominated field within the broader field of power. In one of his earliest formulations of the intellectual field, Bourdieu (1971) examines the historical emergence of intellectuals as they gain relative autonomy from external influences, the internal differentiation among intellectuals as they struggle for cultural recognition and authority, and the ways that certain types of intellectuals intervene in the public arena. Ringer (1992) compares German and French humanists and social scientists around 1890–1920 through the lens of different national intellectual fields. The differences in educational ideals and practices are attributed to differences in intellectual fields and the composition of the two middle classes. Sapiro (2004) employs the concept of field to examine the types of political activism employed by French writers in the twentieth century. She correlates the writer's cultural field position with his conception of literary work and form of politicization and identifies four types of political expression among French writers: 'notabilities','esthetes','avant-garde', and 'writer-journalists'. And Swartz (2003, 2013b) examines Bourdieu's own political activism in his later years relative to his professional career and the changing character of the French intellectual field in relationship to politics and the mass media. His 2013 book offers a field analysis of Bourdieu's own political activism as an engaged sociologist.

Law

Apart from a long theoretical paper, Bourdieu (1987a) published relatively little on law. In that paper he applies the properties of field to jurisprudence to describe it as the site of competition to monopolize the right to determine the law. However, Bourdieu (2014) does devote considerable attention to the historical role of jurists in the development of the modern state. This collection of 23 lectures includes numerous passages where through secondary analysis of several historical studies of modern state formation Bourdieu identifies the key role played by lawyers and law in the development of the modern state as a field of contention to monopolize the means of symbolic as well as physical violence. His field perspective on law has generated some ground-breaking research in that substantive area. Vauchez (2008) looks at the central role played by law and lawyers in the construction of the European Union as a field.

Mass Media

In *On Television* (Bourdieu 1998[1996]), an explosive, polemical, and widely read indictment of media journalism in 1996, Bourdieu clearly marked his interest in the mass media. In that book, he argues that all of the fields of cultural production, including the fields of science, law, and politics, have come to be structurally constrained by the journalistic field which is today dominated by television. Media visibility has come to be a key and constraining standard for modern cultural and political life. As Benson (1999) shows, the concept of field proved to be key in shaping what might be called the distinctly Bourdieusian approach to media sociology. Benson and Neveu (2005) offers the most elaboration and critical evaluation to date of the application of field theory to the mass media in both France and the United States. This book demonstrates methods for measuring field autonomy and spatially mapping journalistic fields and discusses similarities and differences between field theory, new institutionalism, hegemony, and differentiation theory. Couldry (2003) invites consideration of how both the mass media and the state intersect in the field of power. He develops the idea of "media meta-capital" as a conceptual tool for understanding how mass media along with the state exercises power over the rules of the game in the field of power. Krause (2011) applies Bourdieu's idea of fields of cultural production to the history of US journalism. This field analysis historicizes the journalistic ideals of public service through news gathering and reporting as a distinctive cultural practice and identifies their institutional foundation. It examines the changing degree of autonomy of the American journalistic field relative to business interests and politics. And it examines multiple media forms and compares the field properties of journalism to other fields, notably the economic and political fields.

Organizations

Bourdieu's concept of field has found its way into organization sociology largely through the landmark work of DiMaggio and Powell (1983), which draws upon the idea of field in formulating the authors' widely influential neo-institutional perspective. This view offers an expanded view of Bourdieu's concept though one that downplays the dimensions of power and competition (see also Baier and Schmitz, in this volume, for an illustration of field analysis in organizational sociology). Fligstein and McAdam (2012) likewise draws some inspiration from Bourdieu's concept in using the language of field to analyze meso-level organizational realities rather than focusing on just individual organizations as units of analysis. By contrast, Emirbayer and Johnson (2008) offers a more thorough Bourdieusian perspective for analyzing organizations as fields and organizations as units within larger fields. The authors draw on all three of Bourdieu's pillar concepts (habitus, capital, and field) and propose a relational approach to the study of organizations. They argue that field analysis with inattention to habitus and a relational perspective offers a very impoverished view of fields. Using all these concepts, the authors reframe existing thinking about organizations, particularly from the neo-institutional and resource dependence schools. They recommend studying both organizations-in-fields and organizations-as-fields.

Political Field

Bourdieu (1991[1981], 2000) identify the political field as a relatively autonomous subfield within the field of power and distinct from the state. Bourdieu (1991[1981]) identifies distinctive features of the political field and political capital and the problems that professionalization of political leadership pose for genuine democratic representation. Here Bourdieu distinguishes between a political field and an apparatus. Eyal (2005) elucidates the concept of political field for the purpose of analyzing post-communist politics in Czechoslovakia. The empirical analysis focuses on the round-table negotiations between the regime and the opposition in 1989 and the polarization of the political field between the Czech right wing and left wing. Mudge (2011) brings a field perspective to shifts in the traditional left-right political party spectrum in Western democracies due to the rise of neoliberalism. Using an index of neoliberalism based on policy positions, she finds that this historical shift has occurred across the left-right spectrum among mainstream parties and this move has been particularly the case in 'third wave' policies of left parties. The field perspective highlights how political categories in electoral politics are contested and whose historical meanings can shift over time, most notably in what it means to be 'left' politically. And Ray (1999) uses the concept of political field to illuminate differences in women's protest movements in Calcutta and Bombay. She finds that differences in ideology, mobilization issues, tactics, and successes are better explained by a field analytical framework than by opportunity structures or general structural trends such as general living conditions (similar for women in both cities), modernization, and demographic variables like education, fertility, and labor force participation.

Religion

While Bourdieu drew extensively from Marx's, Durkheim's, and Weber's respective analyses of religion to develop his sociology of culture (Dianteill 2003; Rey 2007; Swartz 1996), he himself wrote only ten texts that address religion more or less centrally. The conceptually most important are Bourdieu (1987b, 1991). In the 1987b text Bourdieu reconceptualizes Weber's classic types of religious leaders (prophet, priest, and magician) to show that their interactions need to be understood in terms of their structured interests in the religious field. The 1991 text is Bourdieu's most widely cited analysis of religion. It examines the historical origins of an autonomous religious field and explores its structure and social functions. Bourdieu and de Saint Martin (1982) is the most extensive empirical study in religion. This study offers a field analysis of French Catholic bishops and documents, despite official claims of unity, a fundamental polarity between those for whom the church provides a channel for upward social mobility and those who enter their religious vocation as heirs of considerable social and cultural capital. The former identify more with the institution than the latter. Nonetheless, the sociology of religion has drawn significantly from Bourdieu's writings including his concept of field. Dianteill (2003) documents the origins of Bourdieu's concept of field in Weber's sociology of religion and explores the way it was employed by Bourdieu in his analysis of institutions, particularly the Catholic Church, and how Bourdieu's thinking can be a rich source of theoretical inspiration for students of religion. Rey (2007) introduces Bourdieu's theory of practice as it pertains to the study of religion and includes a detailed discussion of the religious field with a substantive example from colonial New England. Swartz's (1996) essay examines key features of Bourdieu's sociology of culture, particularly how he elaborates from Marx's and Weber's sociologies of religion, to offer a political economy of religious practices. Particular attention is given to the concept of field as the most relevant of Bourdieu's concepts for this undertaking.

Social Movements

Bourdieu did not systematically engage social movement research with his concept of field, though social movements and a field perspective did inform his political activism (Bourdieu 2008). Nonetheless, several features of his field perspective are applicable to social movement research, as the programmatic article *Esquisse d'une théorie de la contestation: Bourdieu et le modèle du processus politique* by Ancelovici (2010) suggests. Ancelovici brings the concept of field to the political opportunity/process framework of social movements as developed by Sidney Tarrow, Charles Tilly, and Doug McAdam. The concept of opportunity structures is redefined as "field opportunity structures" to permit their application to a far greater range of sites of social mobilization, such as religion, that are carriers of political consequences but not directly linked to the state or political field. Crossley (2003) sees fields of protest as emerging around specific forms of capital that actors use to launch campaigns directed at other fields. Fields of protest are also important sites of socialization for movement activists. Yadgar (2003) offers an interesting field analysis of the SHAS political/religious movement in Israel. Fligstein and McAdam (2012) draw on selected features of Bourdieu's concept to analyze the civil rights struggle for racial equality in the United States. Bloemraad (2001) applies the concept to the 1995 Quebec independence movement to develop the idea of "mobilization playing fields" to argue that collective identity cannot be separated from political mobilization. And Ray (1999) finds that differences in ideology, mobilization issues, tactics, and successes of women's protest movements in Bombay and Calcutta are better explained by a field analytical framework than by the popular opportunity structures framework in social movements or by general structural trends that are popular in modernization perspectives, such as general living conditions (similar for women in both cities) and demographic variables like education, fertility, and labor force participation.

Stratification, Field of Power, and the State

Bourdieu's sociology is having a growing influence on social stratification research, particularly his landmark book *Distinction: A Social Critique of the Judgement of Taste* (Bourdieu 1984[1979]) and his study of elite educational institutions in relation to structures of power, *The State Nobility: Elite Schools in the Field of Power* (Bourdieu 1996[1989]). *Distinction* is the most detailed empirical field analysis of social class lifestyles in France and considered one of Bourdieu's most significant contributions to stratification research. One of Bourdieu's most cited works, *Distinction* lays out his conception of the social class structure as a multidimensional social space, which he also considers as the field of social classes. Fields also designates arenas of taste that mediate social class relations.

Both Bourdieu's field of power and his view of the modern state are central to how he thinks power is distributed in modern stratified societies. The field of power is conceptually elaborated and empirically informed in Bourdieu's (1996[1989]) analysis of the *grandes écoles* and corporate elites in France. In this book Bourdieu replaces the language of "dominant class" or "upper class" with "field of power" to offer a more differentiated and multidimensional view of the concentrations of power in modern societies. The field of power is that arena of struggle among the different power fields themselves (particularly the economic and cultural fields) for the right to dominate throughout the social order. In modern capitalist societies the field of power is bifurcated by the poles of economic and cultural capital. In an interview with Wacquant (1993), Bourdieu identifies key features of the field of power and specifies the central role that elite educational institutions (*grandes écoles*) play in the field of power in France. The field of power informs Medvetz's (2012: 23) study of the historical formation and current form and functioning of think tanks as "a constitutively blurry network of organizations, themselves internally divided by the opposing logics of academic, political, economic, and media production."

Bourdieu (1994[1993], 2014) theorizes a field perspective on the modern state as that ensemble of bureaucratic fields that monopolizes the means of symbolic as well as physical violence and regulates relations within the field of power. The 1994 text conceptualizes the state as an ensemble of bureaucratic fields of struggle among different governmental agencies rather than as a unitary actor. The 2014 book assembles Bourdieu's 1989–1992 Collège de France lectures on the rise of the modern state, its field structure, and social functions. Bourdieu (1996[1989]) conceptualizes and empirically analyzes the central place of the French state in providing elite educational channels and social networks in the formation of public leadership in France. Swartz (2013b) shows the relevance of Bourdieu's field analysis of the modern state for political sociology.

Transnational and Global Fields

Bourdieu himself confined most of his empirical research employing the concept of field to France but offered suggestions here and there in his writings for how the concept of field might be applied beyond national borders (see, for example, Bourdieu 2005[2000]) where in sharp criticism of globalization he sees national economic fields increasingly subordinated to a "global financial field" largely controlled by American financial institutions). As Sapiro (2014) points out, while Bourdieu usually employed his concept within the framework of a single national state, nowhere in his writings does Bourdieu delimit the concept of field by a methodological nationalism.

Numerous scholars have explored how fields of power transcend national boundaries. Cohen (2011) applies the concept of the field of power to the "expanding constellation of national and supranational institutions and agents" that are forming a "nascent European field of power." To use Bourdieu's terminology these agents are engaged in the struggle over the "dominant principle of domination" or the "legitimate principle of legitimation" at the level of the European Union. Cohen (2013) stresses the strategic role of elites, particularly professionals of politics/law, in shaping an emerging European field of power at the expense of traditional political monopolies. Kauppi (2003) applies the concept of political field and political capital to the European Union. He argues that the European Union is a transnational political field in formation, taking on some of the functions of the nation-state but slow to develop a European civil society and effective democracy. Dezalay and Garth (2002) shows how the imperial processes of exporting neoliberal economics and the US concept of the rule of law (an independent judiciary) to Latin America are mediated by national fields of struggle for state power. In what they dub "palace wars," Dezalay and Garth examine intertwining power struggles within national fields and between national fields as elites pursue multifaceted strategies of internationalization and nationalization. This work looks at the case of the field strategies of North American lawyers and economists in four Latin American countries: Argentina, Brazil, Chile, and Mexico. Go (2008) proposes the idea of "global fields" to compare and contrast two hegemonic empires, that of Great Britain in the nineteenth century and that of the United States in the post–World War II period. Steinmetz (2007) uses the German case to examine the colonial state in relation to the metropolitan country. This work applies the concept of field to study the colonial state in southwest Africa, Oceania, and Qingdao (Kiaochow in China) under imperial Germany in the late nineteenth and early twentieth centuries. Steinmetz (2017: 376) extends the field concept to colonial states and empires while noting that the latter are *"not* unified fields but congeries of fields that coexisted in less integrated formations that I will call imperial *spaces* (following Bourdieu's distinction between social space and social field)." Go and Krause (2016) offers a collective of original essays that draws explicitly on the Bourdieusian concept of field to explore transnational social spaces of exchange, struggle, and interaction that are not monopolized by states. Several cases explore the emergence, extension, effects, and limits of the concept. And Adler-Nissen (2012) shows how a Bourdieusian field perspective can enrich international relations theory.

Conclusion

These selected works employing Bourdieu's concept of field are but illustrations of the rapidly expanding use of Bourdieu in the Anglo-Saxon world. These English language publications are increasingly being complemented by works in several other languages,—not withstanding French - such as German, Spanish, Italian, Japanese, and Chinese. Bourdieu's concept of field is indeed finding global application. While there is debate over whether Bourdieu's original formulation and application privilege the nation-state as a unit of analysis, clearly researchers are elaborating and deploying the concept in a wide variety of other national contexts and cross-national relations. As research moves forward more attention will be given to the issues of boundaries between fields, how fields intersect and overlap, and the social spaces constituting the interstitial holes between fields—all issues that illustrate the fecundity of Bourdieu's original thinking for advancing new social scientific investigations.

References

Adler-Nissen, R. (Ed.). (2012). *Bourdieu in international relations*. London/New York: Routledge.

Ancelovici, M. (2010). Esquisse d'une théorie de la contestation: Bourdieu et le modèle du processus politique. *Sociologie et Sociétés, 41*(2), 39–62.

Anheier, H., Gerhards, J., & Romo, F. P. (1995). Forms of capital and social structure in cultural fields: Examining Bourdieu's social topography. *American Journal of Sociology, 100*(4), 859–903.

Benson, R. (1999). Field theory in comparative context: A new paradigm for media studies. *Theory and Society, 28*, 463–498.

Benson, R., & Neveu, È. (Eds.). (2005). *Bourdieu and the journalistic field*. Cambridge, UK/Malden: Polity.

Bloemraad, I. (2001). Outsiders and insiders: Collective identity and collective action in the Quebec Independence Movement, 1995. In B. A. Dobratz, L. K. Waldner, & T. Buzzell (Eds.), *The politics of social inequality* (pp. 271–305). New York: JAI.

Bourdieu, P. (1964). The attitude of the Algerian peasant toward time. In J. Pitt-Rivers (Ed.), *Mediterranean countrymen* (pp. 55–72). Paris/The Hague: Mouton.

Bourdieu, P. (1971). Intellectual field and creative project. In M. F. D. Young (Ed.), *Knowledge and control: New directions for the sociology of education* (pp. 161–188). London: Collier-Macmillan.

Bourdieu, P. (1975). The specificity of the scientific field and the social conditions of the progress of reason. *Social Science Information, 14*(6), 19–47.

Bourdieu, P. (1983). The field of cultural production, or the economic world reversed. *Poetics, 12*, 311–356.

Bourdieu, P. (1984[1979]). *Distinction: A social critique of the judgement of taste*. Cambridge, MA: Harvard University Press.

Bourdieu, P. (1985). The market of symbolic goods. *Poetics, 14*, 13–44.

Bourdieu, P. (1987a). The force of law: Toward a sociology of the juridical field. *Hastings Journal of Law, 38*, 209–248.

Bourdieu, P. (1987b). Legitimation and structured interests in Weber's sociology of religion. In S. Lash & S. Whimster (Eds.), *Max Weber, rationality and irrationality* (pp. 119–136). Boston: Allen & Unwin.

Bourdieu, P. (1988[1984]). *Homo academicus*. Stanford: Stanford University Press.

Bourdieu, P. (1991). Genesis and structure of the religious field. *Comparative Social Research, 13*, 1–43.

Bourdieu, P. (1991[1981]). Political representation: Elements for a theory of the political field. In J. B. Thompson (Ed.), *Language and symbolic power* (pp. 171–202). Cambridge, MA: Harvard University Press.

Bourdieu, P. (1993a). *The field of cultural production: Essays on art and literature*. New York: Columbia University Press.

Bourdieu, P. (1993b). *Sociology in question*. Thousand Oaks/London: Sage Publications.

Bourdieu, P. (1994). Rethinking the state: Genesis and structure of the bureaucratic field. *Sociological Theory, 12*(1), 1–18.

Bourdieu, P. (1996[1992]). *The rules of art. Genesis and structure of the literary field*. Stanford: Stanford University Press.

Bourdieu, P. (1996[1989]). *The state nobility: Elite schools in the field of power*. Stanford: Stanford University Press.

Bourdieu, P. (1998[1996]). *On television*. New York: New Press.

Bourdieu, P. (2000). *Propos sur le Champ Politique*. Lyon: Presses Universitaires de Lyon.

Bourdieu, P. (2005[2000]). *The social structures of the economy*. Cambridge: Polity.

Bourdieu, P. (2008). *Political interventions: Social science and political action*. London/New York: Verso.

Bourdieu, P. (2014). *On the state: Lectures at the Collège de France, 1989–1992*. Cambridge, UK/Malden: Polity.

Bourdieu, P., & de Saint Martin, M. (1982). La sainte famille. L'épiscopat français dans le champ du pouvoir. *Actes de la recherche en sciences sociales, 44/45*, 2–53.

Bourdieu, P., & Sayad, A. (1964). *Le déracinement. La crise de l'agriculture traditionnelle en Algérie*. Paris: Editions de Minuit.

Bourdieu, P., & Wacquant, L. J. D. (1992). *An invitation to reflexive sociology*. Chicago: The University of Chicago Press.

Brosnan, C. (2010). Making sense of differences between medical schools through Bourdieu's concept of 'Field'. *Medical Education, 44*(7), 645–652.

Cassirer, E. (1953). *Substance and function, and Einstein's theory of relativity*. New York: Dover.

Cohen, A. (2011). Bourdieu hits Brussels: The genesis and structure of the European field of power. *International Political Sociology, 5*(3), 335–339.

Cohen, A. (2013). The genesis of Europe: Competing elites and the emergence of a European field of power. In N. Kauppi & M. Rask Madsen (Eds.), *Transnational power elites: The new professionals of governance, law and security* (pp. 103–120). London and New York: Routledge.

Couldry, N. (2003). Media meta-capital: Extending the range of Bourdieu's field theory. *Theory and Society, 36*(5/6), 653–677.

Crossley, N. (2003). From reproduction to transformation: Social movement fields and the radical habitus. *Theory, Culture, & Society, 20*(6), 43–68.

Dezalay, Y., & Garth, B. G. (2002). *The internationalization of palace wars: Lawyers, economists, and the contest to transform Latin American states*. Chicago: University of Chicago Press.

Dianteill, E. (2003). Pierre Bourdieu and the sociology of religion: A central and peripheral concern. *Theory and Society, 32*(5/6), 529–549.

DiMaggio, P., & Powell, W. (1983). The Iron cage revisited: Institutional isomorphism and collective rationality in organizational fields. *American Sociological Review, 48*, 147–160.

Emirbayer, M., & Johnson, V. (2008). Bourdieu and organizational analysis. *Theory and Society, 37*(1), 1–44.

Eyal, G. (2005). The making and breaking of the Czechoslovak political field. In L. Wacquant (Ed.), *Pierre Bourdieu and democratic politics: The mystery of ministry* (pp. 151–177). Cambridge, UK/Malden: Polity Press.

Fantasia, R. (2010). "Cooking the books" of the French gastronomic field. In E. Silva and A. Warde (Eds.), *Cultural analysis and Bourdieu's Legacy: Settling accounts and developing alternatives* (pp. 28–44). London/New York: Routledge/Taylor & Francis Group.

Ferguson, P. P. (1998). A cultural field in the making: Gastronomy in 19th-century France. *American Journal of Sociology, 103*, 597–641.

Ferguson, P. P. (2006). *Accounting for taste: The triumph of French cuisine*. Chicago: University of Chicago Press.

Ferrare, J. J., & Apple, M. W. (2015). Field theory and educational practice: Bourdieu and the pedagogic qualities of local field positions in educational contexts. *Cambridge Journal of Education, 45*(1), 43–59.

Fligstein, N., & McAdam, D. (2012). *A theory of fields*. Oxford/New York: Oxford University Press.

Go, J. (2008). Global fields and Imperial forms: Field theory and the British and American Empires. *Sociological Theory, 26*(3), 201–229.

Go, J., & Krause, M. (2016). *Fielding transnationalism: An introduction*. New York: Wiley-Blackwell.

Grenfell, M., & James, D. (2004). Change in the field: Changing the field: Bourdieu and the methodological practice of educational research. *British Journal of Sociology of Education, 25*(4), 507–523.

Hanappi, D. (2011). Economic action, fields and uncertainty. *Journal of Economic Issues, 45*(4), 785–803.

Heilbron, J. (2015). *French sociology*. Ithaca/London: Cornell University Press.

Heise, T., & Tudor, A. (2007). Constructing (Film) art: Bourdieu's field model in a comparative context. *Cultural Sociology, 1*(2), 165–187.

Hilgers, M., & Mangez, E. (Eds.). (2015). *Bourdieu's theory of social fields: Concepts and applications.* New York: Routledge/Taylor & Francis Group.

Karabel, J. (2005). *The chosen: The hidden history of admission and exclusion at Harvard, Yale, and Princeton.* Boston: Houghton Mifflin.

Kauppi, N. (2003). Bourdieu's political sociology and the politics of European integration. *Theory and Society, 32*(5–6), 775–789.

Krause, M. (2011). Reporting and the transformations of the journalistic field: US News Media, 1890–2000. *Media, Culture & Society, 33*(1), 89–104.

Lewin, K. (1951). *Field theory in social science.* New York: Harper.

Ley, D. (2003). Artists, aestheticisation and the field of gentrification. *Urban Studies, 40*(12), 2527–2544.

Lipstadt, H. (2003). Can 'art professions' be Bourdieuean fields of cultural production? The case of the architecture competition. *Cultural Studies, 17*(3–4), 390–419.

Martin, J. L., & Gregg, F. (2015). Was Bourdieu a field theorist? In M. Hilgers & E. Mangez (Eds.), *Bourdieu's theory of social fields* (pp. 39–61). London/New York: Routledge/Taylor & Francis Group.

Martin, J. L. (2003). What is field theory? *American Journal of Sociology, 109*(1), 1–49.

Medvetz, T. (2012). *Think tanks in America.* Chicago/London: The University of Chicago Press.

Meuleman, R., & Savage, M. (2013). A field analysis of cosmopolitan taste: Lessons from the Netherlands. *Cultural Sociology, 7*(2), 230–256.

Mudge, S. L. (2011). What's left of leftism?: Neoliberal politics in Western party systems, 1945–2004. *Social Science History, 35*(3), 337–380.

Oware, M. (2014). (Un)conscious (popular) underground: Restricted cultural production and underground Rap music. *Poetics, 42*, 60–81.

Rawlings, C. M., & Bourgeois, M. D. (2004). The complexity of institutional niches: Credentials and organizational differentiation in a field of U.S. Higher Education. *Poetics, 32*(6), 411–437. https://doi.org/10.1016/j.poetic.2004.09.002.

Ray, R. (1999). *Fields of protest: Women's movements in India.* Minneapolis: University of Minnesota Press.

Rey, T. (2007). *Bourdieu on religion: Imposing faith and legitimacy.* London/Oakville: Equinox.

Ringer, F. (1992). *Fields of knowledge: French academic culture in comparative perspective, 1890–1920.* New York: Cambridge University Press.

Sapiro, G. (2003). The literary field between the state and the market. *Poetics, 31*(5,6), 441–464.

Sapiro, G. (2004). Forms of politicization in the French literary field. In D. L. Swartz & V. L. Zolberg (Eds.), *After Bourdieu: Influence, critique, elaboration* (pp. 145–164). Dordrecht/Boston/London: Kluwer Academic Publishers.

Sapiro, G. (2010). Globalization and cultural diversity in the book market: The case of literary translations in the US and in France. *Poetics, 38*(4), 419–439.

Sapiro, G. (2014). Le champ est-il national? *Actes de la recherche en sciences sociales, 200*, 70–85.

Savage, M., & Silva, E. B. (2013). Field analysis in cultural sociology. *Cultural Sociology, 7*(2), 111–126. https://doi.org/10.1177/1749975512473992.

Steinmetz, G. (2007). *The Devil's handwriting: precoloniality and the German Colonial State in Quingdao, Samoa, and Southwest Africa.* Chicago: The University of Chicago Press.

Steinmetz, G. (2017). The Octopus and the Hekatonkheire: On many-armed states and Tentacular Empires. In K. J. Morgan & A. Shola Orloff (Eds.), *The many hands of the state: Theorizing political authority and social control* (pp. 369–393). New York: Cambridge University Press.

Swartz, D. (1996). Bridging the study of culture and religion: Pierre Bourdieu's political economy of symbolic power. *Sociology of Religion, 57*, 71–85.

Swartz, D. (1997). *Culture and power: The sociology of Pierre Bourdieu.* Chicago: The University of Chicago Press.

Swartz, D. (2003). From critical sociology to public intellectual: Pierre Bourdieu and politics. *Theory and Society, 32*(5–6), 791–823.

Swartz, D. (2013a). Metaprinciples for sociological research in a Bourdieusian perspective. In P. S. Gorski (Ed.), *Bourdieu and historical analysis* (pp. 19–35). Durham/London: Duke University Press.

Swartz, D. (2013b). *Symbolic power, politics, and intellectuals: The political sociology of Pierre Bourdieu.* Chicago/London: University of Chicago Press.

Swedberg, R. (2011). The economic sociologies of Pierre Bourdieu. *Cultural Sociology, 5*(1), 67–82.

Vauchez, A. (2008). The force of a weak field: Law and lawyers in the government of the European Union (For a Renewed Research Agenda). *International Political Sociology, 2*(2), 128–144.

Wacquant, L. J. D. (1993). From ruling class to field of power: An interview with Pierre Bourdieu on *La noblesse d'etat. Theory, Culture, & Society, 10*(3), 19–44.

Yadgar, Y. (2003). SHAS as a struggle to create a new field: A Bourdieuan perspective of an Israeli phenomenon. *Sociology of Religion, 64*(2), 223–246.

Chapter 12
Transformation and Heteronomization of the Academic Field

From Scientific Competition to Economic Struggle

Richard Münch

Introduction

If we apply a field-theoretical perspective to the academic field, it can be understood as "the locus of a competitive struggle, in which the specific issue at stake is the monopoly of scientific authority, defined inseparably as technical capacity and social power" (Bourdieu 1975: 19). Across different nation-states, and indeed in concerted international collaboration, numerous researchers have begun to analyze and criticize a specific recent transformation which is altering the academic field, the character of scientific competition, and the sources of power that are constitutive for modern science. Two of the most striking features of the changing scientific field and academic practice in our time are the substantially increased significance of international university rankings, with an academic 'Champions League', and the global expansion of New Public Management. Both of these new features of the academic work represent a particular colonization of the individual scientific competition for genuinely scientific and symbolic capital, i.e. for progress in knowledge and recognition by the scientific community. This colonization – or heteronomization – manifests itself in the form of the *institutional economic* competition between universities for *institutional* capital, i.e. for research funds, successful researchers, gifted students, and positions of power facilitating the realization of competitive advantages (Wildavsky 2010; Münch 2014, 2016; Münch and Baier 2012; Baier and Schmitz 2012; Baier and Münch 2013; Wieczorek et al. 2017; Baier and Schmitz in this volume).

Robert K. Merton's (1973 [1942]) basic norms of scientific practice – universalism, organized scepticism, intellectual communism, and disinterestedness –

R. Münch (✉)
Zeppelin University, Friedrichshafen, Germany
e-mail: richard.muench@zu.de

© Springer Nature Switzerland AG 2019
J. Blasius et al. (eds.), *Empirical Investigations of Social Space*,
Methodos Series 15, https://doi.org/10.1007/978-3-030-15387-8_12

under the trusteeship of the scientific community and the individual professional associations at the autonomous pole of the scientific field are superimposed by the economic rules of striving for monopoly rents from competitive advantages and market power at the heteronomous pole. Thus, the transformation of the academic field can be described by a particular form of intrusion (Bourdieu 1998): the economic nomos invades the academic field not only at the level of the agent's habitus and practice, but also – and increasingly – at the level of the agents' institutions: the universities.

In this chapter, I will emphasize three core characteristics of the university in this struggle for achievement and their impact on scientific practice and the openness of knowledge evolution: the *entrepreneurial* university striving for competitive advantages, the *audit* university applying measures of quality management from the world of business, and the *strategically planning* third-party funded university, extensively focused on the acquisition of extensive third-party funding for large scale collaborative research (cf. Münch 2014, 2016; Münch and Baier 2012; Baier and Münch 2013; Wieczorek et al. 2017).

The Entrepreneurial University and the Rule of Numbers

According to Bourdieu (1975, 1988), scientific practice can be localized in a scientific or academic field. In an ideal-typical way, this field can be characterized by a horizontal axis with the two poles of autonomy and heteronomy, and by a vertical axis referring to the availability of more or less scientific or institutional capital. In this field, genuine scientific capital (such as publications) and symbolic capital (such as citations, honors, awards) founded on scientific capital are located at the autonomous pole, while institutional capital (research funds, institutional networks, positions of power) and the related symbolic capital (prestige) are situated at the heteronomous pole. I contend that the researchers' and research teams' individual competition for advances in scientific knowledge and recognition for their contributions from the scientific community take place rather at the autonomous pole, while the universities' battle for the accumulation of material and symbolic institutional capital is above all fought at the heteronomous pole.

Remarkably, in his early conceptualization of academic fields, Bourdieu took institutions into account: "The structure of the scientific field at any given moment is defined by the state of the power distribution between the protagonists in the struggle (agents or institutions), i.e. by the structure of the distribution of the specific capital, the results of previous struggles which are objectified in institutions and dispositions and command the strategies and objective chances of the different agents or institutions in the present struggles." (Bourdieu 1975: 27). It is a typical feature of the global expansion and increased importance of rankings and New Public Management (NPM) that universities are addressed as actors who have to position themselves in globalized fields of science and nation-states (Hazelkorn 2011). As a consequence, we can observe a process of encroachment, or superimposition, upon individual scientific competition between scientists of the institutional competition between universities. Universities see themselves increasingly as enterprises striving for competitive advantages, i.e., monopoly rents enabling them to accumulate institutional capital. In the first instance, these institutional struggles for positions in rankings which are fought at the heteronomous pole of the field also change the rules of scientific practice at the autonomous pole. Applying Bourdieusian field theory to Merton's basic norms of science may lead to the contention that resources and scientific knowledge are shared as public goods at the autonomous scientific pole. In the Mertonian ideal world, and a large portion of the Western academic field of the twentieth century, this involves an awareness of the fact that the progress of knowledge is based on a great variety of altruistic cooperation that depends both on smaller and larger contributions. In contrast, the heteronomous pole has always had the role of providing a platform for the exclusive utilization of resources and knowledge which are solely shared within strategic alliances. This, indeed, is the very characteristic of entrepreneurial universities that contributes to this specific type of academic capitalism (Slaughter and Leslie 1997; Slaughter and Rhoades 2004; Radder 2010; Ginsberg 2011; Berman 2012; Münch 2014).

What appears illegitimate at the autonomous pole possesses a distinct status of legitimacy at the heteronomous one; here, the economic field intrudes into the academic field, giving rise to an understanding of universities as enterprises. Resistance against this transformation, fed by the scientific nomos, and represented by the autonomous pole in particular, has little chance of success. Today, the institutional competition between the entrepreneurially managed universities prevails in large parts of national scientific fields. This leads to increasing differentiation between internationally interconnected elite institutions, which at the same time benefit from more capable local and global business partners. Without strong international networking, the remaining universities see themselves reduced to the status of institutions that are only interconnected in their own regions, positions that they are unable to change. This regional aspect corresponds to the logics of economic competition, but not to the requirements of scientific competition. The latter aims for an open evolution of knowledge, which requires utmost diversity. This is driven more by small teams of researchers at a great variety of locations than by the large scale collaborative research that can only be maintained at huge sites without internal displacement effects (Münch 2014).

We can clearly see here what Mathias Binswanger (2010: 44ff.) describes as *market illusion*. The transformation of public services into competitive processes does not usually entail the development of markets in the ideal sense. In the private sector, markets are also distorted by cartels, monopolies, and oligopolies. Such distortion easily occurs in the provision of public services, since better equipped providers can obtain privileged access to central public demanders of services and thus manage to secure a dominating competitive position. This is also entirely applicable to the presence of dominant universities in the committees of public funding institutions like the German Research Foundation (DFG) and their influence on the funding programs, as well as on the distribution of research funds. In other words: The economic illusio that intrudes into the scientific field does not result in a straightforward marketization of science, but rather in a violation of the market principle. The tendency towards overinvestment at the top and underinvestment among the wide mass of universities is thus a counterproductive consequence of the increasing concentration of research funding on elite institutions – not only in the scientific regard, but also from the economic point of view.

Research shows a curvilinear, inverted u-shaped relationship between investment and returns in the sense of publications. In minimally capital-intensive disciplines like microeconomics, the optimal point of the critical mass of equipment is reached much earlier than in very capital-intensive disciplines such as, for instance, particle physics (Jansen et al. 2007). The optimal point of investment is achieved earlier the stronger the related output is relativized in terms of investments. It is reached at the latest point of ongoing investment for the absolute output, is found in a median position with regard to the output per scientist, and is hit very early for the output per one million Euro research funds. Beyond this optimal point, the law of falling marginal utility becomes effective. Every further unit of investment yields less output. We can demonstrate for the discipline of chemistry in Germany that – under the condition of the curvilinear, inverted u-shaped causal relationship between investment and returns – the increasing concentration of research funding on elite institutions results in numerous institutions remaining below an optimal equipment threshold, while the elite institutions enjoy facilities that surpass the optimal level by far (Münch 2014: 223ff.). The overall scientific output, not to mention economic efficiency, would be much higher if more institutions were equipped exactly at the critical point of optimality. Large investments of institutional capital might enhance absolute publication output, but they do not improve relative publication output per scientist or the relative output per invested amount of money.

Despite the developments outlined so far, the forces which counteract the concentration processes of elite competition have not been eliminated completely. In Germany, federalism is such a force. The eagerness of 16 federal states to distinguish themselves with excellent universities results in a broader distribution of at least adequately equipped universities than, for instance, in France and Great Britain. These universities have been proven to perform well in the competition for scientists, students, and third-party funds. Among other things, this is evidenced by the research rating of the German Science Council (WR 2008) pertaining to the two subjects of chemistry and sociology. In chemistry, at least one internationally visible research unit assessed as very good or excellent was found at as many as 34 out of 57 universities, and at 14 out of 20 non-university research institutions. As far as sociology is concerned, 34 out of 54 universities and 3 non-university sites achieved such assessments.

A network analysis of first appointments to a professorship in the field of chemistry confirms that, (unlike in the United States, where alumni of the larger institutions are at a considerable advantage) even young scientists trained at smaller locations in Germany have certain chances of being appointed as professors at smaller, middle-sized and larger locations (Baier and Münch 2013). However, it is undeniable that large locations provide an extremely high number of first professorial appointments from their own ranks for the entire system. In Germany, one must additionally consider the relatively high number of non-university research institutions, which spend about 40% of the public research budget. They also develop a large number of first-appointment professors.

Also, in contrast to the United States, where the top 20 departments in the field of sociology, for example, recruit 88% of their assistant professors from among themselves (Burris 2004), the training and placement of junior researchers is subject to broader distribution and variation in Germany. However, there is still a considerable concentration of institutional capital and of purely scientific capital in the field, which cannot be disregarded. If the memberships of academies, the DFG, and German Council of Science and Humanities were taken into account, they would concentrate at the top, thus multiplying the institutional capital gathered there.

Nevertheless, the German political field tends to abide by the global agenda by institutionalizing heteronomous principles of differentiation within the scientific field. I contend that generalized mistrust in the performance of public institutions is a basic characteristic of this global agenda. The paradigm of basic mistrust in the performance of public institutions, globally spread by the neoliberal reform agenda, is theoretically rooted in public choice theory and particularly in the principal-agent model of institutional economics (Meyerson 1982; Laffont and Martimort 2009). The principal delegates tasks which they are unable or unwilling to accomplish themselves to an agent. It is assumed that both principal and agent are rational utility maximizers. Accordingly, the agent has to be paid an appropriate remuneration for their services. The rarer the skills, the higher the enforceable wage demands. More common qualifications entail the need for collective support from trade unions. As both are utility maximizers, the principal must be careful not to be outsmarted by the agent, who might exploit the principal by achieving the required minimum output with the lowest effort, or by performing a task to their own satisfaction, but not to the satisfaction of the principal. The principal is thus primarily confronted with a control problem: All efforts must be concentrated on making the work of the agent observable and controllable. One extreme method would place the agent in a market where they have to sell their services on their own, thus being paid by revenues. The other drastic approach involves agreeing on a piece rate. There is basically no trust between the principal and the agent. Everything has to be regulated by a contract that specifies the services to be performed and the payable remunerations very closely. Should this be impossible, the contract is incomplete and contains more or less serious information asymmetries (Tirole 1999). Both parties are never fully aware of what the other side is doing; not upon conclusion of the contract, nor during the performance of the delegated tasks, nor when the rendered service – regarding which the agent is better informed than the principal – is assessed.

The application of the principal-agent model entails a permanent search for possibilities to eliminate information asymmetries between the two parties. The steadily increasing advancement of information technologies, of instruments for the collection and evaluation of data, has made a substantial contribution to this phenomenon. The digitalization of work has unquestionably promoted the efforts to observe work performances and services, and to fine-tune them down to the tiniest details. Today, principals can monitor the work performances and services of their agents online in real time and guide their behavior with the help of incentive systems (Therefore, every principal who is advised by McKinsey & Co. dreams of digitalized fine-tuning). One tool which has created great expectations in this regard is the Balanced Scorecard (Kaplan and Norton 1993), which is designed to log even complex activities aimed at optimizing several goals at the same time into a digitalized incentive and control system. It requires a growing amount of data evaluated with increasingly efficient computers.

Without this progress in information technology, no one would have expected that the completion of even complex tasks could be subject to monitoring in even the most minute detail. Once available, every application of this instrument at one site entails an increasing pressure to apply it at other sites, too, in order to fine-tune complex, interrelated performances. This development also affects academic activities that must likewise be captured by information technological methods which use indicators. The issued performance records, completed written and oral examinations, PhD graduates, habilitations, publications, and acquired third-party funds are to be counted, credit points have to be assigned, and the attained credit points have to be linked to payments. In order to leave nothing to chance, target agreements have to be negotiated pertaining to the acquisition of external funding and to the number and volume of publications. Research and teaching are thus turned into a calculable and controllable process for the university administration. Presenting the relevant indicators, the university administration can explain itself to external parties, to government ministries, the university council, to sponsors, and to the public. And since this need for justification from third parties has only grown in significance in face of the general suspicion that public institutions are prone to waste tax money – a suspicion itself inspired by neoliberalist impulses and the economic principal-agent model – the new control and monitoring system based on scores is sprawling relentlessly and inexorably in the field of academia. The scores are intended to visualize what had never before been visible from the outside.

The visualization of the previously invisible is in the best interest of the media; it can much better fulfill its informative duties towards the general public, and indeed has a whole new field for reporting that now delivers interesting news, because the increases or losses in numbers evinced by the indicators are attractive even for the inattentive reader. We must be aware that the fulfillment of the increased informative duties towards the outside world – that is, media reporting on universities – affects research and teaching within universities, as they are in consequence driven to provide data and events in a form easily presentable to the public by the media. At first glance, this appears to be a sound representation of what is done in research and teaching anyway; it should not present any problems. For this purpose, the public relations department is expanded, followed by the publication of an impressive high-gloss magazine and increasing attempts to furnish the audience with data on the services performed in the field of teaching and research. However, success in reporting is determined by the laws of impression management. At this point, the external criteria of successful reporting begin to exert their influence on research and teaching within the university. This might be mitigated by constructing a media-compatible facade behind which teaching and research can continue to follow their own rules without being disturbed (Meyer and Rowan 1977). However, public relations strategies can also colonize the field of teaching and research, at least to the extent to which they are subject to the production of medially well exploitable events and scores (cp. Bourdieu 1998). Especially these scores will then turn into a reality sui generis, a social fact subjecting teaching and research to its own regime. At this point, the rule *by* numbers turns into a rule *of* numbers from which no one can escape (Porter 1995).

The rule of the numbers is fueled by the fact that the university, acting as an enterprise towards the outside world, at the same time requires internal quality management capable of steering the field of teaching and research in a way that ensures for the university the best possible conditions in its confrontation with other universities. The illusion of measurability identified by Mathias Binswanger (2010: 67ff.) comes into effect here. Since the competition between universities lacks any price-performance mechanism, scores have to be applied in order to make the performances rendered at universities, or individual faculties and departments, comparable – and to enable decision-making based on these comparisons, such as, for instance, government funding, allocation of third-party funds, sponsorship money, or taking up studies. Making this kind of commensuration possible is the function of rankings (Espeland and Sauder 2007).

The Audit University and Standardization

In his description of the scientific field, Bourdieu put a particular emphasis on the special relationship in the sciences between the expert and the layman: "The struggle for scientific authority [...] owes its specificity to the fact that the producers tend to have no possible clients other than their competitors" (Bourdieu 1975: 23). In this view, "this means that in a highly autonomous scientific field a particular producer cannot expect recognition of the value of his products ('reputation', 'prestige', 'authority', 'competence', etc.) from anyone except other producers, who, being his competitors, too, are those least inclined to grant recognition without discussion and scrutiny" (Bourdieu 1975: 23). He contends: "This is true de facto: only scientists involved in the area have the means of symbolically appropriating his work and assessing its merits. And it is also true de jure: the scientist who appeals to an authority outside the field cannot fail to incur discredit" (Bourdieu 1975: 23).

Applying this view, I contend that the ongoing transformation of the scientific field also manifests itself in a particular transformation of the specific expert-layman relation Bourdieu identified for the scientific field: Just as there is a genuinely scientific form of competition, there is also the genuinely scientific process of quality assurance situated at the autonomous pole of the academic field. In an ideal-typical scientific field, intra-scientific quality assurance provides the basis upon which scientific communities build their professional trusteeship. Their vitality, cultivated in annual conventions and in many individual conferences and workshops, has always been an important prerequisite for scientific progress.

Another crucial factor is the socialization process, compelling junior scientists to incorporate the search for truth for its own sake and the desire for recognition from the scientific community into their habitus. Every statement made in science calls on the addressee to subject this statement to a thorough critical investigation. Every thesis provokes an antithesis, every assertion elicits criticism. The ideal speech situation as a regulative idea ensures that no statement can claim to be true simply because of the speaker's authority; only the better argument counts. Enrolling in university study programs means becoming integrated in and getting used to this process of assertion and criticism, and the more advanced the student is, the better he or she masters the necessary methodical tools. Peer review as a genuinely scientific quality assurance tool is rooted in the process of criticism between peers. Scientific journals, publishers, and editors of anthologies subject each contribution to a more or less systematically organized peer review (Bornmann 2010).

When scientists in Germany are appointed to a professorship at the average age of 41 years, they have incorporated the critical examination of statements to a degree that every thought internally follows this procedure, and possible objections are anticipated far in advance. The larger part of scientists has made this process a habitus; they belong to the cautious species who critically investigate each thought from all perspectives before putting it up for discussion. They pursue their research activities under a strictly controlled risk. Those scientists who take greater risks differ from this approach: This starts with the spontaneous expression in a workshop and ends with the draft of a new theory. However, these adventurous researchers constitute a small minority of scientists. It could even be said that the hindrance of too much self-criticism presents the greatest obstacle to those academic careers that aim to go beyond mere quality improvement and actually create new knowledge. From the point of view of science itself at the autonomous pole, we might claim that it suffers rather from too much than from too little quality assurance.

Against this backdrop, there can hardly be said to be a lack of genuine scientific procedures for quality assurance that would explain the current movement professing to provide better quality assurance in science. The reason for this movement must thus have its origin outside science, or at least outside the autonomous pole of the academic field supervised by the scientific community. It is the neoliberal agenda, encouraged by the media that puts public institutions under general suspicion of wasting taxpayer's money. The traditional control ensured by the Court of Auditors is considered insufficient in this context. The auditors only specialize in looking at the adherence to laws and regulations, which does not in the least guarantee that tax money is spent for society in an economically efficient way, supplying "value for money". What can be observed here is an *economic turn* in scientific quality assurance (cp. Münch 2014: 53ff.).

The Court of Auditors has not traditionally based its inspection on scientific criteria either, but solely on bureaucratic ones, which are progressively being replaced by economic principles in the hope of an increased supply of "value for money". At this point, monitoring undergoes an essential change. While the bureaucratic control exerted by the Court of Auditors has left the scientific field completely unaffected, economic control intervenes much more strongly in the field of teaching and research.

The characteristic neoliberal mistrust in the performance and capacity of public institutions, exacerbated by the media, requires a system of indicators permitting the observation and control of performances and accomplishments in order to provide a legitimation towards the general public in the external relationship, and to ensure the monitoring of teaching and research with the help of quality management tools in the internal relationship. Since, unlike traditional bureaucratic control, quality management seeks to produce performances and achievements in the field of teaching and research that can be visualized by scores, the process of scientific quality assurance tends to be superimposed or colonized – or even completely displaced – by the economic one (Janssen and Sass 2008). In other words: Bourdieu's homo academicus turns into a homo oeconomicus. Biswanger's (2010: 67–91) measurability illusion is corroborated by the fact that the score-based control does not involve a continuous readjustment of supply and demand, as would be the case on an ideal market, facilitated by such a market's price-performance mechanism. Instead, the activities are strongly focused on the fulfilment of the requirements set by central instances and implemented in the scores. The more complex the performances to be achieved, and the farther they go beyond the items measured by the scores, the greater the resulting performance deficits. This culminates in exactly those mismanagements familiar to us from centralized socialist planned economies. Too many of the items set and rewarded by the scores are produced, while many other items are not produced at all, despite being in demand. As long as there are still chances to maintain inward scope for variation while simultaneously presenting scores to the outside world, scientific practice preserves at least a part of its genuine quality. The tighter the control, the more scientific practice becomes colonized and disciplined by the score system (Power 1997). It ultimately turns into a Foucaultian panopticon of science (Foucault 1977; Sauder and Espeland 2009).

The university then approaches the model of a total organization observing and controlling the lives of its members, right down to the smallest detail. Whatever fails to comply with this schematism is forced to disappear, unless it is maintained in unobserved 'preservation' zones in the underground life of the organisation. In science, these zones include all those teaching and research activities that do not yield any points, e.g., the composition of expertises, papers in edited volumes, reviews, newspaper articles, and monographs, or simply discussions with students in the cafeteria. As Parsons and Platt (1973) made unmistakeably clear, learning, teaching, and research can only occur in a protected space under the trusteeship of an autonomous academic community (cp. Bourdieu 1989: 660f.). The panopticon of external quality assurance currently under construction is the death of academic freedom and of the unhindered progress of knowledge.

No system of scores is able to sufficiently reflect the continuously changing performance spectrum of fairly complex activities; it will invariably lag behind the requirements. And as this is an immutable fact, it has a restricting effect on the activities themselves, ossifying them, forming a schematism that results in massive performance deficits. This is especially true in the context of teaching and research.

Rankings in particular aggravate the constrictive effects of scoring systems on academic practice. Their addressee is the public, which means that they are part of the media system and subject to its laws (Münch 1991, 1995; Luhmann 1996; Franck 1998; Bourdieu 1998). They must produce sets of scores that are comprehensible at a single glance, enabling the transmission of readily intelligible messages. They require tables that display the individual ranks of the universities, schools, or departments, which is more interesting and easier to understand than excessive information on their specific unique features. With the help of rankings, the investors (the state, private contributors and students paying their tuition fees) receive publicly consecrated assessments on the return on investment to be expected of a specific university degree. Since rankings create a social fact reproducing itself from publication to publication, they provide investors with sufficiently reliable information. They also largely generate the reality they pretend to measure. They produce the same effects as self-fulfilling prophecies (Merton 1968), creating reactivity in the sense that everybody, producers and consumers, adapts their behavior to the figures, and everything else becomes invisible (Espeland and Sauder 2007, 2009). Therefore, there are no noteworthy positional changes in the ranking over time once it has been set. An essential function of rankings is thus to ensure for investors stable returns on their commitment. Correspondingly, they are also of considerable and verifiable appeal to potential investors, thus countering academic criticisms of their over-simplification of reality.

In Germany, this was the reply given by the Bertelsmann Foundation's Center for University Development (CHE) and their media collaborator ZEIT-Campus to the criticism of their university ranking system expressed by the Executive Board of the German Sociological Association (DGS 2012; CHE Ranking 2012). The fact that the CHE university ranking is carried out on behalf of the German Rectors' Conference reveals a growing conflict between the scientific community and university management departments. The main authorities at the autonomous pole of the academic field are forced to fend off the invasion of schematised and rankable performance assessments encouraged by the German Rector's Conference and university management. They are developed according to media logic, and are unable to fulfill the actual requirements of intra-academic performance assessment. Rankings in the academic field give credence to Campbell's Law (1976), which states that performance assessment based on scores corrupts behavior to the extent to which status and remuneration are linked to the parameters of the performance assessment. This corruption of behavior becomes more widespread the more distant the performance assessment is from the activity itself, and the more status and remuneration are linked to it. Since rankings are largely subject to the attention economy (Franck 1998) of the media system, and have to work with simple scores, they are especially distant from 'real' academic practice.

In his presidential address at the annual meeting of the American Sociological Association (ASA), Michael Burawoy (2005) complained that American sociology was dominated by only one of four equally important variants of sociology, namely by the professional sociology of peer reviewed journals – pure sociology for sociologists, and scarcely relevant for questions going beyond the specialist field, let alone for questions of public and further societal interest. According to Burawoy, it has displaced all other variants of sociology: critical sociology, with a focus on concept and theory work and on the self-reflection of the discipline; policy-oriented sociology aiming at a transfer of knowledge to practice; and public sociology, which addresses the communication of knowledge to the public and provides analyses of contemporary culture (*Zeitdiagnosen*).

The sociology research rating reveals that these variants are still present in Germany, but it also indicates that a consistent and continuous adherence to the rating's dominant standard is destroying any chance of their survival. Research institutions that have afforded plurality of practice to all these variants of sociology were clearly at a disadvantage compared to research institutions that had one-dimensionally specialized in professional sociology. The assessments of research institutions which facilitated conceptual and theoretical work, the transfer of knowledge to practice, and cultural analysis; all clearly suffered in comparison to research institutions that had practiced purely professional sociology. Practicing these kinds of sociology drags down the overall assessment of research institutions, so that they are in danger of being closed by a strategically active management department: What has saved them so far is only the continued existence of a disconnection between formal structure and actual active structure (Meyer and Rowan 1977). The research rating of the Science Council that is particularly close to science thus cannot evade the maelstrom of destroying diversity through standardization. This adherence to the scientific logic is an important factor in enablings the uniform and standardized side of science to dominate over its diverse and creative side, since – unlike the diverse side – it is much easier to assess *with the tools of science themselves*, i.e., according to uniform standards.

So, if even a laborious and relatively complicated procedure such as research rating represents a substantial obstruction to diversity, this will be even more true of any type of ranking that inevitably has to standardize and simplify the process even further. What is hindered in its further development by standardization and simplification is nothing less than the progress of knowledge itself (Espeland and Sauder 2009). Here, we observe a variant of Mathias Binswanger's (2010: 92ff.) motivation illusion involved in the implementation of standardized assessment procedures. The competition for scores, encouraged by incentives, replaces intrinsic motivation with its extrinsic form (Frey 2006). This entails a loss of the creative potential involved in intrinsic motivation and thus a libido transformation of scientists' habitus.

From Research in Small Teams to Research in Large Scale Collaborative Units: The Third-Party Funded University

In the United States, the major responsibility of university administrations today are raising sponsorship money for asset growth, its profitable investment, and its investment in the improvement of their department's prestige through the appointment of promising junior scientists and renowned professors. Their achievements are measured by the amount of funding attained yearly, and by the return on investment in terms of enhanced prestige, measured in the ranking position of the university's departments and schools. The intensification of the competition for funds entails an increasing interest on the part of university management in capital growth, fueled by extensive third-party fund raising. Industrial funds have proven to be particularly lucrative in this regard: The US $500 million invested by BP into the establishment of an Energy Bioscience Institute at UC Berkeley in 2007 are evidence of the success of this strategy (Sanders 2007). As a result, there is a tendency towards a targeted support of departments capable of attracting such amounts with their research activities. What is researched therefore depends increasingly on the third-party funding it yields. When looking for funds from industry, support is preferably allocated to those projects that promise economic benefits. Consequentially, research occurs in great proximity to the existing industrial structure, and thus loses part of its potential to renew science in and of itself, independent of any industrial structure. An environment conducive to such renewal would necessitate greater distance from existing external interests and heteronomous demands. Any type of research activity with no immediate relevance for industry is marginalized all the more. This problematic side of the growth of third-party funds as the primary target of the departments' research agenda has been investigated in the USA under the keyword of "academic capitalism" (Slaughter and Leslie 1997; Slaughter and Rhoades 2004; Berman 2012; Münch 2016). In this context, the contract concluded between UC Berkeley and the Swiss pharmaceutical group Novartis in 1998, spanning a 5-year duration and involving US $25 million, attracted particular attention (Rudy et al. 2007); this was still a modest amount compared with the US $500 million contract concluded with BP in 2007 (Sanders 2007). Particular criticism was provoked by the fact that Novartis was represented in the five-person research committee of the microbiology department by two members.

However, funds from industry are not generally more restrictive with regard to freedom of research than public funds. Applying for funds from the American National Science Foundation (NSF) typically requires one to comply with strict rules, which may actually result in less freedom for exploration than industrial funds given to a renowned scientist without obligation to describe exactly what he or she wants to investigate and how he or she plans to proceed (cp. Evans 2010). Greater leeway in research funded by industry seems to be a privilege of scientists at the most prestigious institutions and represents high institutional symbolic capital, while their colleagues at the less prestigious institutions are forced to provide services which are more directly oriented to the interests of the sponsor (cp. Wieczorek et al. 2017).

Particular criticism against the backdrop of the increasing pressure of acquiring external funds is directed at the extraordinary growth of an expensive university administration with presidents, provosts, deans and "deanlings" pursuing their own accumulation of power and wealth, with the help of a subordinated and disempowered research and teaching staff. Some critical voices have determined that scientists have to generate a research funding overhead of up to 80%, to allow the administration to glorify in with prestigious construction projects, and to increase their salaries way above the salaries of average professors (Tuchman 2009; Ginsberg 2011).

Unlike their US counterparts, university management in Germany does not have the opportunity to raise funds from sponsors on a large scale. Under public pressure – exacerbated by the neoliberal reform agenda – they are all the more reliant on their faculty professors to present visible success in order to acquire third-party funds. For this purpose, quality management based on economic logic provides instruments for target agreements and the performance-oriented distribution of financial means (performance-oriented remuneration). The coordinated programs of the German Research Foundation (DFG) and the Excellence Initiative of the federal and state governments have supplied the tools for raising third-party funds on a large scale. Altogether, 59% of the DFG budget is spent on collaborative research (DFG 2012: 37). Such collaborative research can best be realized at larger sites, since they are the ones who possess the required critical mass. Accordingly, the quality of equipment available to scientists is highly correlated with the generation of third-party funds, which means that the competition for third-party funds is frequently decided in advance and thus unnecessary, needed only for legitimation purposes, if at all (Münch 2014: 190ff.).

One serious effect of this preference for large scale collaboration in research in the allocation of major third-party funding are the growing legions of research assistants, who conduct their research work over many years under the direction of their professors with only meagre prospects of being promoted to a professorship. In the first round of the excellence initiative, 92% of the staff resources were invested in junior staff positions, mostly for professorial research assistants. At German universities, we find a personnel structure comprising only 15% professorships, but 85% positions for research and/or teaching assistants, which is unique in international comparison. In the USA, the proportion is reversed, according to a recent publication of the *Konsortium Bundesbericht wissenschaftlicher Nachwuchs* (*Federal Report on Junior Academics*) (2013: 15, Fig. A1–8). (However, in the USA, the so-called adjunct faculty – fixed-term teaching staff – has substantially grown with the expansion of business managerialism, which is not represented in the statistics of this report. It is estimated that the ratio between regular faculty and adjunct faculty at US research universities has inverted from 70:30 to 30:70). In Germany, the enormous increase in third-party university funding achieved by strategic management therefore engenders a structure which inhibits innovation more than at any time in the past, namely the oligarchy of university chair holders, who have increasingly turned into managers, no longer performing their own research activities, but chiefly involved in the acquisition of third-party funds for the further employment of their staff. This is contrary to two requirements essential for the continuous renewal of science: early independence for junior researchers, with rapid generational change (Ben-David 1971[1984]), and research in small teams with secure and flexibly applicable funding (Heinze et al. 2009).

Conclusion

Just like any other field, science develops between two poles: the pole of autonomy and the pole of heteronomy. In the scientific field, the pole of autonomy is supervised by the scientific community, and this is where genuinely scientific competition takes place; internal quality assurance is situated at this pole, and research advances the progress of knowledge. It provides the basis for science to unfurl in the tension between two inner poles: The competition for both progress of knowledge and for reputation, driven by the tension between collegiality and competition; for both equality and differentiation of reputation based on performance; for quality assurance derived from the tension between the diversity of ideas and the uniformity of the methodical standards; in sum, research which balances equality and hierarchy, spontaneous and strategic cooperation, freedom and constraint resulting from the subordination to methodologically standardized research programs.

The pole of heteronomy is home to the entrepreneurial universities involved in the institutional competition for monopoly rents, to the audit university, which aims to establish external quality assurance through indicators, and to the third party-funded university, which subjects research to strategic planning, strict management, and forced cooperation within large scale collaborative units. The neoliberal agenda assigns more significance to the heteronomous side leading to a situation in which – from the perspective of the autonomous pole –those strategies which are adjacent to the heteronomous pole gain in importance: Competition takes precedence over collegiality, uniformity over diversity, and constraint over freedom.

References

Baier, C., & Münch, R. (2013). Institutioneller Wettbewerb und Karrierechancen von Nachwuchswissenschaftlern in der Chemie. *Kölner Zeitschrift für Soziologie und Sozialpsychologie,* 65(1), 129–155.

Baier, C., & Schmitz, A. (2012). Organisationen als Akteure in sozialen Feldern – Eine Modellierungsstrategie am Beispiel deutscher Hochschulen. In S. Bernhard & C. Schmidt-Wellenburg (Eds.), *Feldanalyse als Forschungsprogramm – Der programmatische Kern* (pp. 191–220). Wiesbaden: VS.

Ben-David, J. (1971/1984). *The scientist's role in society.* Chicago: University of Chicago Press.

Berman, E. P. (2012). *Creating the market university: How academic science became an economic engine*. Princeton: Princeton University Press.

Binswanger, M. (2010). *Sinnlose Wettbewerbe. Warum wir immer mehr Unsinn produzieren*. Freiburg: Herder.

Bornmann, L. (2010). Scientific peer review. *Annual Review of Information Science and Technology, 45*, 199–245.

Bourdieu, P. (1975). The specificity of the scientific field and the social conditions of the progress of reason. *Social Science Information, 14*(6), 19–47.

Bourdieu, P. (1988). *Homo Academicus*. Stanford: Stanford University Press.

Bourdieu, P. (1989). The corporatism of the universal: The role of intellectuals in the modern world. *Telos, 81*, 99–110.

Bourdieu, P. (1998). *On Television* (P. P. Ferguson, Trans.). London: New Press.

Burawoy, M. (2005). For public sociology. *American Sociological Review, 70*(1), 4–28.

Burris, V. (2004). The academic caste system. Prestige hierarchies in PhD exchange networks. *American Sociological Review, 69*(2), 239–264.

Campbell, D. T. (1976). *Assessing the impact of planned social change*. (Occasional Paper Series No. 8). Western Michigan University, Kalamazoo. Evaluation Center. Retrieved July 17, 2012, from www.eric.ed.gov/PDFS/ED303512.pdf

CHE-Ranking. (2012). *Methodische Genauigkeit und öffentlicher Nutzen des CHE-Hochschulrankings. Erwiderung des CHE auf die Stellungnahme der DGS zum CHE Hochschulranking*. Gütersloh: CHE.

DFG (Deutsche Forschungsgemeinschaft) (Ed.). (2012). Förderatlas 2012. Kennzahlen zur öffentlich finanzierten Forschung in Deutschland. Bonn.

DGS (Deutsche Gesellschaft für Soziologie) (Ed.). (2012). *Wissenschaftliche Evaluation Ja – CHE-Ranking Nein*. Retrieved July 29, 2013, from http://www.soziologie.de/de/nc/aktuell/che/aktuelles-single-view/archive/2012/06/01/article/wissenschaftliche-evaluation-ja-che-ranking-nein-1.html

Espeland, W. N., & Sauder, M. (2007). Rankings and reactivity. How public measures recreate social worlds. *American Journal of Sociology, 113*(1), 1–40.

Espeland, W. N., & Sauder, M. (2009). Rankings and diversity. *Southern California Review of Law and Social Justice, 18*(3), 401–435.

Evans, J. (2010). Industry induces academic science to know less about more. *American Journal of Sociology, 116*(2), 389–452.

Foucault, M. (1977). *Discipline and punish*. London: Penguin Books.

Franck, G. (1998). *Ökonomie der Aufmerksamkeit: ein Entwurf*. München: Carl Hanser.

Frey, B. S. (2006). *Evaluitis – Eine neue Krankheit* (Working Paper No. 293). Institut für empirische Wirtschaftsforschung Zürich.

Ginsberg, B. (2011). *The fall of the faculty*. Oxford: Oxford University Press.

Hazelkorn, E. (2011). *Rankings and the reshaping of higher education: The Battle for world class excellence*. Basingstoke: Palgrave Macmillan.

Heinze, T., Shapira, P., Rogers, J. D., & Senker, J. M. (2009). Organizational and institutional influences on creativity in science. *Research Policy, 38*(4), 610–623.

Jansen, D., Wal, A., Franke, K., Schmoch, U., & Schubert, T. (2007). Drittmittel als Performanzindikator der wissenschaftlichen Forschung. Zum Einfluss von Rahmenbedingungen auf Forschungsleistungen. *Kölner Zeitschrift für Soziologie und Sozialpsychologie, 59*(1), 125–149.

Janssen, J., & Sass, E. (2008). Strategisches prozessorientiertes Qualitätsmanagement an der Hochschule (Fuldaer Modell). *QiW-Qualität in der Wissenschaft, 2*, 8–12.

Kaplan, R. S., & Norton, D. P. (1993, September/October). Putting the balanced scorecard to work. *Harvard Business Review*, 2–16.

Konsortium Bundesbericht wissenschaftlicher Nachwuchs (Ed.). (2013). *Bundesbericht wissenschaftlicher Nachwuchs*. Bielefeld: W. Bertelsmann Verlag.

Laffont, J. J., & Martimort, D. (2009). *The theory of incentives: The principal agent model*. Princeton: Princeton University Press.

Luhmann, N. (1996). *Die Realität der Massenmedien*. Wiesbaden: Westdeutscher Verlag.

Merton, R. K. (1968). The self-fulfilling prophecy. In R. K. Merton (Ed.), *The sociology of science* (pp. 424–436). Chicago: University of Chicago Press.

Merton, R. K. (1973[1942]). The normative structure of science. In R. K. Merton (Ed.), *The sociology of science* (pp. 267–278). Chicago: University of Chicago Press.

Meyer, J. W., & Rowan, B. (1977). Institutionalized organizations. Formal structures as myth and ceremony. *American Journal of Sociology, 83*(2), 340–363.

Münch, R. (1991). *Dialektik der Kommunikationsgesellschaft*. Frankfurt am Main: Suhrkamp.

Münch, R. (1995). *Dynamik der Kommunikationsgesellschaft*. Frankfurt am Main: Suhrkamp.

Münch, R. (2014). *Academic capitalism. Universities in the global struggle for excellence*. London/New York: Routledge.

Münch, R. (2016). *Academic capitalism*. Retrieved August 11, 2017, from http://politics.oxfordre.com/view/10.1093/acrefore/9780190228637.001.0001/acrefore-9780190228637-e-15.

Münch, R., & Baier, C. (2012). Institutional struggles for recognition in the academic field: The case of university departments in German chemistry. *Minerva, 50*(1), 97–126.

Meyerson, R. B. (1982). Optimal coordination mechanisms in generalized principal-agent problems. *Journal of Mathematical Economics, 10*(1), 67–81.

Parsons, T., & Platt, G. (1973). *The American University*. Cambridge, MA: Harvard University Press.

Porter, T. M. (1995). *Trust in Numbers: The pursuit of objectivity in science and public life*. Princeton: Princeton University Press.

Power, M. (1997). *The audit society: Rituals of verification*. Oxford: Oxford University Press.

Radder, H. (2010). *The commodification of academic research*. Pittsburgh: University of Pittsburgh Press.

Rudy, A. P., Coppin, D., Konefal, J., Shaw, B. T., Eyck, T. T., Harris, C., & Bush, L. (2007). *Universities in the age of corporate science. The UC Berkeley – Novartis controversy*. Philadelphia: Temple University Press.

Sanders, R. (2007, February 1). BP selects UC Berkeley to lead $ 500 million energy research consortium with partners. Lawrence Berkeley National Lab, University of Illinois. *UC Berkeley News*.

Sauder, M., & Espeland, W. N. (2009). The discipline of rankings: Tight coupling and organizational change. *American Sociological Review, 74*(1), 63–82.

Slaughter, S., & Leslie, L. L. (1997). *Academic capitalism: Politics, policies, and the entrepreneurial university*. Baltimore/London: The Johns Hopkins University Press.

Slaughter, S., & Rhoades, G. (2004). *Academic capitalism and the new economy. Markets, state, and higher education*. Baltimore/London: The Johns Hopkins University Press.

Tirole, J. (1999). Incomplete contracts: Where do we stand? *Econometrica, 67*(4), 741–781.

Tuchman, G. (2009). *Wannabe U: Inside the corporate university*. Chicago: University of Chicago Press.

Wieczorek, O., Beyer, S., & Münch, R. (2017). Fief and benefice feudalism. Two types of academic autonomy in US chemistry. *Higher Education, 73*(6), 887–907.

Wildavsky, B. (2010). *The great brain race. How global universities are reshaping the world*. Princeton: Princeton University Press.

WR (Wissenschaftsrat). (2008). *Pilotstudie Forschungsrating. Empfehlungen und Dokumentation*. Köln: Wissenschaftsrat.

Chapter 13
For or Against the European Banking Union: How Internationalisation Affects the Position-Takings of 'German-Speaking Economists' on Crisis Issues

Christian Schmidt-Wellenburg

Introduction: Taking Positions on Different Forms of Crisis

In today's world, economists are not only academic specialists of economic behaviour but have turned into public and media mediated authorities that shape what political and other social agents know about the world (Maeße 2015a). The ivory tower may still function as their home and powerbase, but their scope of action is global and their expertise has performative effects on the whole of society (MacKenzie 2007). Economic ideas and concepts structure how we see human behaviour and social life, how we think we could and should influence it and to what purpose (Vogl 2010).

Consequently, when crisis struck in 2008, economists were involved on all fronts at the same time. The financial instruments that failed only existed because financial economics had become highly mathematised over the years. The people made redundant were experts trained in economics and socialised as professionals in business schools and economic departments. Those who had deregulated financial markets in the years prior to this had been deeply absorbed by a basic set of economic ideas tightly interwoven in the overarching neoclassical paradigm: that unhampered (particularly financial) markets create optimal results, further the public good and are consequently of general public interest. At the same time, political action had to be taken, policies to counter the crisis were needed, and economists' expertise was sought by those in charge. As a result of this, the crisis did not

Electronic supplementary material The online version of this chapter (https://doi.org/10.1007/978-3-030-15387-8_13) contains supplementary material, which is available to authorized users.

C. Schmidt-Wellenburg (✉)
Faculty of Economic and Social Sciences, University of Potsdam, Potsdam, Germany
e-mail: cschmidtw@uni-potsdam.de

© Springer Nature Switzerland AG 2019
J. Blasius et al. (eds.), *Empirical Investigations of Social Space*,
Methodos Series 15, https://doi.org/10.1007/978-3-030-15387-8_13

diminish the importance of the profession of economics for modern economies and states alike (Mudge and Vauchez 2018). Instead it turned into a catalytic moment because it gave different factions within economics a chance to reposition themselves in order to gain or preserve their influence and their careers.

Statements and position-takings by economists in this situation roughly fall into two main categories. On the one hand, economists engage in detecting causes of the economic crisis and framing them as problems, proposing solutions to solve these problems and naming agents responsible for taking action (or accusing them of inaction). In June 2012, for example, the European Council decided to go ahead with forming the Single Supervisory Mechanism (SSM) and the European Stability Mechanism (ESM) because they saw it as "imperative to break the vicious circle between banks and sovereigns" (Euro Area Summit Statement on 29 June 2012). The announcement of effectively creating a European banking union was immediately met by resistance not only by German politicians, but also by German-speaking economists. Within less than a week, an open letter opposing an EU banking union was written and ultimately signed by 274 "German speaking economists" (Krämer et al. 2012). This almost instantaneously triggered a response by another group of economists in favour of a European solution to the banking crisis, who issued an open letter signed by 221 economists (Burda et al. 2012). Here, we have two opposing and strong statements on the feasibility of a European solution to a certain dimension of the economic crisis.

On the other hand, economists take issue with their own discipline and profession (Caspari and Schefold 2011), asking the question: "Why didn't we see this coming?" Reactions fell into two large camps that shared the perception that something has to change and aired their views in two open letters in 2009. The first letter was signed by 83 economists and pleaded to "Rescue 'Wirtschaftspolitik' at German Universities" (Aberle et al. 2009). It called for a renaissance of economics as a discipline geared towards consulting government on creating and maintaining institutions, a view deeply rooted in the tradition of German ordoliberalism (Pahl 2011a). The second letter was signed by 188 economists and strongly opposed this view, appealing to "Restructuring German Economics According to International Standards" (Adam et al. 2009). It argues that more internationalisation and mathematization is needed and attributes many of the failures of German academic economics to it lagging behind international developments.

Taking position on either the economic crisis or the crisis of economics is part of daily academic life for economists and the two are interconnected as shown by those 104 economists that signed one of the letters on the EU banking union as well as one of the letters on the state of the discipline. Opinions expressed are understood by other economists as statements made in certain economic discourses and used to locate speakers, to understand what certain speakers stand for and to position themselves in relation to them (Angermüller 2013). The magnitude of statements is estimated with reference to the speaker's position in relation to other economists, drawing on the knowledge of their achievements and career trajectories. At the same time, this kind of understanding is only possible because those observing and reacting to these statements have the ability to 'read' each other, always in perspective, due to their own professional socialisation.

If this holds true, an epistemological conclusion has to be drawn and a basic research hypothesis can be proposed. In order to explain opposing statements on either of the crises, we have to consider not only political, bureaucratic and economic circumstances but also the relationships between economists. This can be done by reconstructing the field of economists, by capturing the historical changes it underwent or is currently undergoing and by grasping how involvement in academic, political and professional practices is structured. Starting from these epistemological premises, it becomes possible to formulate the general hypothesis that position-takings on either of the crises are interconnected and both differences between and similarities of the statements can be seen as having structural homologies to the positions of the agents uttering them (Lebaron 2000).

German Economics as a Discipline in the Academic Field

The space of economists reconstructed here is part of the academic world and, as such, all agents in it hold the shared perception that they are engaging in scientific practices in order to produce true statements. Their work is driven by an interest in disinterestedness, as is the case in any field in which symbolic forms are produced (Bourdieu 1998a): The descriptions and explanations of economic phenomena are published as contributions to the imagined pool of objective knowledge, not as moves in the struggles to improve one's position, although they always also have this effect. The disinterestedness guarantees the autonomy of the academic field and, at the same time, the double-faced character of academic practices is an open secret known to anyone engaging in science (Bourdieu 2004: 25). This not only leads to many practices aimed at upholding disinterestedness but also results in two kinds of habitual abilities needed to engage in this practice and two kinds of objectified forms of such abilities – scientific and academic capital – that structure this field.

Scientific capital is a special form of symbolic capital that depends on the general cultural and more specific academic merits that agents have acquired (see also Münch in this volume). Such symbolic capital is the ability to objectify certain aspects of the world, to produce doxical categories and worldviews used throughout society as basic and natural ontologies (Bourdieu 1989). Symbolic capital materialises in publications and statistics which in turn indicate a scientist's reputation to his or her peers. This is at the heart of his or her ability to continue to produce scientific statements. This makes publications a form of scientific capital in two ways: each publication notes the historically objectified value-form prized at that very moment and becomes a sought-after resource for future engagement (Bourdieu 2004: 55). Hence, scientists struggle not only to produce these statements but also to influence how such statements should be legitimately made. At the same time, publications have a wide societal impact and contribute to symbolic domination beyond the academic field: they inform legitimate descriptions of the world, state what the facts are, what has to be done and who can do what.

Academic capital consists of academic merits in the form of qualifications obtained, the organisational influence and manpower one commands due to one's position in academic institutions such as universities, research institutes or academies and the financial resources one is able to thus mobilise. Here, the links with other forms of capital and hence other fields becomes apparent, particularly politics and the economy (Bourdieu 1998b: 36). In general, economic capital transfers into academic capital in the form of university and research funding, whereas political capital transfers into academic capital by deeming certain disciplines to be researching subjects of general public interest or directly contributing to the common good, which will again translate into funding. All positions in the academic field integrate scientific as well as academic capital and agents constantly engage in practices that transfer one into the other. The type of statements and the symbolic capital making them possible are the stakes fought over and, at the same time, statements translate into political influence, income, social prestige and social structural position. Practising science is a constant quest for knowledge and, at the same time, it is a struggle over legitimate forms of cognition and one's place in the social space.

Economists distinguish themselves from other disciplines through the theoretical assumptions and methods they use to produce true statements about economic phenomena other disciplines cannot produce (Schmidt-Wellenburg and Lebaron 2018). They share a mind-set that they have incorporated through their scientific socialisation in the PhD phase, a not only reflexive but in many ways tacit knowledge that allows them to produce economic research questions, utilise mathematical techniques in order to analyse data so as to reach economists' conclusions. Being a member of this tribe not only means being able to engage in the tribe's practice but, at the same time, being able to show the legitimate, objectified symbolic tokens associated with membership. It is those tokens that can be used to trace the differences between different agents: official qualifications including a hierarchy of institutions awarding these, publications including a hierarchy of types of publishing and outlets, membership of academic circles and associations and working for or consulting with political and economic agencies. All the different tokens can be used to envisage relationships of power as well as of meaning between economists, making it possible to trace the forms and distributions of scientific and academic capital in this specific disciplinary space.

Since World War II, German economics has become more and more internationalised. What was once "Nationalökonomie", a science closely associated with the nation state and focused on understanding the economy as a national-bound system, became linked to the US field of economists, when the US government and various philanthropic organisations such as the Ford Foundation became involved in rebuilding German academia (Hesse 2012). Exchanges of lecturers, researchers and students with the US were academic merits in their own right. Over time, together with US PhDs, these changed from being something extraordinary into common career opportunities, very often opening up possibilities for top German economists to pursue a career in the US. From the 1990s onwards, German PhD education was reinvented along the US paradigm of graduate schools, departments were restructured by denominating chairs along the trinity of mic-mac-metrics (micro-economics, macro-economics and econometrics) with assorted applied specialisations, and teaching today follows the global textbook canon (Colander 2008; Pahl 2011b; Maeße 2015b).

The potential for transnationalisation is linked to the universal languages of English and mathematics, modelling and statistics in economics. In addition, the focus of economics as a universal science attending to an anthropologically universal phenomenon, market exchange, and presenting general solutions for how to further and govern markets, frees academic economics from much of its historical rooting (Fourcade 2006). As a result, some areas of German economics became sucked into the transnational academic field of economists dominated by US-based academic institutions and international organisations. It is important not to forget, however, that this does not mean that all German academic economists hold a Chicago or Harvard PhD and publish in the American Economic Review. As Marion Fourcade (2009) has shown for the US, UK and France, the national pathways and institutional characteristics prevail to this day, but in each of the various national contexts, a transnational part of the field of economists has developed.

From this setting, we can derive the main hypothesis to be examined here: the politico-economic statements on the European banking union aired through the media and aimed at the field of politics are linked to the positions held by German economists, positions that have been greatly affected by the internationalisation of the field. Those who have profited from internationalisation and have been involved in recent years in researching transnational and European phenomena are those who opt for a European banking union. Those who opt for a national solution to the banking crisis, conversely, are those who have not profited from internationalisation because their careers are inextricably linked to the older and more nationally anchored areas of the field more closely associated with classic ordoliberal positions aimed at the nation state. Practice theory is at the base of the argument: the practical sense inherent to agents lets them engage in practices and produce behaviour with "family resemblances" (Wittgenstein 1980: 67) even across different social settings, ranging from research projects and publishing to engagement in politico-economic discourse. Hence, the task is to reconstruct the practical sense by showing the family resemblances and uncovering the main structural dimensions of the space occupied by economists underlying them.

Generating the Data

The individuals observed are the 480 signatories of the two letters on the EU banking union. The threshold that needs to be overcome to sign one of the letters (or indeed both, as 15 signatories did) is relatively low compared to other forms of taking sides on the issue. Hence, not only those who routinely engage in public discourse but also many academic backbenchers signed. This enables us to examine more than just the discursively highly vibrant areas of the German-speaking field of economists (cf. Hirte 2013), although it is not possible to quantify exactly who has self-selected him or herself from the overall population of economists. The reference made in all letters to the German language points to the high level of integration of German, Austrian and Swiss academia in which 82.9% of the signatories are employed as professors, with 74.6% having been born in or holding the citizenship of one of the three countries and 82.3% having received their PhD from a German-speaking university. The position of professor is held by a total of 90.6% of those in our study and lies at the basis of their ability to publicly voice their opinions and actually be heard (Schmidt-Wellenburg 2013: 342 ff.).

Curricula Vitae as Sources of Information

Indicators for the amount and composition of capital that economists hold can best be observed in their curricula vitae (CVs). Writing a CV enables academics to objectify their positions using standard means of evaluating their achievements and closely associated legitimate ambitions that make up their careers. At the same time, CVs are used in the field of economists to measure the worth of academic agents and to judge their potential. Standard evaluative practices involving CVs are hiring, applying for funding, and awarding grants and prizes. CVs are a synopsis of all different types of practices that are highly objectified, legitimated and worthy, in other words, the forms of capital in the field that empower those who hold them and position them in relation to others. At the same time, a CV reveals the standards of valuation used by the person writing it. As a result, differences between CVs become very important and should not be glossed over; they should not be aligned to one ideal model.

In addition to the CVs, alternative sources accessible online were used to gather information included in some CVs but not all: membership lists, Kürschners Deutscher Gelehrten-Kalender Online and Deutsches Hochschullehrerverzeichnis (both online databases on German-speaking academics), Munzinger Online (biographical database of German speakers), GEPRIS (German Project Information System, a database on academic research funding in Germany), Deutsche Nationalbibliothek (the German National Library), www.econbiz.de (database on publications in economic sciences) and the Social Science Citation Index (SSCI). Information from CVs and other sources was taken into account for up until the end of 2013, in order to document agents' properties held in summer 2012.

Grounded Theory Coding and Multiple Correspondence Analysis

In order to capture the practical sense inherent in a certain practice, the behaviour of various agents has to be closely monitored and compared to each other. The aim is to reconstruct the rules that make the communalities and differences intelligible to an observer. These reconstructed rules should not be confused with the habitual dispositions that effectively structure behaviour. They much more resemble a possible hypothesis about what happens that can be used to understand the situation (Schmidt 2012). If they cannot make what is observed intelligible, they need to be adjusted in the process of research. In order to create such a hypothesis, it is necessary to break with the everyday perception of reality (Bachelard 1978). The intuitive habitual understanding of practice has to be replaced by a reflected reconstruction of our understanding and the understanding of others. It helps here to concentrate not on the dispositions inherent in habitus, but on externalized, objectified and often directly exhibited properties of agents, which in turn correspond to their dispositions. These social properties have to be scientifically reconstructed by developing categories that order individual characteristics into collective properties (Bourdieu and Wacquant 1992).

This can be done by using grounded theory methodology (GTM). Here, hermeneutic interpretation structured by reflexive steps of open coding, contrasting codes and recoding is used to unearth the main meaning structures behind a certain class of social phenomena (Corbin and Strauss 2008). GTM and field analysis when seen in a practice theoretical framework share the basic methodological concept of creating knowledge by breaking with presuppositions, by reconstructing categories using the idea of maximal or minimal differences between observations, by reconstructing rules as observed sense and attempting to refine or redesign these by taking on more and different material, trying to adjust scientific statements and observed behaviour in a fitting process (Kelle 1994; Diaz-Bone 2007).

The system of codes developed from coding CVs and additional sources using the qualitative software MAXQDA links each economist to certain codes and hence properties. This information was exported and then examined and quantified using geometric data analysis (GDA). GDA allows us to explore the relationships between the properties of individuals in order to find the main structures in a given group of individuals (Le Roux and Rouanet 2004: 10ff.). It ideally complements GTM because it also uses cross tabulations of properties but to an extent that could never be checked by hand nor interpreted using a method that does not use chi-square statistics, dimension reduction using least square techniques and graphical representations of multidimensional spaces. On the other hand, without a controlled construction of categories as proposed by GTM, these instruments may well construct either meaningless or distorted spaces representing only official meanings because they are based on official categories.

GDA was used at two stages of the project. First, hierarchical agglomerative clustering (HAC, taken from SPAD 8.2), which follows the same inductive logic as GTM, was used to construct variables with multiple but mutually exclusive categories in a certain area of practice, plus one category for individuals who do not share any properties coded for this area. For this, the codes initially generated using GTM were subjected to a multiple correspondence analysis (MCA) including only individuals that had at least been assigned 'yes' for one of the codes examined. The cloud of individuals was then partitioned into sub-clouds using HAC (Le Roux and Rouanet 2004: 106). The decision where to cut the hierarchical tree and, consequently, how many partitions to use was made on the basis of three criteria. First, a big loss in inter-cluster inertia by the fusion of two clusters is seen as an indicator to use the prior partition. Second, properties that characterise the clusters had to be interpretable in context of the CVs in order to be able to formulate cluster characterizations that can then be assigned to each one of the economists as his or her property. Third, the number of individuals assigned to each cluster should not vary too much between classes making it it possible to capture differences between all individuals and not only between one major and a few minor classes, so as not to lose too much information for the final MCA.

Second, specific MCA (taken from SPAD 8.2) was used to reconstruct the space of properties and individuals because it allows us to set certain categories of active variables as passive, which is very useful for preventing an overrepresentation of some characteristics of individuals that are described by more than one modality. In addition, the individuals were weighted according to their stance towards the European banking union, since both camps were not equally present in the data set and this would have distorted the space towards the preferences of the larger group.

The categories used as active variables in the MCA fall into four broad classes that are important throughout the historical period of all careers observed: academic merits, scientific practices, academic memberships, and scientific funding or generating income by consulting or working in politics or business. In addition, two groups of passive variables were used. The first group encloses variables that further characterise individuals' scientific positions in more detail, but would add unnecessary complexity to the construction of the space, such as age. The second group consists of variables that allow us to describe the engagement of economists in politico-economic struggles, such as having affiliations with political parties and partisan foundations or as taking position on current political issues, or that enable us to pinpoint their stance on internationalising the discipline of economics. See the Online Appendix for a more detailed description of all variables.

Reconstructing the Space of German Economists in 2012

On the basis of the data described above, a specific MCA was conducted using 78 active properties grouped into 20 variables. The first three axes capture 77.66% of the overall variance when corrected using Benzécri's method (Le Roux and Rouanet

2004: 200 ff.; to calculate the correction by means of Benzécri's method for a specific MCA using SPAD 8.2 see the Excel macro accessible at www.cevipof.com/fr/l-equipe/l-equipe-administrative/bdd/equipe/43 written by Flora Chanvril.). Here, I will focus on the first (53.55%) and second axis (17.49%) in detail, since the third axis (6.72%) has only an indirect relationship to the position-takings of economists on the issue of the European banking union. The objective is to make sense of the main structural dimensions that organise the data by examining the categories that contribute to a large extent to the orientation of the axes (Le Roux and Rouanet 1998; Le Roux and Rouanet 2004: 217 f.). In a second step, I will present a theoretical argument that attempts to spell out the logic that links these properties together (Duval 2013: 115 f.).

Interpretation of Axis

The first axis can be interpreted as depicting the volume of capital and hence power in this space of economists. It constitutes a hierarchy of positions with lower, less well-equipped positions to the right and higher, better equipped positions to the left. The following seven variables account for approximately three quarters of the axis orientation and describe academic practices and achievements: average journal ranking 14.46%, current university 10.15%, type of funding 9.49%, non-German research institutes 9.35%, form of academic engagement 9.24%, PhD 8.87%, German research institute 8.43%. Engagement with governmental institutions or business hardly contributes. For a more detailed interpretation, I will take a closer look at those 17 modalities that contribute between 2.0% and 7.5% each to the axis and fall into two large groups, situated on both sides of the first axis running from right to left (Fig. 13.1).

Modalities that describe a low overall volume of capital, for instance, not having obtained funding (3.5%), never having being affiliated with a research institute (2.6%), and never having published an article in a journal that is ranked in the *Handelsblatt*-ranking (4.5%) are located to the right. Individuals situated here put their academic efforts into publishing monographs (2.9%) and engage in the areas of general economics and economic education, in management and financial sciences as well as statistics (3.6%). Those with a profile like this are most certainly not at the forefront of scientific progress as understood by the majority of economists in the field. Two other categories suggest why this could be the case: being an emeritus (2.1%) and being employed by a university of applied sciences (2.4%), which means much more teaching and often working in business or closely with businesses.

On the left-hand side, we see those that publish in journals ranked in the highest quartile of the *Handelsblatt*-ranking (7.3%), the other quartiles not contributing as much to the first axis, but nicely ordered from high to low along it. High-end journals such as *American Economic Review*, *Econometrica*, or *The Journal of Finance* are all in English, mostly US based and seen as the main outlets of current high-profile economic research, whereas non-US-based or even non-English-language

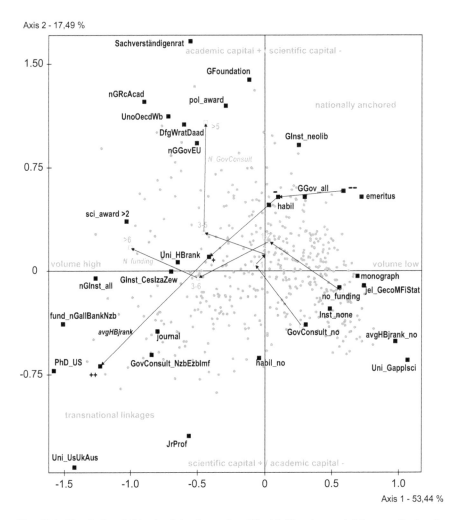

Fig. 13.1 Cloud of modalities in plain of axes 1 and 2 with 33 active modalities contributing the most to the plain and passive projection of the number of political consulting engagements and the number of funded research projects

journals rank in the lowest quartile. Publishing mainly in high ranking journals goes hand in hand with focusing academic production on publishing journal articles (5.1%). Economists located here have affiliations to non-German research institutes (7.5%) such as the US National Bureau of Economic Research and special German research institutes (3.1%) such as the CES-Ifo Institute in Munich, Institute of Labour Economics (IZA) in Bonn and the Centre for European Economic Research (ZEW) in Mannheim, all of which are internationally renowned for their scientific reputation and less for a certain ideological imprint.

Consulting or working at another type of internationally acclaimed research institution can also be seen here: national central banks, the European Central

Bank or the International Monetary Fund (2.3%). This goes hand in hand with acquiring funding from non-German research institutions, national central banks and other banks (5.0%). The career paths of economists located here often include a PhD from a US university (4.0%) as well as being employed by a US, UK or Australian university (2.2%) or at a German economics department ranked in the top 27 departments by the 2011 *Handelsblatt*-ranking (2.3%). It seems natural that having received more than two scientific awards (3.7%) can also be seen here, being both a form of symbolic recognition and masking of how this space works as a scientific universe: all the other forms of capital mentioned above, the struggles to obtain them and the positioning of those who do not fare well in these games to the right of the axis are forgotten when scientific genius is marked and put on display by bestowing some with many prizes (Lebaron 2006).

The capital volume interpretation is supported by the location of the passive categories that depict the amount of funding acquired: they run from right to left in rank order starting with no funding and ending with more than six projects. Funding of projects is important, since it is a basic requirement for employing people to work on one's own research agenda and enables them and oneself to publish and gain a good reputation. At the same time, obtaining funding in itself discloses to the community the economist's ability to produce important research; this then becomes a basis for accumulating further funding and a catalyst for transforming scientific into academic capital and vice versa. Positioned close to the first axis, it shows quite nicely who has acquired more or less capital applicable in this universe and how the different forms acquired are transformed into one another through research projects.

The second axis distinguishes the practices and accompanying properties connected to academic, educational and state bureaucratic institutions at the top – the heteronomous pole – from those that are more focused on research and the purely scientific universe at the bottom – the autonomous pole. Eight out of 20 active variables account for approximately three quarters of the axis inertia. They all have a link to national institutions such as being a member of German (7.19%) or other national (6.15%) scientific academies and learned societies or institutions of academic self-governance, being affiliated to German foundations (5.55%), consulting or having worked for government institutions (12.27%). Other variables describe a direct connection such as committing oneself or not to a career as civil servant by acquiring a *Habilitation* (10.70%) or holding a position (6.62%) at a state-funded university (5.55%). Other variables are explicitly denoted as purely scientific such as – again – publishing in high ranking journals (9.62%). In order to illustrate this dimension, I will refer to the 16 properties that contribute the most to the second axis, ranging between 2.1% and 6.1% each. They fall into two large groups, one located at the top and the other at the bottom of the two-dimensional space depicted here.

Prestigious academic positions can be found at the top, often seen as bestowing whoever holds them with high academic honours and, at the same time, the opportunity to continuously exert power in this space and on the set-up of this space. These include membership in the German Research Foundation (DFG) the German Council of Science and Humanities (WR) or the German Academic Exchange Service (DAAD) (7.19%), or membership of a non-German research council, academy or learned society (6.15%), or affiliation to a German philanthropic foundation mostly with a business background (5.55%). These are all institutions deeply anchored in the nation state context and responsible for directing funding, setting research agendas and structuring the allocation of academic capital. In addition, a *Habilitation* (5.17%) indirectly links up with nation state bureaucracies. Even more directly linked to national bureaucracies are those working for or consulting local, regional or national government institutions (2.18%), the German Council of Economic Experts (*Sachverständigenrat*) (3.38%), non-German governments or EU Commission or EU Parliament (3.54%), or international governance institutions such as the United Nations, the Organisation for Cooperation and Development (OECD) and the World Bank (2.1%). Being given political awards (2.27%), such as the *Bundesverdienstkreuz*, and having worked for or being affiliated to an ordoliberal or neoliberal institute or think tank (2.28%) such as the Walter Eucken Institute, the Initiative Neue Soziale Marktwirtschaft or the Mont Pelerin Society can also be seen as stemming from an engagement overlapping with the field of politics.

The economists located at the bottom are distinguished from the ones closely linked to state institutions at the top by not having acquired a *Habilitation* (6.09%) and currently holding or having held a junior professorship (3.8%). Again, these are the ones who also tend to publish in the top journals (3.38%) and concentrate on publishing journal articles (2.3%) in general. They are located at the autonomous pole and hence are also characterised by not consulting or having worked for any government institutions (2.62%). At the same time, the dimension is characterised by currently working at a US, UK or Australian university (3.25%), most of the universities in question being at the centre of internationalised economics.

The main characteristic of the second axis can be illustrated by plotting the number of consulting or job engagements with government institutions, one of the supplementary variables not used to construct the space itself. It runs from the lower right quadrant to the upper left quadrant and nicely illustrates how the importance of bureaucratic capital stemming from or linked to political institutions increases as a source of power in the academic context. The third axis will only be touched upon. It is again constructed by opposing scientific autonomy and academic heteronomy, although heteronomy is this time created by an overlap with the business world. Interestingly enough, this axis does not correspond to either a positive or negative stance towards the European banking union as a solution to the politico-economic crisis and since it only accounts for 6.72% of the total variance, it will not be examined any further.

Overall, the first axis can be interpreted as distinguishing positions by the overall amount of capital potent in this space. The second axis then distinguishes between academic capital built on positions in academic and, in the wider sense, state-bureaucratic institutions, and scientific capital as a reputation built on publishing research results acknowledged as new and well-founded. As is the case with many analyses that focus on hierarchies and diversity of certain social areas, the diversity documented at the higher end seems to be greater than at the lower end. This is not due to ignorance, but is in itself a symptom of the prevailing domination: it is created by observing practices such as CVs that are drenched with symbolic power and function as important instruments of symbolic violence. Bearing this in mind, we can use the attributes that objectify the different forms and amounts of capital in certain areas of this space to understand the basic differences and communalities between economists located within it.

In the bottom right quadrant, we find those who rank low in today's internal hierarchy of economics, have not published much after their first book, generally their PhD, do not publish in internationally acclaimed journals and have only obtained minor positions in academic institutions or are located at the margins of economics proper. Economists in the top right quadrant have a fair amount of academic capital as emeriti and engage with local, regional and national institutions of government and especially ordoliberal and neoliberal think tanks. Economists in the top left quadrant are highly active in national and international government institutions and, at the same time, in national academic institutions, from where their high amount of academic capital stems. Their scientific counterparts in the lower left quadrant are located close to sources of scientific reputation and autonomy as well as government institutions autonomous from national and everyday politics such as the IMF and the ECB.

The space is structured by transnationalisation increasing from top right to bottom left and opposing nationally anchored economists with those with transnational linkages. These transnational linkages are accompanied by an increase in autonomy to follow the latest research programmes and to detach oneself from producing practically applicable governmental insights, ideal typically located at the other side of the space with the *Sachverständigenrat*. It is important to bear in mind that economists with transnational linkages do not need to be firmly rooted in other nationally anchored fields, for example, the US or French field of economists that are structured along the same logics (Lebaron 2001: 103) but would in other similar contexts most probably also be located at the transnational fringes. The transnationalisation of this space is also a generational phenomenon, as can be ascertained by the passive PhD cohorts (see Fig. 13.2): younger generations without a *Habilitation* and holding junior professorships benefit from changed rules of the game that go hand in hand with the internationalisation of the discipline, whereas older generations – emeriti with *Habilitation* qualifications – might lose out as change sweeps through the space and pushes them into the top right-hand corner.

Grounding Statements on European Banking Union and Future of Economics in the Space

In general, one can observe that the position-takings on the issue of the EU banking union are located in the midst of the cloud of individuals, since it is a property many share: those in favour of it are located in the top right and those against in the bottom left quadrant, with those having signed both letters closer to the barycentre. Similar to these other non-active properties depicting economists' stance on the future of

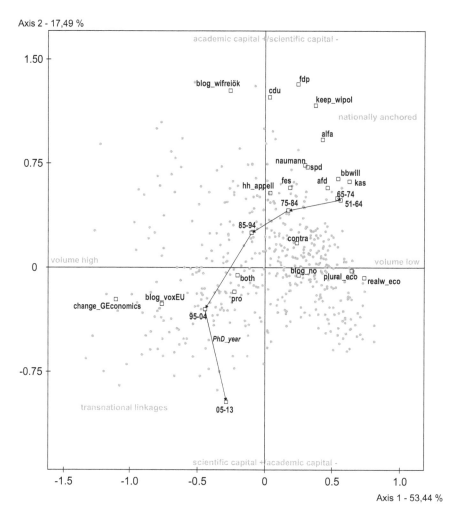

Fig. 13.2 Cloud of modalities in plain of axes 1 and 2 with passive projection of PhD cohorts and of position-takings on EU banking union, future of economics, political engagement and publishing in blogs

the discipline, their political engagment and writing in blogs are also arranged along the descending years of PhD thesis (see Fig. 13.2) and the ascending rank of journals in which articles are published (see Fig. 13.1), making the process of the transnationalisation of the space of economists the main indicator for understanding these position-takings in the politico-economic discourse.

Towards the bottom left we have economists who have built their careers on engaging with international institutions governing an internationalised economy as well as with international research institutes and universities, coming from generations of economists that did not confine their research to national economies. At the top right we have older economists from generations, mostly past the peak of their careers, that research national economies, engage with national political institutions, and produce as well as continue to apply insights into how to govern these on the national, regional and local level. This is also evident from their engagement with political parties ranging from neoliberal and nationalist populist movements to all the established parties, and it shows in their work for party foundations. Engagement for the first wave of neoliberal restructuring of Germany, illustrated here by signing the Hamburger Appell in 2005, is also located in this area. It follows the national logic anchored in this region of space, since it was directed at national policies to reduce regulation, the cost of labour, state exposure and involvement in order to increase productivity and understood in the framework of nation states competing. The logic behind it portrayed the EU as a competitive arena in which the current state of struggles was objectified by EU or OECD rankings and the underlying imperative was to 'do better than the other nations' in order not to fall behind and become last in line: "Die rote Laterne [back light]" (Sinn 2003). When taking into account that writing in a blog involves more than signing letters and that a higher position transfers better into symbolic capital, which can be used to do just that, the location of writing for one of the neoliberal blogs at the top or writing for one of the pro-European blogs in the bottom left quadrant – both left of the barycentre – becomes apparent.

The stances taken towards the future of economics correspond well with the position-takings on the European banking union. Having signed to "Rescue 'Wirtschaftspolitik' at German Universities" is located in the top right quadrant, "Restructuring German Economics According to International Standards" in the bottom left quadrant. These differences can also be understood by reference to economists' careers in either internationalised economics or nationally anchored ordoliberalism. That the economists located in the bottom right quadrant are not engaged much in these debates seems obvious for two reasons. They are either located at the fringes of economics as a university discipline having no PhD, hardly publishing or not publishing at all, or working at a university for applied sciences, or they come from or are closely associated with other disciplines. It is at this point in space that the properties of engaging in the movement for "Real World Economics" and "Plurale Ökonomie" are located; heretics who would like to change much more than just replacing an older orthodoxy with a new international one (cf. Davis 2008).

Conclusion

The results presented show that position-takings by German-speaking economists on two issues still highly contested today – the 'internationalisation' of German-speaking economics and the EU banking union as a solution to the EU banking crisis – were structured in 2012 by the positions held in the German-speaking field of economists. The positions are made intelligible by reconstructing the space of economists using GTM and MCA to unearth the main dimensions that structure relationships between economists. The main axes – capital volume and the opposition of academic and scientific capital – resemble structures of hierarchy and differentiation between heteronomy and autonomy found in other academic fields (Bourdieu 1988; see also Münch and Baier & Schmitz in this volume). They intersect with two historical developments outside of but influencing the field. The first is the emergence of a European field of bureaucracy (Georgakakis and Rowell 2013) that offers not only new objects of research but also new opportunities for economists to engage with politics and hence access to new sources of academic capital. The second is the emergence of a new class of international research institutes, some located close to Eurocracy, others beyond it such as scientised national central banks, the ECB, and above all the IMF (Mudge and Vauchez 2016), that offer new sources of scientific capital to economists and integrate them into transnational linkages.

During the economic crisis that has prevailed since 2009, both developments have not declined but picked up momentum, leading to a situation where ever more possibilities open up for economists in the transnational realm (Schmidt-Wellenburg 2017). This contributes to an increase of autonomy from political institutions anchored in nation states and to a transnationalisation of the field (see also Swartz in this volume) and it creates the two opposing 'camps' of economists, one higher in the field hierarchy with international linkages, the other lower in the field hierarchy and anchored in the nation state, that make the different position-takings intelligible. At the same time, the crisis has not led to a fundamental overhaul, neither with reference to the politico-economic discourse on banking regulation nor on the future of the discipline of economics itself, but to incremental changes. It seems as if a transnational pragmatism, already strong before in both of the discursive realms, has managed to become the new general guiding principle. The high hopes associated with heterodox economic policies and heterodox economists at the beginning of the crisis were grounded by the forces of the field.

References

Aberle G., et al. (2009, May 5). Rettet die Wirtschaftspolitik an den Universitäten! *Frankfurter Allgemeine Zeitung*.

Adam, K., et al. (2009, June 14). Baut die deutsche Volkswirtschaft nach internationalen Standards um! *Handelsblatt*.

Angermüller, J. (2013). How to become an academic philosopher. *Sociología Historíca, 2*, 263–288.

Bachelard, G. (1978). *Die Bildung des wissenschaftlichen Geistes*. Frankfurt am Main: Suhrkamp.

Bourdieu, P. (1988). *Homo Academicus*. Stanford: Stanford University Press.

Bourdieu, P. (1989). Social space and symbolic power. *Sociological Theory, 4*, 18–26.

Bourdieu, P. (1998a). *Practical reason*. Cambridge: Polity Press.

Bourdieu, P. (1998b). *Vom Gebrauch der Wissenschaft*. Konstanz: Universitätsverlag Konstanz.

Bourdieu, P. (2004). *Science of science and reflexivity*. Cambridge: Polity Press.

Bourdieu, P., & Wacquant, L. (1992). *An invitation to reflexive sociology*. Cambridge: Polity Press.

Burda, M., et al. (2012, July 9). Ökonomenaufruf im Wortlaut. Zur Europäischen Bankenunion. *Frankfurter Allgemeine Zeitung*.

Caspari, V., & Schefold, B. (Eds.). (2011). *Wohin steuert die ökonomische Wissenschaft?* Campus: Frankfurt am Main.

Colander, D. (2008). The making of a global European economist. *KYKLOS, 61,* 215–236.

Combes P. P., & Linnemer, L. (2010). *Inferring missing citations: A quantitative multi-criteria ranking of all journals in economics.* CREQAM Document de Travail.

Corbin, J., & Strauss, A. (2008). *Basics of qualitative research. Techniques and procedures for developing grounded theory.* London: Sage.

Davis, J. (2008). The turn in recent economics and return of orthodoxy. *Cambridge Journal of Economics, 32,* 349–366.

Diaz-Bone, R. (2007). Die französische Epistemologie und ihre Revision. Zur Rekonstruktion des methodologischen Standortes der Foucaultschen Diskursanalyses. *Forum Qualitative Sozialforschung, 8*(2), Art. 24.

Duval, J. (2013). L'analyse des correspondences et la construction des champs. *Actes de la Recherche en Sciences Sociales, 200,* 111–123.

Fourcade, M. (2006). The construction of a global profession: The transnationalization of economics. *American Journal of Sociology, 112,* 145–194.

Fourcade, M. (2009). *Economists and societies.* Princeton: Princeton University Press.

Georgakakis, D., & Rowell, J. (Eds.). (2013). *The field of Eurocracy.* Houndsmill: Palgrave Macmillan.

Hesse, J. O. (2012). The 'Americanisation' of West German economics after the second world war: Success, failure, or something completely different? *The European Journal of History of Economic Thought, 19,* 67–98.

Hirte, K. (2013). *ÖkonomInnen in der Finanzkrise. Diskurse. Netzwerke. Initiativen.* Marburg: Metropolis-Verlag.

Kelle, U. (1994). *Empirisch begründete Theoriebildung. Zur Logik und Methodologie interpretativer Sozialforschung.* Weinheim: Deutscher Studien Verlag.

Krämer, W., et al. (2012). *Bankenkrise. Aufruf von 273 deutschsprachigen Wirtschaftsprofessoren.* Retrieved Janurary 8, 2015, from https://www.statistik.tu-dortmund.de/kraemer.html.

Le Roux, B., & Rouanet, H. (1998). Interpreting axes in multiple correspndence analysis. In J. Blasius & M. Greenacre (Eds.), Visualization of categorical data (pp. 197–220). San Diego: Academic.

Le Roux, B., & Rouanet, H. (2004). *Geometric data analysis. From corrspondence analysis to structural data analysis.* Dordrecht: Kluwer Academic Publishers.

Lebaron, F. (2000). *La croynace économique. Les économistes entre science et politique.* Paris: Le Seuil.

Lebaron, F. (2001). Economists and the economic order. The field of economists and the field of power in France. *European Societies, 3,* 91–110.

Lebaron, F. (2006). Nobel' economists as public intellectuals: The circulation of symbolic capital. *International Journal for Contemporary Sociology, 43,* 88–101.

MacKenzie, D. (Ed.). (2007). *Do economists make markets? On the performativity of economics.* Princeton: Princeton University Press.

Maeße, J. (2015a). Economic experts: A Discoursice political economy of economics. *Journal of Multicultural Discourses, 10,* 279–305.

Maeße, J. (2015b). *Eliteökonomen.* Wiesbaden: Springer VS.

Mudge, S., & Vauchez, A. (2016). Fielding supernationalism: The European Central Bank as a field effect. *The Sociological Review Monographs, 64,* 146–169.

Mudge, S., & Vauchez, A. (2018). Too embedded to fail: The ECB and the necessity of calculating Europe. *Historical Social Research, 43*(3), 248–273.

Pahl, H. (2011a). Die Wirtschaftswissenschaften in der Krise. Vom massenemdialen Diskurs zu einer Wissenssoziologie der Wirtschaftswissenschaften. *Schweizer Zeitschrift für Soziologie, 37,* 259–281.

Pahl, H. (2011b). Textbook Economics: Zur Wissenschaftssoziologie eines Wirtschaftswissenschaftlichen Genres. *PROKLA, 41*(164), 369–387.

Schmidt, R. (2012). *Soziologie der Praktiken.* Frankfurt am Main: Suhrkamp.

Schmidt-Wellenburg, C. (2013). *Die Regierung des Unternehmens. Managementberatung im neoliberalen Kapitalismus*. Konstanz: Universitätsverlag Konstanz.

Schmidt-Wellenburg, C. (2017). Europeanisation, stateness and professions: What role do economic expertise and economic experts play in European political integration? *European Journal of Cultural and Political Sociology, 4*, 1–27.

Schmidt-Wellenburg, C., & Lebaron, F. (2018). There is no such thing as "the Economy". Economic phenomena analysed from a field-theoretical perspective. *Historical Social Research, 43*(3), 7–38.

Sinn, H. W. (2003). *Die rote Laterne. Die Gründe für Deutschlands Wachstumsschwäche und die notwendigen Reformen*. Paderborn: Schöningh.

Vogl, J. (2010). *Das Gespenst des Kapitals*. Zürich: Diaphanes.

Wittgenstein, L. (1980). *Philosophische Untersuchungen*. Frankfurt am Main: Suhrkamp.

Chapter 14
Mapping the Public of a Literature Festival with MCA: Overall Cultural Capital vs. Specific Literary Capital

Myrtille Picaud, Jérôme Pacouret, and Gisèle Sapiro

Introduction

In France, festival audiences offer a space in which to examine the transformations of cultural practices in the last 20 years, besides the national quantitative surveys on these issues. The first important research on festivals was dedicated to the theater festival in Avignon (Ethis 2002; Fabiani 2008). Since then, other surveys have been conducted on music festivals (Négrier et al. 2010; Wynn 2015). However, despite the growing prominence of literature festivals since the 1990s, until recently their audiences have been subject to little research. Apart from our own survey on the French festival *Les Correspondances de Manosque*, few academic surveys have been conducted on these events (Giorgi et al. 2011; Giorgi 2011; Driscoll 2014; Kulkarni et al. 2017).

The sociological survey that we undertook during the 2011 edition of the *Les Correspondances de Manosque* festival[1] (see next section) aimed to explore this new form of cultural mediation in the reading sector and its role in the literary field (Sapiro et al. 2015; Sapiro 2016). *Les Correspondances de Manosque* was one of the first literature festivals to be organized in France. Founded in 1999, it

Electronic supplementary material The online version of this chapter (https://doi.org/10.1007/978-3-030-15387-8_14) contains supplementary material, which is available to authorized users.

[1] The authors would like to thank the festival's organizers for their help, as well as Brigitte Le Roux, Jean-Louis Fabiani and Julien Duval for their insightful comments on the questionnaire and MCA. Hélène Seiler-Juilleret, Aude Servais, and Jasmine Van Deventer contributed to the survey, and Pernelle Issenhuth helped prepare and analyze the data.

M. Picaud (✉) · J. Pacouret · G. Sapiro
Centre d'Etudes Européennes et de Politique Comparée (CEE), Paris, France
e-mail: sapiro@ehess.fr

© Springer Nature Switzerland AG 2019
J. Blasius et al. (eds.), *Empirical Investigations of Social Space*,
Methodos Series 15, https://doi.org/10.1007/978-3-030-15387-8_14

focuses on contemporary French literature. Taking place in the southern town of Manosque, close to Marseille, at the end of September, the festival is visited mostly by local residents (7 out of 10 live in the region Provence-Alpes-Côte d'Azur), but it also attracts people from other parts of France, as shown by our results, attesting to the legitimacy it has acquired at a national level. This legitimacy is confirmed by the fact that one of its founders and main organizers, Olivier Chaudenson, was appointed director of the *Maison de la poésie* in Paris in 2015. The festival runs from Wednesday to Sunday and encompasses around 60 events. Most of these events are free events: interviews or debates given on the city's public squares by the invited authors, or readings of their works, but there are also paying literary concerts each night in the local theater. These are conceived of as a way of broadening the audience's social origins, by inviting musicians who mainly perform *chanson française*, a middlebrow musical genre. The festival events are attended by a large and diverse audience, whose numbers are difficult to estimate, but we counted between 170 and 250 persons at free events taking place on the Hôtel-de-Ville square, between 60 and 150 on the smaller squares (Herbès and Marcel Pagnol), and observed that the Manosque theater, which seats 700, is usually full for the paying events.

Like earlier literary gatherings, festivals fulfill a ritual function, which consists in reinforcing the *illusio*, i.e. a belief in the value of literature (Bourdieu 1993; Bourdieu 1995). However, unlike their predecessors – in particular the Parisian *cénacles*, which sustained the cohesion of a group of peers, all professional writers – literature festivals aim above all to support the belief of the public of laypersons. Regarding the prevailing cultural function of literature festivals and their programming, we can thus expect the audience to be, on average, endowed with more cultural capital compared to more commercial events, such as book fairs for instance.

While analyzing the festival's organization and settings enabled us to display the modern ways in which the broader public's belief in the symbolic value of literature is sustained, our survey of its audience, and more specifically our multiple correspondence analysis (MCA), reveals a particular kind of cultural capital: literary capital. This capital is characterized by regular cultural practices focused on literature (reading literary works and critics, knowing about authors, attending literary events), and supported by dispositions related to literary education and/or to occupations such as teaching literature or working as a librarian. The public endowed with specific literary capital differs in its cultural practices from the audience members endowed with other forms of cultural capital, who attend all kinds of festivals or performances (theater, music), but whose reading practices are less intense. Thus we distinguish reading practices from cultural entertainment ('going out').

After a presentation of the survey and of the construction of the variables, the three first axes of the MCA are analyzed. They show the different ways in which audience members engage with the festival, as well as with other literary and cultural practices.

The Survey and the Definition of the Variables

The research during the festival included interviews with the organizers, observation of the events, and a survey of audience members, on which we focus here. A questionnaire was distributed to festivalgoers over the festival's 5 day duration, be it before, during, or after the events taking place in the city's public squares and at Manosque's theater (for more details on the survey, see Sapiro et al. 2015). Written after exploratory interviews with the festival's organizers, the questionnaire also draws on French national surveys (Donnat 2009, in particular) on cultural practices to allow for comparison. This enables a better evaluation of the volume of cultural capital that the festival's audiences are endowed with, and of the intensity of their cultural practices. It covers three main topics: the participation in the festival (13 closed-ended questions, 4 open-ended questions); cultural practices, including reading, writing, and going out (18 closed-ended questions, 2 open-ended questions); and socio-demographic characteristics (17 questions). 467 questionnaires were filled in before, during, or after events. Because the questionnaire was quite long (around 30 minutes), most of the forms were filled in directly by audience members, sometimes with assistance from our research team; 10 percent were administered directly.

Our quantitative study is based on these questionnaires. We applied MCA to 460 of these questionnaires. Each individual in the MCA attended at least one event during the festival. 445 of them are included as active individuals and 15 of them are supplementary individuals. This small group of supplementary individuals comprises high school students accompanied by their teachers, whose answers differed strongly from the other individuals'. They were excluded from the group of active individuals in order to prevent their answers from contributing disproportionately to the formation of the axis.

The MCA has 81 active variables and 191 active modalities (see the Appendix for a complete presentation of the variables, Tables 14.O2, 14.O3, 14.O4, and 14.O5). In order to prepare and read the MCA, these variables are divided into three groups. A first set of active variables describes the respondents' knowledge of the festival and their attendance practices: the first time they came; why they came; how many and what kind of events they attended; which events they preferred; whether or not they talked to other audience members, to authors or to critics; how many and which guest writers they knew prior to the festival, etc. This group has 26 active variables and 77 active modalities.

A second set of questions is dedicated to the attendance of other cultural events. 16 active variables and 32 modalities concern the respondents' other cultural practices during the previous year: whether they went to theatrical plays or movie screenings, attended concerts of various music styles (such as jazz, rock, classical, world music, etc.), or visited other music, theater, or film festivals.

The last group of active questions focuses on their activities related to literature – that is their reading and writing practices – as well as their participation in other literary events. This set of questions was more detailed, comprising 39 active variables and 82 active modalities. It included questions such as how many books were read during the previous year; what kind of books and novels were most often read; what newspapers and journals were read; attendance of any other literature festivals, book fairs, public readings, literature conferences, or writing workshops during the previous year; whether they write novels, short stories, plays, poetry, or journals; whether any of their texts was published and where. Respondents were also asked Yes/No questions about the types of books they read (from contemporary French or foreign literature to comics, cooking and gardening manuals, or scientific books) – that is, reading practices pointing to different levels of cultural legitimacy, and different kinds of novels, ranging from highbrow to lowbrow fiction.

We used the specific MCA method to transform some modalities in the active variables into supplementary modalities (for more on this method, see Le Roux 2004: 378–394; Le Roux and Rouanet 2004; Lebaron and Le Roux 2015). These are mostly 'junk categories', i.e. answers left blank by the respondents. However, non-responses are sometimes as interesting as answers. Two exceptions were made to categorizing missing answers as supplementary modalities: One question asked about the number of events respondents thought they would attend. The answer 'don't know' was made into an active modality, because it sheds light on the respondents' level of interest and knowledge about the festival. The second question pertains to knowledge of the authors: Respondents were asked whether they knew any prior to the festival, and then asked to write down names. When audience members stated that they knew guest writers but wrote no names, their response was made into an active modality. Of course, they could simply have been too lazy to write any names, but they could also be pretending to know these authors, an element that we analyzed as an indicator for cultural 'good will'.

The MCA also includes 10 supplementary variables, adding up to 74 supplementary modalities. These questions regard the socio-demographics, careers, and social origins of the attendees: sex, age, city of residence, family and marital status, occupational status, levels and types of academic degrees (see Appendix, Table 14.O1). These are used as supplementary variables because our aim was to see how the respondents differ according to their cultural and literary practices and tastes, as well as their participation in the festival, and then to test the hypothesis that these oppositions are linked to social and economic characteristics. This group of supplementary variables is thus used here as explanatory factors for the geometric distribution of the cultural practices.

Compared to other kinds of festivals, the audience of this literature festival has specific characteristics. Close to 75 percent of the respondents were women. This proportion of women can be explained by the gendering of literature reading among the French population: according to the last national survey (2008), twice as many women as men read novels (other than crime novels). The respondents' average age is 51 years old. Elderly people are overrepresented, with 52.2% of the respondents being between 35 and 64 years old, and 22 percent older than 65. The overrepresentation can be explained by the free time necessary to attend the festival, which also takes place on weekdays that are not holidays. This hypothesis is confirmed by the fact that the average age of respondents decreases during the weekend, and by the overrepresentation of retirees: 37.1 percent of the respondents are retirees, which is twice their share of the French population in 1999, and much more than their percentage (2.1 percent) amongst the audience members at the theater festival in Avignon in 2004 (Ethis et al. 2008).

Similarly to Avignon, respondents belonging to the upper middle and upper classes are overrepresented, compared to their share in the French society: 44.6 percent are high-status occupations (the French *cadres et professions intellectuelles* category), with many civil servants and teachers, intellectual or artistic professions, and fewer private sector managers, engineers, and representatives of the medical and law professions. Respondents with intermediary positions (*professions intermé-diaires*), mostly working in the fields of health, social work or teaching, represent 27.6 percent, whereas service workers (*employés*) comprise only 7.1 percent (around a quarter of their share in the French working population in 2012). Businessmen and women, skilled crafts workers, and shop-owners represent 4.1 percent (a little more than their national share), and fewer than 2 percent of respondents are blue collar workers, although 20.8 percent belong to this category amongst French workers in 2012. 11.3 % have never worked (students belong to this modality).

The role that cultural capital plays in attendance of the Manosque festival can also be seen in the high levels of educational achievement amongst the respondents. These are comparable to those at Avignon, but given the difference in age between festivalgoers, audience members at Manosque appear to have even higher academic credentials: 57.4 percent have at least a bachelor's degree (a similar percentage compared to Avignon in 2004), 17.6 percent have a two-year higher education diploma, 10.9 percent have a high school diploma (baccalaureate) and 8 percent have not graduated from high school. More than half of the respondents with a university degree have studied literature, foreign languages or social sciences and humanities. This suggests a specific type of cultural capital, as we will see later.

Applying MCA to the questionnaire reveals more clearly the diversity within the respondents' cultural and literary practices, and enables us to link these practices to the diverse ways in which the audience members engage with the festival. It also allows us to show how these cultural practices and festival attendance patterns are inscribed in different occupational and social backgrounds.

To interpret each axis, we selected only the modalities whose contributions exceed the average contribution. We present the first three axes, which account for 12 percent of the total MCA variance, or 67 percent according to Benzécri's modified rate. The latter gives an idea of the importance of all three axes (Le Roux and Rouanet 2004).

Frequency of Cultural Practices and Overall Volume of Cultural Capital

The first factor of the MCA shows that the attendees' cultural and literary practices vary in their frequency and also in their cultural legitimacy. Their engagement with the festival (number and types of events attended) is correlated to these other cultural and literary practices.

This factor helps to identify a first group of participants who know the guest writers and attend many events of various kinds during the festival (Fig. 14.1, on the right). These audience members also state that they discussed literary issues with guest writers and literature professionals (such as publishers and critics) while at Manosque. Their reading practices are well adjusted to the festival's program; they read several books every month and enjoy French contemporary literature. The year before this festival, they attended other literature-related events, such as public readings and other literary festivals, and they also read literary magazines or supplements. Some of them write poetry, short stories, or novels. These literature

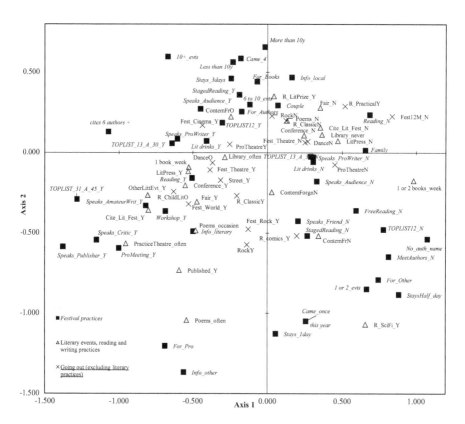

Fig. 14.1 Axes 1 and 2: active modalities with above-average contribution

enthusiasts also enjoy other highbrow cultural practices: they attend festivals, concerts, plays, movie screenings, and dance performances. Unsurprisingly, higher-ranking civil servants, librarians, people working in the media or the cultural fields, and (to a lesser extent) teachers are overrepresented in this group of respondents with high cultural capital and frequent highbrow cultural and literary practices. The fact that the respondents most engaged with the festival are endowed with high volumes of cultural capital is a result of Manosque's specific literary line-up: The festival focuses on living authors, many of them quite young. These writers are located at the pole of small-scale circulation of the literary field: They do not write bestsellers, but have won literary awards (though not the most prestigious ones) and are recognized by their peers and by literary critics (Bourdieu 1993; Bourdieu 1995). The festival's events also take a specific form, which also explains this social selection amongst attendees; events are not academic courses *per se*, but they require listening skills comparable to the ones people learn at university or at the library.

On the other side of axis 1, we find people who spend little time at the festival, who do not know the guest writers, and who do not attend the festival's main events (that is, interviews with writers). These audience members read fewer books than other participants (one or two per semester). Some of them declare less legitimate literary tastes. These can be oriented towards forms of literature that are absent from the festival (science fiction for example). On this side of axis 1, we also find people who attend neither movie screenings nor theatrical plays. Most of these participants belong to the working class or lower middle class, which are underrepresented among the festival audience.

This axis shows that attending the Manosque festival usually correlates with having a great amount of cultural capital (Figs. 14.2 and 14.3).

Differentiated Forms of Participation

The second axis of the MCA reveals the intensity and duration of respondents' participation in the festival. These various ways of engaging with the festival are related to different writing and reading habits. They are also distinguished by age groups (the supplementary variable about age is dispersed alongside axis 2, with the youngest at the bottom and the oldest on top, Fig. 14.3).

At the top of axis 2 (Figs. 14.1 and 14.3), we find people who participated in many festival events, over a period of several days. They have been attending the festival for many years. The guest writers and their books are their main interest in the festival. They often come with their husbands or wives, although women respondents are overrepresented on this side of axis 2. These longtime attendees are older than the average respondent (who is 51 years old). In summary, the group of participants at the top of axis 2 represents the core of the audience (Fig. 14.1), whose literary tastes are well adapted to the festival's literary line-up. But this core faithful group is not necessarily composed of audience members whose cultural and literary practices are the most intense and diverse.

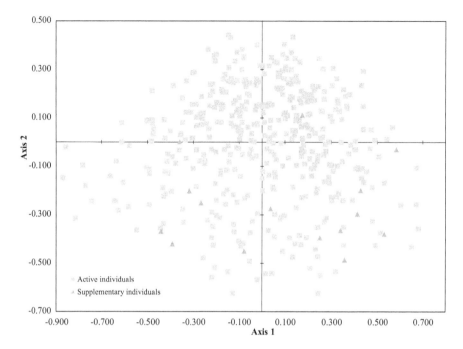

Fig. 14.2 Axes 1 and 2: active and supplementary individuals (Individuals are represented without using the transition formula)

At the bottom of axis 2, the participants' cultural practices and social backgrounds are quite diverse, as shown by the dispersal of individuals on Fig. 14.2. Several types of attendees can be identified. Some of them are librarians, who know many of the guest authors, including those that the rest of the respondents fail to mention. Librarians attend the festival for several days, and also attend other events related to literature. Students form another group of participants (the supplementary individuals that are in high school also appear here) whose literary tastes are quite different from the festival's line-up; consequently, they attend the festival only for a short period of time. Lastly, some participants state that their presence at Manosque is determined by work-related reasons. They only attend a few events, and generally work in the cultural and media fields or are students. The modalities for those not knowing the invited authors prior to the festival, as well as those referring to personal writing practices (writing novels or poetry, having been published), also appear at the bottom of axis 2. These categories point to a group amongst respondents who attend the festival for work-related reasons, engage in conversations with literary critics and professionals, and express an interest in the way authors work. Writing also plays a part in their presence at the

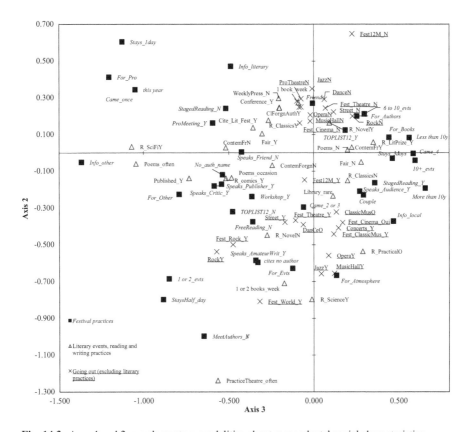

Fig. 14.3 Axes 1 and 2, supplementary modalities about respondents' social characteristics

festival. However, amateur writing is not central in the festival's self-presentation and organization; on the contrary, this variable actually contributes to the divide between professional and amateur participants.

While many of the participants come to the festival because they have intense reading practices and share the festival's literary tastes, some respondents' attendance is also motivated by multiple factors, such as one's own writing project.

The Specificity of Literary Practices: Reading vs. Going Out

It is on the third axis of the MCA that what we have termed 'literary capital' appears most clearly (see Figs. 14.4 and 14.6). As shown in Table 14.01 (Appendix), the third axis distinguishes between two groups of festivalgoers according to

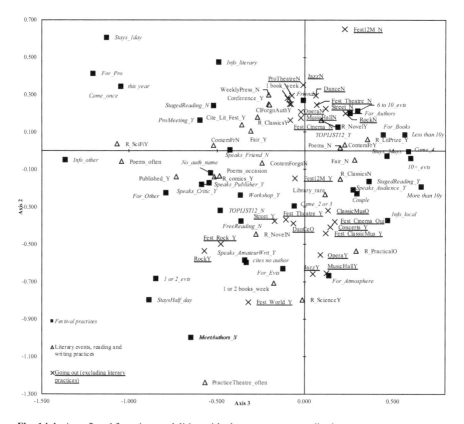

Fig. 14.4 Axes 2 and 3: active modalities with above-average contribution

their cultural practices and the events they favor during the festival. The first group comprises respondents more likely to attend performances (music concerts, theatrical plays etc.), the second those for whom reading literature is more central to their cultural practices. However, rather than clearly separating the audiences at the festival into two distinct poles, the respondents appear to be spread out on a continuum between both, because many tend to accumulate different types of cultural practices.

On the right are individuals whose cultural practices generally revolve around 'going out': they attend festivals, dance and theatre performances, and concerts of both highbrow and lowbrow music genres (jazz, rock, music-hall, opera and operetta, world and traditional music). This preference for performance is also attested by the events they attend during the festival, namely the concerts and staged readings. Their appreciation for the artists and comedians during the festival's events, or the fact that they come to the festival primarily for its atmosphere, rather than for the authors, also singles them out. Contrary to a large majority of the respondents to the questionnaire (88 percent), some of them declare that they do not intend to or have not participated in the interviews with writers. On this right-hand side of the axis, we also see the modalities signaling respondents who read less frequently than others (no more than 3 or 4 books a year), and whose literary tastes are less legitimate and/or more distant from the festival's choice of books, such as scientific, technical or professional books, practical books, comics, or self-help books. Citing contemporary novels amongst one's reading preferences does not appear on this side of the axis, nor does knowing the names of many authors on the festival program.

On the other, left-hand side of axis 3, the respondents rarely attend performances but read often, citing literary supplements and magazines, and their literary prefer-ences include novels, and also books by important foreign authors. These different literary practices testify to the possession of specific literary capital. This is also apparent in the events that they attend during the festival, both encounters with the authors as well as professional gatherings. Outside of this festival, they also go to conferences or classes on literature, an indication of the perpetuation and enrichment of this literary capital through participation in other collective events. The festival *Les Correspondances* thus appears as one of many different places in which this capital may be reinvested and yield a profit.

The supplementary variables show that respondents are distributed along this axis according to their age, professional status, gender, education levels, and occupations. The older they are, the more likely it is that their cultural practices revolve around literature, rather than going to performances or activities such as taking theater lessons. On the other hand, men tend to be situated closer to the group of performance-goers than women, controlling for age.

The difference between both groups of audience members is also strongly linked to educational levels and professional occupation. Indeed, literature teachers and librarians (they comprise 1 out of 3 respondents) seem especially willing to attend the interviews with writers. This can be explained by a large amount of literary capital, but also because of their professional interest and habitus, both well-adjusted to this type of event. Indeed, half of the librarians surveyed and one out of ten teachers declare that they attend the festival for professional reasons, even when it takes place during their free time.

For that part of the audience possessing this literary capital, the festival offers a space for the accumulation of capital, and for perspectives of distinction, as is the case for some librarians or teachers in their professional sphere. It also creates a place similar to concert venues for music-lovers, allowing a collective celebration of literature and the enjoyment of literary sociability and exchange. In this space, specific literary capital, less valued or visible elsewhere, can be actualized and establish distinction.

However, the results of the MCA also show that *Les Correspondances de Manosque* bring together individuals whose social characteristics and cultural practices are diverse, some of them being endowed with less literary capital. The individuals keener to attend concerts and staged readings rather than interviews with writers are also more often medical or law professionals and engineers, or people who have graduated in law or economics, but also those participants who have working class backgrounds and low levels of education. They tend to prefer the artists and musicians rather than the literary works presented during the events. This may indicate that performances offer more attractive and generally 'safer' situations for festivalgoers endowed with less legitimate cultural capital and/or literary capital than the other respondents (Figs. 14.5 and 14.6).

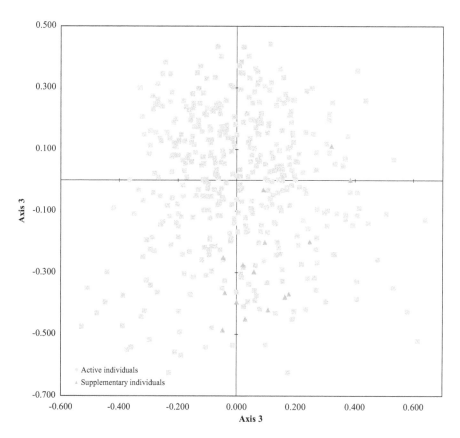

Fig. 14.5 Axes 2 and 3: active and supplementary individuals

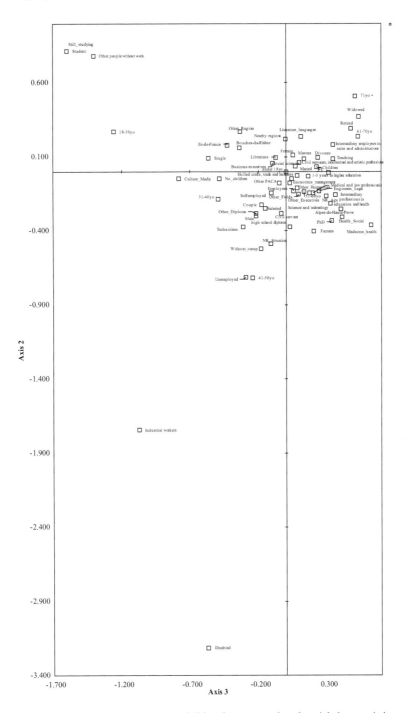

Fig. 14.6 Axes 2 and 3: supplementary modalities about respondents' social characteristics

Conclusion

The festival *Les Correspondances de Manosque* enables different types of mediation between the literary market and audiences who, on the whole, are endowed with a considerable amount of cultural capital – both reading a great deal as well as frequently going out – but whose types of cultural capital and practices differ. The interviews with writers draw on a specifically literary cultural capital, which can be found mainly amongst people who studied literature or whose occupation is linked to literature. The meetings with writers create a space to share this capital, and allow its development and upkeep, so that it might be converted and redeployed in the professional space or in moments of private social exchange. Mediating literature through well-known artists makes the staged readings and literary concerts accessible to other audiences less endowed with literary capital, and whose social characteristics and cultural practices are more diverse.

This research has thus allowed us to distinguish a specific kind of cultural capital: literary capital. Acquired during literary education of all kinds, this specific capital is becoming increasingly devalued in the French social space due to the growing importance allocated to economic and financial capital (Denord et al. 2011), as well as the devaluation of literary education itself, and the rivalry with other forms of cultural expression (see also Bennett et al. 2010). Invested in contemporary literature and shared during the festival, this capital finds a space where it is valued and exchanged, not just upheld, but even yielding a profit. The worth of new works is difficult to assess in an autonomous literary field where competition is harsch and this can further complicate the process of measuring one's own literary capital. The festival enables comparisons of this personal capital with that of other well-read individuals. Furthermore, meeting in person with the sanctified figures of the writers adds value to the consumption of cultural goods for those audiences best endowed with specific literary capital. Thriving on the "self-actualizing experiences" described by Holt (1998)[2], this capital thus enables the appreciation of the authenticity derived from meeting with the authors, discussing their works, and listening to staged and musical readings, all of which contrast with the usual isolation and asceticism associated with reading a book.

References

Bennett, T., Warde, A., Silva, E., Savage, M., Gayo-Cal, M., & Wright, D. (2010). *Culture, class, distinction*. London: Routledge.

Bourdieu, P. (1993). *The field of cultural production. Essays on Art and literature* (R. Johnson, Ed.). Cambridge: Polity Press.

---

[2]These elements are characteristic of the consumption habits of people with important amounts of cultural capital: "they seek out diverse, educational, informative experiences that allow them to achieve competence, acquire knowledge, and express themselves creatively" (Holt 1998: 17).

Bourdieu, P. (1995). *The rules of Art: genesis and structure of the literary field* (S. Emmanuel, Trans.). Stanford: Stanford University Press.

Denord, F., Lagneau-Ymonet, P., & Thine, S. (2011). Le champ du pouvoir en France. *Actes de la recherche en sciences sociales, 190*(5), 24–57.

Donnat, O. (2009). *Les Pratiques culturelles des Français à l'ère numérique, Enquête 2008*. Paris: Ministère de la Culture et de la Communication / La Découverte.

Driscoll, B. (2014). *The New Literary Middlebrow*. London: Palgrave Macmillan UK.

Ethis, E. (Ed.). (2002). *Avignon, le public réinventé. Le festival sous le regard des sciences sociales*. Paris: Ministère de la Culture – DEPS.

Ethis, E., Fabiani, J. L., & Malinas, D. (Eds.). (2008). *Avignon ou le public participant*. Montpellier: L'Entretemps.

Fabiani, J. L. (2008). *L'Éducation populaire et le théâtre. Le public d'Avignon en action*. Saint Martin d'Hères: Presses Universitaires de Grenoble.

Giorgi, L. (2011). Literature festivals and the sociology of literature. *The International Journal of Arts in Society, 4*, 317–316.

Giorgi, L., Sassatelli, M., & Delanty, G. (Eds.). (2011). *Festivals and the Cultural Public Sphere*. London/New York: Routledge.

Holt, D. B. (1998). Does cultural capital structure American consumption. *Journal of Consumer Research, 25*, 1–25.

Kulkarni, S., Dhanamjaya, M., & Preedip Balaji, B. (2017). Do literature festivals promote reading and public libraries? A survey. *Library Hi Tech News, 34*, 13–15.

Lebaron, F., & Le Roux, B. (Eds.). (2015). *La Méthodologie de Pierre Bourdieu en action. Espace culturel, espace social et analyse des données*. Paris: Dunod.

Le Roux, B. (2004). *Analyse géométrique des données multidimensionnelles*. Paris: Dunod.

Le Roux, B., & Rouanet, H. (2004). *Geometric Data Analysis. From Correspondence Analysis to Structured Data Analysis*. Dordrecht: Kluwer Academic Publishers.

Négrier, E., Djakouane, A., & Jourda, M. (2010). *Les Publics des festivals*. Paris: Michel de Maule.

Sapiro, G. (2016). The Metamorphosis of modes of consecration in the literary field: Academies, literary prizes, festivals. *Poetics, 59*, 5–19.

Sapiro, G., Picaud, M., Pacouret, J., & Seiler, H. (2015). L'amour de la littérature : le festival, nouvelle instance de production de la croyance. Le cas des Correspondances de Manosque. *Actes de la recherche en sciences sociales, 206–207*, 108–137.

Wynn, J. R. (2015). *Music/City: American Destivals and Placemaking in Austin, Nashville, and Newport*. Chicago: University of Chicago Press.

Chapter 15
Education as Field and Market: The Case of Upper Secondary School in Stockholm, 2006–2008

Håkan Forsberg, Mikael Palme, and Mikael Börjesson

Introduction

In the last three decades, Swedish education has undergone profound transformations, including a gradually increased degree of privatization, commodification and marketization. For instance, the number of children in private preschools has risen from 10,000 in 1998 to 50,000 in 2014, and children in non-public compulsory schools have increased from 30,000 in 1998 to 134,000 in 2014. The corresponding figures for upper secondary school are 11,000 in 1998 and 83,000 in 2014. Furthermore, there are substantial regional differences. The larger metropolitan regions have developed more private options and formed larger educational markets, the most extensive one to be found in the Stockholm region. Today, at the upper secondary level where the tendencies are most pronounced, this market includes more than 130 private schools and 65 public schools competing for 75,000 pupils. In the central city of Stockholm, private schools dominate, constituting the major share, 70%, of the schools, and representing half of the pupils.

The implications of privatization, commodification and marketization of the public sector have been a major concern for research in different disciplines focusing on different aspects. In studies in economics, market reforms are largely understood within the framework of a deregulation of supply and demand in sectors such as education and health care enabling schools, hospitals and care centers and their owners to compete in offering services to families who make more or less well-informed choices based on their interest and willingness to invest in available options. By examining what is understood as correlations of causality between a market-based system, built on the choices of providers and customers, and outcomes

H. Forsberg (✉) · M. Palme · M. Börjesson
Department of Education, Sociology of Education and Culture (SEC), Uppsala University,
Uppsala, Sweden
e-mail: hakan.forsberg@edu.uu.se; mikael.palme@edu.uu.se; mikael.borjesson@edu.uu.se

© Springer Nature Switzerland AG 2019
J. Blasius et al. (eds.), *Empirical Investigations of Social Space*,
Methodos Series 15, https://doi.org/10.1007/978-3-030-15387-8_15

such as economic efficiency, pupils' study results, social inequality or accessibility, this research seeks to determine the societal impact of market reforms (Böhlmark and Lindahl 2007; Bradley and Taylor 2010; Francois and Vlassopoulos 2008; Gaynor et al. 2013; Hoxby 2003; Propper et al. 2004). In another vein of research, common in social sciences, the introduction of market models in the public sector is seen as part of a neoliberal shift in society. Here, marketization is perceived as a new mode of governance, the market becoming a force in itself that penetrates social welfare, causing the decline of equity and the transformation of values traditionally connected to the public sector into market relations (See Ball 2007; Gewirtz 2002; Harvey 1989; Lubienski 2003; Reay 2004; Whitty and Power 2000).

In this chapter[1], we suggest that Bourdieusean sociology offers an alternative, more fruitful understanding of marketization as embedded in social fields with a particular history and structure (see also Lidegran et al., Chap. 3 and Dalberg, Chap. 17, in this volume). The distribution of material and symbolic assets in these fields, among producers as well as consumers, set the conditions for how 'economic' markets in the restricted sense of the word operate (Bourdieu 1979: 93–94, Bourdieu 2000: 113–114). Taking market-oriented reforms in Swedish upper secondary education as our point of departure, we attempt to contribute to the sociology of educational markets by focusing on one of these conditions, the social character of the 'demand' for education. We argue that far from being explained by the calculated choices of interchangeable consumers or by influences from market forces themselves, this demand is shaped by the long history lying behind the volume and structure of social groups' assets and the dispositions vis-à-vis education that the same history has produced. We relate the supply-side, the educational programmes and the schools, to the demand-side and conclude that marketization, privatization and commodification are unevenly distributed in the field.

Privatization, Commodification and Marketization of Upper Secondary Education in Sweden and in Stockholm

In order to understand the deregulation of state and public controlled upper secondary education in Stockholm, we need to differentiate between three different mechanisms, or dimensions: privatization, commodification and marketization (cf. Börjesson 2016). Firstly, it is important to note the difference between privatization and marketization. Privatization relates both to the control of how education is supplied and to its funding. While, in the Swedish case, the control of the provision of education was increasingly privatized in the early 1990s by improving the

---

[1] The article draws on the dissertation by Håkan Forsberg (2015) and is written within the context of the research programme *Families in the new educational landscape. Paths, assets and strategies 1985 to 2016*, directed by Mikael Palme and funded by the Swedish Research Council.

conditions for non-public so called independent schools at various levels, funding remained public through the implementation of a voucher system. Marketization, on the other hand, denotes a particular regulation of the educational offer vis-à-vis the demand for education in which schools compete for pupils and pupils (or families) compete for entry into schools (cf. Engwall 2007).

Furthermore, marketization does not necessarily presuppose privatization. One can create a market in the sense of a deregulated offer and supply-structure while maintaining public control and public funding of the supply. However, a deregulated relation between the offer and demand for education is likely to bring about what is often referred to as a commodification of education (cf. Ball 2009; Lynch and Moran 2006), in particular when it is combined with privatization and the growth of private, profit-run educational companies. Less clear as a concept, commodification has had profound effects on how schools and teaching are organised, how the educational offer is packaged and what working conditions for teachers look like.

Thus, we need to distinguish between three dimensions of state deregulation in education: privatization, commodification and marketization. To each one we can relate specific indicators:

1. The level of privatization of schools (How many are private and how large a share do they represent?)
2. The level of marketization (How many pupils are included in the market, do they all have the same possibilities to choose freely?)
3. The level of commodification (Are profits allowed? To what extent is market-orientation reflected in how schools and teaching operate and in teachers' conditions? How important are marketing instruments?)

In the following, we will analyse how privatization, marketization and commodification of upper secondary education in Stockholm have developed.

As regards privatization, it is clear that the number of private or independent institutions rose dramatically, especially during the early 2000s; see Fig. 15.1. The number of independent schools doubled from 10 to 20 during the 1990s, and doubled again up to 2003, just to double once more in the following 5 years (from 40 to almost 70). At the same time, the number of public schools remained fairly stable, around 30. In 2001, the independent schools surpassed public ones in number, and in 2007 they were twice as many. However, a notable characteristic of these independent schools was their relatively small size, in average approximately a third of that of public schools. Small size provided greater flexibility in finding suitable facilities and a possibility to establish new niches on the expanding educational market, offering profiled study programmes and small-scale educational settings that could be marketed as more 'personal' than those of the anonymous public schools (Palme 2008). Even if the rise in number of independent schools was not matched by their share of pupils, the proportion of pupils attending non-public institutions grew from around 10% in the late 1990s to 55% in 2016.

For commodification purposes, we will here use a simple indicator that has the merit of being easily accessible in public statistics: the number of schools owned by educational companies with for-profit status. Before the market reforms in the

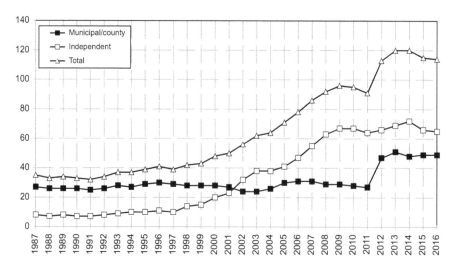

Fig. 15.1 Number of municipal/county and independent schools in Stockholm city, 1987 to 2011. (Note: The counting of schools managed by municipalities/counties changed in 2012. Source: Forsberg 2015)

early 1990s, 11 independent schools existed in Stockholm County, all of which were owned by non-profit organisations or foundations. From, 1992 to 1998, 14 new independent schools were established – 8 in the form of share-holder companies. After 2000, when the vast expansion of independent schools occured, share-holder companies became the dominant form, constituting 38 out of 43 independent schools created in the period 2006 to 2008.

Let us finally turn to the rise of the educational market. During the 1990s and the first decade of the 2000s, upper secondary education in Stockholm developed in the direction of becoming a cohesive educational market with increasingly less formal obstacles for families' and pupils' choice of secondary education. At the beginning of this development, independent schools were few and pupils could choose between study programmes, but the ruling proximity principle did not allow a choice of which public school to attend. With the accelerating surge of independent schools challenging the public ones, municipalities had to reconsider the proximity principle. While it was abolished in the City of Stockholm in 2000/2001, surrounding municipalities engaged in facilitating inter-municipal pupil mobility in order to protect their public schools from the exodus to independent schools. For some years, the only remaining restriction prevented pupils living outside of the City of Stockholm from applying to the much sought-after study programmes provided by public schools in the city and oriented towards higher education. Finally, in 2011, this restriction was also eliminated, turning upper secondary education in Stockholm County into a unified market. From being limited to study programmes offered by the closest public schools and a few independent schools, families' and pupils' options, in 20 years' time, came to include the choice between over 200 schools, whereof approximately 75 were public and close to 130 independent ones. In 2011 alone, municipal and independent schools competed for 75,000 upper secondary pupils representing an annual economic value in terms of school vouchers corresponding to roughly 900 million EUR (Forsberg 2015).

Marketization was not limited to school choice. The reforms of the early 1990s' also launched three innovations: the so called 'individual programme', the 'specially designed programme' and local profiles of the national study programmes. These changes made it possible to adjust the educational offer to both individual and local market demands, creating new niches in the educational landscape. In the period from 1987 to 2008, the total educational offer in the Stockholm region, grew from 650 to 850 educational options (study programme by school) (Forsberg 2015).

The expansion of schools and educational programmes coincided with a demographic increase of pupils, especially after the millennium shift. However, the growth in pupil numbers is far from explaining the proportionally larger surge in the number of schools, which suggests that the proliferation of independent (non-public) school operators was an effect of the market reforms. The new possibility to compete for the funding that pupils' school vouchers represented stimulated the establishment of schools increasingly owned by and operated as commercial companies. Further, competition between schools took the form of an expansion of tailored courses and study programmes as a central element for attracting potential pupils.

Field and Market

In a series of studies assembled as a book published in 2000, Bourdieu analyses the French housing market as being embedded in overlapping social fields (Bourdieu 2000). One of his major conclusions is that what economists call a 'market', regulated by the logic of supply and demand, only represents a small part of the social order in which the production and purchase of houses is inserted, and a part that cannot be understood by reference to itself. The 'economic' market, in the restricted sense of the word, presupposes a world of production that has a history of its own. This world comprises not only companies of different seniority, size and profile, but also the involvement of government agencies, stakeholder organizations and financing institutes, all inhabited by persons with a certain symbolic capital with regard to defining acceptable housing policies and with a different habitus depending on the positions they have come to occupy. Moreover, the market necessarily involves consumers whose preferences cannot be reduced to the economic resources they possess or to purely economic calculations, but make part of their reproduction strategies, tastes and lifestyles. For Bourdieu, the order that regulates the purely economic market depends not only on economic power, but as much on the distribution of symbolic power, accumulated under the condition that it is not connected to economic gains.

The social field approach applied here to the marketization of Swedish upper secondary education bears many resemblances with Bourdieu's study of the French house market. The educational market is to a large extent shaped by the State through government regulations, the most obvious example being the public funding of the school voucher that creates the market as such. It is further managed by municipalities with varying demographic compositions, political majorities and bureaucratic traditions. Organizations for different stakeholders play an important role in shaping policies at both national and municipal levels. Far from operating as a pure market defined by the interplay between offer and demand, its mode of functioning is the object of struggles between conflicting political, administrative and commercial interests. The outcomes of these struggles define the rules for the functioning of the 'market' in a narrow sense of the word. In the social field of producers of education, municipality owned schools compete for pupils with schools owned by foundations and, above all, commercial companies.

However, in this study, we do not set out to analyse the field of production of upper secondary education, considering various types of symbolic, social and economic capital at stake in the field, as in the fairly abundant analyses of social fields in the Bourdieusean tradition after *Le patronat* (Bourdieu and De Saint Martin 1978) and *Homo academicus* (Bourdieu 1984), such as those of Lebaron (2010) or Denord et al. (2011). Instead, we focus on one particular, but crucial aspect of the conditions for the competition between educational institutions: the social character of the audience attending the hugely increased number of schools and educational options that these institutions offer. While this indicator has obvious limitations, putting other types of institutional assets in the dark, it has the advantage of being accessible through statistical data. Moreover, as an indicator it has the merit of connecting the supply of education to the character of the demand. Focusing on the pattern of relations between social groups and the education offered by educational institutions, the analysis aligns to an existing tradition of studies in sociology of education (cf. Bertilsson 2014; Felouzis et al. 2013; Forsberg 2015; Lidegran 2009; Palme 2008; Poupeau et al. 2007). However, with the exception of Poupeau et al. (2007), Felouzis et al. 2013, and Forsberg (2015), educational markets have so far not been a major concern in this tradition.

We try to answer three sets of questions:

I. Firstly, how is the field of upper secondary education in Stockholm structured with regard to, on the one hand, gender and social origin, and, on the other hand, educational programmes at schools with geographical locations?

II. Secondly, where is the most obvious expression of privatization, the independent schools, located in the space? Do their positions differ from the public schools? And what internal differences among independent schools can be identified? Do for profit-driven schools attract other audiences than schools owned by non-profit organisations or foundations?

III. Thirdly, if we assume, with Bourdieu, that the educational demand is the expression of accumulated resources and socially shaped dispositions (habitus) which have taken time to develop and cannot be separated from other social reproduction strategies, to what extent has the marketization of upper secondary education transformed the preferences for education as these are expressed in educational choices after the market reforms? In other words, does the structure of the educational field differ from earlier stages in the history of the field?

Applying Correspondence Analysis

In the competition for pupils brought about by the market reforms, upper secondary schools needed to shape the study programmes they offered so as to distinguish themselves from other schools. This competition is expressed in the growth of educational profiles that multiplied the possible educational choices (study programme per school) at upper secondary level. In the analysis presented here, correspondence analysis (CA) and agglomerative hierarchical classification (AHC), also called Euclidian classification (Le Roux and Rouanet 2004: 105ff.) were used for exploring the social structure of the educational choices made by all pupils at upper secondary level in 2006–2008, that is, at a time when the marketization, privatisation and commodification of the field had reached a certain magnitude and presence in the field. Using the 'bottom up' approach of Euclidian classification enables a more thorough investigation of how the recruitment to different study programmes and schools is related to their position in the constructed social space.

The analysis departs from individual data for the total pupil population in these years. Individual pupils are characterized by information on the choice of school and study programme (educational options), as well as on gender and social origin, the latter classified in 27 categories. In order not to treat gender and social origin as separate qualities, the 27 social groups in the social classification were divided according to gender, creating a total of 54 categories (daughter as opposed to sons of physicians, secondary teachers, small entrepreneurs, etc.). In addition, other statistically available information on pupils was included as supplementary variables in the analysis, for example on the grades received at the end of compulsory education, parents' educational level; the income and type of residential area of the household of origin, and on whether the pupil or parents had a migration background. The target population consisted of all students in Grade 2 in upper secondary education, representing a total of 71,000 individual pupils. Out of these, 62,000 were included in the analysis since information on their on social origin was available. In order to make the analysis more stable, educational options recruiting 35 pupils during the 3 years in consideration were omitted. As a consequence, 522 out of a total of 766 existing educational options were active in the analysis, attended by 57,660 pupils or 93% of the approximately 62,000 pupils.

In the analysed contingency table, the rows or 'individuals' represented the variable education, separating between all existing study programmes per school, i.e. all educational options. The columns, characterizing all existing educational options (rows), represented, firstly, social origin and gender put together, or more precisely, the number of daughters and sons from each of the 27 social groups attending each educational option. These four dimensions – educational programme and school, on the one hand, and social origin by gender on the other hand – represented the two *active* variables in the construction of the space. The structure of the space is, then, an expression of the relationships between these active variables, for example the proximity or distance between educational options where daughters of lawyers or sons of blue-collar workers tend to be found. In addition, this structure of relations was further explored using supplementary variables, or non-active columns in the contingency table, whose position in the space was projected into the structure without affecting it. As indicated above, these supplementary variables provided information of both acquired and inherited assets among the pupils attending the various educational options. Finally, the distribution of modalities or categories pertaining to each variable was thoroughly analysed using Euclidean Clustering (see above).

The correspondence analysis generated 49 axes of which the first one had an eigenvalue of 0.267, corresponding to 25.8% of the total variance. The second axis contributed somewhat less to the variance with an eigenvalue of 0.180 (17.4%). Combined, the first two axes explained 43.3% of the total variance. The third axis had a much lower eigenvalue value, 0.047, explaining only 4.6% of the variance.

The Social Structure of Upper Secondary Education in Stockholm in the Wake of the Market Reforms

The result of the correspondence analysis uncovers two distinct dimensions of the social space of upper secondary education in Stockholm, when pupils' social origin and gender are taken as the point of departure and other characteristics mentioned above are used as supplementary variables. Since the educational options, study programmes per school attended by the pupils are many, they are omitted in Fig. 15.2 but will be briefly described in the following. The first and most significant polarity (opposition left to right in the figure, first axis) differentiates between educational options primarily chosen by girls and those almost solely populated by boys. The second polarity (opposition top to down, second axis) reflects a social class-related division, distinguishing between schools and programmes receiving pupils rich in inherited as well as acquired assets and educational options accommodating pupils with weak assets.[2]

If one considers the two polarities mentioned above in the multidimensional space generated by the correspondence analysis – one gender-distinctive and the other socially distinctive –, a triangular structure emerges. At the base of the triangle, pupils' inherited and acquired assets are small. Here, boys and girls are separated into preparatory vocational programmes with very different specialisations: edu-

---

[2]See Appendix Table 15.1 for the categories that contribute over the mean on the 3 first axis of the CA.

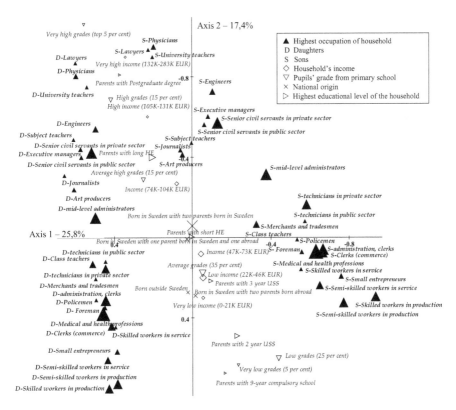

Fig. 15.2 Correspondence Analysis (CA) – the social space of upper secondary education in Stockholm 2006–2008, axes 1 and 2

cation oriented towards manual work in areas such as construction or industrial production opposes orientations towards caring professions. The further up towards the peak of the triangle one moves, the more evenly distributed boys and girls become. Study programmes preparing for higher education dominate at the same time as the importance of inherited assets, indicated by pupils' high social origin, increases.

Domains of Privatization in the Field of Upper Secondary Education

So far, the social structure of the field of upper secondary education has been analysed in terms of the social character of the demand. Let us now turn the attention to the educational programmes and schools, the 'supply' side. A first question to address is the extension of private/public options in the space (see Fig.

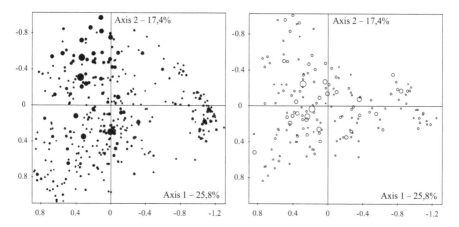

Fig. 15.3 (**a, b**) Study programmes at municipal (**a**) and independent (**b**) upper secondary schools in Stockholm County, 2006–2008. Axes 1 and 2. Study programmes at schools managed by municipalities ○ Study programmes at independent schools. (Note: The size of the symbols is proportional to frequencies, i.e. study programmes with many pupils have larger size)

15.3a, b). The study programmes at municipal upper secondary schools are spread across the whole spatial structure, ranging from the elite schools in the inner city of Stockholm with a highly selective social and merit-based recruitment to the schools in the suburban municipalities offering vocational education that mainly recruit either girls or boys with small volumes of inherited and acquired assets. The independent schools show an almost opposite dispersion in the field. With a few important exceptions, the educational options offered by independent upper secondary schools recruit most of their pupils from a broad middle tier, considering social class origin and previously acquired school assets. These educational options are also more frequently attended by girls than boys, as is testified to by the strong presence of 'daughters' pertaining to the various social categories.

Further, a distinction needs to be made among independent schools between those run by for-profit companies and those owned by foundations and non-profit organisations (see Fig. 15.4). As argued above, this distinction serves as an indicator of the degree of commodification of education, here represented by the for-profit companies. As mentioned before, this category of owners has rapidly increased over the last decade. When the distribution of the two types of independent schools in the field is considered, it becomes obvious that the type of ownership divides the field. The educational options at schools run by for-profit companies are oriented towards the middle and lower part of the field, while they are completely absent at the socially and scholarly dominating part of the field in the upper regions of the figure. In contrast, in this upper region we find a concentration of educational options at schools owned by foundations and non-profit organisations. In reverse, these schools are rare in the lower, socially and scholarly dominated parts of the field.

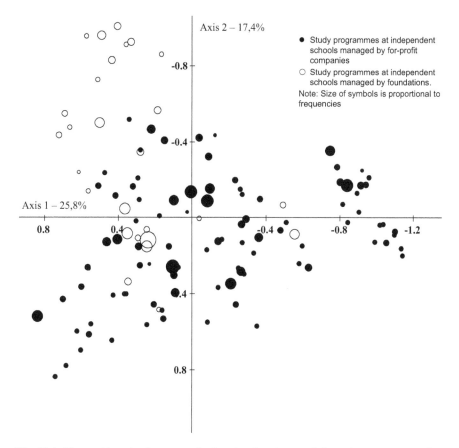

Fig. 15.4 The positions in the space of educational options at independent upper secondary schools by type of owner in Stockholm County, 2006–2008. Axes 1 and 2. Study programmes at schools managed by municipalities ○ Study programmes at independent schools. (Note: The size of the symbols is proportional to frequencies, i.e. study programmes with many pupils have larger sizes)

While the for-profit companies orient themselves towards the most populated areas of the field, where the largest number of pupils and thus the best conditions for profit are to be found, non-profit independent schools, often characterized by having a long history as institutions, are oriented towards a considerably narrower, small-scale social audience with abundant assets. Besides being non-public, these two types of independent schools have little in common. While independent schools owned by foundations and non-profit organisations primarily constitute a challenge to prestigious, traditional public grammar schools in the inner city and the wealthier suburbs, the for-profit schools compete among themselves and with public schools in socially heterogeneous municipalities in the suburbs.

In terms of geographic spread, the City of Stockholm has the largest proportion of educational options situated in the upper part of the structure where we also find pupils with the strongest inherited and acquired assets. Similarly, educational programmes offered by schools in the comparatively well-off northern suburban municipalities are mainly concentrated in the upper part of the structure. In contrast, very few educational programmes at upper secondary schools located in the poorer southern suburban municipalities can be found in this part of the space.

Nine Clusters of Educational Options (Study Programme per School)

While the structure disclosed by the correspondence analysis provides a general map of the upper secondary education landscape in 2006–08, Euclidean clustering makes it possible to take the analysis of this map a step further. By taking into account the coordinate positions of the educational options (rows) along the axes or planes produced by the CA, these options can be grouped together according to the principle that, at any given level of division (partitions), those that are closest to each other in terms of distance are grouped together in a cluster and separated from those pertaining to other clusters at the same level (Le Roux and Rouanet 2004). Starting from the bottom, with many divisions, this grouping creates a hierarchical tree of partitions in which, at the top, all educational options belong to the same class. In the tree of partitions, each level explains, to varying degrees, the total variance of the data, while taking into account both the within and between variance of the hierarchy classes. The choice of partitions has to be weighed against the importance of making a sociological interpretation of the concerned clusters. In the present case, we choose a partition that explains 71% of the total variance in the data and that generates nine classes of educational options (study programme in combination with school). Including still more partitions would not add anything to the sociological analysis. The distribution of these nine classes or clusters is displayed in Fig. 15.5.

By considering the modalities that are over- or underrepresented in each one of the identified nine clusters (see Appendix, Table 15.2, for an inventory of these modalities), we can make a more detailed sociological analysis of what characterizes the educational options in each cluster in relation to those in other clusters. In Fig. 15.5, the clusters are projected into the first and second planes of the space created by the CA.

Just below the center, we find educational options oriented towards business and dominated by pupils from the lower-middle classes and working classes or by pupils with migrant background (Cluster 5). Overlapping and slightly above, a cluster of educational options are located that prepare for higher education while being especially sought-after by lower middle class pupils (Cluster 6). It is noteworthy that one third of the educational options in this cluster are offered by profit-oriented independent schools run by business corporations. Moving further left, slightly

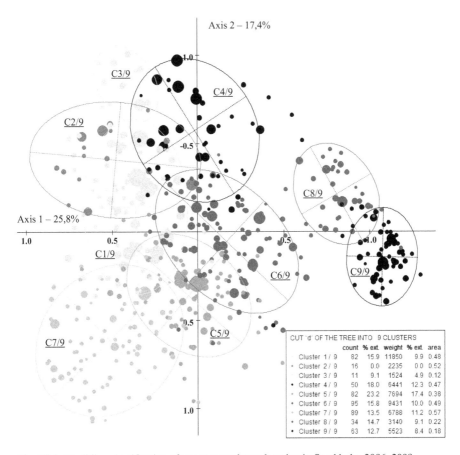

Fig. 15.5 Euclidian classification of upper secondary education in Stockholm 2006–2008

higher up in the spatial structure, we find a cluster of educational study programmes oriented towards social sciences and recruiting especially the daughters of the middle classes (Cluster 1). While here, too, the proportion of independent schools is large, 45%, a significant number of these schools are run by foundations or non-profit organisations. To the right, there is a cluster of educational options oriented towards technology, the vast majority of which are situated at public, municipal schools, and populated by the sons of the middle and working classes, (Cluster 8). The area at the bottom of the space is dominated by the opposition between a cluster of vocational study programmes inhabited by the daughters of the working classes on the left (Cluster 7), a cluster of male dominated vocational programmes inhabited by the sons from the same classes (Cluster 9). The latter cluster is the one most separated from others.

Moving to the upper part of the space, clusters comprising educational options favoured by fractions of the upper middle class appear. The most distinguished cluster is found highest up in the structure and consists of the elite educational options recruiting both sons and daughters of highly educated fractions of the upper middle class, the *Bildung*-fractions (Cluster 3). Here, the over-representation is strongest not only of sons and daughters of physicians, lawyers and parents with postgraduate degrees, but also of pupils with the highest grades from compulsory education, the scholastic elite. The traditional inner-city public schools occupy dominating positions, but we also find the largest proportion of educational options provided by independent schools (54%). However, all of these are owned by non-profit organisations or foundations and none by commercial educational companies. On the right, we find a cluster of educational options oriented towards science that are characterized by a particularly strong recruitment of sons from economically wealthy upper-middle class families (Cluster 4). This cluster is less homogenous than the previous one (Cluster 3) in terms of its distribution in the space. Finally, slightly below on the left side, we find a cluster of educational study programmes and schools dominated by daughters to cultural fractions of the middle class (Cluster 2).

The Euclidian classification brings forward differences underlying the axes discovered by the original correspondence analysis providing us with a more detailed understanding of its outcomes. The differences between the clusters – in terms of particular recruitment profiles to the educational options that they bring together, as well as with respect to the nature of these educational options themselves (vocational as opposed to preparatory programmes, social sciences as opposed to science, etc.) and the type of schools they are located at – suggest fine but systematic social distances that make up the educational landscape of upper secondary education in which the educational market operates.

A Stable Social Structure

Let us return to the third research question concerning the stability of the field and, in a concluding step, reconnect to the concept of education as social field.

The correspondence analysis that revealed the basic polarities of upper secondary education in 2006–2008 can be compared to similar analyses that had been preceding the market reforms for years (cf. Börjesson 2004; Palme 2008). It is notable that the basic oppositions between schools and study programmes ('educational options') are very similar. While on a first axis, female dominated programmes oppose male dominated ones, a second axis distinguishes education with selective social and scholarly recruitment to those with less selective recruitment profiles. The same triangular structure can be observed. At its base, girls and boys of working class and lower middle class origin are separated in different types of vocational study programmes, while at the top of the triangle sons and daughters from upper-middle class families and with high grades from compulsory school meet in study programmes preparing for higher education.

At this level of analysis, the introduction of an educational market based on free choice and school vouchers does not seem to have transformed the basic social polarities in upper secondary education. Much to the contrary, the 'supply' of education under the market regime appears to have adapted to the pre-existing social balances between social groups with different assets and different dispositions towards education. A likely explanation is that the dispositions vis-à-vis education, as inseparable part of the life trajectories that shape the assets of which social groups dispose, are subject to an inertia that the educational market cannot but recognize. Moreover, the stability of the social structure reminds us of the fact that far from being 'free' in more than a juridical, formal sense, the choice of upper secondary education remains determined by the volume and structure of the assets or capital that social groups possess, not the least the probability of their offspring receiving high grades in compulsory education.

However, the Euclidean classification indicates that certain significant transformations probably do have occurred, although we lack comparable studies from previous years. The substantial expansion of schools and locally designed study programmes brought about by the reforms have likely resulted not only in an increased educational competition, but also in more stratified educational market niches of the type revealed by the analysis of the nine clusters. As could have been anticipated, inherited resources indicated by the social origin go along with acquired educational resources (high grades) in the selection to the most selective educational options in niches pertaining to the clusters in the upper region.

These results shed light on the transformation of the 'demand' on the educational market. What about the educational institutions providing the 'supply', pertaining to the field of production of upper secondary education? In the absence of a more thorough field analysis, we argued that the character of the recruitment to the educational options on offer could serve as a viable indicator of the structure of this field. In supplementation to the previous characterisation of the nine clusters, it can be noted that 10 years after the introduction of the educational market in Stockholm County, a substantial part of middle tiers pupils in upper secondary education tend to attend private commercial schools where the entry requirements are less competitive than at schools of elite character. The underachieving pupils of the working classes, including pupils with migration background from families without high levels of education, are relegated to what can be characterized as 'exposed' schools with low-performing pupils. While many of these schools are municipal, some are commercially driven. Finally, the children of the highly-educated 'Bildungs-bourgeoisie' stick to highly selective elite schools, many of which are public schools in the inner city of Stockholm and some more recently established independent schools owned by foundations or non-profit organisations.

Conclusions: An Educational Market Embedded in an Educational Field

The analysis suggests that, in the Stockholm region, the educational market created in upper secondary education through state intervention resulted in a heavy expansion of the 'supply' of education in terms of schools and study programmes. We can note an increase as regards all three dimensions that we initially outlined: a proliferation of privatization by means of a rapid expansion of independent, non-public, schools; full-fledged marketization through the deregulation of the relation between the educational offer and the educational demand; and, finally, strengthened commodification in the form of for-profit educational companies rapidly expanding their share of the educational offer.

However, while these transformations can be experienced as dramatic, as the heated debate on education testifies, too, there is, at the same time, stability and continuity. As the analysis reveals, the relation between the supply of education and the 'demand' obeys social forces similar to those that structured the field of upper secondary education before the reforms, opposing higher social classes to lower ones and creating class-specific gender balances. While the strengthened segmentation and branding of schools indicated by the Euclidean classification have probably increased competition among educational institutions and their owners, as well as between pupils, families and social groups, the particular shape that this segmentation takes aligns to oppositions between social classes and class fractions. The social character of the demand sets limits for the options of the suppliers, relegating the commodified, for-profit schools to an audience with substantially weaker assets than the audience whose favours public and non-profit schools of elite character compete for. This stability reminds of the fact that the educational market is embedded in a wider social field of education with a historically developed structure of relations between educational institutions and the social groups using education, a structure to which the market and the ensuing commodification adapt. As the social field perspective suggests, the concept of educational market has limited explanatory value as such, since the rules regulating the market, as well as the forces shaping the character of both supply and demand, need sociological and historical explanations.

Appendix

Table 15.1 Correspondance Analysis (CA). Active categories (columns) contributing over mean of 2.0

Axis 1	Ctr	Crd	Axis 2	Ctr	Crd	Axis 3	Ctr	Crd
D-physicians	2.06	0.63	D-skilled workers in production	10.46	0.75	S-executive managers	3.14	0.38
D-senior civil servants in private sector	4.66	0.53	D-semi-skilled workers in production	10.11	0.73	S-senior civil servants in private sector	13.37	0.36
D-class teachers	2.06	0.48	D-semi-skilled workers in service	5.75	0.64	S-engineers	4.17	0.30
D-mid-level administrators	4.09	0.48	D-small entrepreneurs	2.74	0.59	S-mid-level administrators	4.40	0.20
D-technicians in private sector	2.41	0.43	D-clerks (commerce)	3.53	0.47	D-skilled workers in production	2.51	0.18
D-medical and health professions	4.05	0.42	D-medical and health professions	5.33	0.40	S-technicians in private sector	2.18	0.16
D-administration, clerks	2.50	0.40	D-administration, clerks	2.48	0.33	S-semi-skilled workers in production	2.94	−0.19
S-technicians in private sector	4.13	−0.55	S-mid-level administrators	2.91	−0.34	S-semi-skilled workers in service	2.48	−0.20
S-medical and health professions	8.62	−0.61	S-senior civil servants in private sector	3274	−0.37	S-skilled workers in production	6.17	−0.27
S-semi-skilled workers in service	4.27	−0.65	D-engineers	2.85	−0.51	D-physicians	4.08	−0.37
S-clerks (commerce)	4.32	−0.65	S-senior civil servants in private sector	8.2	−0.57	S-art producers	6.20	−0.47
S-administration, clerks	7.11	−0.66	S-engineers	6.29	−0.74	D-subject teachers	6.91	−0.65
S-small entrepreneurs	3.20	−0.75	D-physicians	4.20	−0.76	D-journalists	8.17	−0.70
S-semi-skilled workers in production	8.40	−0.79	D-lawyers	2.10	−0.80	D-art producers	18.29	−0.82
S-skilled workers in production	12.53	−0.94	S-lawyers	2.60	−0.92			
			S-physicians	6.63	−0.93			

Table 15.2 Euclidean classification. Characteristics of 9 clusters based on the 10 most over-represented categories

	% of in total population	Frequency in cluster	Over-representation
Cluster 1 – Social Science SPs of the daughters of the middle classes			
Daughters of senior civil servants in public sector	1,0	1,9	1,9
Daughters of executive managers	0,9	1,7	1,8
Daughters of journalists	0,7	1,3	1,8
Daughters of lawyers	0,6	1,0	1,8
Daughters of senior civil servants in private sector	4,2	7,2	1,7
Daughters of art producers	1,2	0,2	1,6
Daughters of midlevel administrators	4,5	7,2	1,6
Daughters of subject teachers	0,7	1,1	1,6
Students with medium to high grades (245–270)	20,1	31	1,5
Daughters of class teachers	2,2	3,4	1,5
Cluster 2 – Art SPs of the daughters of the cultural fractions of the middle classes			
Daughters of subject teachers	0,7	3,4	4,6
Daughters of art producers	1,2	5,5	4,5
Daughters of journalists	0,7	3,3	4,4
Very high grades (310–320)	6,6	23,8	3,6
Sons of art producers	1,3	3,9	3,1
Sons of subject teachers	0,7	2,3	3,1
Daughters of physicians	1,3	3,8	2,9
Sons of university teachers	0,5	1,3	2,8
Daughters of university teachers	0,4	1,3	2,8
Daughters of lawyers	0,6	1,6	2,8
Cluster 3 – Elite SPs of Bildung-fractions of the upper middle class			
Very high grades (310–320)	6,6	50,1	7,6
Daughters of physicians	1,3	7,3	5,6
Sons of lawyers	0,5	2,7	4,9
Daughters of lawyers	0,6	2,7	4,7
Sons of physicians	1,4	6,3	4,6
Parents with PhD	3,6	14,6	4,1
Parents with very high incomes (140,000–300,000 EUR)	6,3	25,7	4,1
Daughters of university teachers	0,4	1,8	4,0
Daughters of executive managers	0,9	2,8	3,1
Sons of university teachers	0,5	1,2	2,7

(continued)

Table 15.2 (continued)

	% of in total population	Frequency in cluster	Over-representation
Cluster 4 – science SPs of the sons of the wealthy upper middle classes			
Sons of university teachers	0,5	1,4	3,0
Sons of engineers	2,1	6,1	2,9
Sons of physicians	1,4	3,9	2,8
Sons of lawyers	0,5	1,5	2,7
Parents with very high incomes (140,000–300,000 EUR)	6,3	15,6	2,5
Sons of executive managers	1,0	2,2	2,2
Sons of senior civil servants in private sector	4,6	10,1	2,2
Parents with PhD	3,6	7,9	2,2
Sons of senior civil servants in public sector	1,0	2,1	2,1
Very high grades (310–320)	6,6	13,5	2,0
Cluster 5 – economy-oriented SPs of the sons and daughters of the lower middle classes, the working class and migrants			
Parents with 9-year compulsory school	6,2	11,6	1,9
Daughters of small entrepreneurs	1,4	2,5	1,8
Daughters of semi-skilled workers in service	2,4	4,2	1,7
Daughters of tradesmen	0,5	0,9	1,7
Daughters of semi-skilled workers in production	3,3	5,7	1,7
Born in Sweden with two parents born abroad	15,1	25,1	1,7
Daughters of skilled workers in service	0,7	1,2	1,7
Low grades (90–185)	28,0	43,5	1,6
Born outside Sweden	10,6	15,6	1,5
Very low grades (0–85)	5,0	7,7	1,5
Cluster 6 – University preparatory SPs of the sons and daughters of the lower middle classes			
Sons of law enforcement	0,6	0,8	1,4
Daughters of technicians in public sector	0,6	0,8	1,4
Sons of foreman	1,0	1,3	1,3
Sons of medical and health professions.	5,8	7,5	1,3
Sons of technicians in public sector	0,6	0,7	1,3
Sons of class teachers	2,3	2,9	1,3
Sons of clerks	4,1	5,2	1,3
Sons of technicians in private sector	3,4	4,3	1,3
Sons of semi-skilled workers in production	3,4	4,2	1,2
Sons of midlevel administrators	4,6	5,6	1,2

(continued)

Table 15.2 (continued)

	% of in total population	Frequency in cluster	Over-representation
Cluster 7 – vocational SPs of the daughters of the working class			
Daughters of skilled workers in production	3,2	9,3	2,9
Daughters of semi-skilled workers in production	3,3	9,1	2,7
Daughters of semi-skilled workers in service	2,4	6,1	2,5
Daughters of foreman	0,9	1,9	2,1
Daughters of small entrepreneurs	1,4	2,9	2,1
Daughters of clerks (commerce)	2,8	5,5	2,0
Daughters of clerks	3,9	7,7	2,0
Daughters of medical and health professions.	5,7	11,3	2,0
Daughters of skilled workers in service	0,7	1,4	1,9
Parents with 9-year compulsory school	6,2	11,5	1,8
Cluster 8 – technical SPs of the sons of the middle classes and the working class			
Sons of technicians in private sector	3,4	10,1	2,9
Sons of law enforcement	0,6	1,3	2,4
Sons of midlevel administrators	4,6	0,10	2,2
Sons of technicians in public sector	0,6	1,2	2,2
Sons of clerks	4,1	8,7	2,1
Sons of skilled workers in service	0,6	1,3	2,0
Sons of skilled workers in production	3,6	7,1	2,0
Sons of engineers	2,1	3,9	1,9
Sons of medical and health professions.	5,8	10,4	1,8
Sons of class teachers	2,3	4,0	1,8
Cluster 9 – vocational SPs of sons of the working class			
Sons of skilled workers in production	3,6	12,8	3,6
Sons of small entrepreneurs	1,4	4,4	3,0
Sons of semi-skilled workers in production	3,4	9,7	2,9
Sons of clerks (commerce)	2,6	6,8	2,6
Sons of semi-skilled workers in service	2,5	6,6	2,6
Sons of medical and health professions	5,8	14,3	2,5
Sons of clerks	4,1	10,1	2,4
Low grades (90–185)	28,0	66,2	2,4
Sons of foreman	1,0	2,2	2,2
Sons of skilled workers in service	0,6	1,3	2,0

In all the interpretation of the 9 clusters is based on 85 categories from 1 active and 6 supplementary variables (columns) together with information from the active row variable that includes school, municipality, study programme and specialization. For more information on interpretation of this data, please contact the authors

References

Ball, S. J. (2007). *Education PLC: Understanding private sector participation in public sector education*. London/New York: Routledge.

Ball, S. J. (2009). Privatising education, Privatising education policy, Privatising educational research: Network governance and the 'competition state'. *Journal of Education Policy, 24*(1), 83–99.

Bertilsson, E. (2014). *Skollärare: rekrytering till utbildning och yrke 1977–2009*. Uppsala: Acta Universitatis Upsaliensis.

Böhlmark, A., & Lindahl, M. (2007). *The impact of school choice on pupil achievement, segregation and costs: Swedish evidence* (IZA Discussion Papers). Bonn: The Institute for the Study of Labor (IZA).

Börjesson, M. (2004). *Gymnasieskolans sociala struktur och sociala gruppers utbildningsstrategier: tendenser på nationell nivå 1997–2001* (Rapporter från forskningsgruppen för utbildnings- och kultursociologi, Vol. 32). Uppsala: SEC, ILU, Uppsala universitet.

Börjesson, M. (2016). Oraison funèbre du modèle suédois. Trois dimensions de la marchandisation de l'enseignement supérieur. In C. Charle & C. Soulié (Eds.), *La dérégulation académique: la construction étatisée des marchés universitaires dans le monde* (pp. 287–307). Paris: Syllepse.

Bourdieu, P. (1979). *La distinction: Critique sociale du jugement de goût*. Paris: Minuit.

Bourdieu, P. (1984). *Homo academicus*. Paris: Editions de Minuit.

Bourdieu, P. (2000). *Les structures sociales de l'économie*. Paris: Seuil.

Bourdieu, P., & De Saint Martin, M. (1978). Le patronat. *Actes de la recherche en sciences sociales, 20*(1), 3–82.

Bradley, S., & Taylor, J. (2010). Diversity, choice and the quasi-market: An empirical analysis of secondary education policy in England. *Oxford Bulletin of Economics and Statistics, 72*(1), 1–26.

Denord, F., Lagneau-Ymonet, P., & Thine, S. (2011). Le pouvoir économique. Classes sociales et modes de domination. *Actes de la recherche en sciences sociales*, (190), 24–57.

Engwall, L. (2007). Universities, the state and the market. *Higher Education Management and Policy, 19*(3), 1–18.

Felouzis, G., Henriot-Van Zanten, A., & Maroy, C. (2013). *Les marchés scolaires: sociologie d'une politique publique d'éducation*. Paris: Presses Univ. de France.

Forsberg, H. (2015). *Kampen om eleverna: Gymnasiefältet och skolmarknadens framväxt i Stockholm, 1987–2011* (Studier i utbildnings- och kultursociologi 7 och Södertörn Doctoral Dissertations, Vol. 112). Uppsala: Acta Universitatis Upsaliensis.

Francois, P., & Vlassopoulos, M. (2008). Pro-social motivation and the delivery of social services. *CESifo Economic Studies, 54*(1), 22–54.

Gaynor, M., Moreno-Serra, R., & Propper, C. (2013). Death by market power: Reform, competition, and patient outcomes in the National Health Service. *American Economic Journal: Economic Policy, 5*(4), 134–166.

Gewirtz, S. (2002). *The managerial school: Post-welfarism and social justice in education. The state of welfare*. London: Routledge.

Harvey, D. (1989). From managerialism to entrepreneurialism: The transformation in urban governance in late capitalism. *Geografiska Annaler. Series B, Human Geography, 71*(1), 3–17.

Hoxby, C. M. (2003). *The economics of school choice*. Chicago: University of Chicago Press.

Le Roux, B., & Rouanet, H. (2004). *Geometric data analysis: From correspondence analysis to structured data analysis*. Dordrecht: Kluwer Academic.

Lebaron, F. (2010). European Central Bank leaders in the global space of central bankers: A geometric data analysis approach. *French Politics, 8*(3), 294–320.

Lidegran, I. (2009). *Utbildningskapital: om hur det alstras, fördelas och förmedlas*. Uppsala: Acta Universitatis Upsaliensis:

Lubienski, C. (2003). Innovation in education markets: Theory and evidence on the impact of competition and choice in charter schools. *American Educational Research Journal, 40*(2), 395–443.

Lynch, K., & Moran, M. (2006). Markets, schools and the convertibility of economic capital: The complex dynamics of class choice. *British Journal of Sociology of Education, 27*(2), 221–235.

Palme, M. (2008). *Det kulturella kapitalet: studier av symboliska tillgångar i det svenska utbildningssystemet 1988–2008*. Uppsala: Acta Universitatis Upsaliensis.

Poupeau, F., François, J., & Couratier, E. (2007). Making the right move: How families are using transfers to adapt to socio-spatial differentiation of schools in the Greater Paris Region. *Journal of Education Policy, 22*(1), 31–47.

Propper, C., Burgess, S., & Green, K. (2004). Does competition between hospitals improve the quality of care? *Journal of Public Economics, 88*(7–8), 1247–1272.

Reay, D. (2004). Exclusivity, exclusion, and social class in urban education markets in the United Kingdom. *Urban Education, 39*(5), 537–560.

Whitty, G., & Power, S. (2000). Marketization and privatization in mass education systems. *International Journal of Educational Development, 20*(2), 93–107.

Chapter 16
The Social Space of Work Orientations: The Case of Nursing

Michael Gemperle

Introduction

Work orientations have attracted increased attention in recent years. The shift in focus away from manual factory workers, rising levels of qualification (e.g. Gallie and White 1998; Rose 2005), and intensified attempts by management to exert more control over workers' subjectivity (e.g. Baldry et al. 2007) have led to a growing interest in the factors that produce and reproduce work attitudes and behavior. However, despite numerous studies – for example on job satisfaction (Kalleberg 1977) and work commitment (Lincoln and Kalleberg 1985) – knowledge of the significance of work orientations for the social relations within professional groups themselves remains limited.

This is especially the case with regard to health care professionals, particularly nurses. Numerous studies characterize nurses as being one of the occupations most likely to prioritize the intrinsic rewards of their job over extrinsic rewards. Furthermore, this tendency is reported especially in association with poor working conditions, suggesting that work orientations are relatively independent of the work environment (cf. Morgan et al. 2013). At the same time, research on specific professions repeatedly shows that occupational groups are characterized by diverging theoretical and practical conceptions of work and that these divergences go hand in hand with social differences within the groups (cf. Boltanski 1982; Dubois 2013; Lehmann 2005; Muel-Dreyfus 1983; Serre 2009). The questions we intend to answer here are: Which work orientations can be distinguished for nurses? How are these orientations related to the professionals' social characteristics?

M. Gemperle (✉)
Institute of Sociology, University of St. Gallen, St. Gallen, Switzerland
e-mail: michael.gemperle@unisg.ch; michael.gemperle@zhaw.ch

© Springer Nature Switzerland AG 2019

J. Blasius et al. (eds.), *Empirical Investigations of Social Space*,
Methodos Series 15, https://doi.org/10.1007/978-3-030-15387-8_16

Theory

Following several decades during which work attitudes and behavior were discussed almost exclusively in terms of the workplace (e.g. Blauner 1964; Lockwood 1966), the focus of attention increasingly shifted to "*independent* [. . .] [factors] relative to the in-plant situation" (Goldthorpe et al. 1968: 183, emphasis in original), leading to the emergence of the concept of work orientation in sociological research. Since the 1980s, authors have increasingly argued for the significance of individuals' embodied characteristics and have often conceptualized these as being independent of social conditions (e.g. Hakim 1995). By contrast, however, several studies have demonstrated that work orientations vary according to, for instance, age, stages in the family life cycle (e.g. Crompton and Harris 1998a), occupational sectors (e.g. Procter and Padfield 1999) and countries (e.g. Crompton and Harris 1998b).

Pierre Bourdieu's (1985) concept of social space makes it possible to system-atically include the material and symbolic resources available to individuals in a given social sphere, enabling us to understand work orientations as an integral part of the system of social relations under consideration. As a result, differences in work attitudes and behaviors can be understood, on the one hand, as an expression of the power relations within the social sphere under consideration. The space of professionals' possible attitudes and behaviors is structured by the relative importance of their cultural, economic and other resources. On the other hand, work orientations are seen as being a source of division and alliance themselves. Work orientations express a vision of the social world and its functioning, representing as such the positions taken by the actors in the symbolic struggles of the sphere in question.

This study applies the concept of social space to an occupational group. Occu-pational groups count among the most important institutions of modern societies according to the sociology of professions (cf. Abbott 1988). Due to their selection and socialization, the members of an occupational group have a series of properties in common, as is to be expected as members of a shared denomination. At the same time, the members of an occupational group also have characteristics that set them apart from one another. These are related to secondary properties such as age, gender, and social and ethnic origin (Bourdieu 1984: 102f.). For this reason, occupational groups consist of subgroups, characterized by different ways and possibilities of investing in the occupational activity, but also by diverging approaches to deriving benefits from their investment. A comparative assessment of research on occupational groups (e.g. Boltanski 1982; Dubois 2013; Lehmann 2005; Muel-Dreyfus 1983; Serre 2009) shows that work attitudes and behaviors go hand in hand with major divergences between professionals. Occupational groups are a "space of competition and struggle" (Bourdieu and Wacquant 1992: 243) over symbolic and material resources (on income and career differences within nursing, cf. Pudney and Shields 2000); it is ultimately the legitimate forms of classification (*doxa*) which are at stake (cf. Bourdieu 1990a: 66).

This chapter aims to contribute to the debate on the social significance of work orientations in paid care work. A major point of reference within the emerging theories of care (England 2005) is the (relative) importance of intrinsic and extrinsic attitudes and behaviors. On the one hand, many studies highlight the contradictions between, as Lyon (2010: 170) put it, "care as love and care as labour" (e.g. Held 2002; Himmelweit 1999; Hochschild 1983). On the other hand, a dichotomizing interpretation of this tension is questioned on the grounds of principal arguments (Nelson 1999; Zelizer 2002) and empirical evidence (Hebson et al. 2015; Morgan et al. 2013). One particularly promising avenue seems to be the characterization of work orientations "as a continuum upon which both remuneration and vocation feature and whose relative importance is determined by the personal circumstances of the individual workers" (Kaine 2012: 325), when these personal circumstances are defined in terms of economic and cultural resources within a social space (Bourdieu 1990).

Data

This analysis is based on data collected by a survey of nurses working in the canton of St. Gallen, in the eastern part of Switzerland. The author administered the survey in the summer of 2014 in all of the region's general hospitals. The survey formed part of the project *Nursing ethics in transition*, subsidized by the Swiss National Science Foundation. The 12 clinics participating in the survey forwarded the letter of invitation to participate in the survey to the nurses in their employ, and made the questionnaire available to them. In the questionnaire, I was careful to use items that measure the identification with and inclination towards concrete forms of behavior in routine work (rather than abstract principles). Moreover, the questionnaire captured information on social demographic characteristics and education.

The present analysis refers to 499 individuals. To keep positional characteristics as constant as possible, the analysis looks only at nurses working in acute care hospitals; this means that nurses working in outpatient care institutions are not part of the sample, nor are professionals working in nursing homes, rehabilitation clinics, and psychiatric hospitals. Furthermore, in order to keep the professional position constant, within this group the analysis takes into account only registered staff nurses, that is to say, professionals mainly working with patients. Nurses in management positions, such as ward managers and nursing directors, were excluded. In order to capture the relative position of an individual within the group, the answers were recoded according to the dispersion of all answers in two modalities (*high* and *low*) or three modalities (*high*, *middle*, and *low*), pooling infrequent categories (<5%) in other categories. Previous specific multiple correspondence analyses conducted with recoded data (recoded into three modalities with regard to the content of answers on the five-point Likert scale), as well as correspondence factor analyses, have both shown a Guttman effect on the second axis, which is not unusual in analyses of scales data (Le Roux 1999; Le Roux and Rouanet 2010).

To construct the space of work orientations, I used nine questions from the organizational citizenship behavior scale (Organ 1988), capturing the level of respondents' agreement or disagreement with statements regarding their work style. The sample gathers 18 modalities (two each for the nine questions); five *middle* and nine *missing* modalities were excluded.

The Space of Work Orientations

A specific multiple correspondence analysis was performed for the analysis. If we look at the modified rates (Benzécri 1992: 412) of the axes, we see that we can interpret the first two axes, which together have an importance of over 99% in explaining the variance in the cloud. This number can be considered to be high, since we are comparing attitudes and behaviors that are quite complex. Most of the variance is accounted for by axis 1 (67%), whereas axis 2 accounts for 32% of the variance.

If we look at the cloud of individuals, no noticeable irregularities can be identified (see Fig. 16.3). As the baseline criterion for retaining modalities to interpret the axes, we apply the standard measure and take the average contribution of the modalities to the axis, which lies at $100/18 = 5.5\%$.

Axis 1 ($\lambda 1 = 0.164$, 67.3%). Occupational Commitment: High Commitment vs. Low Commitment

Eight modalities fulfill the baseline criterion of 5.5% (see Table 16.1), they contribute to 71% of the variance of axis 1. All modalities expressing relatively low levels of commitment to work-related behaviors lie to the right of axis 1 (see Fig. 16.1). They indicate comparatively low levels of commitment to helping coworkers to improve their work (HelCow-), keeping up with developments in the organization (KeepDvp-), and continuing learning in order to improve their work (LearnCo-), as well as lower levels of making innovative suggestions for improving the quality of the organization (InnSugg-) and taking the initiative to protect the organization (ProInst-). On the left side of axis 1, by contrast, we see the modalities indicating higher levels of commitment to these activities: higher degrees of continued learning (LearnCo+), keeping up with developments (KeepDvp+), and protecting the institution (ProInst+). The other variables (below the baseline criterion) show the same pattern. Overall, axis 1 appears to group together different aspects of occupational commitment, with low occupational commitment on the right side and high occupational commitment on the left side.

Table 16.1 Active categories: frequencies, principal coordinates and contributions to the first two axes

	Frequencies	Coordinates		Contributions (in %)	
		Axis 1	Axis 2	Axis 1	Axis 2
I keep up with developments in the organization.					
KeepDvp-	83	1.164	−0.621	**11.6**	3.9
KeepDvp+	88	−1.209	0.060	**13.2**	0.0
I learn continuously to make my work better.					
LearnCo-	90	0.993	−0.282	**9.1**	0.9
LearnCo+	84	−1.032	0.390	**9.2**	1.6
I take steps to protect the organization from possible problems.					
ProInst-	216	0.589	−0.278	**7.7**	2.0
ProInst+	272	−0.460	0.214	**5.9**	1.5
I make innovative suggestions for improving the quality of the organization.					
InnSugg-	129	0.806	−0.676	**8.6**	**7.1**
InnSugg+	360	−0.290	0.241	3.1	2.5
I help coworkers to improve their work.					
HelCow-	114	0.704	−0.366	**5.8**	1.9
HelCow+	61	−0.839	0.525	4.4	2.0
I'm absent only when it is absolutely impossible for me to get to work.					
AbsONec-	207	0.442	0.831	4.1	**17.3**
AbsONec+	284	−0.324	−0.610	3.1	**12.8**
I take off only in very urgent situations.					
OffOUrg-	168	0.379	0.665	2.5	**9.0**
OffOUrg+	134	−0.614	−1.033	5.2	**17.3**
I do not take extra breaks.					
NoEBrks-	104	0.519	0.849	2.9	**9.1**
NoEBrks+	174	−0.433	−0.565	3.4	**6.7**
I'm worried about changes in the organization.					
WryChgs-	330	−0.044	0.187	0.1	1.4
WryChgs+	161	0.088	−0.391	0.1	3.0
I keep up with developments in the organization.					
KeepDvp-	83	1.164	−0.621	11.6	3.9
KeepDvp+	88	−1.209	0.060	13.2	0.0
I learn continuously to make my work better.					
LearnCo-	90	0.993	−0.282	9.1	0.9
LearnCo+	84	−1.032	0.390	9.2	1.6
I take steps to protect the organization from possible problems.					
ProInst-	216	0.589	−0.278	7.7	2.0
ProInst+	272	−0.460	0.214	5.9	1.5
I make innovative suggestions for improving the quality of the organization.					
InnSugg-	129	0.806	−0.676	8.6	7.1
InnSugg+	360	−0.290	0.241	3.1	2.5

(continued)

Table 16.1 (continued)

	Frequencies	Coordinates		Contributions (in %)	
		Axis 1	Axis 2	Axis 1	Axis 2
I help coworkers to improve their work.					
HelCow-	114	0.704	−0.366	5.8	1.9
HelCow+	61	−0.839	0.525	4.4	2.0
I'm absent only when it is absolutely impossible for me to get to work					
AbsONec-	207	0.442	0.831	4.1	17.3
AbsONec+	284	−0.324	−0.610	3.1	12.8
I take off only in very urgent situations.					
OffOUrg-	168	0.379	0.665	2.5	9.0
OffOUrg+	134	−0.614	−1.033	5.2	17.3
I do not take extra breaks.					
NoEBrks-	104	0.519	0.849	2.9	9.1
NoEBrks+	174	−0.433	−0.565	3.4	6.7
I'm worried about changes in the organization.					
WryChgs-	330	−0.044	0.187	0.1	1.4
WryChgs+	161	0.088	−0.391	0.1	3.0

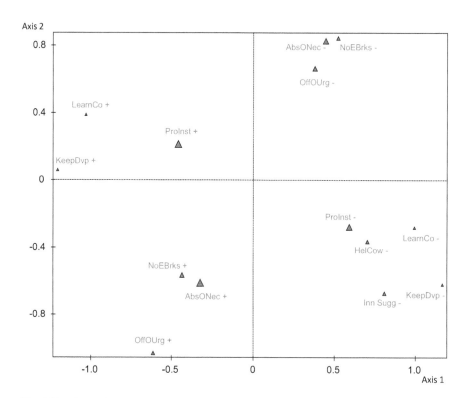

Fig. 16.1 Plane 1–2. Interpretation of axis 1 and 2: the 14 modalities contributing most to the axes

Table 16.2 Coordinates of supplementary categories

	Frequencies	Axis 1	Axis 2
Gender			
Women	484	0.023	−0.006
Men	15	−0.732	0.191
Age			
18–24	32	0.263	−0.055
25–34	200	0.183	0.040
35–44	125	−0.047	−0.004
45–54	95	−0.271	−0.084
55–64	47	−0.284	0.049
Household income			
<5200 CHF	55	0.258	−0.128
5200–9899 CHF	249	−0.018	−0.097
9900–15,099 CHF	128	0.005	0.193
≥CHF15100 CHF	19	−0.539	0.197
Education level			
compuls.	307	0.082	−0.019
postcomp.	139	−0.104	−0.129
≥*Matura*	47	−0.182	0.457
Work experience			
0–16 year	308	0.123	0.025
17–33 year	153	−0.208	−0.084
34–45 year	14	−0.443	0.281

Axis 2 (λ2 = 0.139, 32.1%). Occupational Dimensions: Activity vs. Employment

Axis 2 is dominated by seven modalities of four variables that together contribute to 79% of the variance. At the top of axis 2 (see Fig. 16.1) are modalities expressing lower degrees of the behaviors to avoid extra breaks (NoEBrks-), to leave work early only in very urgent situations (OffOUrg-), and to be absent from work only if necessary (AbsONec-). At the bottom of this axis, we find modalities indicating higher levels of these kinds of behavior (NoEBrks+, OffOUrg+, AbsONec+) as well as lower levels of making suggestions for improving the quality of the organization (InnSugg-). This opposition may be interpreted as an antagonism between two fundamentally different stances towards work: between work orientations that tend to focus on the activity as a vocation, on the one hand (at the top in Fig. 16.1), and attitudes and behaviors that tend to focus on aspects of employment and employee status, on the other (at the bottom). This opposition is familiar from the literature of industrial and work sociology, which distinguishes the producer's perspective (*Produzentenperspektive*) from the wage laborer's perspective (*Arbeitnehmerperspektive*). The former is mainly preoccupied with the activity itself, its content and meaning, while the latter focuses on the ability to work, remuneration, and job security (cf. Schumann et al. 1982). In total, the modalities suggest that axis 2 seems to capture the differences which distinguish those staff nurses who are more oriented towards the activity itself (top) from staff nurses more oriented towards employment in general (bottom).

Socio-demographics

We will now take a look at the socio-demographic variables associated with the first two axes structuring the space of work orientations. These socio-demographic variables do not contribute to the construction of the space of distances between the individuals, and thus have an illustrative character. The variable *gender* is not taken into account because there are very few men in the sample (3.0%). For *age*, the modalities are ordered on axis 1, and the deviation between the extreme modalities (*18–24* and *55–64*) is notable (d = 0.5). The modalities for *household income* are ordered on axis 1 and axis 2. The extreme modalities (*<CHF 5200* and ≥ *CHF 15,100*) show a large deviation (d = 0.8) on axis 1. *General education* levels are essentially ordered on axis 1, but show a small deviation (d = 0.3). However, the difference between *compuls.* (9 years of education) and *postcomp.* (9 years of compulsory education plus 1 to 3 years specialized education) on the one hand and ≥ *Matura* (academic upper secondary school, total of 12 years of education) on the other shows a notable (d = 0.5) correlation with axis 2. The modalities for *work experience* show a notable deviation (d = 0.6) between the modalities *0-16y* and *34-45y* on axis 1.

Overall, axis 1 is determined by the factors *age, work experience* and *household income* (see Fig. 16.2). The factor income indicates that nurses with greater household income exhibit stronger occupational commitment. Age and work experience (occupational tenure) result in older (and more experienced) staff nurses being notably more engaged with their occupation than younger (and less experienced) professionals. Older (and more experienced) professionals tend to have a greater household income. In sum, axis 1 seems to capture predominantly the volume of (economic) resources.

Axis 2 is determined by the factor *education* (see Fig. 16.2). Staff nurses with a *Matura* (academic upper secondary school education) tend to be more oriented towards the activity itself, and less towards the employment side of their occupation than their colleagues with lower education. Overall, axis 2 captures differences in cultural resources.

Axis 1 distinguishes the staff nurses according to their occupational commitment. The analysis shows that different forms of occupational commitment are positively correlated. All the modalities manifesting higher levels of occupational commitment are on the left side of the origin, and the modalities expressing lower levels are on the right side (see Fig. 16.1). Evidently, the same individuals tend to display either high levels or low levels of engagement for multiple behaviors. Occupational commitment seems to constitute a major source of the differences between nurses. At the same time, it is striking that the different forms of commitment point in the same direction, although they do not necessarily express identical behaviors. Occupational commitment is a complex phenomenon comprising different dimensions,

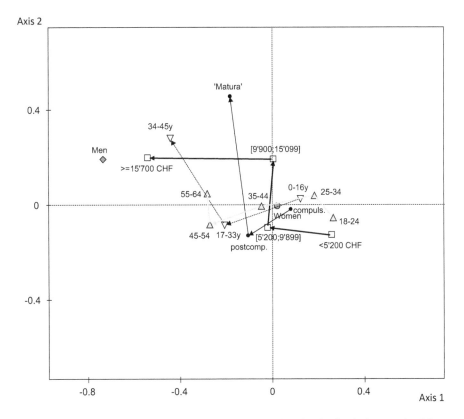

Fig. 16.2 Age, work experience, household income and education in cloud of categories (plane 1–2)

including one's relationship with one's colleagues, one's conscientiousness, and one's importance for the institution.

To fully understand the significance of axis 1, we take closer look at the most characteristic forms of occupational commitment. We can see that for two of the three questions contributing most to axis 1, social status is particularly relevant: learning to improve one's work, and taking the initiative to protect the organization. It seems as if by indicating their occupational commitment, the respondents tended to assert (amongst other things) their own social status, increasingly so the more resources they had at their disposal. The analysis of axis 1 shows that age and work experience have a notable effect on work commitment, and that the effect of household income is even larger. This is in line with the literature, which demonstrates that occupational commitment is not only often associated with occupational tenure, but is also determined by economic resources – besides education level and occupational position (Baudelot and Collac 2003: 222), which here are both constant.[1]

Axis 2 differentiates nurses according to their orientation towards their employment in general and the activity itself. Nurses with a strong orientation towards their occupational activity are located at the top of axis 2, whereas those who tend to be oriented towards employment are found at the bottom of it (Fig. 16.1). The analysis shows a notable effect of the difference between the education levels below academic upper secondary school education (*compuls.*, *postcomp.*), and academic upper secondary school education and above ('*≥Matura*') on axis 2. Nurses who have completed academic upper secondary school tend to have a stronger orientation towards the activity than their colleagues and a less strong orientation towards employment.

With an academic upper secondary school qualification, nurses not only acquire further general education, which provides them with additional knowledge and techniques. Nurses with these qualifications have also been socially and symbolically separated from the occupational field (before entering the profession) for a longer period than their colleagues, and have thus acquired different dispositions. They were still going to school while their colleagues were already beginning their careers (cf. Bourdieu 1992). We have every reason to believe that an academic upper secondary school qualification in particular provides nursing professionals with resources for taking a more distanced stance towards their employment and its constraints. Conversely, nurses without an academic upper secondary school education enter the world of work much earlier, sometimes straight after compulsory schooling, and tend to interiorize the expectations of a subaltern workforce (availability, conscientiousness, etc.) much more easily, especially as they generally lack experience of the alternatives.

Individuals Within the Space of Work Orientations

To assess the validity of the results and to refine the interpretation of the axis, we now turn to individual sample members with whom interviews were conducted. Following the survey, a total of 46 respondents were investigated. The interviews took place in 2015 in a location chosen by the interviewees, either at their place of work (in a quiet room), at a restaurant, or at the University of St. Gallen. The conversation consisted of a semi-structured interview, generally one hour in length, and focused upon their trajectory, work experience, perception of nursing work,

---

[1]Complementary specific multiple correspondence analyses conducted including nurses at higher levels in the hierarchy (ward managers, nursing directors) produce a space with not only a similar structure to the present analysis, but also with a strong association on axis 1 between institutional hierarchies and responsibilities.

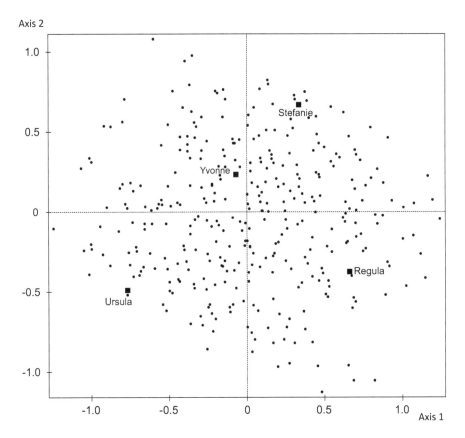

Fig. 16.3 Cloud of individuals (plane 1–2) with the position of the 4 interviewees

and relationship to colleagues. Figure 16.3 shows the position of the four selected individuals within the cloud of individuals.

- Ursula is one of the nurses with a high occupational commitment with more economic than cultural resources at their disposal. Ursula is 57 years old and lives with her husband and their four grown-up children in the city in which the clinic she works at is located. Working in a surgery unit, she increased her employment level to 70% a few years ago to cover the study-related costs of their children. Ursula comes from a farming family, and in the interview she stresses that access to higher education is "difficult" under such "family circumstances". Her husband is a graduate from the local business school and works as a banking professional.

According to the information she shared in the survey, Ursula shows particularly high occupational commitment in seven of the nine categories: She is characterized by high conscientiousness and does not take extra breaks, is absent from work only if necessary, and leaves work early only in very urgent situations. In addition, she keeps up to date, learns continually, and takes the initiative to protect the institution more than her colleagues do. Furthermore, she is more worried than others about changes at the institution.

Ursula "has always worked alongside" her family duties. Thus it is little surprise that she notes in the interview that what "gives her ultimate contentment at work" is when she "can draw on her experience" vis-à-vis younger nurses and medical assistants. Ursula clearly distances herself from "helper's syndrome types", who she believes will "very likely become exhausted sometime". At the same time, she emphasizes (not without pride) that during her years at work she "has never been absent from work, not even due to sickness". Ursula is most bothered by her colleagues when they are not cooperative and hard-working, as described in the following statement:

> It bothers me if someone is indifferent. [. . .] Or do not help each other enough. Those who are more idle than others, and so on. Just recently, I had another conversation with a colleague, who told me: "This colleague never helps at night and I had to do everything alone . . . ". And then I always say: "Oh! I would never want people to say such things about me (*laughs*) – absolutely not! (*guffaws*)"

- Yvonne can be considered a representative of the nurses with high occupational commitment who have more cultural than economic resources at their disposal. Her father was a journalist at a (church-oriented) newspaper and her mother, who held a commercial qualification, worked mainly in the household. Yvonne is 40 years old, is married, with two children of school age, and has a part-time position (40%) in Accident and Emergency (A&E). Yvonne completed upper secondary specialized school (Diplommittelschule), but makes clear that she could have obtained a higher general education degree ("my teachers actually wanted me to go into an academic upper secondary school"). Yvonne's husband works in marketing and the monthly household income is about 10,000 CHF (roughly 10,000 $ monthly).

Yvonne has some points in common with Ursula. She is also characterized by higher levels of taking the initiative to improve the workplace and protect the institution. And, like Ursula, she worries more than others about changes in the institution. Unlike Ursula, however, Yvonne tends towards higher levels of taking extra breaks and being absent from work.

Yvonne is certainly one of the more experienced nurses in her specialist field and, like Ursula, has the impression that she has more knowledge and skills than the "younger ones" as a result of her experience. In contrast to Ursula, Yvonne shows very high motivation for the content of her work. Although she stopped working in the profession for almost a decade when she became a mother and claims she will not be able to increase her employment level "for the next ten years" because of her children, Yvonne says in the interview that she finds working in A&E "very exciting", quite unlike other areas, even though it involves shift and weekend work. Not only has Yvonne moved to another city to remain working in this special area; she has also completed additional training, is involved with a national association of other professionals in the field ("I'm doing this voluntarily, I'm paying for it by myself"), and meets colleagues privately. And she emphatically distances herself from the economic rewards of her activity:

> I got pregnant, I had the first child. I then stayed at home – voluntarily, quite deliberately actually! After two years, I had the second child. Then, after one and a half years I realized I would love to go back to work, because I would otherwise be bored at home – quite honestly!

• Stefanie belongs to the group of nurses with a relatively low occupational commitment with more cultural than economic resources at their disposal. She is 26 years old, childless and married to a salesman. Her monthly household income lies at approximately 9000 CHF. Stefanie completed her professional training 3 years ago and has a full-time position in the neurological unit of a larger hospital. In the interview, Stefanie expresses great disappointment with nursing work, and states that she is considering professional alternatives. Stefanie's father is a plant manager, her mother is a doctor's receptionist and her elder sister a registered nurse.

Stefanie has some points in common with Yvonne. She takes the initiative to improve the workplace and to protect the institution. Furthermore, she takes more breaks and is absent from work more than her colleagues on average. However, Stefanie also shows a higher level of ongoing learning. On the other hand, she takes more time off than others, is less worried about changes in the institution, keeps herself less informed, and supports colleagues less.

Like Yvonne, Stefanie is also concerned with the content of her work. She says in the interview that "the medical aspect" gives her "great joy" and is what "fulfills" her. Even more strongly than Yvonne, her objectives and aspirations seem to be defined by medicine, and she says that "there is really a fascination [for medicine]". She considers colleagues who do not have an affinity for people and do not think and act professionally to be in the wrong place.

> If you do not have that patience with a sick person. Or, if you cannot look at it as a disease with a dementia patient, but get agitated, for example: "Look, he's done it again... wet the bed, he's doing this on purpose!" [...] If you're not able to do that, then you shouldn't be doing the job!

Stefanie shows great dissatisfaction with her professional environment. She is looking for an activity in which she "still has the medical aspect, but no longer in that style". It seems that her opportunities for qualifying herself further are considerably limited because of the costs. So she goes about her occupation without great commitment, hoping to soon find a way out of her situation ("I might know where to go in 10 years").

• Regula is a representative of the nurses with low occupational commitment who have more economic than cultural resources at their disposal. Regula is 44 years old, childless and single. In addition to her occupational work, she volunteers at a Sunday school. She recently reduced her employment level to 70% to start training as an acupuncturist. The household income is close to 5000 CHF. Regula's father is a businessman, her mother is a hairdresser.

In the survey, Regula shows particularly low commitment in six of the nine categories: keeping up to date, protecting the institution, worrying about changes in the institution, helping coworkers, and continued learning. On the other hand, Regula is more engaged than her colleagues in improving the quality of the workplace, not taking extra breaks, and being absent from work only if necessary.

Regula has worked in an interdisciplinary ward in a mid-sized clinic for more than 20 years. During this time, she has held various management positions and completed a range of further training. However, as her account suggests, her desire to be a good employee seems to have been more important in this than her identification with the activity itself ("I had the impression someone had to do it", "I slipped into it"). She is religiously motivated and is bothered by "competitiveness" and "performance mentality". However, in the interview the main focus of her resentment are the material and symbolic rewards the clinic has withheld from her, and in this regard she reports multiple "defiant phases" in her working life. At present, Regula seems to be committed above all to her acupuncture training and to building up an alternative occupational existence, which was also the goal of her earlier training as an advisory pastor.

Conclusion

This study aimed to investigate how the work orientations of staff nurses vary with their position within the occupational group's social space. The Specific Multiple Correspondence Analysis showed that occupational commitment constitutes a major source of differences between nurses and is positively associated with (economic) resources. Moreover, staff nurses with higher levels of education tended to display an orientation towards the activity of caregiving itself, whereas their colleagues with fewer cultural resources were more closely oriented towards seeing nursing as a form of employment. The results suggest that work orientations vary considerably dependent on the volume and composition of cultural and economic resources.

The analysis of the four selected portraits demonstrated that with work orientations, the beliefs of a social space are also relevant. As nursing is an occupational group in a subordinate relationship with medical doctors, these beliefs are partially determined by the field of medicine. Notably, the interviewees who are oriented towards the actual activity of providing care seem to exhibit many more beliefs that are dominant within the medical field than the interviewees oriented towards the dimension of employment. Moreover, the analysis showed that the likelihood of expressing these beliefs (and thus distinguishing oneself from the wage laborer's perspective) vary considerably in proportion to cultural resources. This can be interpreted in the light of the opposition between (bourgeois) inheritors and parvenus, which is characteristic of many occupational groups according to Bourdieu (1984); its significance has been shown for different occupational groups (e.g. Boltanski 1982; Dubois 2013; Lehmann 2005; Muel-Dreyfus 1983; Serre 2009). Consequently, this analysis seems to provide evidence for the opposition between two fundamentally distinct occupational attitudes and behaviors, which are rooted in different occupational fractions. On a more general level, the analysis shows that with every space of work orientations, the properties of the social space in question have to be taken into consideration.

The results of this study can also be discussed in terms of the dual categories of intrinsic and extrinsic orientations, a central reference point in the contemporary discourse on nurses' work orientations (see introduction). In conceptual terms, the opposition intrinsic-extrinsic seems close to that between the producer's and the wage laborer's perspective. Intrinsic motivation refers to satisfaction found in the work activity itself, and the producer's perspective to the use value of work; conversely, extrinsic motivation refers to material rewards (income, promotion) and the wage laborer's perspective to the exchange value of the activity. If we accept this connection, this analysis is empirical evidence – consistent with recent studies (Hebson et al. 2015; Morgan et al. 2013) – that the categories intrinsic and extrinsic address important differences and should be seen as two ends of a continuum. However, in referring mainly to employees' conscious intentions, the categories intrinsic orientation and extrinsic orientation seem to conceptually capture only part of the opposition between the producer's perspective and the wage laborer's perspective.

Further work will be necessary to clarify the mechanisms underlying the relation between occupational positions and work orientations. In particular, it would be interesting to investigate other occupational spaces and compare them with the group scrutinized here. For this purpose, occupational groups with great autonomy in terms of the social macrocosm seem particularly appropriate (see Lebaron & Bonnet in this volume on class-specific analysis). This would also enable the more precise identification of those characteristics of work orientations which are universal, and those which are specific to a certain group – thus contributing to a sounder understanding of the relation between social structure and work orientations. A closer examination of different generations could also open up new perspectives. Furthermore, the inclusion of other types of behavior might help to improve the dimensionality of the model and thus lead to a more refined picture of the significance of work orientations for the social space of occupational groups.

References

Abbott, A. (1988). *The system of professions: An essay on the division of expert labor*. Chicago: University of Chicago Press.

Baldry, C., Bain, P., Taylor, P., Hyman, J., Scholarios, D., Marks, A., Watson, A., Gilbert, K., Gall, G., & Bunzel, D. (2007). *The meaning of work in the new economy*. Basingstoke: Palgrave Macmillan.

Baudelot, C., & Gollac, M. (2003). *Travailler pour être heureux? Le bonheur et le travail en France*. Paris: Fayard.

Benzécri, J. P. (1992). *Correspondence analysis handbook*. New York: Dekker.

Blauner, R. (1964). *Alienation and freedom. The factory worker and his industry*. Chicago: University of Chicago Press.

Boltanski, L. (1982). *Les cadres: la formation d'un group social*. Paris: Éditions de Minuit.

Bourdieu, P. (1984). *Distinction: A social critique of the judgement of taste*. London: Routledge & Kegan Paul.

Bourdieu, P. (1985). The social space and the genesis of groups. *Theory and Society, 14*(6), 723–744.

Bourdieu, P. (1990). *The logic of practice*. Cambridge: Polity Press.

Bourdieu, P. (1992). *Questions de sociologie*. Paris: Éditions de Minuit.

Bourdieu, P., & Wacquant, L. (1992). *An invitation to reflexive sociology*. Cambridge: Polity.

Crompton, R., & Harris, F. (1998a). Explaining women's employment patterns: 'Orientations to work' revisited. *The British Journal of Sociology, 49*(1), 118–136.

Crompton, R., & Harris, F. (1998b). Gender relations and employment: The impact of occupation. *Work, Employment & Society, 12*(2), 297–315.

Dubois, V. (2013). *La culture comme vocation*. Paris: Raisons d'agir.

England, P. (2005). Emerging theories of care work. *Annual Review of Sociology, 31*, 381–399.

Gallie, D., & White, M. (1998). *Restructuring the employment relationship*. Oxford: Clarendon Press.

Goldthorpe, J., Lockwood, D., Bechhofer, F., & Platt, J. (1968). *The affluent worker: Industrial attitudes and behaviours*. London: Cambridge University Press.

Hakim, C. (1995). Five feminist myths about women's employment. *The British Journal of Sociology*, 429–455.

Hebson, G., Rubery, J., & Grimshaw, D. (2015). Rethinking job satisfaction in care work: Looking beyond the care debates. *Work, Employment & Society, 29*(2), 314–330.

Held, V. (2002). Care and the extension of markets. *Hypatia, 17*(2), 19–33.

Himmelweit, S. (1999). Caring Labor. *The ANNALS of the American Academy of Political and Social Science, 561*(1), 27–38.

Hochschild, A. R. (1983). *The managed heart: Commercialization of human feeling*. Berkeley: University of California Press.

Kaine, S. (2012). Regulation and employee voice in the residential aged care sector. *Human Resource Management Journal, 22*(3), 316–331.

Kalleberg, A. L. (1977). Work values and job rewards: A theory of job satisfaction. *American Sociological Review, 42*(1), 124–143.

Le Roux, B. (1999). Analyse spécifique d'un nuage euclidien: application à l'étude des questionnaires. *Mathématiques et sciences humaines*, (146), 65–83.

Le Roux, B., & Rouanet, H. (2010). *Multiple correspondence analysis*. Thousand Oaks: Sage.

Lehmann, B. (2005). *L'orchestre dans tous ses éclats: ethnographie des formations symphoniques*. Paris: La Découverte.

Lincoln, J. R., & Kalleberg, A. L. (1985). Work organization and workforce commitment: A study of plants and employees in the U.S. and Japan. *American Sociological Review, 50*(6), 738–760.

Lockwood, D. (1966). Sources of variation in working class images of society. *The Sociological Review, 14*, 249–267.

Lyon, D. (2010). Intersections and boundaries of work and non-work. *European Societies, 12*(2), 163–185.

Morgan, J. C., Dill, J., & Kalleberg, A. L. (2013). The quality of healthcare jobs: Can intrinsic rewards compensate for low extrinsic rewards? *Work, Employment & Society, 27*(5), 802–822.

Muel-Dreyfus, F. (1983). *Le métier d'éducateur: les instituteurs de 1900, les éducateurs spécialisés de 1968*. Paris: Éditions de Minuit.

Nelson, J. (1999). Of Markets and Martyrs: Is it OK to Pay well for Care? *Feminist Economics, 5*(3), 43–59.

Organ, D. W. (1988). *Organizational citizenship behavior: The good soldier syndrome*. Lexington Books/DC Heath and Com.

Procter, I., & Padfield, M. (1999). Work orientations and women's work: A critique of Hakim's theory of the heterogeneity of women. *Gender, Work & Organization, 6*(3), 152–162.

Pudney, S., & Shields, M. (2000). Gender, race, pay and promotion in the British nursing profession: Estimation of a generalized ordered probit model. *Journal of Applied Econometrics, 15*(4), 367–399.

Rose, M. (2005). Do rising levels of qualification alter work ethic, work orientation and organizational commitment for the worse? evidence from the UK, 1985–2001. *Journal of Education and Work, 18*(2), 131–164.

Schumann, M., Einemann, E., Siebel-Rebell, C., & Wittemann, K. P. (1982). *Rationalisierung, Krise, Arbeiter: eine empirische Untersuchung der Industrialisierung auf der Werft*. Frankfurt am Main: Europäische Verlagsanstalt.

Serre, D. (2009). *Les coulisses de l'État social. Enquête sur les signalements d'enfant en danger*. Paris: Raisons d'agir.

Zelizer, V. (2002). How care counts. *Contemporary Sociology, 31*(2), 115–119.

Chapter 17
Structure and Change in the Field of Mid-Twentieth Century Human Scientists in Sweden

Tobias Dalberg

Introduction

The middle decades of the twentieth century were central to the development of the modern human sciences in many ways. In Sweden, like in most other western states where the intensity of reform increased (Smith 1997), most of the disciplines we see as core components of the social sciences today established their position and expanded over the course of the 1940s to the 1960s. This development took a very concrete form in the government commissions launched in late 1943 (by minister of education and economics professor Gösta Bagge) and in the middle of 1945 (by the new minister of education and *Filosofie Kandidat* – FK, the Swedish equivalent of a Bachelor's degree – in statistics and economics Tage Erlander). The directive of the first commission was to investigate the possibility of establishing a research council for the social sciences, a form of organization that became very fashionable during the 1940s. Over the course of 5 years, a research council would be established for each of the main research domains, beginning with the research council for technology in 1942, and continuing with medicine in 1945 and natural science 1946, with social science finally getting a research council in 1947 after a heated debate over the proposals of the first commission in particular. The same year, the Humanities Fund, created to support research in the humanities, began receiving most of its annual budget from direct government funds.

Electronic supplementary material The online version of this chapter (https://doi.org/10.1007/978-3-030-15387-8_17) contains supplementary material, which is available to authorized users.

T. Dalberg (✉)
Graduate School of Education, Stanford University, Stanford, California
e-mail: tobias_dalberg@hotmail.com

© Springer Nature Switzerland AG 2019
J. Blasius et al. (eds.), *Empirical Investigations of Social Space*,
Methodos Series 15, https://doi.org/10.1007/978-3-030-15387-8_17

Since the social sciences had been neglected in terms of resources, a proposition that would increase such funds through a research council might initially be seen as something that most could agree upon. It was not well-received, however, as many of the professors who had not been part of the commission were critical of the way the proposal unquestioningly embraced the idea of social research being governed by its relevance to society and the political field. They would rather have seen increased basic funding of the social sciences with more chairs in general, and particularly in the most recent disciplines of the social sciences. A third position was taken by economist Gunnar Myrdal who, while also acknowledging the neglect in resources, argued in favor of the autonomy of the social sciences, and indeed of science in general. On the face of it, this stance would seem put him in the same position as the "protectionist professors" arguing for more basic funding (Nybom 1997: 92). Myrdal would, however, go further and attack this stance too, warning of the dangers that are involved in providing young and immature fields with additional resources without letting them first grow into strong disciplines themselves. By establishing chairs in disciplines without a critical mass of competent candidates, one would, according to Myrdal, "risk having witless holders of the new chairs. This would be most dangerous, if they, in addition, were young . . . " (Myrdal 1944: 255).

Among other things, this debate highlights a trait fundamental to the basic analytical model underpinning this paper: The organizational structure of the human sciences, including the careers within them, is itself an essential component of the contest for positions in the university field in general and in the relatively autonomous subsystem of human sciences in particular. Continuing this line of argument, one of the main functions of this subsystem could be regarded as providing and distributing career opportunities to human scientists. Furthermore, since it is populated by social agents with certain attributes, an analysis of the formation of these social agents and of how they are linked to other fields or subsystems should be an integral part of any description of the functioning of this subsystem (cf. Gingras 1991: 4). The aim of this paper is to begin such an analysis, with a particular focus on (1) the career patterns of Swedish human scientists in 1945, and on (2) how these patterns developed over the following two decades as the social sciences expanded.

Since this chapter deals with the structure of the subsystem of human sciences and how this structure may have changed over time, a central question that will be discussed in this analysis is: Under which conditions one would expect stable and changing structures, respectively? In the method section I argue that, depending on how the empirical analysis is designed, the patterns resulting from the analysis will likely follow one of only a limited set of models of change.

In brief, I approach this question using a prosopography of the human scientists who held some kind of position at Swedish universities and university colleges in 1945 and 1965. This includes those who held a chair (*professur*) and those who were employed on temporary scholarships and contracts (*docent*) or held the teaching position of university lecturer (*universitetslektor*, since 1959). With the concepts of capital and field as my starting point, I use geometric data analysis (GDA) to explore the distribution of career patterns and resources in the human sciences, conceived of as a relatively autonomous subsystem of the university field and the scientific field.

The structure of the aforementioned distribution of career patterns and resources has not previously been investigated empirically by way of a multivariate statistical approach. Consequently, there are no studies with such an approach to the Swedish case which examine how this structure might change over time. Indeed, for a long time, it seemed inconceivable to conduct studies of change within the GDA paradigm with the same meticulous approach applied to the study of structures. In recent times, though, there has been an upsurge in works attempting to solve this issue among those scholars who combine the concepts of capital and field with GDA.

Next, I provide an overview of the Swedish academic career system and how I use concepts like capital and field to analyze it. This is followed by a section on the methodological considerations, i.e. the sources and indicators used and how to compare structures over time. The next section compares two separate multiple correspondence analyses (MCA) of the field of human sciences in 1945 and 1965. In the concluding section, I discuss some of the results in relation to some more general trends in the history of human sciences in Sweden.

Becoming a Human Scientist

During the first half of the 1900s, there was basically one form of tenured teaching position at Swedish universities (and the country's two private colleges): the professor, equivalent to the German *Lehrstuhl*. As Swedish higher education, like in the rest of the industrialized world, expanded in the middle decades of the century, a new position solely for teaching was created in 1959, the university lecturer. As of 1852, university statutes had obliged the professors to carry out both teaching and research.

The single most important qualification required to become eligible for a professorship was the doctoral degree. If one wanted to pursue a university career, one would need to qualify as a docent, something which required one of the three highest grades (*Laudatur* to *Cum laude approbatur*). For those who passed, but still failed to reach the top three grades, a university career was practically impossible. Those whose disciplines were taught at the *läroverk* (upper secondary schools) could, however, pursue a career as a teacher at these schools.

On average, just over six professors a year were appointed in human sciences between 1925–1965 (*Sveriges statskalender* 1925, 1945, 1965), with fewer in the first decades and more after the late 1940s. The principle was that there should be at most one professor in each discipline at each faculty. A discipline could be fully represented when it had one professor each at the universities in Uppsala and Lund and at the university colleges (later on universities) in Göteborg and Stockholm. This organization was very similar to the German and Austrian model (Fleck 2011: 18).

These constrained numbers set the basis for what might be considered the peculiarities of the Swedish system. Becoming professor at a young age meant that you were one of just a select few who could influence the developments in your discipline from an advanced position. Being a professor meant, for the social scientists in particular, that you were the 'go-to guy' whenever the government launched a commission and needed commissioners or experts. As Bo Sandelin (2000: 67) pointed out, the commission on monetary value in 1918 commissioned half of all economics professors – active and retired – at the time, with half in this case meaning a total of three persons.

In this setting, the typical career pattern of the human scientists would begin with a successful journey through the educational system. It started with a maturity exam from the Latin track at the *läroverk* (upper secondary school), continued with a *Filosofie Kandidat* after about two and half years at university, followed by a *Filosofie Licentiat* (FL) degree 6 years after the FK degree, and a *Filosofie Doktor* (FD) an additional 4 years later. Provided that the defense yielded a docent grade, one could be in possession of a docent scholarship within 2 years after the defense. Since the professor was influential in allocating these scholarships within his discipline, being a holder of such scholarship put you in a favorable position in the competition for the professor chair once its holder retired.

Careers as Accumulation and Conversion of Resources

The social selection taking place en route to the professor position can be neatly illustrated by a comparison of the social origins of the human scientists in my data and the population in general at the times in question. In 1911, three clerks at the Swedish statistical agency (SCB) created a classification scheme based on the social groups I, II, and III, or "higher class", "middle class", and "manual workers' class", to be used in the studies of poll results (Andersson et al. 1981: 113). In general elections in 1928, the higher class consisted of about 5% of the adult population, the middle class of about 39%, and the workers' class of about 56% (*Statistisk årsbok för Sverige* 1931: 336–337). Grouping academics by their fathers' occupations in 1945 and 1965 provides almost the exact inverse proportions of social groups: Just over one half originated from social group I, almost 40% from social group II, and less than 10% from the manual workers' class.

Their social selectivity apart, other indicators suggest the human scientists – at least the professors – occupied a prominent position in the contemporary social space. They were, as a consequence of their educational qualification criteria, perhaps the richest in terms of institutionalized cultural capital. In addition, being holders of a university diploma, they were placed in the most highly remunerated group among the diploma holders in state service (SCB 1959). This suggests that it might be reasonable to place them in a position analogous to that of the French university teachers in *Homo Academicus*, where they occupied a position in the dominated pole of the field of power, while at the same time – due to their wealth in institutionalized cultural capital – occupying a temporally dominant position in the field of cultural production (Bourdieu 1996: 71).

The involvement of human scientists in the state apparatus through the government commissions certainly places them close to the field of power, but what about the relation of the human scientists to the field of cultural production? By virtue of their research object, art and literature historians are more or less connected to the cultural domain. But as Bourdieu (1998: 59–60) suggested, the relations between the fields of science and of journalism, in his case, depend also on the power relations between the fields and on the degree of independence of the scientific disciplines (see also Münch, Chap. 12 and Baier and Schmitz, Chap. 18, in this volume). The bottom line is that while a scientist's position depends on recognition in various forms, this recognition could either rest more upon validation from their peers or from the media. As an indicator of this, we might consider whether an individual wrote for the cultural journal *Ord och Bild*, chosen because of its centrality in the cultural field and its longevity – it is the oldest still active cultural journal in Sweden and has been distributed since 1892. Apart from art and literary criticism, it frequently published a wider range of scientific contributions from both the human and the natural sciences. At least a quarter of the 1945 cohort once or occasionally wrote for this journal. This share dropped to one eighth for the 1965 cohort.

Both participation in commissions and contribution to cultural journals may be considered, to borrow from Bourdieu (1975: 25), a conversion of the specific kind of authority that is bestowed upon those who establish themselves in the field of human sciences. The alternative, of course, is that they have somehow accumulated the necessary political or literary capital required to be a commission expert or a literary critic elsewhere. The latter is, however, less likely, due to the fact that it takes a substantial amount of time to accumulate the resources needed to become established in any field, and the simultaneous accumulation of literary and scientific capital would be rare indeed. There are obviously exceptions, for instance a dissertation in history of literature that transgresses the genres of science and literary criticism.

In capital terminology, the form of the struggles in the field of science are, according to Bourdieu, determined by the accumulation and distribution of two types of power associated with two species of scientific capital: the intellectual power of scientific prestige and the temporal power of institutional scientific capital (Bourdieu 1997: 28–30; see also Münch, Chap. 12, in this volume). Transporting and translating this terminology from France to Sweden, one must be cautious not to set these concepts in stone before they can be applied. There was, for instance, a strong geographical concentration of intellectual life in Paris, where most of the effective agents of the intellectual field were geographically located (Bourdieu and Passeron 1967: 202), which does not easily translate into Swedish conditions in the mid-twentieth century. Swedish scientists were scattered over the four cities of Uppsala, Stockholm, Göteborg, and Lund. The small size of the system was a condition not only for interdisciplinary collaborations but also for keeping track of one's disciplinary (and other) colleagues at the other institutions.

Accumulation of the resources specific to the field of science can certainly be facilitated by having a position in the field. This is why entering the field at a young age could be an advantage (Graf 2015: 165), especially for reaping the temporal rewards associated with the occupational passage of time. In addition, having a position at the university was basically a precondition for being elected to other institutions like the royal academies and the learned societies. In terms of resource accumulation, these extra-university institutions served at least three functions. First of all, being accepted was an acknowledgement of one's work, when it comes to both the royal academies and the learned societies. Second, since they gathered a number of acknowledged researchers from Sweden and from abroad, the academies and societies could provide what Randall Collins (1975: 494–495) refers to as a power base of information and communication channels. Because of their exclusive membership roster, the academies and societies provided a source of information not available to all. A third function was the allocation of opportunities to conduct research. The royal academies were perhaps more important agents than the learned societies in this respect, with the Royal Academy of Letters and its establishment of the Humanities Foundation in 1928 as an example. This foundation would later be reorganized in 1959 to become the humanities research council. In some sense, the research councils established in the 1940s supported many of the same activities as the academies and the learned societies, like furthering this or that science by financing and publishing research, and by promoting communication between researchers, although the financing was by far the research councils' more important role.

Most of the above description of the Swedish case is well known. How these aspects of the human scientist's career (or all scientists' careers, for that matter) are connected has so far received little attention. Previous studies have focused on physicists (Kaiserfeld 1997), women in academia (Markusson Winkvist 2003), and careers of doctors in selected disciplines (Blom and Pikwer 1976; Dahllöf 1987). By studying the career patterns and taking a closer look at how their different attributes – like social origin, age of entering the field, or memberships in academies and societies – are related, it will be possible to analyze the distribution of power in the field of human science using geometric data analysis.

Data and Method

In order to capture the accumulation of resources briefly described above – or perhaps, more accurately, to capture the effects of this accumulation process – I have collected them in an objectified state as a set of indicators to be investigated by statistical analysis. This is obviously a significant reduction in detail, as inherited properties are indicated by social origin, and effects of accumulation processes are indicated by age of dissertation defense, participation in government commissions, writing for a cultural journal, and by being learned society memberships. It is a necessary reduction all the same, as it allows for a simultaneous analysis of the distribution of all these various effects, which would be practically impossible using other methods.

The population was selected based on being listed in the state register for 1945 and 1965 at the universities in Uppsala and Lund and the university colleges (universities in 1965) in Göteborg and Stockholm. Since they were the four institutions with research and teaching positions involving human sciences at the time, the population includes all human scientists holding a position at these two cross-sections. These scientists add up to 891 in total. In addition to information on the positions, the state calendars provide membership information and indicate whether individuals received any awards.

Because they had a rather prominent position, as suggested in previous sections, the human scientists are highly visible in biographical dictionaries. While the information provided by these may vary from one person to another, the minimum usually comprises year and place of birth, name of parents and their occupation (usually only the father, as the mothers were seldom paid for their daily work at home and therefore not awarded an occupational title), year of maturity exam, year of dissertation defense, and position at the time of the entry in the dictionary (e.g. Boëthius et al. 1918, *Vem är det?* 1942). For the 1945 cohort and a majority of the 1965 cohort, it is also possible to use the printed university matricules of the staff as a source (Adelsköld 1978, 1984; Dintler and Grönberg 1975; Dintler and Lindqvist 1953; Hellstrand 1987; Olsson and Norlind 1940; Persson and Norlind 1951, 1962; Sandberg 1957). These are often to a large extent based on self-reported information unless the matriculated person has deceased. The matricules and the dictionaries have been used to gather the information on the basic social and demographic properties. There were only 31 of 891 positions whose holders left no trace in any of the above sources or in any other similar printed source, but a non-response rate of 3.5% must be considered negligible.

The doctorate dissertation was, as I mentioned earlier, at the focal point of socially determined educational trajectories and their projected paths into the academic and, to a large extent, scientific field. I have therefore used the Libris library catalog to obtain information on the places of and ages at dissertation defense, as well as on the style of the dissertation in terms of language and the number of pages. There are only 43 positions for which I have not used information on the dissertation, mainly because at the time they had not defended one.

Those individuals for whom I had no basic social and demographic information and those who had not defended a dissertation were excluded from the statistical analysis, since they would constitute a simultaneously specific and yet monotonous contribution to the variance of the cloud. In total, 830 positions were retained for the statistical analysis, which amounts to a non-response rate of 6.8%.

For publishing activities in *Ord och Bild*, the article database of the journal was used and the numbers of articles authored by the human scientists holding a position in 1945 or 1965 were counted. There is no similar database for the participation in government commissions, and while all reports since 1922 have been made available in digital format, the amount of reports, i.e. 2388 from 1922 to 1965, make a manual lookup a laborious task. The solution I chose was to search for each name in the documents, a method which misses out on some names that have not been properly recognized by the OCR process. Because of the lack of precision in attaining the raw data for commission participation, in the analyses below this indicator was binary coded (either *have* or *have not* participated).

Table 17.1 Active variables in the multiple correspondence analysis. (8 variables: 28 active and 4 passive modalities)

Q	K	N 1945	%	N 1965	%
Social group	SGI	141	53.8	283	49.8
	SGII	94	35.9	236	41.5
	SGIII	27	10.3	49	8.6
	SGN/A[a]	0	0.0	0	0.0
Fraction	Economic	33	12.6	59	10.4
	Educated	42	16.0	122	21.5
	Religious	32	12.2	35	6.2
	Professional	23	8.8	50	8.8
	State	27	10.3	48	8.5
	X[b]	105	40.1	254	44.7
Dissertation length	19–200 pp	83	31.7	107	18.8
	201–300 pp	84	32.1	187	32.9
	301–400 pp	57	21.8	135	23.8
	401–750 pp	36	13.7	134	23.6
	NoDissLength[b]	2	0.8	5	0.9
PhD defending age	22–29yo	96	36.6	85	15.0
	30–34yo	100	38.2	223	39.3
	35–39yo	51	19.5	140	24.6
	40–62yo	15	5.7	120	21.1
	NoDdegree[a]	0	0.0	0	0.0
PhD institution	DefUppsala	129	49.2	204	35.9
	DefLund	61	23.3	148	26.1
	DefStockholm	35	13.4	131	23.1
	DefGothenburg	30	11.5	57	10.0
	DefNoDissertation[a]	0	0.0	0	0.0
	DefForeign[b]	7	2.7	19	3.3
	DefBusiness[b]	0	0.0	9	1.6
Member scientific society	2–5SciSocityMemb	17	6.5	26	4.6
	SciSocietyMemb	50	19.1	77	13.6
	NoSciSociety	195	74.4	465	81.9
Participation in committee	SOU	86	32.8	167	29.4
	no_SOU	176	67.2	401	70.6
Writing in Ord och Bild	Freq	22	8.4	27	4.8
	Yes	44	16.8	47	8.3
	No	196	74.8	494	87.0
Total		262	100.0	568	100.0

[a]Not included
[b]Passive modality

A total of 8 variables with 32 categories (cp. Table 17.1) were selected for a MCA, a technique well suited for analyzing relationships between categorical data and, as in this case, discrete and continuous numerical data (e.g. number of memberships, age at dissertation defense). Because some of the modalities have very low frequencies, they risk becoming, as Le Roux and Rouanet write, "too influential to the determination of axes" (Le Roux and Rouanet 2004: 203). This is true for the modalities 'No dissertation length' and having defended the dissertation at a business school or at a foreign university. The first step is always to try and pool these infrequent modalities. If that is not possible, one can set them as passive modalities. This is why I opted for a specific MCA. In addition, because it was basically only the occupations in the highest social group (I) that could be assigned as belonging to a specific social fraction, the modality that indicates no fraction ("X") has been set as supplementary to avoid amplifying certain traits due to redundancy in the different variables.

Comparing the two spaces produced by the specific MCA raises issues of both methodological and theoretical concern. Two recent dissertations have dealt with this problem. One of them compared two social spaces based on two cohorts of Swedish 40 year olds in 1990 and 2008 by performing a separate specific MCA for each cohort and comparing the structures of the distribution of social, educational, and economic properties. Melldahl calls this a sociological comparison based on reasoning. His main objection to, for instance, using one of the cross-sections as reference space and projecting the other cross-section into this space as a supplementary cloud (cf. Lidegran 2009: 175–180) is that this method, by forcing the same variables and modalities on two potentially quite distinct spaces, risks obscuring important and meaningful differences between the spaces (Melldahl 2015: 137–138). The other dissertation compared two spaces of Dutch CEOs in 1976 and 2009, performing both a separate specific MCA for each cross-section and a joint analysis of the two cross-sections with a class specific MCA on the 2009 cross-section (Timans 2015).

I opted for separate specific MCA of each cross-section instead of the so-called class specific analysis, or specific MCA of a subcloud of individuals (Le Roux and Rouanet 2004: 204), where distances are defined by the whole cloud of 1945 and 1965 (for eigenvalues, see Table 17.2, Appendix). A joint analysis would have created a reference space that would have referred to neither 1945 nor 1965, but to a simultaneous construction of two spaces separated by a certain period of time. As the above discussion demonstrates, this would have been problematic.

To compare the two spaces, I have projected the individuals of the non-active cross-section onto the space of the active cross-section. That means I have projected, as supplementary, the individuals of 1965 onto the space of 1945, and vice versa. The coordinates of the supplementary individuals are determined by the active elements of the analysis (active individuals and active modalities) and do not affect the structure itself (Le Roux and Rouanet 2004: 209). The comparison has been interpreted in three steps. First and foremost, the structures of the two separate spaces, 1945 and 1965, were compared to see whether the retained axes represented more or less the same latent variables. If the same modalities are polarized along the same axes in the two separate analyses, the latent variables have probably not changed in any important way.

Secondly, if the axes in the two separate spaces are more or less the same, one can proceed with inspecting the development of single modalities. This can be made by calculating the mean points of modalities from the coordinates of the supplementary individuals.

Thirdly, one can inspect the trajectories of specific individuals who appear both in 1945 and in 1965. I have limited myself to inspecting the trajectories of those individuals who moved the greatest distance along the statistically most important axis, i.e. the first axis.

From a speculative point of view, one would expect patterns resulting from the MCAs to follow one of the following three models and their different scenarios, depending on the design of the analysis.

If the analysis only consisted of temporary variables (variables that change on the individual level over the course of time), it is quite possible that the structure would remain while the individuals move over time. This is the first model.

If the analysis consisted only of permanent variables which remain stable on the individual level over the course of time, and those who entered the property space possessed the same properties as those who left, this space would probably remain stable and the individuals immobile. A variant of this scenario would be that those who entered have other properties than those who leave, leading to a changing structure, and to movement of individuals within this structure.

If the analysis consists of both temporary and permanent variables and the reproduction of the permanent variables is more or less the same, one would probably find a stable structure, but mobile individuals. In a variation of this scenario where, for instance, the demography is different within the various permanent variables, one would probably find cyclical change in the structures due to the movement of the individuals, who in turn affect the movement of the temporary variables.

Comparing Structures

If one agrees that publishing in a cultural magazine, being a member in scientific societies, or being on the board of a research council are to some extent manifestations of resource accumulation, or the conversion of some kind of accumulated resource, a successful accumulation is very much linked to an early entry into the field (cf. Graf 2015: 165). It is understandable that these 'early birds' who defended their dissertation at 22–27 years of age rarely had time to write more than 200 pages. In opposition to these early birds are the 'late bloomers', who seem to be deprived of all those attributes that mark the established. What stands out the most, though, is their late age of dissertation defense (35–39 years old), having no memberships in learned societies, and having never written for the cultural journal *Ord och Bild*. This axis may be summarized by the corresponding opposition between professors and docents, although with an η^2 just over 0.30 (the ratio between variance on this item and total variance), the variance within each of these two groups is greater than

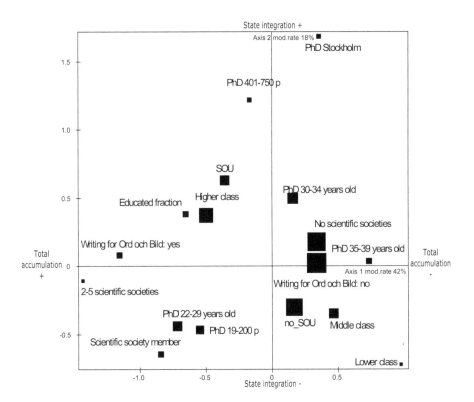

Fig. 17.1 Modalities contributing above average to axis 1 and 2 in 1945

the variance between them. These are also the two supplementary modalities with the greatest test-values: 8.9 on both the positive and negative side, respectively.

The second axis distinguishes in multiple ways those who are more integrated from those who are less integrated into the state apparatus. Participating in committees (SOU) is the most obvious sign for this. Defending the dissertation at Stockholm University College is closely related to participating in committees in the upper part of Fig. 17.1. This is another sign of state integration. Writing long dissertations was, in addition, confined mostly to historians, political scientists, and historians of literature. They had, respectively, national history, the national constitution, and national literature as their main research objects.

We also know, especially from statistician Paul Dahn's (1936: 334–367) studies conducted in the mid-1930s on the social background of upper secondary and university students, that Stockholm University College, at least in the 1920s, had an overrepresentation of sons of state officials. And from a strictly geographical point of view, Stockholm was the center of the state apparatus.

Twenty years on, the basic structure, with its key differentiation between accumulation conditions, i.e. between defending a dissertation earlier or later in ones' life, remains the same. If anything, defending a dissertation late in life has

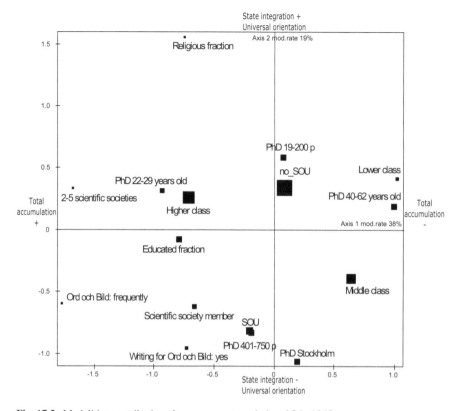

Fig. 17.2 Modalities contributing above average to axis 1 and 2 in 1965

become even clearer an obstacle to accumulating and converting resources into memberships in learned societies and positions in research councils.

In 1965, being integrated into the state apparatus is still a distinguishing trait of the second axis (cp. Fig. 17.2). Also, the social sciences are closer to the more state integrated pole than the humanities, and looking at the individual disciplines, we find that those whose objects are more universal in nature, or which deal with international or foreign objects, are located further from the state integrated pole than the disciplines that have a more distinctly national research object. In the upper part of the graph in Fig. 17.4, the philologists, ancient historians, orientalists, philosophers, comparative ethnographers, and statisticians are located far from the state integrated pole, where the economists, historians of literature, political scientists, sociologists, and law scientists reside. One should remember though, that these are not all philologists or all economists, as there is also great dispersion within these disciplines.

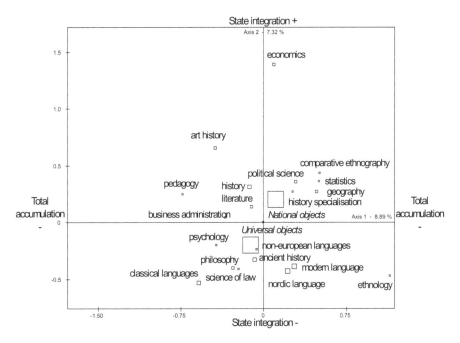

Fig. 17.3 Disciplines of the docents, professors and university lecturers projected as supplementary categories in 1945

In summary, the first axes in 1945 and 1965 (cp. Figs. 17.3 and 17.4) are more or less the same, whereas the second axes both exhibit integration into the state apparatus, but are certainly not identical.

Comparing Properties

In Fig. 17.5, each of the modalities contributing most to the plane of axis 1 and 2 in 1945 have been plotted together with its counterpart among the supplementary individuals from the 1965 cross-section (see Table 17.3 and 17.4, Appendix). There has been a general shift towards the right (positive) along the first axis, since the mean point of the 1965 cross-section is located at about 0.21 on the this axis. In other words, there is nothing in the individual modality trajectories that deviates in any remarkable way from the movement of the entire cloud of supplementary individuals.

The largest shifts (larger than average) have been observed for the modalities *2–5 scientific society memberships, scientific society membership, short dissertation length, writing for Ord och Bild: yes, higher* and *middle class*, and the *educated fraction*. The difference, in other words, is larger between those individuals who had one or more of these properties in 1945 and those who had one or more of

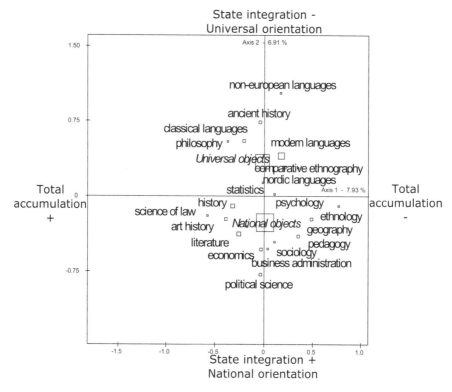

Fig. 17.4 Disciplines of the docents, professors and university lecturers projected as supplementary categories in 1965

them in 1965 than between those who had one or more of the other properties in 1945 and in 1965. The major reason behind this is the scarcity of the property, since numerically larger properties are less sensitive to small changes.

Individual Trajectories

A clear pattern emerges among those scholars who had moved the greatest distance in 1965 with reference to the structure of the space in 1945. We are dealing with persons who moved from a position as a docent to professor (supplementary variable), a move which has opened up possibilities for membership in scientific societies. We can see this for the ancient historian Holger Arbman, the business economist Sune Carlson, the intellectual historian Sten Lindroth, the historian Jerker Rosén, and the economist Ingvar Svennilson.

We also find similar trajectories among the following three scholars, but it is worth highlighting the differences here in more detail. The philosopher Ingemar

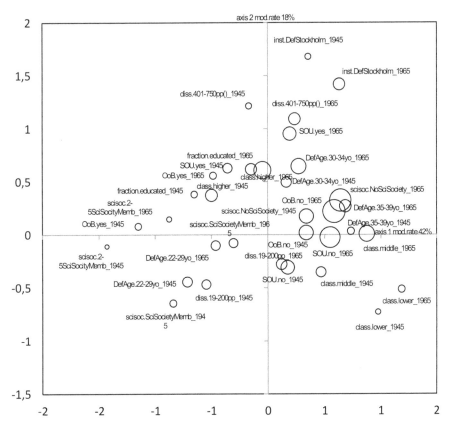

Fig. 17.5 Active modalities with an above-average contribution to axis 1 (a1) and 2 (a2) in the 1945 reference space and coordinates based on the same category mean points of supplementary individuals (1965)

Hedenius not only a became professor and a member of more scientific societies, but also became a frequent writer in *Ord och Bild*. Karl Gustav Ljunggren, professor in Nordic languages both in 1945 and in 1965, accumulated more memberships over time. Dag Strömbäck, who seemed destined for a trajectory in Nordic languages in 1945, had acquired a position as professor of ethnology by 1965.

It is clearly the membership variable that changes over time, whereas others do not (see Table 17.5, Appendix). This is both a social fact and an artifact of the design of the analysis. The number of memberships is a variable in both space and time while the occupation of the father, for instance, as given in biographical dictionaries, only varies in space and is constant for the individual over time.

One needs to keep in mind that the visualization of the individual trajectories in Fig. 17.6 only holds under the assumption that the individuals change whereas everything else is the same. This assumption holds true to some extent, and at least for the first axis, but it should nonetheless be considered as being constructed in

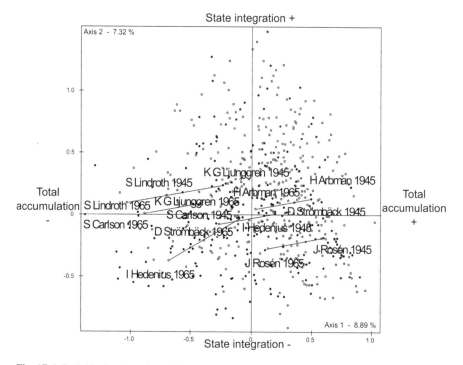

Fig. 17.6 Individual trajectories with 1945 as reference cloud

this experimental analysis; further investigations are needed to confirm whether this assumption really holds true or not.

Concluding Remarks

Due to a limitation of variables for reasons of comparability, the multiple correspondence analyses presented in this contribution should be considered as kind of a pilot study, where a number of methodological tools for a rigorous empirical comparison of structures were tested. Based on those results that enable statistically sound comparisons, it seems safe to say that the main differentiating principle among careers in the subsystem of human sciences (having more or fewer accumulated resources), and its relation to the condition of entry (defending a dissertation at a younger or older age), remained stable over the time span of 20 years compared in this paper.

Because this dimension is so often found in various MCAs of different populations, it seems almost trivial to establish a distinction between those who have and those who have not accumulated a large amount of resources. However, one only has to consider the meaning of this distinction, which in this case is a distinction between those who hold many memberships in various scientific societies (to name just one property) and those who have no memberships: Attending meetings or corresponding with fellow members is undoubtedly an asset in various situations one encounters in the university field.

As for the second dimension in the two separate analyses, which turned out to be about degree of integration into the state apparatus, I would like to return to the opening paragraphs of this paper, that is, the setting of the analysis.

Although Gunnar Myrdal, the protectionist professors, and the commission on the creation of a social science research council disagreed upon how to shape the relations between the social sciences and social and political agendas, they were all of the opinion that the social sciences were nonetheless vital to the solution of social problems and social planning. The government commissions were not the only concrete link between science and state in policy making (Nybom 1997: 98); the new social science research council was also to become such a link as it gathered researchers, politicians, and representatives of the industrial and business sectors. This pertains to what I have described in the empirical analysis as "state integration", i.e. that some parts of the field of human science are more integrated in this policy-making process than others. What Per Lundin and Niklas Stenlås (2015) call "reform technocrats" – those academics that were central in initiating commissions, leading commissions, and then in some cases becoming heads of agencies created on the suggestion of these commissions – is most likely the extreme form of state integration.

I suggest that state integration is a case of the conversion of scientific authority accumulated in the scientific field and its relatively autonomous subsystem of human sciences (cf. Bourdieu 1975: 25). Because a successful accumulation of this authority usually takes time, the most important immediate condition for it to be successful is entering the field at an early age. This would eventually grant you the time to become a professor once one of the few positions opened up; with luck, you might even become a professor almost immediately, thus influencing the direction of your discipline for a whole generation of scholars.

Being a professor meant that you gained access not only to the power resources that were inherent to the role itself – deciding on doctoral dissertations, docent scholarships, expert opinions on other professorial appointments – but also other resources like public acknowledgment, the recognition of being a member of a learned society or a royal academy, or the power to allocate funds to research by belonging to the board of a research council. In order to become a professor and gain access to these resources at the time in question, however, it would undeniably have been helpful to be the son or daughter of a professor.

References

Adelsköld, E. (1978). *Stockholms högskolas matrikel 1888–1927*. Stockholm: Univ.
Adelsköld, E. (1984). *Stockholms högskolas matrikel 1928–1950*. Stockholm: Univ.
Andersson, L. G., Erikson, R., & Wärneryd, B. (1981). Att beskriva den sociala strukturen. Utvärdering av 1974 års förslag till socio-ekonomisk indelning. *Statistisk Tidskrift, Tredje följden, 19*(2), 113–136.
Blom, C., & Pikwer, B. (1976). *Vem blev forskare och vad blev forskaren?*. Lund: Historiska inst., Lunds univ.
Boëthius, B., Hildebrand, B., & Nilzén, G. (1918). *Svenskt biografiskt lexikon*. Stockholm: Svenskt biografiskt lexikon. Retrieved April 8, 2015, from http://www.nad.riksarkivet.se/sbl/Start.aspx
Bourdieu, P. (1975). The Specificity of the Scientific Field and the Social Conditions of the Progress of Reason. *Social Science Information, 14*(6), 19–47.
Bourdieu, P. (1996). *Homo Academicus*. Moderna franska tänkare, 99-0818927-1; 27, Eslöv: B. Östlings bokförl. Symposion.
Bourdieu, P. (1997). *Les usages sociaux de la science : pour une sociologie clinique du champ scientifique*. Paris: Institut national de la recherche agronomique.
Bourdieu, P. (1998). *On television*. New York: New Press.
Bourdieu, P., & Passeron, J. C. (1967). Sociology and philosophy in France since 1945: Death and resurrection of a philosophy without subject. *Social Research, 34*(1), 162–212.
Collins, R. (1975). *Conflict sociology: Toward an explanatory science*. New York: Academic.
Dahllöf, U. (1987). *Disputationerna och specialarbetsmarknaden för doktorer i skolväsendets undervisningsämnen 1890–1939*. Uppsala: Uppsala universitet.
Dahn, P. (1936). *Studier rörande den studerande ungdomens sociala och geografiska härkomst*. Lund: Fahlbeckska stiftelsen.
Dintler, Å., & Grönberg, L. (1975). *Uppsala universitets matrikel 1951–1960*. Uppsala: Almqvist & Wiksell.
Dintler, Å., & Lindqvist, S. (1953). *Uppsala universitets matrikel 1937–1950*. Uppsala: Almqvist & Wiksell.
Fleck, C. (2011). *A Transatlantic history of the social sciences: Robber Barons, the Third Reich and the invention of empirical social research*. London: Bloomsbury Academic.
Gingras, Y. (1991). *Physics and the rise of scientific research in Canada*. Montreal: McGill-Queen.
Graf, A. (2015). *Die Wissenschaftselite Deutschlands : Sozialprofil und Werdegänge zwischen 1945 und 2013*. Frankfurt am Main: Campus.
Hellstrand, A. (1987). *Stockholms högskolas matrikel 1951–1960*. Stockholm: Univ.
Kaiserfeld, T. (1997). *Vetenskap och karriär : svenska fysiker som lektorer, akademiker och industriforskare under 1900-talets första hälft*. Trita-HOT, 0348-4696; 2033, Lund: Arkiv.
Le Roux, B., & Rouanet, H. (2004). *Geometric data analysis: From correspondence analysis to structured data analysis*. Dordrecht: Kluwer Academic.
Lidegran, I. (2009). *Utbildningskapital: om hur det alstras, fördelas och förmedlas*. Uppsala: Acta Universitatis Upsaliensis.
Lundin, P., & Stenlås, N. (2015). The Reform Technocrats: The Strategists of the Swedish Welfare State, 1930–60. In J. Vandendriessche, E. Peeters, & K. Wils (Eds.), *Scientists' Expertise as Performance: Between State and Society, 1860–1960* (pp. 135–146). London: Pickering & Chatto Ltd.
Markusson Winkvist, H. (2003). *Som isolerade öar : de lagerkransade kvinnorna och akademin under 1900-talets första hälft*. Eslöv: B. Östlings bokförl. Symposion.
Melldahl, A. (2015). *Utbildningens värde: Fördelning, avkastning och social reproduktion under 1900-talet*. Uppsala: Acta Universitatis Upsaliensis.
Myrdal, G. (1944). Samhällsvetenskapernas utbyggnad vid universiteten och de fria högskolorna. *Ekonomisk Tidskrift, 46*(4), 245–272.
Nybom, T. (1997). *Kunskap, politik, samhälle : essäer om kunskapssyn, universitet och forskningspolitik 1900–2000*. Hargshamn: Arete.

Olsson, B., & Norlind, W. (1940). *Lunds universitets matrikel. 1939.* Lund: Gleerup.

Persson, M., & Norlind, W. (1951). *Lunds universitets matrikel. 1949–50.* Lund: Gleerup.

Persson, M., & Norlind, W. (1962). *Lunds universitets matrikel. 1959/60.* Lund: Gleerup.

Sandberg, N. (1957). *Göteborgs högskolas matrikel 1942–1954.* Göteborg: Wettergren & Kerber.

Sandelin, B. (2000). Nationalekonomin i Sverige uner 100 år. *Ekonomisk Debatt, 28*(1), 59–69.

SCB. (1959). *Tjänstemän inom statlig och statsunderstödd verksamhet. 1954–1957.* Stockholm: Statistiska centralbyrån.

Smith, R. (1997). *The Fontana history of the human sciences.* London: Fontana Press.

Statistisk årsbok för Sverige. (1931). Stockholm: SCB

Sveriges statskalender 1945. (1945). Stockholm: Fritze.

Sveriges statskalender 1965. (1965). Stockholm: Fritzes offentliga publikationer.

Sveriges statskalender för året 1925. (1925). Uppsala: Almqvist & Wiksell.

Timans, R. (2015). *Studying the Dutch Business Elite: Relational concepts and methods.* Rotterdam: Mediview.

Vem är det? Svensk biografisk handbok 1943. (1942). Stockholm: Norstedt.

Chapter 18
Organizational Environments and Field Theory: The Example of the Field of German Universities 2002–2014

Christian Baier and Andreas Schmitz

Introduction

Since its early days, the sociology of organization has been conceiving of organizations as part of larger social contexts that provide both opportunities and constraints for internal processes. Parsons (1956) addressed the adaption of organizations towards societal subsystems such as economy or culture. Stinchcombe (1965) focused on the effects of societal conditions such as class structure and status stratification on organizations and vice versa. From these early approaches to organization-environment relations, two major paradigms have emerged: population ecology and neo-institutionalism. They conceptualize the environments in which organizations can be located as 'organizational populations' or 'organizational fields' respectively. Traditionally, population ecology has focused mainly on the *material* resources which organizations obtain from their environment, as well as on the requirements for adapting to ecological conditions which foster the diversification and specialization of organizations. Inspired by biology, population ecology argues that organizations are compelled to find niches within a common 'resource space' and that organizations within different niches will be distinguished from each other due to different resources, different stresses and compulsions, and, ultimately, different internal adaptions. Neo-institutionalism, in contrast primarily conceives of organizational environments as *cultural* sources of legitimization and de-legitimization. Here, external context is assumed to exert a standardizing pressure on all organizations within the field, so that organizations in a shared

C. Baier (✉)
Bayerisches Landesamt für Statistik Nürnberg, Nürnberg, Germany
e-mail: christian.baier@posteo.de

A. Schmitz
Department of Sociology, University of Bonn, Bonn, Germany
e-mail: andreas.schmitz@uni-bonn.de

© Springer Nature Switzerland AG 2019
J. Blasius et al. (eds.), *Empirical Investigations of Social Space*,
Methodos Series 15, https://doi.org/10.1007/978-3-030-15387-8_18

environment tend to become more similar over time. Evidently then, population ecology and neo-institutionalism address two different but complementary aspects of organizational environments and tendencies in organizational development: variation induced by material opportunities on the one hand, similarity induced by cultural pressures on the other hand. Although both approaches have proven valuable concepts for the analysis of organization-environment relations, they also exemplify a rift within modern organizational sociology, which undermines comprehensive descriptions of organizations-in-environments that include cultural as well as material factors and allow for outcomes involving both variation and standardization.

We argue that a Bourdieusian approach can serve to integrate these seemingly incompatible approaches (cp. Baier and Schmitz 2012). Although Bourdieu himself did not develop an explicit sociology of organizations (see Swartz, Chap. 11, in this volume), two perspectives valuable for organizational sociology can be derived from his theory. In this contribution, we want to demonstrate the *theoretical* capacity of field theory with regard to the conceptualization of organizational environments and the interplay between environment and intra-organizational structures. In order to illustrate this field-theoretical approach to organizational environments, we use the *empirical* example of the field of German universities and its ongoing drift toward academic capitalism (Baier & Schmitz 2012; Münch, Chap. 12, in this volume).

Conceptualizations of Organization-Environment Relations

Organizational Ecology and Neo-institutionalism

Population ecology or organizational ecology (OE) and neo-institutionalism (NI), two important research traditions in organizational sociology, are both concerned with questions of organizations within their contexts. However, there exists a peculiar form of analytical specialization between the two approaches: They seem to have divided up the study of organizations into two incompatible axiomatic systems and corresponding bodies of research. The stated goal of OE is to explain *why there are different kinds of organizations* (Hannan and Freeman 1977) and how niches in organizational ecologies develop (Dobrev et al. 2002). Organizational ecology studies emphasize the importance of the distribution of material resources that act as opportunities for and constraints on organizational development and survival (Hannan and Freeman 1977). According to OE, organizations are different because they occupy diverse positions in the ecology and therefore have access to different types of resources, which encourages the emergence of varying organizational forms.

Conversely, NI sets out to explain *why organizations are so similar* and tend to become even more so over time (DiMaggio and Powell 1983: 148).

Neo-institutional organizational fields are understood as structures of formal and informal rules and standards; reputation and legitimation according to these rules are the most important organizational resources. Organizations have high amounts of behavioral discretion, but can only be successful if they (appear to) act and interact according to the dominant rules in their field.

Both approaches assume specific causal mechanisms that lead to the differentiation of organizational forms or organizational isomorphism respectively. OE postulates that organizations are extremely inert and cannot purposefully adapt to their environment, and therefore, environmental conditions determine which organizational forms evolve and survive (Hannan and Freeman 1977, 1984: 151ff.). In contrast, NI argues that organizations tend to establish webs of relations and sets of rules and procedures that put pressure on those who diverge from these standards (DiMaggio and Powell 1983: 148ff.). Therefore, in OE the critical question is whether the environment supplies enough material resources for survival in different niches, while in NI cultural conditions like legitimation and reputation are the *sine qua non* conditions for an organization's subsistence.

If we look at these two frameworks in this way, we see that the field of organizational sociology has become infested with various 'false dualisms': Material pressures and diversity on the one hand are pitted against socio-cultural forces and standardization on the other. However, it should be evident that organizations are subject both to isomorphic pressures and mechanisms of differentiation; they depend both on material and on social and symbolic resources; they are subject to both cultural and structural logics, and exhibit practices of cooperation as well as competition; they are simultaneously affected by members' activities, the activities of other organizations, etc. Additionally, questions about the interaction of these two sides of organizational life might be among the most interesting topics of organizational sociology: How is the identity of an organization influenced by both its material and its cultural environment? How do social bonds between organizations affect their ability to adapt to changing environmental conditions? Questions like these are hard to answer given the peculiar division of analytic labor between these two frameworks.

Abandoning these dualisms represents an important step toward the development of an integrative theoretical model of organizations in their environments. Accordingly, such an approach should comprise the main theoretical ideas and insights of both OE and NI. As recognized in the literature, Bourdieu's relational theory offers a potential framework for a comprehensive sociology of organizations in environments (Emirbayer and Johnson 2008). Therefore, we shall now outline the core principles of a field-theoretical sociology of organizations and relate them to the central ideas of neo-institutionalism and organizational ecology. In doing so, we illustrate in what ways Bourdieu's ideas can help to subvert and overcome the restrictive tendencies toward specialization outlined here.

A Field Theoretical Approach to Organizations

The concept of 'field' refers to the structure of objective relations between a set of positions. More concretely, fields are understood as sets of relations between the agents (people as well as organizations) and between the relevant practices and (material and symbolic) resources or capital forms of a social sphere (Bourdieu and Wacquant 1992: 94ff.). Fields are – in an ideal-typical view – structured by the distribution of specific objects of interest, as well as by the symbolic dimension of these objects. For example, an academic field is structured by scientific capital, which comprises various kinds of knowledge and skills or reputation among peers through publications and citations, and institutional capital, which entails the ability to influence the distribution of departmental funding and other resources such as research assistants, labs, machines, or buildings (cp. Münch, Chap. 12, in this volume). Thus, the concept of capital encompasses material resources, which OE focuses on, as well as symbolic resources like reputation and legitimation, which are given more emphasis in NI.

From a Bourdieusian perspective, all agents in a field are, consciously or not, engaged in a *struggle for power* over field-specific goods, the capital structure of the field, and the symbolic value of the different capital forms. Fields are conceptualized as arenas where agents compete and fight to maintain and improve their own positions. In the case of organizations, aspects of this competition are easy to recognize. Every organization is, to some extent, interested in its own survival, and therefore threatened by the existence of competing organizations. Not only business enterprises, but many other organizations – universities not least among them – openly compete for members, resources, and symbolic assets like awards and public recognition. Thus, field theory is not only clearly more agonistic than NI, but it is also more general than OE, conceptualizing conflict and competition as questions of cultural legitimation, and ultimately as power struggles.

Furthermore, field theory, due to its relational epistemology, differs from NI in that it does not reduce this competition (and cooperation) to direct or network-mediated interactions. Agents need not even be aware of each other's existence. From the viewpoint of field theory, manifest interactions are merely *one* emanation of relations within fields. Similar to their conceptualization in OE, competition (and cooperation) also include latent and indirect mechanisms such as competition over the value of capital forms. In doing so, field theory differs from OE in that it emphasizes the issue of strategic re-definition of legitimate capital forms beyond the mere struggle for given resources.

An issue of paramount relevance for the operation of a field is the question of the field's environment. Whereas OE tends to restrict itself to resource spaces that consist of similar organizations and economic resources, NI is sensitive regarding the effects of a potentially changing political climate on organizations (Dobrev 2001). More strongly than both OE and NI, however, the field concept asserts that any social sphere – albeit with its individual structures and dynamics – is only *relatively* autonomous from external contexts. For example, the academic field may well be seen as being structured by academic capital, a field-specific illusio (truth), and academic habitus. However, this field is, just as any field, affected by other fields, such as the field of the nation-state or the political field. Ultimately, field theory cannot conceive of an (organizational) field without its embeddedness in the social space. Whereas OE and NI do not offer an elaborated theory of the context of an organization, field theory conceptualizes the totality of interdependent fields as the 'field of power' (Bourdieu 1998; Schmitz et al. 2017). Organizational fields, as well as quasi-functionally differentiated fields are seen as mutually constitutive and restrictive, independent of their content: A field is located within the field of power. The field of German universities, for example, cannot be understood without reference to its relations with the broader academic field, the German nation state, the transnational academic field, the economic field, organizational fields such as the field of publishing houses, and so on.

Not least as a consequence of the relevance of contextual embeddedness, organizational sociology is interested in the historical preconditions and temporal developments of organizations and their exogenous contexts. For example, the emphasis on temporality can be identified both in OE, where the age of organizations plays an important role, and in NI, where arbitrary modes of behavior gain binding power to the extent that these processes are time-consuming. The Bourdieusian concept of social fields is even more sensitive than OE and NI towards questions of time and historicity: Fields are seen as the product of historical developments, where the outcomes of past struggles continually feed back into the status quo and agents and classes show a certain temporal trajectory through the field of power.

When conceptualizing fields, one can distinguish between *synchronous* and *diachronous* models: A synchronous model of the field describes the positions of agents, resources, and practices at a given point in time and thereby gives the analyst an overwiew of the state of affairs in the field at that time. A diachronous model is more comprehensive, as it describes the development of a field over two or more points in time. This enables the analyst to assess the degree of stability of observed field structures as well as the trajectories of organizations in the field. The issue of time and temporal development is addressed in field theory by the concepts of a field's genesis and an organization's trajectory. The issue of relative stability over time and resilience towards exogenous influences can be addressed by the concepts of relative autonomy and habitus. In the case of German universities presented below, for example, state reforms induce massive change in the field structure. One crucial aspect of this change is that some universities which, before the reforms, were positioned very closely to one another embarked on quite different trajectories and ended up in different regions of the field. This kind of diversification from a homogenous position can only be explicitly analyzed with a diachronous model.

Amongst others, field theory addresses the synchronic and diachronic conditions observed in human and organizational agents with the concept of *habitus*. Habitus refers to a set of dispositions that agents acquire in their ongoing involvement in social fields: The opportunities and constraints encountered in the past shape the agents' perceptions, evaluations, and actions in the present, as well as their objective and subjective prospects. Habitus is, on the one hand, structured by the objective conditions of the field, while on the other hand habitus itself structures the ways in which the objective conditions are perceived, evaluated, and acted upon. Analogously, *organizational habitus* can be understood as a set of dispositions (formal and informal rules, routines, procedures, methods, organizational cultures, hierarchies, material and cultural constitution, etc.) (Meyer and Rowan 1977). Due to the abstract nature of field theory, practices and processes in organizations can be seen as being shaped by these embedded dispositions, just as human action can be seen as being shaped by (semi-conscious) dispositions engrained in the body. The concept of *practice* (instead of action) then emphasizes the fact that not only human social agency can be interpreted as being guided by (conscious, semi-conscious, and unconscious) dispositions and 'habits'.

These organizational dispositions develop as responses to past opportunities and constraints; they are inert and relatively autonomous from exogenous intrusion. Organizational practice is affected by the structure of power relations inside the organization that mediate these forces. This inert organizational core, whose importance is recognized in both NI and OE, determines how external influences and opportunities are perceived, evaluated, and acted upon. These internal structures of organizations are notorious for their pervasive influence on organizations' performance, as well as for their high resistance to intervention and change. In the NI tradition, the idea of decoupling between inert organizational core structures on the one hand and various volatile forms of organizational practice and self-presentation on the other has been very influential (Meyer and Rowan 1977). Likewise in OE, inertia is a core theoretical assumption, i.e. it is listed as a major reason why organizations are unable to purposefully adapt to their environment (Hannan and Freeman 1977, 1984). From a Bourdieusian perspective, the considerable inertia of organizational cultures, identities, and styles can be explained by the fact that organizations are not simply aggregates of human agents, but function as fields that are relatively autonomous (Bourdieu 2005: 205). Nonetheless, organizational fields are continuously, subtly, and selectively affected, not only by the present state of affairs inside the organization, by the habitus of its personnel, and by society in its widest sense, but by the surrounding organizational field. The structure and character of the field of universities, for example, may exert a sui generis influence on the organizations it comprises.

The relational structure of a field comprises material and cultural dimensions as well as the competition for resources and legitimacy. In doing so, Bourdieu's concept of fields allows analysts to examine and describe the dimensionality and topology of fields, as well as the relations between different positions or 'niches'. This means that where NI focuses on the global isomorphic field effect, which is similar for every organization, and OE focuses on differentiated positions in the overall field, the Bourdieusian concept allows for the integration of both ideas: Fields affect all of their agents in certain ways, and can thus encourage isomorphy, but because of differences in agents' resources and habitus, the global field effect can produce quite different results in different agents, thus encouraging diversification.

Field theory addresses the very relation of material and cultural aspects, the connection between niches and the emergence of cultural hegemony in a field, the endogenous transformation of an organization in reaction to both isomorphism and ecological pressure, and ultimately, the changes in the organizational field itself.

Field theory does not impute the operation of singular mechanisms, or the relevance of a singular form of capital, before – or worse, without – the work of empirical construction. Thus, in the subsequent chapter we intend to *empirically* analyze whether isomorphic effects and niches can be observed within the same organizational field.

Data and Methods

For the purpose of constructing the field of German universities, we carried out three iterations: We began by collecting different types of data that depict the main differences in the field. The original data set contained various types of publication and funding data, as well as variables that captured key institutional and historical characteristics, e.g. founding dates, or whether the university was located in the former states of West or East Germany. However, upon closer consideration, we found that organizational habitus and practice, as well as the effects of recent reforms, were not yet adequately represented in the data. Therefore, we proceeded to add further information: We investigated the universities' involvement in the Excellence Initiative,[1] and we acquired data on the universities' memberships in strategic associations that have emerged over the past few years as a reaction to increasing competition. Additionally, we gathered data on various aspects of the universities' internal structure that might have emerged in reaction to the reforms. In many universities, special organizational units have been formed to deal with issues such as the Excellence Initiative, fundraising, internationalization, strategy, and quality management. These data are of special interest for our analysis because they refer to our concept of organizational habitus outlined above, as they represent an internalization of objective, external pressures and opportunities into the institutional structure of the organization itself.

The final data set is based on 58 of 108 German universities. The most important variables concern two of the basic structural properties of the field: input, i.e. funding, on the one hand, and output, i.e. published research papers, on the other. As a data source for the operationalization of research output, we use data from the Web of Science (WoS), a database that indexes scientific publications. WoS provides broad categories – called 'research areas' – into which research journals and articles are sorted. For each university we recorded the 12 most important research areas, i.e. those to which most of the papers published by a university belong. These 12 research areas are subsequently referred to here as 'publication profiles'. For a few

---

[1] Incentive program for German universities (cp. Münch, Chap. 12, in this volume).

universities, especially smaller ones and those with strong profiles in the humanities, there were few publications listed in the WoS and thus, fewer than 12 research areas emerged. On average, 80 percent of a university's publications fall into its 12 most prominent research areas. Therefore, by considering these, we are confident in having covered the most important differences that structure the output side of the field. Table 18.1 (Appendix) summarizes selected items we use for operationalizing the publication profiles of universities. It is apparent that in this area, complex changes happen over time. On the one hand, there are central research areas that are widespread and remain so over time, e.g. physics and chemistry. On the other hand, changes do occur, as evidenced for example by the rapid spread of computer science and environmental science, and the moderate decline of cell biology and surgery. Regarding methods, geometric data analysis provides various approaches that are well-suited for this type of analytical task. Geometric statistics is a group of scaling methods which includes principal component analysis, multidimensional scaling, and simple and multiple correspondence analysis, as well as the multiple factor analysis (MFA) approach used in the following (Escofier and Pagès 1994; see also Robette and Roueff, Chap. 8, in this volume). Ratios between regular (i.e. state) funding and third-party funding, and the publication profiles extracted from WoS, are used as active variables (see Table 18.1 Appendix). The other variables that concern organizational practice and habitus (see Table 18.2, Appendix) are treated as outcomes of field effects, as discussed in the last section of this article.

Findings

The Structure of the Field of German Universities

Analyzing the data described, we are able to model the dynamic development of the German field of universities for two periods or 'time slices', namely 1995–2000 and 2007–2012.

As a first step, we present a plot of the first time slice. It represents the categorical active variables (i.e. universities' research profiles) in relation to the first and second dimension of the MFA. If research areas are located close to each other on the plot, they are 'similar' to the extent that 'similar' universities publish in these areas. Conversely, if categories are far from each other, it is unlikely that universities will produce significant amounts of publications in more than one of these categories.

Investigating the distribution of active variables (funding type and research profiles) in Fig. 18.1, one can identify a specific structure: Publications in natural sciences are principally produced in the upper region of the field, while social sciences and related disciplines are located in the field's lower region. Horizontally, we find agents with a broad research focus centering on the life sciences on the left and a narrow research focus centered on technology and applied sciences on the right. The ratio of third-party funds correlates with this structure: Universities that

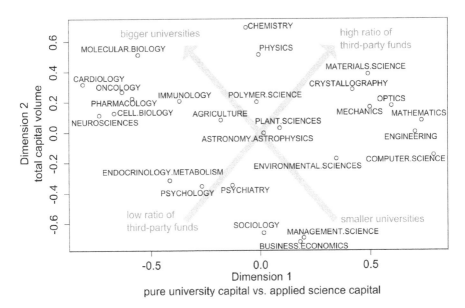

Fig. 18.1 The field of German universities – T1

are focused on natural sciences as well as those that specialize in applied sciences like engineering and materials science tend to be largely financed through third-party funds, while those that focus on other topics, especially social sciences and psychology, are chiefly financed through regular funds. As indicated in Fig. 18.1, university size is woven into this structure, in such a way that smaller universities are situated in the lower right and larger ones in the upper left.

Building on our conceptual apparatus, we provide the following interpretation: Dimension 1 represents the distribution of two kinds of capital that are available in the field. We call these forms of capital *traditional university capital* on the one hand and *applied science capital* on the other. Agents with a high amount of traditional university capital tend to be larger universities which are mainly financed by regular funds (that is, from the field of the nation-state), and have broad research profiles, ranging from biology and other natural sciences to various strands of medicine and psychology. Agents with lots of applied scientific capital rely more strongly on third-party funding (which often comes from non-academic sources, such as the economic field) and have more narrow research profiles that are oriented towards technological, economic, or political expectations from outside the academic field. The term 'applied scientific capital' is meant to emphasize the fact that the strength of these universities lies in their ability to combine academic and non-academic resources and motivations: Science made applicable for non-scientific concerns.

Dimension 2 represents the total volume of capital. This means that agents located in the upper parts of the field possess more of their respective resources than those located in the lower part of the field. The sizes of the universities, the degree to which they publish in core natural sciences (physics and chemistry), as well as

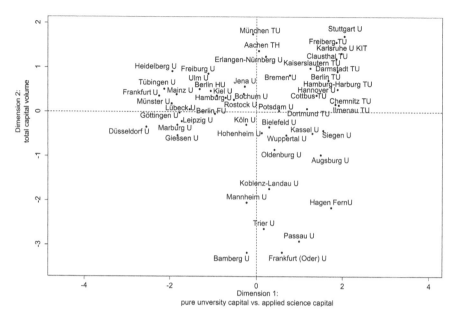

Fig. 18.2 The field of German universities – T1 – agents' positions

the third-party funding ratio, are correlated with capital volume. In sum, then, we see that dimension 2 represents overall power, whereas dimension 1 distinguishes between two different and competing types of power in the field.

Figure 18.2 shows the positions of the universities in the field constructed in our MFA. While research subjects in Fig. 18.1 are distributed fairly evenly, universities cluster in the upper half, and only a few are found at the bottom of the plot. Thus, we conclude that the field of German universities consists of a large number of 'standard' agents and a smaller number of 'special' agents. Members of the latter group stand out because they specialize in humanities and social sciences and publish little in disciplines like physics and chemistry. Indeed, many of the universities in the lower half of Fig. 18.2 are known as 'reform universities', which were founded (or re-founded) in the 1960s and early 1970s, the main phase of educational expansion in Germany, initiated by the field of the German nation-state. Many of these younger universities were not yet fully established when the economic stagnation of the 1970s and the 1980s restricted state investment in high-cost disciplines like medicine, biology, chemistry, or physics. As a result, many younger universities in Germany do not have natural sciences and medical departments and focus instead on less costly types of research, e.g. on psychology and the social sciences. As Fig. 18.2 shows, in the period between 1995 and 2000 the difference between the few special universities and all the others was the main dividing line in the field – the line between the dominant and the dominated.

The other major divide, separating the left from the right side of the field, results from the distinction between natural and life sciences (left) and applied, technological sciences (right). This distinction also originates from a special type of university, namely the Technical Universities (TU), many of which can be found in the right half of the field. Most of these universities were founded as advanced schools for technicians and engineers in the nineteenth century, sometimes gaining full university status as late as the beginning of the twentieth century. Since that time, many of them have become important agents in the German university field; for example, the TU Munich and TU Aachen are often considered to be at the top of the German university system. Still, because of their unique organizational heritage, TUs remain distinct and assume a special role in the university system. Thus, we can summarize the positions of agents in Fig. 18.2 as displaying three groups of universities: The classic, 'full universities'[2] which aspire to the Humboldtian ideal, located in the upper left quadrant of the field; the TUs, with their special focus on technology and application, located on the right side; and the younger 'reform universities' that focus on social sciences, management sciences, and humanities, located at the bottom of Fig. 18.2.

Trajectories Within the Field of German Universities

While this synchronous analysis is necessary and insightful, an analysis of organizational fields should be aiming for more. We need to look not only at the structure of a field at a given moment, but also at the temporal dynamic underlying that structure. If we fail to do so, we might be tempted into various kinds of oversimplification, for example interpreting the activities of organizations as mechanically emerging from their position in the field, or regarding as 'similar' agents who in fact move through the field along different trajectories which only coincidentally intersect at the moment of observation. Worst of all, we might be tempted to view the structure outlined above as relatively stable, an assumption which will be thoroughly refuted in the subsequent diachronic analysis.

Figure 18.3 illustrates this point: It shows the trajectories that the 58 universities have taken through the field from the late 1990s to the late 2000s. These trajectories are due to changes in the publication output of the universities, as well as the relative amounts of regular state funding and competitive third-party funding they receive. The circles in the figure roughly indicate the three groups of universities mentioned above – full, technical, and reform universities.

If we take into account that universities in general are relatively inert organizations, and in particular that the degree of organizational autonomy and competition among German universities is still fairly low, such massive and varied movement in the field is remarkable. There are agents with similar starting positions who move in different directions with different velocities. Consider for example the University of Mannheim, marked 43 in Fig. 18.3, and the University of Frankfurt/Oder, marked

---

[2] *Volluniversitäten* in German.

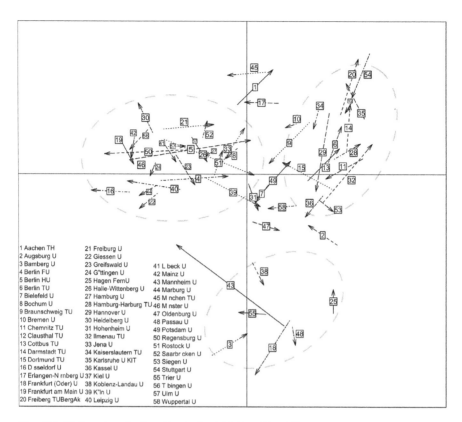

Fig. 18.3 Trajectories of universities in the field, from T1 to T2

18. Both start at roughly the same position, but their development over time differs hugely, so that by 2012 the University of Mannheim has moved far to the left and upward, thus becoming similar to the full universities, while the University of Frankfurt/Oder has moved farther away from the mainstream and became an even more exceptional case (developments than can be understood by recourse to the respective organizations' dispositions and strategies to a changing environment).

An observation like this is very hard to explain with recourse to the standard concepts of organization studies. For example, isomorphic pressure fails to hold up as an interpretation, because there is apparent diversification among formerly similar agents. Examples for the reverse case, where agents move towards each other from distant regions of the field, can also be found in Fig. 18.2. From the perspective of organizational ecology this result is perplexing, because organizations that share a position in the ecology are expected to behave in largely similar ways.

A close examination of the dynamic structure of the field shows that we cannot explain the movements of the universities with recourse to a general, causal mechanism exerted by one or a few manifest variables. From a Bourdieusian point of view, we can expect that there exists a connection between a university's trajectory and its starting position in the field. To examine this idea, we can look at correlations between the starting position on the first dimension and the movement along that dimension (Pearson's $r = .159$), as well as the starting position and the movement along the second dimension (Pearson's $r = .181$). Yet, these correlations are much lower than a deterministic reading of Bourdieu might suggest, where future developments are purportedly determined by past and present positions. Given the pattern of movement in Fig. 18.3, the idea that there exists a clear linear relation between the starting position and the trajectory does not seem plausible. If such an overarching relation does exist, we can assume that it is complex and not linear, because it results from the interaction between intra-organizational and extra-organizational field effects, from influences from other social fields, and, ultimately, from the overarching field of power. Thus, moving on from the trajectories of singular agents, we shall now turn to the changing structure of the field's topology.

The Changing Topology of the German University Field

Up to this point, the analysis was concerned with individual organizational agents or groups of universities in relation to each other. Now, we turn our attention from these individual agents in order to elucidate the topological structure of the social space that lies behind specific positions and movements. The relationship between social spaces and the entities in them is one of mutual structuration: Agents bend and shape social space through their presence and their movement, while social space, through its slopes and gradients, encourages and constrains different types of movement and positioning. In order to identify the topological structure of the field, we interpret the positions of agents in the field as sample points of measurement, and apply a two-dimensional kernel density model (Venables and Ripley 2013) in order to estimate the overall shape of the field on the basis of these measurements. As a result, we get a graphical representation of the field space that can be interpreted like a two-dimensional histogram, i.e. a model of the likelihood of positions in the given field. This model makes the power of fields over their members tangible as a kind of social topology: In regions of the field where agents are close together, social space is bent into curvatures that can divert the trajectories of those who move through this region. In densely populated regions, niches can form that severely constrain agents' mobility. In other regions of the field where agents are widely dispersed, social space remains relatively flat and thus trajectories are less constrained by the field's force. Looking at fields' topologies in this way, we can incorporate both the idea of isomorphic pressure and of ecological niches: In densely populated regions of social space, isomorphic pressures are at work that drive agents toward similarity, while these densely populated areas themselves can be viewed as ecological niches that differ remarkably from each other.

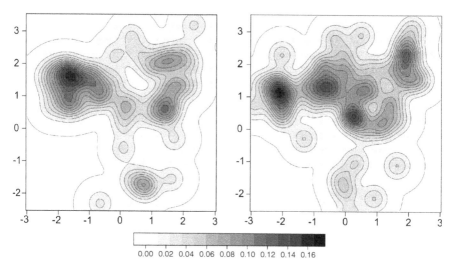

Fig. 18.4 The spatial structure of the field, T1 and T2

We visualize the spatial characteristics of the field of German universities by applying a two-dimensional kernel density model to the coordinates of the individual agents on the first and second dimension of the MFA. Figure 18.4 shows two level-plots of two kernel density models, each calculated for one of the time slices in the field's development. These plots can be interpreted like topological maps: Lighter regions of the map are flat, i.e. social space in these regions is not bent by the presence of agents. Conversely, the darker the plot, the more agents are located there.

With the aid of this model, we can begin to describe the field's spatial structure as a whole. The traditional approach to field structure works by identifying structuring axes and grouping agents into classes and describing the relation between classes (e.g. Bourdieu 1988). With the shift of focus away from the dimensions and classes of agents we propose here, we can interpret field structure without having to concern ourselves with the whereabouts of individual agents.

In the model of the first time period (T1, left side side of Fig. 18.4), three main regions of the field can be discerned. These correspond with the classical three-part grouping of universities mentioned previously: the tightly integrated group of full universities leaves a clear mark on the field space in the upper left region; the more dispersed group of universities with a focus on applied sciences impacts the field on the upper right, and the smaller indentation created by the reform universities can be seen in the lower region of the plot.

Inspecting the model of the second time period (T2), we see the disruption of this classical three-part structure that has taken place: On the left side, the formerly homogenous position of full universities has broken apart, with one group drifting toward the center and another remaining in the upper left. On the right side, a similar process has taken place and has further intensified the scattering of the TUs, with some of them forming a new distinct niche further to the right, while another group gravitates towards the center. In the lower part of the field, the formerly distinct position of the reform universities has evaporated almost completely, with single agents moving in opposite directions. In terms of capital, the three niches that existed in the 1990s were reasonably homogenous: only full universities (on the right side of the field) possessed significant amounts of traditional university capital, while TUs on the right side had the monopoly on applied science capital, and the reform universities in the lower part of the field had relatively small amounts of both types of capital.

In the second time period, the isomorphic pull of these three niches has been weakened through various policy reforms, most notably through the Excellence Initiative and the increasing importance of competitive third-party funding. As a consequence, agents in all regions of the field have begun to pursue types of capital that were previously unavailable and unattractive to them. On the organizational side, universities are transformed into 'complete organizations', becoming actual 'organizational actors'. Consequently, universities leave the institutional categories that have previously structured the field and develop individual strategies and practices, so that today a growing variety of organizational forms exists in the field and distinctions are less clear-cut. The two forms of capital that were previously monopolized by one type of university are nowadays combined more often and begin to lose their distinctive value. Instead of three types of universities with respective niches and two distinct types of capital, we now have an amalgam of different organization types that cluster around the center of the field, but have arrived there from opposite poles, as well as two groups of organizations that still keep their tight research focus on either basic or applied research.

These changes are, to a large extent, reactions toward intrusions from other fields, namely the economic, bureaucratic and especially the field of the German nation-state and the political field (Münch 2014). External forces interact with established structures in the field and produce outcomes that only ostensibly resemble their initial motivations: while the reforms are intended to govern the whole field in a more effective way and to improve its overall performance, we can see that the main outcomes in terms of field structure are increased complexity, heterogeneity, and thus insecurity. While some universities clearly benefit from this development, the overall tendency is that universities need more and more resources to adapt to the changing conditions and secure their positions in the face of competition. Altogether, the 'governability' of the field, be it from within or from without, has clearly been diminished through the reforms. Additionally, it is questionable whether the reforms have improved scientific performance sufficiently to compensate for the growing amount of resources spent on management, image-building, and competition.

The changes we observe here are just the first step toward the establishment of a more competitive field dynamic. We expect that the ability to simultaneously acquire large amounts of both types of capital will, over time, become the new mode of domination in the field. In the course of this development, the instability and complexity of the field structure are likely to increase, and further new organizational forms will emerge. The dissolution of clear-cut institutional boundaries causes universities to change more rapidly than in the past. In the wake of accelerated change, new practices like fundraising and 'friend-raising' that are presently taking root in the field will become more important. Dominant universities which excel at combining basic research and applied sciences will be the major beneficiaries of these developments, while universities that continue to orient their practice toward the traditional three-part field structure and the Humboldtian ideals embedded therein will be continually challenged.

Conclusion

The concept of an organizational field *sensu* Bourdieu has decisive analytical advantages which have been demonstrated in the example of the structure and ongoing transformation of the field of German universities. While the organizational ecology approach overemphasizes variation and tends to neglect cultural adaptation, and the neo-institutional approach overemphasizes the standardizing effects of legitimacy and culture, Bourdieusian field theory offers a balanced model, combining the insights of both approaches.

The construction of the German academic field revealed both the tendency of organizations to diversify into niches as well as the tendency toward isomorphism. For example, the recent reforms in German research policy have put particular pressure on the so-called reform universities, so that the niche in which these organizations were positioned is in decline, with its various occupants moving to different parts of the field. On the other hand, a new dominant organizational form, positioned in the center of the field, seems to have emerged in the wake of the reforms, which brings together universities that formerly belonged to distinct types – traditional full universities as well as universities with an applied focus – into a new isomorphic position. Furthermore, differentiation and isomorphism can not only both be modeled, but can also be theoretically related to each other through field-theoretical concepts: In the case of the German university field, we see reforms which push traditionally quite distinct types of universities to compete for the same resources in an increasingly homogenous arena. This change in the environment on the one hand causes a new dominant niche to emerge, which can exert isomorphic pressures on the field; on the other hand, established niches, especially in the already dominated part of the field, are disintegrating. In this sense, field theory enables us to see how both the standardization and the de-standardization of organizational forms emerge from the transformation of the organizational environment in terms of material resources, administrative rules, and cultural expectations.

Appendix: Tables

Table 18.1 Dispersion of ten selected WoS research areas among German universities

	1995–2000		2007–2012	
	N	Percent (%)	N	Percent (%)
Phyics	59	100.0	59	100.0
Chemistry	58	98.3	59	100.0
Biochemistry & molecular biology	48	81.4	46	78.0
Computer science	39	66.1	49	83.1
Psychology	25	42.4	38	64.4
Cell biology	22	37.3	15	25.4
Plant sciences	13	22.0	9	15.3
Environmental sciences	12	20.3	25	42.4
Business economics	7	11.9	21	35.6
Geology	5	8.5	10	16.9

Table 18.2 Universities' practices and internal structures

Excellence initiative applications	N	Percent (%)
Research clusters	34	57.6
Graduate schools	35	59.3
Future concept	13	22.0
University associations		
German U 15	12	20.3
TU9	8	13.6
Mid-sized universities	15	25.4
Intra-organizational structures (Staffs)		
Fundraising	33	55.9
Strategy	50	84.7
International affairs	44	74.6
Quality management	55	93.2

References

Baier, C., & Schmitz, A. (2012). Organisationen als Akteure in sozialen Feldern–Eine Model-lierungsstrategie am Beispiel deutscher Hochschulen. *Feldanalyse als Forschungsprogramm, 1*, 191–220.
Bourdieu, P. (1988). *Homo Academicus*. Stanford: Stanford University Press.

Bourdieu, P. (1998). *The state nobility: Elite schools in the field of power*. Stanford: Stanford University Press.

Bourdieu, P. (2005). *The social structures of the economy*. Cambridge: Polity.

Bourdieu, P., & Wacquant, L. J. D. (1992). *An invitation to reflexive sociology*. Chicago: University of Chicago Press.

DiMaggio, P. J., & Powell, W. W. (1983). The iron cage revisited: Institutional isomorphism and collective rationality in organizational fields. *American Sociological Review, 48*(2), 147–160.

Dobrev, S. D. (2001). Revisiting organizational legitimation: Cognitive diffusion and sociopolitical factors in the evolution of Bulgarian newspaper enterprises, 1846–1992. *Organization Studies, 22*(3), 419–444.

Dobrev, S. D., Kim, T., & Carroll, G. R. (2002). The evolution of organizational niches: U.S. automobile manufacturers, 1885–1981. *Administrative Science Quarterly, 47*(2), 233.

Emirbayer, M., & Johnson, V. (2008). Bourdieu and organizational analysis. *Theory and Society, 37*(1), 1–44.

Escofier, B., & Pagès, J. (1994). Multiple Factor Analysis (AFMULT package). *Computational Statistics & Data Analysis, 18*(1), 121–140.

Hannan, M. T., & Freeman, J. (1977). The population ecology of organizations. *American Journal of Sociology, 82*(5), 929–964.

Hannan, M. T., & Freeman, J. (1984). Structural inertia and organizational change. *American Sociological Review, 49*(2), 149–164.

Meyer, J. W., & Rowan, B. (1977). Institutional organizations: formal structure as myth and ceremony. *American Journal of Sociology, 83*, 340–363.

Münch, R. (2014). *Academic capitalism: Universities in the global struggle for excellence*. London: Routledge.

Parsons, T. (1956). Suggestions for a sociological approach to the theory of organizations I. *Administrative Science Quarterly, 1*, 63–85.

Schmitz, A., Witte, D., & Gengnagel, V. (2017). Pluralizing field analysis: Toward a relational understanding of the field of power. *Social Science Information, 56*(1), 49–73.

Stinchcombe, A. L. (1965). Social structure and organizations. In J. G. March (Ed.), *Handbook of organizations*. Chicago: Rand McNally.

Venables, W. N., & Ripley, B. D. (2013). *Modern applied statistics with S-Plus*. New York: Springer.

Part III
Methodology and Methods

Chapter 19
Assigning Changes Over Time Using Geometric Data Analysis Methods: Application to the French "Barometer of Political Trust"

Frédérik Cassor and Brigitte Le Roux

Introduction

This chapter has a methodological objective. We deal with the following issues:

First, we present a geometric method for the analysis of a questionnaire with bipolar questions (Likert-type scale). More precisely, we undertake a coding of questions, namely the doubling procedure, then we proceed to a correspondence analysis (CA).

Second, we give guidance on how to balance the headings of the questionnaire when the numbers of questions per headings are very different. The principle is to put weights on questions so that headings contribute equally to the total variance.

Third, in the framework of geometric data analysis (GDA), we develop a procedure based on transition formulas, to compare questions that are measured upon different samples of individuals on a regular basis over time and to inspect trajectories of questions.

Fourth, we propose a new method for assigning supplementary individuals to clusters produced by Euclidean ascending hierarchical clustering (AHC); the procedure is based on the successive dichotomies of the hierarchy, and takes into account the geometric properties of the clusters, particularly their shape.

F. Cassor
Centre for Political Research in Sciences Po (CEVIPOF), SciencesPo Paris, France
e-mail: frederik.cassor@sciencespo.fr

B. Le Roux (✉)
MAP5, Université Paris Descartes & CEVIPOF, SciencesPo Paris, France
e-mail: Brigitte.LeRoux@mi.parisdescartes.fr

© Springer Nature Switzerland AG 2019
J. Blasius et al. (eds.), *Empirical Investigations of Social Space*,
Methodos Series 15, https://doi.org/10.1007/978-3-030-15387-8_19

All procedures are illustrated using data stemming from the *barometer survey* on levels of trust among French citizens, carried out by CEVIPOF (Center for Political Research in Sciences-Po Paris) each year since 2009 (see www.cevipof.com/fr/le-barometre-de-la-confiance-politique-du-cevipof/).

Trust is a complex and multidimensional phenomenon. There are two constituent elements of the bond of trust, namely 'being trusting' and 'being trustworthy'. Furthermore, beyond this double aspect of trust, it is usual to distinguish trust in persons from trust in institutions. The second form is much more uncertain and evanescent than the first (Hardin 2002). Research into the roles of trust in our society has offered a broad range of often conflicting theories. Some theorists maintain that trust is a social virtue that cannot be reduced to strategic self-interest; others claim that trusting another person is ultimately a rational calculation based on information about that person. It can be assumed that the main incentive for trust is to maintain a relationship with those whom we trust – be it for reasons of economic benefit or for friendship.

Regarding the CEVIPOF barometer data, we aim to answer the following research questions (Le Roux and Perrineau 2011):

1. What is the organization of the components of trust? What is the structure of the French space of trust?
2. Are there groups of French citizens who exhibit different kinds of trust?
3. What are the changes in trust year on year from 2012 to 2016?

In order to answer these questions, the statistical analysis comprises three steps. The first step is the *construction of the space of trust* based on 2016 data, using CA after doubling and weighting of questions. The second step consists in studying the *distribution of individuals in the multidimensional space of trust*: Firstly, we study a structuring factor; secondly, we perform a clustering of individuals. The third step deals with the *study of change* in answers to questions and the variability of groups of individuals.

Data and Elementary Statistics

We base our study on barometer data stemming from online surveys about levels of trust among French citizens, carried out by CEVIPOF. Samples (about 1500 persons) are designed to be representative of the French citizens registered to vote, by using the quota method (gender, age, occupation) and categorization by type of agglomeration and size of the home town. The data were collected by the polling institute OpinionWay using a CAWI (Computer Assisted Web Interview) system.

Individuals

To construct the space of trust and to make a typology of the French citizens according to their levels of trust, we choose to take the interviewees of the 2016 survey as a reference sample. This means that, in the analyses, the individuals of this survey are put as *active elements*, and the ones of the four surveys from 2012 to 2015 are put as *supplementary elements*.

The number of respondents to the survey taken as a reference is 2044. We discard from the analysis the respondents who did not answer more than one question in each component of trust. We also discard individuals with paradoxical answers. In the end, 1963 respondents are retained for the analysis. We have verified that they still constitute a representative sample.

Questions

We selected four components of trust (political, institutional, economic, interpersonal) that are measured by 19 questions. Among them, 18 are coded on a rating scale with four levels, and one is dichotomous. An example of a question is: "How much do you trust in the following political persons? (your mayor, the Prime Minister, etc.)". The possible answers are *very trustful* (coded ++), *fairly trustful* (coded +), *not very trustful* (coded –), and *not at all trustful* (coded – –); in addition, there is one category for *no answer* or *don't know*, which is recoded according to the respondent's answers to the other questions of the component.

The questions that we use in this study can be summarized as follows:

1. *Political trust*: trust in political roles (7 questions): Presidential institution, Prime Minister, your Member of Parliament (MP), your Mayor, your General Councillor, political parties, European Union;
2. *Institutional trust*: trust in large public or private institutions (5 questions): hospitals, police, media, trade unions, World Trade Organization (WTO);
3. *Economic trust*: trust in economic organizations (4 questions, one of which is dichotomous): banks, public firms, private firms, 'the State must trust/control firms';
4. *Interpersonal trust* (3 questions): neighbors, people we first meet (strangers), foreigners.

Table 19.1 shows the frequencies (in %) of the categories of the 19 questions. A perfunctory review of Table 19.1 shows that the level of trust in all political items is very low. From an economic perspective, the trust in public and private firms is mixed, and there is considerable distrust in banks; however, 66% of the respondents choose 'the State must trust firms' versus 'the State must control and regulate firms more closely'. Regarding institutional trust, the level is quite high for hospitals and the police, and rather bad for the media, trade unions, and the WTO. Interpersonal trust is good, even though it does not necessarily attain high levels (except for the respondents' own family – consequently, this weakly selective question is not included in the analyses).

The main topic of this chapter is to study trust by taking account of its full multidimensionality. To do that, we construct the space of trust by using Geometric

Table 19.1 Frequencies (in %) of categories of the 19 questions

	++	+	−	− −
Pres. institution	3	31	42	24
Prime Minister	4	31	35	30
Member of Parliament	3	42	40	15
Mayor	12	52	25	11
General councillor	2	48	38	12
Political parties	1	10	47	42
European Union	3	34	39	24
	++	+	−	− −
Hospitals	16	68	13	4
Police	16	62	16	6
Media	1	23	46	30
Trade unions	3	26	40	32
WTO	1	25	49	24
	++	+	−	− −
Banks	2	28	42	28
Public firms	2	44	40	14
Private firms	3	40	39	17
The state must trust firms and give them more freedom	66	The state must control and regulate firms more closely		34
	++	+	−	− −
Neighbors	24	52	20	4
People we first meet	4	42	44	10
Foreigners	15	50	26	9

Data Analysis; then, we inspect groups of individuals in the space of trust, establish a typology of individuals, and examine the location of the groups of individuals in the space of trust. Lastly, we show the changes in trust from 2012 to 2016.

The Space of Trust

Data Coding

The 19 questions chosen for constructing the space are bipolar. We construct the space of trust using correspondence analysis (CA) after doubling (see Appendix). Moreover, the number of questions is not the same for each component of trust, so we have weighted each question by the inverse of the number of questions of its component (see Appendix). Thus, the components are roughly balanced in the analysis (see Table 19.3). We then proceed to the CA of the weighted doubled table (see Appendix).

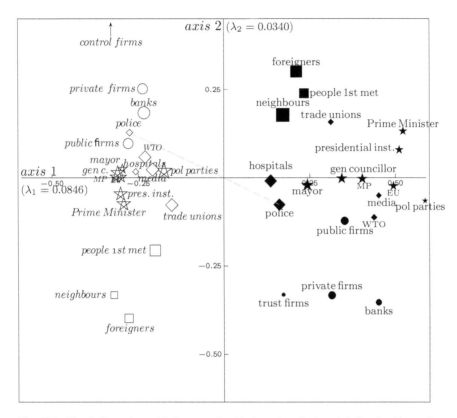

Fig. 19.1 Cloud of questions with the two poles: black markers for 'trust', italics & white markers for '*distrust*'; sizes of markers are proportional to mean scores

Main Results of the CA of Doubled Table

The main results of the analysis are the variances of axes (eigenvalues), the cloud of questions, the cloud of individuals, and the contributions of questions to axes.

The variances of axes are given in Table 19.2 and the diagram of variances of axes is depicted in Fig. 19.3. There are five axes whose variances are greater than the mean ($0.2939/19 = 0.0155$). We can see that the first axis is by far the most important axis. With three axes, we have almost half of the total variance; therefore, we interpret three axes.

Table 19.3 gives the contributions (in %) of the components of trust to the cloud, and to the first three axes.

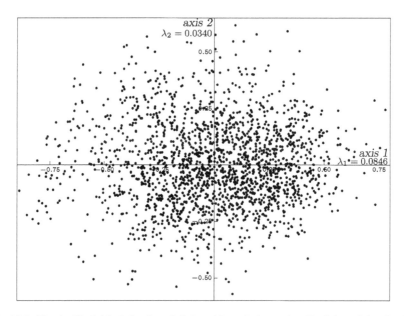

Fig. 19.2 Cloud of individuals in plane 1–2 (graphic scale is equal to ¾ of that of the cloud of questions)

Table 19.2 Variance of axes

Axis	Variance	Variance rate
1	0.08464	28.8
2	0.03401	40.3
3	0.02744	49.7
4	0.01784	55.7
5	0.01605	61.2
6	0.01368	65.9
7	0.01268	70.2
8	0.01125	74.7
9	0.01095	77.7
10	0.00966	81.0

We see on Table 19.3 that contributions to the cloud are almost balanced. Axis 1 is primarily a political axis (44% for political trust). Axis 2 is related to interpersonal (52%) and economic trust (42%). Axis 3 combines institutional, economic, and interpersonal trust.

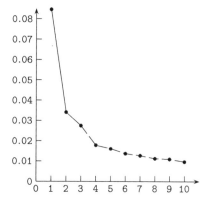

Fig. 19.3 Diagram of variances of axes

Table 19.3 Contributions (in %) of components of trust to the cloud and to the first three axes

Contribution (in %)	Cloud	Axis 1	Axis 2	Axis 3
Political trust	29.9	**44.0**	2.0	13.4
Institutional trust	24.0	19.9	4.6	**30.6**
Economic trust	24.1	21.5	**41.7**	27.2
Interpersonal trust	22.0	14.6	**51.7**	**28.7**

Interpretation of Axes

The interpretation of axes is based on the contribution of questions, that is, the sum of contributions of the two poles of questions. The questions retained for interpretation are the ones whose contribution is greater than the average contribution (basic criterion); here we take 5%.

Axis 1 accounts for 29% of the variance of the cloud. It opposes all trust categories (located on the right in Fig. 19.1) to all distrust categories (located on the left): It is therefore an axis indicating the *general level of trust*.

The 14 questions whose contributions are greater than 5% contribute as a whole 97% of the variance of axis 1 (see Table 19.4). They constitute a fairly good summary of axis 1. As already noted, the political component of trust is the one that contributes more to axis 1 (44%); all questions of this component (except the one regarding respondents' levels of trust in their mayors) satisfy the criterion, with the highest contribution from the questions about 'Prime Minister' and 'presidential institution', then from the EU and MPs. Then, there is the economic component, with three questions about banks and large public and private firms, whose contribution is 22%; then comes the institutional component, which contributes 20% with the WTO and the media; and lastly, we have the interpersonal component (neighbors, foreigners).

Table 19.4 Contributions (in %) of questions to the first three axes, in bold those that satisfied the criterion

	Cloud	Axis 1	Axis 2	Axis 3
Presidential institution	4.4	**7.8**	0.5	2.5
Prime Minister	5.2	**7.8**	1.2	3.6
MP	3.8	**6.4**	0.0	0.0
mayor	4.5	3.7	0.1	1.6
General councillor	3.4	**5.2**	0.0	0.0
political parties	4.1	**5.2**	0.2	3.9
European Union	4.5	**7.8**	0.0	1.8
total	29.9	44.0	2.0	13.4
hospitals	3.7	2.2	0.0	0.3
police	4.5	2.8	1.5	3.9
trade unions	6.0	2.9	1.9	**20.3**
media	5.1	**5.8**	0.2	**5.0**
WTO	4.7	**6.2**	1.0	1.0
total	24.0	19.9	4.6	30.6
banks	6.4	**7.6**	**11.8**	0.0
public firms	5.0	**7.1**	2.2	0.3
private firms	5.8	**5.4**	**15.2**	3.2
trust/control firms	7.0	1.4	**12.6**	**23.7**
total	24.1	21.5	41.7	27.2
neighbors	7.8	**5.0**	**13.4**	**20.9**
strangers	6.1	4.3	**11.2**	4.5
foreigners	8.1	**5.3**	**27.2**	3.2
Total	22.0	14.6	51.7	28.7

To sum up: Axis 1 can be interpreted as indicating a general level of trust/distrust, especially with regards to politics and economic institutions.

Axis 2 accounts for 12% of the variance of the cloud. Its interpretation is based on 6 questions that together account for 91% of its variance (see Table 19.4). The contribution of the interindividual component is the most important one (52%).

Axis 2 depicts an opposition between (at the top of Fig. 19.4) interpersonal trust (neighbors, foreigners, strangers) and distrust with respect to economic institutions and, at the bottom of Fig. 19.4, interpersonal distrust associated with economic trust (banks, large firms).

Axis 3 accounts for 9% of the variance of the cloud. Six questions meet the criterion and together contribute 78% of the variance of axis 3 (see Table 19.4). The institutional component is the most important one (31%), with a large contribution from the responses regarding trust in trade unions (20%) and to a lesser degree the media (5%). Next, we find one economic question (the State must trust/control firms) whose contribution is equal to 24%. After that, we have the interpersonal component with two questions about neighbors (21%) and strangers (5%).

Axis 3 establishes that there is an opposition between, on the one hand, trust in firms as well as a trust in neighbors (at the bottom of Fig. 19.5) and, on the other,

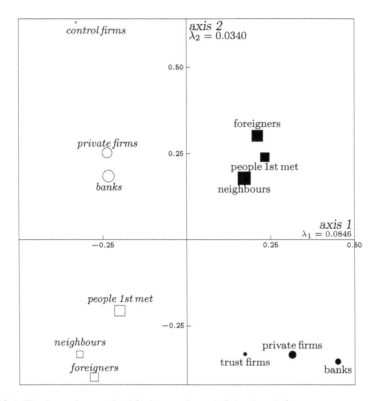

Fig. 19.4 The 6 questions retained for interpreting axis 2, in plane 1–2

trust in trade unions as well as close control of firms by the state (in order to confront economic difficulties), associated with distrust in neighbors (at the top of Fig. 19.5).

To sum up: Axis 3 presents an opposition between freedom and constraints related to control and regulation.

Study of a Structuring Factor: Closeness of a Political Party

As an example of a *structured data analysis* (see Appendix), we choose, as a *structuring factor,* the following question: "Is there any particular party you feel closer to than others?" We will briefly study the spread of individuals in the space of trust according to their closeness to a political party. From this question, we delineate groups of individuals in the geometric space.

A subcloud of the cloud is associated with each group of individuals. In Table 19.5, we give the calibrated deviation from mean points of subclouds to the origin (coordinate of the mean point divided by the standard deviation ($\lambda^{1/2}$) of the axis), and the variances of subclouds along the axes.

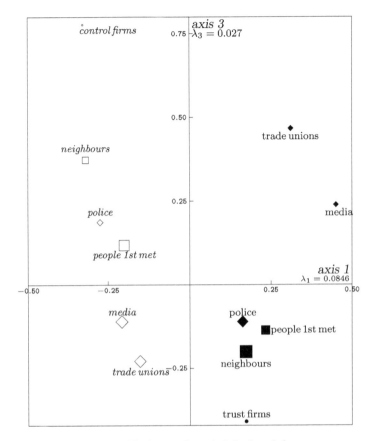

Fig. 19.5 The 6 questions retained for interpreting axis 3, in plane 1–3

Table 19.5 Calibrated deviations and variances of each group on the first three axes

	n	Axis 1 ($\lambda_1 = 0.085$)		Axis 2 ($\lambda_2 = 0.034$)		Axis 3 ($\lambda_3 = 0.027$)	
		Calibrated deviation	Variance	Calibrated deviation	Variance	Calibrated deviation	Variance
far left	136	−0.051	0.072	**0.903**	0.040	**0.512**	0.022
PS	263	**0.633**	0.054	0.368	0.023	**0.437**	0.019
LR (UMP)	310	0.296	0.060	**−0.503**	0.021	**−0.458**	0.025
FN	291	**−0.640**	0.075	**−0.476**	0.029	0.024	0.028
none	556	−0.269	0.084	0.068	0.031	0.035	0.026

In the analysis, we consider the four main political groups, namely the "far left" (grouping of parties on the left of PS, namely, LO, NPA, PCF, PG, $n = 136$), the Socialist party (PS, n $= 263$), the center right party (LR, $n = 310$), and the extreme right party (FN, $n = 291$), as well as the group of 'closeness to no party' ($n = 556$), hence a subset of 1556 respondents.

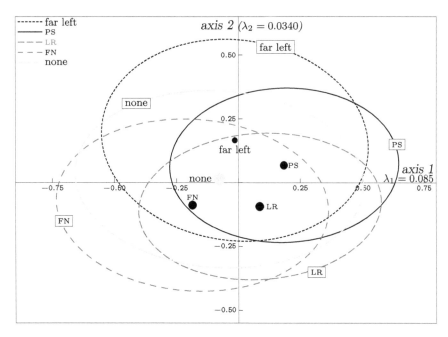

Fig. 19.6 Plane 1–2. Concentration ellipses of the groups of individuals according to closeness to the five main political parties and *no closeness* (*none*) (legend on the top left corner of the figure)

Table 19.6 Double breakdown of variances on the first three axes

Variances	Axis 1	Axis 2	Axis 3
total	0.0872	0.0345	0.0270
between groups	0.0157	0.0064	0.0026
within groups	0.0716	0.0281	0.0244
η^2	0.18	0.19	0.10

We consider a deviation to be notable if the absolute value of the calibrated deviation is greater than 0.4 (Le Roux and Rouanet 2010: 59). From Table 19.5, we see that deviations are notable for PS and FN on axis 1, for the far left, LR, and FN on axis 2, and for the far left, PS, and LR on axis 3. Considering the sign of the deviation, we notice there is an opposition between PS and FN on axis 1, and a clearcut opposition between the far left and LR and FN on axis 2 (Fig. 19.6). The traditional political divide between left and right is found on the third axis.

From Table 19.6, we note that variances within groups are much larger than variances between groups on the three axes; the coefficient η^2 (see Appendix) is less than 20% on the two first axes, and is even smaller on axis 3. This result leads us to consider only the first two axes for a more detailed study of the closeness to political parties.

In Fig. 19.6, we depict, in plane 1–2, the concentration ellipses of groups of citizens according to the particular party they feel closer to. Each concentration ellipse is a *geometric summary* of the group of individuals (if the group is normally

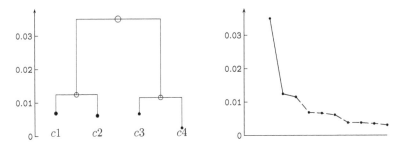

Fig. 19.7 Superior hierarchical tree and diagram of level indices of the hierarchy

shaped, its concentration ellipse contains about 86% of individuals, Le Roux 2010: 69–70). As expected, the sympathizers of PS (the ruling party at that time) are located on the side of trust (on the right in Fig. 19.6). Those who feel closer to the center right party (LR) are also located on the side of trust, but mainly in the bottom right quadrant, on the side of trust in economics. We notice also that the far left concentration ellipse is widely dispersed throughout in the plane, albeit mainly located in the upper side of the figure; that is, as a whole, the sympathizers of the far left distrust economic institutions. As we will also see in the clustering analysis, the sympathizers of the extreme right party (FN, $n = 291$) are clearly located on the side of distrust.

Clustering of Individuals

Euclidean ascending hierarchical clustering of active individuals is performed on the first five principal axes (whose variances are greater than the average and where the sum of contributions is equal to 61%, see Table 19.2).

It can be seen in Fig. 19.7 that the level indices of the hierarchy slowly decrease from the fourth onward; therefore we interpret a partition in four clusters. The superior hierarchical tree, whose number of terminal nodes is equal to four, is shown in Fig. 19.7; the concentration ellipses of clusters in plane 1–2 are shown in Fig. 19.8.

To interpret the clusters of the partition, we apply the method that involves selecting categories of active questions that are overrepresented in the cluster (Le Roux 2014: 335–337). A category is overrepresented in the cluster if:

1. The relative frequency of the category in the cluster is 5% greater than the one in the reference set (set of all active individuals);
2. The hypergeometric test comparing the relative frequency in the cluster to the reference one is significant (Rouanet et al. 2000: 102).

Firstly, we interpret clusters from active questions (before doubling, that is, using the four levels of the scales). Secondly, we study the usual socio-demographic variables.

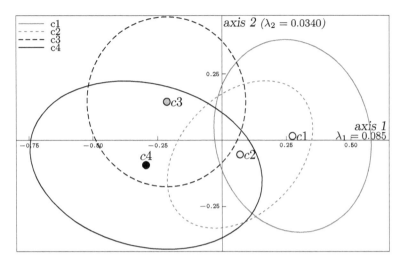

Fig. 19.8 Concentration ellipses of the four clusters in plane 1–2 of the space of trust (legend on the top left corner of the figure)

Cluster 1: The "Hyper-Trusters" (666 Respondents, 34%)

In this cluster, the overrepresented categories are the ones of relatively high trust (see table below).

Pres.inst	+	Hospitals	+	Banks	+
Prime Minister	+	Police	+	Public	+
MP	+	Media	+	Private firms	+
mayor	++,+	Trade unions	+	Trust/control	
Gen.councillor	+	WTO	+	Neighbors	++
Pol. parties	+,−			Strangers	+
EU	+			Foreigners	++,+

NB: If for a question no category is indicated, this means that no category is either overrepresented either underrepresented.

Furthermore, considering the socio-demographic variables, we find an overrepresentation of respondents with a high educational level (more than 2 years after *Baccalauréat*: 36% compared to the global rate of 29%), then an overrepresentation of retired persons (32% vs 28%), and of those with no financial difficulty (49% vs 38%). We also observe an overrepresentation of citizens close to the socialist party (PS) (25% vs 13%), and an underrepresentation of those close to the *Front National* (FN) (7% vs 15%). In this cluster, 29% of individuals trust the Left to rule the country (vs 14%). Moreover, more than half of respondents who are close to the socialist party (PS) are found in this cluster.

Cluster 2: The "Moderate Trusters" (463 Respondents, 23%)

The overrepresented categories are the ones with moderate trust (+) in economic institutions, and in interindividual items, with a mixed trust in public and private institutions, and with moderate distrust (−) in politics (except for their mayor).

Pres.inst	−	Hospitals	+	Banks	+,−
Prime Minister	−	Police	+	Public firms	+
MP	−	Media	−	Private firms	+
Mayor	+	Trade unions	− −	Trust	
Gen.councillor	−	WTO	−	Neighbors	+,++
Pol. parties	−			Strangers	+
EU	−			Foreigners	+

Furthermore, we observe an overrepresentation of persons aged over 65 (36% compared to the overall rate of 25%), of retired persons (41% vs 30%), and of practicing Catholics (20% vs 13%). The individuals belonging to this cluster position themselves on the right of the political spectrum (31% vs 19%); they are fairly close to the main center right party (LR) (25% vs 16%), and trust the right-wing parties to rule the country (33% vs 21%).

Cluster 3: The "Distrusters" (388 Respondents, 20%)

The overrepresented categories are those with moderate (−) or high (− −) distrust in political, institutional and ecomomic components; a moderate trust (+) in neighbors and strangers (interindividual component).

Pres.inst	−,− −	Hospitals	−	Banks	− −
Prime Minister	− −	Police	−	Public firms	−,− −
MP	−,− −	Media	− −	Private firms	− −
Mayor	−,− −	Trade unions	− −	Control	
Gen.councillor	−,− −	WTO	− −	Neighbors	+
Pol. parties	− −			Strangers	
EU	− −			Foreigners	+

Furthermore, there is an overrepresentation of persons aged 35–49 (31% vs 27%), and of individuals in a precarious financial position (56% of respondents in this cluster are struggling economically, which is only 47% of the overall set of respondents). 42% of individuals belonging to this cluster (vs 29%) say "when they think of politics, they feel repulsed"; 82% (vs 64%) trust neither the right nor the left to rule the country.

Cluster 4: The "Hyper-Distrusters" (446 Respondents, 23%)

The overrepresented categories are ones displaying a very high level of distrust
(− −) in all domains (see table below).

pres.inst	− −,−	Hospitals	− −,−	Banks	− −,−
Prime Minister	− −	Police	− −,−	Public firms	− −,−
MP	− −,−	Media	− −	Private firms	− −,−
Mayor	− −,−	Trade unions	−	Control	
Gen.councillor	− −,−	WTO	− −,−	Neighbors	− −,−
Pol. parties	− −			Strangers	− −,−
EU	− −,−			Foreigners	− −,−

Furthermore, social groups overrepresented are: women (61% vs 50%), workers
(27% vs 20% for employees, 20% vs 13% for unskilled workers), persons in
precarious financial positions (28% vs 18% for those at greatest risk of becoming
unemployed and 17% vs 9% for those struggling economically), and those who are
close to the main extreme right party (FN, 28% vs 15%).

In addition, 80% (vs 64%) of individuals of this cluster trust neither the right nor
the left to rule the country; 86% (vs 71%) think that, in France, democracy either
does not work well and or not at all; and 61% (vs 43%) think that France must be
protected more from the today's world.

Changes in Trust Between 2012 and 2016

In order to show changes over time, we develop two methods: defining trajectories of
questions in the space of trust, and assigning supplementary individuals to clusters.

Trajectory of Questions

In the construction of the space of trust, the respondents of the survey of 2016 are
made active elements, and the others are put as supplementary elements. Then, from
each supplementary survey, points associated with the two poles of questions are
constructed using transition formulas from CA (see Appendix); we then compare
their locations to those from the 2016 survey.

From Fig. 19.9, we can interpret the changes in trust as follows. Excluding the
trajectories for trust in the PM and the presidential institution, we notice that, in
general, the trajectories point towards the lower left quadrant until 2014, which
means a general decrease of the level of trust over this period. Specifically, we see a
more distrust towards strangers, although more trust in economic institutions. This
result is slightly modified after the relative rebound of the level of trust that we
observe in 2015 (the year of the terrorist attacks in Paris).

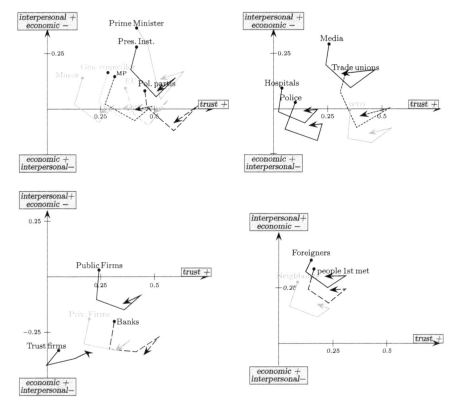

Fig. 19.9 Trajectories of the poles *"trust"*[+] of questions from 2012 (bullet-point) to 2016 (point of arrow) in plane 1–2

Assigning Supplementary Individuals to Clusters

We propose a new method to assign individuals of the surveys from 2012 to 2015 to the clusters obtained previously from the ascending hierarchical clustering (AHC) of the active individuals (2016 survey). This method takes into account successive dichotomies within the hierarchy, as well as the shape of clusters.

Following the method described in Appendix, we assign the respondents of surveys from 2012 to 2015 to the clusters that have been previously defined.

For each cluster, the percentages of individuals are given in the following table, according to years.

Clusters		2012 ($n = 1456$)	2013 ($n = 1733$)	2014 ($n = 1782$)	2015 ($n = 1974$)	**2016** ($n = 1963$)
c1	Hyper-trusters	33	29	35	39	**34**
c2	Moderate trusters	20	23	22	22	**23**
c3	Distrusters	19	18	17	17	**20**
c4	Hyper-distrusters	28	30	26	22	**23**
		[100%]	[100%]	[100%]	[100%]	[100%]

Conclusion

Trust is not something that appears to be widespread in French society. Trust itself is split into a range of components that have their relative autonomy. These various components of trust do not necessarily overlap neatly. Furthermore, during the period 2012–2017 (when François Hollande was the President of the Republic), the overall level of trust remained low, although there was a shift towards more economic trust, accompanied by a decrease in levels of interpersonal trust. Trust in general begins to increase in 2015, the year when Paris was hit by several terrorist attacks (the survey was conducted in December 2015, one month after the Bataclan attacks).

In most poll surveys, especially in electoral surveys, the basic data concern individuals and provide traditional, elementary analyses, but they are not really scrutinized from a multidimensional perspective. With multivariate methods (construction of scales, analysis of variance, classical variance analysis, etc.), the modeling is focused on the structural relations between variables (properties, opinions); the individuals are only 'bearers of variables'. Even in multiple correspondence analysis, only the cloud of categories is depicted. From this perspective, individuals' answers do not appear as fundamental elements of analysis. In this study, however, we focus on the benefits of studying in detail the data at an individual level.

As we have seen, our methods of assigning individuals to clusters, and of calculating the trajectory of questions are of particular interest for the study of data tables that are indexed by time. These methods can also be used when investigating clouds of individuals equipped with structuring factors, for instance when comparing, as Pierre Bourdieu stated, "positions in the field and position taking", which in our illustrative study here are the respondents' locations in the 'trust space' and their political choices, respectively.

Appendix

Doubling Procedure

The doubling procedure consists in assigning two scores per individual instead of a single score (see Benzécri et al. 1973, pp 25–27). We coded the four levels of each scale with (3,0), (2,1), (1,2) and (0,3), respectively, and the two levels of dichotomous question with (1,0), (0,1).

For example, in our study, the table is doubled with a "trust pole" (denoted q+) and a "distrust pole" (denoted q–) for each question.

Weighting Procedure

In order to balance each heading we weight each one here with the inverse of the number of questions the heading contains; consequently, the weight of a question is that of its heading.

Technically, the weighting procedure for CA consists in multiplying the two columns of each question by the weight.

Correspondence Analysis After Doubling

- In the CA of a doubled table (Le Roux 2014a: 206–209) all the rows of the table have the same total, hence each individual receives the same weight.
- In the CA display, we obtain two points for each question and one point for each individual. The line joining the two poles of one question passes through the origin (as shown in Fig. 19.1 for the question "trust in police"), and the distances of poles to origin are inversely proportional to the means of the scores of the pole.
- The distance between two individuals resulting from a question depends on the number of levels between their answers. The global distance is a weighted mean of the distances resulting from questions.
- The weight of the question has the following property: The greater the deviation from the mean of the question to the mid-point of the scale, the greater the weight of the question.

Nevertheless, it worth noting that, for a dichotomous question, the formula is exactly the same as that of MCA (Le Roux and Rouanet 2010: 35).

- The contribution of a question to the variance of cloud depends on:
  the dispersion of responses around the mean;
  the number of levels of the scale (questions will preferably be coded on scales with the same number of levels).

To sum up: Questions with extreme answers create greater distances, and questions exhibiting great agreement make a small contribution to the total variance.

For examples of CA after doubling, see Benzécri (1973, three studies in Tome 2, Part C) and Benzécri (1992: chapter 12).

Structured Data Analysis

A structuring factor generates a partition of the cloud of individuals (Le Roux and Rouanet 2004; Le Roux 2014b: Chapter 12). By plotting the mean point of each subcloud, we get a derived cloud of mean points whose variance defines the between-variance of the partition. The average variance of the subclouds defines the within-variance of the partition.

The coefficient η^2 (eta square: squared coefficient ratio) is equal to the between-variance divided by the total variance (between plus within).

Useful geometric summaries of subclouds in the plane are provided by concentration ellipses (Le Roux and Rouanet 2010: 69–71).

Trajectory of Questions (Coordinates of the Poles of Questions in CA)

The transition formulas for doubling CA are similar to the ones of MCA. The location of the pole of a question can be reconstituted from the cloud of individuals.

Given an axis, for each pole and each question, we compute the coordinates as follows. The coordinate of q^+ is equal to the weighted mean of the coordinates of individuals divided by the standard deviation of the axis ($\sqrt{\lambda}$). The weight of an individual (denoted ω_i^+) depends on the coded score of the individual to the question, denoted x_q^i, and of the mean ($\bar{x}_q$) of the coded scores of the questions. For the pole q^-, the width of the scale (denoted e) intervenes in the formula (here, $e = 3$).

$$y^{q+} = \frac{1}{\sqrt{\lambda}} \sum_{i \in I} \omega_i^+ y^i \text{ with } \omega_i^+ = \frac{x_q^i}{n\bar{x}_q} \quad y^{q-} = \frac{1}{\sqrt{\lambda}} \sum_{i \in I} \omega_i^- y^i \text{ with } \omega_i^- = \frac{e - x_q^i}{n\left(e - \bar{x}_q\right)}$$

The coordinates of the two poles of each question are calculated from the individuals of each supplementary survey; we can then depict the trajectory of each question.

Assigning Object to Clusters of a Euclidean AHC

In a Euclidean AHC (Ward's method), the usual method for allocating a supplementary object to a cluster is based on the geometric distance from the object-point to the barycenter of the cluster. The main drawback of this method is that it does not take into consideration that clusters differ with regard to weights, shapes, and dispersions. Neither does it take into account successive dichotomies of the hierarchy of classes. This is why we propose a new ranking rule adapted to geometric data analysis that takes the shape of clusters into account.

From a set of supplementary objects, we propose a strategy for assigning these objects to clusters stemming from an AHC. The idea is to assign supplementary objects at the local level of a node to one of its two successors until a cluster of the partition under study is reached. We define a criterion based on the ratio of Mahalanobis distances from the object-point to barycenters of the two clusters that make up the node (Le Roux and Cassor 2015; Le Roux 2014a, b; Benzécri 1977).

R script Interfaced with Coheris SPAD is available from the authors.

References

Benzécri, J.-P., et al. (1973). *L'analyse des données, 2. L'analyse des correspondances*. Paris: Dunod.

Benzécri, J.-P. (1977). Analyse discriminante et analyse factorielle. *Les Cahiers de l'Analyse des Données, 2*(4), 369–406.

Benzécri, J.-P. (1992). *Correspondence analysis handbook*. New York: Dekker.

Hardin, R. (2002). *Trust and trustworthiness*. New York: Russell Sage Foundation.

Le Roux, B. (2014a). *Analyse géométrique des données multidimensionnelles*. Paris: Dunods.

Le Roux, B. (2014b). Structured data analysis. In J. Blasius & M. Greenacre (Eds.), *Visualisation and verbalisation of data* (pp. 185–204). London: Chapman & Hall.

Le Roux, B., & Cassor, F. (2015). Assigning Objects to Classes of a Euclidean Ascending Hierarchical Clustering. In *International symposium on statistical learning and data sciences* (pp. 389–396). Springer.

Le Roux, B., & Perrineau, P. (2011). *Les différents types d'électeurs au regard de différents types de confiance* (Vol. 54, pp. 5–35). Les Cahiers du CEVIPOF. Retrieved from http://www.cevipof.com/fr/les-publications/les-cahiers-du-cevipof/.

Le Roux, B., & Rouanet, H. (2004). *Geometric data analysis: From correspondence analysis to structured data analysis*. Dordrecht: Kluwer.

Le Roux, B., & Rouanet, H. (2010). *Multiple correspondence analysis* (Series QASS) (Vol. 163). Thousand Oaks: SAGE.

Rouanet, H., Bernard, J.-M., Bert, M.-C., Lecoutre, B., Lecoutre, M.-P., & Le Roux, B. (2000). *New ways in statistical methodology* (2nd ed.). Berne: Peter Lang.

Chapter 20
The Geometry and Topology of Data and Information for Analytics of Processes and Behaviours: Building on Bourdieu and Addressing New Societal Challenges

Fionn Murtagh

Introduction

We begin by summarizing the relevance and importance of inductive analytics based on the geometry and topology of data and information. Contemporary issues are then discussed. These include how sampling data for representativity is increasingly to be questioned. While we can always avail of analytics from a "bag of tools and techniques", in the application of machine learning and predictive analytics, nonetheless we present the case for Bourdieu and Benzécri-based science of data, as follows. This is to construct bridges between data sources and position-taking, and decision-making. There is summary presentation of a few case studies, illustrating and exemplifying application domains.

From the data analytics viewpoint, a summary of the main procedural principles and features of the analytical methodology arising out of Pierre Bourdieu's work is provided in Lebaron (2015). The following points are related to that summary, and some important implications are noted also.

1. Determine and display social field structure, or even more comprehensively, social space configuration.
2. Show structural homologies between fields or social spaces, based on axis, or factor, interpretation.
3. So, this is reasoning by analogy, therefore inductive reasoning, but in a context that can use, in an integral manner, statistical modelling and predictive learning.

F. Murtagh (✉)
School of Computing and Engineering, University of Huddersfield, Huddersfield, UK
e-mail: fmurtagh@acm.org; f.murtagh@hud.ac.uk

© Springer Nature Switzerland AG 2019   345
J. Blasius et al. (eds.), *Empirical Investigations of Social Space*,
Methodos Series 15, https://doi.org/10.1007/978-3-030-15387-8_20

The former, statistical modelling, includes regression, and the latter, all of machine learning. The point at issue here is that there is no opposition or counterposing to inductive reasoning by such other analytical methods.

4. Determine relative autonomy between fields or social spaces. This is through use of comparative procedures, and causal hypotheses on the relations between fields.
5. Study sub-spaces in a global social space. This is through use of class specific analysis, or MCA, Multiple Correspondence Analysis of sub-clouds of subjects.
6. Informed by statistics, and supervised (with training set, test set) machine learning, explain social practice and position-taking, and it can be derived that associated decision-making can ensue.
7. Effects and consequences, thus predictive field-related outcomes. Here, there may be integrated use of analysis of variance (ANOVA) or regression, or of supervised machine learning methods.
8. Study field dynamics using hierarchical classification, in factor space, use of appropriate supplementary or contextual elements (attributes, subjects) that can form structuring factors, and fully integrate time-evolving data.

This comprehensive and far-reaching data analysis methodology, will encompass statistical modelling, machine learning, predictive analytics, and visualization analytics, whenever these are relevant and appropriate. Relative to current machine learning practice that can be characterized as the "bag of tools and techniques" approach to analytics, the following are unquestionably major benefits. Field and homology, and underpinning these, geometry and topology, employed for inductive reasoning, and relating such reasoning with position-taking or decision making.

Themes of this article encompass the following: application of analytics drawing on social fields and homology, and beyond; general and broad relevance and applicability; underpinning the analytics, we may consider that we have: data leading to information, leading to knowledge, leading to wisdom. Geometric data analysis (GDA), and based on GDA, topology, is the essential basis for all such work.

In section "New Challenges and Opportunities in the Context of Big Data Analytics", we both justify and strongly motivate Bourdieu-related analytics for contemporary data analytics problems.

In section "Narrative Analytics, and Narrative Synthesis", in our analytics, we are seeking explanatory or elucidatory narratives. Three case studies are at issue. Firstly, there is the expression or manifestation of underlying emotions. Secondly, there is the convergence of events or activities, expressing causal or consequential outcomes. Thirdly, there are the most influential patterns and trends in very large data sources.

Section "Towards Behaviour and Activity Analytics, for Mental Health, Depres-66 sion, and Lifestyle Analytics" introduces particular issues in, and perspectives on, the analytics of behaviour and activity. This is pursued with a preliminary study of mental health issues.

New Challenges and Opportunities in the Context of Big Data Analytics

The following expands on our contribution to the discussion in Keiding and Louis (2016). The comprehensive survey (with 141 references) of Keiding and Louis (2016) sets out new contemporary issues of sampling and population distribution estimation. An important take-home message is this: "There is the potential for big data to evaluate or calibrate survey findings ... to help to validate cohort studies". Examples are discussed of "how data ... tracks well with the official", and contextual, repository or holdings. It is well pointed out how one case study discussed "shows the value of using 'big data' to conduct research on surveys (as distinct from survey research)". This arises from what has been discussed by Japec et al. (2015, p. 10): "The new paradigm means it is now possible to digitally capture, semantically reconcile, aggregate, and correlate data."

Limitations though are clear: "Although randomization in some form is very beneficial, it is by no means a panacea. Trial participants are commonly very different from the external ... pool, in part because of self-selection, ...". This is due to, "One type of selection bias is self-selection (which is our focus)".

Important points towards addressing these contemporary issues include the following. "When informing policy, inference to identified reference populations is key". This is part of the bridge which is needed, between data analytics technology and deployment of outcomes. "In all situations, modelling is needed to accommodate non-response, dropouts and other forms of missing data."

While "Representativity should be avoided", here is an essential way to address in a fundamental way, what we need to address: "Assessment of external validity, i.e. generalization to the population from which the study subjects originated or to other populations, will in principle proceed via formulation of abstract laws of nature similar to physical laws".

Interesting perspectives that support Keiding and Louis (2016), include Friedman et al. (2015), and the following, from Laurison and Friedman (2015): "... the GBCS [Great British Class Survey] data have three important limitations. First, the GBCS was a self-selecting web-based survey, ... This means it is not possible to make formal inferences. ... the nationally representative nature of the Labour Force Survey (LFS) along with its detailed and accurate measures ... facilitates a much more in-depth investigation ..." In a blog posting, Laurison (2015) points very clearly to how, just "Because the GBCS is not a random-sample or representative survey", other ways can and are being found to draw great benefit.

Another different study on open, free text questionnaires (Züll and Scholz 2011, see also 2015) notes selection bias, but also: "However, the reasonable use of data always depends on the focus of analyses. So, if the bias is taken into account, then group-specific analyses of open-ended questions data seem appropriate".

The bridge between the data that is analyzed, and the calibrating Big Data, is well addressed by the geometry and topology of data. Those form the link between sampled data and the greater cosmos. Bourdieu's concept of field is a prime exemplar. Consider, as noted by Lebaron (2009), how Bourdieu's work, involves "putting his thinking in mathematical terms", and that it "led him to a conscious and systematic move toward a geometric frame-model". This is a multidimensional, "structural vision". Bourdieu's analytics "amounted to the global [hence Big Data] effects of a complex structure of interrelationships, which is not reducible to the combination of the multiple [... effects] of independent variables". The concept of field, here, uses Geometric Data Analysis that is core to the integrated data and methodology approach used in the Correspondence Analysis platform (used, in general, in Murtagh 2010; and comprehensively in Le Roux and Rouanet 2004; Le Roux 2014).

An approach to drawing benefit from Big Data is precisely as described in Keiding and Louis (2016). The noting of the need for the "formulation of abstract laws" that bridge sampled data and calibrating Big Data can be addressed, for the data analyst and for the application specialist, as geometric and topological.

The principles and practice following from the Big Data setting for our analytics can also be linked to ethical issues. Consider, for example, that sources of data start with: interviews, online media, and big data including data that is unstructured, structured, heterogeneous multimedia, open linked, and so on. One example is to consider the long term prediction of criminal activity, versus the prediction of exposure or vulnerability to crime. The latter can lead to preemptive and preventative action, with no ethical aspects involved. A narrative approach, therefore using analytical field dynamics, offers a practical and effective alternative (Harcourt 2002, 2006). Over and above the sole use of quantitative prediction, we are noting the importance of integrated qualitative and quantitative analytics.

In line with Harcourt's work (Harcourt 2002), with the central role of Correspondence Analysis, this programme of work encompasses: not "content analysis" but rather "map analysis". I.e. "cognitive mapping, relational analysis, and meaning analysis" among other names. Harcourt notes the need "to visually represent the relationship between structures of social meaning and the contexts and practices within which they are embedded".

Harcourt's work has case studies related to sexual activity, and activities with firearms. We would propose the great importance of pursuing field and homology analytics, of underpinning geometric and topological data analysis, for all levels of digital, online or cyber crime and misdemeanour. From Harcourt (2005): "Where do we stake the boundary of the criminal law – or, more importantly, how? How do we decide what to punish? Do we distribute these vices, these recreations, these conducts – what do we even call these things? – into two categories, the passable and the penal, and then carve some limiting principle to distinguish the two? Are we, in the very process, merely concocting some permeable line – a Maginot line – to police the criminal frontier?"

In this section, we have noted the contemporary very wide-ranging, and comprehensive, applicability of analytics that come from the work of Pierre Bourdieu, taking the integral theory and practice of Jean-Paul Benzécri's life work. Note has also been made of how this can incorporate and include the mostly sole use of "bag of tools and techniques" (informally expressed in this way) characterization of unsupervised and supervised machine learning.

Narrative Analytics, and Narrative Synthesis

A key aim of this work is to situate or locate Pierre Bourdieu's work, and related work, in current fields of analytical work. This is in a practical sense, i.e. oriented towards new application domains, but certainly exploiting and benefiting from multidisciplinarity, regarding methodology. A crucially important aspect is what data is at issue.

Data potentially encompasses all that there is both quantitatively and qualitatively. Qualitative data may constitute the ambient information. In mainstream statistics, qualitative data is often a synonym for categorical data. An open issue in practice will, of course, be such issues as data precision or data trustworthiness, or the lack of statistical bias of the data, and how data is best encoded (Murtagh 2005, 2016b). Current trends may be expressed, and profiled, as follows: (i) the Big Data epoch implies ancillary, contextual and underlying data sources, in addition to the core subject of interest (Murtagh and Farid 2017), and (ii) data science, the aim of which, we would state, is to effectively integrate data and appropriate methodology. In this section there is a short review of narrative analytics. It is to be noted that Bourdieu et al. (1979) treats semantic underpinning of socio-economic developments.

In Bécue-Bertaut et al. (2014), the semantic trajectory of a prosecutor speech in a murder-related court case is at issue. From the Correspondence Analysis that maps the semantic content into the factor space, i.e. the latent semantic space, there follows: chronological hierarchical clustering. This yields the cluster segments of the discourse. In Murtagh and Farid (2015), such work is carried out in one US Supreme Court case, in order to study through semantic mapping, "the structure of argument".

We consider a complex web of relationships. Semantics include web of relationships – thematic structures and patterns. Structures and interrelationships evolve in time. Semantics include time evolution of structures and patterns, including both: threads and commonality; and change, the exceptional, the anomalous. Narrative can suggest a causal or emotional relationship between events. A story is an expression of causality or connection. Narrative connects facts or views or other units of information.

In Murtagh et al. (2009), there is stochastic analysis of structure and style, of the film script of the movie, Casablanca, shot by Warner Brothers between May and August 1942. This both statistically and qualitatively supports McKee's (1999) statement that the composition of Casablanca is "virtually perfect".

An application that resulted from this work was visualization of narrative, supporting collective, collaborative narrative construction. This related to collective book authoring by literature students in university, and for many books published, by school children, following this narrative display and support framework. See Reddington et al. (2013).

In the tracking of emotion, we are determining and tracking emotion in an unsupervised way. (This is not machine learning like in sentiment analysis, which is supervised.) Emotion is understood as a manifestation of the unconscious. Social activity causes emotion to be expressed or manifested. (Cf. Murtagh 2014).

We used chapters 9, 10, 11, 12 of Gustave Flaubert's nineteenth century novel, Madame Bovary. This concerns the three-way relationship between Emma Bovary, her husband Charles, and her lover Rodolphe Boulanger. In Murtagh and Ganz (2015) we look at, firstly, emotional interaction in the Casablanca movie, using dialogue (and dialogue only) between main characters Ilsa and Rick. Secondly, we look at all of the text in chapters 9–12 of the novel, Madame Bovary. In both studies, we used the same methodology, i.e. cross-tabulation of word sets, comprising the entire universe of discourse, and including function and grammar words that characterized textual "texture". We find the latter to be very useful for expression of emotion.

Figure 20.1 displays the evolution of sentiment, expressed by (or proxied by) the terms "kiss", "tenderness", and "happiness". There are 22 text segments crossed

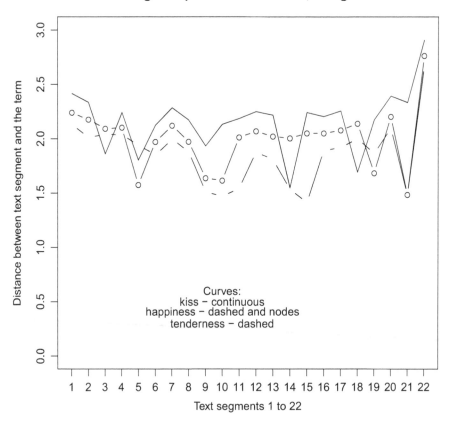

Fig. 20.1 The chronology of sentiment tracks the closeness of these different sentimental terms relative to the narrative, represented by the text segment

by the word set, termed word corpus, that is obtained from the book's text. The Correspondence Analysis factor space provides the Euclidean metric-endowed space that can be characterized as the latent semantic space. We see that these three terms are fairly similar in their semantic proximity to the text segments, allowing relative emotional content to be quantified. But we also see that the word "happiness" is more likely to be semantically closer to text segments than the word "kiss".

Themes here are arising out of the framework provided by the Correspondence Analysis analytics platform, or, alternatively expressed, framework, or methodological basis. This encompasses both quantitative and qualitative analytics.

A particular narrative pattern is at issue now, arising out of a social media case study, and motivated by Jürgen Habermas's communicative action, in the sense that communication can be associated with convergence or net outcomes. For impact of actions, here based on initiating tweets on Twitter, related to environmental issues, this is considered as: semantic distance between the initiating action, and the net aggregate outcome. This can be statistically modelled and tested. See Murtagh et al. (2016).

Figure 20.2 shows the 8 tweets that initiated the campaigns, and the net aggregate campaigns, given by the centres of gravity of the 8 campaigns. Please note that while this is fully based on Murtagh et al. (2016) the enhancing of good environmental citizenship through initiating tweets, what is presented here is based on a slightly different word corpus extracted from the Twitter data, compared to the foregoing reference.

The centres of gravity of the campaigns, i.e. the net aggregate of the campaigns, have an arrow to them from the initiating tweet. All is displayed here in the principal factor plane. For quantifying distance between initiating tweet and net outcome, and even statistically testing that, it may be desirable to use the selected factor projections, or perhaps even the full dimensionality factor space.

We see here that campaigns 3, 5, 8 have initiating tweets that are fairly close to the net overall campaign in these cases. By looking at all tweets, and all terms, it is seen that the campaign initiating tweets, and the overall campaign means, are close to the origin, i.e. the global average. That just means that they (respectively, initiating tweets, and means) are relatively unexceptional among all tweets. While the information that we find in our data is very faint, nonetheless we have an excellent visualization of this information, that in Murtagh et al. (2016) is statistically tested for the relationship between the initiating action and the outcome.

A further study is at issue, next, with a far larger Twitter data source. In Murtagh (2016a), we are concerned with social and community aspects of cultural festivals. Our data is about 12 million Twitter tweets, in the time period, May to December 2015. (Further data will be analysed by us in the future.) Included are such events as the following: Cannes Film Festival (13–24 May 2015); Fèis Ìle, Isle of Islay (Scotland) Festival (23–31 May 2015); Berlin Film Festival (19–21 May 2015); CMA, Country Music Association (Nov. 2015); Yulin Dog (June 2015); and Avignon Theatre Festival (4–25 July 2015). In our initial exploratory analyses, the critical Twitter debate in regard to the Yulin Dog Meat Festival meant that Twitter

Campaign initiating tweets, and net campaigns (centres of gravity)

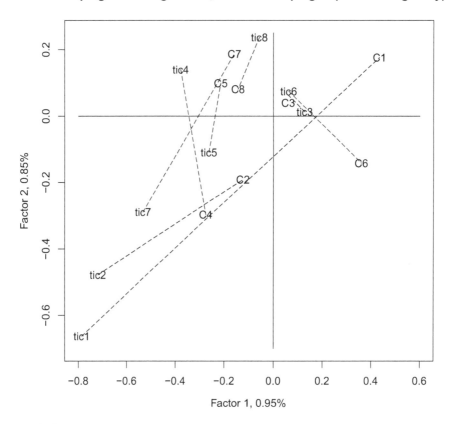

Fig. 20.2 This is a principal factor plane displaying initiating tweets (labelled "tic1" to "tic8") and net outcomes (labelled "C1" etc.)

data was quite distinct. A sufficiently used word set was derived from the Twitter tweet set. For the data used here, a 5815 word corpus was used, from the 32,507,477 words in the data. Occurrence of 1000 uses of a word was required. Filtering was also carried out of prepositions, parts of verbs, just some abbreviations or partial words, and non-Roman scripts including Cyrillic, Chinese, Japanese, and Greek. In what was retained, English, French and Spanish dominated.

An initial analytics decision to be made is what is the principal set of individuals or records to be used, with other such objects being supplementary elements; and similarly, what is the principal attribute or variable or variable modality set to be used, with other variables being supplementary elements. Contextual attributes will naturally be supplementary elements. We can have the following analytics perspective: we use an analytics resolution scale, that is such that tweets per day are considered. Thus the principal data crosses the set of 233 days (from 11 May

2015 to 31 December 2015) by the retained word corpus. That is under investigation in Murtagh (2016a).

One study was of the principal variables being the five festivals. Factor 1 is dominated by (contribution to the axis inertia) the Avignon Theatre Festival, factor 2 is dominated by the Nashville, Tennessee, Country Music Association, factor 3 is dominated by the Berlin Film Festival. (The numbers of occurrences of these festival names, which could have multiple occurrences in a single tweet, and certainly possibly lots of occurrences in a day's tweets, are: Cannes, 1,615,550; Avignon, 102,499; CMA, 9407; Berlin, 5557; and Île, 1998.)

From the point of view of analytical procedure, in the foregoing summary, we have made use of the following: resolution scale of the analysis, and our primary focus in the analysis; contextual or ancillary information associated as supplementary elements; and selective pattern determination and trend following.

Towards Behaviour and Activity Analytics, for Mental Health, Depression, and Lifestyle Analytics

We are using Euclidean geometry for semantics of information. In the referenced articles, in previous sections, we used hierarchical topology for other aspects of semantics, and in particular how a hierarchy expresses anomaly or change. A further useful case is when the hierarchy respects chronological or other sequence information. Analytics based on Bourdieu's work, based on MCA, Multiple Correspondence Analysis, (encompassing e.g. field, homology, habitus, etc.) should be a main analytics approach in many current areas of work, including smarter cities, analytics of Internet of Things, security and forensics (including trust and identity), Big Data, etc. Associated with MCA, of course, when domains other than questionnaire analytics are at issue, are Correspondence Analysis and related geometric mapping, and associated topological perspectives, from the mathematical and computational perspectives. Also supported and aided in such analytics are visualization, interpretation and further outcomes, and prediction and related statistical testing.

This is motivated by what has been at issue in section "New Challenges and Opportunities in the Context of Big Data Analytics" above; and in section "Narrative Analytics, and Narrative Synthesis" how the following can be applied: narratives of behaviour and both qualitative and quantitative effectiveness and outcomes of actions and behaviour.

It is noted in Kleinman et al. (2016) how relevant and important mental health is, given the integral association with physical health. From Kleinman et al. (2016) there is the following: "... parity between mental and physical health conditions remains a distant ideal". "The global economy loses about $1 trillion every year in productivity due to depression and anxiety". "Next steps include ... integration of mental health into other health and development sectors".

In Cooper et al. (2016), page 4, under the heading of "Five Ways to Wellbeing", reference is made to "mental capital and wellbeing". On page 14, a section is entitled "The 'mental capital' values of the outdoors". There is no doubt that a Bourdieu-based analytical methodology can be of relevance and potential importance here.

Initial analysis relating to mental health is at issue here. This is using data from the Adult Psychiatric Morbidity Survey, England, 2007. Essentially one viewpoint is obtained here, relating to what can be, or might be, contextualized.

A periodic survey of mental health, HSCIC (2009), is used. There are 1704 variables, including questioning of the subjects about symptoms and disorders, psychoses and depression characteristics, anti-social behaviours, eating characteristics and alcohol consumption, drug use, and socio-demographics, including gender, age, educational level, marital status, employment status, and region lived in.

As a first analysis, the following variables were selected: 14 questions, hence 14 categorical variables, relating to "Neurotic symptoms and common mental disorders". These are described in HSCIC (2009, Appendix C). Almost all of these variables had as question responses, whether or not there were symptoms or disorders in the past week, one question related to one's lifetime, and one question related to the age of 16 onwards. Another question set was selected, relating to socio-demographic variables, noted in the foregoing paragraph. In this set of socio-demographic variables, there were 9 variables.

An initial display of the neurotic symptoms and common mental disorders sought to have socio-demographic variables as supplementary. But these were projected close to the origin, therefore showing very little differentiation or explanatory relevance for the symptoms and disorders data.

Next, it was sought to characterize the socio-demographic data, and then to see if the neurotic symptoms and common mental disorders data could be explanatory and contextual for the socio-demographic data. But no differentiation was found for these supplementary variables, indicating no particular explanatory capability in this particular instance.

It may be just noted how the main and supplementary variables were interchanged. Respectively, the symptoms and demographic variables were main and supplementary; then the main and supplementary variables were the demographic variables and symptoms. This was done in order to explore the data.

Finally, it was checked whether neurotic symptoms and common mental disorders data should be jointly analysed with the socio-demographic data.

One aim that we have in future work is to see if we can formulate forms and expressions of "mental capital". This concept was noted above in this section where an example of it was going for a walk, therefore taking exercise, in the countryside or parkland.

The analytical outcomes that were summarized in this section are in Murtagh and Farid (2017).

Conclusions

As presented in section "New Challenges and Opportunities in the Context of Big Data Analytics", many pending issues to address, and problems to solve, that arise from Big Data, can be, and certainly we wish to indicate, they will be, addressed through multidisciplinary analytical research. Motivation, and indeed justification, are provided. This is the viewpoint here that we should not simply automate all of analytics, which would necessarily lead to what is termed "black box" analytical methods. That is to express the fact that only quantitative outcomes are desired. However our analytical methodologies should pay attention to the underpinning mathematics and other procedural properties of what is done in carrying out the analytics. Thus, to be emphasized are: cross-disciplinarity, qualitative as well as quantitative observation of underlying reality, and new potential, and never to entirely replace analysis and research work with automated systems for doing that.

A conclusion is that Bourdieu's work is to have a central role in the rapidly growing discipline of Data Science, and in the evolving domain of Big Data, with associated ethical questions. All of these issues are included in Murtagh (2017).

In this work, we have essentially sought to provide perspectives and focus for the analytics of behaviours and activities, practices and discourses. These can be related to individuals, and to social groupings or collectivities. We will, in such analytics, work towards responding to the problem of bias in big data sampling and related representativity. We also seek to bridge the data with decision-making information. In the sense of the latter, we are bridging data analytics with position-taking.

Procedurally, the following can be noted. Methodology and implementation are quite integral to the analytics described here. This is counterposed to having methods used as "black boxes", which was a term used, occasionally, in the early days of neural network methods, typically for supervised classification, or nonlinear regression.

In this work, there is direct relationship also with psycho-analytical issues, with the same geometric and topological data analytics for the bi-logic that is manifested by the integral human reasoning and thought processes, both conscious and unconscious. For background on this, and case studies, detailing the Correspondence Analysis platform, and ultrametric (hierarchical) topology that is central to unconscious thought processes, see Murtagh (2014).

References

Bécue-Bertaut, M., Kostov, B., Morin, A., & Naro, G. (2014). Rhetorical strategy in forensic speeches: Multidimensional statistics-based methodology. *Journal of Classification, 31*, 85–106.

Bourdieu, P., Aymard, M., Revel, J., & Wallerstein, I. (1979). *Algeria 1960: The disenchantment of the world, the sense of honour. The Kabyle house or the world reversed*. Cambridge: Cambridge University Press.

Cooper, C., Wilsdon, J., & Shooter, M. (2016). Making the case for the social sciences, No. 9 mental wellbeing. 28 pp. BACP, British Association for Counselling and Psychotherapy. Available at: http://www.acss.org.uk/wp-content/uploads/2013/09/Making-the-Case-9-Mental-Wellbeing-Web.pdf

Friedman, S., Laurison, D., & Miles, A. (2015). Breaking the 'class' ceiling? Social mobility into Britain's elite occupations. *The Sociological Review, 63*, 259–289.

Harcourt, B. E. (2002). Measured interpretation: Introducing the method of correspondence analysis to legal studies. *University of Illinois Law Review, 4*, 979–1017.

Harcourt, B. E. (2005). Carceral imaginations. *Carceral notebooks, 1.* Available at: http://www.thecarceral.org/imaginations.pdf

Harcourt, B. E. (2006). *Against prediction. Profiling, policing, and punishing in an actuarial age.* Chicago: University of Chicago Press.

HSCIC, Health and Social Care Information Centre (National Health Service, UK). (2009). National Statistics Adult Psychiatric Morbidity in England – 2007, Results of a Household Survey, Appendices and Glossary, p. 174. Available at: http://www.hscic.gov.uk/pubs/psychiatricmorbidity07

Japec, L., Kreuter, F., Berg, M., Biemer, P., Decker, P., Lampe, C., Lane, J., O'Neil, C., & Usher, A. (2015). *AAPOR report on big data.* Technical report. AAPOR, American Association for Public Opinion Research, p. 50. Available at: http://www.aapor.org/getattachment/Education-Resources/Reports/BigDataTaskForceReport_FINAL_2_12_15_b.pdf.aspx

Keiding, N., & Louis, T. A. (2016). Perils and potentials of self-selected entry to epidemiological studies and surveys. *Journal of the Royal Statistical Society, Series A, 179, Part 2,* 319–376.

Kleinman, A., Lockwood Estrin, G., Usmani, S., Chisholm, D., Marquez, P. V., Evans, T. G., & Saxena, S. (2016). Time for mental health to come out of the shadows. *The Lancet, 387,* 2274–2275.

Laurison, D. (2015). Blog, three myths and facts about the Great British Class Survey. Available at: http://www.thesociologicalreview.com/information/blog/three-myths-and-facts-about-the-great-british-class-survey.html

Laurison, D., & Friedman, S. (2015). *Introducing the class ceiling: Social mobility and Britain's elite occupations* (LSE (London School of Economics) sociology department working paper series). Available at: http://www.lse.ac.uk/sociology/pdf/Working-Paper_Introducing-the-Class-Ceiling.pdf

Lebaron, F. (2009). How Bourdieu 'quantified' Bourdieu: The geometric modelling of data (Chapter 2). In K. Robson & C. Sanders (Eds.), *Quantifying theory: Pierre Bourdieu.* Heidelberg: Springer.

Lebaron, F. (2015). L'espace social. Statistique et analyse géométrique des données dans l'œuvre de Pierre Boudieu. (Social space. Statistics and geometric data analysis in the work of Pierre Bourdieu) (Chapter 3). In F. Lebaron & B. Le Roux (Eds.), *La Méthodologie de Pierre Bourdieu en Action, Espace Culturel, Espace Social et Analyse des Données (The methodology of Pierre Bourdieu in action, cultural space, social space and data analysis).* Paris: Dunod.

Le Roux, B. (2014). *Analyse Géométrique des Données Multidimensionnelles.* Paris: Dunod.

Le Roux, B., & Rouanet, H. (2004). *Geometric data analysis: From correspondence analysis to stuctured data analysis.* Dordrecht: Kluwer Academic.

McKee, R. (1999). *Story, substance, structure, style, and the principles of screenwriting.* London: Methuen.

Murtagh, F. (2005). *Correspondence analysis and data coding with R and Java.* Boca Raton: Chapman and Hall/CRC Press.

Murtagh, F. (2010). The correspondence analysis platform for uncovering deep structure in data and information. Sixth Boole Lecture. *Computer Journal, 53*(3), 304–315.

Murtagh, F. (2014). Mathematical representations of Matte Blanco's bi-logic, based on metric space and ultrametric or hierarchical topology: Towards practical application. *Language and Psychoanalysis, 3*(2), 40–63.

Murtagh, F. (2016a). Semantic mapping: Towards contextual and trend analysis of behaviours and practices. In K. Balog, L. Cappellato, N. Ferro, & C. MacDonald (Eds.), *Working Notes of CLEF 2016 – Conference and Labs of the Evaluation Forum*, Évora, September 5–8, 2016, pp. 1207–1225. Available at: http://ceur-ws.org/Vol-1609/16091207.pdf

Murtagh, F. (2016b). Sparse p-adic data coding for computationally efficient and effective big data analytics. *p-Adic Numbers, Ultrametric Analysis and Applications, 8*(3), 236–247.

Murtagh, F. (2017). *Data science foundations: Geometry and topology of complex hierarchic systems and Big Data analytics*. Boca Raton: Chapman and Hall/CRC Press.

Murtagh, F., & Farid, M. (2015). The structure of argument: Semantic mapping of US supreme court cases. In A. Gammerman, V. Vovk, & H. Papadopoulos (Eds.), *Statistical learning and data sciences* (Lecture Notes in Artificial Intelligence (LNAI), vol. 9047, pp. 397–405). Cham: Springer.

Murtagh, F., & Farid, M. (2017). Contextualizing geometric data analysis and related data analytics: A virtual microscope for big data analytics. *Journal of Interdisciplinary Methodologies and Issues in Science, 3.* Available at: https://jimis.episciences.org/2570

Murtagh, F., & Ganz, A. (2015). Pattern recognition in narrative: Tracking emotional expression in context. *Journal of Data Mining and Digital Humanities, 2015*, 21. Available at: http://arxiv.org/abs/1405.3539

Murtagh, F., Ganz, A., & McKie, S. (2009). The structure of narrative: The case of film scripts. *Pattern Recognition, 42*, 302–312. (Discussion in Merali Z (June 2008) Here's looking at you, kid. Software promises to identify blockbuster scripts, *Nature*, 453).

Murtagh, F., Pianosi, M., & Bull, R. (2016). Semantic mapping of discourse and activity, using Habermas's theory of communicative action to analyze process. *Quality and Quantity, 50*(4), 1675–1694.

Reddington, J., Murtagh, F., & Cowie, D. (2013). Computational properties of fiction writing and collaborative work. In D. J. Hand et al. (Eds.), *Advances in intelligent data analysis XII* (Lecture Notes in Computer Science, vol. 8207, pp. 369–379). Berlin/New York: Springer.

Züll, C., & Scholz, E. (2011). Who took the burden to answer on the meaning of left and right? Response behaviour on an open-ended question. In *Conference Proceedings of the 64th Annual Conference of WAPOR: Public Opinion and the Internet.* Available at: http://wapor.unl.edu/wp-content/uploads/2011/09/Zuell_Scholz.docx

Züll, C., & Scholz, E. (2015). Who is willing to answer open-ended questions on the meaning of left and right? *Bulletin of Sociological Methodology, 127*(1), 26–42.

Chapter 21
Class-Specific Analysis: Methodological and Sociological Reflections

Frédéric Lebaron and Philippe Bonnet

Introduction

When studying a particular field or social space, sociologists increasingly use geometric data analysis (GDA) (for example: Lebaron and Le Roux 2015). However, analyzing a subset of a whole sample or a population with this kind of method raises several sociological and methodological questions, which will be the focus of this chapter.

From a sociological point of view, this approach raises the question of how we can represent the complex structures of a society, a group, or a subgroup of individuals, while simultaneously taking into account the existence of different *levels* of social entities. GDA techniques allow us to construct social spaces of any kind, but social reality, as a set of interdependent and nested social structures, is theoretically difficult to reduce to isolated entities which could be studied separately, taken as a series of independent social spaces. Overcoming this simplification and taking into account the existence of these interdependences would require a method which allows us to study 'embedded' social spaces: provided that the whole reference has first been constructed, all other spaces can then be analyzed as subspaces, while still remaining situated *inside* this global space, and studied as such.

From a methodological point of view, which is our main focus in this chapter, we can assume that the data have first been analyzed with the use of multiple correspondence analysis (MCA), and that variables and individuals were correctly

F. Lebaron (✉)
Department of Social Sciences, Ecole normale supérieure Paris-Saclay, Cachan, France
e-mail: frederic.lebaron@uvsq.fr

P. Bonnet
Paris Descartes University, Paris, France
e-mail: philippe.bonnet@parisdescartes.fr

© Springer Nature Switzerland AG 2019   359
J. Blasius et al. (eds.), *Empirical Investigations of Social Space*,
Methodos Series 15, https://doi.org/10.1007/978-3-030-15387-8_21

chosen. Results of this 'global' MCA have been interpreted, so that the next step of the study is to analyze a subset of individuals taken from the whole sample or population. How do we approach this? A usual and routine answer to this question is to perform, separately, another MCA on the data of this subgroup. Results are then interpreted for themselves and sometimes also compared to those of the global MCA. As the first and crucial step of MCA is the specification of a distance between individuals – this distance being defined based on their responses and depending on the frequency of these in the sample – there is no reason why the distance defined in the analysis of the subgroup should be the same as the one defined in the analysis of the whole sample or population. Therefore, how are we to assess whether the first dimension of the subgroup MCA is *the same* as the first one of the global MCA? This is formally impossible, except in the very unrealistic case of the distances being identical in the two analyses. First proposed in the seminal work of Rouanet and Le Roux (2004, 2010), a variant of MCA called Class Specific Analysis (CSA) can be used to study a class (subset or subcloud) of individuals, with reference to the whole set of active individuals.

MCA, one of the main paradigms of GDA, is a very efficient method for the analysis of large questionnaires. Besides standard MCA, two variants of MCA have been developed: specific MCA consists in restricting the analysis to the categories of interest, and has been largely used to overcome issues related to missing or junk categories; Class Specific Analysis (CSA) consists in analyzing a subcloud of individuals, and represents the methodological solution to our methodological and sociological problem here.

We will present here the example of the European judicial space, as studied in a pluri-disciplinary prosopographical research project (Mégie and Sacriste 2009). Beginning with a standard MCA of the entire data set, we will perform a CSA of three subsets of individuals (and compare the results with standard MCA of these subsets) before concluding with a discussion of the general advantages of the method and its sociological relevance.

The European Judicial Space: Data and Research Questions

The judicial sphere can be seen as a major subfield within the field of power and, indeed, as an essential condition for the emergence of the nation-state (Bourdieu 2012). Just as the actors from the judicial field contribute to the emergence of the nation-state, one can obviously argue that these actors strongly contribute to the consolidation and formation of the European Union, which manifests itself mainly as a judicial construction (Cohen and Vauchez 2010, Vauchez and de Witte 2012). In the subsequent analyses, we shall focus on the specific group of European law professionals who have in common their participation to the legal construction of the EU since the 1950s.

In the Polilexes prosopographical survey, the starting point was consequently a set of questions about the structuring role of law in the construction of the

European Union. The study examines historical evolutions, and is intended to investigate in detail the biographical trajectories of efficient 'judicial' agents inside the European space: it has then both a socio-historical and biographical dimension. The studied population was restricted to the law professionals in a broad sense from the beginning of the European project (1950) to the last major enlargement (2004): after methodological discussions, we obtained a set of n = 442 actors, comprising judges at different courts, law clerks, members of European Parliament, and other public agents of the EU since the Treaty of Rome. Our aim was to understand the way the European judicial space is structured, how this structure has been constituted and transformed since the beginning of the European Union, and, finally, what kinds of social and professional trajectories define the contours, the lines of division and stress inside this space.

The analyzed space is built on data from respondents' answers to 15 questions (54 categories):

- Sex, size of country (2 questions, 4 categories).
- Level of education, place of diploma completion, US university, College of Bruges, Parisian university, Oxford/Cambridge (6 questions, 18 categories).
- Age of the first time in a European institution, first professional sector, last professional sector, number of sectors over whole career, number of positions in European institutions, activity in private sector, political activity (7 questions, 32 categories).

Out of the 442 individuals selected, 160 can be classified as Members of European Parliament (MEP), 125 as law clerks, and 90 as judges; the other individuals are other law professionals, who will be present in the global analysis but not studied specifically.

The European Judicial Space: Results of the Global MCA

We performed a specific MCA of the global population (N = 442), with 15 questions yielding 54 active categories, nine of which we set as passive. Therefore, there are 45 active categories. Two axes will be interpreted (63.9% of importance as measured with the cumulated modified rates, see Table 21.1).

Table 21.1 Eigenvalues, variance rates, modified rates (Benzécri and Benzécri 1984) of the global MCA first five axes

Eigenvalues	Variance rates	Modified rates	Cumulated modified rates
$\lambda_1 = 0.18404$	9.1	49.8	49.8
$\lambda_2 = 0.12421$	6.1	14.1	63.9
$\lambda_3 = 0.10984$	5.4	8.8	72.1
$\lambda_4 = 0.10705$	5.3	7.9	80.5
$\lambda_5 = 0.09989$	4.9	5.8	86.3

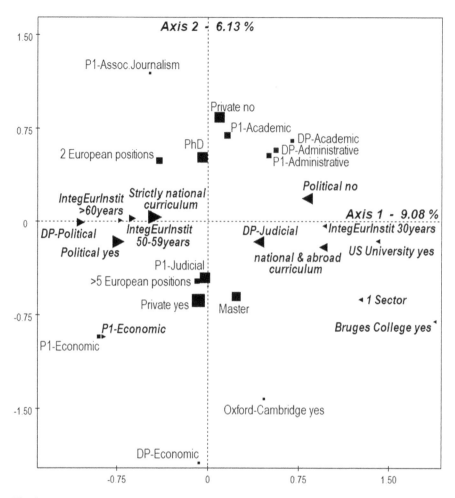

Fig. 21.1 Contributing categories to axis 1 [triangles] and axis 2 [squares], (global MCA)

Interpretation of Axis 1: Axis of Professional Trajectory (Fig. 21.1, triangles)

The first axis is predominantly an axis of professional and educational trajectories. On this axis, one finds an opposition between categories on the negative, left-hand side of the axis such as 'last position in political sector', 'strictly national curriculum', and 'integration in European institutions between 50 and 59 years', and categories on the positive, right-hand side of the axis like 'no experience in political sector', 'national and international curriculum', 'US university', 'Bruges College', 'one sector for the whole career', and 'integration in the European institutions before the age of 30'.

This axis is mostly determined by the two factors of respondents' links with politics and by their academic trajectories. These trajectories can take place in various countries and international institutions, or they can be strictly limited to one country. There is an opposition between national academic capital and forms of international academic capital, and between political capital and other kinds of capital. It is also an axis in which age is involved.

Global MCA: Interpretation of Axis 2 (Fig. 21.1, squares). Private-Economic Versus Academic-Administrative

This axis distinguishes types of professional trajectories. At the bottom, one finds categories such as 'private sector', 'economy as last professional sector', 'master', 'Oxford/Cambridge', 'first professional sector: economy, judicial'. At the top, one can find categories such as 'no private sector', 'PhD', 'academic sector', 'administrative sectors as first profession', 'associative sector or journalism as first profession', '2 European positions'. This axis clearly opposes a private and economic pole (at the bottom) to a public and academic or administrative pole (at the top).

Global MCA: Cloud of Individuals

Individuals are distributed fairly equally throughout in the plane (see Fig. 21.2). We can consider some of them to be typical individuals of one pole in the space. For instance, at the extreme left of the first axis, Antonio Fantini is a member of the European Parliament. Born in 1936, he started as union member; he entered European institutions in 1956. He has a relatively low level of education and a strictly national curriculum. On the other side, Christine Stix-Hackl, born in 1957, has a high level of education. She obtained a master's at the University of Vienna and then went to the United States. She was educated as a lawyer and entered European institutions in 1982 before becoming a judge.

In the plane of the first two axes (Fig. 21.2), one can distinguish the three categories of individuals studied in this chapter: members of the European parliament, law clerks, and judges. For each group, we give its concentration ellipsis, showing its dispersion along the first two axes. There is a clear distinction between members of Parliament (left side) and law clerks (right side), judges being situated in between.

We find here a classical opposition inside the field of power, between young, educated and internationalized professionals and older, more nationally-oriented holders of political capital. On the second axis, the three groups are not strongly differentiated, except by a small deviation in the judges' mean-point toward the top, on the side of administrative-academic capital.

Class Specific Analyses of the Three Subgroups

The three groups of individuals are clearly distinguished according to their status: members of European Parliament, law clerks, and judges inhabit three distinct social universes, related to different institutions and professional roles. Sociologically, one can say they are relatively heterogeneous, but they are all involved in the same global

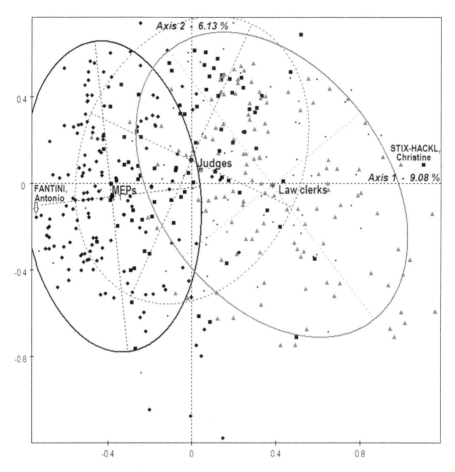

Fig. 21.2 The three groups (MEPs, Law clerks and Judges) in the plane of axes 1 and 2 (global MCA)

field, which is defined by a certain *illusio*, a sense of the game, which is the definition of European legal institutions and 'laws'.

As we saw with the global MCA, MEPs and law clerks are relatively separated in the plane of the first two axes, whereas judges are less distinguished from these two groups. Now we shall try to answer the following question: how is each of these groups structured, within the European judicial space? This needs a specific analytic approach, and we will perform a CSA of each group.

If we admit they are part of the same field, then for each group, the distance between two individuals inside that group only really makes sense in this global field, and not in an artificial space restricted to the individuals of the group. The distance is computed with reference to the frequency of categories chosen in the whole sample, and the distance between categories is of course dependent on their frequency in the subgroup, albeit still in reference to their frequency in the whole sample (see short presentation in the Appendix).

To operationalize this idea, CSA consists in searching the principal dimensions of the subcloud of interest without 'extracting' it from the global space. This means that we keep the distance as defined in the global space. We 'see' the subcloud inside the global space, but projected on its own principal dimensions. Then we apply the usual GDA methodology: interpretation of axes and structured data analysis.

As we can see in Table 21.2, the total variance of the different subgroups is not very different from the one of the entire set, except for the judges.

Moreover, for each CSA, the variance rate of the first plane (axes 1 and 2) is greater than the one of the global MCA. For each CSA, we interpret the first two axes.

Members of European Parliament

Examining the first results of the CSA, we can see that the variance in the group of MEPs is smaller than the one of the whole population. The variance rates of the five first axes are greater than those of the global MCA (see Table 21.2).

CSA of MEPs: Interpretation of Axis 1 ($\lambda_1 = 0.1925$, 10.18%, Fig. 21.3, Triangles)

The first axis of the CSA for MEPs distinguishes two major types of trajectories: on one side (the left), respondents are likely to have held many positions at the European level, but always in an economic framework (P1-Economic, DP-Economic), and in the private sector, and exhibit prestigious academic vitae (Oxford/Cambridge); on the other side (the right), respondents hold fewer positions (two European positions), are unlikely to have worked in the private sector, and come from the political world or the associative sector and journalism, with general basic academic vitae (licence).

CSA of MEPs: Interpretation of Axis 2 ($\lambda_2 = 0.1806$, 9.55%, Fig. 21.3, Squares)

This second axis shows an opposition between categories referring to age at the first time in European institutions, sex, and first and last professional sector. On

Table 21.2 Eigenvalues and variance rates for the global MCA and the three CSA

	Global MCA		MEPs CSA		Law clerks CSA		Judges CSA	
Total variance	2.0273		1.8920		1.9100		1.6432	
N°	Eigenvalue	%	Eigenvalue	%	Eigenvalue	%	Eigenvalue	%
1	0.1840	9.08	0.1925	10.18	0.2533	13.26	0.1968	11.97
2	0.1242	6.13	0.1806	9.55	0.1744	9.13	0.1623	9.88
3	0.1098	5.42	0.1597	8.44	0.1617	8.47	0.1432	8.71
4	0.1071	5.28	0.1335	7.06	0.1485	7.78	0.1179	7.17
5	0.0999	4.93	0.1197	6.33	0.1148	6.01	0.1073	6.53

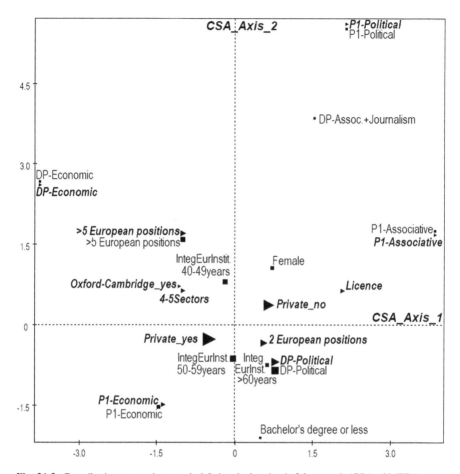

Fig. 21.3 Contributing categories to axis 1 [triangles] and axis 2 [squares], (CSA of MEPs)

the negative side of the axis (the bottom) we find relatively late-starting careers (integrating into European institutions at 50–59 and more than 60 years) with low-level degrees (Bachelor's), and with the respondents' last professional sector being in the political world. On the positive side (the top), we find longer careers (integrating into European institutions at 40–49 years) with several positions in European institutions (five European positions). Still in this top half of the axis, the respondents' first professional sector is politics and/or the associative field. The last professional sector can be either political or associative, or journalism. It is also on this side that we see contribution of the female category, illustrating the fact that women's entry in the European judicial field is quite recent, and still at a less established pole, relatively speaking.

Sociologically, this opposition illustrates a very well-known classical opposition between incumbents and newcomers in the political field, which correlates with

Table 21.3 Angles between global MCA axes and MEPs' CSA axes

Angles	CSA Axis 1	CSA Axis 2	CSA Axis 3
ACM axis 1	99°	74°	101°
ACM axis 2	49°	91°	103°
ACM axis 3	96°	119°	75°
ACM plane 1–2	48°	74°	
ACM plane 1–3	79°	56°	

various social characteristics, such as age, sex, educational level, etc. (see for example: Hjellbrekke et al. 2007).

CSA and MCA

When interpreting the results of the CSA, one has to locate axes of the CSA in reference to the axes of the global MCA. Among the results, cosines of the angles between CSA axes and MCA axes are available tools to assess the degree of specific refraction of the sub-field. The first CSA axis makes a 99 degrees angle with the first MCA axis, which means that it is nearly orthogonal to the first MCA axis. It makes a 49 degrees angle with the second axis of MCA and a 48 degrees angle with plane 1–2 of MCA (see Table 21.3). The second CSA axis makes a 91 degrees angle with the second MCA axis, which means again that it is orthogonal to the second MCA axis. Furthermore, the second CSA axis makes a 74 degrees angle with the plane 1–2 of the MCA.

These results show strong specificity in the subcloud of MEPs, which clearly relates to its particular features as an autonomous field. Hence, CSA is actually able to reveal specificity, and does not presuppose it as it is the case when performing a separate MCA on the sub-data set.

CSA of MEPs: Cloud of Individuals, Fig. 21.4

The cloud of individuals is still, for the most part, equally distributed in the plane. Among the MEPs, 22 are women. Most of them appear in the positive, upper half of the second axis of the CSA. We highlight them here:.

Law Clerks

CSA of Law Clerks: Interpretation of Axis 1 ($\lambda_1 = 0.2533$, 13.26%, Fig. 21.5, Triangles)

This first axis opposes two types of trajectories: one whose respondents display national and international vitae (Bruges College, US university), first and last

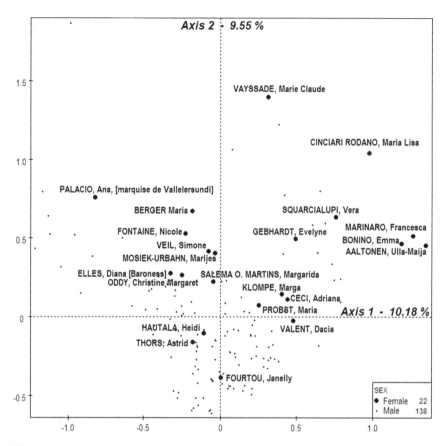

Fig. 21.4 Cloud of individuals in the plane of the first two axes (CSA of MEPs) with all women highlighted

professional sectors in the judicial sphere, one sector for their whole careers, and activity in private sector (on the left side of the axis); the other type (on the right side of the axis) is characterized by strictly national vitae, with respondents' last professional sector being in the administrative sector, and no activity in private sector.

It is clearly an axis showing the important division of the group between a set of very internationalized and economically-embedded actors and the more classical administrative-national profiles of law professionals. Law clerks could thus be described as a professional *avant-garde* in the legal field, and as a group they embody a specific pole which is typical for the possession of the most *avant-garde* properties.

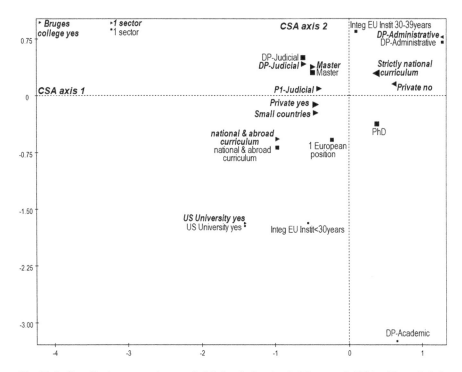

Fig. 21.5 Contributing categories to axis 1 [triangles] and axis 2 [squares], (CSA of Law clerks)

CSA of Law Clerks: Interpretation of Axis 2 ($\lambda_2 = 0.1744$, 9.13%, Fig. 21.5, Squares)

The second axis opposes two types of position one (at the top of the axis) characterized by a master's level of education, working in one sector for the whole career, the last professional sector being in the judicial or administration sphere, and entering European institutions between the age of 30 and 39; the other position (at the bottom of the axis) is more open to international vitae (US university), PhD levels of education, entering European institutions before the age of 30, and respondents whose last professional sector was in the academic field. One finds here an opposition between a bureaucratic and an academic pole.

Here, the first axis of the CSA makes a 122 degrees angle with the first MCA axis and a 44 degrees angle with the plane 1–2 of the MCA (cp. Table 21.4). This means that the first principal dimension of the law clerks subcloud is clearly not the same as the first axis of the global cloud; nevertheless, it is not wholly different, as we observed in the case of the MEPs, which points here to a more mixed or hybrid situation.

Assessing the degree of 'refraction' of a subspace or field by the use of cosines and angles between dimensions can be interpreted, from a sociological point of view, as a way to study empirically the issue of 'homology' between subspaces or

Table 21.4 Angles between global MCA axes and Law clerks' CSA axes

Angles	CSA Axis 1	CSA Axis 2	CSA Axis 3
ACM axis 1	122°	103°	99°
ACM axis 2	60°	101°	102°
ACM axis 3	99°	100°	71°
ACM plane 1–2	44°	73°	75°
ACM plane 1–3	57°	73°	69°

fields. We can say in the case of law clerks that the level of this refraction is less important; this result is consistent with our interpretation of the first axis, revealing an opposition that is not very different from the one found in the global space, and showing a general tension between highly internationalized and more national profiles.

Judges

CSA of Judges: Interpretation of Axis 1 ($\lambda 1 = 0.1968$, 11.97%, Fig. 21.6, Triangles)

The first axis opposes two types of trajectories: one (at the right side of the horizontal axis) is characterized by respondents with a master's level of education, mostly achieved at Parisian universities, who are involved in political activity, have their first professional sector in the judicial sphere, four to five sectors throughout their whole careers, and who enter European institutions relatively late (between the ages of 40 and 49 or 50 and 59); the other (at the left side of the axis) includes the categories 'international vitae' (US university), 'coming from small countries', 'first professional sector in the academic field', 'no political activity', 'entering European institutions before the age of 30' and 'two positions in these institutions'.

We see here a strong opposition between a political, multi-sectorial and France-centred career on one side, and a more American and academic type of trajectory with early European involvement on the other, a biography which also appears to be more specific to small European countries.

CSA of Judges: Interpretation of Axis 2 ($\lambda 2 = 0.1623$, 9.88%, Fig. 21.6, Squares)

The second axis opposes two types of trajectories: one (at the top of the axis) is made up of respondents with national and international vitae (Paris, Oxford/Cambridge), activity in the private sector, and origins in small countries and entering European institutions late (50–59 years); the other (at the bottom of the axis) is composed of those with no activity in private sector, a last professional sector in the academic field, two positions in European institutions, four or five sectors for the whole career, and who enter European institutions between the age of 40 and 49 years.

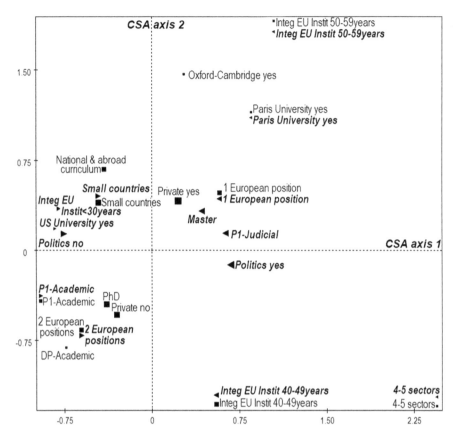

Fig. 21.6 Contributing categories to axis 1 [triangles] and axis 2 [squares] (CSA of judges)

Again, one finds a public/private opposition, which is related to other indicators of specific integration inside the field, like the link to prestigious European academic institutions, a late arrival in the European field, and an origin in small countries (which is more frequent on the private side).

The first axis of the CSA makes a 26 degrees angle with the first axis of the MCA and a 29 degrees angle with the second axis of the MCA (cp. Table 21.5). It also makes a 50 degrees angle with the plane 1–2 of MCA, which means that this first CSA axis is not situated in this plane. The second axis of CSA makes a 73 degrees angle with the first axis of MCA and a 112 degrees angle with the second axis of MCA. Finally, this second CSA axis makes a 62 degrees angle with the plane 1–2 of MCA (Table 21.5).

Table 21.5 Angles between global MCA axes
and Judges' CSA axes

Angles	CSA Axis 1	CSA Axis 2	CSA Axis 3
ACM axis 1	116°	73°	95°
ACM axis 2	119°	112°	70°
ACM axis 3	78°	96°	88°
ACM plane 1–2	50°	62°	69°
ACM plane 1–3	61°	72°	85°

Table 21.6 Eigenvalues and variance rates for the three analyses (global MCA, CSA and MCA)

Global MCA			MEPs CSA			MEPs MCA		
Total variance: 2.02730			Total variance: 1.89203			Total variance: 2.17644		
N°	Eigenvalue	%	N°	Eigenvalue	%	N°	Eigenvalue	%
1	0.1840	9.08	1	0.1925	10.18	1	0.1941	8.92
2	0.1242	6.13	2	0.1806	9.55	2	0.1791	8.23
3	0.1098	5.42	3	0.1597	8.44	3	0.1451	6.66
4	0.1071	5.28	4	0.1335	7.06	4	0.1362	6.26
5	0.0999	4.93	5	0.1197	6.33	5	0.1194	5.48

Standard MCA of the Members of European Parliament

In order to discuss the relevance of CSA, one must compare its results with at least
one case where the alternative solution of a separate analysis seems reasonable,
taking into account the strong relative autonomy of the political field.

To that end, we perform a standard MCA on the subgroup of MEPs without any
reference to the whole population. Examining the first results, we can see that the
total variance is not the same as that established by the CSA. The individuals are
the same, and so are the questions; this difference simply means that the distances
between individuals are not the same from one analysis (CSA) to the other (MCA
of the subgroup).

*MCA of MEPs Group: Interpretation of Axis 1 ($\lambda 1 = 0.1941$, 8.92%, Fig. 21.7,
Triangles)*

The first axis opposes different types of trajectory. We find on the left side of
the axis categories referring to international trajectories (US university, Oxford-
Cambridge, national and international vitae) with many positions (more and more)
in the European institutions, and early starts to institutional careers (30–39), with
the last employment being in the judicial sector. On the opposite side, we can see
short vitae (the category 'licence'), few positions in the European institutions, most
recent employment in the political world, and no work in private sector.

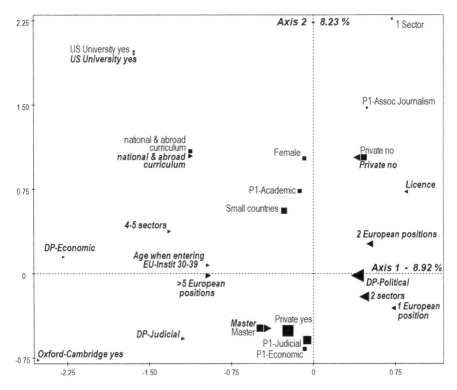

Fig. 21.7 Contributing categories to axis 1 [triangles] and axis 2 [squares], (MCA of MEPs)

MCA of MEPs Group: Interpretation of Axis 2 ($\lambda2 = 0.1791$, 8.23%, Fig. 21.7, Squares)

This axis opposes two types of trajectories: on the one hand (at the bottom of the axis) we find categories referring to a profile more widespread among MEPs: a master's level of education and a history of work in the private, economic, or judicial sectors; on the other hand (at the top of the axis) we see a more unusual profile, with international vitae (US university), origins in small countries, and having worked in one sector, academic, associative or journalistic sector, without working in private sector. On this same side, we can find most of the few women belonging to this subgroup (see Fig. 21.8).

MCA of MEPs Group: Individuals

If we compare the results from the CSA to those of the MCA of MEPs, we first observe that the axes of the CSA are axes of trajectories, as are those of the MCA of MEPs. But the variables characterizing the axes differ from one analysis to the other.

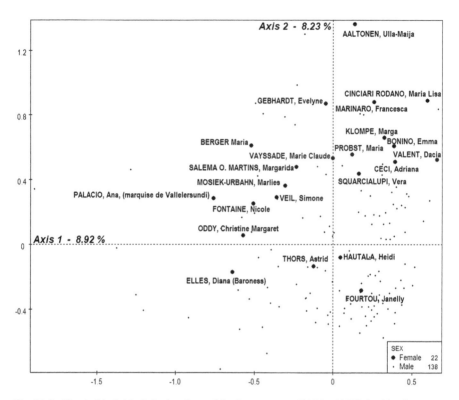

Fig. 21.8 Cloud of individuals in the plane of the first two axes (MCA of MEPs) with all women highlighted

Axis 1 differentiates between long and internationalized careers in the European institutions, starting young from shorter careers, more closely linked to politics, as is, generally speaking, the first axis of the CSA. But, comparing both analyses more closely, we can argue that the MCA of the subgroup seems less clearly distinct from the global MCA than is the CSA. The second axis of the CSA, for example, exhibit an opposition between older MEPS with later entries into European institutions, on the one hand, and younger ones on the other, among whom are numerous women who have already had a career in the European institutions. Conversely, the second axis of the MCA of MEPs depicts the opposition between those MEPs from the economic or judicial sectors, with a master's level of education, and career experience in the private sector and those MEPs with international vitae and origins in small countries, many of whom are women, giving much strength to the economic/non-economic division. Interpretations of the second axis differ substantially, and the CSA ultimately reveals patterns that seem to allow us to 'control', or at least distinguish more clearly, the effects of the insertion in a more global field. In any case, the initial distances within the global cloud are maintained with the use of the CSA, which gives greater strength to any argument about the importance of the autonomy of the subspace. Actually, CSA is the only way to assess this autonomy from a quantitative point of view: a comparison between a global and a separate MCA can only lead to qualitative comments about the interpretation of the axes.

Conclusion

We have shown that it is possible to analyze a subgroup within a population in order to examine more precisely and specifically its structure, taking into account the fact that this subgroup is *at the same time* a subset of a global – or a larger – population. The CSA is a method which allows us to preserve the initial distance that has been defined in the whole population, and, simultaneously, to study the specific dimensions of the subcloud of interest, and assess quantitatively, and more precisely, this specificity.

From a sociological point of view, we can argue that this method allows us, in theory, to provide an appropriate formalization and operational study of any subfield or subspace inside a broader field or social space, giving direct geometric – and numerical – substance to the notion of homology (Bourdieu 1992). This means that, with this method, we can theoretically overcome a lot of the difficult methodological issues generated by the operational use of the notions of field and social space.

The appropriate use of CSA makes it possible to advance a generalized conception of the social space (which always has to be constructed from the existing data) and a pragmatic assessment of the autonomy of any subspace inside this constructed social space. The notion of the field can then be defined from a systematic and relational point of view, as the expression of a certain degree of autonomy or refraction (measurable in terms of angles between axes) inside a broader multidimensional structure.

Appendix: What Is Class Specific Analysis (CSA)?

This form of MCA is useful when one wishes to study a subcloud of individuals, while still preserving the distances defined for the whole cloud. Specific MCA differs from the simple MCA applied to the relevant subtable, in which distances between points and weights of points are defined from the margins of the data subtable, and consequently differ from those of the MCA of the overall data table. By contrast, in a specific analysis, both distances and weights are defined from the initial complete table.

Notations:

N: number of elements of I (total number of individuals);
N_k: number of individuals in I who have chosen category k;

$F_k = N_k/N$: frequency of category k in the whole sample;
I': subset of individuals of the class, n its number of elements;
n_k: number of individuals in I' who have chosen category k;
$f_k = n_k/n$: frequency of category k in the class;
$n_{kk'}$: number of individuals in I' who have chosen both categories k and k'

- Specific cloud of individuals. The distance between two individuals i and i' of the class is the one defined from the whole cloud, for question q: $d_q^2(i, i') = \frac{1}{F_k} + \frac{1}{F_{k'}}$
- Specific cloud of categories. The distance between 2 categories is such that:
$d'^2(k, k') = \frac{f_k(1-f_k)}{F_k^2} + \frac{f_{k'}(1-f_{k'})}{F_{k'}^2} - 2\frac{f_{kk'}-f_k f_{k'}}{F_k F_{k'}}$
- Properties
  - Variance: $V_{spe} = \frac{1}{Q} \sum_{k \in K} \frac{f_k(1-f_k)}{F_k}$
  - Contribution of category point: M^k: $Ctr_k = \frac{\frac{1}{Q}\frac{f_k(1-f_k)}{F_k}}{V_{spe}}$
  - The principal variables on I' are centered and their variances are equal to the specific eigenvalues (μ_l).
  - The principal variables on K, weighted by $p_k = F_k/Q$, are centered and their variances are equal to the specific eigenvalues.

References

Benzécri, F., & Benzécri, J.-P. (1984). *Pratique de l'analyse des données. 1 Analyse des correspondances*. Paris: Dunod.

Bourdieu, P. (1992). *Les règles de l'art. Genèse et structure du champ littéraire*. Paris: Seuil.

Bourdieu, P. (2012). *Sur l'État. Cours au Collège de France (1989–1992)*. Paris: Seuil.

Cohen, A., & Vauchez, A. (2010). Sociologie politique de l'Europe du droit. *Revue française de science politique, 60*(2), 223–226.

Hjellbrekke, K., Le Roux, B., Korsnes, O., Lebaron, F., Rosenlund, L., & Rouanet, H. (2007). The Norwegian field of power anno 0. *European Societies, 9*(2), 245–273.

Le Roux, B., & Rouanet, H. (2004). *Geometric data analysis; from correspondence analysis to structured data analysis*. Dordrecht: Kluwer.

Le Roux, B., & Rouanet, H. (2010). *Multiple Correspondence Analysis. QASS n° 163*. Thousand Oaks: SAGE.

Lebaron, F., & Le Roux, B. (Eds.). (2015). *La méthodologie de Pierre Bourdieu en action. Espace culturel, espace social et analyse des données*. Paris: Dunod.

Mégie, A., & Sacriste, G. (2009). Polilexes: champ juridique européen et *polity* communautaire. *Politique européenne, 28*, 157–162.

Vauchez, A., & de Witte, B. (2012). *The European legal field*. Oxford: Hart Publishing.

Chapter 22
Establishing Correspondence Analysis in Sociological Curricula in German-Speaking Academia

Rainer Diaz-Bone and Katharina Manderscheid

Introduction

For most social scientists outside France, multiple correspondence analysis (MCA) is familiar from, and was made popular by, the works of Pierre Bourdieu, especially the analysis and presentation of the social space of lifestyles in *Distinction* (Bourdieu 2000). The unique strength of this statistical technique lies especially, but not exclusively, in its ability to analyze categorical data, the most common format of social science survey data. What is more, the two-dimensional plots of patterned modalities which constitute the heart of multiple correspondence analysis are easily comprehensible.

Whereas in French sociology *l'analyse des données* represents a well-established procedure in statistics (Lebaron 2006, Lebaron and Le Roux 2015, Robson and Sanders 2009, Grenfell and Lebaron 2014), this is still not the case in German sociology. Consequently, the topic of our contribution consists of an analysis of the partial establishment of MCA in German language sociology curricula.

Especially in the context of the two following, closely-linked arguments, it may be assumed that multiple correspondence analysis is a widely-implemented method in sociological study programs:

This publication has been supported by funds of the Forschungskommission, Universität Luzern.

R. Diaz-Bone (✉)
Department of Sociology, University of Lucerne, Lucerne, Switzerland
e-mail: rainer.diazbone@unilu.ch

K. Manderscheid
Department of Socioeconomics, Universität Hamburg, Hamburg, Germany
e-mail: Katharina.manderscheid@uni-hamburg.de

© Springer Nature Switzerland AG 2019   377
J. Blasius et al. (eds.), *Empirical Investigations of Social Space*,
Methodos Series 15, https://doi.org/10.1007/978-3-030-15387-8_22

(1) Bourdieu is one of the most renowned sociologists worldwide (Grenfell et al. 1993; Fowler 1997; Shusterman 1999; Susen and Turner 2011). In the tradition of French structuralism and epistemology, Bourdieu's work integrates the development of theory and empirical research by translating his conceptual assumptions into methods. From this basis, drawing mainly on Jean-Paul Benzécri (1977, 1992), Bourdieu and his collaborators made correspondence analysis popular in French sociology after the 1970s. In *Distinction* (Bourdieu 2000), one of the most important post-war sociological monographs, multiple correspondence analysis is presented as *the* new tool of contemporary sociological analysis, transforming Bourdieu's relational thinking into statistical data analysis.

(2) The epistemological basis of Bourdieu's sociology are the theories of Gaston Bachelard (1986, 2002, see also Wacquant, Chap. 2, in this volume). Bachelard postulated the need for an epistemological break, realized by applying methods and instruments to the construction of the scientific object. From the late 1920s onward, Bachelard called not only for the coherency of theory and methods, but more radically stated that real science had to transform its conceptual elements into methods – this position can be labelled 'methodical holism', which is not to be confused with methodological holism (see the respective entries in Diaz-Bone and Weischer 2015). By applying these methods in empirical research (which Bachelard labelled *phenomenotechnique*), new phenomena can be examined in greater detail; crucial is that the methods and instruments mirror the theoretical approach of the research.

Bourdieu's work (and that of Michel Foucault) has increasingly made German-speaking sociologists aware of the influence of the philosophy of science developed by Bachelard (Lepenies 1978; Tiles 1986; Dosse 1998a, b; Diaz-Bone 2007, 2010). For Bourdieu, multiple correspondence analysis, developed by Benzécri (Greenacre and Blasius 1994; Blasius 2001; Le Roux and Rouanet 2010; Greenacre 2017), represented a method suitable for the production of sociological research objects – namely social fields, as relational, non-substantial, and latent realities.

Based on these two arguments, combined with the widespread knowledge of Bourdieu's theories, one should expect a similarly well-established expertise in correspondence analysis, and a broad application of this method. What is more, the multivariate procedure of correspondence analysis would seem to be an ideal type of sociological instrument, detecting social structures, dimensions, and groups. Seen from the French point of view, correspondence analysis is not only a special form of factorial analysis, but a general tool for analyzing categorical data.

Yet there seem to be some striking differences between the German sociological tradition and those of other language communities. German-language sociology appears to be divided into two cultures, one oriented toward social theory without strong links to empirical research, and the other grounded mainly in social data analysis, without strong roots in the different strands of social theory. The resulting separation of theory and methods is broadly institutionalized in many sociology departments, with the clear profiling of professorships and chairs as representing either sociological theory or methods of social research.

Against this background, our interest is focused on analyzing the distribution of correspondence analysis training in the curricula of sociology or social science departments in the three (mainly) German-speaking countries Germany, Switzerland, and Austria.

This study can be conceived of as part of a series of sociological analyses which have gathered data on the quantity and structure of methodological training in BA and MA programs in sociology (see the contributions in Engel 2002; Eifler et al. 2011, 2015). However, in most cases these studies advance no real claims, recommendations, or standards with regard to the amount and the content of methodological training in sociology (cf. Schimank 2006; Shostak et al. 2010; Pfeffer and Rogalin 2012; Bögelein and Serrano-Velarde 2012). Furthermore, these studies are characterized by broad categorizations of (statistical) methods, so that no clear picture of MCA training in BA and MA programs can be established (cf. Blanchard et al. 2016). We consider MCA as an essential statistical tool for sociologists useful to analyze the most important kind of sociological data, categorical data, and we apply MCA to analyze the structure of statistical training in BA and MA programs in the German-speaking sociology departments.

Expectations and Hypotheses

Deduced from the arguments outlined above, we formulate and propose two key opposing expectations.

(1) The first expectation asserts that correspondence analysis should be widely implemented in contemporary university sociology curricula in these three countries, due to the broad acceptance of Bourdieu's theories in German-speaking sociology (Schultheis 2007; Fröhlich and Rehbein 2009; Müller 2014). The wide presence of Bourdieu's work in the teaching of sociology is mirrored in the findings of a recent study on theoretical preferences amongst sociology students in Germany: Bourdieu ranks amongst the three most well-known sociologists, and his concepts are the most often applied in student essays and theses (Lenger et al. 2014: 452–455).

Bourdieu emphasized the relational and structural character of social phenomena as distinction, classes, fields, and social spaces which, if they are to be empirically studied, require identification and construction via the application of suitable research methods. The consequence is that social scientists, who apply Bourdieu's theory should also apply correspondence analysis as the statistical tool that corresponds to Bourdieu's theory. In line with this expectation, we can thus formulate the hypothesis that correspondence analysis should be a part of the methods/methodological training in many sociology or social science departments. Especially large departments and departments with scholars oriented towards the work of Bourdieu should offer courses in correspondence analysis as part of their BA or MA sociology programs.

(2) The second and opposite expectation draws on the unique character of German sociology: its separation into two cultures. The reception of Bourdieu's work in German-speaking countries consists mainly of a limited, close reading of his theoretical arguments, which reduces it to a contribution to social theory. In fact, Bourdieu's work is almost fully translated into German (unlike for example the seminal sociological writings of Emile Durkheim). Some of Bourdieu's texts were even published in German first, before being published in French (e.g. Bourdieu 2002, cf. Schultheis 2007: 11). This is taken as evidence for the intense interest in the work of Pierre Bourdieu in German-speaking sociology. However, many leading theorists conduct very little or no empirical research – some even lack a fundamental training in research methods – and social research and sociological data analysis are characterized by a dominance of US sociologists, with their methodological standards and regression analytical techniques, which are currently particularly dominant in German quantitative sociological research. The statistical logic of these methods and the dominance of this specific empirical tradition could be seen to be impeding a broader adaptation of correspondence analytical techniques. Furthermore, the widespread use of IBM SPSS as the standard software for statistical analyses in the social sciences can be seen as influencing or even determining the kinds of quantitative methods which are being taught and implemented (Uprichard et al. 2008). IBM SPSS allows MCA only as a syntax-based analysis of stacked tables, which impacts negatively upon its accessibility and its analytical power.

In this context, we find the 'paradox of the German position': theorists reading and teaching Bourdieu's theory without applying and teaching his methods. It should be added that this diagnosis is restricted to quantitative social research. There is a growing movement in qualitative research applying Bourdieu's methods (Brake et al. 2013).

Based on this expectation, we can develop the hypothesis that even large departments and departments with scholars oriented towards the work of Bourdieu will not necessarily include MCA in their BA or MA curricula.

Data Collection and Analysis

In order to construct a field of German-speaking methods and methodology training, in 2015, we collected data on 57 departments which offer programs with sociology as a main subject, with a total of 43 German, eight Swiss, and six Austrian sociology or social science departments. Departments offering sociology only as a secondary subject were excluded. Our sample includes also the French-speaking sociology departments of Switzerland (Geneva, Lausanne, Neuchâtel, and Fribourg), which, through the exchange of personnel, is in parts influenced by German sociology. Of course, we expect these departments to also be influenced by French social sciences. The basis for our data collection comprised the internet presence of these departments, the profiles of their chairs, as well as the module descriptions of the study programs. Also, we examined the list of courses of the last two semesters for entries containing Bourdieu or correspondence analysis. In a second step, we contacted several experts in the field in order to validate the data through additional insights.

Our data collection included the size (number of professors) of the sociology departments as a whole, the number of professors with an interest in Bourdieu's work (as stated on their website), and the number of professorships dedicated to research methods. Furthermore, we focused on the methods training at the BA and MA levels. In addition to the attempt to establish whether correspondence analysis is part of the training – either mandatory or optional – on the basis of study regulations, we counted the number of compulsory method courses in the different programs and whether research seminars were offered. In addition, we checked the courses offered during the last terms for explicit references to Bourdieu in their description. Of course, we are aware of the range of possible error sources in our procedure of data sampling and we do not claim that our data encompasses the entire field of taught sociology and research methods, which is constantly changing; however, it goes some way toward capturing and illustrating the field's structural shape.[1]

Our main tool to identify patterns in the study programs and departmental structures is – of course – MCA. Yet before discussing our findings in regard to the field of taught methods, we want to summarize the main characteristics descriptively.

Taking Stock: Empirical Results and Interpretations

Descriptives

The departmental size measured in professorships is categorized into four groups, with most departments having between six and nine sociology professors (Table 22.1). Only two sociology departments in Germany have more than 20 professors.

The majority of all sociology departments (82%) have at least one professorship dedicated to methodology, and one third have two or more. The departments with more than one methodology chair are also the ones with the highest number of professorships in total (Table 22.2).

In approximately half of the departments, at least one professor expresses an explicit interest in the works of Pierre Bourdieu, and also in approximately half

---

[1] Due to the very heterogeneous character of university websites and university calendars, the data collection may not perfectly represent the actual field of methods training. Furthermore, we are aware that statistics are often taught by PhD students and lecturers below professorship level, and that the content of these courses may also depend on their personal preferences and competences, which are often not mirrored in the regulations or course descriptions.

Table 22.1 Number of professors per department and by country

| | Number of professorships per department by country | | | |
| | Germany | Switzerland | Austria | Total |
	Percent	Percent	Percent	Percent
5 or fewer	37.2	25.0	50.0	36.8
6 to 9	46.5	62.5	33.3	47.4
10 to 20	11.6	12.5	16.7	12.8
More than 20	4.7	0.0	0.0	3.5
Sum	100 (n = 43)	100 (n = 8)	100 (n = 6)	100 (n = 57)

Table 22.2 Number of methodology professorships

| | Number of methodology professorships by country | | | |
| | Germany | Switzerland | Austria | Total |
	Percent	Percent	Percent	Percent
0	9.3	50.0	33.3	17.5
1	48.8	50.0	50.0	49.1
2	30.2	0.0	16.7	24.6
3	9.3	0.0	0.0	7.0
4	2.3	0.0	0.0	1.8
Sum	100 (n = 43)	100 (n = 8)	100 (n = 6)	100 (n = 57)

Table 22.3 Number of courses with Bourdieu reference by number of professors with Bourdieu interest, in percent

| | | Professors with explicit Bourdieu interest | | |
		None	1 or more	Sum
Courses offered with Bourdieu reference	None	61.5	41.9	50.9
	1 or more	38.5	58.1	49.1
	Sum	45.6 (n = 26)	54.4 (n = 31)	100 (n = 57)

of the departments, courses with an explicit reference to Bourdieu are offered. However, these two modalities seem almost unconnected (Table 22.3), which can probably be explained by the fact that it is the teaching faculty subordinate to the professorship which actually offers the larger part of teaching.

Despite this widespread research interest in and teaching of Bourdieu's concepts, of the 57 sociology or social science departments, only 16 demonstrably offer correspondence analysis in their methods training – be it mandatory (six departments) or optional (ten). Interestingly, it is not the departments with the largest number of methodology chairs where correspondence analysis is most likely to be taught, but the ones with only one methodology chair (Table 22.4).

Table 22.4 Teaching offer MCA by number of methodology professorships

		Number of methodology professorships							
		0		1		2 or more		Sum	
		n	%	n	%	n	%	n	%
MCA teaching	Obligatory	2	20.0	4	14.3	0	0.0	6	10.5
	Optional	1	10.0	6	21.4	3	15.8	10	17.5
	Not at all	7	70.0	18	64.3	16	84.2	41	72.0
	Sum	10	100	28	100	19	100	57	100

Multiple Correspondence Analysis

In order to map the field of methods training in German-speaking sociology departments, we use MCA. As indicators of the structure of the sociology departments, we decided on the following active variables in order to define the geometry:

– number of sociology professors ("Chairs") and number of methodology professors ("MethChairs")
– an explicit interest in Bourdieu's work ("Prof. with B.-interest")
– number of obligatory BA methodology courses ("Meth.courses BA")
– number of obligatory MA methodology courses ("Meth.courses MA")
– whether research seminars are part of the BA ("BA research sem.") or MA training ("MA research sem.")
– number of courses offered in the current and past semester with explicit Bourdieu reference ("Bourdieu courses").

The information regarding whether correspondence analysis is part of the methods training – obligatory, optional, or not at all – is projected into the space thus defined as a supplementary variable. This way, we intend to establish whether the number of professors, their interest in Bourdieu, and the structure of the methods training can offer an explanation for the teaching of correspondence analysis.[2]

Our analysis results in three dimensions, which combined explain 94% of the inertia. The first dimension explains 50.4% and the second 28.1%. The variables "number of professorships", "number of methodology professorships", "number of methods courses in the BA curriculum" and "number of methods courses in the MA curriculum" have a share of 17% each of the variance, while information on research and Bourdieu-related seminars only constitute 8% each (Fig. 22.1).

---

[22] All computation was done using the soc.ca R-package (Grau Larsen 2016). See also Murtagh (2005), Husson et al. (2011) and Pagès (2015) for R-packages related to MCA.

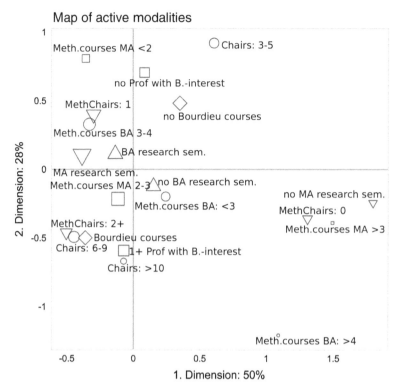

Fig. 22.1 The structure of methods teaching. Map of the active modalities, Data: Own collection 2015

Table 22.5 Dimension1: contributions above average

	Contribution (Ctr)	Coordinates
Dimension 1 (+)		
Method professorships: 0	27.4	1.80
MA research seminars: no	18.9	1.31
MA method courses: >3	11.4	1.49
Professors: 3 to 5	6.5	0.60
BA method courses: >4	6.1	1.09
Dimension 1 (−)		
MA research seminar	5.6	−0.39

Interpretations of Axes

The *first axis* covers a share of about half of the explained variance. The map – together with the information on the most important modalities on the first dimension with a contribution above the average of five (Table 22.5) – suggests an opposition between small-sized departments on the right hand side and larger departments on the left.

Table 22.6 Dimension 2: contributions above average

	Contribution (Ctr)	Coordinates
Dimension 2 (+)		
Professors: 3 to 5	17.4	0.92
Profs with Bourdieu interest: None	12.7	0.71
Method courses MA: <2	8.3	0.81
Courses with Bourdieu: None	6.6	0.48
Dimension 2 (−)		
Profs with Bourdieu interest: 1 or more	10.6	−0.59
Method course BA: >4	8.6	−1.21
Courses with Bourdieu: Yes	6.8	−0.50
Professors: 6 to 9	6.4	−0.49

This opposition is further characterized by the lack of methodology chairs but the presence of many obligatory methods courses on the right hand side, and the existence of methodology chairs in the department and a stronger orientation towards social research on the left. We interpret this axis as an opposition between *integrated*, more modern forms of teaching (such as research seminars) on the left side and more traditional forms of methods training on the right side. Amongst the latter, there may be departments with external methods training, for example together with economy or statistics departments. The *second axis* explains less than one third of the share of the total variance (Table 22.6).

The underlying opposition could be described as small departments without any interest in Bourdieu at the top of the Figure, in contrast to middle-sized sociology departments employing professors interested in Bourdieu at the bottom of the Figure.

The *third axis* has a 15.1% share of explained variance. It covers the influences of departments with a large number of sociology professors. In fact, we are skeptical about this axis. We guess it could be a transformation of the same principle as the second axis.

We then project the supplementary or passive variable into the plot, stating whether correspondence analysis is part of the methods training or not (Fig. 22.2).

The distribution of departments offering courses in correspondence analysis seems to follow the second dimension, which we described as differentiating between medium and large departments with an interest in Bourdieu at the bottom of the axis, and smaller departments without an emphasis on Bourdieu's works at the top. In addition, mapping the individual departments (labelled with the town of the university), shaded according to whether or not they teach of correspondence analysis, shows that the majority of the departments that do offer training in MCA lie on the side of the *integrated* teaching approach, that is, the left side of the plot (Fig. 22.3). At the top right quadrant, however, MCA is obviously not

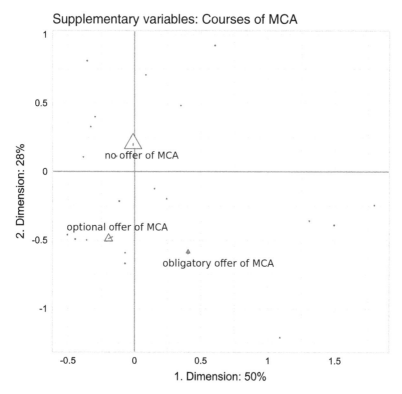

Fig. 22.2 Supplementary variable: correspondence analysis as part of the curriculum. The unlabelled dots mark the location of the active variables. Data: Own collection 2015

part of the curricula. This quadrant is defined by small departments without their own methodology chairs, but with many obligatory methodological courses and without a clear emphasis on Bourdieu's work amongst the faculty. Of the four universities offering MCA located at the bottom right, two are French-speaking Swiss universities, which may indicate their proximity to the French sociology tradition (Fig. 22.3).

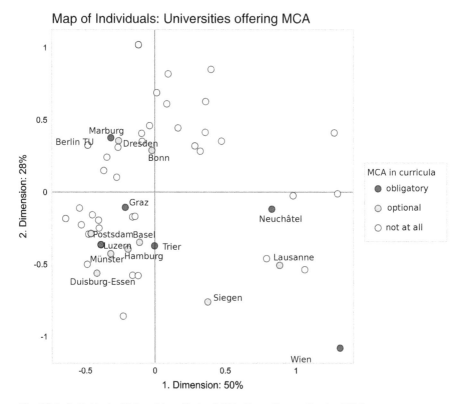

Fig. 22.3 Individuals: Universities offering MCA, Data: Own collection 2015

Conclusions

Our data suggest a series of conclusions, which can be synthesized into four main statements.

(1) One can conclude that, on the one hand, the obligatory teaching of MCA is more probable in sociology departments, which practice integrated methodological training, and, on the other, that selective MCA training will more likely be on offer in larger sociology departments. The explanation could be that a more heterogeneous group of social science researchers is necessarily more likely to include members who have themselves been trained in MCA techniques. These researchers are more likely in larger, more differentiated departments where MCA can be offered as a specialization in (later) methods training.

(2) It seems to us to be evident that MCA has not contributed to the integration of theoretical training and methods training so far. This finding supports our second expectation; that there is a division between theorists who read the works of Bourdieu and methodologists who are more influenced by the American

traditions of research methods. This is clearly a missed opportunity in German sociology departments.

(3) MCA is not correlated with research seminars (which are an essential characteristic of integrated methodological training and) which could otherwise represent a learning platform for the integration of theory and methods training. Again, this can be considered a missed opportunity: As a result of its potential to integrate theory, methodology, and research, MCA could be an excellent tool for research seminars, not only to support Bourdieusian research but also to support any kind of exploratory sociological training. MCA is more suited to the exploratory usage of sociological data than testing procedures as regression analysis.

(4) There is only a small correlation between interest in Bourdieu and MCA training. We assume that theoretical interest prevails over the actual application of MCA as a Bourdieusian method. This assumption also supports our observation of a division between theoretically-oriented social science and empirical research in German sociology.

All in all, we can see more evidence for our second hypothesis: That there is neither a correlation between the prevalence of the teaching of MCA and the size of a department, or between MCA and the level of interest in Bourdieu expressed by a sociology department's professor. Because of sociology's separation into two cultures, the German reception of Bourdieu's work appears to be mainly restricted towards a close reading of its theoretical ingredients without a consideration of its methodology. As early as 1959, C.P. Snow asserted that this is the main divide in western sciences: the rift between the humanities and the empirical (and social) sciences. In fact, many German sociologists exhibit a rather humanities-oriented scientific habitus; many of these social theory professors never received a sound methodological training. This manifests itself in research understood as reading and writing, without standalone elements of data collection and data analysis. On the other hand, quantitative social research methods appear to be shaped by an American, economics-based tradition of statistics teaching which is dominated by regression models and their derivates. Especially this strand of statistics is often reduced to a positivist or empiricist approach to research, which in turn results in a perceived incompatibility between constructivist and post-structuralist theory and statistics (cf. Schwanen and Kwai 2009, Manderscheid 2016a, b). This widespread conflation of quantitative methods with positivism may also be one reason for the limited reception of Bourdieu's work. The consequence for German sociology is that there is almost no established obligatory MCA training today. MCA is still not established in sociology and social sciences methods training in German-speaking countries.

How can one explain the small number of sociology departments which do offer MCA training as part of their BA and MA programs? We surmise that the social networks of early MCA adopters and their students will offer an explanation. Researchers who were influenced early on by Bourdieusian sociology – or who have had early contact with statisticians in the field of MCA – bring MCA training to their departments.

Discussion of Possible Data Flaws and Limitation of Findings

Our findings are possibly negatively affected by different factors of which we are aware, and which impact the validity and the scope of our conclusions.

(1) Although MCA as an explanatory procedure does not demand specific requirements with regard to distributions and levels of measurement, we have a skewed distribution because only a few sociology departments offer MCA courses. Consequently, our picture will be limited, because we have a situation with mainstream methodological training on the one hand and MCA as a more marginal subject on the other.

(2) Our data source is the online presence of departments, their curricula, and their faculty. Although many departments maintain a detailed and up-to-date internet presence, some departmental websites only contain very limited information about the content of method seminars and method lectures. Accordingly, we may have missed some of the MCA courses in the field of German sociology BA and MA programs.

(3) Also, we could have overlooked additional and exceptional courses offering MCA training. We used the search options of the different department sites to detect such additional or irregular courses. However, the searches of the course list function differently for different universities, leading to different findings.

(4) In fact, there seem to be more MCA courses for PhD students and postdocs than for BA and MA students. Currently, many advanced methods are taught at workshops, conferences, and summer schools. In Germany there are some researchers who offer MCA courses or present their MCA-based research at these kinds of occasional events. Correspondingly, our findings are limited to the conditions of the basic training of sociology students, but it cannot be inferred that they apply to doctoral students and postdocs.

Future Needs

For us, as sociologists who appreciate Bourdieusian and French post-Bourdieusian sociology (we both make extensive use of MCA; cf. Diaz-Bone 2015, Manderscheid 2016a, b) as the most innovative and promising strands of contemporary sociology, the situation in German sociology departments is evidently not satisfying.

There is consequently a need for resources supporting the integration of empirical and theoretical research using Bourdieusian methods and MCA.

Firstly, German written introductory statistics textbooks for sociologists should include chapters on MCA. At present, however, there is a visible divide, with specialized statistical textbooks presenting MCA (e.g. Blasius 2001, Wolf and Best 2010, Diaz-Bone 2019) and established ('standard') introductory statistical textbooks excluding MCA. Exceptions are the textbooks written by German economists, which only present bivariate CA (e.g. Backhaus et al. 2015, 2016).

The availability of MCA in German standard textbooks would reduce the barriers for students and teachers to include MCA in their sociology programs. In addition, strengthening the usage of alternative and open statistical software solutions in methods teaching, such as R, would allow researchers to work with more than the statistical techniques prescribed by commercial software (e.g. Manderscheid 2017). The dynamic development of the R environment offers many more options for statistical calculations and analyses than any other available statistical software. Currently, there are several packages available for running MCA analyses with different emphases – on visualization, statistical output, or model specification options. As such, it is hardly surprising that researchers doing MCAs at present mostly work with R.

Secondly, among German sociologists who make reference to the works of Bourdieu in their research and training, there is a need for an improved awareness that this should be combined with MCA training to fully realize the epistemological potential of Bourdieu's work. Instead of reading Bourdieu like a mere philosopher, his work should be read as a guideline for empirical research, one in which MCA is the preeminent analytical tool for transforming Bourdieu's theoretical concepts into a coherent research approach.

References

Bachelard, G. (1986). *The new scientific spirit*. Boston: Beacon Press.

Bachelard, G. (2002). *Formation of the scientific mind*. Manchester: Clinamen.

Backhaus, K., Erichson, B., & Weiber, R. (2015). *Fortgeschrittene multivariate Analysemethoden. Eine anwendungsorientierte Einführung* (3rd ed.). Wiesbaden: Springer.

Backhaus, K., Erichson, B., & Weiber, R. (2016). *Multivariate Analysemethoden. Eine anwendungsorientierte Einführung* (14th ed.). Wiesbaden: Springer.

Benzécri, J. P. (1977). Histoire et préhistoire de l'analyse des données. Partie V: l'analyse des correspondances. *Les Cahiers de l'analyse des données, 2*(1), 9–40.

Benzécri, J. P. (1992). *Correspondence analysis handbook*. New York: Marcel Dekker.

Blanchard, P., Rihoux, B., & Álamos-Concha, P. (2016). Comprehensively mapping political science methods: An instructors' survey. *International Journal of Social Research Methodology, 20*(2), 209–224.

Blasius, J. (2001). *Korrespondenzanalyse*. München: Oldenbourg.

Bögelein, N., & Serrano-Velarde, K. (2012). Qualitative Methodenlehre in Zeiten der Modularisierung. Einführung eines anwendungsorientierten Lehrkonzeptes für die Sozialwissenschaften. *Qualitative Social Research, 13*(1). Retrieved from http://nbn-resolving.de/urn:nbn:de:0114-fqs120290.

Bourdieu, P. (2000). *Distinction. A social critique of the judgment of taste*. Cambridge: Harvard University Press.

Bourdieu, P. (2002). *Ein soziologischer Selbstversuch*. Frankfurt: Suhrkamp.

Brake, A., Bremer, H., & Lange-Vester, A. (Eds.). (2013). *Empirisch arbeiten mit Bourdieu. Theoretische und methodische Überlegungen, Konzeptionen und Erfahrungen*. Weinheim und Basel: Juventa.

Diaz-Bone, R. (2007). Die französische Epistemologie und ihre Revisionen. Zur Rekonstruktion des methodologischen Standortes der Foucaultschen Diskursanalyse. *Qualitative Social Research, 8*(2). Retrieved from http://www.qualitative-research.net/index.php/fqs/article/view/238/528.

Diaz-Bone, R. (2010). *Kulturwelt, Diskurs und Lebensstil. Eine diskurstheoretische Erweiterung der Bourdieuschen Distinktionstheorie* (2nd ed.). Wiesbaden: VS.

Diaz-Bone, R. (2015). *Die "Economie des conventions". Grundlagen und Entwicklungen der neuen französischen Wirtschaftssoziologie*. Wiesbaden: Springer.

Diaz-Bone, R. (2019). *Statistik für Soziologen* (5th ed.). Konstanz: UVK.

Diaz-Bone, R., & Weischer, C. (Eds.). (2015). *Methoden-Lexikon für die Sozialwissenschaften*. Wiesbaden: Springer.

Dosse, F. (1998a). *History of structuralism*. (Vol 1: The rising sign, 1945–1966). Minneapolis: University of Minnesota Press.

Dosse, F. (1998b). *History of structuralism* (Vol 2: The sign set, 1966–Present). Minneapolis: University of Minnesota Press.

Eifler, S., Hoffmeyer-Zlotnik, J. H. P., & Krebs, D. (2011). Die Methodenausbildung in sozialwissenschaftlichen BA-Studiengängen. *Soziologie, 40*(4), 443–465.

Eifler, S., Hoffmeyer-Zlotnik, J. H. P., & Krebs, D. (2015). Die Methodenausbildung in soziologischen MA-Studiengängen: Bestandsaufnahme und Diskussion. *Soziologie, 44*(3), 292–313.

Engel, U. (Ed.). (2002). *Praxisrelevanz der Methodenausbildung* (Sozialwissenschaftliche Tagungsberichte 5). Bonn: Informationszentrum Sozialwissenschaften.

Fowler, B. (1997). *Pierre Bourdieu and cultural theory: Critical investigations*. London: Sage.

Fröhlich, G., & Rehbein, B. (Eds.). (2009). *Bourdieu-Handbuch: Leben – Werk – Wirkung*. Stuttgart: Metzler.

Grau Larsen, A. (2016). *Package 'soc.ca'. Specific Correspondence analysis for the social sciences*. R Package Version 0.7.1 Retrieved from https://cran.r-project.org/web/packages/soc.ca/soc.ca.pdf

Greenacre, M. (2017). *Correspondence Analysis in practice* (3rd ed.). Boca Raton: Taylor & Francis.

Greenacre, M., & Blasius, J. (Eds.). (1994). *Correspondence Analysis in the social sciences*. London: Academic Press.

Grenfell, M., & Lebaron, F. (Eds.). (2014). *Bourdieu and data analysis. Methodological principles and practice*. Bern: Peter Lang.

Grenfell, M., LiPuma, E., & Postone, M. (1993). *Pierre Bourdieu: Critical perspectives*. Chicago: University of Chicago Press.

Husson, F., Lê, S., & Pagès, J. (2011). *Exploratory multivariate analysis by examples using R*. Boca Raton: CRC Press.

Le Roux, B., & Rouanet, H. (2010). *Multiple correspondence analysis* (Vol. 163). Sage.

Lebaron, F. (2006). *L'enquête quantitative en sciences sociales: Recueil et analyse des données*. Paris: Dunod.

Lebaron, F., & Le Roux, B. (Eds.). (2015). *La méthodologie de Pierre Bourdieu en action. Espace culturel, espace social et analyse des données*. Paris: Dunod.

Lenger, A., Rieder, T., & Schneickert, C. (2014). Theoriepräferenzen von Soziologiestudierenden. Welche Autor*innen Soziologiestudierende tatsächlich lesen. *Soziologie, 43*(4), 450–467.

Lepenies, W. (1978). Vergangenheit und Zukunft der Wissenschaftsgeschichte – Das Werk Gaston Bachelards. In G. Bachelard (Ed.), *Die Bildung des wissenschaftlichen Geistes. Beitrag zu einer Psychoanalyse der objektiven Erkenntnis* (pp. 7–34). Frankfurt: Suhrkamp.

Manderscheid, K. (2016a). Quantifying mobilities? Reflections on a neglected method in mobilities research. *Applied Mobilities, 1*(1), 43–055.

Manderscheid, K. (2016b). Mobile Ungleichheiten. Eine sozial- und infrastrukturelle Differenzierung des Mobilitätstheorems. *Österreichische Zeitschrift für Soziologie, 41*(1), 71–96.

Manderscheid, K. (2017). *Sozialwissenschaftliche Datenanalyse mit R*. 2nd rev. ed. Wiesbaden: Springer VS.

Müller, H. P. (2014). *Pierre Bourdieu. Eine systematische Einführung*. Berlin: Suhrkamp.

Murtagh, F. (2005). *Correspondence analysis and data coding with Java and R*. Boca Raton: Chapman & Hall.

Pagès, J. (2015). *Multiple factor analysis by examples using R*. Boca Raton: CRC Press.

Pfeffer, C. A., & Rogalin, C. (2012). Three Strategies for Teaching Research Methods: A Case Study Teaching Sociology. *Teaching Sociology*, 40(4), 368–376.

Robson, K., & Sanders, C. (Eds.). (2009). *Quantifying theory: Pierre Bourdieu*. Heidelberg: Springer.

Schimank, U. (2006). Empfehlungen der Deutschen Gesellschaft für Soziologie (DGS) zur Ausgestaltung soziologischer Bachelor- und Master-Studiengänge. *Soziologie, 35*(1), 80–84.

Schultheis, F. (2007). *Bourdieus Wege in die Soziologie: Genese und Dynamik einer reflexiven Sozialwissenschaft*. Konstanz: UVK.

Schwanen, T., & Kwan, M. P. (2009). "Doing" critical geographies with numbers. *The Professional Geographer, 61*(4), 459–464.

Shostak, S., Girouard, J., Cunningham, D., & Cadge, W. (2010). Teaching graduate and under-graduate research methods: A multipronged departmental initiative. *Teaching Sociology, 38*(2), 93–105.

Shusterman, R. (1999). *Bourdieu: A critical reader*. Oxford: Blackwell Publishers.

Snow, C. P. (1959). *The two cultures*. Cambridge: Cambridge University Press.

Susen, S., & Turner, B. S. (Eds.). (2011). *The legacy of Pierre Bourdieu*. London: Anthem Press.

Tiles, M. (1986). *Bachelard: Science and objectivity*. Cambridge: Cambridge University Press.

Uprichard, E., Burrows, R., & Byrne, D. (2008). SPSS as an 'Inscription Device': From causality to description? *The Sociological Review, 56*(4), 606–622.

Wolf, C., & Best, H. (Eds.). (2010). *Handbuch der sozialwissenschaftlichen Datenanalyse*. Wiesbaden: VS Verlag für Sozialwissenschaften.

Chapter 23
Traveling with Albert Gifi: Nominal, Ordinal and Interval Approaches in Comparative Studies of Social and Cultural Spaces

Dominique Joye, Gunn Elisabeth Birkelund, and Yannick Lemel

Introduction

In the social sciences, researchers who address the same topic of investigation and even use the same data might prefer to apply different methods when analysing these data. The methodological consequences of the choice of research design are often not fully evaluated. In this article, we detail the consequences of methodological choices, in particular between techniques related to nominal (MCA), ordinal (CatPCA) and metric (PCA) variables. All of these are integrated in the Gifi framework (Gifi 1990). Even if it is rarely used in sociology, such a framework is an elegant solution for comparing different methodological designs applied to the same data.

Earlier versions of this paper were presented at different conferences, and we thank the participants and discussants for their comments. Part of this work was also realised in the framework of the National Centre of Competence in Research LIVES. We would also like to thank Jan de Leeuw, Julie Falcon, John Eriksen and Amal Tawfik for their discussions and comments. The content of this paper, however, is our own responsibility

Electronic supplementary material The online version of this chapter (https://doi.org/10.1007/978-3-030-15387-8_23) contains supplementary material, which is available to authorized users.

D. Joye (✉)
Faculty of Social and Political Sciences, Institute for Social Sciences, University of Lausanne, Lausanne, Switzerland
e-mail: Dominique.joye@unil.ch

G. E. Birkelund
University of Oslo, Oslo, Norway
e-mail: g.e.birkelund@sosgeo.uio.no

Y. Lemel
GEMASS, Sorbonne Université, Paris, France
e-mail: Yannick.Lemel@ensae.fr

© Springer Nature Switzerland AG 2019
J. Blasius et al. (eds.), *Empirical Investigations of Social Space*,
Methodos Series 15, https://doi.org/10.1007/978-3-030-15387-8_23

Our empirical topic of investigation is studying social spaces and cultural activities in modern societies, and we will compare outcomes in three countries: France, Norway and Switzerland. Inspired by the homology thesis of Bourdieu (1984), some researchers in the field of social stratification and cultural consumption generate latent dimensions by means of multiple correspondence analyses (MCA) (Lebaron and Le Roux 2015), whereas other researchers generate latent dimensions by means of other multivariate methods, such as principal component analysis (PCA) or multidimensional scaling (Chan 2010). These methodological choices are associated with different ways of considering the data: MCA refers to nominal variables, while PCA and multi-dimensional scaling are based on higher-level measurements, such as interval- or ordinal-level variables. Therefore, even when researchers use the same original data, the choice of method and associated assumptions about the level of measurement of the variables might have implications for how well the models fit the data as well as – perhaps – for the substantial outcomes of the analyses. To our knowledge, there is no study discussing these issues or comparing different methods and measurements applied to the same data. In addition, there is no consensus on how we might best compare different models in terms of how well they fit the data. In this paper, we begin to undertake this extensive task by testing empirically different methods with associated assumptions about variable measurements and scaling applied to the same data. Comparative studies of methodological choices have been rare – even more so in this field of research – so it is often unclear if differences in outcomes are driven by methodology or are meaningful in terms of substantial results.

From a substantial point of view, the main research question addressed in this literature is how cultural consumption is associated with social position. In Bourdieu's tradition, social space can be defined as a two-dimensional space where the first dimension captures the overall volume of capital and the second dimension captures the composition of capital (Bourdieu 1985: 724). This is also in line with the "Japanese lesson" where Bourdieu wrote: "Social space is constructed in such a way that agents or groups are distributed in it according to their position in the statistical distribution based on two differentiation principles which, in the most advanced societies, such as the United States, Japan, or France, are undoubtedly the most efficient: economic capital and cultural capital" (Bourdieu 631). But the omnivore thesis, associated with Peterson (1992) and later with Chan and Goldthorpe (2007), is less explicit about the number of stratification dimensions, even if these analyses mainly operate with one principal dimension. We will use comparable data from national representative surveys on cultural consumption in France, Norway and Switzerland to determine the association between a set of variables measuring cultural consumption and that of a set of variables measuring social position. In particular, we will discuss the methodological aspects of these comparisons.

Theoretically, according to Bourdieu's proposition, the social and cultural spaces *symmetrically* shape each other, yet the most common approach to this type of investigation treats the two sets of variables in a *pre-defined order*: first, a cultural space is constructed, and then the social position variables are 'added', or the reverse, such as, for example, Prieur et al. (2008). There are a number of examples for such a strategy in the literature, such as in Coulangeaon and Duval (2015), Lebaron and Le Roux (2015), Rosenlund (2015) and Bennett et al. (2015), to mention just a few. In our case, to find the best association between the two sets of variables, we will apply a canonical correlation design which generates latent dimensions that are the best possible representation of the two sets of manifest variables under the constraint of maximum correlation between the two-by-two sets of latent dimensions. We apply the canonical correlation methods, giving the same weight to both sets of variables, within the framework of Gifi (1990), which allows flexibility in terms of the levels of measurements for all of the included variables, that is nominal, ordinal and interval. Thus, our paper has three intertwined contributions, both methodological and substantial. First, we believe our discussion contributes to the theory of measurement by demonstrating the usefulness of explicit considerations regarding different levels of measurements. Second, we also believe that reintroducing the canonical correlation design to generate latent dimensions is useful, particularly for this topic of investigation. Third, by comparing three countries, we provide a robust test of our findings to see if the associations between cultural consumption and social position are affected by different national contexts. Although our chapter addresses a particular substantive topic – the homology thesis – we hope that our discussions and analyses might be helpful for other topics of investigation as well, in which one of the main purposes is to identify meaningful latent dimensions in different social contexts.

This chapter is organized in the following way: first, we present the methodological framework of our analyses, which includes a discussion on the scaling of variables and the canonical correlation design. We then present the results of our analysis, in which we report different scaling models. And we finally discuss the models' explanatory power, taking into account their complexity. The implications of the substantive results as well as the methodological consequences are discussed in a last conclusive part.

Methods

Jan de Leeuw and colleagues at the University of Leiden developed the Gifi framework (Gifi 1990; de Leeuw 1984). The Albert Gifi team[1] developed a system of nonlinear multivariate analysis that extends various techniques, such as principal component and canonical correlation analysis (Cox and Cox 1994, see also http:// gifi.stat.ucla.edu). The Gifi framework is relevant to us because it is a general way to present different multivariate techniques. For example, multiple correspondence analysis, often used in the French tradition of 'Analyse des données', as well

---

[1] Albert Gifi was the servant of Galton, the latent helper, whose contribution was large but mainly unknown to the outside world (Gifi 1990; Van der Heijden and Sijtsma 1996).

as principal component analysis could be seen as particular cases of the Gifi framework. The Gifi framework considers a continuum of restrictions ranging from MCA, in which there is no restriction on scaling, to PCA, in which an equal distance between categories is defined, with CatPCA as an intermediate solution, in which the order between categories has to be respected. The Gifi framework consequently allows us to consider variables as interval, ordinal and nominal and to appreciate the *loss of fit* that such a situation implies. In other words, we will find an optimal coding of the variables to maximize an indicator of quality of the model. This is what we mean by 'scaling'.

Scaling

The nominal, ordinal or interval characteristic of variables is a complicated topic. For instance, consider the following question, as translated from one of our surveys: "How often do you go to the opera?" The questionnaire includes the following possible answers: (1) never; (2) not often; (3) sometimes; and (4) often. The variables could be treated at face value, which means that the codes 1, 2, 3 and 4 would be used directly, with 1 measuring the distance between the responses (constant intervals between the categories). This is in fact an identity transformation, which in the Gifi framework is called the 'single interval' solution.

However, this strategy is not necessarily the best solution. For example, if we suppose that going to the opera or not determines cultural behaviour, we might argue that the distance between *never* and *not often* is greater than that between *not often* and *sometimes*. In this case, a scaling giving a value of 0 for *never* and 1 for the other categories would respect the order and be a better fit for the underlying scale.

Such a solution preserves the ordinal measurements of the variables by applying an external criterion to find an optimal transformation of the scaling of the variable. Thus, what Gifi calls a 'single ordinal' solution builds interval variables from ordinal ones, with the help of additional information.

We can, of course, also imagine a more complex transformation that not only allows the values to change but also the order of the categories. This can be seen as consuming more 'degrees of freedom', but this kind of transformation can give a better fit. Such a case is called the 'single nominal' one.

In the terminology proposed by Gifi (1990), the examples given so far are *"single" scaling models*, as only one transformation is used for each variable – the same for any dimension. This will necessarily be the case if the solution of the multivariate analysis is unidimensional. However, if, as in our case (and many others), the analysis implies generating more than one latent dimension, then the manifest variables involved might be scaled differently when estimating each latent dimension. This is the *'multiple' scaling solution*, which is in fact an alternative way of presenting multiple correspondence analysis.

We will return to the difference between "single" and "multiple" scaling models when we present the results of the analysis. It is nevertheless important to underline that if we have - until now - only discussed a model composed of a single set of variables, like in PCA or MCA, this logic can of course be generalized to two or more sets of variables, like in the family of canonical analysis, which we will soon address.

In other words, the measurements of the variables – nominal, ordinal and interval, which are often discussed from a rather 'mechanistic perspective' in statistical textbooks for the social sciences – could sometimes be seen as partially misleading. However, this does not mean there is complete freedom in the choices of measurements and scaling. Adopting a nominal strategy, for example, adds complexity by implying the need to estimate more parameters. In other words, using more 'degrees of freedom' means that there is a price to pay. In order to choose between different models, we apply the well-known principle of Occam's razor (*Lex parsimoniae*). If two models are alike in terms of how well they describe the data, but one is more complicated than the other, we should prefer the simplest/least complicated model. We will consider what this principle means when discussing results, after presenting canonical correlations in more detail.

Canonical Correlation

Hotteling initiated the canonical correlation method as early as in 1938 (Gittins 1985). Canonical correlation measures the relationship between two sets of variables by searching for the best linear combinations of variables in the first set that could be related to the best linear combinations of the variables in the second set (Levine 1977). The underlying idea is the following: Suppose two sets of manifest variables are associated with each other. The two sets of manifest variables are measured for the same observations, with the dimensionality of the first and second sets being l (for the left side) and r (for right side), respectively. Then, l and r latent variables (factors) can be calculated (subject to various assumptions and standardizations) respecting the following constraints:

- The l latent variables are uncorrelated, and the r latent variables are also uncorrelated;
- the first of the l latent variables is maximally correlated to the first of the r variables;
- the second of the l latent variables is maximally correlated to the second of the r variables, and this is the same for the third dimension of each set, and so on.

To summarize, the constructed latent dimensions are explanatory factorial dimensions of the two respective original variable sets with the strongest possible correlations between each set of latent dimensions. As in factor analysis, the first dimension (here, the first pair of dimensions) will carry most of the meaningful information, and we can neglect the last dimensions. In our case, the manifest variables on the left side measure social position, and the manifest variables on the right side measure cultural activities. Thus, L1 and L2 refer to the first two

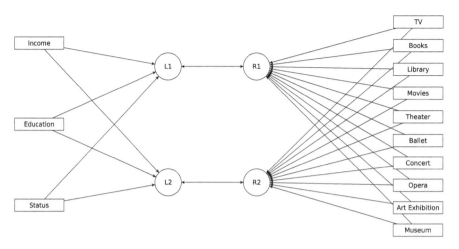

Fig. 23.1 Schema of canonical correlation analysis considered in the three countries

latent dimensions of social space, whereas R1 and R2 refer to the first two latent dimensions of cultural consumption (Fig. 23.1).

Canonical correlation will generate as many pairs of latent dimensions as the minimum number of manifest variables (i.e., with three variables for social position and 10 variables for cultural consumption, canonical correlation will generate no more than three pairs of latent variables: L1 and R1; L2 and R2; L3 and R3). In fact, the criterion to choose for – considering the number of dimensions – is analogous to the one used in PCA, looking to the change of explained variance from one solution to the other.

The canonical correlation analysis takes the central hypothesis proposed by Bourdieu into account, namely that social positions cannot be defined without simultaneously considering the lifestyles that may be associated with them. By correlating two sets of variables – one measuring social space (such as education, income, status, etc.) and the other measuring cultural activities (such as attending the opera or ballet, etc.) – the canonical correlation method offers a fairly direct way of assessing the relevance of the theory of structural homology. The magnitude of the correlation between the two latent dimensions/canonical components (built on each of the two sets of manifest variables) is a direct evaluation of the homology hypothesis. Despite all of these advantages, we are aware of only one text (Frie and Janssen 2009) that applied the canonical correlation method, in a work inspired by *La Distinction*. Here, we will use this method systematically by varying the measurement level attributed to the variables. In the Gifi framework, this means recalculating the scaling of the variables under the assumption that the two sets of variables, respectively measuring social and cultural space, should be as highly correlated as possible (in line with the homology hypothesis of Bourdieu).

From a practical point of view, if the different software developed in the Gifi framework share one characteristic – a name ending with ALS – then we can distinguish at least three implementations, with a fourth one called GIFI actually being rewritten in C for use inside R.

- A set of FORTRAN programs (that were still available 2 years ago under the address http://gifi.stat.ucla.edu). For technical reasons, we used "CANALS" (CANonical Alternative Linear Scaling) for some analyses, as it is the easiest way to obtain the canonical correlation coefficient between two sets in the traditional way.
- An implementation mainly from the original OVERALS FORTRAN program in the SPSS Categories module.
- An implementation in R allowing a large set of models to be analysed in the HOMALS package. This was also used in many of our analyses.

Data and Variables

The three countries we compared are similar enough to make comparisons meaningful, yet different enough to provide contextual variation. These countries are all located in Europe and are relatively wealthy. They all have a long tradition of democratic institutions, and all three countries have high scores on the UN's well-being indexes. Furthermore, these three countries have also been more frequently investigated in this research perspective than other European countries, outside the Bourdieusian tradition of France. This is the case, for example, of Rosenlund (2015) in Norway and Tawfik (2013) in Switzerland. Looking at differences, Norway and Switzerland are both outside the EU and have relatively small populations, whereas France is one of the founders of the EU and has a large population. In addition to geographical, historical and demographic diversity, the three countries also differ in cultural terms. According to Hofstede's model on cultural dimensions (http://geert-hofstede.com/dimensions.html), France, Norway and Switzerland are similar in some respects (*individualism* and *long-term orientation*), but different in other dimensions (*power distance, uncertainty avoidance* and *masculinity*). An important reason for comparing these three countries is the available survey data, which allow for a detailed comparative analysis. As we will see, even if these surveys are fairly comparable, there are still some variations between them.

Surveys[2]

The French survey, *Participation Culturelle et Sportive*, was part of the May 2003 issue of *The Continuous Survey of Living Conditions* carried out by the French

---

[2]We would like to very warmly thank the institutions that put their data at our disposal for this study.

Statistical Office. The random sample, with a response rate of 67 percent, was representative of individuals aged 15 and over who lived in private households in metropolitan France. The Norwegian survey, *Kultur og mediebruksundersøkelsen*, was carried out in 2004 by Statistics Norway. The sample was representative of the Norwegian resident population aged 19–79 years. The response rate was 70 percent. The Swiss survey, *Pratiques culturelles en Suisse*, was conducted in 2008 by the Swiss Statistical Office with a CATI procedure and obtained a 66 percent response rate. For comparative purposes, we limited the samples in all three countries to include only occupationally active individuals between 20–64 years of age, which leaves us with a sample of 3744 individuals in France, 1005 in Norway and 2442 in Switzerland. Although these data are not entirely fresh, we note that Tawfik (2013) has concluded that the relation between social and cultural spaces is probably stable in the long run.

Variables

The variables we included as well as the characteristics of these variables are important for testing differences in methods and measurements. Can we plausibly argue a priori that variables pertinent for analysing social space should be seen as nominal, ordinal or interval alternatives? Some components of social position, such as education, are sometimes treated as interval-level variables, yet they are often measured at less precise levels in surveys. This may be problematic in countries with a vocational training system and an academic track at the same level, with different implications for human capital. Nominal variables, such as respondents' occupations, are often grouped into categories such as social classes, or they are ranked according to an interval-level socio-economic scale or other scales (such as Treiman's prestige scale and status scales). Furthermore, these variables can be linked to the individual or the household, leaving room for a very vivid debate on the 'proper' unit of analysis in social stratification, which we will not engage in here except of saying that if we use individuals as the basic unit of analysis, we also include a measure of economic capital based on the household's income. All of this will be important when discussing the links between social and cultural spaces in the concluding part.

   In our analysis, three variables are used to describe the social space: *education*, *household income* and *occupation*. *Education* in Norway is measured by the number of years necessary to get the highest diploma, with 10 categories. In the Swiss and French data, education has six categories; in Switzerland, these categories also include information on vocational training. In all three countries, *household income* is measured as the logarithm of household income per capita. *Occupation* is measured according to the ISEI scale in Switzerland (Joye and Chevillard 2011) and the Chan and Goldthorpe social status scale in France and Norway (France: Cousteaux and Lemel 2004, Norway: Chan et al. 2011). Ideally, we would have supplemented these variables with other indicators of social structure, such as home or stock ownership. Unfortunately, this information is not available in our three surveys. However, it is clear that income, education and occupation are basically the three most important indicators used by stratification and social mobility researchers and they are also correlated with other measures of social position. We are therefore confident that this set of manifest variables can fruitfully be used to describe the social structure and form the basis of constructing the social space. All of these variables were recoded into a smaller number of categories after considering their distribution. Table 23.5 in the appendix recapitulates the number of categories used for each variable in each country. For previous analyses using the French and Norwegian parts of these data, please see Birkelund and Lemel (2013).

The three surveys include a variety of questions about cultural practices, such as reading, listening to music, visiting museums, going to the opera and other cultural outings, television viewing, artistic hobbies and sports activities, allowing us to form a set of variables measuring *cultural consumption*. These questions are retrospective in nature and ask about the respondents' activity over the past 12 months (excluding professional and school obligations). Ten cultural activities were similarly fielded in the three countries: watching TV, reading books and visiting the library, movies, theatres, the ballet, concerts, operas, art exhibitions and museums. The cultural consumption variables are usually measured at an ordinal level, using a scale of ranked values. Nevertheless, such variables are often analysed as interval ones, with the justification that they measure an unobserved latent continuous dimension. Our survey data include rather small samples. In addition, we have limited our analyses to occupationally active respondents between 20 and 64 years of age. To avoid excluding too many individuals, for variables that had many individuals with missing values, we decided to impute new values for the missing cases using auxiliary information.

Results

In the methodological part, we have introduced the difference between 'single scaling', in which the scale transformation is the same for all dimensions, and 'multiple scaling', in which the transformation can be different for each dimension, like in MCA.

In a country-by-country strategy, we will start by introducing *single scaling models*. For each country, a table comparing the canonical correlation between the latent dimensions generated by the three *single-scale models* – the single nominal, the single ordinal and the single interval – was computed. Two models that provide a similar level of explanation will have similar canonical correlation coefficients, and the simplest model should be preferred (based on Occam's razor). We therefore adjudicated – separately for each country – which of the single-scaling models were the most efficient ones for maximizing the correlation between the two sets measuring social and cultural space.

We then move on to the *multiple scaling models*, which imply that we allow the values of each variable to be transformed differently for each dimension within the same canonical correlation analysis. We only consider one multiple nominal model, and we will compare the outcomes of this model with the 'best' single scaling solution.

In order to evaluate the goodness of fit, we constructed R^2-like statistics, which will be used later, together with the potential degrees of freedom, to measure the models' overall fit to the data.

Single Scaling Models

We only considered the most meaningful latent dimensions, since keeping all latent dimensions means no reduction of information compared to the original manifest variables (with three variables in the smallest data set, there will be at most three dimensions to consider). Using a traditional criterion like the decrease of the canonical correlations between the two variable sets, we decided to continue with two latent dimensions.

Each estimated model has manifest social position variables on the left side and manifest cultural consumption variables on the right side. Table 23.1 shows the canonical correlations between the left- and right-side latent dimensions as well as the sum of their squared value, which gives an indication of the explained variance.

In Table 23.1, we of course have a better fit at the nominal level, confirming that the more degrees of freedom we use, the higher the fit will be. For each country, there are hardly any detectable differences between the canonical correlations (correlation 1, correlation 2) associated with the nominal and ordinal levels of measurements, respectively. Comparing the ordinal and interval levels, we found slightly lower canonical correlations associated with the interval level in each country, which indicates that the ordinal level of measurement seems more

Table 23.1 Canonical correlations in the single interval, ordinal and nominal solutions

	Correlation 1	Correlation 2	R^2
Switzerland			
Single interval	0.47	0.19	0.25
Single ordinal	0.49	0.20	0.28
Single nominal	0.49	0.20	0.28
France			
Single interval	0.60	0.14	0.38
Single ordinal	0.61	0.24	0.43
Single nominal	0.61	0.24	0.43
Norway			
Single interval	0.53	0.23	0.33
Single ordinal	0.55	0.26	0.37
Single nominal	0.56	0.26	0.38

appropriate: The ordinal-level models are associated with higher explanatory power than the interval-level models, and the ordinal-level models utilize fewer degrees of freedom than the nominal-level models. In addition to the canonical correlations, we note that the R^2 values for each country are slightly lower for the interval-level models. The strength of the relation as measured by this R^2 between the left and right-side latent variables or social and cultural spaces, respectively, is strongest in France and weakest in Switzerland, as a consequence of a higher canonical correlation for the first dimension.

The Single Ordinal Model in Detail

The best single scaling model according to the number of parameters is the ordinal one. But what is the interpretation of the dimensions obtained in this case? We first look at the two left-side dimensions of social space and then at the two right-side dimensions of cultural activity.

Loadings of the Left Set – Social Space

There are four latent variables associated with two sets of canonical correlation solutions; see Table 23.2. On each side of the canonical correlation model, the latent variables are constructed from the manifest variable sets, and the correlations between each manifest and latent variable show their relations. These correlations are called loadings, as in PCA. Note that the algorithm generating these latent variables is set up so that they are defined to maximize the correlation between the right side (R) and the left side (L). In our analysis, this means that the two latent variables measuring "social space" are generated simultaneously with the two latent variables measuring cultural activities. We adhered to a common practice of only emphasizing loadings above 0.4 when interpreting the results.

   In the three countries, all of the manifest variables have negative loadings on the first latent dimension (L1). Thus, the first latent variable on the left side appears to be an indicator of global capital, where a high score implies a low volume of capital and vice versa. This pattern is the same in all three countries.

Table 23.2 Loadings on the left set, ordinal measurement

	Switzerland		France		Norway	
	L1	L2	L1	L2	L1	L2
Isei	−0.65	0.08	−0.85	0.52	−0.77	−0.04
Income	−0.63	0.76	−0.82	−0.25	−0.96	0.01
Education	−0.93	−0.29	−0.67	−0.52	−0.21	−0.97

In the second latent dimension (L2), the three variables have different loadings by country. In Switzerland, income has the highest loading in the second latent variable; in France, social status is opposed to education; and in Norway, education is the only manifest variable with a noticeable loading on the second latent variable (L2). These latent variables appear to differ partly from the usual Bourdieusian interpretation of the second latent dimension of the social space (i.e., the capital composition). One reason for this result might be that we have only crude measurements of income (only at the household level), whereas education and social status are measured at the individual level. Another reason could be that the Bourdieusian interpretation of the second dimension of social space is not relevant, at least not with these data. A third reason might be that we generated the latent dimensions of the social space simultaneously with the latent dimension of the cultural space, based on the manifest variables of cultural activities. For now, we note that the second latent variable differs between the countries. We will discuss these possible interpretations later.

Loadings of the Right Set – Cultural Space

In all of the countries, nine out of the 10 manifest variables have negative loadings on the first latent dimension (R1); see Table 23.3. In all countries, R1 captures an opposition between TV and all of the other cultural activity variables. This means that this dimension could be interpreted as a kind of omnivore dimension contrasting TV with all of the other cultural activities.

The second dimension of the right set is more difficult to interpret. In Norway and Switzerland, visiting libraries has the largest loadings on R2. This aspect also appears in France, albeit weaker. However, none of these cultural activities seems to have a strong discriminating power (higher loadings than .40) in France.

In other words, the first latent dimension shows a relatively strong relation between a global capital and a cultural composition, with a relatively high canon-

Table 23.3 Loadings on the right set, ordinal measurement

| | Switzerland | | France | | Norway | |
	R1	R2	R1	R2	R1	R2
TV	0.41	0.38	0.37	−0.15	0.29	−0.26
Book	−0.70	−0.09	−0.63	0.28	−0.39	−0.19
Library	−0.23	−0.83	−0.37	0.36	−0.41	0.72
Movie	−0.55	−0.09	−0.63	0.52	−0.57	0.16
Theatre	−0.47	0.06	−0.56	−0.37	−0.52	−0.13
Ballet	−0.27	−0.16	−0.26	−0.19	−0.27	0.30
Opera	−0.55	−0.26	−0.38	−0.24	−0.39	−0.01
Concert	−0.48	0.04	−0.53	−0.18	−0.17	−0.02
Museum	−0.74	−0.17	−0.71	−0.32	−0.75	−0.2
Exhibition	−0.53	−0.02	−0.76	−0.31	−0.56	−0.15

ical correlation reinforcing the homology hypothesis, whereas the second latent dimension seems more particular with reference to the use of libraries, with a lower canonical correlation. This implies that the homology is stronger in a unidimensional perspective within the single scaling models.

Multiple Scaling Model

Until now, the scaling of the manifest variables have been considered "single", meaning that each manifest variable has kept the same scaling when constructing the different latent dimensions. This restriction might be relaxed to allow for multiple transformations, one for each dimension. In fact, such a multiple nominal scaling corresponds to MCA, as used in Bourdieu's tradition. We will do the same in the context of canonical correlation and see whether the difference between single and multiple scaling models is important.

Table 23.4 compares the previous canonical correlations of the single scaling models (as presented in Table 23.1) with the canonical correlations obtained in the multiple scaling models. We include the same R^2-like statistic, defined as the sum of the square of the canonical correlations, to assess the global 'quality' of the link between the two sets.

When comparing the models in Table 23.4, we first appreciate the increase in the R^2 from one model to the other in each country, which is of course linked to the characteristics of the solutions: As the multiple nominal model uses the maximum number of degrees of freedom, it is therefore to be expected that the R^2 will always be increasing, but according to Table 23.4, this increase is either non-existent (in Switzerland) or relatively minor (in France and Norway).

The question, however, is how to balance this change in degrees of freedom in relation to the models' explanatory power. In order to measure these degrees of freedom, we propose a rule, based on the following reasoning.

- First, in single interval models, the model uses no extra degrees of freedom for the scaling of the categories, as the codes are used directly in the analysis.

Table 23.4 Canonical correlations in the three countries and according to scaling

	Switzerland					France					Norway				
	C1	C2	R^2	PDF	RD	C1	C2	R2	PDF	RD	C1	C2	R2	PDF	RD
SI	.47	.19	.25	0		.60	.14	.38	0		.53	.23	.33	0	
SO	.49	.20	.28	30	.10	.61	.24	.43	30	.17	.55	.26	.37	27	.15
SN	.49	.20	.28	43	.00	.61	.24	.43	43	.00	.56	.26	.38	40	.08
MN	.49	.23	.29	86	.02	.62	.28	.47	86	.09	.56	.29	.40	80	.05

C1 first canonical correlation, *C2* second canonical correlation, *R2* explained variance, *PDF* pseudo-degrees of freedom or number of parameters to estimate, *RD* relative difference or change in R2 by change in pseudo-degrees of freedom

- Second, in single ordinal models, the ranking of the values is based on fixing the extreme values and then letting the intermediate categories vary while respecting their order. This means that the degree of freedom in such a case can be approximated by the sum of the number of categories minus two (i.e., the two fixed extremes) for each variable.
- Third, in the single nominal case, the degrees of freedom, as defined here, are based on the number of categories minus one serving as a reference.
- Finally, in the multiple nominal models, the degrees of freedom will be twice that of the single nominal in the case of two dimensions, three times more in case of three dimensions and so on.

In Table 23.4, the estimated R^2 values associated with these four models are corrected by this indicator of degrees of freedom. Based on this estimation, we now have a comparison of *the gain in the R^2 according to the increase in the degrees of freedom*, which we use to compare the three single scaling models and the multiple nominal models. In each case, when we take into account the growth of the number of parameters, the single ordinal model seems to be the most efficient solution. This does not mean that it is not interesting to consider, particularly in the case of France, the information added by the multiple nominal models.

One way to do this is to look at the rescaling proposed by the multiple nominal solution, as presented in the Appendix, where Figs. 23.2 (France, Online Appendix), 23.3 (Norway, Online Appendix) and 23.4 (Switzerland, Online Appendix) show the original and the transformed values for each manifest variable for the first latent dimension (in black) and the second latent dimension (in red). Interestingly, for the cultural space (see the lowest 10 sub-figures), all of the transformations (rescaling) are in line with the original order of the values, confirming the idea that ordinal transformation is optimal. In other words, in each country, the cultural activity variables would best be considered as ordinal variables.

When we look at the scaling of the three variables describing the social space, we see that there are more differences for some categories according to scaling. These differences are found among values/categories in the middle rank and not in the upper-rank categories. If we had found a particular pattern for the upper positions, we might have argued that we need to differentiate the ranking of the elite from the other categories. This might justify a different ordering that distinguishes cultural and economic elites. We will not comment in further detail on the multiple nominal solution, but the correlations between the canonical variates in the single and multiple nominal cases show that the differences are extremely small – which is a further argument for sticking to the simplest solution: the single ordinal one.

In summary, the Gifi framework applied to the canonical correlation analysis and the principle of parsimony provides us with a clear conclusion: Keep the most parsimonious models, which in our case are the single ordinal models. Second, we have seen that the outcomes of the other models are rather similar. This demonstrates the general robustness of the methods used. It also shows that, with these data, a simple ordinal model dominates the structure even though multiple scaling might be appropriate for some particular variables.

Discussion and Conclusions

We have analysed social and cultural spaces in three countries: France, Norway and Switzerland. In each country, we used survey data to construct the social space associated with and according to the homology thesis – theoretically defined by cultural activities and socio-economic position. Our main topic of investigation was to consider the choices of methodology related to previous analyses of this topic. In particular, we have discussed two issues: first, the overall methodology of these analyses, and second, the scaling of the variables used in these analyses.

Previous studies on social and cultural space have started by first representing a cultural 'space' based on a multiple correspondence analysis of one set of manifest variables (most often the cultural consumption variables) before adding indicators of social position as supplementary variables (based on a set of variables measuring social position). The reasons for such methodological choice are seldom explicated in detail. Within the Gifi framework, in line with the theoretical argument of the homology thesis, we decided to treat the social and cultural spaces in a direct, symmetrical way, which is in line with the homology thesis.

On the scaling of the variables, we explored different possibilities to see if the established research praxis of assuming, without discussion, that all variables are scaled at the nominal level of measurement (as in MCA) or at the interval level of measurement (as in PCA) is justified. Thus, we have explored nominal, ordinal and interval levels of measurements within the canonical correlation design to see which level of scaling is most appropriate for the associations among social and cultural sets of manifest variables, given the principle of parsimony in science. The transformation of the original codes was the same across all latent dimensions. In addition, we have also explored the outcome when our choice of scaling for the manifest variables differed across different latent dimensions, as it would be in a comparison between PCA and CatPCA on the one side and MCA on the other.

In summary, we would like to underline three points:

- Whatever scaling we applied, in all of the analyses, two latent canonical dimensions emerged in all three countries, with the first set of dimensions being most important. In the French case, the relationship between the social and cultural spaces was stronger than in Switzerland and Norway. In France, the importance of the second dimension was larger than in Switzerland and Norway. In other words, the homology thesis is sustained in all three countries, but appears stronger in France.
- In all three countries, the solutions obtained were very close to each other. Thus, the idea that a particular method will induce a particular kind of representation, showing results that would not have been possible to observe with another model, is not confirmed. On the contrary, the results between the different models used in this analysis had great coherence.
- However, the "single" ordinal model was slightly more adapted to our data than the others; thus, following the idea of parsimony as stated in the Occam's razor principle, we suggest that the "single" ordinal model is the best in terms of

explanatory economy. Of course, some interesting details can only be discovered by carefully looking at the transformation of the variables. In particular, we have seen that a precise description of the social space could imply a close examination of the relative positions of education and income for some categories.

More generally, we believe that reintroducing the canonical correlation design is useful, particularly for this topic of investigation. However, we also suggest applying such a design for other topics in which two sets of manifest variables are theoretically symmetrically associated. We also believe that "travelling with Gifi" has contributed to the theory of measurement by demonstrating the usefulness of explicit considerations of different scalings. Furthermore, we have provided a more robust test of our findings by comparing three countries. We have seen that the associations between cultural consumption and social position are relatively similar across these countries. This result is well in line with the conclusion of Falk and Katz-Gerro (2015) regarding cultural behaviour: "There is surprisingly little variation in the influence of education and income across countries". It is also in line with other comparative studies mentioned by Coulangeon and Duval (2015) and Lebaron and Le Roux (2015), which also show fairly similar strengths of homology between social and cultural spaces across different national contexts. In the case studied here, our approach is more appropriate, given Bourdieu's homology hypothesis and the theoretical definition of social space.

The canonical correlation analysis is also a general analytical and methodological approach that is independent of researchers' choice of scaling. The Gifi framework integrates different strategies for variable transformations within each model. In line with the usual rules of empirical research, we emphasize this framework as being flexible and allowing researchers to decide which method to use, given the characteristics and properties of the data.

This discussion can be framed in a more general debate on the links between methods and results. For example, some researchers have argued that the MCA method allows social scientists to find a particular category of results and to "discover" otherwise invisible phenomena. In this context, Philippe Cibois (1981, our translation) recalls a very illuminating quote of Jean-Paul Benzecri, the "father" of the correspondence analysis method: "[if we make such analyses], it is in the hope of discovering the very axes of a truly existing equilibrium in the world (...), we aspire to discover the hidden properties placed higher in the natural hierarchy of causes than those that are obvious". By opposition, the use of a broad range of models, like in the Gifi framework, puts this discussion on a more empirical level by testing the results of alternatives and judging them by using a relation between explanation and complexity. In this line, we would argue in favour of pragmatism when choosing the most appropriate methodological design, given the theoretical ambition, the data and their measurements.

Appendix

Table 23.5 Variables and number of categories, by country

Switzerland		France		Norway	
N	2442	N	3744	N	1005
Income	5	Education	6	Status	6
Education	6	Status	6	Education	10
Status	6	Income	6	Income	6
TV	4	TV	4	TV	5
Books	5	Books	3	Books	3
Library	5	Library	4	Library	3
Movies	5	Movies	4	Movies	4
Theatre	3	Theatre	4	Theatre	3
Ballet	2	Ballet	4	Ballet	3
Opera	4	Opera	3	Concert	3
Concert	4	Concert	4	Opera	2
Art exhibition	4	Art exhibition	4	Art exhibition	3
Museum	3	Museum	4	Museum	3

References

Bennett, T., Bustamante, M., & Frow, J. (2015). The Australian space of lifestyles in comparative perspective. In P. Coulangeon & J. Duval (Eds.), *The Routledge companion to Bourdieu's distinction*. London: Routledge.

Birkelund, G. E., & Lemel, Y. (2013). Lifestyles and social stratification: An explorative study of France and Norway. *Comparative Social Research, 30*, 189–220.

Bourdieu, P. (1984). *Distinction: A social critique of the judgement of taste*. London: Routledge & Keagan Paul.

Bourdieu, P. (1985). The social space and the genesis of groups. *Theory and Society, 14*, 723–744.

Bourdieu, P. (1991). First lecture. Social space and symbolic space: Introduction to a Japanese reading of distinction. *Poetics Today, 12*, 627–638.

Chan, T. W. (Ed.). (2010). *Social status and cultural consumption*. Cambridge: Cambridge University Press.

Chan, T. W., & Goldthorpe, J. H. (2007). Social stratification and cultural consumption: The visual arts in England. *Poetics, 35*, 168–190.

Chan, T. W., Birkelund, G. E., Aas, A. K., & Wiborg, Ø. (2011). Social status in Norway. *European Sociological Review, 27*, 451–468.

Cibois, P. (1981). Analyse des données et sociologie. *L'Année sociologique, 31*, 333–348.

Coulangeon, P., & Duval, J. (2015). *The Routledge companion to Bourdieu's distinction*. London: Routledge.

Cousteaux, A. S., & Lemel, Y. (2004). *Etude de l'homophilie socioprofessionnelle à travers l'enquête contacts* (CREST Working Paper, 2004–2010).

Cox, T. F., & Cox, M. A. A. (1994). *Multidimensional Scaling*. London: Chapman and Hall.

De Leeuw, J. (1984). The Gifi system of nonlinear multivariate analysis. *Data Analysis and Informatics III*, 415–424.

Falk, M., & Katz-Gerro, T. (2015). Cultural participation in Europe: Can we identify common determinants? *Journal of Cultural Economics, 40*(2), 127–162.

Frie, K. G., & Janssen, C. (2009). Social inequality, lifestyles and health – A non-linear canonical correlation analysis based on the approach of Pierre Bourdieu. *International Journal of Public Health, 54*, 213–221.

Gifi, A. (1990). *Nonlinear multivariate analysis*. Hoboken: Wiley.

Gittins, R. (1985). *Canonical analysis. A review with applications in ecology*. Berlin: Springer.

Joye, D., & Chevillard, J. (2011). Identités, inégalités et changement social: les enjeux de la mesure. In C. Burton-Jeangros & C. Maeder (Eds.), *Identité et transformation des modes de vie. Identität und Wandel der Lebensformen* (pp. 184–207). Zurich: Seismo.

Lebaron, & Leroux (Eds.). (2015). *La méthodologie de Pierre Bourdieu en action. Espace culturel, espace social et analyse des données*. Paris: Dunod.

Levine, M. S. (1977). *Canonical analysis and factor comparison*. Beverly Hills/London/New Delhi: Sage.

Peterson, R. A. (1992). Understanding audience segmentation: From elite and mass to omnivore and Univore. *Poetics, 21*, 243–258.

Prieur, A., Rosenlund, L., & Skjott-Larsen, J. (2008). Cultural capital today: A case study from Denmark. *Poetics, 36*, 45–71.

Rosenlund, L. (2015). Working with distinction: Scandinavian experiences. In P. Coulangeon & J. Duval (Eds.), *The Routledge companion to Bourdieu's distinction*. London: Routledge.

Van der Heijden, P. G. M., & Sijtsma, K. (1996). Fifty years of measurement and scaling in the Dutch social sciences. *Statistica Neerlandica, 50*(1), 111–135.

Chapter 24
Habitus as the "Third Layer": Qualitative Data Analysis by Habitus Analysis

Heinrich Wilhelm Schäfer, Leif-Hagen Seibert, and Adrián Tovar Simoncic

Introduction: A Third Layer

What is it that the concept of habitus has in common with models of the social space and of fields of praxis? Pierre Bourdieu gives a glimpse of an answer to this question in a chapter of *Distinction* pivotal to the development of his social space model. Constructing a model of a social space of lifestyles, he writes, is like superimposing transparent sheets of the diagram of social conditions on another one of lifestyles. "Finally, between the two previous diagrams one ought to insert a third, presenting the theoretical space of habitus, that is, of the generative formulae (. . .) which underlie each of the classes of practices and properties (. . .)" (Bourdieu 2010: 120).

One "ought to insert" a structured set of markers that represents the generative cognitive, emotional, and bodily processes of perception, judgment, and action by which actors, individually or collectively, transform their experiences in specific social conditions into visible lifestyles, proclaimed identities, and appropriate strategies. Coherent with his wider social theory, Bourdieu conceives of the habitūs of actors as structured generative processes that articulate the distribution of goods and opportunities with the attitudes and capabilities of social actors. Indeed, following the above quoted text, and with regard to a model of the social space – or of a field – one can conceive the habitūs of the actors as such a "third layer". Bourdieu makes

Electronic supplementary material The online version of this chapter (https://doi.org/10.1007/978-3-030-15387-8_24) contains supplementary material, which is available to authorized users.

H. W. Schäfer (✉) · L.-H. Seibert · A. Tovar Simoncic
Center for the Interdisciplinary Research on Religion and Society (CIRRuS), Bielefeld University, Bielefeld, Germany
e-mail: heinrich.schaefer@uni-bielefeld.de; leif.seibert@uni-bielefeld.de; atovar@uni-bielefeld.de

© Springer Nature Switzerland AG 2019
J. Blasius et al. (eds.), *Empirical Investigations of Social Space*,
Methodos Series 15, https://doi.org/10.1007/978-3-030-15387-8_24

the insertion of the habitūs into geometric models of social relations a desideratum for praxeological sociology. Notwithstanding, in his further methodological work, Bourdieu concentrates on field and space analyses (Bourdieu 1996, 2010), while developing the concept of habitus from a predominantly theoretical perspective (Bourdieu 1990, 2000). He does not develop a methodological approach to the habitus, nor does he insert the "third layer" into the models of fields and space.

HabitusAnalysis is the attempt to do so. As a method for qualitative data analysis that tries to operationalize the crux of Bourdieu's theoretical underpinnings on habitus theory, HabitusAnalysis serves as a sociological tool for the reconstruction of empirical habitūs from ordinary language texts (such as interviews) by modeling them as logical networks of dispositions.

The initial idea and the corresponding models, which we will discuss in this article, were developed during field research on religious movements in counter-insurgency warfare (Schäfer, Central America, 1980s). In wartime, the differences and antagonisms between social, political, and military positions has a strong impact on individuals. Thus, it became immediately obvious that the – then state of the art – phenomenological and subjectivistic approach (Berger and Luckmann 1966) was not adequate, since it did not account for the nexus between cognitive schemes and social context. In contrast, the concept of habitus as developed in *Esquisse d'une théorie de la pratique* grasps precisely this nexus and therefore was developed further (Schäfer 2005; Schäfer et al. 2015a, b).

We take a decidedly relationist approach to praxeology, which links Habitus-Analysis to the logic of Bourdieu's models of social relations in general. Thus, with regard to Bourdieu's desideratum of a "third layer," we see the following opportunities to integrate HabitusAnalysis with models of social conditions and lifestyles: HabitusAnalysis provides insights into the networks of dispositions of actors clustered in models of social space or fields; HabitusAnalysis functions as an explorative technique clustering actors of similar dispositions, even taking into account membership of multiple groups or institutions. Network models of cognitive dispositions provide the actors' perspective on the different fields of praxis they are involved in or, at least, affected by. Thus, the models serve for comparison with the sociologists' construction of social differentiation.

First, we will interpret the habitus as a network of dispositions. Second, we develop corresponding models for the schemes of the practical sense: the praxeological square and the network. Third, we sketch these models, which relate dispositional networks with the positions these actors occupy in different fields and in the overall social distribution of opportunities and constraints.

Habitus as Network of Dispositions

Two philosophical sources of Bourdieu's theory of meaning are pivotal for the epistemological premises of HabitusAnalysis (Schäfer 2015a): First, Cassirer's relationist concept of perceptional schemes enables an understanding of habitual operations as *logical series*, combined according to the practical logic of a given actor. Second, Wittgenstein underscores the instrumental character of linguistic signals, and their use in propositions and in life-forms, so as to highlight the constitutive role of context for meaning.

In consequence, praxeological research on language is not interested in words (in the sense of universal semantics) but in the meaning of natural language utterances for the actors involved. From the actors' perspective, the *relation* between their experiences and their interpretations of these experiences is what produces meaning – whereby 'interpretation' is not conceived of as an intellectual exercise but as the mainly unconscious operation of habitualized dispositions: "Social reality exists, so to speak, twice, in things and in minds, in fields and in habitus, outside and inside of agents" (Bourdieu and Wacquant 1992: 127). For social actors, the connections between "telling things" and "practical signs" (Schäfer 2015a: 175ff.) are the transformative operations generated between "things and signs" by dispositions of perception, judgment, and action. Already habitualized experiences take the shape of perceptional and axiological schemes that interpret new experiences, sometimes confirming the settled structure, sometimes changing it.

The aspects of habitus theory significant for our approach are the following. First and foremost, the concept of habitus denotes a vast cognitive (emotional and bodily) network of dispositions or 'schemes' (Cassirer, Bourdieu) of perception, judgment, and action orientation. Bourdieu repeatedly highlights the *ars combinatoria* of the habitus, which generates "an infinity of practices adapted to endlessly changing situations" (Bourdieu 1977: 16, 20) with a relatively small number of schemes. Such "transformational schemes" operate in relation to and between "diverse fields of practice" with a "'fuzzy' logic of approximation" (Bourdieu 1977: 122). From these ideas, Bourdieu proceeds to what he calls a "dispositionalist theory" of the habitus (Bourdieu 2017). While he does not elaborate in detail on a relational and fuzzy dispositional "composition" of habitus, he nevertheless posits a dispositional "deconstruction" of the concept of habitus in *Logic of Practice*. He describes practical logic and with it the dispositions of habitūs as fuzzy, flexible, only partially logical networks of semantic oppositions (Bourdieu 1990: 267–269).

Our understanding of the habitus as a network of dispositions stems from this approach (as well as, to a certain extent, from Max Weber's concept of *Sinnzusammenhang*, 1978: 9). The notion of a network of semantic oppositions – and dispositions – highlights a research experience that can be made during the structured analysis of a given text. Texts like interviews or sermons include both references to experiences and the ascription of interpretative terms to these experiences; they reveal positive and negative value judgments; and – above all and almost by themselves – the relations between semantic terms extend into vast networks of meaning related to any field of praxis relevant for the respective interviewee. This can be taken as sufficient reason for developing a theory of *identity as a network* (Schäfer 2005, 2015b), based upon a relational theory of the habitus as a simultaneously individual and collective network of dispositions. (Lahire (2011), on the other hand, opts for an individualist approach.)

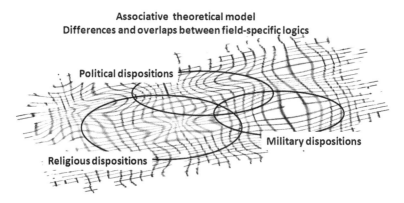

Fig. 24.1 Network of dispositions

As depicted in our purely associative theoretical model (Fig. 24.1), we conceive of cognitive dispositions that organize experiences and interpretations as
linked together in networks composed of logical (albeit fuzzy) relations between
(semantic) terms. The dispositions in the network combine experience and its
interpretation according to different but partly overlapping fields relevant for the
actors (exemplified in Fig. 24.1 by politics, the military, and religion). The networks
include both dense and scattered areas, which correspond to more or less knowledge,
or more or less intensely held convictions. The frayed fringes in the model represent
the openness and lasting incompleteness of dispositional networks.

It is necessary to treat the schemes of perception, judgment, and action orientation as operators with an "infinite yet strictly limited generative capacity" (Bourdieu
1990: 55). Instead of the ready-made *opus operatum*, the *modus operandi* is of
interest, but it can only be reconstructed by way of the *opus operatum*. We regard the
interest in modes of operation as a crucial trait of praxeological theory in general.
Even in his early work (1977: 97), Bourdieu states that praxis always "implies a
cognitive operation" that transforms the experience of "practical functions" into
"systems of classification (taxonomies)", which, for their part, "organize perception
and structure practice." "[S]chemes of perception, appreciation, and action," are
formed by this process of production, which in turn "function as practical operators"
of further production of meaning and practices.

In consequence, Bourdieu understands these schemes as "instruments of cognition and communication which are the precondition for the establishment of meaning and the consensus on meaning." Habitus is thought of not as a fixed cognitive
structure but as a generator of meaning through the ever-changing combination of
experiences with cognitive dispositions. The semantic terms ascribed to experiences
are conceived of as operating agents: A word works like a lever, Wittgenstein would
say. Semantic terms operate by integrating elemental experiences (like military
violence) into the complex of embodied experience (dispositions of the habitus)
that serve for interpretation (like an apocalyptic belief in the imminent end of the
world), thus transforming both elemental experiences and the complex of experience

present in the dispositions (the habitus), and consequently generating a new concept of the elemental experience (violence as an apocalyptic sign).

First, we distinguish analytically between semantic terms according to the different relations in which they 'labor': the reference to experiences and the production of interpretation – both, in mutual relation, generate meaning. These relations can be modeled as transformations in the model of the praxeological square, a model of an *opus operatum* that facilitates reconstruction of the *modus operandi* of meaning generation (see below). Second, we also distinguish between dispositions and schemes (Schäfer 2015a: 116ff.).

Bourdieu uses both terms with slight differences. We distinguish clearly, and understand "schemes of practical sense" to be dispositions that have become manifest in speech and action. 'Disposition' refers to the latent state of schemes; 'scheme' refers to the manifest state of dispositions. We can empirically reconstruct schemes by analyzing and modeling the observable utterances and practices of the respective actors. The results of the reconstruction allow us to draw conclusions about the dispositions of these actors. This knowledge facilitates not only the empirical reconstruction of the *modus operandi* of the embodied structures that relate experience and interpretation to each other; it also allows a very fine-grained assessment of the practical operations between the dispositions of the actors and the social positions of the actors in the dynamics of different fields and the social space.

Models of Dispositions: The Sense for Praxis

Our two models for cognitive schemes, the praxeological square and the network, can be triangulated with two other models for positions: fields and the social space. In this article, we put the emphasis on cognitive schemes (i.e. the manifest dispositions). The dispositional models we outline here will

- address the cognitive schemes as structured practical operators that transform an actor's experience of social conditions into cognitive orientation;
- distinguish between (but not separate) experience and interpretation, positive and negative evaluations,
- reconstruct the generation of meaning (as identity and strategies) through the relations that the labor of language, by means of cognitive operators, establishes between complex experiences and clear-cut judgments and value ascriptions;
- be suitable for situating these processes within a sociological framework that does justice to the social conditions of complex societies, modeled e.g. as positions in fields and the social space or as relations of symbolic power and violence.

Our basic model is that of the praxeological square. The network iterates the square by homologous schemes, which means that it is possible to link multiple praxeological squares according to logical rules; once connected, an isomorphism between different squares in the same network highlights semantic homologies in the underlying empirical material.

The Praxeological Square

The model of the praxeological square is the core tool of HabitusAnalysis. Based upon the insight that "the real is relational" (Bourdieu), the praxeological square arranges qualitative data by logical relations in a classical format based upon the square of oppositions from propositional logic (Apuleius: *Peri hermeneias* V, in Londey and Johanson 1987: 87ff.). Thus, the square serves as a formal frame to analyze the utterances of actors as practical operators according to the way in which they are logically interconnected, thus highlighting the relational nature of the dispositions underlying these expressions (Schäfer 2003: 229). However, we do not suppose that each and every operation involved in generating perception, judgment, and action can be modeled by the praxeological square and the network. We only consider that, in the framework of praxeological theory, some important operations certainly can be. The model is based upon the following assumptions: Social actors' perceptions, judgments, and actions can be understood by their underlying positive and negative value ascriptions, as well as the distinction between experience and interpretation in a very general sense. This simple observation already leads to four terms: negative experience, positive experience, interpretation of negative experience, and interpretation of positive experience. In the tradition of logic, a model of four terms, based on Aristotle and compiled by Apuleius, has been used to organize propositions according to four forms of opposition: subalterns, contraries, sub-contraries, and contradictories (tacitly including a fifth: equivalence).

These basic relations are culturally universal since they organize fundamental logical relations; in any culture people know that rain *implies* wet streets (subaltern opposition), friendly and unfriendly behavior are *different* (subcontrary opposition), and in real darkness, there is *no* light (contrary opposition). The syllogistic square was handed down in two different lines of tradition to medieval philosophy, where it served as an important tool for logics and the organization of propositions, as well as being an indispensible part of philosophical propaedeutics (Fig. 24.2).

We follow the classical model and focus on the logic of *propositions* (Bochenski 1961: §24.29). From this point of view, the praxeological square as presented below facilitates insights into the regularities of cognitive transformations in individual and collective actors (Schäfer 2009: 6), as well as into the processes of transformation from perception, through judgment, to action (Schäfer 2005: 267), and finally – by the square's transformation into a network –into the 'cognitive maps' of the actors.

Propositions and terms: From a praxeological perspective, it is simply not sufficient to restrict the analysis of interviews to a model that relies on formal combinations of concepts and their negation (e.g. masculine/non-masculine, feminine/non-feminine). Instead, propositions or 'judgments' – composed of a subject and an attribute (predicate) – and syllogistic transformations bind elemental signs into complex expressions (see Fig. 24.3 in comparison to Fig. 24.2). In consequence, the terms of the square can be reconstructed with much more semantic content; that is, not just concepts but propositions and their equivalences (Fig. 24.6). Moreover, all terms in the praxeological square are aligned with contextual logical properties beyond their intrinsic meaning.

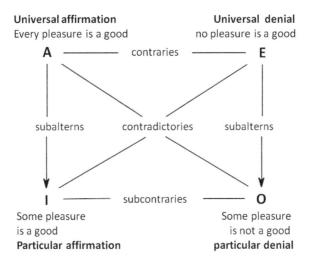

Traditional propositional square

Universal affirmation
Every pleasure is a good

Universal denial
no pleasure is a good

A ——————— contraries ——————— E

subalterns   contradictories   subalterns

I ——————— subcontraries ——————— O

Some pleasure
is a good
Particular affirmation

Some pleasure
is not a good
particular denial

Fig. 24.2 Logical relations

Experience and interpretation

Axis of clear-cut judgments

Interpretation
(positive)
PI

Interpretation
(negative)
NI

Positive
Experience
PE

Negative
Experience
NE

Axis of complex contexts of action

——————▶ = Implication   ▬ ▬ ▬ ▬ = Sub-contrariness
——————— = Contrariness   ◆———◆ = Contradiction

Fig. 24.3 Praxeological square: logical relations

In consequence, the relations between the terms can be understood as operations that generate practical meaning. In this context, the distinction between universal ("every pleasure . . .") and partial propositions ("some pleasure . . .") becomes a useful systematic distinction between the reference to complex and always specific experiences, and to the interpretative categories that structure these experiences according to clear-cut categorical value judgments, and even names. Thus, the axis of universal affirmation versus universal denial can be treated as the axis of interpretation, where only one of both can be true; whereas the axis of particular judgments can be treated as axis of experience, where both experiences may be true. Similarly, the logical notions of affirmation and negation are adopted as positive and negative evaluations. Thus, we take the step from logics to socio-logics by applying the model to natural language in practical contexts. By making the model praxeological, it becomes socio-logical. As a result of this adaptation to a sociological logic, we obtain four terms that the corresponding propositions uttered by a given actor may be ascribed to: negative experience (NE), positive experience (PE), negative interpretation (NI), and positive interpretation (PI).

Terms and relations: For the following, it is important to realize that the arrangement of terms in these four positions (NE, PE, NI, PI) is a technical shorthand for propositional properties derived from the context in which the terms are used; logical quality (negation vs. affirmation) translates into negative and positive evaluation, logical quantity (particular vs. universal) derives from the difference between experience and interpretation. For instance, the subaltern relation (PI, PE) can be read as follows: Both affirmations PI and PE, (and both negations NI and NE) appear in such a relation to each other that the universal affirmation is a condition of the partial affirmation. Thus, for our model construction, the relation of subalternity can be understood as implication: A (true) clear cut judgment implies a certain position in complex social relations. Moreover, the schemes between NE and PI can be interpreted as a characteristic way of making sense out of negative experiences. Likewise, the transformation between PE and NI indicates strategic perspectives.

Empirically, the logical relations capture syntactic (syntagmatic) relations. Theoretically, these relations represent schemes of perception, judgment, and action orientation. Methodologically, the relations serve a double purpose. First, they constitute meaning by means of relation. Second, they enable the tagging of logical relations with semantic content. The social meaning of the term 'poverty' (constituted by its use) is completely different in the following two examples: It is one thing if an actor sees the reasons for 'poverty' (NE) in the "greed of *latifundistas (owner of large estates or ranches)*" (NI) (relation: 'exploitation') and contrasts it with the utopia of a 'society without classes' (PI) (R: 'abolition of poverty'). It is another social reality if an actor sees the cause of 'poverty' (NE) in the 'approaching end of the world' (NI) (R: 'divine lawfulness') and contrasts it with the hope for a 'rapture into heaven' (PI) (R: 'withdrawal from the world'). In the first case, the actor most probably 'goes into the mountains' (i.e. joins the guerrilla) (PE); in the second case, the actor prepares for the rapture by 'church attendance' (PE).

Relations and semantics: For relational qualitative sociology, the structure of the square conveys various benefits. First, it provides a formal structure in which the practical semantics of given actors can emerge without the interference of any content premeditated by the researcher. The model of the square is a theoretically and methodologically justified matrix for establishing and arranging the semantic contents used by the actors. As the model is extremely open (only basic logical connectors), the input of semantic contents is not predetermined by, for instance, the questions of an interviewer regarding certain semantic content. Hence, through a strongly inductive procedure, the terms of the square are 'filled' with content uttered by the actors.

This means, second, that the formal model serves as an instrument for the "epistemological break" and the "construction of the object" Bourdieu et al. (1991: 13ff.; see also Wacquant, Chap. 2, in this volume),[1] avoiding a naïve identification of the scientific view with social reality. It is the very abstractness and formality of the model that enables its use *as a model*, avoiding the temptations of mimesis. Third, it provides terms (PI, NE . . .) that address basic human modes of cognitively categorizing experiences. Fourth, the relations between terms enable two further analytical operations: As formal relations, fixed by the logic of the square, they facilitate conclusions on the effective meaning of the relation between two terms (e.g. NE 'poverty', PI 'rapture'). Beyond formal logical connections, it is possible to tag relations with semantic content according to syntagmatic relations and similar cognitive associations (syntagmatic linkage, verbs, conjunctions, ...).

Transformation and meaning: The sociologically most fruitful adaptation of propositional logic to modeling may be generative transformations (Fig. 24.5). To sociological observers, the relations modeled by the square give an account of the deep transformational structure that operates between an actor's experiences and their interpretations. The logical operation to proceed from A to B passes by Non-A. From PE, one has to pass by NI in order to end up in NE (examples below). Given the fact that the terms of the square are linked by logical relations, the relations serve to describe the transformational path. From a sociological point of view, these are not simply logical relations in a universe of abstract semantic terms (as in Greimas 1983). Rather, the relations of the square – in their formality, as well as when they are semantically tagged – serve to systematically capture basic syntagmatic transformations and the generation of practical meaning (in the pragmatist, Wittgensteinian, and Bourdieusian sense).

The praxeological square is an observational model that reveals the transformations of the practical logic that prevail in the deep structures of natural language (e.g. interviews or other genres of texts), and thus provides insight regarding the *modus operandi* of the practical sense of given actors. It serves to model basic operations of "*the internalization of externality and the externalization of internality*" (Bourdieu 1977: 72, emphasis in original) with regard to any kind of social actor. The strictly formal operation of the model makes it widely applicable, allowing the contents (semantics, practices) relevant for the specific collective or individual actor under scrutiny to emerge. Over the following pages, we transform the logical structure into a model of cognitive and finally of sociological operations (see Fig. 24.4).

Cognitive operations: *perception and action orientation*. Bourdieu often mentions the triad of perception, judgment, and action – a notion that invites methodological formalization. In a first step we narrow our focus to examine cognitive

---

[1] If one considers the German tradition of hermeneutics, the square is a methodological instrument to solve the problem of preconceptions (Gadamer 2006); however, Gadamer himself does not consider the problem to have been solved by this method.

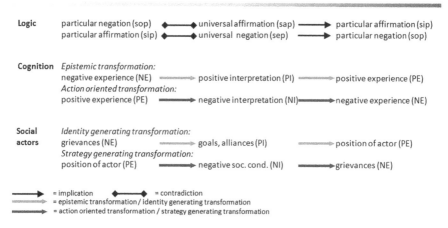

Fig. 24.4 Praxeological square: transformation from logic to socio-logic

operations. With regard to the cognitive operations modeled by the square (and the network), there are two transformations of special interest: We can call them epistemic and action-oriented transformations. We conceive of the epistemic transformation as an operation by which actors perceive and evaluate problems (NE), counter them with their own ideals (PI), and thus derive their self-image (PE). The epistemic transformation enables the reconstruction of the positions the actors themselves take within their experiential contexts. From there, the action-oriented operation that facilitates strategic action can be observed. Action-orientation depends on the self-positioning of an actor; from their own position (PE), the actors are modeled with reference to causes of negative experience. From this evaluation, they are modeled to deduce opportunities of action to cope with their problems (NI), and to orientate their action according to their goals (PI). Interpretation and experience are combined in such a way that the meaning of experiences is elaborated by clear-cut judgment, and the effective meaning of interpretation is constituted by its relation to the complex context of experiences and action (see Fig. 24.5).

Social operations: *Identity and strategy.* The decisive step from propositional logics to sociology is taken by modeling the generation of identity and strategy (see Fig. 24.5). The square allows us to model the generation of a collective identity in the following way: The terms of NE can be understood as perceived crises or grievances. Social movements or groups counter their grievances with a programmatic goal (PI), thus generating a meaningful relation between negative experiences and projections of a positive alternative. From these factors, the movement or group derives its own position in relation to the crisis (PE in sub-contrary relation to NE).

Strategy generation is taken into account in the model by two relations. Primarily, this is the complementary transformation to identity generation: From its own position, a movement or group analyzes the reasons for its grievances, such as "neg-

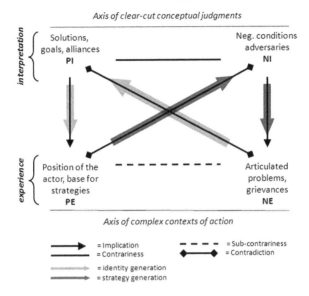

Fig. 24.5 Praxeological square: social actors in general

ative social conditions, adversaries" (NI), and fights the grievances by addressing their cause (PE, NI, NE). The second relation models teleological motivation: The terms of PI (read as 'solutions, goals, alliances') can be understood as perceived opportunities and goals towards which the action of the collective actor (PE) is directed. Correspondingly, the model allows for a systematic empirical integration of identity and strategy-oriented approaches to collective action. Moreover, the model allows us to distinguish between clear-cut judgments (level of interpretation), which are helpful for the mobilization of a movement, and the complex contexts of action, enabling both the practical implementation of judgments and, usually, their relativization.

Thus, the model can be read as a process by which social actors position themselves within their social context. Actors articulate grievances, imagine and formulate solutions, and affirm their position. The model allows us to reconstruct the process of interpretation through which the actors cognitively elaborate their experiences, making clear-cut judgments in order to position themselves in their fields of action and generate an *identity* as a social actor. The actors also are described as developing *strategies* to cope with the 'structural conditions' and 'adversaries' that cause their 'grievances' – while 'solutions' and 'adversaries' model the notions of opportunities and constraints. The model does not exclude the possibility of strategic calculus – but it excludes the illusion that calculi are free from contingent (habitual) dispositions. It thus articulates schemes of perception and judgment as conditions for the design of strategies that allow conclusions regarding dispositions.

Data: The data needed for HabitusAnalysis are both qualitative and quantitative. The analysis of the practical sense according to the logic of the praxeological square and the network focuses on utterances of the actors. Taking into account the specific hermeneutic dynamics of different genres of texts (political discourses, religious sermons, Twitter communications, website texts etc.), virtually every natural language product may be analyzed. However, the best source is habitus interviews: These begin with an open biographic narrative, as a warm-up, leading into a freely developed account. The second part follows the transformational logic of the square by combining questions about experiences with those regarding interpretation.

All questions avoid any semantic content possibly relevant for the interviews, but are strictly formal in terms of negative and positive experience and its interpretation. For instance, "What do you experience as particularly negative in our world [this society]?" (NE) is followed by "What do you think causes the negative things you referred to?" (NI), and so forth for PI and PE. Hence, the interviewees can fill in whatever semantic content they consider relevant. Follow-up questions may enlarge upon any thematic field the research project is investigating. "What do members of your political party (movement, institution, neighborhood initiative, labor union . . .) think causes the problems . . . ", etc.

Example: *Religious praxis.* Although we designed our models to be applied mutatis mutandis to any kind of social actors and conditions, after our highly abstract introduction we will now present empirical examples from the field of research we have examined the most: religion, and more specifically the Pentecostal movement in conditions of counter-insurgency war in Guatemala in 1985/86. During this period, Guatemala was extremely polarized in terms of the distribution of economic and cultural capital, as well as in terms of opportunities of action in the face of a very violent counter-insurgency campaign. Both religious groupings sketched here are rooted in US-American Pentecostalism, and they use the same religious-symbolic repertoire. However, the reconstruction by means of the model reveals that each cluster of actors develops a completely different practical logic out of an identical stock of religious symbols. By localizing the clusters of different religious practical logics in the social space according to the economic and cultural capital held by their members, we see that a social divide exists which mirrors this symbolic distinction.

Since we have already explained the formal operations of our model we will only contrast the results for both groups: the lower class Pentecostals (so-called "classical Pentecostals") and the upper-middle class and upper class ("Neopentecostals").

For the lower class Pentecostals (Fig. 24.6), the experiences of economic misery, repression, and war cumulate in a sensation of having lost all opportunities for a better future (NE). Their religious response is apocalyptic; they hope for the rapture of their Church to heaven (PI), thus negating their current grievances (NE), and simultaneously laying the symbolic base for a collective identity in preparation for the rapture (by attendance, prayer, communitarian solidarity etc. – PE). From this point of view (PE), the very cause for their grievances is also seen in the end of the world drawing near (NI). The strategic consequence is to withdraw into the religious group, ignoring worldly issues like politics or social commitments. The effect of

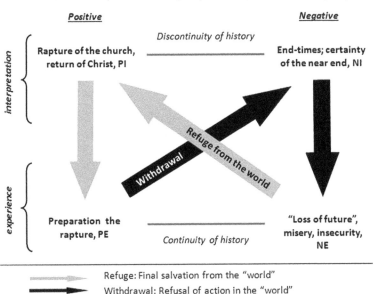

Fig. 24.6 Classical Pentecostals – Guatemala 1985

this practical logic in the context of a counter-insurgency war is survival without losing self-esteem. The discontinuity of imagined history facilitates the continuity of experienced history.

In contrast, the Neopentecostals (Fig. 24.7) in the urban modernizing upper-middle class suffered from economic decline and increasing public violence, accompanied by symptoms such as alcoholism and bulimia – in short, a sense of a generalized threat (NE) to the power these actors had acquired during the 1970s as a result of their swift upward mobility. Their religious response is the recourse to the power of God in the Holy Spirit (PI). For example, God's power incorporates itself in the believers in ecstatic sessions. Thus, the believers understand themselves as individuals empowered (PE) by both spiritual and social capabilities, for instance miracles and self-discipline, respectively. The threat to power (NE) is interpreted as caused by demons (NI), acting through the competitors of these modernizing social climbers, such as unionists, guerrillas, indigenous people, and some politicians. Hence, exorcism, the exclusion of the competing other, is the favored strategy for problem-solving in virtually all areas of life. The central issue at stake is not history but power: While the struggle for power is continuously experienced in society, the religious interpretation generates believers who are confident in God's victory over their own foes.

Since the square condenses the results of detailed semantic analyses into four quintessential positions, it may seem too austere to model the wide array of cognitive dispositions. Therefore, one can use the analytic material stored in the quintessential propositions to construct a more fine-grained (and thus less condensed) network model of linguistic operators.

Upper middle class (relatively high cultural capital)

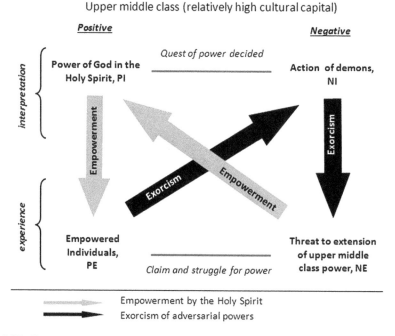

Fig. 24.7 Neopentecostalism – Guatemala 1985

The Praxeological Network

Modeling a network of cognitive operators is an attempt at a methodological operationalization of Bourdieu's theoretical remarks on dispositional networks (see Sect. 24.2). As such, a praxeological network is constructed by unfolding the analytically condensed content of a given square into a large number of interconnected squares.[2] It represents a reconstructed 'mental map' of the actors in question. It is important to note that such a network preserves all properties of the square: the references to experience and interpretation in careful distinction, the production of meaning by linguistic transformations between terms, as well as the

---

[2]The process of unfolding originates from a *central* square (see Fig. 24.7). Its centrality is, methodologically, the result of the frequency of iterations in the analyzed corpus of texts of the practical-logical scheme it models. Theoretically, centrality relates here to the distinction between 'secondary' and 'main/central' oppositions (Bourdieu 1990: 269–270). Nonetheless, one should be aware here of two things. First, we stress again a statement of Bourdieu's quoted above, that "in practice only one sector of a system of schemes is mobilized at a time" (Bourdieu 1990: 269); second, we emphasize that every interview practice is prone to bias depending on which sector is mobilized, if only by the knowledge of the interviewee of the research topic. Alternatively, it is of course also possible to reconstruct many single squares, for instance with different thematic foci, and to combine them later. See Online Appendix 1 for an exemplary network graph.

generation of identities and strategies. However, all these operations are now visible in a way that allows detailed assessments with regard to different linguistic domains or fields of praxis, as the case may be.

A network of dispositions models the embodied vision of social divisions – the actors' view of the different fields of praxis relevant for them and the dispositions of perception, judgment, and action orientation these actors consider appropriate to different fields: e.g. prosperity versus laziness for economic relations. Hence, a praxeological network also serves to model the transpositions (Bourdieu calls it "reconversion" 2010: 119ff.) of embodied schemes of perception, judgment, and action from one field to another – e.g. making plausible a strategy of exorcism as a response counter-insurgency warfare, even when, as in Guatemala, it involves the use of napalm.

Dense and scattered areas of the network indicate more or less reliable schemes of convictions and action, respectively, and also indicate stronger or weaker levels of significance for the identity of the actor. Since different areas of the cognitive network are shown as related to determinate areas of social experience – that is, to different fields of praxis – the embeddedness of the embodied processing of experience in objectified structures may be reconstructed with more specificity.

Models of Positions: The Conditions of Praxis

In order to complete the program of HabitusAnalysis, the analysis of practical sense (the dispositions of an actor) has to be complemented by an analysis of the objectified factors of praxis; these social structures were modeled by Bourdieu – in the context of stratification – as social space (mainly in *Distinction*), and – in the context of functional differentiation – as fields (in *Rules of Art*). Models of fields and of the social space are suitable for the projection of habitus-specific groups of actors onto corresponding positions in different distributional structures of diverse capitals. In our research, we consider this aspect mainly via the application of two models.

Fields: With regard to the struggles among experts in functionally differentiated fields, we draw upon Bourdieu's field of cultural production (Bourdieu 1993, 1996; Seibert 2010, 2018). We consider many traits of this construct to be helpful for modeling other fields as well. Bourdieu constructs the field of art as a two-dimensional model, with one axis representing *arrivée* (the achievement of eminence) and the other reflecting authenticity. Obviously, there are certain traits of this model that are characteristic for the arts; on the other hand, Bourdieu's two-dimensional design can be generalized to a certain degree.

Concerning organizations, *achievement of eminence* can be described as their complexity. In religion and in democratic politics, complexity may be understood as a logarithmic relationship between the performers and the audience of an organization. Our approach establishes a continuum between highly institutionalized organizations with large audiences and assemblies of activists without a passive audience as this first dimension.

Authenticity is a less objectively addressable notion, as it mostly stands for the image of being an agent of the 'true' arts, politics, or religion. The dimension thus revolves around the credibility of experts in the eyes of the public. In democracies, opinion polls serve as instruments to gauge the credibility of politicians. Similarly, for our research in religion, we determine the perceived authenticity of any given religious actor by randomized household surveys.

Located in a field model, the objective positions of different clusters of habitūs facilitate conclusions about functionally differentiated competitive dynamics that influence the identities and strategies of the actors in question.

Space: Alongside the triangulation of the models of the practical sense (square and network) with the model of differentiated competition, it is of analytical interest to examine the connection between the habitūs and the power structures of the social space. Hitherto, we have worked with simplified models of social space. This allowed for a heuristics of basic distributions of economic and cultural capital (see Schäfer 2015b). For our examples of churches in Guatemala, the distinction between the lower classes and the upper-middle and upper classes has proved of great benefit for understanding the bewildering differences in the religious practical sense of Pentecostals and Neopentecostals. Using just two socio-demographic variables is nothing more than an auxiliary construction with limited explanatory value; however, similar to the combination of HabitusAnalysis with a field model constructed via PCA, the combination of HabitusAnalysis with MCA promises to be very useful.

Conclusion: HabitusAnalysis as the Third Layer

HabitusAnalysis provides the data to insert a "third layer" between social structure and (life)styles. Thus, using HabitusAnalysis for an in-depth breakdown of the semantics that correspond to a specific societal position can significantly augment our understanding of the actors in question. However, it stands to reason that the successful amalgamation of HabitusAnalysis and MCA should provide even more research opportunities, because the results of the former are, in essence, well-grounded sets of categorical data that may in turn be used to inform the latter. For instance, each detected habitus formation – a set of different religious groups, political activists, occupational groups etc. – can be used as an active variable.

Thus, reconstructed sets of dispositions can be seen in correspondence with political inclination, gender, favorite media, etc. A more sophisticated and explorative approach could treat single terms (e.g. NE 'war' or NE 'crime') as categorical variables to study their distribution. This approach could be enhanced by transforming single *relations* of the square into categorical variables, such as the relation 'crime (NE) versus the law of God (PI)'. Here, one could look for the combination of an identity focusing on "law" with different political inclinations, and then examine whether the causal ascription to 'crime' varies for different actors ('NI = unjust social conditions' or 'NI = sin' or 'NI = bad character' etc.); if so, the expected strategies should also differ. Examples such as these show that, for the analysis of dispositions as a 'third layer' between social structures and styles, the combination of HabitusAnalysis with the sophisticated tools and techniques of MCA promises real innovation.

References

Berger, P. L., & Luckmann, T. (1966). *The social construction of reality. A treatise in the sociology of knowledge*. Garden City: Doubleday.

Bochenski, I. M. (1961). *A history of formal logic*. New York: Chelsea Pub.

Bourdieu, P. (1977). *Outline of a theory of practice*. Cambridge: Cambridge University Press.

Bourdieu, P. (1990). *The logic of practice*. Stanford: Stanford University Press.

Bourdieu, P. (1993). *The field of cultural production. Essays on art and literature*. New York: Columbia University Press.

Bourdieu, P. (1996). *The rules of art. genesis and structure of the literary field*. Stanford: Stanford University Press.

Bourdieu, P. (2000). *Pascalian meditations*. Stanford: Stanford University Press.

Bourdieu, P. (2010). *Distinction. A social critique of the judgement of taste*. London: Routledge.

Bourdieu, P. (2017). *Manet: A symbolic revolution*. Malden: Polity (forthcoming).

Bourdieu, P., & Wacquant, L. J. D. (1992). *An invitation to reflexive sociology*. Cambridge: Polity Press.

Bourdieu, P., Chamboredon, J. C., & Passeron, J. C. (1991). *The craft of sociology: Epistemological preliminaries*. Berlin: de Gruyter.

Gadamer, H. G. (2006). *Truth and method*. London: Continuum.

Greimas, A. J. (1983). *Structural semantics: An attempt at a method*. Lincoln: University of Nebraska Press.

Lahire, B. (2011). *The plural actor*. Cambridge/Malden: Polity Press.

Londey, D., & Johanson, C. (Eds.). (1987). *The logic of Apuleius. Including a complete Latin text and English translation of the Peri Hermeneias of Apuleius of Madaura*. Leiden: Brill.

Schäfer, H. W. (2003). *Zur Theorie von kollektiver Identität und Habitus am Beispiel sozialer Bewegungen. Eine Theoriestudie auf der Grundlage einer interkulturellen Untersuchung zweier religiöser Bewegungen*. Berlin: Humboldt Universität.

Schäfer, H. W. (2005). Identität als Netzwerk. Ein Theorieentwurf am Beispiel religiöser Bewegungen im Bürgerkrieg Guatemalas. *Berliner Journal für Soziologie, 15*(2), 259–282.

Schäfer, H. W. (2009). The praxeological square as a method for the intercultural study of religious movements. In S. Gramley & R. Schneider (Eds.), *Cultures in process: Encounter and experience* (pp. 5–19). Bielefeld: Aisthesis.

Schäfer, H. W. (2015a). *HabitusAnalysis, Vol. 1. Epistemology and language*. Wiesbaden: Springer VS.

Schäfer, H. W. (2015b). *Identität als Netzwerk. Habitus, Sozialstruktur und religiöse Mobilisierung*. Wiesbaden: Springer VS.

Schäfer, H. W., Seibert, L. H., Tovar Simoncic, A., & Köhrsen, J. (2015a). Towards a praxeology of religious life 1: Modes of observation. In F. Wijsen & K. von Stuckrad (Eds.), *Making religion: Theory and practice in the discursive study of religion* (pp. 147–171). Leiden: Brill.

Schäfer, H. W., Seibert, L. H., Tovar Simoncic, A., & Köhrsen, J. (2015b). Towards a praxeology of religious life 2: Tools of observation. In F. Wijsen & K. von Stuckrad (Eds.), *Making religion: Theory and Practice in the discursive study of religion* (pp. 175–202). Leiden: Brill.

Seibert, L. H. (2010). Glaubwürdigkeit als religiöses Vermögen: Grundlagen eines Feldmodells nach Bourdieu am Beispiel Bosnien-Herzegowinas. *Berliner Journal für Soziologie, 20*(1), 89–117.

Seibert, L. H. (2018). *Religious credibility under fire. A Praxeological analysis of the determinants of religious legitimacy in Postwar Bosnia and Herzegovina*. Wiesbaden: Springer VS.

Weber, M. (1978). *Economy and society: An outline of interpretive sociology*. Berkeley: University of California Press.

Chapter 25
Conclusion: State of the Art and Future of Bourdieusian Relational Methodology

Jörg Blasius, Frédéric Lebaron, Brigitte Le Roux, and Andreas Schmitz

More than 15 years after his passing, Pierre Bourdieu continues to be one of the most important figures in the field of social sciences. His oeuvre, his analytical concepts, and, his methods of conducting empirical research are still gaining in relevance. Much of this success, both within and outside the field of social sciences, can be traced back to the unique way Bourdieu combined (or rather: related) traditionally distinct scientific cultures and tools (such as spatial concepts and geometric data analysis, qualitative and quantitative techniques, as well as empirical and critical research, etc.).

With a great number of illustrative examples, this book covers a variety of investigations into social spaces and fields, exploring and understanding societal logics and dynamics within a common, elaborated analytical and methodological framework. The contributions discuss the conceptualization of social spaces and social fields, the intimately associated relational methodology, and the constitutive role of GDA as a method of objectifying social phenomena. A core aspect is Bourdieu's method of constructing social spaces and fields using Geometric Data Analysis (GDA), or in French *analyse des données*, an approach that was developed

J. Blasius (✉)
Institut für politische Wissenschaft und soziologie, University of Bonn, Bonn, Germany
e-mail: jblasius@uni-bonn.de

F. Lebaron
Department of Social Sciences, Ecole normale supérieure Paris-Saclay, Cachan, France
e-mail: frederic.lebaron@uvsq.fr

B. Le Roux
CRNS, Université Paris Descartes, Paris, France
e-mail: Brigitte.LeRoux@mi.parisdescartes.fr

A. Schmitz
Department of sociology, University of Bonn, Bonn, Germany
e-mail: andreas.schmitz@uni-bonn.de

© Springer Nature Switzerland AG 2019
J. Blasius et al. (eds.), *Empirical Investigations of Social Space*,
Methodos Series 15, https://doi.org/10.1007/978-3-030-15387-8_25

in the 1970s (Benzécri et col 1973; Le Roux and Rouanet 2010) for exploring large and complex data tables. GDA comprises several methods of multivariate data analysis, such as Simple and Multiple Correspondence Analysis (SCA, MCA), Principal Component Analysis (PCA), and Multiple Factor Analysis (MFA), which are important tools for the social sciences.

As the authors demonstrate throughout this book, GDA can be understood as a direct way of constructing multidimensional spaces that can be interpreted for example, to explore what the French call the "cloud of modalities", i.e. the visualization of the variable categories, and the "cloud of individuals", i.e. showing the locations of the individuals in the social space. Both the simplicity and homogeneity of the mathematical framework, derived from linear algebra, and the innovative tools of data visualization, based on structured data analysis, make GDA methods a powerful exploratory tool with a large variety of inferential and explanatory applications (Le Roux and Rouanet 2010). The authors of this edited volume make extensive use of this methodological approach of applying GDA as a means of field construction and field analysis. They also discuss further developments of GDA, other methods within Bourdieu's relational framework, and elaborations of concepts such as symbolic domination, social fields, habitus, and practice – which achieve their full analytical power when they are combined and applied relationally. Before we give an outlook, we offer a brief overview on the specific contributions of the authors and their particular analytical and methodical approaches that lead them to their insights.

Social Spaces

The opening section of the book (Section A) is on the theoretical conceptualization and construction of social spaces, class relations, and capital distributions. It starts with *Loïc Wacquant's* contribution; he argues that the analytical dyad of 'social space and symbolic power' is a more appropriate representation of Bourdieusian theory than the widespread triad of 'habitus, capital, and field'. By way of shifting from this triad to the dyad, this contribution yields a parsimonious analytical framework within which different relational concepts can be used, be it in terms of analytical or in terms of empirical research. While doing so, Wacquant also stresses that social spaces and social fields (as treated in section two of the book) are two sides of the same coin (cp. Schmitz et al. 2016).

Using specific Multiple Correspondence Analysis (specific MCA), a further development within the GDA framework that enables the handling of missing data without excluding the cases and without considering separate categories for them (for details, see Le Roux and Rouanet 2004, 2010, or for an alternative approach that has the same features, called subset MCA, Greenacrce and Pardo 2006), *Ida Lidegran, Mikael Börjesson, Donald Broady & Ylva Bergström* analyzed the field of elite education in Uppsala (Sweden). This technique allows the authors to empirically construct a space of the educational orientations of upper secondary school pupils, thus revealing a dimensional structure of a 'general axis of educational commitment', an axis of 'subjects and studies: easiness versus difficultness', and an axis of 'studies and teaching: large versus minor investments'. *Johs. Hjellbrekke & Olav Korsnes* apply MCA and class specific MCA (Le Roux and Rouanet 2010; Hjellbrekke 2018) in order to explore the relation between the field of power and its subfields to test Bourdieu's homology thesis. Using the case of the Norwegian field of power, the use of specific MCA enables them to empirically model Bourdieu's theoretical proposition that sub-field possess a relative autonomy and thus relatively autonomous orientations and axes of capital. The contribution by *Jörg Blasius & Jürgen Friedrichs* uses MCA, albeit not with human actors but dwellings; more precisely, with those households living in the dwellings, as analytical entities. On the basis of a dwelling panel (for constructing such a panel, see Friedrichs and Blasius 2015), the authors show how these entities change over time. Using as an example the process of gentrification while applying Bourdieu's lifestyle approach to a neighborhood in Cologne (Germany), they illustrate how changes over time can be modelled based on stationary units (dwellings). Likewise, *Nora Waitkus & Olaf Groh-Samberg* focus on an issue of dynamics within the Bourdieusian framework: class mobility over time. Using latent class analysis on disaggregated measures they construct nine classes based on previously defined capital portfolios. This approach allows them to, among other things, illustrate a basic assumption of Bourdieu's habitus concept, namely that actors rarely change their investment and accumulation strategies.

Using the concept of social classes, *Stine Thidemann Faber, Annick Prieur, Lennart Rosenlund & Jakob Skjøtt-Larsen* give another example of both analytical reasoning within the Bourdieusian framework and the further development of this paradigm. They theoretically disentangle five ways to think of social classes: as structures of distribution, as forms of the habitus, as symbolic boundaries, as symbolic structures of domination, and as consciousness or identity. Also in the context of the homology problem, *Nicolas Robette & Olivier Roueff* propose another promising methodological development: Analyzing a survey on cultural practices, they first use MCA in order to compare four different tastes' spaces, and subsequently MFA (Escofier and Pagès 1988; Pagés 2014) in order to test the homology of these spaces. Yet another methodological proposal is given by *Martin Munk*, who models Relative Risk Ratios (RRR), a generalization of odds ratios to multinomial models within the framework of Bourdieusian sociology. This approach enables him to show the differences between children of different parental backgrounds when it comes to seeking elite education abroad. Amongst other things, he shows that the children of upper-class parents with university degrees have a considerably higher probability of attending a higher-ranked university either at home or abroad, when compared to children with a lower class background. The concluding paper of Section A, given by *Magne Flemmen, Vegard Jarness & Lennart Rosenlund*, also uses specific MCA in order to give an account of Bourdieu's homology thesis. Their approach enables them to reveal empirically structural similarities in both the space of lifestyles and the space of political stances.

Social Fields

Section B of this volume assesses the different, relatively autonomous rent forms of societalization within the overall social space: social fields. The section starts with a theoretical work by *David Swartz*, who gives an overview of the use of Bourdieu's field concept in the Anglophone literature. His contribution presents the multitude of different possible ways of using the concept of field, and, at the same time, it motivates the following chapters (e.g. from the European discourse) that extend the already wide scope. The first social field that is discussed is the academic field of science, presented by *Richard Münch*. Although his paper is also of theoretical nature, it actually comprises the manifold results of Münch's empirical work of the last decade on academic capitalism and the numerous transformations the scientific world has been experiencing. With the example of an economic field, *Christian Schmidt-Wellenburg* uses specific MCA in order to construct a field of German-speaking economists. By way of passive projection of their statements on the recent financial crisis, he shows how internationalization affects actors' position-takings. *Myrtille Picaud, Jérôme Pacouret & Gisèle Sapiro* deal with a cultural field: the field of visitors of a festival. Constructing a social space of the public of a literary festival, implementing specific MCA, they illustrate that cultural capital has a twofold form here: cultural capital in the classical sense, and literary capital as characterized by regular cultural practices focused on literature, and by dispositions related to literary education and occupations in affiliated fields. To sum up, this paper gives an example for the context-specificity of capital structure and capital content.

The field of education is analyzed by the contribution of *Håkan Forsberg, Mikael Palme & Mikael Börjesson*. The authors use MCA in order to reveal the structure of the field of upper secondary education in Stockholm, structured with regard to gender and social origin, and educational programs at schools in combination with their geographical locations. This (re-)construction allows them to analyze in a second step how independent schools and public schools differ in their particular attractiveness to school audiences. *Michael Gemperle* analyzes a specific sub-field: nurses working in the canton of St. Gallen (Switzerland). Using specific MCA, he shows that work orientations of nurses correspond to their position within the occupational group's social space, thereby showing that even in small, relatively homogenous contexts, the homology of position and disposition can indeed be a strong analytical perspective. The contribution by *Tobias Dalberg* deals with another specific sub-population: Swedish human scientists. Dalberg conducts a prosopography of human scientists who held some kind of position at Swedish universities and university colleges between 1945 and 1965. He uses specific MCA in order to explore the distribution of career patterns and resources in the human sciences. Thereby, Dalberg exemplifies the genuinely dynamic (and anything but static) nature of Bourdieu's theory, as well as the use of specific MCA for the assessment of research questions including developmental aspects. The final contribution in Section B, by *Christian Baier & Andreas Schmitz*, also deals with the field of science. The focus is on institutional rather than individual entities in their field construction. Using the example of German universities, they apply MFA, which allows them to illustrate changes within this institutional field from 1995 to 2012 in reaction to heteronomous intrusions from the overarching field of power (national and transnational fields, such as nation-states, political fields, and economic fields).

Methodology and Methods

Section C, the last part of the book, focuses on methodology and methods within the Bourdieusian framework. In doing so, it comprises both quantitative and qualitative contributions. This section begins with the paper from *Brigitte Le Roux & Frédérik Cassor*. Analyzing the *French Barometer*, using questions of *Political Trust*, they show how to describe changes over time by combining various GDA methods, including the assignment of supplementary individuals to clusters produced by Euclidean ascending hierarchical clustering.

Fionn Murtagh gives three examples of modern applications of GDA: the challenges and opportunities presented by big data analysis, the narrative analysis of sentiments, and the sphere of mental health and depression. He shows that one can extend the realm of the methodological perspective, as set up by the French tradition of statistics, to a virtually unlimited number of social phenomena, thereby underlining the fundamental epistemological and methodological scope of both GDA and relational reasoning. *Frédéric Lebaron & Philippe Bonnet* provide one of the first illustrations on class-specific MCA to show the benefits of this method. Class specific MCA allows us to identify autonomous sub-groups within an overall social space. Using the European judicial field as an example, they show how to differentiate subgroups, such as members of the European Parliament and law clerks affiliated with different institutions and professional roles. *Rainer Diaz-Bone & Katharina Manderscheid* use MCA to map the field of methods training in German-speaking sociology departments. While MCA and other GDA methods are well established in French-speaking and many other European countries, these methods are not well established in Germany, Austria, and Switzerland. This is rather problematic as Bourdieusian sociology is of particular relevance in these countries; therefore, its methodological impact is largely ignored. *Dominique Joye, Gunn Elisabeth Birkelund & Yannick Lemel* assess a fundamental question of quantitative social research (within and outside the Bourdieusian tradition): the problem of different scale levels of data. Using the Gifi approach (Gifi 1990; Heiser and Meulman 1994), which also combines different scaling methods and which can be seen as the Netherlands' alternative to GDA, they compare methods of analyzing nominal, ordinal, and metric data. This includes MCA (for analyzing nominal data): In previous publication it was referred to as *homogeneity analysis*, but it provides the same solutions as MCA, *categorical* (or nonlinear) *principal component analysis*, and PCA for metric data. The Gifi approach is especially applicable in cases when the input data consists of different scale levels without categorizing metric information. *Heinrich Schäfer, Leif-Hagen Seibert & Adrian Tovar Simoncic* conclude Section C and the entire book with a qualitative contribution: They derive from Bourdieu's relational epistemology and methodology a conceptualization of the habitus as an analytical third layer of 'socioanalysis'. They vote for an integrative use of qualitative constructed habitus-types and for a quantitative construction of social spaces and fields using GDA.

In sum, the different contributions of this volume represent both the plurality of Bourdieusian research today and the common analytical framework that links these different ways of conducting a modern, relational approach to social science. Furthermore, readers should be motivated to engage themselves with the approaches as presented in this book and to mobilize relational methodology in the context of their own research. They should also be encouraged to reflect on the limitations of each method, and thus to find adequate solutions (be they of theoretical, quantitative, or qualitative nature) to their particular problems; often they can use existing conceptual and methodical approaches. Above all, when it comes to the process of objectification of spaces and fields, the use of GDA is indispensable. Nevertheless, there are many challenges social sciences have to face, challenges that often necessitate and inspire variations of already existing methods (such as variants of GDA), sometimes new methods, and sometimes combinations (i.e. acts of relating) of seemingly incompatible methods. Thus, finally, we shall orient our perspective towards the future, and assess some foreseeable new steps in the empirical study of social spaces. In which directions might empirical analyses of social spaces and fields, as well as the appurtenant relational methodology and methods, be expected to develop in the coming years?

Outlook

Applying an *externalist view* to the development of society, we can surely expect the proliferation and institutionalization of processes we can already observe (and which are also treated within this volume): for example, globalization and transnationalization, and at the same time counter-developments such as localization and re-traditionalization. It is a particular strength of Bourdieusian sociology that one can use the basic concepts of this approach for a constantly changing world. Thus, on the one hand, the theoretical foundations of sociological relationalism will not be invalidated due to developments in society itself. One the other hand, Bourdieusian sociology implies the use of 'open concepts', that is, the adaptation and elaboration of analytical tools such as 'field', 'habitus', or 'capital' for the relevant societal conditions. Thus, concepts such as 'transnational' or 'global' fields are currently in the process of development and discussion (cp. Schmitz et al. 2015; Schneickert 2015; Schmidt-Wellenburg and Bernhard 2019).

Applying a more *internalistic view*, i.e. a scientific perspective on the question of future developments, we anticipate that sociology will change its appearance: Different scientific disciplines will become more relevant for sociology (for example data science), whereas other streams of sociology may shift towards other disciplines (for example hermeneutic approaches). Observable trends of this kind illustrate that any genuine development in (Bourdieusian) sociology will also take the form of methodological and methodical developments. Although it is quite difficult to predict the exact constitution of future social sciences, we can base our reflections on some cutting-edge analysis of current research that has been carried out in the field of Bourdieusian sociology. Also, it is to be expected that sociology as a whole will experience the same regular oscillations it has since its beginnings: a return to the actor, a return to structure (and function!), a return to things, a return to norms, a return to economy, etc. Whatever 'turn' may be proclaimed in the future, Bourdieu's relational perspective will always (and sometimes tediously) remind us that we shall not forsake one analytical aspect in favor of another, more 'zeitgeisty', option.

We shall now briefly touch on three more specific that will surely affect the near future of our discipline: comparisons and generalizations of results and concepts, social scientists' dialog with disciplines from other areas of research, and the growing need for linking empirical investigations into social spaces with the dynamics of data sciences in the sphere of Big Data.

Comparison and Generalization of Results and Concepts

A first evolution in the research of social spaces is the further growth in the number of explorations in different areas. In the future, we expect an increasing number of attempts to produce syntheses through systematic comparisons, over regions (neighborhoods, districts, cities, counties, and countries) and over time. Meta-studies and replication studies, which are still rare in this area of research, are another possible approach for further investigation. However, a core task for future research is to take into account empirical developments that dissect and dissolve formerly recognized levels and borders: new forms of societalization ('*Vergesellschaftung*') and new social spaces (e.g. empires, economically or religiously structured groups that make claims to controlling and integrating regions and inhabitants). Yet, in times of dramatic societal changes and challenges, the function of social sciences is not to propose ever-new analytical tools, but to refocus on the existing analytical tool kit and to refine it according to scientific (as opposed to populist) demands.

Among various issues, another cutting-edge problem is the convergence of studies around the multidimensionality of social spaces. Above all, there is a need to develop an abstract vision of social differentiation and inequality. What has been coined the "capital composition" principle (Rosenlund 2009), following Bourdieu's seminal analyses in *Distinction* (Bourdieu 1984 [1979]), remains a central topic in social science discussions on the fundamental structures of the social space: To what extent are the structures of contemporary societies similar and comparable (cp. Blasius and Winkler 1989)? What kinds of latent capital compositions can be observed in Western and non-Western societies? And how stable are the differences in capital compositions over time (cp. Rosenlund 2015; Flemmen et al. 2017)? Such questions will inevitably require the selection of indicators derived in accordance with societal developments (that is: they cannot be specified a priori).

Social Sciences' Dialog with Other Disciplines

At least some of the rejuvenation of empirical studies of social spaces will rely on our capacity to engage in dynamic interactions with other scientific fields. We shall mention three domains with considerable potential for future investigations.

First, applied statistics – in light of developments in data science but also in various sectors of statistical modeling – will certainly remain central to the dynamics of scientific progress in the empirical analysis of social spaces. The main issue we are facing in this area is to condense complexity through the use of GDA tools. Computational capacity, both storage and speed, has increased drastically over time, and will continue to do so. Although many of the older techniques for simplifying data via visualization used by the early Bourdieu (1962), for example the ones he applied for his Algerian studies, are now obsolete, other tools are still being applied to visualize the complexity of life. While earlier applications of SCA and especially MCA were limited to a relatively small number of variables and individuals, which was the reason that Bourdieu used SCA for his early empirical investigations into the social space (Blasius and Schmitz 2014), nowadays MCA applications are limited by the availability of data and theoretical considerations.

MCA has been included since the late 1980s in all major statistical packages such as SPSS, Stata, and SAS. Further, there is an increasing use of R packages (R Core Team 2016); among others there are the packages 'ca' (Greenacrce et al. 2018), 'soc.ca' (Larson 2016), and 'FactoMineR' (Husson et al. 2018). They include procedures to run different forms of SCA and MCA, including specific or subset MCA, just as they provides us with the different variants of GDA. Thus, sociologists can utilize many concepts and tools that are important for Bourdieusian field construction.

As mentioned earlier, MCA is only one variant of GDA: With increasingly complex data and increasing computing capacity, other variants of GDA will become more relevant, such as, for example, multilevel models (e.g. actors nested in geographic areas), models testing for significance (e.g. the reliability of the position of category in the space), models specifying causal relations (e.g. combining regression models with social space models, as Bourdieu envisioned), or non-linear spaces and axes. It is to be expected that, as part of this change, formal social space applications of this kind will increasingly be based on process data, and modelled in their temporal dynamics (e.g. temporal development of social spaces and/or positions); in fact, this corresponds to Bourdieu's view of the social, which is – despite some misunderstandings in secondary literature – a genuinely dynamic one.

Second, cognitive sciences that investigate 'neuronal' and 'mental' spaces could be more strongly associated with social spaces in order to study, for example, phenomena such as fear or anxiety, both combined with individual behavior but above all based on the concept of habitus. Again, this represents not only an empirical class of questions; on the contrary, the basic insight of Bourdieusian (and other) views is that society itself manifests below the 'level' of an (ostensibly) autonomous actor. Collaboration between Bourdieusian sociologists and neuroscientists might initiate systematic collective research that builds on that insight by collecting information below the 'micro-level' and analyzing it by means of habitus, social field, social space, and other perspectives. This field of research is dynamic and complex, and it will include the social sciences only if sociologists prove themselves to be open to new technical developments and, at the same time, willing to actively contribute their reflections and knowledge.

Third, further developments could come from the growing interactions between the studies of social and physical spaces. Geographical and environmental studies investigating physical spaces can (or rather: should) also consider social spaces, as has already been discussed by Bourdieu (1996). Furthermore, indicators from the physical space, for example, the various locations in a city, as well as access to public transport and to cultural events (opera, concerts, etc.), can be included as lifestyle indicators and assigned to individuals, as it is done in the field of gentrification (Zukin 1982; Bridge 2001). In future, social space applications will surely include the interrelations between physical and digital spaces.

Data Science and Sociological Data in the Digital Era

Among social scientists, process-generated data are often considered a way to make accessible the large micro-datasets collected by national statistical offices (Ollion and Boelert 2015). Such data corresponds to a practice of research rooted in countries where official statistics provide comprehensive and relatively simple access to very large register databases, such as those provided by the Scandinavian countries. In other European countries, for example in France, there are official data sources such as the EU-SILC dataset. Both sources allow researchers to construct a variety of social spaces and to perform various configurations of comparisons between countries, regions, socio-occupational groups, etc. Similar developments are occurring in the United States with projects on social mobility and stratification (Grusky et al. 2015).

Process-generated data today is most frequently discussed in the context of Big Data: With the increasing amount of data that individuals disclose on the internet every second (every minute, every hour, every day ...), a great deal of new interdisciplinary work becomes possible. Textual data is a particularly relevant example here; this is a kind of unstructured information that contains words, sentences, and symbols, which have to be converted into a structured form (cp. Benzécri et col 1981; Pêcheux 1995; Lebart 1998) according to a particular research question. It can found both off and online: With increasing digitalization and storage capacities of text footprints of online communication, the availability of textual data is continually growing. The formal construction of social spaces based on new data sources does not – in principle – constitute a new problem. In fact, one of the earliest presentations of correspondence analysis by Benzécri (Benzécri et col 1981) was based on textual data.

Apart from textual data, a core source of information that can be derived from online sources is interactional data (cp. Bergström 2011; Schmitz 2012, 2017). For example, classical sociological (and Bourdieusian) questions regarding partnership formation can be assessed based on a mass of interactions that are observed in real-time. Information on interaction processes between two actors, as well as their personal traits and practices, can be combined and will provide a richer source of information than classical survey data. Furthermore, such data often include a large amount of lifestyle and socio-economic information, and they have proven to be valuable for analysis in the context of the social space framework.

Using such data and combining it with other data is commonly understood as a kind of *El Dorado* for modern social sciences. Combining individual data on lifestyles, preferences, and political convictions – for example, with data from social media such as Facebook – allows for precise investigations of human practices, a reconstruction of their habitus, their trajectories and, eventually, their position within different social fields.

However, the use of Big Data and other new types of data does not guarantee good data quality; currently, the opposite is often the case. Although there has already been some preliminary research concerning the data quality issues of web-generated process data, more effort is required from a large number of researchers to solve problems such as the representativeness of samples and the definition of the population. What is more, the concept of data quality itself needs a revision in light of new types of data and their technical characteristics.

Not least among these 'technicalities' is the fact that this kind of data and data combination allow for personalized canvassing, as everybody was made aware of when, in November 2016, Donald Trump became elected president of the United States. Bourdieusian sociology and methodology will not only be useful in systematically (far beyond mere 'explorative' approaches) analyzing such data. On the contrary, the intimate nexus between social science theory and empirical research will remind us of the societal implications and consequences of such data, ranging from a power shift towards technical experts right through to a reconfiguration of the social space towards the logics of the digital sphere.

Regardless of how future developments regarding the scope of data volume and relational complexity and the statistical and technical tools for handling them evolve, a core element of Bourdieusian sociology is reflexivity: Social scientists should keep in mind that they are part of the social world they think they are analyzing. Even, and indeed especially, if they are armed with ever new information and tools, they should be particularly cautious regarding not only the validity of their data, but more importantly the recursive effects such data (and its analysis) can have on society itself.

References

Benzécri, J. P., et al. (1973). *L'analyse des données. L'analyse des correspondances*. Paris: Dunod.

Benzécri, J. P., et al. (1981). *Pratique de l'analyse des données: Linguistique et lexicologie. Vol 3*. Paris: Dunod.

Bergström, M. (2011). La toile des sites de rencontres en France. *Réseaux, 166*(2), 225–260.

Blasius, J., & Schmitz, A. (2014). Empirical construction of Bourdieu's social space. In J. Blasius & M. Greenacre (Eds.), *Visualization and verbalization of data* (pp. 205–222). Boca Raton: Chapman & Hall.

Blasius, J., & Winkler, J. (1989). Gibt es die ‚feinen Unterschiede "? Eine empirische Überprüfung der Bourdieuschen Theorie. *Kölner Zeitschrift für Soziologie und Sozialpsychologie, 41*, 72–94.

Bourdieu, P. (1962). *The Algerians*. Boston, MA: Beacon Press.

Bourdieu, P. (1984[1979]). *La distinction*. Paris: Les éditions de minuit. (Distinction. A social critique of the judgement of taste. 1984. Cambridge, MA: Harvard University Press).

Bourdieu, P. (1996). Physical space, social space and habitus. *Vilhelm Aubert Memorial lecture, Report, 10*.

Bridge, G. (2001). Estate agents as interpreters of economic and cultural capital: The gentrification premium in the Sydney housing market. *International Journal of Urban and Regional Research, 25*, 87–101.

Escofier, B., & Pagès, J. (1988). *L'analyse factorielles simples et multiples: objectifs, méthodes et interpretation*. Paris: Dunod. EU-SILC: https://www.eui.eu/Research/Library/ResearchGuides/Economics/Statistics/DataPortal/EU-SILC.

Flemmen, M., Jarness, V., & Rosenlund, L. (2017). Social space and cultural class divisions: The forms of capital and contemporary lifestyle differentiation. *The British Journal of Sociology, 69*, 124–153.

Friedrichs, J., & Blasius, J. (2015). The dwelling panel – A new research method for studying urban change. *Raumforschung und Raumordnung, 73*, 377–388.

Gifi, A. (1990). *Nonlinear multivariate analysis*. Hoboken: Wiley.

Greenacrce, M., & Pardo, R. (2006). Multiple correspondence analysis of subsets of response categories. In M. Greenacre & J. Blasius (Eds.), *Multiple correspondence analysis and related methods* (pp. 197–217). San Diego: Academic.

Greenacrce, M., Nenadić, O., & Friendly, M. (2018). *Package 'ca'*. https://cran.r-project.org/web/packages/ca/ca.pdf. Access 10 Nov 2018.

Grusky, D. B., Smeeding, T. M., & Snipp, C. M. (2015). A new infrastructure for monitoring social mobility in the United States. *The Annals of the American Academy of Political and Social Sciences, 657*, 63–82.

Heiser, W. J., & Meulman, J. J. (1994). Homogeneity analysis: Exploring the distribution of variables and their nonlinear relationships. In M. Greenacre & J. Blasius (Eds.), *Correspondence analysis in the social sciences* (pp. 179–209). London: Academic.

Hjellbrekke, J. (2018). *Multiple correspondence analysis for the social sciences*. London: Routledge.

Husson, F., Josse, J., Le, S., & Mazet, J. (2018). *FactoMineR: Multivariate exploratory data analysis and data mining*. https://cran.r-project.org/web/packages/FactoMineR/index.html. Access 10 Nov 2018.

Larson, A. G. (2016). *soc.ca: Specific correspondence analysis for the Social sciences*. https://cran.r-project.org/web/packages/ca/ca.pdf. Access 10 Nov 2018.

Le Roux, B., & Rouanet, H. (2004). *Geometric data analysis. From correspondence analysis to structured data analysis*. Dordrecht: Kluwer.

Le Roux, B., & Rouanet, H. (2010). *Multiple correspondence analysis*. London: Sage.

Lebart, L. (1998). Visualizations of textual data. In J. Blasius & M. Greenacre (Eds.), *Visualization of catgorical data* (pp. 133–147). San Diego: Academic.

Ollion, É., & Boelert, J. (2015). Au delà des *big data*. Les sciences sociales et la multiplication des données numériques. *Sociology, 6*, 295–310.

Pagés, J. (2014). Multiple factor analysis; General presentation and comparison with STATIS. In J. Blasius & M. Greenacre (Eds.), *Visualization and verbalization of data* (pp. 223–253). Boca Raton: Chapman & Hall.

Pêcheux, M. (1995). *Automatic discourse analysis* (Vol. 5). Amsterdam: Rodopi.

R Core Team. (2016). *R: A languge and environment for statistical computing*. Vienna: R Foundation for Statistical Computing. https://www.R-project.org/

Rosenlund, L. (2009). *Exploring the city with Bourdieu: Applying Pierre Bourdieu's theories and methods to study the community*. Saarbrücken: VDM Verlag.

Rosenlund, L. (2015). Working with distinctions. Scandinavian experiences. In P. Coulangeon & J. Duval (Eds.), *The Routledge companion to Bourdieu's distinction* (pp. 157–187). New York: Routledge.

Schmidt-Wellenburg, C., & Bernhard, S. (Eds.). (2019). *Charting transnational fields. Methodology for a political sociology of knowledge*. New York: Routledge.

Schmitz, A. (2012). Elective affinities 2.0? A Bourdieusian approach to couple formation and the methodology of E-dating. *RESET. Social Science Research on the Internet, 1*, 175–202.

Schmitz, A. (2017). *The structure of digital partner choice. A Bourdieusian perspective*. Amsterdam: Springer International.

Schmitz, A., Heiberger, H., & Blasius, J. (2015). Das globale Feld der Macht als ‚Tertium Comparationis". *Österreichische Zeitschrift für Soziologie, 40*, 247–263.

Schmitz, A., Witte, D., & Gengnagel, V. (2016). Pluralizing field analysis: Toward a relational understanding of the field of power. *Social Science Information/Information sur les sciences sociales, 56*, 49–73. https://doi.org/10.1177/0539018416675071. (Online first).

Schneickert, C. (2015). *Nationale Machtfelder und globalisierte Eliten*. Konstanz: UVK.

Zukin, S. (1982). *Loft-living: Culture and capital in urban change*. New Brunswick: Rutgers University Press.

9 783030 153861